HOLT SCIENCE & TECHNOLOGY

Physical Science

HOLT, RINEHART AND WINSTON

A Harcourt Classroom Education Company

Austin · New York · Orlando · Atlanta · San Francisco · Boston · Dallas · Toronto · London

Acknowledgments

Contributing Authors

Christie Borgford, Ph.D.
Professor of Chemistry
University of Alabama
Birmingham, Alabama

Andrew Champagne
Former Physics Teacher
Ashland High School
Ashland, Massachusetts

Mapi Cuevas, Ph.D.
Professor of Chemistry
Santa Fe Community College
Gainesville, Florida

Leila Dumas
Former Physics Teacher
LBJ Science Academy
Austin, Texas

William G. Lamb, Ph.D.
Science Teacher and Dept. Chair
Oregon Episcopal School
Portland, Oregon

Sally Ann Vonderbrink, Ph.D.
Chemistry Teacher
St. Xavier High School
Cincinnati, Ohio

Lab Writers

Phillip G. Bunce
Former Physics Teacher
Bowie High School
Austin, Texas

Kenneth E. Creese
Science Teacher
White Mountain Junior High School
Rock Springs, Wyoming

William G. Lamb, Ph.D.
Science Teacher and Dept. Chair
Oregon Episcopal School
Portland, Oregon

Alyson Mike
Science Teacher
East Valley Middle School
East Helena, Montana

Joseph W. Price
Science Teacher and Dept. Chair
H. M. Browne Junior High School
Washington, D.C.

Denice Lee Sandefur
Science Teacher and Dept. Chair
Nucla High School
Nucla, Colorado

John Spadafino
Mathematics and Physics Teacher
Hackensack High School
Hackensack, New Jersey

Walter Woolbaugh
Science Teacher
Manhattan Junior High School
Manhattan, Montana

Academic Reviewers

Paul R. Berman, Ph.D.
Professor of Physics
University of Michigan
Ann Arbor, Michigan

Russell M. Brengelman, Ph.D.
Professor of Physics
Morehead State University
Morehead, Kentucky

John A. Brockhaus, Ph.D.
Director, Mapping, Charting and Geodesy Program
Department of Geography and Environmental Engineering
United States Military Academy
West Point, New York

Walter Bron, Ph.D.
Professor of Physics
University of California
Irvine, California

Andrew J. Davis, Ph.D.
Manager, ACE Science Center
Department of Physics
California Institute of Technology
Pasadena, California

Peter E. Demmin, Ed.D.
Former Science Teacher and Department Chair
Amherst Central High School
Amherst, New York

Roger Falcone, Ph.D.
Professor of Physics and Department Chair
University of California
Berkeley, California

Cassandra A. Fraser, Ph.D.
Assistant Professor of Chemistry
University of Virginia
Charlottesville, Virginia

L. John Gagliardi, Ph.D.
Associate Professor of Physics and Department Chair
Rutgers University
Camden, New Jersey

Gabriele F. Giuliani, Ph.D.
Professor of Physics
Purdue University
West Lafayette, Indiana

Roy W. Hann, Jr., Ph.D.
Professor of Civil Engineering
Texas A&M University
College Station, Texas

John L. Hubisz, Ph.D.
Professor of Physics
North Carolina State University
Raleigh, North Carolina

Samuel P. Kounaves, Ph.D.
Professor of Chemistry
Tufts University
Medford, Massachusetts

Acknowledgments (cont.)

Karol Lang, Ph.D.
Associate Professor of Physics
The University of Texas
Austin, Texas

Gloria Langer, Ph.D.
Professor of Physics
University of Colorado
Boulder, Colorado

Phillip LaRoe
Professor
Helena College of Technology
Helena, Montana

Joseph A. McClure, Ph.D.
Associate Professor of Physics
Georgetown University
Washington, D.C.

LaMoine L. Motz, Ph.D.
Coordinator of Science Education
Department of Learning
Services
Oakland County Schools
Waterford, Michigan

R. Thomas Myers, Ph.D.
Professor of Chemistry, Emeritus
Kent State University
Kent, Ohio

Hillary Clement Olson, Ph.D.
Research Associate
Institute for Geophysics
The University of Texas
Austin, Texas

David P. Richardson, Ph.D.
Professor of Chemistry
Thompson Chemical
Laboratory
Williams College
Williamstown, Massachusetts

John Rigden, Ph.D.
Director of Special Projects
American Institute of Physics
Colchester, Vermont

Peter Sheridan, Ph.D.
Professor of Chemistry
Colgate University
Hamilton, New York

Vederaman Sriraman, Ph.D.
Associate Professor of Technology
Southwest Texas State
University
San Marcos, Texas

Jack B. Swift, Ph.D.
Professor of Physics
The University of Texas
Austin, Texas

Atiq Syed, Ph.D.
*Master Instructor of Mathematics
and Science*
Texas State Technical College
Harlingen, Texas

Leonard Taylor, Ph.D.
Professor Emeritus
Department of Electrical
Engineering
University of Maryland
College Park, Maryland

Virginia L. Trimble, Ph.D.
*Professor of Physics and
Astronomy*
University of California
Irvine, California

Martin VanDyke, Ph.D.
Professor of Chemistry Emeritus
Front Range Community
College
Westminster, Colorado

Gabriela Waschewsky, Ph.D.
Science and Math Teacher
Emery High School
Emeryville, California

Safety Reviewer

Jack A. Gerlovich, Ph.D.
Associate Professor
School of Education
Drake University
Des Moines, Iowa

Teacher Reviewers

Barry L. Bishop
Science Teacher and Dept. Chair
San Rafael Junior High School
Ferron, Utah

Paul Boyle
Science Teacher
Perry Heights Middle School
Evansville, Indiana

Kenneth Creese
Science Teacher
White Mountain Junior High
School
Rock Springs, Wyoming

Vicky Farland
Science Teacher and Dept. Chair
Centennial Middle School
Yuma, Arizona

Rebecca Ferguson
Science Teacher
North Ridge Middle School
North Richland Hills, Texas

Laura Fleet
Science Teacher
Alice B. Landrum Middle
School
Ponte Vedra Beach, Florida

Jennifer Ford
Science Teacher and Dept. Chair
North Ridge Middle School
North Richland Hills, Texas

Susan Gorman
Science Teacher
North Ridge Middle School
North Richland Hills, Texas

C. John Graves
Science Teacher
Monforton Middle School
Bozeman, Montana

Dennis Hanson
Science Teacher and Dept. Chair
Big Bear Middle School
Big Bear Lake, California

David A. Harris
Science Teacher and Dept. Chair
The Thacher School
Ojai, California

Norman E. Holcomb
Science Teacher
Marion Local Schools
Maria Stein, Ohio

Kenneth J. Horn
Science Teacher and Dept. Chair
Fallston Middle School
Fallston, Maryland

Tracy Jahn
Science Teacher
Berkshire Junior-Senior High
School
Canaan, New York

Kerry A. Johnson
Science Teacher
Isbell Middle School
Santa Paula, California

Drew E. Kirian
Science Teacher
Solon Middle School
Solon, Ohio

Harriet Knops
Science Teacher and Dept. Chair
Rolling Hills Middle School
El Dorado, California

Scott Mandel, Ph.D.
*Director and Educational
Consultant*
Teachers Helping Teachers
Los Angeles, California

Thomas Manerchia
Former Science Teacher
Archmere Academy
Claymont, Delaware

Edith McAlanis
Science Teacher and Dept. Chair
Socorro Middle School
El Paso, Texas

Kevin McCurdy, Ph.D.
Science Teacher
Elmwood Junior High School
Rogers, Arkansas

Alyson Mike
Science Teacher
East Valley Middle School
East Helena, Montana

Donna Norwood
Science Teacher and Dept. Chair
Monroe Middle School
Charlotte, North Carolina

Joseph W. Price
Science Teacher and Dept. Chair
H. M. Browne Junior High
School
Washington, D.C.

Terry J. Rakes
Science Teacher
Elmwood Junior High School
Rogers, Arkansas

Beth Richards
Science Teacher
North Middle School
Crystal Lake, Illinois

Elizabeth J. Rustad
Science Teacher
Crane Middle School
Yuma, Arizona

Acknowledgments (cont.)

Rodney A. Sandefur
Science Teacher
Naturita Middle School
Naturita, Colorado

Helen Schiller
Science Teacher
Northwood Middle School
Taylors, South Carolina

Bert J. Sherwood
Science Teacher
Socorro Middle School
El Paso, Texas

Patricia McFarlane Soto
Science Teacher and Dept. Chair
G. W. Carver Middle School
Miami, Florida

David M. Sparks
Science Teacher
Redwater Junior High School
Redwater, Texas

Larry Tackett
Science Teacher and Dept. Chair
Andrew Jackson Middle School
Cross Lanes, West Virginia

Elsie N. Waynes
Science Teacher and Dept. Chair
R. H. Terrell Junior High School
Washington, D.C.

Sharon L. Woolf
Science Teacher
Langston Hughes Middle
School
Reston, Virginia

Alexis S. Wright
*Middle School Science
Coordinator*
Rye Country Day School
Rye, New York

Lee Yassinski
Science Teacher
Sun Valley Middle School
Sun Valley, California

John Zambo
Science Teacher
Elizabeth Ustach Middle School
Modesto, California

Staff Credits

Editorial

Robert W. Todd, Associate
Director, Secondary Science
Debbie Starr, Managing Editor
Anne Engelking, Senior Editor
Michael Mazza, Editor

ANNOTATED TEACHER'S EDITION

Ken Shepardson, Amy James,
Michael Mazza, Kelly Rizk,
Bill Burnside

COPYEDITORS

Dawn Spinozza, Copyediting
Manager

EDITORIAL SUPPORT STAFF

Jeanne Graham, Mary Helbling,
Kenneth G. Raymond, Tanu'e
White

EDITORIAL PERMISSIONS

Cathy Paré, Permissions Manager
Jan Harrington, Permissions
Editor

Art, Design, and Photo

BOOK DESIGN

Richard Metzger, Design Director
Marc Cooper, Senior Designer
Ron Bowdoin, Designer
David Hernandez, Designer
Alicia Sullivan, Designer (ATE),
Cristina Bowerman, Design
Associate (ATE)

IMAGE ACQUISITIONS

Elaine Tate, Art Buyer Supervisor
Sean Moynihan, Art Buyer
Tim Taylor, Photo Research
Supervisor
Stephanie Morris, Assistant
Photo Researcher

PHOTO STUDIO

Sam Dudgeon, Senior Staff
Photographer
Victoria Smith, Photo Specialist
Lauren Eischen, Photo
Coordinator

Production

Mimi Stockdell, Senior
Production Manager
Adriana Bardin Prestwood,
Senior Production Coordinator
Beth Sample, Production
Coordinator
**Suzanne Brooks, Sara Carroll-
Downs**

Contents in Brief

LabBook **620**

Contents

Unit 1 ··· Introduction to Matter

The more labs, the better!

Take a minute to browse the **LabBook** located at the end of this textbook. You'll find a wide variety of exciting labs that will help you experience science firsthand. But please don't forget to be safe. Read the "Safety First!" section before starting any of the labs.

Start your engines with an activity!

Science is an activity in which investigation leads to information and understanding. The **Start-Up Activity** at the beginning of each chapter helps you gain scientific understading of the topic through hands-on experience.

START-UP Activity

QuickLab

Not all laboratory investigations have to be long and involved.

The **QuickLabs** found throughout the chapters in this book require only a small amount of time and limited equipment. But just because they are quick, don't skimp on the safety.

$\div\ 5\ \div\ \ ^{\Omega}\ _\leq\ \infty\ +_\Omega\ ^\surd\ 9\ _\infty\ ^\leq\ \Sigma\ 2$

MATH BREAK

Science and math go hand in hand.

The **MathBreaks** in the margins of the chapters show you many ways that math applies directly to science and vice versa.

Connections

One science leads to another.

You may not realize it at first, but different areas of science are related to each other in many ways. Each **Connection** explores a topic from the viewpoint of another science discipline. In this way, areas of science merge to improve your understanding of the world around you.

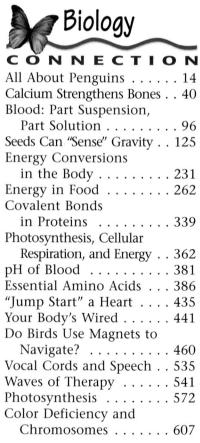

Biology
CONNECTION

Oceanography
CONNECTION

Environment
CONNECTION

Physics
CONNECTION

Meteorology
CONNECTION

Astronomy
CONNECTION

Geology
CONNECTION

Feature Articles

Feature articles for any appetite!

Science and technology affect us all in many ways. The following articles will give you an idea of just how interesting, strange, helpful, and action-packed science and technology are. At the end of each chapter, you will find two feature articles. Read them and you will be surprised at what you learn.

How to Use Your Textbook

Your Roadmap for Success with *Holt Science & Technology*

Study the Terms to Learn

Key Terms are listed for each section. Learn the definitions of these terms because you will most likely be tested on them. Use the glossary to locate definitions quickly.

STUDY TIP If you don't understand a definition, reread the page where the term is introduced. The surrounding text should help make the definition easier to understand.

Read What You'll Do

Objectives tell you what you'll need to know.

STUDY TIP Reread the objectives when studying for a test to be sure you know the material.

Take Notes and Get Organized

Keep a science notebook so that you are ready to take notes when your teacher reviews the material in class. Keep your assignments in this notebook so that you can review them when studying for the chapter test. In addition, you will be asked to keep a *ScienceLog*, in which you will write your answers to certain questions. Your *ScienceLog* may be a section of your science notebook.

Section 1

Terms to Learn

states of matter   pressure
solid   Boyle's law
liquid   Charles's law
gas   plasma

What You'll Do

◆ Describe the properties shared by particles of all matter.
◆ Describe the four states of matter discussed here.
◆ Describe the differences between the states of matter.
◆ Predict how a change in pressure or temperature will affect the volume of a gas.

Four States of Matter

Figure 1 shows a model of the earliest known steam engine, invented about A.D. 60 by Hero, a scientist who lived in Alexandria, Egypt. This model also demonstrates the four most familiar states of matter: solid, liquid, gas, and plasma. The **states of matter** are the physical forms in which a substance can exist. For example, water commonly exists in three different states of matter: solid (ice), liquid (water), and gas (steam).

Figure 1 *This model of Hero's steam engine spins as steam escapes through the nozzles.*

Moving Particles Make Up All Matter

Matter consists of tiny particles called atoms and molecules (MAHL i KYOOLZ) that are too small to see without an amazingly powerful microscope. These atoms and molecules are always in motion and are constantly bumping into one another. The state of matter of a substance is determined by how fast the particles move and how strongly the particles are attracted to one another. **Figure 2** illustrates three of the states of matter—solid, liquid, and gas—in terms of the speed and attraction of the particles.

Figure 2 Models of a Solid, a Liquid, and a Gas

Particles of a solid do not move fast enough to overcome the strong attraction between them, so they are held tightly in place. The particles vibrate in place.

Particles of a liquid move fast enough to overcome some of the attraction between them. The particles are able to slide past one another.

Particles of a gas move fast enough to overcome nearly all of the attraction between them. The particles move independently of one another.

60   Chapter 3

⤴ Be Resourceful, Use the Web

Internet Connect boxes in your textbook take you to resources that you can use for science projects, reports, and research papers. Go to **scilinks.org** and type in the SciLinks code to get information on a topic.

Visit go.hrw.com Find worksheets and other materials that go with your textbook at **go.hrw.com**. Click on the textbook icon and the table of contents to see all of the resources for each chapter.

Second Class Levers With a second class lever, the load is between the fulcrum and the input force, as shown in **Figure 11**. Second class levers do not change the direction of the input force, but they allow you to apply less force than the force exerted by the load. Because the output force is greater than the input force, you must exert the input force over a greater distance. Some examples of second class levers are shown at right.

Figure 11 A Second Class Lever

Examples of Second Class Levers

Using a second class lever results in a **mechanical advantage of greater than 1.** The closer the load is to the fulcrum, the more the force is increased and the greater the mechanical advantage.

Third Class Levers With a third class lever, the input force is between the fulcrum and the load, as shown in **Figure 12**. Third class levers do not change the direction of the input force. In addition, they do *not* increase the input force. Therefore, the output force is always less than the input force. Some examples of third class levers are shown at right.

Figure 12 A Third Class Lever

Examples of Third Class Levers

Using a third class lever results in a mechanical advantage of less than 1 because force is decreased. But third class levers are helpful because they increase the distance through which the output force is exerted.

Work and Machines **199**

REVIEW

1. Name the parts of a cell, and explain how they work together to produce an electric current.

2. How do the currents produced by a 1.5 V flashlight cell and a 12 V car battery compare?

3. **Inferring Conclusions** Why do you think some solar calculators contain batteries?

internet connect

SciLINKS.
NSTA

TOPIC: Electrical Energy
GO TO: www.scilinks.org
sciLINKS NUMBER: HSTP410

432 Chapter 17

Use the Illustrations and Photos

Art shows complex ideas and processes. Learn to analyze the art so that you better understand the material you read in the text.

Tables and graphs display important information in an organized way to help you see relationships.

A picture is worth a thousand words. Look at the photographs to see relevant examples of science concepts you are reading about.

Answer the Section Reviews

Section Reviews test your knowledge over the main points of the section. Critical Thinking items challenge you to think about the material in greater depth and to find connections that you infer from the text.

STUDY TIP When you can't answer a question, reread the section. The answer is usually there.

Do Your Homework

Your teacher may assign worksheets to help you understand and remember the material in the chapter.

STUDY TIP Don't try to answer the questions without reading the text and reviewing your class notes. A little preparation up front will make your homework assignments a lot easier. Answering the items in the Chapter Review will help prepare you for the chapter test.

Holt Online Learning

Visit Holt Online Learning
If your teacher gives you a special password to log onto the **Holt Online Learning** site, you'll find your complete textbook on the Web. In addition, you'll find some great learning tools and practice quizzes. You'll be able to see how well you know the material from your textbook.

Visit CNN Student News
You'll find up-to-date events in science at **cnnstudentnews.com**.

TIMELINE

Introduction to Matter

In this unit, you will explore a basic question that people have been pondering for centuries: What is the nature of matter? You will learn how to define the word *matter* and how to describe matter and the changes it goes through. You will also learn about the different states of matter and how to classify different arrangements of matter as elements, compounds, or mixtures. This timeline shows some of the events and discoveries that have occurred throughout history as scientists have sought to understand the nature of matter.

1712
Thomas Newcomen invents the first practical steam engine.

1661
Robert Boyle, a chemist in England, determines that elements are substances that cannot be broken down into anything simpler by chemical processes.

1949
Silly Putty® is sold in a toy store for the first time. The soft, gooey substance quickly becomes popular because of its strange properties, including the ability to "pick up" the print from a newspaper page.

1957
The space age begins when the Soviet Union launches *Sputnik I,* the first artificial satellite to circle the Earth.

1971
The first "pocket" calculator is introduced. It has a mass of more than 1 kg and a price of about $150—hardly the kind of pocket calculator that exists today.

1766
English chemist Henry Cavendish discovers and describes the properties of a highly flammable substance now known as hydrogen gas.

1800
Current from an electric battery is used to separate water into the elements hydrogen and oxygen for the first time.

1920
American women win the right to vote with the ratification of the 19th Amendment to the Constitution.

1937
The *Hindenburg* explodes while docking in Lakehurst, New Jersey. The airship was filled with flammable hydrogen gas to make it lighter than air.

1928
Sir Alexander Fleming discovers that the mold *Penicillium notatum,* shown here growing on an orange, is capable of killing some types of bacteria. The antibiotic penicillin is derived from this mold.

1989
An oil tanker strikes a reef in Prince William Sound, Alaska, spilling nearly 11 million gallons of oil. The floating oil injures or kills thousands of marine mammals and seabirds and damages the Alaskan coastline.

2000
The World's Fair, an international exhibition featuring exhibits and participants from around the world, is held in Hanover, Germany. The theme is "Humankind, Nature, and Technology."

The World of Physical Science

Pre-Reading Questions

1. What are scientific methods?

2. What is a model, and what are the limitations of models?

3. What tools are used to measure mass and volume?

SHOULD A SHIP HAVE FLIPPERS?

Putting flippers on a ship may seem like a strange idea. But think about how well penguins use flippers to move through the water. Maybe flippers could help ships too. This is exactly what two scientists from the Massachusetts Institute of Technology have been trying to find out. In this chapter, you will learn how these scientists have used scientific methods to answer their questions. Maybe, as a result of these investigations, ships will have flippers someday!

START-UP Activity

FIGURE IT OUT

In this activity, you will do some things scientists do—make observations and use them to solve a puzzle.

Procedure

1. Get the **five shapes** shown below from your teacher.

2. Observe the drawing below. Predict how the five shapes could be arranged to make the fish.

3. Test your idea. You may have to try several times. (Hint: Shapes can be turned over.) Record notes about each try in your ScienceLog.

Analysis

4. Did you solve the puzzle just by making observations? What observations helped the most?

5. How did testing your ideas help?

Exploring Physical Science

It's Monday morning. You're eating breakfast and trying to pull yourself out of an early morning daze. As you eat a spoonful of Crunch Blasters, your favorite cereal, you look down and notice your reflection in your spoon. Something's funny about it—it's upside down! "Why is my reflection upside down even though I'm holding the spoon right side up?" you wonder. Is your spoon playing tricks on you? Next you look at the back of the spoon. "A-ha!" you think, "Now my reflection is right side up!" However, when you look back at the inside of the spoon, your reflection is upside down again. What is it about the spoon that makes your reflection look right side up on one side and upside down on the other?

That's Science!

You may not realize it, but you were just doing science. Science is all about being curious, making observations, and asking questions about those observations. For example, you noticed your reflection in your spoon and became curious about it. You observed that it was upside down, but that when you looked at the back of the spoon, your reflection was right side up. Then you asked what the two sides of the spoon had to do with your reflection. So you were definitely doing science!

Everyday Science Science is all around you, even if you're not thinking about it. Everyday actions such as putting on your sunglasses when you're outside, timing your microwave popcorn just right, and using the brakes on your bicycle all use your knowledge of science. But how do you know how to do these things? From experience—you've gained an understanding of your world by observing and discovering all your life.

Because science is all around, you might not be surprised to learn that there are different branches of science. This book is all about physical science. So just what is physical science?

Matter + Energy → Physical Science

Physical science is the study of matter and energy. Matter is the "stuff" that everything is made of—even stuff that is so small you can't see it. Your shoes, your pencil, and even the air you breathe are made of matter. And all of that matter has energy. Energy is easier to describe than to explain. For example, energy is partly responsible for rainbows in the sky, but it isn't the rainbow itself. When you throw a ball, you give the ball energy. Moving objects have energy, as you can see in **Figure 1.** Food also has energy. When you eat food, the energy in the food is transferred to you, and you can use that energy to carry out your daily activities. But energy isn't always associated with motion or food. All matter has energy, even matter that isn't moving, like that shown in **Figure 2.**

As you explore physical science, you'll learn more about the relationship between matter and energy by answering questions such as the following: Why does paper burn but gold does not? Why is it harder to throw a bowling ball than a baseball? How can water turn into steam and back to water? All of the answers have to do with matter and energy. And although it is difficult to talk about matter without talking about energy, sometimes it is useful to focus on one or the other. That's why physical science is often divided into two categories—chemistry and physics.

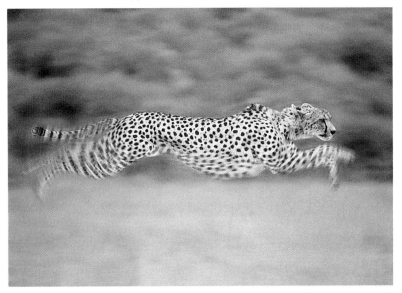

Figure 1 *The cheetah, the fastest land mammal, has a lot of energy when running full speed. The cheetah also uses a lot of energy to run so fast. But a successful hunt will supply the energy the cheetah needs to live.*

Figure 2 *All matter has energy—even this monumental stone head that is over 1.5 m tall!*

Chemistry Studying all forms of matter and how they interact is what chemistry is all about. You'll learn about the properties and structure of matter and how different substances behave under certain conditions, such as high temperature and high pressure. You'll also discover how and why matter can go through changes, such as the one shown in **Figure 3.** Check out the chart below to find out what you can learn by studying chemistry.

Figure 3 *When you wash your clothes, the detergent and the stains interact. The result? Clean clothes!*

By studying chemistry, you can find out . . .

- why yeast makes bread dough rise.

- how the elements chlorine and sodium combine to form table salt, a compound.

- why water boils at 100°C.

- why sugar dissolves faster in hot tea than in iced tea.

- how pollution affects our atmosphere.

Physics Like chemistry, physics deals with matter. But unlike chemistry, physics is mostly concerned with energy and how it affects matter. Studying different forms of energy is what physics is all about. When you study physics, you'll discover how energy can make matter do some interesting things, as shown in **Figure 4.** You'll also begin to understand aspects of your world such as motion, force, gravity, electricity, light, and heat. Check out the chart below to find out what you can learn by studying physics.

Figure 4 *When you study physics you'll learn how energy causes the motion that makes a roller coaster ride so exciting.*

By studying physics, you can find out . . .

- why you move to the right when the car you're in turns left.

- why you would weigh less on the moon than you do on Earth.

- why you see a rainbow after a rainstorm.

- how a compass works.

- how your bicycle's gears help you pedal faster or slower.

Physical Science Is All Around You

Believe it or not, the things that you'll learn about matter and energy by studying physical science are important for what you'll learn in other science classes, too. Take a look below to see the role of physical science in areas that you might have thought only involved Earth science or life science.

Astronomy uses physical science to explain the composition of planets, the light given off by stars, and the motion of different galaxies in the universe.

Meteorology applies physical science in its study of the movement of air masses, weather patterns, and the composition of the atmosphere.

Botany, the study of plants, uses physical science to explain how plants use carbon dioxide and water to make food.

Geology uses physical science to explain earthquake waves and rock composition.

Oceanography uses physical science to explain waves, currents, and the chemistry of ocean water.

Ecology uses physical science to explain the nitrogen cycle and the transfer of energy between organisms in a food chain.

Biology uses physical science to explain how the heart pumps blood, how the eyes and ears work, and how the brain sends electrical impulses throughout the body.

Physical Science in Action

Now that you know physical science is all around you, you may not be surprised to learn that a lot of careers rely on physical science. What's more, you don't have to be a scientist to use physical science in your job! On this page, you can see some career opportunities that involve physical science.

Gene Webb is an auto mechanic. He understands how the parts of a car engine move and how to keep cars working efficiently.

Shirley Ann Jackson has done research in the semiconductor and optical physics industries. She became president of Rensselaer Polytechnic Institute in 1999.

Roberto Santibanez is a chef. He knows how ingredients interact and how energy can cause the chemical changes that produce his delicious meals.

Julie Fields is a chemist who studies chemical substances found in living organisms. She investigates how these substances can be made into products such as medicines.

Other Careers Involving Physical Science

- Architect
- Pharmacist
- Firefighter
- Engineer
- Construction worker
- Optician
- Pilot
- Electrician
- Computer technician

REVIEW

1. What is physical science all about?

2. List three things you do every day that use your experience with physical science.

3. **Applying Concepts** Choose one of the careers listed in the chart at left. How do you think physical science is involved in that career?

Using the Scientific Method

Terms to Learn

scientific method   data
technology   theory
observation   law
hypothesis

What You'll Do

- Identify the steps used in the scientific method.
- Give examples of technology.
- Explain how the scientific method is used to answer questions and solve problems.
- Describe how our knowledge of science changes over time.

When you hear or read about advancements in science, do you wonder how they were made? How did the scientists make their discoveries? Were they just lucky? Maybe, but chances are that it was much more than luck. The scientific method probably had a lot to do with it!

What Is the Scientific Method?

The **scientific method** is a series of steps that scientists use to answer questions and solve problems. The chart below shows the steps that are commonly used in the scientific method. Although the scientific method has several distinct steps, it is not a rigid procedure whose steps must be followed in a certain order. Scientists may use the steps in a different order, skip steps, or repeat steps. It all depends on what works best to answer the question.

Do you remember James Czarnowski and Michael Triantafyllou, the two scientists discussed at the beginning of this chapter? What scientific problem were they trying to solve? In the next few pages, you'll learn how they used the scientific method to develop new technology—*Proteus,* the penguin boat.

The Scientific Method

- Ask a question.
- Form a hypothesis.
- Test the hypothesis.
- Analyze the results.
- Draw conclusions.
- Communicate results.

Spotlight on Technology

Technology is the application of knowledge, tools, and materials to solve problems and accomplish tasks. Technology can also refer to the objects used to accomplish tasks. For example, computers, headphones, and the Internet are all examples of technology. But even things like toothbrushes, light bulbs, and pencils are examples of technology.

Science and technology are not the same thing. The goal of science is to gain knowledge about the natural world. The goal of technology is to apply scientific understanding to solve problems. Technology is sometimes called *applied science.*

Figure 5
Stopwatches and rulers are some of the many tools used to make observations.

Ask a Question

Asking a question helps you focus your investigation and identify what you want to find out. Usually, scientists ask a question after they've made a lot of observations. An **observation** is any use of the senses to gather information. Measurements are observations that are made with instruments, such as those shown in **Figure 5.** The chart below gives you some examples of observations. Keep in mind that you can make observations at any point while using the scientific method.

Examples of Observations	
■ The sky is blue.	■ He is 125 centimeters tall.
■ The ice began to melt 30 seconds after it was taken out of the freezer.	■ Adding food coloring turned the water red. Adding bleach made the water clear again.
■ This soda bottle has a volume of 1 liter.	■ This brick feels heavier than this sponge.
■ Cotton balls feel soft.	■ Sandpaper is rough.

A Real-World Question So what question did the scientists who made *Proteus* ask? Czarnowski and Triantafyllou, shown in **Figure 6,** are engineers, scientists who put scientific knowledge to practical human use. Engineers create technology. While a graduate student at the Massachusetts Institute of Technology, Czarnowski worked with Triantafyllou, his professor, to observe boat propulsion systems and investigate how to make them work better. A propulsion (proh PUHL shuhn) system is what makes a boat move; most boats are driven by propellers.

One thing that Czarnowski and Triantafyllou were studying is the efficiency of boat propulsion systems. *Efficiency* (e FISH uhn see) compares energy output (the energy used to move the boat forward) with energy input (the energy supplied by the boat's engine). Czarnowski and Triantafyllou learned from their observations that boat propellers, shown in **Figure 7** on the next page, are not very efficient.

Figure 6 *James Czarnowski (left) and Michael Triantafyllou (right) made observations about how boats work in order to develop* Proteus.

Figure 7 Observations About the Efficiency of Boat Propellers

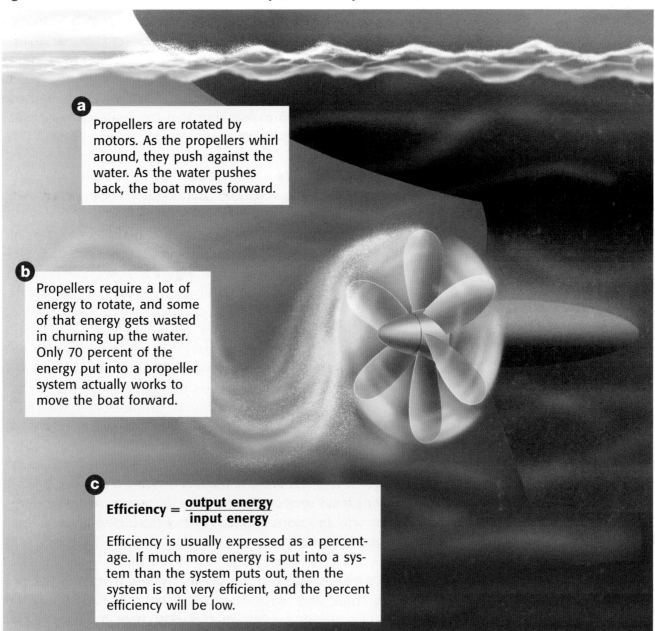

a Propellers are rotated by motors. As the propellers whirl around, they push against the water. As the water pushes back, the boat moves forward.

b Propellers require a lot of energy to rotate, and some of that energy gets wasted in churning up the water. Only 70 percent of the energy put into a propeller system actually works to move the boat forward.

c
$$\text{Efficiency} = \frac{\text{output energy}}{\text{input energy}}$$

Efficiency is usually expressed as a percentage. If much more energy is put into a system than the system puts out, then the system is not very efficient, and the percent efficiency will be low.

Why is boat efficiency important? Most boats are only about 70 percent efficient. Making only a small fraction of the United States' boats and ships just 10 percent more efficient would save millions of liters of fuel per year. Saving fuel means saving money, but it also means using less of the Earth's supply of fossil fuels. Based on their observations and all of this information, Czarnowski and Triantafyllou knew what they wanted to find out.

Ask some questions of your own on page 626 in the LabBook.

The Question:

How can boat propulsion systems be made more efficient?

Form a Hypothesis

Once you've asked your question, your next step is forming a hypothesis. A **hypothesis** is a possible explanation or answer to a question. You can use what you already know and any observations that you have made to form a hypothesis. A good hypothesis is testable. If no observations or information can be gathered or if no experiment can be designed to test the hypothesis, it is untestable.

Figure 8 Penguins use their flippers almost like wings to "fly" underwater. As they pull their flippers toward their body, they push against the water, which propels them forward.

Nature Provides a Possible Answer
Czarnowski and Triantafyllou were also looking for an example from nature on which to base their hypothesis. Czarnowski had made observations of penguins swimming at the New England Aquarium. **Figure 8** shows how penguins propel themselves. He observed how quickly and easily the penguins moved through the water. He also observed that penguins have a rigid body, similar to a boat. These observations led the two scientists to a possible answer to their question: a propulsion system that works the way a penguin swims!

Hypothesis:
A propulsion system that mimics the way a penguin swims will be more efficient than propulsion systems that use propellers.

Before scientists test a hypothesis, they often make predictions that state what they think will happen during the actual test of the hypothesis. Scientists usually state predictions in an "If . . . then . . ." format. The engineers at MIT might have made the following prediction: *If* two flippers are attached to a boat, *then* the boat will be more efficient than a boat powered by propellers.

Biology
CONNECTION

Penguins, although flightless, are better adapted to water and extreme cold than any other bird. Most of the world's 18 penguin species live and breed on islands in the subantarctic waters. Penguins can swim as fast as 40 km/h, and some can leap more than 2 m above the water.

REVIEW

1. How do scientists and engineers use the scientific method?

2. Give three examples of technology from your everyday life.

3. **Analyzing Methods** Explain how the accuracy of your observations might affect how you develop a hypothesis.

Test the Hypothesis

After you form a hypothesis, you must test it to determine whether it is a reasonable answer to your question. In other words, testing helps you find out if your hypothesis is pointing you in the right direction or if it is way off the mark. Often a scientist will test a hypothesis by testing a prediction.

One way to test a hypothesis is to conduct a controlled experiment. In a controlled experiment, there is a control group and an experimental group. Both groups are the same except for one factor in the experimental group, called a *variable*. The experiment will then determine the effect of the variable.

Sometimes a controlled experiment is not possible. Stars, for example, are too far away to be used in an experiment. In such cases, you can test your hypothesis by making additional observations or by conducting research. If your investigation involves creating technology to solve a problem, you can make or build what you want to test and see if it does what you expected it to do. That's just what Czarnowski and Triantafyllou did— they built *Proteus*, the penguin boat, shown in **Figure 9.**

Figure 9 Testing Penguin Propulsion

Quick Lab

That's Swingin'!

1. Make a pendulum by tying a **piece of string** to a **ring stand** and hanging a **small mass,** such as a washer, from the end of the string.

2. Form a hypothesis about which factors (such as length of string, mass, etc.) affect the rate at which the pendulum swings.

3. In your ScienceLog, record what factors you will control and what factor will be your variable.

4. Test your hypothesis by conducting several trials, recording the number of swings made in a given time, such as 10 seconds, for each trial.

5. Was your hypothesis supported? In your ScienceLog, analyze your results.

ⓐ *Proteus* is only 3.4 m long and 50 cm wide, too narrow for even a single passenger.

ⓑ *Proteus* has two flipper-like paddles, called *foils*. Both foils move out and then in, much as a penguin uses its flippers underwater.

ⓔ Each of *Proteus*'s flapping foils is driven by a motor that gets its energy from two car batteries.

ⓓ A desktop computer programs the number of times the foils flap per second.

ⓒ As the foils flap, they push water backward. The water pushes against the foils, propelling the boat forward.

Self-Check

What variable were Czarnowski and Triantafyllou testing? *(See page 724 to check your answer.)*

Testing *Proteus* Czarnowski and Triantafyllou took *Proteus* out into the open water of the Charles River when they were ready to collect data. **Data** are any pieces of information acquired through experimentation. The engineers did several tests, each time changing only the flapping rate. For each test, data such as the flapping rate, energy the motors used, and the speed achieved by the boat were carefully recorded. The input energy was determined by how much energy was used. The output energy was determined from the speed *Proteus* achieved.

Analyze the Results

After you collect and record your data, you must analyze them to determine whether the results of your test support the hypothesis. Sometimes doing calculations can help you learn more about your results. Organizing numerical data into tables and graphs makes relationships between information easier to see.

Analyzing *Proteus* Czarnowski and Triantafyllou used the data for input energy and output energy to calculate *Proteus*'s efficiency for different flapping rates. These data are graphed in **Figure 10.** The scientists compared *Proteus*'s highest level of efficiency with the average efficiency of a propeller-driven boat. Look at the bar graph in Figure 10 to see if their data support their hypothesis—that penguin propulsion would be more efficient than propeller propulsion.

Figure 10 Graphs of the Test Results

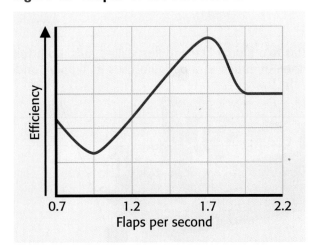

This line graph shows that *Proteus* was most efficient when its foils were flapping about 1.7 times per second.

This bar graph shows that *Proteus* is 17 percent more efficient than a propeller-driven boat.

Draw Conclusions

At the end of an investigation, you must draw a conclusion. You could conclude that your results supported your hypothesis, that your results did *not* support your hypothesis, or that you need more information. If you conclude that your results support your hypothesis, you can ask further questions. If you conclude that your results do not support your hypothesis, you should check your results or calculations for errors. You may have to modify your hypothesis or form a new one and conduct another investigation. If you find that your results neither support nor disprove your hypothesis, you may need to gather more information, test your hypothesis again, or redesign the procedure.

The *Proteus* Conclusion After Czarnowski and Triantafyllou analyzed the results of their test, they conducted many more trials. Still they found that the penguin propulsion system was more efficient than a propeller propulsion system. So they concluded that their hypothesis was supported, which led to more questions, as you can see in **Figure 11.**

Figure 11 *Could a penguin propulsion system be used on large ships, such as an oil tanker? The research continues!*

Communicate Results

One of the most important steps in any investigation is to communicate your results. You can write a scientific paper, make a presentation, or create a Web site. Telling others what you learned is how science keeps going. Other scientists can conduct their own tests, modify your tests to learn something more specific, or study a new problem based on your results.

Communicating About *Proteus* Czarnowski and Triantafyllou published their results in academic papers, but they also displayed their project and its results on the Internet. In addition, science magazines and newspapers have reported the work of these engineers. These reports allow you to conduct some research of your own about *Proteus.*

Breaking the Mold of the Scientific Method

Not all scientists use the same scientific method, nor do they always follow the same steps in the same order. Why not? Sometimes you may have a clear idea about the question you want to answer. Other times, you may have to revise your hypothesis and test it again. While you should always take accurate measurements and record data correctly, you don't always have to follow the scientific method in a certain order. **Figure 12** shows you some other paths through the scientific method.

Figure 12 *Scientific investigations do not always proceed from one step of the scientific method to the next. Sometimes steps are skipped, and sometimes they are repeated.*

Building Scientific Knowledge

Using the scientific method is a way to find answers to questions and solutions to problems. But you should understand that answers are very rarely *final* answers. As our understanding of science grows, our understanding of the world around us changes. New ideas and new experiments teach us new things. Sometimes, however, an idea is supported again and again by many experiments and tests. When this happens, the idea can become a theory or even a law. As you will read on the next page, theories and laws help to build new scientific knowledge.

Turn to page 33 to discover a tale of young Einstein's encounter with some other science heavyweights.

Scientific Theories You've probably heard a detective on a TV show say, "I've got a theory about who committed the crime." Does the detective have a scientific theory? Probably not; it might be just a guess. A scientific theory is more complex than a simple guess.

In science, a **theory** is a unifying explanation for a broad range of hypotheses and observations that have been supported by testing. A theory not only can explain an observation you've made but also can predict an observation you might make in the future. Keep in mind that theories, like the one shown in **Figure 13,** can be changed or replaced as new observations are made or as new hypotheses are tested.

Scientific Laws What do you think of when you hear the word *law*? Traffic laws? Federal laws? Well, scientific laws are not like these laws. Scientific laws are determined by nature, and you can't break a scientific law!

In science, a **law** is a summary of many experimental results and observations. A law tells you how things work. Laws are not the same as theories because laws only tell you *what* happens, not *why* it happens, as shown in **Figure 14.** Although a law does not explain why something happens, the law tells you that you can expect the same thing to happen every time.

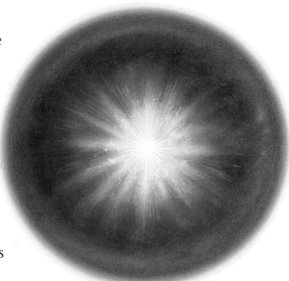

Figure 13 *According to the big-bang theory, the universe was once a small, hot, and dense volume of matter. About 10 to 20 billion years ago, an event called the big bang sent matter in all directions, forming the galaxies and planets.*

Figure 14 *Dropping a ball illustrates the law of conservation of energy. Although the ball doesn't bounce back to its original height, energy is not lost—it is transferred to the ground.*

REVIEW

1. Name the steps that can be used in the scientific method.

2. How is a theory different from a hypothesis?

3. **Analyzing Ideas** Describe how our knowledge of science changes over time.

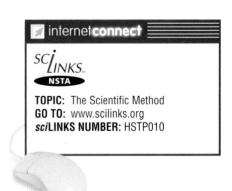

internet connect

SC*i*LINKS.
NSTA

TOPIC: The Scientific Method
GO TO: www.scilinks.org
*sci*LINKS NUMBER: HSTP010

What You'll Do

◆ Explain how models represent real objects or systems.
◆ Give examples of different ways models are used in science.

Using Models in Physical Science

Think again about *Proteus*. How much like a penguin was it? Well, *Proteus* didn't have feathers and wasn't a living thing, but its "flippers" were designed to create the same kind of motion as a penguin's flippers. The MIT engineers built *Proteus* to mimic the way a penguin swims so that they could gain a greater understanding about boat propulsion. In other words, they created a *model*.

What Is a Model?

A **model** is a representation of an object or system. Models are used in science to describe or explain certain characteristics of things. Models can also be used for making predictions and explaining observations. A model is never exactly like the real object or system—if it were, it would no longer be a model. Models are particularly useful in physical science because many characteristics of matter and energy can be either hard to see or difficult to understand. You can see some examples of scientific models below.

Examples of Models

A model rocket is much smaller than a real rocket, but launching one in your backyard can help you understand how real rockets blast off into space.

You can't see the tiny parts that make up matter, but you can make a model that shows how the parts fit together.

A model of a building can be designed on a computer before money is spent constructing the actual building.

A cell diagram is a model that lets you look at all the parts of a cell up close—without using a microscope.

Models Help You Visualize Information

When you're trying to learn about something that you can't see or observe directly, a model can help you visualize it, or picture it in your mind. Familiar objects or ideas can help you understand something a little less familiar.

Objects as Models When you use an object as a model for something you cannot see, the object must have characteristics similar to those of the real thing. For example, a coiled spring toy is often used as a model of sound waves. You've probably used this kind of spring toy before, so it's a familiar object. Sound waves are probably a little less familiar—after all, you can't see them. But the spring toy behaves a lot like sound waves do. So using the spring toy as a model, as shown in **Figure 15,** can make the behavior of sound waves easier to understand.

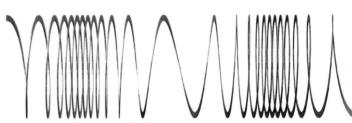

Figure 15 *A coiled spring toy can show you how air particles crowd together in parts of a sound wave.*

Ideas as Models When you're trying to understand something but don't have an object to use as a model, you can create a model from an idea. For example, when sugar dissolves in iced tea, it seems to disappear. To try to understand where the sugar goes, imagine a single drop of tea magnified until it is almost as big as you are, with tiny spaces between the particles of water in the tea. Using this model, as shown in **Figure 16,** you can understand that the sugar seems to disappear because the sugar particles fit into spaces between the water particles in the tea.

Figure 16 *Just by imagining a big drop of tea, you are creating a model!*

Models for Weather Forecasting

You've probably seen a weather report on television. Think about the models that a weather reporter uses to tell you about the weather: satellite pictures, color-coded maps, and live radar images. How are these models used to represent the weather? Why do you think that sometimes weather forecasts are wrong?

Models Are Just the Right Size

How can you observe how the phases of the moon occur? That's a tough problem, because you're on Earth and you can't easily get off of the Earth to observe the moon going around it. But you can observe a model of the moon, Earth, and sun, as shown in **Figure 17.** As you can see, models can represent things that are too large to easily observe.

Figure 17 *Using this model, you can see how the Earth's rotation, in addition to the moon's revolution around the Earth as the Earth revolves around the sun, results in the different phases of the moon.*

Figure 18 *The particles of matter in a grain of salt connect in a continuous pattern that forms a cube. That's why a grain of salt has a cubic shape.*

Models are also useful for understanding things that are too small to see. For example, you can tell just by looking that a grain of salt has a definite shape, but you may not know why. A model of the structure of salt, as shown in **Figure 18,** can help you understand how the arrangement of tiny particles accounts for its shape.

Models Build Scientific Knowledge

Models not only can represent scientific ideas and objects but also can be tools that you can use to conduct investigations and illustrate theories.

Testing Hypotheses The MIT engineers were trying to test their hypothesis that a boat that mimics the way a penguin swims would be more efficient than a boat powered by propellers. How did they test this hypothesis? By building a model, *Proteus.* When using the scientific method to develop new technology, testing a hypothesis often requires building a model. By conducting tests with *Proteus,* the MIT engineers tested their hypothesis and found out what factors affected the model's efficiency. Using the data they collected, they could consider building a full-sized penguin boat.

Build a model car and test its speed on page 627 in the LabBook.

Illustrating Theories Recall that a theory explains why things happen the way they do. Sometimes, however, a theory is hard to picture. That's where models come in handy. A model is different from a theory, but a model can present a picture of what the theory explains when you cannot actually observe it. You can see an example of this in **Figure 19.**

Models Can Save Time and Money

When creating technology, scientists often create a model first so that they can test its characteristics and improve its design before building the real thing. You may recall that *Proteus* wasn't big enough to carry even a single passenger. Why didn't the MIT engineers begin by building a full-sized boat? Imagine if they had gone to all that trouble and found out that their design didn't work. What a waste! Models allow you to test ideas without having to spend the time and money necessary to make the real thing. In **Figure 20,** you can see another example of how models save time and money.

Figure 19 *This model illustrates the atomic theory, which states that all matter is made of tiny particles called atoms.*

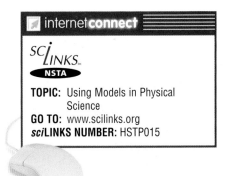

Figure 20 *Car engineers can conduct cyber-crashes, in which computer-simulated cars crash in various ways. Engineers use the results to determine which safety features to install on the car—all without damaging a single automobile.*

REVIEW

1. What is the purpose of a model?

2. Give three examples of models that you see every day.

3. **Interpreting Models** Both a globe and a flat world map model certain features of the Earth. Give an example of when you would use a globe and an example of when you would use a flat map.

internetconnect

SC*L*INKS.
NSTA

TOPIC: Using Models in Physical Science
GO TO: www.scilinks.org
*sci*LINKS NUMBER: HSTP015

Measurement and Safety in Physical Science

Terms to Learn

meter   temperature
volume   area
mass   density

What You'll Do

◆ Explain the importance of the International System of Units.
◆ Determine the appropriate units to use for particular measurements.
◆ Describe how area and density are derived quantities.

Hundreds of years ago, different countries used different systems of measurement. In England, the standard for an inch used to be three grains of barley placed end to end. Other standardized units of the modern English system, which is used in the United States, used to be based on parts of the body, such as the foot. Such units were not very accurate because they were based on objects that varied in size.

Eventually people recognized that there was a need for a single measurement system that was simple and accurate. In the late 1700s, the French Academy of Sciences began to develop a global measurement system, now known as the International System of Units, or SI.

The International System of Units

Today most scientists in almost all countries use the International System of Units. One advantage of using SI measurements is that it helps scientists share and compare their observations and results. Another advantage of SI is that all units are based on the number 10, which makes conversions from one unit to another easy to do. The table in **Figure 21** contains the commonly used SI units for length, volume, mass, and temperature.

Figure 21 *Prefixes are used with SI units to convert them to larger or smaller units. For example* kilo *means 1,000 times, and* milli *indicates 1/1,000 times. The prefix used depends on the size of the object being measured.*

Common SI Units		
Length	**meter (m)**	
	kilometer (km)	1 km = 1,000 m
	decimeter (dm)	1 dm = 0.1 m
	centimeter (cm)	1 cm = 0.01 m
	millimeter (mm)	1 mm = 0.001 m
	micrometer (µm)	1 µm = 0.000 001 m
	nanometer (nm)	1 nm = 0.000 000 001 m
Volume	**cubic meter (m³)**	
	cubic centimeter (cm³)	$1\ cm^3 = 0.000\ 001\ m^3$
	liter (L)	$1\ L = 1\ dm^3 = 0.001\ m^3$
	milliliter (mL)	$1\ mL = 0.001\ L = 1\ cm^3$
Mass	**kilogram (kg)**	
	gram (g)	1 g = 0.001 kg
	milligram (mg)	1 mg = 0.000 001 kg
Temperature	**Kelvin (K)**	0°C = 273 K
	Celsius (°C)	100°C = 373 K

Length   How long is an Olympic-sized swimming pool? To describe its length, a physical scientist would use **meters (m)**, the basic SI unit of length. Other SI units of length are larger or smaller than the meter by multiples of 10. For example, 1 kilometer (km) equals 1,000 meters. If you divide 1 m into 1,000 parts, each part equals 1 mm. This means that 1 mm is one-thousandth of a meter. Although that seems pretty small, some objects are so tiny that even smaller units must be used. To describe the length of a grain of salt, micrometers (μm) or nanometers (nm) are used.

Volume   Imagine that you need to move some lenses to a laser laboratory. How many lenses will fit into a crate? That depends on the volume of the crate and the volume of each lens. **Volume** is the amount of space that something occupies.

Volumes of liquids are expressed in liters (L). Liters are based on the meter. A cubic meter (1 m³) is equal to 1,000 L. So 1,000 L will fit into a box 1 m on each side. A milliliter (mL) will fit into a box 1 cm on each side. So 1 mL = 1 cm³. Graduated cylinders are used to measure the volume of liquids.

Volumes of solid objects are expressed in cubic meters (m³). Volumes of smaller objects can be expressed with cubic centimeters (cm³) or cubic millimeters (mm³). To find the volume of a crate, or any other rectangular shape, multiply the length by the width by the height. To find the volume of an irregularly shaped object, measure how much liquid that object displaces. You can see how this works in **Figure 22.**

Activity

Pick an object to use as a unit of measure. It could be a pencil, your hand, or anything else. Find how many units wide your desk is, and compare your measurement with those of your classmates. What were some of the units that your classmates used?

70 mL

80 mL

Figure 22 *When the rock is added, the water level rises from 70 mL to 80 mL. Because the rock displaces 10 mL of water, and because 1 mL = 1 cm³, the volume of the rock is 10 cm³.*

Mass How many cars can a bridge support? That depends on the strength of the bridge and the mass of the cars. **Mass** is the amount of matter that something is made of. The kilogram (kg) is the basic SI unit for mass and would be used to express the mass of a car. Grams (one-thousandth of a kilogram) are used to express the mass of small objects. A medium-sized apple has a mass of about 100 g. Masses of very large objects are expressed in metric tons. A metric ton equals 1,000 kg.

Temperature How hot is melted iron? To answer this question, a physical scientist would measure the temperature of the liquid metal. **Temperature** is a measure of how hot (or cold) something is. You are probably used to expressing temperature with degrees Fahrenheit (°F). Scientists often use degrees Celsius (°C), but the kelvin (K) is the SI unit for temperature. The thermometer in **Figure 23** compares °F with °C, the unit you will most often see in this book.

Figure 23 Measuring Temperature

212°F — Water boils ---- 100°C Water boils
98.6°F — Normal body temperature ---- 37°C Normal body temperature
32°F — Water freezes ---- 0°C Water freezes

Derived Quantities

Some quantities are formed from combinations of other measurements. Such quantities are called *derived quantities*. Both area and density are derived quantities.

Area How much carpet would cover the floor of your classroom? It depends on the area of the floor. **Area** is a measure of how much surface an object has. To calculate the area of a rectangular surface, measure the length and width, then use this equation:

$$\text{Area} = \text{length} \times \text{width}$$

The units for area are called square units, such as m^2, cm^2, and km^2. The area of the rectangle in **Figure 24** is 20 cm^2.

MATH BREAK

Using Area to Find Volume

Area can be used to find the volume of an object according to the following equation:

$$\text{Volume} = \text{Area} \times \text{height}$$

1. What is the volume of a box 5 cm tall whose lid has an area of 9 cm^2?

2. A crate has a volume of 48 m^3. The area of its bottom side is 16 m^2. What is the height of the crate?

3. A cube with a volume of 8,000 cm^3 has a height of 20 cm. What is the area of one of its sides?

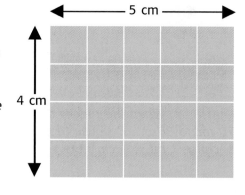

Figure 24 *If you count the smaller squares within the rectangle, you'll count 20 squares that each measure 1 cm².*

5 cm

4 cm

Density Another derived quantity is density. **Density** is mass per unit volume. So an object's density is the amount of matter it has in a given space. To find density (*D*), first measure mass (*m*) and volume (*V*). Then use the following equation:

$$D = \frac{m}{V}$$

For example, suppose you want to know the density of the gear shown at right. Its mass is 75 g and its volume is 20 cm³. You can calculate the gear's density like this:

$$D = \frac{m}{V} = \frac{75 \text{ g}}{20 \text{ cm}^3} = 3.75 \text{ g/cm}^3$$

Safety Rules!

Physical science is exciting and fun, but it can also be dangerous. So don't take any chances! Always follow your teacher's instructions, and don't take shortcuts—even when you think there is little or no danger.

Before starting an experiment, get your teacher's permission and read the lab procedures carefully. Pay particular attention to safety information and caution statements. The chart below shows the safety symbols used in this book. Get to know these symbols and what they mean by reading the safety information on page 622. **This is important!** If you are still unsure about what a safety symbol means, ask your teacher.

Stay on the safe side by reading the safety information on page 622. **You must do this before doing any experiment!**

Stay on the safe side by reading the safety information on page 622. **You must do this before doing any experiment!**

Safety Symbols

 Eye protection   Clothing protection   Hand safety

Heating safety   Electric safety   Sharp object

 Chemical safety   Animal safety   Plant safety

REVIEW

1. Why is SI important?

2. Which SI unit would you use to express the height of your desk? Which SI unit would you use to express the volume of this textbook?

3. **Comparing Concepts** How is area different from volume?

internet connect

SCi LINKS
NSTA

TOPIC: SI Units
GO TO: www.scilinks.org
*sci*LINKS NUMBER: HSTP020

Chapter Highlights

Vocabulary
physical science (p. 7)

Section Notes

- Science is a process of making observations and asking questions about those observations.

- Physical science is the study of matter and energy and is often divided into physics and chemistry.

- Physical science is part of many other areas of science.

- Many different careers involve physical science.

Vocabulary
scientific method (p. 11)
technology (p. 11)
observation (p. 12)
hypothesis (p. 14)
data (p. 16)
theory (p. 19)
law (p. 19)

Section Notes

- The scientific method is a series of steps that scientists use to answer questions and solve problems.

- Any information you gather through your senses is an observation. Observations often lead to questions or problems.

- A hypothesis is a possible explanation or answer to a question. A good hypothesis is testable.

- After you test a hypothesis, you should analyze your results and draw conclusions about whether your hypothesis was supported.

- Communicating your findings allows others to verify your results or continue to investigate your problem.

- A scientific theory is the result of many investigations and many hypotheses. Theories can be changed or modified by new evidence.

- A scientific law is a summary of many experimental results and hypotheses that have been supported over time.

Labs
Exploring the Unseen (p. 626)

☑ Skills Check

Math Concepts

AREA To calculate the area of a rectangular surface, first measure its length and width, then multiply those values. The area of a piece of notebook paper with a length of 28 cm and a width of 21.6 cm can be calculated as follows:

$$\text{Area} = \text{length} \times \text{width}$$
$$= 28 \text{ cm} \times 21.6 \text{ cm}$$
$$= 604.8 \text{ cm}^2$$

Visual Understanding

SCIENTIFIC METHOD To answer a question in science, you can use the scientific method. Review the flowchart on page 18 to see that the scientific method does not have to follow a specific order.

MODELS A model is a representation of an object or system. Look back at the examples on page 20 to learn more about different models.

SECTION 3

Vocabulary
model *(p. 20)*

Section Notes

- Scientific models are representations of objects or systems. Models make difficult concepts easier to understand.

- Models can represent things too small to see or too large to observe directly.

- Models can be used to test hypotheses and illustrate theories.

Labs
Off to the Races! *(p. 627)*

SECTION 4

Vocabulary
meter *(p. 25)*
volume *(p. 25)*
mass *(p. 26)*
temperature *(p. 26)*
area *(p. 26)*
density *(p. 27)*

Section Notes

- The International System of Units is the standard system of measurement used by scientists around the world.

- Length, volume, mass, and temperature are quantities of measurement. Each quantity of measurement is expressed with a particular SI unit.

- Area is a measure of how much surface an object has. Density is a measure of mass per unit volume.

- Safety rules are important and must be followed at all times during scientific investigations.

Labs
Measuring Liquid Volume *(p. 628)*
Coin Operated *(p. 629)*

---

internetconnect

GO TO: go.hrw.com

Visit the **HRW** Web site for a variety of learning tools related to this chapter. Just type in the keyword:

KEYWORD: HSTWPS

SCILINKS SM
N S T A

GO TO: www.scilinks.org

Visit the **National Science Teachers Association** on-line Web site for Internet resources related to this chapter. Just type in the *sci*LINKS number for more information about the topic:

TOPIC: Matter and Energy	*sci*LINKS NUMBER: HSTP005
TOPIC: The Scientific Method	*sci*LINKS NUMBER: HSTP010
TOPIC: Using Models in Physical Science	*sci*LINKS NUMBER: HSTP015
TOPIC: SI Units	*sci*LINKS NUMBER: HSTP020

Chapter Review

For each pair of terms, explain the difference in their meanings.

1. science/technology

2. observation/hypothesis

3. theory/law

4. model/theory

5. volume/mass

6. area/density

UNDERSTANDING CONCEPTS

Multiple Choice

7. Physical science is the study of
   a. matter and motion.
   b. matter and energy.
   c. energy and motion.
   d. matter and composition.

8. 10 m is equal to
   a. 100 cm.   c. 10,000 mm.
   b. 1,000 cm.   d. Both (b) and (c)

9. For a hypothesis to be valid, it must be
   a. testable.
   b. supported by evidence.
   c. made into a law.
   d. Both (a) and (b)

10. The statement "Sheila has a stain on her shirt" is an example of a(n)
    a. law.
    b. hypothesis.
    c. observation.
    d. prediction.

11. A hypothesis is often developed out of
    a. observations.   c. laws.
    b. experiments.   d. Both (a) and (b)

12. How many milliliters are in 3.5 kL?
    a. 3,500   c. 3,500,000
    b. 0.0035   d. 35,000

13. A map of Seattle is an example of a
    a. law.   c. model.
    b. quantity.   d. unit.

14. Which of the following is an example of technology?
    a. mass
    b. physical science
    c. screwdriver
    d. none of the above

Short Answer

15. Name two areas of science other than chemistry and physics, and describe how physical science has a role in those areas of science.

16. Explain why the results of one experiment are never really final results.

17. Explain why area and density are called derived quantities.

18. If a hypothesis is not testable, does that mean that it is wrong? Explain.

Concept Mapping

19. Use the following terms to create a concept map: science, scientific method, hypothesis, problems, questions, experiments, observations.

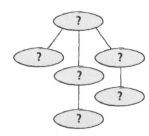

20. A tailor is someone who makes or alters items of clothing. Why might a standard system of measurement be helpful to a tailor?

21. Two classmates are having a debate about whether a spatula is an example of technology. Using what you know about science, technology, and spatulas, write a couple of sentences that will help your classmates settle their debate.

22. Imagine that you are conducting an experiment in which you are testing the effects of the height of a ramp on the speed at which a toy car goes down the ramp. What is the variable in this experiment? What factors must be controlled?

23. Suppose a classmate says, "I don't need to study physical science because I'm not going to be a scientist, and scientists are the only people who use physical science." How would you respond? (Hint: In your answer, give several examples of careers that use physical science.)

24. The cereal box at right has a mass of 340 g. Its dimensions are 27 cm × 19 cm × 6 cm.

  a. What is the volume of the box?

  b. What is its density?

  c. What is the area of the front side of the box?

Examine the picture below, and answer the questions that follow:

25. How similar to the real object is this model?

26. What characteristics of the real object does this model not show?

27. Why might this model be useful?

Reading Check-up

Take a minute to review your answers to the Pre-Reading Questions found at the bottom of page 4. Have your answers changed? If necessary, revise your answers based on what you have learned since you began this chapter.

CAREERS

ELECTRONICS ENGINEER

Julie Williams-Byrd uses her knowledge of physics to develop better lasers. She started working with lasers as a graduate student at Hampton University, in Virginia. Today Williams-Byrd works as an electronics engineer in the Laser Systems Branch (LSB) of NASA. She designs and builds lasers that are used to monitor phenomena in the atmosphere, such as wind and ozone.

*T*he white light we see every day is actually composed of all the colors of the spectrum. A laser emits a very small portion of this spectrum. That is why there are blue lasers, red lasers, and so on. High-voltage sources called laser "pumps" cause laser materials to emit certain wavelengths of light, depending on the material used. A laser material, such as helium neon gas, emits radiation (light) as a result of changes in the electron energy levels of its atoms. This process gives lasers their name: **L**ight **A**mplification of the **S**timulated **E**mission of **R**adiation.

Using Scientific Models

Julie Williams-Byrd uses scientific models to predict the nature of different aspects of laser design. Different laser materials emit radiation at different wavelengths, and specific pump sources must be used to induce "lasing." "Researchers at LSB use laser models to predict output energy, wavelength, efficiency, and a host of other properties of the laser system," Williams-Byrd says.

New Technologies

Her most challenging project has been building a laser-transmitter that will be used to measure winds in the atmosphere. This system, called *Lidar,* is very much like radar except that it uses light waves instead of sound waves to bounce off objects. To measure winds, a laser beam is transmitted into the atmosphere, where it illuminates particles. A receiver looks at these particles over a period of time and determines the changes in position of the particles. Wind velocity is then determined from this information. This new technology is expected to be used in a space shuttle mission called Sparcle.

Lasers All Around Us

Although Williams-Byrd works with high-tech lasers, she points out that lasers are a part of daily life for many people. For example, lasers are used in scanners at many retail stores. Ophthalmologists use lasers to correct near-sightedness. Some metal workers use them to cut metal. And lasers are even used to create spectacular light shows!

Going Further

▶ Can you think of any new uses for lasers? Make a list in your ScienceLog, and then do some research to find out if any of your ideas already exist.

▼ *Julie Williams-Byrd uses laser generators like this one in her work at NASA.*

Science Fiction

"Inspiration"

by Ben Bova

No matter where you are on the face of the Earth, you can pinpoint your location. Most of the time, you use map coordinates, or latitude and longitude readings. And you can give your distance above sea level. With modern technology, you can give an accurate, three-dimensional description of where you are. But what about a fourth dimension? Consider for a moment traveling in *time.* Not just getting through today and into tomorrow but actually being able to leap back and forth through time.

Novelist H. G. Wells imagined such a possibility in his novelette *The Time Machine.* When the story was published in 1895, most physicists said that the notion of traveling in time was nonsense and against all the laws of physics that govern the universe. The idea that *time* was similar to *length, width,* or *height* was foolishness. Or so they thought.

It was up to Albert Einstein, in 1905, to propose a different view of the universe. However, when Wells's story was first published, Einstein was just 16 and not a very good student. What if Einstein had been discouraged and had not pursued his interest in physics? But Einstein did look at the universe and maybe, just maybe, he had an inspiration.

Ben Bova's story "Inspiration" describes just such a possibility. Young Einstein meets Wells and the great physicist of the time, Lord Kelvin. But was the meeting just a lucky coincidence or something else entirely? Escape to the *Holt Anthology of Science Fiction,* and read "Inspiration" to find out.

The Properties of Matter

Pre-Reading
Questions

1. What is matter?
2. What is the difference between a physical property and a chemical property?
3. What is the difference between a physical change and a chemical change?

NICE ICE

You've seen water in many forms: steam rising from a kettle, dew collecting on grass, and tiny crystals of frost forming on the windows in winter. But no matter what its form, water is still water. In this chapter, you'll learn more about the many different properties of matter, such as water. You'll also learn about changes in matter that take place all around you.

SACK SECRETS

In this activity, you will test your skills in determining the identity of an object based on its properties.

Procedure

1. You and two or three of your classmates will receive a **sealed paper sack** containing a **mystery object.** Do not open the sack!

2. For 5 minutes, make as many observations as you can about the object. You may touch, smell, or listen to the object through the sack; shake the sack; and so on. Be sure to record your observations.

Analysis

3. At the end of 5 minutes, discuss your findings with your partners.

4. In your ScienceLog, list the object's properties. Make a conclusion about the object's identity.

5. Share your observations, your list of properties, and your conclusion with the class. Now you are ready to open the sack.

6. Did you properly identify the object? If so, how? If not, why not? Write your answers in your ScienceLog. Share them with the class.

What You'll Do

- ◆ Name the two properties of all matter.
- ◆ Describe how volume and mass are measured.
- ◆ Compare mass and weight.
- ◆ Explain the relationship between mass and inertia.

QuickLab

Space Case

1. Crumple a **piece of paper,** and fit it tightly in the bottom of a **cup** so that it won't fall out.

2. Turn the cup upside down. Lower the cup straight down into a **large beaker or bucket** half-filled with **water** until the cup is all the way underwater.

3. Lift the cup straight out of the water. Turn the cup upright and observe the paper. Record your observations in your ScienceLog.

4. Now punch a small hole in the bottom of the cup with the point of a **pencil.** Repeat steps 2 and 3.

5. How do these results show that air has volume? Record your explanation in your ScienceLog.

What Is Matter?

Here's a strange question: What do you have in common with a toaster?

Give up? Okay, here's another question: What do you have in common with a steaming bowl of soup or a bright neon sign?

You are probably thinking these are trick questions. After all, it is hard to imagine that a human—you—has anything in common with a kitchen appliance, some hot soup, or a glowing neon sign.

Everything Is Made of Matter

From a scientific point of view you have at least one characteristic in common with these things. You, the toaster, the bowl, the soup, the steam, the glass tubing, and the glowing gas are all made of matter. But what is matter exactly? If so many different kinds of things are made of matter, you might expect the definition of the word *matter* to be complicated. But it is really quite simple. **Matter** is anything that has volume and mass.

Matter Has Volume

All matter takes up space. The amount of space taken up, or occupied, by an object is known as the object's **volume.** The sun, shown in **Figure 1,** has volume because it takes up space at the center of our solar system. Your fingernails, the Statue of Liberty, the continent of Africa, and a cloud all have volume. And because these things have volume, they cannot share the same space at the same time. Even the tiniest speck of dust takes up space, and there's no way another speck of dust can fit into that space without somehow bumping the first speck out of the way. Try the QuickLab on this page to see for yourself that matter takes up space.

Figure 1 *The volume of the sun is about 1,000,000 (1 million) times larger than the volume of the Earth.*

Liquid Volume Lake Erie, the smallest of the Great Lakes, has a volume of approximately 483,000,000,000,000 (483 trillion) liters of water. Can you imagine that much liquid? Well, think of a 2 liter bottle of soda. The water in Lake Erie could fill more than 241 trillion of those bottles. That's a lot of water! On a smaller scale, a can of soda has a volume of only 355 milliliters, which is approximately one-third of a liter. You can read the volume printed on the soda can. Or you can check the volume by pouring the soda into a large measuring cup from your kitchen, as shown in **Figure 2.**

Figure 2 *If the measurement is accurate, the volume measured should be the same as the volume printed on the can.*

Measuring the Volume of Liquids In your science class, you'll probably use a graduated cylinder to measure the volume of liquids. Keep in mind that the surface of a liquid in a graduated cylinder is not flat. The curve that you see at the liquid's surface has a special name—the **meniscus** (muh NIS kuhs). When you measure the volume of a liquid, you must look at the bottom of the meniscus, as shown in **Figure 3.** (A liquid in any container, including a measuring cup or a large beaker, has a meniscus. The meniscus is just too flat to see in a wider container.)

Liters (L) and milliliters (mL) are the units used most often to express the volume of liquids. The volume of any amount of liquid, from one raindrop to a can of soda to an entire ocean, can be expressed in these units.

Figure 3 *To measure volume correctly, read the scale at the lowest part of the meniscus (as indicated) at eye level.*

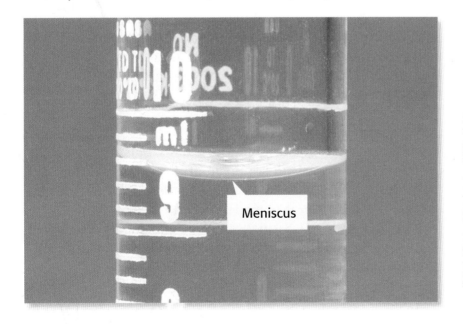

Meniscus

BRAIN FOOD

The volume of a typical raindrop is approximately 0.09 mL, which means that it would take almost 4,000 raindrops to fill a soda can.

MATH**BREAK**

Calculating Volume

A typical compact disc (CD) case has a length of 14.2 cm, a width of 12.4 cm, and a height of 1.0 cm. The volume of the case is the length multiplied by the width multiplied by the height:

14.2 cm × 12.4 cm × 1.0 cm = 176.1 cm³

Now It's Your Turn

1. A book has a length of 25 cm, a width of 18 cm, and a height of 4 cm. What is its volume?

2. What is the volume of a suitcase with a length of 95 cm, a width of 50 cm, and a height of 20 cm?

3. For additional practice, find the volume of other objects that have square or rectangular sides. Compare your results with those of your classmates.

How would you measure the volume of this strangely shaped object? To find out, turn to page 630 in the LabBook.

Solid Volume The volume of any solid object is expressed in cubic units. *Cubic* means "having three dimensions." One cubic unit, a cubic meter, is shown in **Figure 4.** In science, cubic meters (m^3) and cubic centimeters (cm^3) are the units most often used to express the volume of solid items. The *3* in these unit abbreviations shows that three quantities were multiplied to get the final result. For a rectangular object, these three quantities are length, width, and height. Try this for yourself in the MathBreak at left.

1 m

1 m³

1 m 1 m

Figure 4 *A cubic meter has a height of 1 m, a length of 1 m, and a width of 1 m, so its volume is 1 m × 1 m × 1 m = 1 m³.*

Comparing Solid and Liquid Volumes Suppose you want to determine whether the volume of an ice cube is equal to the volume of water that is left when the ice cube melts. Because 1 mL is equal to $1 cm^3$, you can express the volume of the water in cubic centimeters and compare it with the volume of the ice cube. The volume of any liquid can be expressed in cubic units in this way. (However, in SI, volumes of solids are never expressed in liters or milliliters.)

Measuring the Volume of Gases How do you measure the volume of a gas? You can't hold a ruler up to a gas, and you can't pour a gas into a graduated cylinder. So it's impossible, right? Wrong! A gas expands to fill its container, so if you know the volume of the container the gas is in, then you know the volume of the gas.

Matter Has Mass

Another characteristic of all matter is mass. **Mass** is the amount of matter that something is made of. For example, the Earth is made of a very large amount of matter and therefore has a large mass. A peanut is made of a much smaller amount of matter and thus has a smaller mass. Remember, even something as small as a speck of dust is made of matter and therefore has mass.

Is a Puppy Like a Bowling Ball? An object's mass can be changed only by changing the amount of matter in the object. Consider the bowling ball shown in **Figure 5**. Its mass is constant because the amount of matter in the bowling ball never changes (unless you use a sledgehammer to remove a chunk of it!). Now consider the puppy. Does its mass remain constant? No, because the puppy is growing. If you measured the puppy's mass next year or even next week, you'd find that it had increased. That's because more matter—more puppy—would be present.

Figure 5 *The mass of the bowling ball does not change. The mass of the puppy increases as more matter is added—that is, as the puppy grows.*

The Difference Between Mass and Weight

Weight is different from mass. To understand this difference, you must first understand gravity. **Gravity** is a force of attraction between objects that is due to their masses. This attraction causes objects to exert a pull on other objects. Because all matter has mass, all matter experiences gravity. The amount of attraction between objects depends on two things—the masses of the objects and the distance between them, as shown in **Figure 6**.

Figure 6   How Mass and Distance Affect Gravity Between Objects

a Gravitational force (represented by the width of the arrows) is large between objects with large masses that are close together.

b Gravitational force is smaller between objects with smaller masses that are close together than between objects with large masses that are close together (as shown in **a**).

c An increase in distance reduces gravitational force between two objects. Therefore, gravitational force between objects with large masses (such as those in **a**) is less if they are far apart.

Activity

Imagine the following items resting side by side on a table: an elephant, a tennis ball, a peanut, a bowling ball, and a housefly. In your ScienceLog, list these items in order of their attraction to the Earth due to gravity, from least to greatest amount of attraction. Follow your list with an explanation of why you arranged the items in the order that you did.

TRY at HOME

The mineral calcium is stored in bones, and it accounts for about 70 percent of the mass of the human skeleton. Calcium strengthens bones, helping the skeleton to remain upright against the strong force of gravity pulling it toward the Earth.

May the Force Be with You Gravitational force is experienced by all objects in the universe all the time. But the ordinary objects you see every day have masses so small (relative to, say, planets) that their attraction toward each other is hard to detect. Therefore, the gravitational force experienced by objects with small masses is very slight. However, the Earth's mass is so large that the gravitational force between objects, such as our atmosphere or the space shuttle, and the Earth is great. Gravitational force is what keeps you and everything else on Earth from floating into space.

So What About Weight? A measure of the gravitational force exerted on an object is called **weight.** Consider the brick in **Figure 7.** The brick has mass. The Earth also has mass. Therefore, the brick and the Earth are attracted to each other. A force is exerted on the brick because of its attraction to the Earth. The weight of the brick is a measure of this gravitational force.

Now look at the sponge in Figure 7. The sponge is the same size as the brick, but its mass is much less. Therefore, the sponge's attraction toward the Earth is not as great, and the gravitational force on the sponge is not as great. Thus, the *weight* of the sponge is less than the *weight* of the brick.

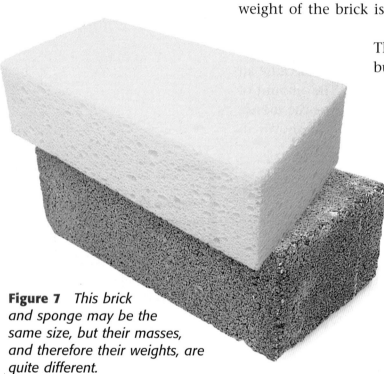

Figure 7 *This brick and sponge may be the same size, but their masses, and therefore their weights, are quite different.*

At a Distance The attraction between objects decreases as the distance between them increases. As a result, the gravitational force exerted on objects also decreases as the distance increases. For this reason, a brick floating in space would weigh less than it does resting on Earth's surface. However, the brick's mass would stay the same.

Massive Confusion Back on Earth, the gravitational force exerted on an object is about the same everywhere, so an object's weight is also about the same everywhere. Because mass and weight remain constant everywhere on Earth, the terms *mass* and *weight* are often used as though they mean the same thing. But using the terms interchangeably can lead to confusion. So remember, weight depends on mass, but weight is not the same thing as mass.

Measuring Mass and Weight

The SI unit of mass is the kilogram (kg), but mass is often expressed in grams (g) and milligrams (mg) as well. These units can be used to express the mass of any object, from a single cell in your body to the entire solar system. Weight is a measure of gravitational force and must be expressed in units of force. The SI unit of force is the **newton (N).** So weight is expressed in newtons.

A newton is approximately equal to the weight of a 100 g mass on Earth. So if you know the mass of an object, you can calculate its weight on Earth. Conversely, if you know the weight of an object on Earth, you can determine its mass. **Figure 8** summarizes the differences between mass and weight.

Figure 8   Differences Between Mass and Weight

Mass is . . .

- a measure of the amount of matter in an object.

- always constant for an object no matter where the object is in the universe.

- measured with a balance (shown below).

- expressed in kilograms (kg), grams (g), and milligrams (mg).

Weight is . . .

- a measure of the gravitational force on an object.

- varied depending on where the object is in relation to the Earth (or any other large body in the universe).

- measured with a spring scale (shown above).

- expressed in newtons (N).

> ✔ **Self-Check**
>
> If all of your school books combined have a mass of 3 kg, what is their total weight in newtons? Remember that 1 kg = 1,000 g. *(See page 724 to check your answer.)*

Mass, Weight, and Bathroom Scales

Ordinary bathroom scales are spring scales. Many scales available today show a reading in both pounds (a common, though not SI, unit of weight) and kilograms. How does such a reading contribute to the confusion between mass and weight?

Mass Is a Measure of Inertia

Imagine trying to kick a soccer ball that has the mass of a bowling ball. It would be painful! The reason has to do with inertia (in UHR shuh). **Inertia** is the tendency of all objects to resist any change in motion. Because of inertia, an object at rest will remain at rest until something causes it to move. Likewise, a moving object continues to move at the same speed and in the same direction unless something acts on it to change its speed or direction.

Mass is a measure of inertia because an object with a large mass is harder to start in motion and harder to stop than an object with a smaller mass. This is because the object with the large mass has greater inertia. For example, imagine that you are going to push a grocery cart that has only one potato in it. No problem, right? But suppose the grocery cart is filled with potatoes, as in **Figure 9.** Now the total mass— and the inertia—of the cart full of potatoes is much greater. It will be harder to get the cart moving and harder to stop it once it is moving.

Figure 9 *Why is a cartload of potatoes harder to get moving than a single potato? Because of inertia, that's why!*

internetconnect

SC*i*LINKS.
NSTA

TOPIC: What Is Matter?
GO TO: www.scilinks.org
*sci*LINKS NUMBER: HSTP030

REVIEW

1. What are the two properties of all matter?

2. How is volume measured? How is mass measured?

3. **Analyzing Relationships** Do objects with large masses always have large weights? Explain your reasoning.

Describing Matter

Have you ever heard of the game called "20 Questions"? In this game, your goal is to determine the identity of an object that another person is thinking of by asking questions about the object. The other person can respond with only a "yes" or a "no." If you can identify the object after asking 20 or fewer questions, you win! If you still can't figure out the object's identity after asking 20 questions, you may not be asking the right kinds of questions.

What kinds of questions should you ask? You might find it helpful to ask questions about the properties of the object. Knowing the properties of an object can help you determine the object's identity, as shown below.

Terms to Learn

physical property   physical change
density   chemical change
chemical property

What You'll Do

◆ Give examples of matter's different properties.
◆ Describe how density is used to identify different substances.
◆ Compare physical and chemical properties.
◆ Explain what happens to matter during physical and chemical changes.

Could I hold it in my hand?   Yes.

Does it have an odor?   Yes.

Is it safe to eat?   Yes.

Is it an apple?   Yes.

Is it orange?   No.
Yellow?   No.
Red?   Yes.

Activity

With a partner, play a game of 20 Questions. One person will think of an object, and the other person will ask yes/no questions about it. Write the questions in your ScienceLog as you go along. Put a check mark next to the questions asked about physical properties. When the object is identified or when the 20 questions are up, switch roles. Good luck!

Physical Properties

Some of the questions shown above help the asker gather information about *color* (Is it orange?), *odor* (Does it have an odor?), and *mass* and *volume* (Could I hold it in my hand?). Each of these properties is a physical property of matter. A **physical property** of matter can be observed or measured without changing the identity of the matter. For example, you don't have to change what the apple is made of to see that it is red or to hold it in your hand.

Physical Properties Identify Matter You rely on physical properties all the time. For example, physical properties help you determine whether your socks are clean (odor), whether you can fit all your books into your backpack (volume), or whether your shirt matches your pants (color). The table below lists some more physical properties that are useful in describing or identifying matter.

More Physical Properties		
Physical property	**Definition**	**Example**
Thermal conductivity	the ability to transfer thermal energy from one area to another	Plastic foam is a poor conductor, so hot chocolate in a plastic-foam cup will not burn your hand.
State	the physical form in which a substance exists, such as a solid, liquid, or gas	Ice is water in its solid state.
Malleability (MAL ee uh BIL uh tee)	the ability to be pounded into thin sheets	Aluminum can be rolled or pounded into sheets to make foil.
Ductility (duhk TIL uh tee)	the ability to be drawn or pulled into a wire	Copper is often used to make wiring.
Solubility (SAHL yoo BIL uh tee)	the ability to dissolve in another substance	Sugar dissolves in water.
Density	mass per unit volume	Lead is used to make sinkers for fishing line because lead is more dense than water.

Spotlight on Density Density is a very helpful property when you need to distinguish different substances. Look at the definition of density in the table above—mass per unit volume. If you think back to what you learned in Section 1, you can define density in other terms: **density** is the amount of matter in a given space, or volume, as shown in **Figure 10.**

Figure 10 *A golf ball is more dense than a table-tennis ball because the golf ball contains more matter in a similar volume.*

To find an object's density (D), first measure its mass (m) and volume (V). Then use the following equation:

$$D = \frac{m}{V}$$

Units for density are expressed using a mass unit divided by a volume unit, such as g/cm^3, g/mL, kg/m^3, and kg/L.

Using Density to Identify Substances Density is a useful property for identifying substances for two reasons. First, the density of a particular substance is always the same at a given pressure and temperature. For example, the helium in a huge airship has a density of $0.0001663 \ g/cm^3$ at 20°C and normal atmospheric pressure. You can calculate the density of any other sample of helium at that same temperature and pressure—even the helium in a small balloon—and you will get $0.0001663 \ g/cm^3$. Second, the density of one substance is usually different from that of another substance. Check out the table below to see how density varies among substances.

Densities of Common Substances*			
Substance	**Density (g/cm³)**	**Substance**	**Density (g/cm³)**
Helium (gas)	0.0001663	Copper (solid)	8.96
Oxygen (gas)	0.001331	Silver (solid)	10.50
Water (liquid)	1.00	Lead (solid)	11.35
Iron pyrite (solid)	5.02	Mercury (liquid)	13.55
Zinc (solid)	7.13	Gold (solid)	19.32

* at 20°C and normal atmospheric pressure

Mass = 96.6 g
Volume = 5.0 cm³

Figure 11 *Did you find gold or fool's gold?*

Do you remember your imaginary attempt at gold prospecting? To make sure you hadn't found more fool's gold (iron pyrite), you could compare the density of a nugget from your sample, shown in **Figure 11,** with the known densities for gold and iron pyrite at the same temperature and pressure. By comparing densities, you'd know whether you'd actually struck gold or been fooled again.

Figure 12 *The yellow liquid is the least dense, and the green liquid is the densest.*

Liquid Layers What do you think causes the liquid in **Figure 12** to look the way it does? Is it magic? Is it trick photography? No, it's differences in density! There are actually four different liquids in the jar. Each liquid has a different density. Because of these differences in density, the liquids do not mix together but instead separate into layers, with the densest layer on the bottom and the least dense layer on top. The order in which the layers separate helps you determine how the densities of the liquids compare with one another.

The Density Challenge Imagine that you could put a lid on the jar in the picture and shake up the liquids. Would the different liquids mix together so that the four colors would blend into one interesting color? Maybe for a minute or two. But if the liquids are not soluble in one another, they would start to separate, and eventually you'd end up with the same four layers.

The same thing happens when you mix oil and vinegar to make salad dressing. When the layers separate, the oil is on top. But what do you think would happen if you added more oil? What if you added so much oil that there was several times as much oil as there was vinegar? Surely the oil would get so heavy that it would sink below the vinegar, right? Wrong! No matter how much oil you have, it will always be less dense than the vinegar, so it will always rise to the top. The same is true of the four liquids shown in Figure 12. Even if you add more yellow liquid than all of the other liquids combined, all of the yellow liquid will rise to the top. That's because density does not depend on how much of a substance you have.

APPLY

Density and Grease Separators

The grease separator shown here is a kitchen device that cooks use to collect the best meat juices for making gravies. Based on what you know about density, describe how a grease separator works. Be sure to explain why the spout is at the bottom.

REVIEW

1. List three physical properties of water.

2. Why does a golf ball feel heavier than a table-tennis ball?

3. Describe how you can determine the relative densities of liquids.

4. **Applying Concepts** How could you determine that a coin is not pure silver?

Chemical Properties

Physical properties are not the only properties that describe matter. **Chemical properties** describe a substance based on its ability to change into a new substance with different properties. For example, a piece of wood can be burned to create new substances (ash and smoke) with properties different from the original piece of wood. Wood has the chemical property of *flammability*—the ability to burn. A substance that does not burn, such as gold, has the chemical property of nonflammability. Other common chemical properties include reactivity with oxygen, reactivity with acid, and reactivity with water. (The word *reactivity* just means that when two substances get together, something can happen.)

Observing Chemical Properties Chemical properties can be observed with your senses. However, chemical properties aren't as easy to observe as physical properties. For example, you can observe the flammability of wood only while the wood is burning. Likewise, you can observe the nonflammability of gold only when you try to burn it and it won't burn. But a substance always has its chemical properties. A piece of wood is flammable even when it's not burning.

Some Chemical Properties of Car Maintenance Look at the old car shown in **Figure 13.** Its owner calls it Rust Bucket. Why has this car rusted so badly while some other cars the same age remain in great shape? Knowing about chemical properties can help answer this question.

Most car bodies are made from steel, which is mostly iron. Iron has many desirable physical properties, including strength, malleability, and a high melting point. Iron also has many desirable chemical properties, including nonreactivity with oil and gasoline. All in all, steel is a good material to use for car bodies. It's not perfect, however, as you can probably tell from the car shown here.

Paint doesn't react with oxygen, so it provides a barrier between oxygen and the iron in the steel.

This hole started as a small chip in the paint. The chip exposed the iron in the car's body to oxygen. The iron rusted and eventually crumbled away.

Figure 13   Rust Bucket
One unfavorable chemical property of iron is its reactivity with oxygen. When iron is exposed to oxygen, it rusts.

This bumper is rust free because it is coated with a barrier of chromium, which is nonreactive with oxygen.

Physical Vs. Chemical Properties

Figure 14 *Substances have different physical and chemical properties.*

You can describe matter by both physical and chemical properties. The properties that are most useful in identifying a substance, such as density, solubility, and reactivity with acids, are its characteristic properties. The *characteristic properties* of a substance are always the same whether the sample you're observing is large or small. Scientists rely on characteristic properties to identify and classify substances. **Figure 14** describes some physical and chemical properties.

It is important to remember the differences between physical and chemical properties. For example, you can observe physical properties without changing the identity of the substance. You can observe chemical properties only in situations in which the identity of the substance could change.

a Helium is used in airships because it is less dense than air and is nonflammable.

b If you add bleach to water that is mixed with red food coloring, the red color will disappear.

Comparing Physical and Chemical Properties		
Substance	**Physical property**	**Chemical property**
Helium	less dense than air	nonflammable
Wood	grainy texture	flammable
Baking soda	white powder	reacts with vinegar to produce bubbles
Powdered sugar	white powder	does not react with vinegar
Rubbing alcohol	clear liquid	flammable
Red food coloring	red color	reacts with bleach and loses color
Iron	malleable	reacts with oxygen

Physical Changes Don't Form New Substances

A **physical change** is a change that affects one or more physical properties of a substance. For example, if you break a piece of chalk in two, you change its physical properties of size and shape. But no matter how many times you break it, chalk is still chalk. The chemical properties of the chalk remain unchanged. Each piece of chalk would still produce bubbles if you placed it in vinegar.

Examples of Physical Changes Melting is a good example of a physical change, as you can see in **Figure 15**. Still another physical change occurs when a substance dissolves into another substance. If you dissolve sugar in water, the sugar seems to disappear into the water. But the identity of the sugar does not change. If you taste the water, you will also still taste the sugar. The sugar has undergone a physical change. See the chart below for more examples of physical changes.

Figure 15 *A physical change turned a stick of butter into the liquid butter that makes popcorn so tasty, but the identity of the butter did not change.*

More Examples of Physical Changes

- Freezing water for ice cubes
- Sanding a piece of wood
- Cutting your hair
- Crushing an aluminum can
- Bending a paper clip
- Mixing oil and vinegar

Can Physical Changes Be Undone? Because physical changes do not change the identity of substances, they are often easy to undo. If you leave butter out on a warm counter, it will undergo a physical change—it will melt. Putting it back in the refrigerator will reverse this change. Likewise, if you create a figure from a lump of clay, you change the clay's shape, causing a physical change. But because the identity of the clay does not change, you can crush your creation and form the clay back into its previous shape.

Chemical Changes Form New Substances

A **chemical change** occurs when one or more substances are changed into entirely new substances with different properties. Chemical changes will or will not occur as described by the chemical properties of substances. But chemical changes and chemical properties are not the same thing. A chemical property describes a substance's ability to go through a chemical change; a chemical change is the actual process in which that substance changes into another substance. You can observe chemical properties only when a chemical change might occur.

QuickLab

Changing Change

1. Place a folded **paper towel** in a **small pie plate.**

2. Pour **vinegar** into the pie plate until the entire paper towel is damp.

3. Place **two or three shiny pennies** on top of the paper towel.

4. Put the pie plate in a place where it won't be bothered, and wait 24 hours.

5. Describe the chemical change that took place.

6. Write your observations in your ScienceLog.

A fun (and delicious) way to see what happens during chemical changes is to bake a cake. When you bake a cake, you combine eggs, flour, sugar, butter, and other ingredients as shown in **Figure 16.** Each ingredient has its own set of properties. But if you mix them together and bake the batter in the oven, you get something completely different. The heat of the oven and the interaction of the ingredients cause a chemical change. As shown in **Figure 17,** you get a cake that has properties completely different to any of the ingredients. Some more examples of chemical changes are shown below.

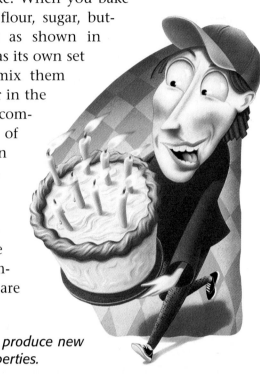

Figure 16 *Each of these ingredients has different physical and chemical properties.*

Figure 17 *Chemical changes produce new substances with different properties.*

Examples of Chemical Changes

Soured milk smells bad because bacteria have formed new substances in the milk.

Effervescent tablets bubble when the citric acid and baking soda in them react with water.

The hot gas formed when hydrogen and oxygen join to make water helps blast the space shuttle into orbit.

The Statue of Liberty is made of shiny, orange-brown copper. But the metal's interaction with carbon dioxide and water has formed a new substance, copper carbonate, and made this landmark lady green over time.

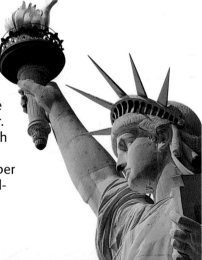

Clues to Chemical Changes Look back at the bottom of the previous page. In each picture, there is at least one clue that signals a chemical change. Can you find the clues? Here's a hint: chemical changes often cause color changes, fizzing or foaming, heat, or the production of sound, light, or odor.

In the cake example, you would probably smell the sweet aroma of the cake as it baked. If you looked into the oven, you would see the batter rise and turn brown. When you cut the finished cake, you would see the spongy texture created by gas bubbles that formed in the batter (if you baked it right, that is!). All of these yummy clues are signals of chemical changes. But are the clues and the chemical changes the same thing? No, the clues just result from the chemical changes.

Can Chemical Changes Be Undone? Because new substances are formed, you cannot reverse chemical changes using physical means. In other words, you can't uncrumple or iron out a chemical change. Imagine trying to un-bake the cake shown in **Figure 18** by pulling out each ingredient. No way! Most of the chemical changes you see in your daily life, such as a cake baking or milk turning sour, would be difficult to reverse. However, some chemical changes can be reversed under the right conditions by other chemical changes. For example, the water formed in the space shuttle's rockets could be split back into hydrogen and oxygen using an electric current.

Environment

CONNECTION

When fossil fuels are burned, a chemical change takes place involving sulfur (a substance in fossil fuels) and oxygen (from the air). This chemical change produces sulfur dioxide, a gas. When sulfur dioxide enters the atmosphere, it undergoes another chemical change by interacting with water and oxygen. This chemical change produces sulfuric acid, a contributor to acid precipitation. Acid precipitation can kill trees and make ponds and lakes unable to support life.

Figure 18 *Looking for the original ingredients? You won't find them—their identities have changed.*

REVIEW

1. Classify each of the following properties as either physical or chemical: reacts with water, dissolves in acetone, is blue, does not react with hydrogen.

2. List three clues that indicate a chemical change might be taking place.

3. **Comparing Concepts** Describe the difference between physical changes and chemical changes in terms of what happens to the matter involved in each kind of change.

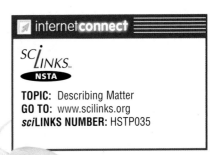

internet**connect**

SC*i*LINKS
NSTA

TOPIC: Describing Matter
GO TO: www.scilinks.org
*sci*LINKS **NUMBER:** HSTP035

Chapter Highlights

Vocabulary

matter *(p. 36)*

volume *(p. 36)*

meniscus *(p. 37)*

mass *(p. 38)*

gravity *(p. 39)*

weight *(p. 40)*

newton *(p. 41)*

inertia *(p. 42)*

Section Notes

• Matter is anything that has volume and mass.

• Volume is the amount of space taken up by an object.

• The volume of liquids is expressed in liters and milliliters.

• The volume of solid objects is expressed in cubic units, such as cubic meters.

• Mass is the amount of matter that something is made of.

• Mass and weight are not the same thing. Weight is a measure of the gravitational force exerted on an object, usually in relation to the Earth.

• Mass is usually expressed in milligrams, grams, and kilograms.

• The newton is the SI unit of force, so weight is expressed in newtons.

• Inertia is the tendency of all objects to resist any change in motion. Mass is a measure of inertia. The more massive an object is, the greater its inertia.

Labs

Volumania! *(p. 630)*

☑ Skills Check

Math Concepts

DENSITY To calculate an object's density, divide the mass of the object by its volume. For example, the density of an object with a mass of 45 g and a volume of 5.5 cm³ is calculated as follows:

$$D = \frac{m}{V}$$

$$D = \frac{45 \text{ g}}{5.5 \text{ cm}^3}$$

$$D = 8.2 \text{ g/cm}^3$$

Visual Understanding

MASS AND WEIGHT
Mass and weight are related, but they're not the same thing. Look back at Figure 8 on page 41 to learn about the differences between mass and weight.

PHYSICAL AND CHEMICAL PROPERTIES All substances have physical and chemical properties. You can compare some of those properties by reviewing the table on page 48.

Vocabulary

physical property *(p. 43)*
density *(p. 44)*
chemical property *(p. 47)*
physical change *(p. 48)*
chemical change *(p. 49)*

Section Notes

- Physical properties of matter can be observed without changing the identity of the matter.

- Density is the amount of matter in a given space, or the mass per unit volume.

- The density of a substance is always the same at a given pressure and temperature regardless of the size of the sample of the substance.

- Chemical properties describe a substance based on its ability to change into a new substance with different properties.

- Chemical properties can be observed only when one substance might become a new substance.

- The characteristic properties of a substance are always the same whether the sample observed is large or small.

- When a substance undergoes a physical change, its identity remains the same.

- A chemical change occurs when one or more substances are changed into new substances with different properties.

Labs

Determining Density *(p. 632)*
Layering Liquids *(p. 633)*
White Before Your Eyes *(p. 634)*

internetconnect

GO TO: go.hrw.com

Visit the **HRW** Web site for a variety of learning tools related to this chapter. Just type in the keyword:

KEYWORD: HSTMAT

GO TO: www.scilinks.org

Visit the **National Science Teachers Association** on-line Web site for Internet resources related to this chapter. Just type in the *sci*LINKS number for more information about the topic:

TOPIC: What Is Matter?	*sci*LINKS **NUMBER:** HSTP030
TOPIC: Describing Matter	*sci*LINKS **NUMBER:** HSTP035
TOPIC: Dark Matter	*sci*LINKS **NUMBER:** HSTP040
TOPIC: Building a Better Body	*sci*LINKS **NUMBER:** HSTP045

Chapter Review

USING VOCABULARY

For each pair of terms, explain the difference in their meanings.

1. mass/volume

2. mass/weight

3. inertia/mass

4. volume/density

5. physical property/chemical property

6. physical change/chemical change

UNDERSTANDING CONCEPTS

Multiple Choice

7. Which of these is *not* matter?
   a. a cloud
   b. your hair
   c. sunshine
   d. the sun

8. The mass of an elephant on the moon would be
   a. less than its mass on Mars.
   b. more than its mass on Mars.
   c. the same as its weight on the moon.
   d. None of the above

9. Which of the following is *not* a chemical property?
   a. reactivity with oxygen
   b. malleability
   c. flammability
   d. reactivity with acid

10. Your weight could be expressed in which of the following units?
    a. pounds
    b. newtons
    c. kilograms
    d. both (a) and (b)

11. You accidentally break your pencil in half. This is an example of
    a. a physical change.
    b. a chemical change.
    c. density.
    d. volume.

12. Which of the following statements about density is true?
    a. Density depends on mass and volume.
    b. Density is weight per unit volume.
    c. Density is measured in milliliters.
    d. Density is a chemical property.

13. Which of the following pairs of objects would have the greatest attraction toward each other due to gravity?
    a. a 10 kg object and a 10 kg object, 4 m apart
    b. a 5 kg object and a 5 kg object, 4 m apart
    c. a 10 kg object and a 10 kg object, 2 m apart
    d. a 5 kg object and a 5 kg object, 2 m apart

14. Inertia increases as ___?___ increases.
    a. time
    b. length
    c. mass
    d. volume

Short Answer

15. In one or two sentences, explain the different processes in measuring the volume of a liquid and measuring the volume of a solid.

16. In one or two sentences, explain the relationship between mass and inertia.

17. What is the formula for calculating density?

18. List three characteristic properties of matter.

Concept Mapping

19. Use the following terms to create a concept map: matter, mass, inertia, volume, milliliters, cubic centimeters, weight, gravity.

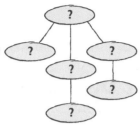

24. What is the volume of a book with the following dimensions: a width of 10 cm, a length that is two times the width, and a height that is half the width? Remember to express your answer in cubic units.

25. A jar contains 30 mL of glycerin (mass = 37.8 g) and 60 mL of corn syrup (mass = 82.8 g). Which liquid is on top? Show your work, and explain your answer.

CRITICAL THINKING AND PROBLEM SOLVING

20. You are making breakfast for your picky friend, Filbert. You make him scrambled eggs. He asks, "Would you please take these eggs back to the kitchen and poach them?" What scientific reason do you give Filbert for not changing his eggs?

Poach these, please!

INTERPRETING GRAPHICS

Examine the photograph below, and answer the following questions:

26. List three physical properties of this can.

27. Did a chemical change or a physical change cause the change in this can's appearance?

28. How does the density of the metal in the can compare before and after the change?

29. Can you tell what the chemical properties of the can are just by looking at the picture? Explain.

21. You look out your bedroom window and see your new neighbors moving in. Your neighbor bends over to pick up a small cardboard box, but he cannot lift it. What can you conclude about the item(s) in the box? Use the terms *mass* and *inertia* to explain how you came to this conclusion.

22. You may sometimes hear on the radio or on television that astronauts are "weightless" in space. Explain why this is not true.

23. People commonly use the term *volume* to describe the capacity of a container. How does this definition of volume differ from the scientific definition?

Reading Check-up

Take a minute to review your answers to the Pre-Reading Questions found at the bottom of page 34. Have your answers changed? If necessary, revise your answers based on what you have learned since you began this chapter.

In the Dark About Dark Matter

What is the universe made of? Believe it or not, when astronomers try to answer this question, they still find themselves in the dark. Surprisingly, there is more to the universe than meets the eye.

A Matter of Gravity

Astronomers noticed something odd when studying the motions of galaxies in space. They expected to find a lot of mass in the galaxies. Instead, they discovered that the mass of the galaxies was not great enough to explain the large gravitational force causing the galaxies' rapid rotation. So what was causing the additional gravitational force? Some scientists think the universe contains matter that we cannot see with our eyes or our telescopes. Astronomers call this invisible matter *dark matter.*

Dark matter doesn't reveal itself by giving off any kind of electromagnetic radiation, such as visible light, radio waves, or gamma radiation. According to scientific calculations, dark matter could account for between 90 and 99 percent of the total mass of the universe! What is dark matter? Would you believe MACHOs and WIMPs?

MACHOs

Scientists recently proved the existence of *MAssive Compact Halo Objects* (MACHOs) in our Milky Way galaxy by measuring their gravitational effects. Even though scientists know MACHOs exist, they aren't sure what MACHOs are made of. Scientists suggest that MACHOs may be brown dwarfs, old white dwarfs, neutron stars, or black holes. Others suggest they

▲ *The Large Magellanic Cloud, located 180,000 light-years from Earth*

are some type of strange, new object whose properties still remain unknown. Even though the number of MACHOs is apparently very great, they still do not represent enough missing mass. So scientists offer another candidate for dark matter—WIMPs.

WIMPs

Theories predict that *Weakly Interacting Massive Particles* (WIMPs) exist, but scientists have never detected them. WIMPs are thought to be massive elementary particles that do not interact strongly with normal matter (which is why scientists have not found them).

More Answers Needed

So far, evidence supports the existence of MACHOs, but there is little or no solid evidence of WIMPs or any other form of dark matter. Scientists who support the idea of WIMPs are conducting studies of the particles that make up matter to see if they can detect WIMPs. Other theories are that gravity acts differently around galaxies or that the universe is filled with things called "cosmic strings." Scientists admit they have a lot of work to do before they will be able to describe the universe—and all the matter in it.

On Your Own

▶ What is microlensing, and what does it have to do with MACHOs? How might the neutrino provide valuable information to scientists who are interested in proving the existence of WIMPs? Find out on your own!

Health WATCH

Building a Better Body

Have you ever broken an arm or a leg? If so, you probably wore a cast while the bone healed. But what happens when a bone is too badly damaged to heal? In some cases, a false bone made from a metal called titanium can take the original bone's place. Could using titanium bone implants be the first step in creating bionic body parts? Think about it as you read about some of titanium's amazing properties.

▲ *Titanium bones—even better than the real thing?*

Imitating the Original

Why would a metal like titanium be used to imitate natural bone? Well, it turns out that a titanium implant passes some key tests for bone replacement. First of all, real bones are incredibly lightweight and sturdy, and healthy bones last for many years. Therefore, a bone-replacement material has to be lightweight but also very durable. Titanium passes this test because it is well known for its strength, and it is also lightweight.

Second, the human body's immune system is always on the lookout for foreign substances. If a doctor puts a false bone in place and the patient's immune system attacks it, an infection can result. Somehow, the false bone must be able to chemically trick the body into thinking that the bone is real. Does titanium pass this test? Keep reading!

Accepting Imitation

By studying the human body's immune system, scientists found that the body accepts certain metals. The body almost always accepts one metal in particular. Yep, you guessed it—titanium! This turned out to be quite a discovery.

Doctors could implant pieces of titanium into a person's body without triggering an immune reaction. A bond can even form between titanium and existing bone tissue, fusing the bone to the metal!

Titanium is shaping up to be a great bone-replacement material. It is lightweight and strong, is accepted by the body, can attach to existing bone, and resists chemical changes, such as corrosion. But scientists have encountered a slight problem. Friction can wear away titanium bones, especially those used near the hips and elbows.

Real Success

An unexpected surprise, not from the field of medicine but from the field of nuclear physics, may have solved the problem. Researchers have learned that by implanting a special form of nitrogen on the surface of a piece of metal, they can create a surface layer on the metal that is especially durable and wear-resistant. When this form of nitrogen is implanted in titanium bones, the bones retain all the properties of pure titanium bones but also become very wear-resistant. The new bones should last through decades of heavy use without needing to be replaced.

Think About It

▶ What will the future hold? As time goes by, doctors become more successful at implanting titanium bones. What do you think would happen if the titanium bones were to eventually become better than real bones?

States of Matter

Pre-Reading Questions

1. What are the four most familiar states of matter?

2. Compare the motion of particles in a solid, a liquid, and a gas.

3. Name three ways matter changes from one state to another.

IT TAKES METTLE TO MELT METAL

If you wanted to make a flavored ice pop, you would pour juice into a mold and freeze it. You are able to make the ice pop into the desired shape because, unlike solids, liquids will take the shape of their container. Metal workers apply this important property of liquids when they create metal parts that have complicated shapes. They melt the metal at extremely high temperatures and then pour it into a mold. In this chapter, you will find out more about the properties of different states of matter.

VANISHING ACT

In this activity, you will use rubbing alcohol to investigate a change of state.

Procedure

1. Pour **rubbing alcohol** into a **small plastic cup** until the alcohol just covers the bottom of the cup.

2. Moisten the tip of a **cotton swab** by dipping it into the alcohol in the cup.

3. Rub the cotton swab on the palm of your hand.

4. Record your observations in your ScienceLog.

5. Wash your hands thoroughly.

Analysis

6. Explain what happened to the alcohol.

7. Did you feel a sensation of hot or cold? If so, how do you explain what you observed?

8. Record your answers in your ScienceLog.

Terms to Learn

states of matter   pressure
solid   Boyle's law
liquid   Charles's law
gas   plasma

What You'll Do

◆ Describe the properties shared by particles of all matter.
◆ Describe the four states of matter discussed here.
◆ Describe the differences between the states of matter.
◆ Predict how a change in pressure or temperature will affect the volume of a gas.

Four States of Matter

Figure 1 shows a model of the earliest known steam engine, invented about A.D. 60 by Hero, a scientist who lived in Alexandria, Egypt. This model also demonstrates the four most familiar states of matter: solid, liquid, gas, and plasma. The **states of matter** are the physical forms in which a substance can exist. For example, water commonly exists in three different states of matter: solid (ice), liquid (water), and gas (steam).

Figure 1 *This model of Hero's steam engine spins as steam escapes through the nozzles.*

Moving Particles Make Up All Matter

Matter consists of tiny particles called atoms and molecules (MAHL i kyoolz) that are too small to see without an amazingly powerful microscope. These atoms and molecules are always in motion and are constantly bumping into one another. The state of matter of a substance is determined by how fast the particles move and how strongly the particles are attracted to one another. **Figure 2** illustrates three of the states of matter—solid, liquid, and gas—in terms of the speed and attraction of the particles.

Figure 2 Models of a Solid, a Liquid, and a Gas

Particles of a solid do not move fast enough to overcome the strong attraction between them, so they are held tightly in place. The particles vibrate in place.

Particles of a liquid move fast enough to overcome some of the attraction between them. The particles are able to slide past one another.

Particles of a gas move fast enough to overcome nearly all of the attraction between them. The particles move independently of one another.

Solids Have Definite Shape and Volume

Look at the ship in **Figure 3.** Even in a bottle, it keeps its original shape and volume. If you moved the ship to a larger bottle, the ship's shape and volume would not change. Scientifically, the state in which matter has a definite shape and volume is **solid.** The particles of a substance in a solid are very close together. The attraction between them is stronger than the attraction between the particles of the same substance in the liquid or gaseous state. The atoms or molecules in a solid move, but not fast enough to overcome the attraction between them. Each particle vibrates in place because it is locked in position by the particles around it.

Figure 3 *Because this ship is a solid, it does not take the shape of the bottle.*

Two Types of Solids   Solids are often divided into two categories—*crystalline* and *amorphous* (uh MOHR fuhs). Crystalline solids have a very orderly, three-dimensional arrangement of atoms or molecules. That is, the particles are arranged in a repeating pattern of rows. Examples of crystalline solids include iron, diamond, and ice. Amorphous solids are composed of atoms or molecules that are in no particular order. That is, each particle is in a particular spot, but the particles are in no organized pattern. Examples of amorphous solids include rubber and wax. **Figure 4** illustrates the differences in the arrangement of particles in these two solids.

Activity

Imagine that you are a particle in a solid. Your position in the solid is your chair. In your ScienceLog, describe the different types of motion that are possible even though you cannot leave your chair.

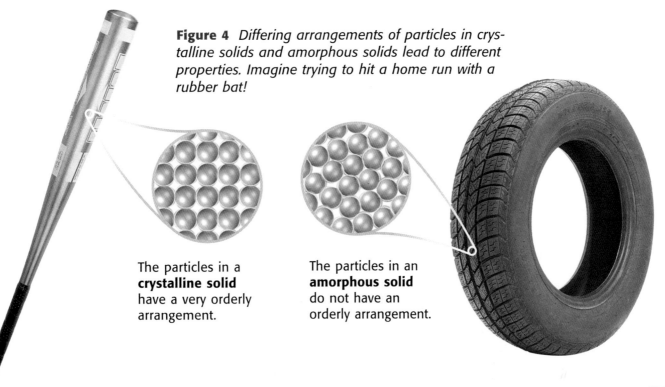

Figure 4 *Differing arrangements of particles in crystalline solids and amorphous solids lead to different properties. Imagine trying to hit a home run with a rubber bat!*

The particles in a **crystalline solid** have a very orderly arrangement.

The particles in an **amorphous solid** do not have an orderly arrangement.

Liquids Change Shape but Not Volume

A liquid will take the shape of whatever container it is put in. You are reminded of this every time you pour yourself a glass of juice. The state in which matter takes the shape of its container and has a definite volume is **liquid.** The atoms or molecules in liquids move fast enough to overcome some of the attractions between them. The particles slide past each other until the liquid takes the shape of its container. **Figure 5** shows how the particles in juice might look if they were large enough to see.

Even though liquids change shape, they do not readily change volume. You know that a can of soda contains a certain volume of liquid regardless of whether you pour it into a large container or a small one. **Figure 6** illustrates this point using a beaker and a graduated cylinder.

Figure 5 *Particles in a liquid slide past one another until the liquid conforms to the shape of its container.*

Figure 6 *Even when liquids change shape, they don't change volume.*

The Squeeze Is On   Because the particles in liquids are close to one another, it is difficult to push them closer together. This makes liquids ideal for use in hydraulic (hie DRAW lik) systems. For example, brake fluid is the liquid used in the brake systems of cars. Stepping on the brake pedal applies a force to the liquid. The particles in the liquid move away rather than squeezing closer together. As a result, the fluid pushes the brake pads outward against the wheels, which slows the car.

BRAIN FOOD

The Boeing 767 Freighter, a type of commercial airliner, has 187 km (116 mi) of hydraulic tubing.

A Drop in the Bucket Two other important properties of liquids are *surface tension* and *viscosity* (vis KAHS uh tee). Surface tension is the force acting on the particles at the surface of a liquid that causes the liquid to form spherical drops, as shown in **Figure 7.** Different liquids have different surface tensions. For example, rubbing alcohol has a lower surface tension than water, but mercury has a higher surface tension than water.

Viscosity is a liquid's resistance to flow. In general, the stronger the attractions between a liquid's particles are, the more viscous the liquid is. Think of the difference between pouring honey and pouring water. Honey flows more slowly than water because it has a higher viscosity than water.

Figure 7 *Liquids form spherical drops as a result of surface tension.*

Gases Change Both Shape and Volume

How many balloons can be filled from a single metal cylinder of helium? The number may surprise you. One cylinder can fill approximately 700 balloons. How is this possible? After all, the volume of the metal cylinder is equal to the volume of only about five inflated balloons.

It's a Gas! Helium is a gas. **Gas** is the state in which matter changes in both shape and volume. The atoms or molecules in a gas move fast enough to break away completely from one another. Therefore, the particles of a substance in the gaseous state have less attraction between them than particles of the same substance in the solid or liquid state. In a gas, there is empty space between particles.

The amount of empty space in a gas can change. For example, the helium in the metal cylinder consists of atoms that have been forced very close together, as shown in **Figure 8.** As the helium fills the balloon, the atoms spread out, and the amount of empty space in the gas increases. As you continue reading, you will learn how this empty space is related to pressure.

Figure 8 *The particles of the gas in the cylinder are much closer together than the particles of the gas in the balloons.*

Gas Under Pressure

Pressure is the amount of force exerted on a given area. You can think of this as the number of collisions of particles against the inside of the container. Compare the basketball with the beach ball in **Figure 9.** The balls have the same volume and contain particles of gas (air) that constantly collide with one another and with the inside surface of the balls. Notice, however, that there are more particles in the basketball than in the beach ball. As a result, more particles collide with the inside surface of the basketball than with the inside surface of the beach ball. When the number of collisions increases, the force on the inside surface of the ball increases. This increased force leads to increased pressure.

Self-Check

How would an increase in the speed of the particles affect the pressure of gas in a metal cylinder? *(See page 724 to check your answer.)*

Figure 9 *Both balls shown here are full of air, but the pressure in the basketball is higher than the pressure in the beach ball.*

The basketball has a higher pressure than the beach ball because the greater number of particles of gas are closer together. Therefore, they collide with the inside of the ball at a faster rate.

The beach ball has a lower pressure than the basketball because the lesser number of particles of gas are farther apart. Therefore, they collide with the inside of the ball at a slower rate.

internet**connect**

SC*i*LINKS
NSTA

TOPIC: Solids, Liquids, and Gases
GO TO: www.scilinks.org
*sci*LINKS NUMBER: HSTP060

REVIEW

1. List two properties that all particles of matter have in common.

2. Describe solids, liquids, and gases in terms of shape and volume.

3. Why can the volume of a gas change?

4. **Applying Concepts** Explain what happens inside the ball when you pump up a flat basketball.

Laws Describe Gas Behavior

Earlier in this chapter, you learned about the atoms and molecules in both solids and liquids. You learned that compared with gas particles, the particles of solids and liquids are closely packed together. As a result, solids and liquids do not change volume very much. Gases, on the other hand, behave differently; their volume can change by a large amount.

It is easy to measure the volume of a solid or liquid, but how do you measure the volume of a gas? Isn't the volume of a gas the same as the volume of its container? The answer is yes, but there are other factors, such as pressure, to consider.

Boyle's Law Imagine a diver at a depth of 10 m blowing a bubble of air. As the bubble rises, its volume increases. By the time the bubble reaches the surface, its original volume will have doubled due to the decrease in pressure. The relationship between the volume and pressure of a gas is known as Boyle's law because it was first described by Robert Boyle, a seventeenth-century Irish chemist. **Boyle's law** states that for a fixed amount of gas at a constant temperature, the volume of a gas increases as its pressure decreases. Likewise, the volume of a gas decreases as its pressure increases. Boyle's law is illustrated by the model in **Figure 10.**

Figure 10 Boyle's Law
Each illustration shows the same piston and the same amount of gas at the same temperature.

Lifting the plunger decreases the pressure of the gas. The particles of gas spread farther apart. The volume of the gas increases as the pressure decreases.

Releasing the plunger allows the gas to change to an intermediate volume and pressure.

Pushing the plunger increases the pressure of the gas. The particles of gas are forced closer together. The volume of the gas decreases as the pressure increases.

See Charles's law in action for yourself using a balloon on page 636 of the LabBook.

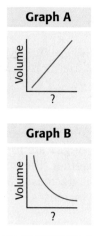

Weather balloons demonstrate a practical use of Boyle's law. A weather balloon carries equipment into the atmosphere to collect information used to predict the weather. This balloon is filled with only a small amount of gas because the pressure of the gas decreases and the volume increases as the balloon rises. If the balloon were filled with too much gas, it would pop as the volume of the gas increased.

Charles's Law An inflated balloon will also pop when it gets too hot, demonstrating another gas law—Charles's law. **Charles's law** states that for a fixed amount of gas at a constant pressure, the volume of the gas increases as its temperature increases. Likewise, the volume of the gas decreases as its temperature decreases. Charles's law is illustrated by the model in **Figure 11.** You can see Charles's law in action by putting an inflated balloon in the freezer. Wait about 10 minutes, and see what happens!

MATH BREAK

Gas Law Graphs

Each graph below illustrates a gas law. However, the variable on one axis of each graph is not labeled. Answer the following questions for each graph:

1. As the volume increases, what happens to the missing variable?

2. Which gas law is shown?

3. What label belongs on the axis?

4. Is the graph linear or non-linear? What does this tell you?

Graph A

Volume
?

Graph B

Volume
?

Figure 11 Charles's Law
Each illustration shows the same piston and the same amount of gas at the same pressure.

Lowering the temperature of the gas causes the particles to move more slowly. They hit the sides of the piston less often and with less force. As a result, the volume of the gas decreases.

Raising the temperature of the gas causes the particles to move more quickly. They hit the sides of the piston more often and with greater force. As a result, the volume of the gas increases.

Charles's Law and Bicycle Tires

One of your friends overinflated the tires on her bicycle. Use Charles's law to explain why she should let out some of the air before going for a ride on a hot day.

Plasmas

Scientists estimate that more than 99 percent of the known matter in the universe, including the sun and other stars, is made of a state of matter called plasma. **Plasma** is the state of matter that does not have a definite shape or volume and whose particles have broken apart.

Plasmas have some properties that are quite different from the properties of gases. Plasmas conduct electric current, while gases do not. Electric and magnetic fields affect plasmas but do not affect gases. In fact, strong magnetic fields are used to contain very hot plasmas that would destroy any other container.

Natural plasmas are found in lightning, fire, and the incredible light show in **Figure 12,** called the aurora borealis (ah ROHR uh BOHR ee AL is). Artificial plasmas, found in fluorescent lights and plasma balls, are created by passing electric charges through gases.

Figure 12 *Auroras, like the aurora borealis seen here, form when high-energy plasma collides with gas particles in the upper atmosphere.*

REVIEW

1. When scientists record the volume of a gas, why do they also record the temperature and the pressure?

2. List two differences between gases and plasmas.

3. **Applying Concepts** What happens to the volume of a balloon left on a sunny windowsill? Explain.

internet**connect**

*sc*LINKS
NSTA

TOPIC: Natural and Artificial Plasma
GO TO: www.scilinks.org
*sci*LINKS NUMBER: HSTP065

Changes of State

Terms to Learn

change of state   boiling
melting   evaporation
freezing   condensation
vaporization   sublimation

What You'll Do

◆ Describe how substances change from state to state.
◆ Explain the difference between an exothermic change and an endothermic change.
◆ Compare the changes of state.

A **change of state** is the conversion of a substance from one physical form to another. All changes of state are physical changes. In a physical change, the identity of a substance does not change. In **Figure 13,** the ice, liquid water, and steam are all the same substance—water. In this section, you will learn about the four changes of state illustrated in Figure 13 as well as a fifth change of state called *sublimation* (SUHB li MAY shuhn).

Figure 13 *The terms in the arrows are changes of state. Water commonly goes through the changes of state shown here.*

Energy and Changes of State

During a change of state, the energy of a substance changes. The *energy* of a substance is related to the motion of its particles. The molecules in the liquid water in Figure 13 move faster than the molecules in the ice. Therefore, the liquid water has more energy than the ice.

If energy is added to a substance, its particles move faster. If energy is removed, its particles move slower. The *temperature* of a substance is a measure of the speed of its particles and therefore is a measure of its energy. For example, steam has a higher temperature than liquid water, so particles in steam have more energy than particles in liquid water. A transfer of energy, known as *heat,* causes the temperature of a substance to change, which can lead to a change of state.

Want to learn how to get power from changes of state? Steam ahead to page 79.

Melting: Solids to Liquids

Melting is the change of state from a solid to a liquid. This is what happens when an ice cube melts. **Figure 14** shows a metal called gallium melting. What is unusual about this metal is that it melts at around 30°C. Because your normal body temperature is about 37°C, gallium will melt right in your hand!

The *melting point* of a substance is the temperature at which the substance changes from a solid to a liquid. Melting points of substances vary widely. The melting point of gallium is 30°C. Common table salt, however, has a melting point of 801°C.

Most substances have a unique melting point that can be used with other data to identify them. Because the melting point does not change with different amounts of the substance, melting point is a *characteristic property* of a substance.

Absorbing Energy For a solid to melt, particles must overcome some of their attractions to each other. When a solid is at its melting point, any energy it absorbs increases the motion of its atoms or molecules until they overcome the attractions that hold them in place. Melting is an *endothermic* change because energy is absorbed by the substance as it changes state.

Figure 14 *Even though gallium is a metal, it would not be very useful as jewelry!*

Freezing: Liquids to Solids

Freezing is the change of state from a liquid to a solid. The temperature at which a liquid changes into a solid is its *freezing point*. Freezing is the reverse process of melting, so freezing and melting occur at the same temperature, as shown in **Figure 15.**

Removing Energy For a liquid to freeze, the motion of its atoms or molecules must slow to the point where attractions between them overcome their motion. If a liquid is at its freezing point, removing more energy causes the particles to begin locking into place. Freezing is an *exothermic* change because energy is removed from, or taken out of, the substance as it changes state.

Figure 15 *Liquid water freezes at the same temperature that ice melts—0°C.*

If energy is added at 0°C, the ice will melt.

If energy is removed at 0°C, the liquid water will freeze.

Vaporization: Liquids to Gases

One way to experience vaporization (VAY puhr i ZAY shuhn) is to iron a shirt—carefully!—using a steam iron. You will notice steam coming up from the iron as the wrinkles are eliminated. This steam results from the vaporization of liquid water by the iron. **Vaporization** is simply the change of state from a liquid to a gas.

Boiling is vaporization that occurs throughout a liquid. The temperature at which a liquid boils is called its *boiling point*. Like the melting point, the boiling point is a characteristic property of a substance. The boiling point of water is 100°C, whereas the boiling point of liquid mercury is 357°C. **Figure 16** illustrates the process of boiling and a second form of vaporization—evaporation (ee VAP uh RAY shuhn).

Evaporation is vaporization that occurs at the surface of a liquid below its boiling point, as shown in Figure 16. When you perspire, your body is cooled through the process of evaporation. Perspiration is mostly water. Water absorbs energy from your skin as it evaporates. You feel cooler because your body transfers energy to the water. Evaporation also explains why water in a glass on a table disappears after several days.

Self-Check

Is vaporization an endothermic or exothermic change?
(See page 724 to check your answer.)

Figure 16 *Both boiling and evaporation change a liquid to a gas.*

Boiling point

Boiling point

Boiling occurs in a liquid at its boiling point. As energy is added to the liquid, particles throughout the liquid move fast enough to break away from the particles around them and become a gas.

Evaporation occurs in a liquid below its boiling point. Some particles at the surface of the liquid move fast enough to break away from the particles around them and become a gas.

Pressure Affects Boiling Point Earlier you learned that water boils at 100°C. In fact, water only boils at 100°C at sea level because of atmospheric pressure. Atmospheric pressure is caused by the weight of the gases that make up the atmosphere. Atmospheric pressure varies depending on where you are in relation to sea level. Atmospheric pressure is lower at higher elevations. The higher you go above sea level, the less air there is above you, and the lower the atmospheric pressure is. If you were to boil water at the top of a mountain, the boiling point would be lower than 100°C. For example, Denver, Colorado, is 1.6 km (1 mi) above sea level and water boils there at about 95°C. You can make water boil at an even lower temperature by doing the QuickLab at right.

Condensation: Gases to Liquids

Look at the cool glass of lemonade in **Figure 17.** Notice the beads of water on the outside of the glass. These form as a result of condensation. **Condensation** is the change of state from a gas to a liquid. The *condensation point* of a substance is the temperature at which the gas becomes a liquid and is the same temperature as the boiling point at a given pressure. Thus, at sea level, steam condenses to form water at 100°C—the same temperature at which water boils.

For a gas to become a liquid, large numbers of atoms or molecules must clump together. Particles clump together when the attraction between them overcomes their motion. For this to occur, energy must be removed from the gas to slow the particles down. Therefore, condensation is an exothermic change.

Figure 17 *Gaseous water in the air will become liquid when it contacts a cool surface.*

Boiling Water Is Cool

1. Remove the cap from a **syringe.**
2. Place the tip of the syringe in the **warm water** provided by your teacher. Pull the plunger out until you have 10 mL of water in the syringe.
3. Tightly cap the syringe.
4. Hold the syringe, and slowly pull the plunger out.
5. Observe any changes you see in the water. Record your observations in your ScienceLog.
6. Why are you not burned by the boiling water in the syringe?

Meteorology CONNECTION

The amount of gaseous water that air can hold decreases as the temperature of the air decreases. As the air cools, some of the gaseous water condenses to form small drops of liquid water. These drops form clouds in the sky and fog near the ground.

Sublimation: Solids Directly to Gases

Look at the solids shown in **Figure 18.** The solid on the left is ice. Notice the drops of liquid collecting as it melts. On the right, you see carbon dioxide in the solid state, also called dry ice. It is called dry ice because instead of melting into a liquid, it goes through a change of state called sublimation. **Sublimation** is the change of state from a solid directly into a gas. Dry ice is colder than ice, and it doesn't melt into a puddle of liquid. It is often used to keep food, medicine, and other materials cold without getting them wet.

For a solid to change directly into a gas, the atoms or molecules must move from being very tightly packed to being very spread apart. The attractions between the particles must be completely overcome. Because this requires the addition of energy, sublimation is an endothermic change.

Figure 18 *Ice melts, but dry ice, on the right, turns directly into a gas.*

Comparing Changes of State

As you learned in Section 1 of this chapter, the state of a substance depends on how fast its atoms or molecules move and how strongly they are attracted to each other. A substance may undergo a physical change from one state to another by an endothermic change (if energy is added) or an exothermic change (if energy is removed). The table below shows the differences between the changes of state discussed in this section.

Summarizing the Changes of State			
Change of state	**Direction**	**Endothermic or exothermic?**	**Example**
Melting	solid ⟶ liquid	endothermic	Ice melts into liquid water at 0°C.
Freezing	liquid ⟶ solid	exothermic	Liquid water freezes into ice at 0°C.
Vaporization	liquid ⟶ gas	endothermic	Liquid water vaporizes into steam at 100°C.
Condensation	gas ⟶ liquid	exothermic	Steam condenses into liquid water at 100°C.
Sublimation	solid ⟶ gas	endothermic	Solid dry ice sublimes into a gas at −78°C.

Temperature Change Versus Change of State

When most substances lose or absorb energy, one of two things happens to the substance: its temperature changes or its state changes. Earlier in the chapter, you learned that the temperature of a substance is a measure of the speed of the particles. This means that when the temperature of a substance changes, the speed of the particles also changes. But while a substance changes state, its temperature does not change until the change of state is complete, as shown in **Figure 19.**

Figure 19 Changing the State of Water

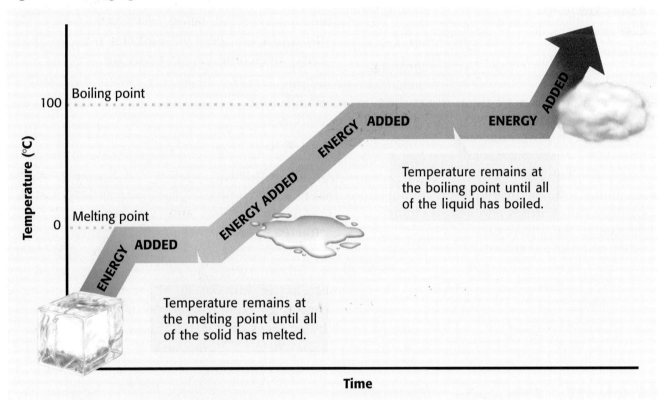

Boiling point

100

Temperature (°C)

Melting point

0

ENERGY ADDED

ENERGY ADDED

ENERGY ADDED

ENERGY ADDED

Temperature remains at the boiling point until all of the liquid has boiled.

Temperature remains at the melting point until all of the solid has melted.

Time

REVIEW

1. Compare endothermic and exothermic changes.

2. Classify each change of state (melting, freezing, vaporization, condensation, and sublimation) as endothermic or exothermic.

3. Describe how the motion and arrangement of particles change as a substance freezes.

4. **Comparing Concepts** How are evaporation and boiling different? How are they similar?

internet**connect**

SC*LINKS*
NSTA

TOPIC: Changes of State
GO TO: www.scilinks.org
*sci*LINKS NUMBER: HSTP070

Chapter Highlights

Vocabulary

states of matter (*p. 60*)

solid (*p. 61*)

liquid (*p. 62*)

gas (*p. 63*)

pressure (*p. 64*)

Boyle's law (*p. 65*)

Charles's law (*p. 66*)

plasma (*p. 67*)

Section Notes

- The states of matter are the physical forms in which a substance can exist. The four most familiar states are solid, liquid, gas, and plasma.

- All matter is made of tiny particles called atoms and molecules that attract each other and move constantly.

- A solid has a definite shape and volume.

- A liquid has a definite volume but not a definite shape.

- A gas does not have a definite shape or volume. A gas takes the shape and volume of its container.

- Pressure is a force per unit area. Gas pressure increases as the number of collisions of gas particles increases.

- Boyle's law states that the volume of a gas increases as the pressure decreases if the temperature does not change.

- Charles's law states that the volume of a gas increases as the temperature increases if the pressure does not change.

- Plasmas are composed of particles that have broken apart. Plasmas do not have a definite shape or volume.

Labs

Full of Hot Air! (*p. 636*)

☑ Skills Check

Math Concepts

GRAPHING DATA The relationship between measured values can be seen by plotting the data on a graph. The top graph shows the linear relationship described by Charles's law—as the temperature of a gas increases, its volume increases. The bottom graph shows the nonlinear relationship described by Boyle's law—as the pressure of a gas increases, its volume decreases.

Visual Understanding

PARTICLE ARRANGEMENT Many of the properties of solids, liquids, and gases are due to the arrangement of the atoms or molecules of the substance. Review the models in Figure 2 on page 60 to study the differences in particle arrangement between the solid, liquid, and gaseous states.

SUMMARY OF THE CHANGES OF STATE Review the table on page 72 to study the direction of each change of state and whether energy is absorbed or removed during each change.

Vocabulary

change of state (p. 68)

melting (p. 69)

freezing (p. 69)

vaporization (p. 70)

boiling (p. 70)

evaporation (p. 70)

condensation (p. 71)

sublimation (p. 72)

Section Notes

- A change of state is the conversion of a substance from one physical form to another. All changes of state are physical changes.

- Exothermic changes release energy. Endothermic changes absorb energy.

- Melting changes a solid to a liquid. Freezing changes a liquid to a solid. The freezing point and melting point of a substance are the same temperature.

- Vaporization changes a liquid to a gas. There are two kinds of vaporization: boiling and evaporation.

- Boiling occurs throughout a liquid at the boiling point.

- Evaporation occurs at the surface of a liquid, at a temperature below the boiling point.

- Condensation changes a gas to a liquid.

- Sublimation changes a solid directly to a gas.

- Temperature does not change during a change of state.

Labs

Can Crusher (p. 637)

A Hot and Cool Lab (p. 638)

internetconnect

GO TO: go.hrw.com

Visit the **HRW** Web site for a variety of learning tools related to this chapter. Just type in the keyword:

KEYWORD: HSTSTA

SCiLINKS

NSTA

GO TO: www.scilinks.org

Visit the **National Science Teachers Association** on-line Web site for Internet resources related to this chapter. Just type in the sciLINKS number for more information about the topic:

TOPIC: Forms and Uses of Glass	sciLINKS NUMBER: HSTP055
TOPIC: Solids, Liquids, and Gases	sciLINKS NUMBER: HSTP060
TOPIC: Natural and Artificial Plasma	sciLINKS NUMBER: HSTP065
TOPIC: Changes of State	sciLINKS NUMBER: HSTP070
TOPIC: The Steam Engine	sciLINKS NUMBER: HSTP075

Chapter Review

USING VOCABULARY

For each pair of terms, explain the difference in meaning.

1. solid/liquid

2. Boyle's law/Charles's law

3. evaporation/boiling

4. melting/freezing

UNDERSTANDING CONCEPTS

Multiple Choice

5. Which of the following best describes the particles of a liquid?
   a. The particles are far apart and moving fast.
   b. The particles are close together but moving past each other.
   c. The particles are far apart and moving slowly.
   d. The particles are closely packed and vibrate in place.

6. Boiling points and freezing points are examples of
   a. chemical properties.   c. energy.
   b. physical properties.   d. matter.

7. During which change of state do atoms or molecules become more ordered?
   a. boiling   c. melting
   b. condensation   d. sublimation

8. Which of the following describes what happens as the temperature of a gas in a balloon increases?
   a. The speed of the particles decreases.
   b. The volume of the gas increases and the speed of the particles increases.
   c. The volume decreases.
   d. The pressure decreases.

9. Dew collects on a spider web in the early morning. This is an example of
   a. condensation.   c. sublimation.
   b. evaporation.   d. melting.

10. Which of the following changes of state is exothermic?
    a. evaporation   c. freezing
    b. sublimation   d. melting

11. What happens to the volume of a gas inside a piston if the temperature does not change but the pressure is reduced?
    a. increases
    b. stays the same
    c. decreases
    d. not enough information

12. The atoms and molecules in matter
    a. are attracted to one another.
    b. are constantly moving.
    c. move faster at higher temperatures.
    d. All of the above

13. Which of the following contains plasma?
    a. dry ice   c. a fire
    b. steam   d. a hot iron

Short Answer

14. Explain why liquid water takes the shape of its container but an ice cube does not.

15. Rank solids, liquids, and gases in order of decreasing particle speed.

16. Compare the density of iron in the solid, liquid, and gaseous states.

Concept Mapping

17. Use the following terms to create a concept map: states of matter, solid, liquid, gas, plasma, changes of state, freezing, vaporization, condensation, melting.

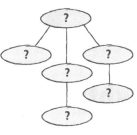

CRITICAL THINKING AND PROBLEM SOLVING

18. After taking a shower, you notice that small droplets of water cover the mirror. Explain how this happens. Be sure to describe where the water comes from and the changes it goes through.

19. In the photo below, water is being split to form two new substances, hydrogen and oxygen. Is this a change of state? Explain your answer.

20. To protect their crops during freezing temperatures, orange growers spray water onto the trees and allow it to freeze. In terms of energy lost and energy gained, explain why this practice protects the oranges from damage.

21. At sea level, water boils at 100°C, while methane boils at –161°C. Which of these substances has a stronger force of attraction between its particles? Explain your reasoning.

MATH IN SCIENCE

22. Kate placed 100 mL of water in five different pans, placed the pans on a windowsill for a week, and measured how much water evaporated. Draw a graph of her data, shown below, with surface area on the *x*-axis. Is the graph linear or nonlinear? What does this tell you?

Pan number	1	2	3	4	5
Surface area (cm²)	44	82	20	30	65
Volume evaporated (mL)	42	79	19	29	62

23. Examine the graph below, and answer the following questions:

   a. What is the boiling point of the substance? What is the melting point?

   b. Which state is present at 30°C?

   c. How will the substance change if energy is added to the liquid at 20°C?

Reading Check-up

Take a minute to review your answers to the Pre-Reading Questions found at the bottom of page 58. Have your answers changed? If necessary, revise your answers based on what you have learned since you began this chapter.

Science, Technology, and Society

Guiding Lightning

By the time you finish reading this sentence, lightning will have flashed more than 500 times around the world. This common phenomenon can have devastating results. Each year in the United States alone, lightning kills almost a hundred people and causes several hundred million dollars in damage. While controlling this awesome outburst of Mother Nature may seem impossible, scientists around the world are searching for ways to reduce the destruction caused by lightning.

Behind the Bolts

Scientists have learned that during a normal lightning strike several events occur. First, electric charges build up at the bottom of a cloud. The cloud then emits a line of negatively charged air particles that zigzags toward the Earth. The attraction between these negatively charged air particles and positively charged particles from objects on the ground forms a *plasma channel*. This channel is the pathway for a lightning bolt. As soon as the plasma channel is complete, BLAM!—between 3 and 20 lightning bolts separated by thousandths of a second travel along it.

A Stroke of Genius

Armed with this information, scientists have begun thinking of ways to redirect these naturally occurring plasma channels. One idea is to use laser beams. In theory, a laser beam directed into a thundercloud can charge the air particles in its path, causing a plasma channel to develop and forcing lightning to strike.

By creating the plasma channels themselves, scientists can, in a way, catch a bolt of lightning before it strikes and direct it to a safe area of the ground. So scientists simply use lasers to direct naturally occurring lightning to strike where they want it to.

A Bright Future?

Laser technology is not without its problems, however. The machines that generate laser beams are large and expensive, and they can themselves be struck by misguided lightning bolts. Also, it is not clear whether creating these plasma channels will be enough to prevent the devastating effects of lightning.

▲ *Sometime in the future, a laser like this might be used to guide lightning away from sensitive areas.*

Find Out for Yourself

► Use the Internet or an electronic database to find out how rockets have been used in lightning research. Share your findings with the class.

Eureka!

Full Steam Ahead!

It was huge. It was 40 m long, about 5 m high, and it weighed 245 metric tons. It could pull a 3.28 million kilogram train at 100 km/h. It was a 4-8-8-4 locomotive, called a Big Boy, delivered in 1941 to the Union Pacific Railroad in Omaha, Nebraska. It was also one of the final steps in a 2,000-year search to harness steam power.

A Simple Observation

For thousands of years, people used wind, water, gravity, dogs, horses, and cattle to replace manual labor. But until about 300 years ago, they had limited success. Then in 1690, Denis Papin, a French mathematician and physicist, observed that steam expanding in a cylinder pushed a piston up. As the steam then cooled and contracted, the piston fell. Watching the motion of the piston, Papin had an idea: attach a water-pump handle to the piston. As the pump handle rose and fell with the piston, water was pumped.

More Uplifting Ideas

Eight years later, an English naval captain named Thomas Savery made Papin's device more efficient by using water to cool and condense the steam. Savery's improved pump was used in British coal mines. As good as Savery's pump was, the development of steam power didn't stop there!

In 1712, an English blacksmith named Thomas Newcomen improved Savery's device by adding a second piston and a horizontal beam that acted like a seesaw. One end of the beam was attached to the piston in the steam cylinder. The other end of the beam was attached to the pump piston. As the steam piston moved up and down, it created a vacuum in the pump cylinder and sucked water up from the mine. Newcomen's engine was the most widely used steam engine for more than 50 years.

Watt a Great Idea!

In 1764, James Watt, a Scottish technician, was repairing a Newcomen engine. He realized that heating the cylinder, letting it cool, then heating it again wasted an enormous amount of energy. Watt added a separate chamber where the steam could cool and condense. The two chambers were connected by a valve that let the steam escape from the boiler. This improved the engine's efficiency—the boiler could stay hot all the time!

A few years later, Watt turned the whole apparatus on its side so that the piston was moving horizontally. He added a slide valve that admitted steam first to one end of the chamber (pushing the piston in one direction) and then to the other end (pushing the piston back). This changed the steam pump into a true steam engine that could drive a locomotive the size of Big Boy!

Explore Other Inventions

▶ Watt's engine helped trigger the Industrial Revolution as many new uses for steam power were found. Find out more about the many other inventors, from tinkerers to engineers, who harnessed the power of steam.

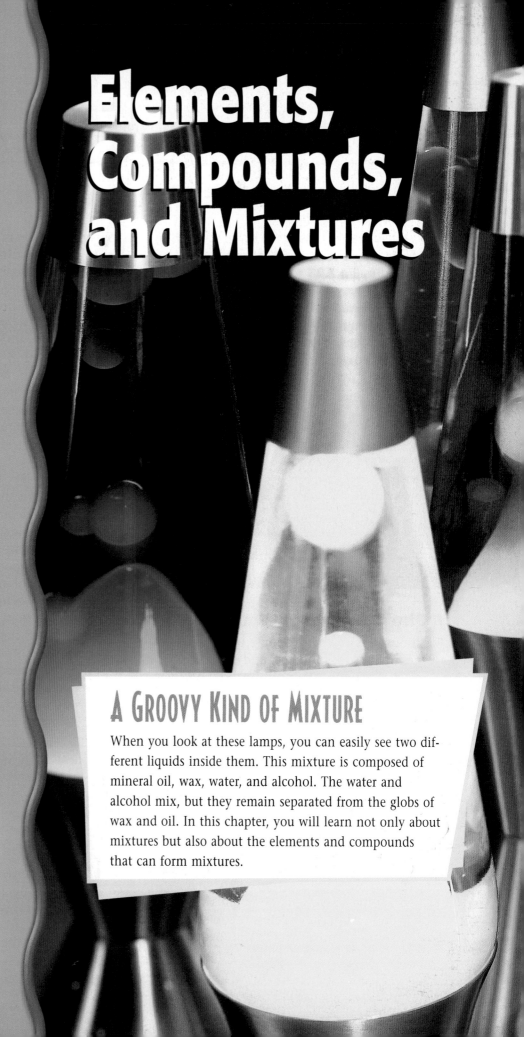

Elements, Compounds, and Mixtures

Pre-Reading Questions

1. What is an element?

2. What is a compound? How are compounds and mixtures different?

3. What are the components of a solution called?

A Groovy Kind of Mixture

When you look at these lamps, you can easily see two different liquids inside them. This mixture is composed of mineral oil, wax, water, and alcohol. The water and alcohol mix, but they remain separated from the globs of wax and oil. In this chapter, you will learn not only about mixtures but also about the elements and compounds that can form mixtures.

MYSTERY MIXTURE

In this activity, you will separate the different dyes found in an ink mixture.

Procedure

1. Tear a strip of paper (about 3 cm × 15 cm) from a **coffee filter.** Wrap one end of the strip around a **pencil** so that the other end will just touch the bottom of a **clear plastic cup.** Use **tape** to attach the paper to the pencil.

2. Take the paper out of the cup. Using a **water-soluble black marker,** make a small dot in the center of the strip about 2 cm from the bottom.

3. Pour **water** in the cup to a depth of 1 cm. Carefully lower the paper into the cup. Be sure the dot is not under water.

4. Remove the paper when the water is 1 cm from the top. Record your observations in your ScienceLog.

Analysis

5. Infer what happened as the filter paper soaked up the water.

6. Which colors were mixed to make your black ink?

7. Compare your results with those of your classmates. Record your observations.

8. Infer whether the process used to make the ink involved a physical or chemical change. Explain.

What You'll Do

◆ Describe pure substances.
◆ Describe the characteristics of elements, and give examples.
◆ Explain how elements can be identified.
◆ Classify elements according to their properties.

Elements

Imagine you are working as a lab technician for the Break-It-Down Corporation. Your job is to break down materials into the simplest substances you can obtain. One day a material seems particularly difficult to break down. You crush and grind it. You notice that the resulting pieces are smaller, but they are still the same material. You try other physical changes, including melting, boiling, and filtering it, but the material does not change into anything simpler.

Next you try some chemical changes. You pass an electric current through the material but it still does not become any simpler. After recording your observations, you analyze the results of your tests. You then draw a conclusion: the substance must be an element. An **element** is a pure substance that cannot be separated into simpler substances by physical or chemical means, as shown in **Figure 1.**

Figure 1 *No matter what kind of physical or chemical change you attempt, an element cannot be changed into a simpler substance!*

Figure 2 *The atoms of the element iron are alike whether they are in a meteorite or in a common iron skillet.*

An Element Has Only One Type of Particle

A **pure substance** is a substance in which there is only one type of particle. Because elements are pure substances, each element contains only one type of particle. For example, every particle (atom) in a 5 g nugget of the element gold is like every other particle of gold. The particles of a pure substance are alike no matter where that substance is found, as shown in **Figure 2.** Although a meteorite might travel more than 400 million kilometers (about 248 million miles) to reach Earth, the particles of iron in a meteorite are identical to the particles of iron in objects around your home!

Every Element Has a Unique Set of Properties

Each element has a unique set of properties that allows you to identify it. For example, each element has its own *characteristic properties*. These properties do not depend on the amount of material present in a sample of the element. Characteristic properties include some physical properties, such as boiling point, melting point, and density, as well as chemical properties, such as reactivity with acid. The elements helium and krypton are unreactive gases. However, the density (mass per unit volume) of helium is less than the density of air. Therefore, a helium-filled balloon will float up if it is released. Krypton is more dense than air, so a krypton-filled balloon will sink to the ground if it is released.

Identifying Elements by Their Properties Look at the elements cobalt, iron, and nickel, shown in **Figure 3.** Even though these three elements have some similar properties, each can be identified by its unique set of properties.

Notice that the physical properties for the elements in Figure 3 include melting point and density. Other physical properties, such as color, hardness, and texture, could be added to the list. Also, depending on the elements being identified, other chemical properties might be useful. For example, some elements, such as hydrogen and carbon, are flammable. Other elements, such as sodium, react immediately with oxygen. Still other elements, such as zinc, are reactive with acid.

Cobalt

Melting point is 1,495°C.
Density is 8.9 g/cm³.
Conducts electric current and thermal energy.
Unreactive with oxygen in the air.

Iron

Melting point is 1,535°C.
Density is 7.9 g/cm³.
Conducts electric current and thermal energy.
Combines slowly with oxygen in the air to form rust.

Nickel

Melting point is 1,455°C.
Density is 8.9 g/cm³.
Conducts electric current and thermal energy.
Unreactive with oxygen in the air.

Figure 3 *Like all other elements, cobalt, iron, and nickel can be identified by their unique combination of properties.*

Elements Are Classified by Their Properties

Consider how many different breeds of dogs there are. Consider also how you tell one breed from another. Most often you can tell just by their appearance, or what might be called physical properties. **Figure 4** shows several breeds of dogs, which all happen to be terriers. Many terriers are fairly small in size and have short hair. Although not all terriers are exactly alike, they share enough common properties to be classified in the same group.

Figure 4 *Even though these dogs are different breeds, they have enough in common to be classified as terriers.*

Elements Are Grouped into Categories

Elements are classified into groups according to their shared properties. Recall the elements iron, nickel, and cobalt. All three are shiny, and all three conduct thermal energy and electric current. Using these shared properties, scientists have grouped these three elements, along with other similar elements, into one large group called metals. Metals are not all exactly alike, but they do have some properties in common.

If You Know the Category, You Know the Properties If you have ever browsed at a music store, you know that the CDs are categorized by type of music. If you like rock-and-roll, you would go to the rock-and-roll section. You might not recognize a particular CD, but you know that it must have the characteristics of rock-and-roll for it to be in this section.

Likewise, you can predict some of the properties of an unfamiliar element by knowing the category to which it belongs. As shown in the concept map in **Figure 5,** elements are classified into three categories—metals, nonmetals, and metalloids. Cobalt, iron, and nickel are classified as metals. If you know that a particular element is a metal, you know that it shares certain properties with iron, nickel, and cobalt. The chart on the next page shows examples of each category and describes the properties that identify elements in each category.

Figure 5 *Elements are divided into three categories: metals, nonmetals, and metalloids.*

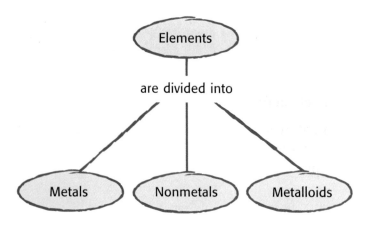

The Three Major Categories of Elements

Metals

Metals are elements that are shiny and are good conductors of thermal energy and electric current. They are *malleable* (they can be hammered into thin sheets) and *ductile* (they can be drawn into thin wires). Iron has many uses in building and automobile construction. Copper is used in wires and coins.

Lead

Tin

Copper

Nonmetals

Sulfur

Nonmetals are elements that are dull (not shiny) and that are poor conductors of thermal energy and electric current. Solid nonmetals tend to be brittle and unmalleable. Few familiar objects are made of only nonmetals. The neon used in lights is a nonmetal, as is the graphite (carbon) used in pencils.

Bromine

Neon

Metalloids

Metalloids, also called semiconductors, are elements that have properties of both metals and nonmetals. Some metalloids are shiny, while others are dull. Metalloids are somewhat malleable and ductile. Some metalloids conduct thermal energy and electric current well. Silicon is used to make computer chips. However, other elements must be added to silicon to make a working chip.

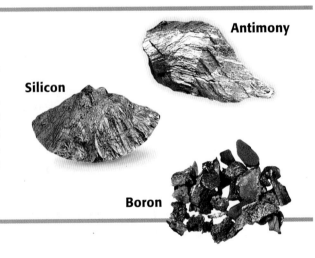
Antimony

Silicon

Boron

internet **connect**

*SCi*LINKS.
NSTA

TOPIC: Elements
GO TO: www.scilinks.org
*sci***LINKS NUMBER:** HSTP085

REVIEW

1. What is a pure substance?

2. List three properties that can be used to classify elements.

3. **Applying Concepts** Which category of element would be the least appropriate choice for making a container that can be dropped without shattering? Explain your reasoning.

Compounds

Most elements take part in chemical changes fairly easily, so few elements are found alone in nature. Instead, most elements are found combined with other elements as compounds.

A **compound** is a pure substance composed of two or more elements that are chemically combined. In a compound, a particle is formed when atoms of two or more elements join together. In order for elements to combine, they must *react*, or undergo a chemical change, with one another. In **Figure 6,** you see magnesium reacting with oxygen to form a compound called magnesium oxide. The compound is a new pure substance that is different from the elements that reacted to form it. Most substances you encounter every day are compounds. The table at left lists some familiar examples.

Familiar Compounds

- **table salt—** sodium and chlorine

- **water—** hydrogen and oxygen

- **sugar—** carbon, hydrogen, and oxygen

- **carbon dioxide—** carbon and oxygen

- **baking soda—** sodium, hydrogen, carbon, and oxygen

Figure 6 *As magnesium burns, it reacts with oxygen and forms the compound magnesium oxide.*

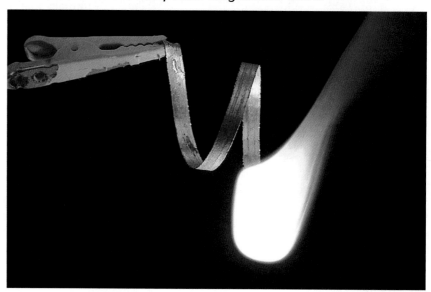

Elements Combine in a Definite Ratio to Form a Compound

Compounds are not random combinations of elements. When a compound forms, the elements join in a specific ratio according to their masses. For example, the ratio of the mass of hydrogen to the mass of oxygen in water is always the same—1 g of hydrogen to 8 g of oxygen. This mass ratio can be written as 1:8 or as the fraction 1/8. Every sample of water has this 1:8 mass ratio of hydrogen to oxygen. If a sample of a compound has a different mass ratio of hydrogen to oxygen, the compound cannot be water.

Every Compound Has a Unique Set of Properties

Each compound has a unique set of properties that allows you to distinguish it from other compounds. Like elements, each compound has its own physical properties, such as boiling point, melting point, density, and color. Compounds can also be identified by their different chemical properties. Some compounds, such as the calcium carbonate found in chalk, react with acid. Others, such as hydrogen peroxide, react when exposed to light. You can see how chemical properties can be used to identify compounds in the QuickLab at right.

A compound has different properties from the elements that form it. Did you know that ordinary table salt is a compound made from two very dangerous elements? Table salt—sodium chloride—consists of sodium (which reacts violently with water) and chlorine (which is poisonous). Together, however, these elements form a harmless compound with unique properties. Take a look at **Figure 7.** Because a compound has different properties from the elements that react to form it, sodium chloride is safe to eat and dissolves (without exploding!) in water.

Compound Confusion

1. Measure 4 g (1 tsp) of **compound A,** and place it in a **clear plastic cup.**

2. Measure 4 g (1 tsp) of **compound B,** and place it in a **second clear plastic cup.**

3. Observe the color and texture of each compound. Record your observations.

4. Add 5 mL (1 tsp) of **vinegar** to each cup. Record your observations.

5. Baking soda reacts with vinegar, while powdered sugar does not. Which of these compounds is compound A, and which is compound B?

Figure 7 *Table salt is formed when the elements sodium and chlorine join. The properties of salt are different from the properties of sodium and chlorine.*

Sodium is a soft, silvery white metal that reacts violently with water.

Chlorine is a poisonous, greenish yellow gas.

Sodium chloride, or table salt, is a white solid that dissolves easily in water and is safe to eat.

✓ Self-Check

Do the properties of pure water from a glacier and from a desert oasis differ? *(See page 724 to check your answer.)*

Compounds Can Be Broken Down into Simpler Substances

Some compounds can be broken down into elements through chemical changes. Look at **Figure 8.** When the compound mercury(II) oxide is heated, it breaks down into the elements mercury and oxygen. Likewise, if an electric current is passed through melted table salt, the elements sodium and chlorine are produced.

Other compounds undergo chemical changes to form simpler compounds. These compounds can be broken down into elements through additional chemical changes. For example, carbonic acid is a compound that helps to give carbonated beverages their "fizz," as shown in **Figure 9.** The carbon dioxide and water that are formed can be further broken down into the elements carbon, oxygen, and hydrogen through additional chemical changes.

Figure 8 *Heating mercury(II) oxide causes a chemical change that separates it into the elements mercury and oxygen.*

Figure 9 *Opening a carbonated drink can be messy as carbonic acid breaks down into two simpler compounds—carbon dioxide and water.*

Physics

CONNECTION

The process of using electric current to break compounds into simpler compounds and elements is known as electrolysis. Electrolysis can be used to separate water into hydrogen and oxygen. The elements aluminum and copper and the compound hydrogen peroxide are important industrial products obtained through electrolysis.

Compounds Cannot Be Broken Down by Physical Changes

The only way to break down a compound is through a chemical change. If you pour water through a filter, the water will pass through the filter unchanged. Filtration is a physical change, so it cannot be used to break down a compound. Likewise, a compound cannot be broken down by being ground into a powder or by any other physical process.

Compounds in Your World

You are always surrounded by compounds. Compounds make up the food you eat, the school supplies you use, the clothes you wear—even you!

Compounds in Nature Proteins are compounds found in all living things. The element nitrogen is needed to make proteins. **Figure 10** shows how some plants get the nitrogen they need. Other plants use nitrogen compounds that are in the soil. Animals get the nitrogen they need by eating plants or by eating animals that have eaten plants. As an animal digests food, the proteins in the food are broken down into smaller compounds that the animal's cells can use.

Another compound that plays an important role in life is carbon dioxide. You exhale carbon dioxide that was made in your body. Plants take in carbon dioxide and use it to make other compounds, including sugar.

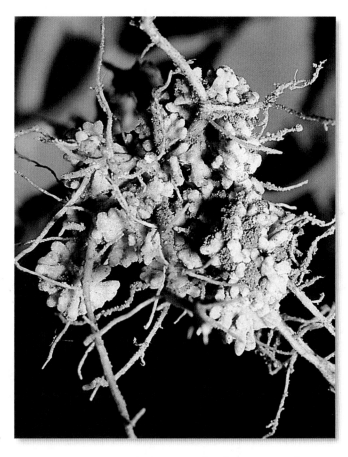

Figure 10 *The bumps on the roots of this pea plant are home to bacteria that form compounds from atmospheric nitrogen. The pea plant makes proteins from these compounds.*

Compounds in Industry The element nitrogen is combined with the element hydrogen to form a compound called ammonia. Ammonia is manufactured for use in fertilizers. Plants can use ammonia as a source of nitrogen for their proteins. Other manufactured compounds are used in medicines, food preservatives, and synthetic fabrics.

The compounds found in nature are usually not the raw materials needed by industry. Often, these compounds must be broken down to provide elements used as raw material. For example, the element aluminum, used in cans, airplanes, and building materials, is not found alone in nature. It is produced by breaking down the compound aluminum oxide.

REVIEW

1. What is a compound?

2. What type of change is needed to break down a compound?

3. **Analyzing Ideas** A jar contains samples of the elements carbon and oxygen. Does the jar contain a compound? Explain.

internet**connect**

SC*LINKS*

NSTA

TOPIC: Compounds
GO TO: www.scilinks.org
*sci*LINKS NUMBER: HSTP090

Mixtures

Have you ever made your own pizza? You roll out the dough, add a layer of tomato sauce, then add toppings like green peppers, mushrooms, and olives—maybe even some pepperoni! Sprinkle cheese on top, and you're ready to bake. You have just created not only a pizza but also a mixture—and a delicious one at that!

What You'll Do

- Describe the properties of mixtures.
- Describe methods of separating the components of a mixture.
- Analyze a solution in terms of its solute, solvent, and concentration.
- Compare the properties of solutions, suspensions, and colloids.

Properties of Mixtures

All mixtures—even pizza—share certain properties. A **mixture** is a combination of two or more substances that are not chemically combined. Two or more materials together form a mixture if they do not react to form a compound. For example, cheese and tomato sauce do not react when they are used to make a pizza.

Figure 11 *Colorless quartz, pink feldspar, and black mica make up the mixture granite.*

Substances in a Mixture Retain Their Identity Because no chemical change occurs, each substance in a mixture has the same chemical makeup it had before the mixture formed. That is, each substance in a mixture keeps its identity. In some mixtures, such as the pizza above or the piece of granite shown in **Figure 11,** you can even see the individual components. In other mixtures, such as salt water, you cannot see all the components.

Mixtures Can Be Physically Separated If you don't like mushrooms on your pizza, you can pick them off. This is a physical change of the mixture. The identities of the substances did not change. In contrast, compounds can be broken down only through chemical changes.

Not all mixtures are as easy to separate as a pizza. You cannot simply pick salt out of a saltwater mixture, but you can separate the salt from the water by heating the mixture. When the water changes from a liquid to a gas, the salt remains behind. Several common techniques for separating mixtures are shown on the following page.

Distillation is a process that separates a mixture based on the boiling points of the components. Here you see pure water being distilled from a saltwater mixture. In addition to water purification, distillation is used to separate crude oil into its components, such as gasoline and kerosene.

A **magnet** can be used to separate a mixture of the elements iron and aluminum. Iron is attracted to the magnet, but aluminum is not.

The components that make up blood are separated using a machine called a **centrifuge.** This machine separates mixtures according to the densities of the components.

A mixture of the compound sodium chloride (table salt) with the element sulfur requires more than one separation step.

1 The **first step** is to mix them with another compound—water. Salt dissolves in water, but sulfur does not.

2 In the **second step,** the mixture is poured through a filter. The filter traps the solid sulfur.

3 In the **third step,** the sodium chloride is separated from the water by simply evaporating the water.

Mixtures vs. Compounds	
Mixtures	**Compounds**
Components are elements, compounds, or both	Components are elements
Components keep their original properties	Components lose their original properties
Separated by physical means	Separated by chemical means
Formed using any ratio of components	Formed using a set mass ratio of components

The Components of a Mixture Do Not Have a Definite Ratio Recall that a compound has a specific mass ratio of the elements that form it. Unlike compounds, the components of a mixture do not need to be combined in a definite ratio. For example, granite that has a greater amount of feldspar than mica or quartz appears to have a pink color. Granite that has a greater amount of mica than feldspar or quartz appears black. Regardless of which ratio is present, this combination of materials is always a mixture—and it is always called granite.

Air is a mixture composed mostly of nitrogen and oxygen, with smaller amounts of other gases, such as carbon dioxide and water vapor. Some days the air has more water vapor, or is more humid, than on other days. But regardless of the ratio of the components, air is still a mixture. The chart at left summarizes the differences between mixtures and compounds.

REVIEW

1. What is a mixture?

2. Is a mixture separated by physical or chemical changes?

3. **Applying Concepts** Suggest a procedure to separate iron filings from sawdust. Explain why this procedure works.

BRAIN FOOD

Many substances are soluble in water, including salt, sugar, alcohol, and oxygen. Water does not dissolve everything, but it dissolves so many different solutes that it is often called the universal solvent.

Solutions

A **solution** is a mixture that appears to be a single substance but is composed of particles of two or more substances that are distributed evenly amongst each other. Solutions are often described as *homogeneous mixtures* because they have the same appearance and properties throughout the mixture.

The process in which particles of substances separate and spread evenly throughout a mixture is known as *dissolving*. In solutions, the **solute** is the substance that is dissolved, and the **solvent** is the substance in which the solute is dissolved. A solute is *soluble,* or able to dissolve, in the solvent. A substance that is *insoluble,* or unable to dissolve, forms a mixture that is not homogeneous and therefore is not a solution.

Salt water is a solution. Salt is soluble in water, meaning that salt dissolves in water. Therefore, salt is the solute and water is the solvent. When two liquids or two gases form a solution, the substance with the greater volume is the solvent.

You may think of solutions as being liquids. And, in fact, tap water, soft drinks, gasoline, and many cleaning supplies are liquid solutions. However, solutions may also be gases, such as air, and solids, such as steel. *Alloys* are solid solutions of metals or nonmetals dissolved in metals. Brass is an alloy of the metal zinc dissolved in copper. Steel, including that used to build the *Titanic,* is an alloy made of the nonmetal carbon and other elements dissolved in iron. Look at the chart below for examples of the different states of matter used as solutes and solvents in solutions.

✔ Self-Check

Yellow gold is an alloy made from equal parts copper and silver combined with a greater amount of gold. Identify each component of yellow gold as a solute or solvent.
(See page 724 to check your answer.)

Examples of Different States in Solutions

Gas in gas	Dry air (oxygen in nitrogen)
Gas in liquid	Soft drinks (carbon dioxide in water)
Liquid in liquid	Antifreeze (alcohol in water)
Solid in liquid	Salt water (salt in water)
Solid in solid	Brass (zinc in copper)

Particles in Solutions Are Extremely Small The particles in solutions are so small that they never settle out, nor can they be filtered out of these mixtures. In fact, the particles are so small, they don't even scatter light. Look at **Figure 12** and see for yourself. The jar on the left contains a solution of sodium chloride in water. The jar on the right contains a mixture of gelatin in water.

Figure 12 *Both of these jars contain mixtures. The mixture in the jar on the left, however, is a solution. The particles in solutions are so small they don't scatter light. Therefore, you can't see the path of light through it.*

Smelly solutions?
Follow your nose and learn
more on page 102.

MATH BREAK

Calculating Concentration

Many solutions are colorless. Therefore, you cannot always compare the concentrations of solutions by looking at the color—you have to compare the actual calculated concentrations. One way to calculate the concentration of a liquid solution is to divide the grams of solute by the milliliters of solvent. For example, the concentration of a solution in which 35 g of salt is dissolved in 175 mL of water is

$$\frac{35 \text{ g salt}}{175 \text{ mL water}} = 0.2 \text{ g/mL}$$

Now It's Your Turn

Calculate the concentrations of each solution below. Solution A has 55 g of sugar dissolved in 500 mL of water. Solution B has 36 g of sugar dissolved in 144 mL of water. Which solution is the more dilute one? Which is the more concentrated?

Concentration: How Much Solute Is Dissolved? A measure of the amount of solute dissolved in a solvent is **concentration.** Concentration can be expressed in grams of solute per milliliter of solvent. Knowing the exact concentration of a solution is very important in chemistry and medicine because using the wrong concentration can be dangerous.

Solutions can be described as being *concentrated* or *dilute.* Look at **Figure 13.** Both solutions have the same amount of solvent, but the solution on the left contains less solute than the solution on the right. The solution on the left is dilute while the solution on the right is concentrated. Keep in mind that the terms *concentrated* and *dilute* do not specify the amount of solute that is actually dissolved. Try your hand at calculating concentration and describing solutions as concentrated or dilute in the MathBreak at left.

Figure 13 *The dilute solution on the left contains less solute than the concentrated solution on the right.*

A solution that contains all the solute it can hold at a given temperature is said to be *saturated.* An *unsaturated* solution contains less solute than it can hold at a given temperature. More solute can dissolve in an unsaturated solution.

Solubility: How Much Solute Can Dissolve? If you add too much sugar to a glass of lemonade, not all of the sugar can dissolve. Some of the sugar collects on the bottom of the glass. To determine the maximum amount of sugar that can dissolve, you would need to know the solubility of sugar. The **solubility** of a solute is the amount of solute needed to make a saturated solution using a given amount of solvent at a certain temperature. Solubility is usually expressed in grams of solute per 100 mL of solvent. **Figure 14** on the next page shows the solubility of several different substances in water at different temperatures.

Figure 14 Solubility of Different Substances

The solubility of most solids increases as the temperature gets higher. Thus, more solute can dissolve at higher temperatures. However, some solids, such as cerium sulfate, are less soluble at higher temperatures.

Sodium chlorate
Sodium nitrate
Potassium bromide
Sodium chloride
Cerium sulfate

Solubility (g/100 mL of water)
Temperature (°C)

Unlike the solubility of most solids in liquids, the solubility of gases in liquids decreases as the temperature is raised. Bubbles of gas appear in hot water long before the water begins to boil. The gases that are dissolved in the water cannot remain dissolved as the temperature increases because the solubility of the gases is lower at higher temperatures.

What Affects How Quickly Solids Dissolve in Liquids?

Many familiar solutions are formed when a solid solute is dissolved in water. Several factors affect how fast the solid will dissolve. Look at **Figure 15** to see three methods used to make a solute dissolve faster. You can see why you will enjoy a glass of lemonade sooner if you stir granulated sugar into the lemonade before adding ice!

Figure 15 *Mixing, heating, and crushing iron(III) chloride increase the speed at which it will dissolve.*

Mixing by stirring or shaking causes the solute particles to separate from one another and spread out more quickly among the solvent particles.

Heating causes particles to move more quickly. The solvent particles can separate the solute particles and spread them out more quickly.

Crushing the solute increases the amount of contact between the solute and the solvent. The particles of solute mix with the solvent more quickly.

Elements, Compounds, and Mixtures **95**

Figure 16 *Dirty air is a suspension that could damage a car's engine. The air filter in a car separates dust from air to keep the dust from getting into the engine.*

Suspensions

When you shake up a snow globe, you are mixing the solid snow particles with the clear liquid. When you stop shaking the globe, the snow particles settle to the bottom of the globe. This mixture is called a suspension. A **suspension** is a mixture in which particles of a material are dispersed throughout a liquid or gas but are large enough that they settle out. The particles are insoluble, so they do not dissolve in the liquid or gas. Suspensions are often described as *heterogeneous mixtures* because the different components are easily seen. Other examples of suspensions include muddy water and Italian salad dressing.

The particles in a suspension are fairly large, and they scatter or block light. This often makes a suspension difficult to see through. But the particles are too heavy to remain mixed without being stirred or shaken. If a suspension is allowed to sit undisturbed, the particles will settle out, as in a snow globe.

A suspension can be separated by passing it through a filter. The liquid or gas passes through, but the solid particles are large enough to be trapped by the filter, as shown in **Figure 16.**

APPLY

Shake Well Before Use

Many medicines, such as remedies for upset stomach, are suspensions. The directions on the label instruct you to shake the bottle well before use. Why must you shake the bottle? What problem could arise if you don't?

Colloids

Some mixtures have properties of both solutions and suspensions. These mixtures are known as colloids (KAWL OYDZ). A **colloid** is a mixture in which the particles are dispersed throughout but are not heavy enough to settle out. The particles in a colloid are relatively small and are fairly well mixed. Solids, liquids, and gases can be used to make colloids. You might be surprised at the number of colloids you encounter each day. Milk, mayonnaise, stick deodorant—even the gelatin and whipped cream in **Figure 17**—are colloids. The materials that compose these products do not separate between uses because their particles do not settle out.

Although the particles in a colloid are much smaller than the particles in a suspension, they are still large enough to scatter a beam of light shined through the colloid, as shown in **Figure 18.** Finally, unlike a suspension, a colloid cannot be separated by filtration. The particles are small enough to pass through a filter.

Figure 17
This dessert includes two delicious examples of colloids—fruity gelatin and whipped cream.

Figure 18 *The particles in the colloid fog scatter light, making it difficult for drivers to see the road ahead.*

Make a colloid found in your kitchen on page 643 of the LabBook.

REVIEW

1. List two methods of making a solute dissolve faster.

2. Identify the solute and solvent in a solution made from 15 mL of oxygen and 5 mL of helium.

3. **Comparing Concepts** What are three differences between solutions and suspensions?

internetconnect

SCILINKS
NSTA

TOPIC: Mixtures
GO TO: www.scilinks.org
*sci*LINKS NUMBER: HSTP095

Chapter Highlights

SECTION 1

Vocabulary

element *(p. 82)*

pure substance *(p. 82)*

metals *(p. 85)*

nonmetals *(p. 85)*

metalloids *(p. 85)*

Section Notes

- A substance in which all the particles are alike is a pure substance.

- An element is a pure substance that cannot be broken down into anything simpler by physical or chemical means.

- Each element has a unique set of physical and chemical properties.

- Elements are classified as metals, nonmetals, or metalloids, based on their properties.

SECTION 2

Vocabulary

compound *(p. 86)*

Section Notes

- A compound is a pure substance composed of two or more elements chemically combined.

- Each compound has a unique set of physical and chemical properties that are different from the properties of the elements that compose it.

- The elements that form a compound always combine in a specific ratio according to their masses.

- Compounds can be broken down into simpler substances by chemical changes.

Labs

Flame Tests *(p. 640)*

✓ Skills Check

Math Concepts

CONCENTRATION   The concentration of a solution is a measure of the amount of solute dissolved in a solvent. For example, a solution is formed by dissolving 85 g of sodium nitrate in 170 mL of water. The concentration of the solution is calculated as follows:

$$\frac{85 \text{ g sodium nitrate}}{170 \text{ mL water}} = 0.5 \text{ g/mL}$$

Visual Understanding

THREE CATEGORIES OF ELEMENTS
Elements are classified as metals, nonmetals, or metalloids, based on their properties. The chart on page 85 provides a summary of the properties that distinguish each category.

SEPARATING MIXTURES   Mixtures can be separated through physical changes based on differences in the physical properties of their components. Review the illustrations on page 91 for some techniques for separating mixtures.

Vocabulary

mixture *(p. 90)*

solution *(p. 92)*

solute *(p. 92)*

solvent *(p. 92)*

concentration *(p. 94)*

solubility *(p. 94)*

suspension *(p. 96)*

colloid *(p. 97)*

Section Notes

- A mixture is a combination of two or more substances, each of which keeps its own characteristics.

- Mixtures can be separated by physical means, such as filtration and evaporation.

- The components of a mixture can be mixed in any proportion.

- A solution is a mixture that appears to be a single substance but is composed of a solute dissolved in a solvent. Solutions do not settle, cannot be filtered, and do not scatter light.

- Concentration is a measure of the amount of solute dissolved in a solvent.

- The solubility of a solute is the amount of solute needed to make a saturated solution using a given amount of solvent at a certain temperature.

- Suspensions are heterogeneous mixtures that contain particles large enough to settle out, be filtered, and block or scatter light.

- Colloids are mixtures that contain particles too small to settle out or be filtered but large enough to scatter light.

Labs

A Sugar Cube Race! *(p. 642)*

Making Butter *(p. 643)*

Unpolluting Water *(p. 644)*

---

internetconnect

GO TO: go.hrw.com

Visit the **HRW** Web site for a variety of learning tools related to this chapter. Just type in the keyword:

KEYWORD: HSTMIX

SCiLINKS sm

N S T A

GO TO: www.scilinks.org

Visit the **National Science Teachers Association** on-line Web site for Internet resources related to this chapter. Just type in the *sci*LINKS number for more information about the topic:

TOPIC: The *Titanic*	*sci*LINKS NUMBER: HSTP080
TOPIC: Elements	*sci*LINKS NUMBER: HSTP085
TOPIC: Compounds	*sci*LINKS NUMBER: HSTP090
TOPIC: Mixtures	*sci*LINKS NUMBER: HSTP095

Chapter Review

Complete the following sentences by choosing the appropriate term from the vocabulary list to fill in each blank:

1. A __?__ has a definite ratio of components.

2. The amount of solute needed to form a saturated solution is the __?__ of the solute.

3. A __?__ can be separated by filtration.

4. A pure substance must be either a(n) __?__ or a(n) __?__.

5. Elements that are brittle and dull are __?__.

6. The substance that dissolves to form a solution is the __?__.

UNDERSTANDING CONCEPTS

Multiple Choice

7. Which of the following increases the solubility of a gas in a liquid?
   a. increasing the temperature
   b. stirring
   c. decreasing the temperature
   d. decreasing the amount of liquid

8. Which of the following best describes chicken noodle soup?
   a. element   c. compound
   b. mixture   d. solution

9. Which of the following does not describe elements?
   a. all the particles are alike
   b. can be broken down into simpler substances
   c. have unique sets of properties
   d. can join together to form compounds

10. A solution that contains a large amount of solute is best described as
    a. unsaturated.   c. dilute.
    b. concentrated.   d. weak.

11. Which of the following substances can be separated into simpler substances only by chemical means?
    a. sodium   c. water
    b. salt water   d. gold

12. Which of the following would not increase the rate at which a solid dissolves?
    a. decreasing the temperature
    b. crushing the solid
    c. stirring
    d. increasing the temperature

13. An element that conducts thermal energy well and is easily shaped is a
    a. metal.
    b. metalloid.
    c. nonmetal.
    d. None of the above

14. In which classification of matter are the components chemically combined?
    a. alloy   c. compound
    b. colloid   d. suspension

Short Answer

15. What is the difference between an element and a compound?

16. When nail polish is dissolved in acetone, which substance is the solute and which is the solvent?

Concept Mapping

17. Use the following terms to create a concept map: matter, element, compound, mixture, solution, suspension, colloid.

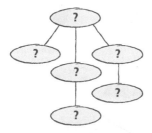

CRITICAL THINKING AND PROBLEM SOLVING

18. Describe a procedure to separate a mixture of salt, finely ground pepper, and pebbles.

19. A light green powder is heated in a test tube. A gas is given off, while the solid becomes black. In which classification of matter does the green powder belong? Explain your reasoning.

20. Why is it desirable to know the exact concentration of solutions rather than whether they are concentrated or dilute?

21. Explain the three properties of mixtures using a fruit salad as an example.

22. To keep the "fizz" in carbonated beverages after they have been opened, should you store them in a refrigerator or in a cabinet? Explain.

MATH IN SCIENCE

23. What is the concentration of a solution prepared by mixing 50 g of salt with 200 mL of water?

24. How many grams of sugar must be dissolved in 150 mL of water to make a solution with a concentration of 0.6 g/mL?

INTERPRETING GRAPHICS

25. Use Figure 14 on page 95 to answer the following questions:
    a. Can 50 g of sodium chloride dissolve in 100 mL of water at 60°C?
    b. How much cerium sulfate is needed to make a saturated solution in 100 mL of water at 30°C?
    c. Is sodium chloride or sodium nitrate more soluble in water at 20°C?

26. Dr. Sol Vent tested the solubility of a compound. The data below was collected using 100 mL of water. Graph Dr. Vent's results. To increase the solubility, would you increase or decrease the temperature? Explain.

Temperature (°C)	10	25	40	60	95
Dissolved solute (g)	150	70	34	25	15

27. What type of mixture is shown in the photo below? Explain.

Reading Check-up

Take a minute to review your answers to the Pre-Reading Questions found at the bottom of page 80. Have your answers changed? If necessary, revise your answers based on what you have learned since you began this chapter.

Science, Technology, and Society

Perfume: Fragrant Solutions

Making perfume is an ancient art. It was practiced, for example, by the ancient Egyptians, who rubbed their bodies with a substance made by soaking fragrant woods and resins in water and oil. From certain references and formulas in the Bible, we know that the ancient Israelites also practiced the art of perfume making. Other sources indicate that this art was also known to the early Chinese, Arabs, Greeks, and Romans.

▲ *Perfumes have been found in the tombs of Egyptians who lived more than 3,000 years ago.*

Only the E-scent-ials

Over time, perfume making has developed into a complicated art. A fine perfume may contain more than 100 different ingredients. The most familiar ingredients come from fragrant plants or flowers, such as sandalwood or roses. These plants get their pleasant odor from their essential oils, which are stored in tiny, baglike parts called sacs. The parts of plants that are used for perfumes include the flowers, roots, and leaves. Other perfume ingredients come from animals and from man-made chemicals.

Making Scents

Perfume makers first remove essential oils from the plants using distillation or reactions with solvents. Then the essential oils are blended with other ingredients to create perfumes. Fixatives, which usually come from animals, make the other odors in the perfume last longer. Oddly enough, most natural fixatives smell awful! For example, civet musk is a foul-smelling liquid that the civet cat sprays on its enemies.

Taking Notes

When you take a whiff from a bottle of perfume, the first odor you detect is called the top note. It is a very fragrant odor that evaporates rather quickly. The middle note, or modifier, adds a different character to the odor of the top note. The base note, or end note, is the odor that lasts the longest.

▲ *Not all perfume ingredients smell good. The foul-smelling oil from the African civet cat is used as a fixative in some perfumes.*

Smell for Yourself

▶ Test a number of different perfumes and colognes to see if you can identify three different notes in each.

Science Fiction

"The Strange Case of Dr. Jekyll and Mr. Hyde"

by Robert Louis Stevenson

A vicious, detestable man murders an old gentleman. A wealthy and respectable scientist commits suicide. Are these two tragedies connected in some way?

Dr. Henry Jekyll is an admirable member of society. He is a doctor and a scientist. Although wild as a young man, Jekyll has become cold and analytical as he has aged and has pursued his scientific theories. Now he wants to understand the nature of human identity. He wants to explore the different parts of the human personality that usually fit together smoothly to make a complete person. His theory is that if he can separate his personality into "good" and "evil" parts, he can get rid of his evil side and lead a happy, useful life. So Jekyll develops a chemical mixture that will allow him to test his theory. The results are startling!

Who is the mysterious Mr. Hyde? He is not a scientist. He is a man of action and anger, who sparks fear in the hearts of those he comes in contact with. Where did he come from? What does he do? How can local residents be protected from his wrath?

Robert Louis Stevenson's story of the decent doctor Henry Jekyll and the violent Edward Hyde is a classic science-fiction story. When Jekyll mixes his "salts" and drinks his chemical mixture, he changes his life—and Edward Hyde's—completely. To find out more, read Stevenson's "The Strange Case of Dr. Jekyll and Mr. Hyde" in the *Holt Anthology of Science Fiction*.

UNIT 2

Motion and Forces

It's hard to imagine a world where nothing ever moves. Without motion or forces to cause motion, life would be very dull! The relationship between force and motion is the subject of this unit. You will learn how to describe the motion of objects, how forces affect motion, and how fluids exert force. This timeline shows some events and discoveries that have occurred as scientists have worked to understand the motion of objects here on Earth and in space.

Around 250 B.C.

Archimedes, a Greek mathematician, develops the principle that bears his name. The principle relates the buoyant force on an object in a fluid to the amount of fluid the object displaces.

Around 240 B.C.

Chinese astronomers are the first to record a sighting of Halley's Comet.

1905

While employed as a patent clerk, German physicist Albert Einstein publishes his special theory of relativity. The theory states that the speed of light is constant, no matter what the reference point is.

1921

Bessie Coleman becomes the first African-American woman licensed to fly an airplane.

1947

While flying a Bell X-1 rocket-powered airplane, American pilot Chuck Yeager becomes the first human to travel faster than the speed of sound.

6062

1519

Portuguese explorer Ferdinand Magellan begins the first voyage around the world.

1687

Sir Isaac Newton, a British mathematician and scientist, publishes *Principia*, a book describing his laws of motion and the law of universal gravitation.

PHILOSOPHIÆ
NATURALIS
PRINCIPIA
MATHEMATICA.

Autore JS. NEWTON, Trin. Coll. Cantab. Soc. Matheseos
Profeſſore Lucaſiano, & Societatis Regalis Sodali.

1846

After determining that the orbit of Uranus is different from what is predicted from the law of universal gravitation, scientists discover Neptune, shown here, whose gravitational force is causing Uranus's unusual orbit.

1764

In London, Wolfgang Amadeus Mozart composes his first symphony—at the age of 9.

1990

The *Magellan* spacecraft begins orbiting Venus for a four-year mission to map the planet. The spacecraft uses the sun's gravitational force to propel it to Venus without burning much fuel.

1971

American astronaut Alan Shepard takes a break from gathering lunar data to play golf on the moon during the *Apollo 14* mission.

1999

NASA launches the Mars *Polar Lander* spacecraft, one of a series sent to explore Mars.

Matter in Motion

Pre-Reading
Questions

1. How is motion measured?
2. What is a force?
3. How does friction affect motion?
4. How does gravity affect objects?

SWOOSH!!

Have you ever watched a speed skating race during the Winter Olympics? Speed skaters are extremely fast. In fact, some speed skaters have been known to skate at a rate of 12 meters per second! Speed skaters, like the one you see in this photograph, must have a great deal of athletic skill and ability. First of all, they have to be very strong in order to exert the force needed to move so fast. Secondly, speed skaters skate on ice, which is very slippery. These athletes must be able to overcome the lack of friction between their skates and the ice—so they won't fall during the race! In this chapter, you will learn more about motion, including speed and acceleration, and the forces that affect motion, such as friction and gravity.

THE DOMINO DERBY

Speed is the rate at which an object moves. In this activity, you will determine the factors that affect the speed of falling dominoes.

Procedure

1. Set up **25 dominoes** in a straight line. Try to keep equal spacing between the dominoes.

2. Using a **meterstick,** measure the total length of your row of dominoes, and write it down.

3. Using a **stopwatch,** time how long it takes for the entire row of dominoes to fall. Record this measurement.

4. Repeat steps 2 and 3 several times, using distances between the dominoes that are smaller and larger than the distance used in your first setup.

Analysis

5. Calculate the average speed for each trial by dividing the total distance (the length of the domino row) by the time taken to fall.

6. How did the spacing between dominoes affect the average speed? Is this result what you expected? If not, explain.

Measuring Motion

Look around you—you're likely to see something in motion. Your teacher may be walking across the room, or perhaps a bird is flying outside a window. Even if you don't see anything moving, motion is still occurring all around you. Tiny air particles are whizzing around, the moon is circling the Earth, and blood is traveling through your veins and arteries!

Terms to Learn

motion   velocity
speed   acceleration

What You'll Do

◆ Identify the relationship between motion and a reference point.
◆ Identify the two factors that speed depends on.
◆ Determine the difference between speed and velocity.
◆ Analyze the relationship of velocity to acceleration.
◆ Interpret a graph showing acceleration.

Observing Motion

You might think that the motion of an object is easy to detect—you just observe the object. But you actually must observe the object in relation to another object that appears to stay in place. The object that appears to stay in place is a *reference point*. When an object changes position over time when compared with a reference point, the object is in **motion.** When an object is in motion, you can describe the direction of its motion with a reference direction, such as north, south, east, west, or up and down.

Common Reference Points The Earth's surface is a common reference point for determining position and motion. Nonmoving objects on Earth's surface, such as buildings, trees, and mountains, are also useful reference points, as shown in **Figure 1.**

A moving object can also be used as a reference point. For example, if you were on the hot-air balloon shown below, you could watch a bird fly by and see that it was changing position in relation to your moving balloon. Furthermore, Earth itself is a moving reference point—it is moving around the sun.

Figure 1 *During the time it took for these pictures to be taken, the hot-air balloon changed position compared with a reference point—the mountain.*

Speed Depends on Distance and Time

The rate at which an object moves is its **speed.** Speed depends on the distance traveled and the time taken to travel that distance. Look back at Figure 1. Suppose the time interval between the pictures was 10 seconds and the balloon traveled 50 m in that time. The speed (distance divided by time) of the balloon is 50 m/10 s, or 5 m/s.

The SI unit for speed is meters per second (m/s). Kilometers per hour, feet per second, and miles per hour are other units commonly used to express speed.

Determining Average Speed Most of the time, objects do not travel at a constant speed. For example, you probably do not walk at a constant speed from one class to the next. Therefore, it is very useful to calculate *average speed* using the following equation:

$$\text{Average speed} = \frac{\text{total distance}}{\text{total time}}$$

Recognizing Speed on a Graph Suppose a person drives from one city to another. The blue line in the graph below shows the distance traveled every hour. Notice that the distance traveled every hour is different. This is because the speed (distance/time) is not constant—the driver changes speed often because of weather, traffic, or varying speed limits. The average speed can be calculated by adding up the total distance and dividing it by the total time:

$$\text{Average speed} = \frac{360 \text{ km}}{4 \text{ h}} = 90 \text{ km/h}$$

The red line shows the average distance traveled each hour. The slope of this line is the average speed.

MATH BREAK

Calculating Average Speed

Practice calculating average speed in the problems listed below:

1. If you walk for 1.5 hours and travel 7.5 km, what is your average speed?

2. A bird flies at a speed of 15 m/s for 10 s, 20 m/s for 10 s, and 25 m/s for 5 s. What is the bird's average speed?

A Graph Showing Distance over Time

Distance ▬▬ Average Distance ▬▬

(Distance (km) vs. Time (h); y-axis marked 0, 100, 200, 300, 400; x-axis marked 1, 2, 3, 4)

Velocity: Direction Matters

Here's a riddle for you: Two birds leave the same tree at the same time. They both fly at 10 km/h for 1 hour, 15 km/h for 30 minutes, and 5 km/h for 1 hour. Why don't they end up at the same destination?

Have you figured it out? The birds traveled at the same speeds for the same amounts of time, but they did not end up at the same place because they went in different directions. In other words, they had different velocities. The speed of an object in a particular direction is the object's **velocity** (vuh LAHS uh tee).

Be careful not to confuse the terms *speed* and *velocity;* they do not mean the same thing. Because velocity must include direction, it would not be correct to say that an airplane's velocity is 600 km/h. However, you could say the plane's velocity is 600 km/h south. Velocity always includes a reference direction. **Figure 2** further illustrates the difference between speed and velocity.

Figure 2 *The speeds of these cars may be similar, but their velocities are different because they are going in different directions.*

Velocity Changes as Speed or Direction Changes You can think of velocity as the rate of change of an object's position. An object's velocity is constant only if its speed and direction don't change. Therefore, constant velocity is always along a straight line. An object's velocity will change if either its speed or direction changes. For example, if a bus traveling at 15 m/s south speeds up to 20 m/s, a change in velocity has occurred. But a change in velocity also occurs if the bus continues to travel at the same speed but changes direction to travel east.

✓ Self-Check

Which of the following are examples of velocity?

1. 25 m/s forward
2. 1,500 km/h
3. 55 m/h south
4. all of the above

(See page 724 to check your answer.)

Combining Velocities If you're riding in a bus traveling east at 15 m/s, you and all the other passengers are also traveling at a velocity of 15 m/s east. But suppose you stand up and walk down the bus's aisle while it is moving. Are you still moving at the same velocity as the bus? No! **Figure 3** shows how you can combine velocities to determine the *resultant velocity.*

Figure 3 Determining Resultant Velocity

15 m/s east

1 m/s east

When you combine two velocities that are **in the same direction,** add them together to find the resultant velocity.

Person's resultant velocity

15 m/s east + 1 m/s east = 16 m/s east

15 m/s east

1 m/s west

When you combine two velocities that are **in opposite directions,** subtract the smaller velocity from the larger velocity to find the resultant velocity. The resultant velocity is in the direction of the larger velocity.

Person's resultant velocity

15 m/s east − 1 m/s west = 14 m/s east

REVIEW

1. What is a reference point?

2. What two things must you know to determine speed?

3. What is the difference between speed and velocity?

4. **Applying Concepts** Explain why it is important to know a tornado's velocity and not just its speed.

BRAIN FOOD

The space shuttle is always launched in the same direction that the Earth rotates, thus taking advantage of the Earth's rotational velocity (over 1,500 km/h east). This allows the shuttle to use less fuel to reach space than if it had to achieve such a great velocity on its own.

Acceleration: The Rate at Which Velocity Changes

Imagine that you are in-line skating and you see a large rock in your path. You slow down and swerve to avoid the rock. A neighbor sees you and exclaims, "That was great acceleration! I'm amazed that you could slow down and turn so quickly!" You're puzzled. Doesn't *accelerate* mean to speed up? But you didn't speed up—you slowed down and turned. So how could you have accelerated?

Defining Acceleration Although the word *accelerate* is commonly used to mean "speed up," there's more to its meaning scientifically. **Acceleration** (ak SEL uhr AY shuhn) is the rate at which velocity changes. To *accelerate* means to change velocity. You just learned that velocity changes if speed changes, direction changes, or both. So your neighbor was right! Your speed and direction changed, so you accelerated.

Keep in mind that acceleration is not just how much velocity changes. It is also *how fast* velocity changes. The faster velocity changes, the greater the acceleration is.

Calculating Acceleration You can calculate acceleration by using the following equation:

$$\text{Acceleration} = \frac{\text{final velocity} - \text{starting velocity}}{\text{time it takes to change velocity}}$$

Velocity is expressed in meters per second (m/s), and time is expressed in seconds (s). Therefore, acceleration is expressed in meters per second per second (m/s/s).

Suppose you get on your bicycle and accelerate southward at a rate of 1 m/s/s. (Like velocity, acceleration has size and direction.) This means that every second, your southward velocity increases by 1 m/s, as shown in **Figure 4** on the next page.

Use this simple device to "see" acceleration on page 647 of the LabBook.

Figure 4 Acceleration at 1 m/s/s South

1 m/s   2 m/s   3 m/s   4 m/s   5 m/s

After 1 second, you have a velocity of 1 m/s south, as shown in Figure 4. After 2 seconds, you have a velocity of 2 m/s south. After 3 seconds, you have a velocity of 3 m/s south, and so on. If your final velocity after 5 seconds is 5 m/s south, your acceleration can be calculated as follows:

$$\text{Acceleration} = \frac{5 \text{ m/s} - 0 \text{ m/s}}{5 \text{ s}} = 1 \text{ m/s/s south}$$

You can practice calculating acceleration by doing the MathBreak shown here.

Examples of Acceleration In the example above, your velocity was originally zero and then it increased. Because your velocity changed, you accelerated. Acceleration in which velocity increases is sometimes called *positive acceleration.*

Acceleration also occurs when velocity decreases. In the skating example, you accelerated because you slowed down. Acceleration in which velocity decreases is sometimes called *negative acceleration* or *deceleration.*

Remember that velocity has direction, so velocity will change if your direction changes. Therefore, a change in direction is acceleration, even if there is no change in speed. Some more examples of acceleration are shown in the chart below.

MATH BREAK

Calculating Acceleration

Use the equation shown on the previous page to do the following problems. Be sure to express your answers in m/s/s and include direction.

1. A plane passes over Point A with a velocity of 8,000 m/s north. Forty seconds later it passes over Point B at a velocity of 10,000 m/s north. What is the plane's acceleration from A to B?

2. A coconut falls from the top of a tree and reaches a velocity of 19.6 m/s when it hits the ground. It takes 2 seconds to reach the ground. What is the coconut's acceleration?

Example of Acceleration	How Velocity Changes
A plane taking off	Increase in speed
A car stopping at a stop sign	Decrease in speed
Jogging on a winding trail	Change in direction
Driving around a corner	Change in direction
Standing at Earth's equator	Change in direction

Figure 5 *The blades of this windmill are constantly changing direction as they travel in a circle. Thus, centripetal acceleration is occurring.*

Circular Motion: Continuous Acceleration   Does it surprise you to find out that standing at Earth's equator is an example of acceleration? After all, you're not changing speed, and you're not changing direction . . . or are you? In fact, you are traveling in a circle as the Earth rotates. An object traveling in a circular motion is always changing its direction. Therefore, its velocity is always changing, so acceleration is occurring. The acceleration that occurs in circular motion is known as *centripetal* (sen TRIP uht uhl) *acceleration.* Another example of centripetal acceleration is shown in **Figure 5.**

Recognizing Acceleration on a Graph   Suppose that you have just gotten on a roller coaster. The roller coaster moves slowly up the first hill until it stops at the top. Then you're off, racing down the hill! The graph below shows your acceleration for the 10 seconds coming down the hill. You can tell from this graph that your acceleration is positive because your velocity increases as time passes. Because the graph is not a straight line, you can also tell that your acceleration is not constant for each second.

A Graph Showing Acceleration

internet**connect**

SC*LINKS*
NSTA

TOPIC: Measuring Motion
GO TO: www.scilinks.org
*sci*LINKS NUMBER: HSTP105

REVIEW

1. What is acceleration?

2. Does a change in direction affect acceleration? Explain your answer.

3. **Interpreting Graphics** How do you think a graph of deceleration would differ from the graph shown above? Explain your reasoning.

What Is a Force?

Terms to Learn

force · net force
newton

What You'll Do

◆ Give examples of different kinds of forces.
◆ Determine the net force on an object.
◆ Compare balanced and unbalanced forces.

You often hear the word *force* in everyday conversation:

"That storm had a lot of force!"
"Our basketball team is a force to be reckoned with."
"A flat tire forced me to stop riding my bicycle."
"The inning ended with a force-out at second base."

But what exactly is a force? In science, a **force** is simply a push or a pull. All forces have both size and direction.

Forces are everywhere. In fact, any time you see something moving, you can be sure that its motion was created by a force. Scientists express force using a unit called the **newton (N).** The more newtons, the greater the force.

Forces Act on Objects

All forces are exerted by one object on another object. For any push to occur, something has to receive the push. You can't push nothing! The same is true for any pull. When doing schoolwork, you use your fingers to pull open books or to push the buttons on a computer keyboard. In these examples, your fingers are exerting forces on the books and the keys. However, just because a force is being exerted by one object on another doesn't mean that motion will occur. For example, you are probably sitting on a chair as you read this. But the force you are exerting on the chair does not cause the chair to move. That's because the Earth is also exerting a force on the chair. In most cases, it is easy to determine where the push or pull is coming from, as shown in **Figure 6.**

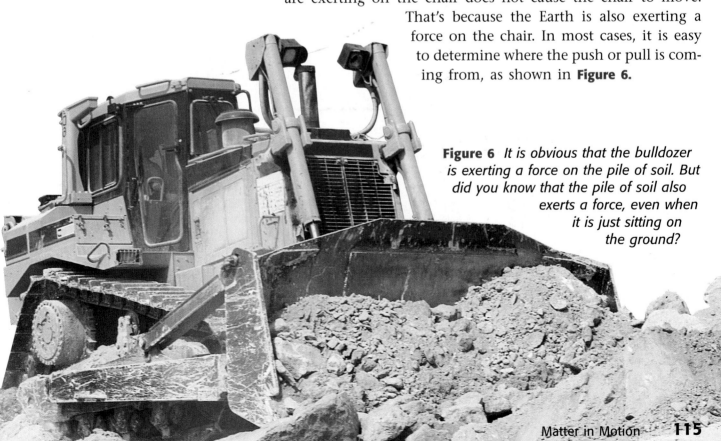

Figure 6 *It is obvious that the bulldozer is exerting a force on the pile of soil. But did you know that the pile of soil also exerts a force, even when it is just sitting on the ground?*

Figure 7
Something unseen exerts a force that makes your socks cling together when they come out of the dryer. You have to exert a force to separate the socks.

It is not always so easy to tell what is exerting a force or what is receiving a force, as shown in **Figure 7.** You cannot see what exerts the force that pulls magnets to refrigerators, and the air you breathe is an unseen receiver of a force called *gravity.* You will learn more about gravity later in this chapter.

Forces in Combination

Often more than one force is exerted on an object at the same time. The **net force** is the force that results from combining all the forces exerted on an object. So how do you determine the net force? The examples below can help you answer this question.

Forces in the Same Direction Suppose you and a friend are asked to move a piano for the music teacher. To do this, you pull on one end of the piano, and your friend pushes on the other end. Together, your forces add up to enough force to move the piano. This is because your forces are in the same direction. **Figure 8** shows this situation. Because the forces are in the same direction, they can be added together to determine the net force. In this case, the net force is 45 N, which is plenty to move a piano—if it is on wheels, that is!

Figure 8 *When the forces are in the same direction, you add the forces together to determine the net force.*

25 N ➡

20 N ➡

Net force
25 N + 20 N = 45 N
to the right

Forces in Different Directions Consider two dogs playing tug of war with a short piece of rope. Each is exerting a force, but in opposite directions. **Figure 9** shows this scene. Notice that the dog on the left is pulling with a force of 10 N and the dog on the right is pulling with a force of 12 N. Which dog do you think will win the tug of war?

Because the forces are in opposite directions, the net force is determined by subtracting the smaller force from the larger one. In this case, the net force is 2 N in the direction of the dog on the right. Give that dog a dog biscuit!

Science
CONNECTION

Every moment, forces in several directions are exerted on the Golden Gate Bridge. For example, Earth exerts a powerful downward force on the bridge while elastic forces pull and push portions of the bridge up and down. To learn how the bridge stands up to these forces, turn to page 135.

←— 10 N   12 N —→

Net force
12 N − 10 N = 2 N
to the right

Figure 9 *When the forces are in different directions, you subtract the smaller force from the larger force to determine the net force.*

Unbalanced and Balanced Forces

If you know the net force on an object, you can determine the effect the force will have on the object's motion. Why? The net force tells you whether the forces on the object are balanced or unbalanced.

Unbalanced Forces Produce a Change in Motion In the examples shown in Figures 8 and 9, the net force on the object is greater than zero. When the net force on an object is not zero, the forces on the object are *unbalanced*. Unbalanced forces produce a change in motion (acceleration). In the two previous examples, the receivers of the forces—the piano and the rope—move. Unbalanced forces are necessary to cause a non-moving object to start moving.

> **✓ Self-Check**
>
> What is the net force when you combine a force of 7 N north with a force of 5 N south? *(See page 724 to check your answer.)*

Unbalanced forces are also necessary to change the motion of moving objects. For example, consider a soccer game. The soccer ball is already moving when it is passed from one player to another. When the ball reaches the second player, the player exerts an unbalanced force—a kick—on the ball. After the kick, the ball moves in a new direction and with a new speed.

Keep in mind that an object can continue to move even when the unbalanced forces are removed. A soccer ball, for example, receives an unbalanced force when it is kicked. However, the ball continues to roll along the ground long after the force of the kick has ended.

Balanced Forces Produce No Change in Motion When the forces applied to an object produce a net force of zero, the forces are *balanced*. Balanced forces do not cause a nonmoving object to start moving. Furthermore, balanced forces will not cause a change in the motion of a moving object.

Many objects around you have only balanced forces acting on them. For example, a light hanging from the ceiling does not move because the force of gravity pulling down on the light is balanced by an elastic force due to tension that pulls the light up. A bird's nest in a tree and a hat resting on your head are also examples of objects with only balanced forces acting on them. **Figure 10** shows another case where the forces on an object are balanced. Because all the forces are balanced, the house of cards does not move.

Figure 10 *The forces on this house of cards are balanced. An unbalanced force on one of the cards would cause motion— and probably a mess!*

REVIEW

1. Give four examples of a force being exerted.

2. Explain the difference between balanced and unbalanced forces and how each affects the motion of an object.

3. **Interpreting Graphics** In the picture at left, two bighorn sheep push on each other's horns. The arrow shows the direction the two sheep are moving. Describe the forces the sheep are exerting and how the forces combine to produce the sheep's motion.

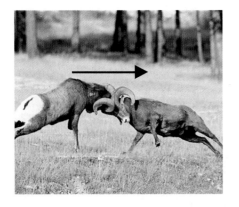

Terms to Learn

friction

What You'll Do

◆ Explain why friction occurs.
◆ List the types of friction, and give examples of each.
◆ Explain how friction can be both harmful and helpful.

Friction: A Force That Opposes Motion

Picture a warm summer day. You are enjoying the day by wearing shorts and tossing a ball with your friends. By accident, one of your friends tosses the ball just out of your reach. You have to make a split-second decision to dive for it or not. You look down and notice that if you dove for it, you would most likely slide across pavement rather than the surrounding grass. What would you decide?

Unless you enjoy scraped knees, you probably would not want to slide on the pavement. The painful difference between sliding on grass and sliding on pavement has to do with friction. **Friction** is a force that opposes motion between two surfaces that are touching.

The Source of Friction

Friction occurs because the surface of any object is rough. Even surfaces that look or feel very smooth are actually covered with microscopic hills and valleys. When two surfaces are in contact, the hills and valleys of one surface stick to the hills and valleys of the other surface, as shown in **Figure 11.** This contact causes friction even when the surfaces appear smooth.

The amount of friction between two surfaces depends on many factors, including the roughness of the surfaces and the force pushing the surfaces together.

Figure 11 *When the hills and valleys of one surface stick to the hills and valleys of another surface, friction is created.*

Quick **Lab**

The Friction 500

1. Make a short ramp out of a **piece of cardboard** and **one or two books** on a table.

2. Put a **toy car** at the top of the ramp and let go. If necessary, adjust the ramp height so that your car does not roll off the table.

3. Put the car at the top of the ramp again and let go. Record the distance the car travels after leaving the ramp. Do this three times, and calculate the average for your results.

4. Change the surface of the table by covering it with **sandpaper** or **cloth.** Repeat step 3. Change the surface one more time, and repeat step 3 again.

5. Which surface had the most friction? Why? What do you predict would happen if the car were heavier? Record your results and answers in your ScienceLog.

TRY at HOME

Rougher Surfaces Create More Friction   Rougher surfaces have more microscopic hills and valleys. Thus, the rougher the surface, the greater the friction. Think back to the example on the previous page. Pavement is much rougher than grass. Therefore, more friction is produced when you slide on the pavement than when you slide on grass. This increased friction is more effective at stopping your sliding, but it is also more painful! On the other hand, if the surfaces are smooth, there is less friction. If you were to slide on ice instead of on grass, your landing would be even more comfortable—but also much colder!

Greater Force Creates More Friction   The amount of friction also depends on the force pushing the surfaces together. If this force is increased, the hills and valleys of the surfaces can come into closer contact. This causes the friction between the surfaces to increase. Less massive objects exert less force on surfaces than more massive objects do, as illustrated in **Figure 12.** However, changing the amounts of the surfaces that touch does not change the amount of friction.

Figure 12 Force and Friction

a There is more friction between the more massive book and the table than there is between the less massive book and the table. A harder push is needed to overcome friction to move the more massive book.

Force needed to overcome friction

Force of friction

b Turning the more massive book on its edge does not change the amount of friction between the table and the book.

Force of friction

Force needed to overcome friction

Types of Friction

The friction you observe when sliding books across a tabletop is called sliding friction. Other types of friction include rolling friction, fluid friction, and static friction. As you will learn, the name of each type of friction is a big clue as to the conditions where it can be found.

Sliding Friction If you push an eraser across your desk, the eraser will move for a short distance and then stop. This is an example of *sliding friction*. Sliding friction is very effective at opposing the movement of objects and is the force that causes the eraser to stop moving. You can feel the effect of sliding friction when you try to move a heavy dresser by pushing it along the floor. You must exert a lot of force to overcome the sliding friction, as shown in **Figure 13.**

You use sliding friction when you go sledding, when you apply the brakes on a bicycle or a car, or when you write with a piece of chalk.

Rolling Friction If the same heavy dresser were on wheels, you would have an easier time moving it. The friction between the wheels and the floor is an example of *rolling friction*. The force of rolling friction is usually less than the force of sliding friction. Therefore, it is generally easier to move objects on wheels than it is to slide them along the floor, as shown at right.

Rolling friction is an important part of almost all means of transportation. Anything with wheels—bicycles, in-line skates, cars, trains, and planes—uses rolling friction between the wheels and the ground to move forward.

Figure 13 Comparing Sliding Friction and Rolling Friction

Moving a heavy piece of furniture in your room can be hard work because **the force of sliding friction is large.**

It is easier to move a heavy piece of furniture if you put it on wheels. **The force of rolling friction is smaller** and easier to overcome.

Figure 14 *Swimming provides a good workout because you must exert force to overcome fluid friction.*

Fluid Friction Why is it harder to walk on a freshly mopped floor than on a dry floor? The reason is that on the wet floor the sliding friction between your feet and the floor is replaced by *fluid friction* between your feet and the water. In this case, fluid friction is less than sliding friction, so the floor is slippery. The term *fluid* includes liquids, such as water and milk, and gases, such as air and helium.

Fluid friction opposes the motion of objects traveling through a fluid, as illustrated in **Figure 14.** For example, fluid friction between air and a fast moving car is the largest force opposing the motion of the car. You can observe this friction by holding your hand out the window of a moving car.

Static Friction When a force is applied to an object but does not cause the object to move, *static friction* occurs. The object does not move because the force of static friction balances the force applied. Static friction disappears as soon as an object starts moving, and then another type of friction immediately occurs. Look at **Figure 15** to understand when static friction affects an object.

Figure 15 Static Friction

Force applied   Static friction

Force applied   Sliding friction

a There is no friction between the block and the table when no force is applied to the block to move it.

b If a small force—shown in blue—is exerted on the block, the block does not move. The force of static friction—shown in orange—exactly balances the force applied.

c When the force exerted on the block is greater than the force of static friction, the block starts moving. Once the block starts moving, all static friction is gone, and the force applied opposes sliding friction—shown in green.

 Self-Check

What type of friction was involved in the imaginary situation at the beginning of this section? *(See page 724 to check your answer.)*

Friction Can Be Harmful or Helpful

Think about how friction affects a car. Without friction, the tires could not push against the ground to move the car forward and the brakes could not stop the car. Without friction, a car is useless. However, friction can cause problems in a car too. Friction between moving engine parts increases their temperature and causes the parts to wear down. A liquid coolant is added to the engine to keep it from overheating, and engine parts need to be changed as they wear out.

Friction is both harmful and helpful to you and the world around you. Friction can cause holes in your socks and in the knees of your jeans. Friction by wind and water can cause erosion of the topsoil that nourishes plants. On the other hand, friction between your pencil and your paper is necessary for the pencil to leave a mark. Without friction, you would just slip and fall when you tried to walk. Because friction can be both harmful and helpful, it is sometimes necessary to reduce or increase friction.

Some Ways to Reduce Friction   One way to reduce friction is to use lubricants. *Lubricants* (LOO bri kuhnts) are substances that are applied to surfaces to reduce the friction between them. Some examples of common lubricants are motor oil, wax, and grease. **Figure 16** shows why lubricants are important to maintaining car parts.

Friction can also be reduced by switching from sliding friction to rolling friction. Ball bearings are placed between the wheels and axles of in-line skates and bicycles to make it easier for the wheels to turn by reducing friction.

Have some fun with friction! Investigate three types of friction on page 650 of the LabBook.

BRAIN FOOD

Lubricants are usually liquids, but they can be solids or gases too. Graphite is a shiny black solid that is used in pencils. Graphite dust is very slippery and is often used as a lubricant for ball bearings in bicycle and skate wheels. An example of a gas lubricant is the air that comes out of the tiny holes of an air-hockey table.

Figure 16 *Motor oil is used as a lubricant in car engines. Without oil, engine parts would wear down quickly, as the connecting rod on the bottom has.*

Figure 17 *No one enjoys cleaning pans with baked-on food! To make this chore pass quickly, press down with the scrubber to increase friction.*

Another way to reduce friction is to make surfaces that rub against each other smoother. For example, rough wood on a park bench is painful to slide across because there is a large amount of friction between your leg and the bench. Rubbing the bench with sandpaper makes it smoother and more comfortable to sit on because the friction between your leg and the bench is reduced.

Some Ways to Increase Friction One way to increase friction is to make surfaces rougher. For example, sand scattered on icy roads keeps cars from skidding. Baseball players sometimes wear textured batting gloves to increase the friction between their hands and the bat so that the bat does not fly out of their hands.

Another way to increase friction is to increase the force pushing the surfaces together. For example, you can ensure that your magazine will not blow away at the park by putting a heavy rock on it. The added mass of the rock increases the friction between the magazine and the ground. Or if you are sanding a piece of wood, you can sand the wood faster by pressing harder on the sandpaper. **Figure 17** shows another situation where friction is increased by pushing on an object.

APPLY

Friction and Tires

The tire shown here was used for more than 80,000 km. What effect did friction have on the rubber? What kind of friction is mainly responsible for the tire's appearance? Why are car owners warned to change their car tires after using them for several thousand kilometers?

🖳 internet**connect**

SC*i*LINKS
NSTA

TOPIC: Force and Friction
GO TO: www.scilinks.org
*sci*LINKS **NUMBER:** HSTP110

REVIEW

1. Explain why friction occurs.

2. Name two ways in which friction can be increased.

3. Give an example of each of the following types of friction: sliding, rolling, and fluid.

4. **Applying Concepts** Name two ways that friction is harmful and two ways that friction is helpful to you when riding a bicycle.

Gravity: A Force of Attraction

Terms to Learn

gravity   mass
weight

What You'll Do

◆ Define gravity.
◆ State the law of universal gravitation.
◆ Describe the difference between mass and weight.

If you watch videotape of astronauts on the moon, you will notice that when the astronauts tried to walk on the lunar surface, they bounced around like beach balls instead.

Why did the astronauts—who were wearing heavy space-suits—bounce so easily on the moon (as shown in **Figure 18**), while you must exert effort to jump a few centimeters off Earth's surface? The answer has to do with gravity. **Gravity** is a force of attraction between objects that is due to their masses. In this section, you will learn about gravity and the effects it has on objects.

Figure 18 *Because gravity is less on the moon than on Earth, walking on the moon's surface was a very bouncy experience for the Apollo astronauts.*

Biology

C O N N E C T I O N

Scientists think seeds can "sense" gravity. The ability to sense gravity is what causes seeds to always send roots down and the green shoot up. But scientists do not understand just *how* seeds do this. Astronauts have grown seedlings during space shuttle missions to see how seeds respond to changes in gravity. So far, there are no definite answers from the results of these experiments.

All Matter Is Affected by Gravity

All matter has mass. Gravity is a result of mass. Therefore, all matter experiences gravity. That is, all objects experience an attraction toward all other objects. This gravitational force "pulls" objects toward each other. Right now, because of gravity, you are being pulled toward this book, your pencil, and every other object around you.

These objects are also being pulled toward you and toward each other because of gravity. So why don't you see the effects of this attraction? In other words, why don't you notice objects moving toward each other? The reason is that the mass of most objects is too small to cause an attraction large enough to move objects toward each other. However, you are familiar with one object that is massive enough to cause a noticeable attraction—the Earth.

Earth's Gravitational Force Is Large Compared with all the objects around you, Earth has an enormous mass. Therefore, Earth's gravitational force is very large. You must apply forces to overcome Earth's gravitational force any time you lift objects or even parts of your body.

Earth's gravitational force pulls everything toward the center of Earth. Because of this, the books, tables, and chairs in the room stay in place, and dropped objects fall to Earth rather than moving together or toward you.

✓ Self-Check

What is gravity? *(See page 724 to check your answer.)*

The Law of Universal Gravitation

For thousands of years, two very puzzling questions were "Why do objects fall toward Earth?" and "What keeps the planets in motion in the sky?" The two questions were treated as separate topics until a British scientist named Sir Isaac Newton (1642–1727) realized that they were two parts of the same question.

The Core of an Idea Legend has it that Newton made the connection when he observed a falling apple during a summer night, as shown in **Figure 19.** He knew that unbalanced forces are necessary to move or change the motion of objects. He concluded that there had to be an unbalanced force on the apple to make it fall, just as there had to be an unbalanced force on the moon to keep it moving around Earth. He realized that these two forces are actually the same force—a force of attraction called gravity.

Figure 19
Newton Makes the Connection

A Law Is Born Newton generalized his observations on gravity in a law now known as the *law of universal gravitation.* This law describes the relationships between gravitational force, mass, and distance. It is called universal because it applies to all objects in the universe.

The law of universal gravitation states the following: All objects in the universe attract each other through gravitational force. The size of the force depends on the masses of the objects and the distance between them. The examples in **Figure 20** show the effects of the law of universal gravitation. It is easier to understand the law if you consider it in two parts.

a Gravitational force is small between objects with small masses.

Figure 20 *The arrows indicate the gravitational force between the objects. The width of the arrows indicates the strength of the force.*

b Gravitational force is larger between objects with larger masses.

c If the distance between two objects is increased, the gravitational force pulling them together is reduced.

Part 1: Gravitational Force Increases as Mass Increases
Imagine an elephant and a cat. Because an elephant has a larger mass than a cat, the amount of gravity between an elephant and Earth is greater than the amount of gravity between a cat and Earth. That is why a cat is much easier to pick up than an elephant! There is gravity between the cat and the elephant, but it is very small because the cat's mass and the elephant's mass are so much smaller than Earth's mass.

The moon has less mass than Earth. Therefore, the moon's gravitational force is less than Earth's. Remember the astronauts on the moon? They bounced around as they walked because they were not being pulled down with as much force as they would have been on Earth.

 Astronomy
C O N N E C T I O N

Black holes are 10 times to 1 billion times more massive than our sun. Thus, their gravitational force is incredibly large. The gravity of a black hole is so large that an object that enters a black hole can never get out. Even light cannot escape from a black hole. Because black holes do not emit light, they cannot be seen—hence their name.

Figure 21 *Venus and Earth have approximately the same mass. However, Venus is closer to the sun. Thus, the gravity between Venus and the sun is greater than the gravity between Earth and the sun.*

Part 2: Gravitational Force Decreases as Distance Increases The gravity between you and Earth is large. Whenever you jump up, you are pulled back down by Earth's gravitational force. On the other hand, the sun is more than 300,000 times more massive than Earth. So why doesn't the sun's gravitational force affect you more than Earth's does? The reason is that the sun is so far away.

You are approximately 150 million kilometers away from the sun. At this distance, the gravity between you and the sun is very small. If there were some way you could stand on the sun (and not burn up), you would find it impossible to jump or even walk. The gravitational force acting on you would be so great that your muscles could not lift any part of your body!

Although the sun's gravitational force does not have much of an effect on your body here, it does have a big effect on Earth itself and the other planets, as shown in **Figure 21.** The gravity between the sun and the planets is large because the objects have large masses. If the sun's gravitational force did not have such an effect on the planets, the planets would not stay in orbit around the sun.

Weight Is a Measure of Gravitational Force

You have learned that gravity is a force of attraction between objects that is due to their masses. **Weight** is a measure of the gravitational force exerted on an object. When you see or hear the word *weight,* it usually refers to Earth's gravitational force on an object. But weight can also be a measure of the gravitational force exerted on objects by the moon or other planets.

You have learned that the unit of force is a newton. Because gravity is a force and weight is a measure of gravity, weight is also expressed in newtons (N). On Earth, a 100 g object, such as a medium-sized apple, weighs approximately 1 N.

Activity

Suppose you had a device that could increase or decrease the gravitational force of objects around you (including small sections of Earth). In your ScienceLog, describe what you might do with the device, what you would expect to see, and what effect the device would have on the weight of objects.

TRY at HOME

Weight and Mass Are Different Weight is related to mass, but the two are not the same. Weight changes when gravitational force changes. **Mass** is the amount of matter in an object, and its value does not change. If an object is moved to a place with a greater gravitational force—like Jupiter—its weight will increase, but its mass will remain the same. **Figure 22** shows the weight and mass of an object on Earth and a place with about one-sixth the gravitational force—the moon.

Gravitational force is about the same everywhere on Earth, so the weight of any object is about the same everywhere. Because mass and weight are constant on Earth, the terms are often used to mean the same thing. This can lead to confusion. Be sure you understand the difference!

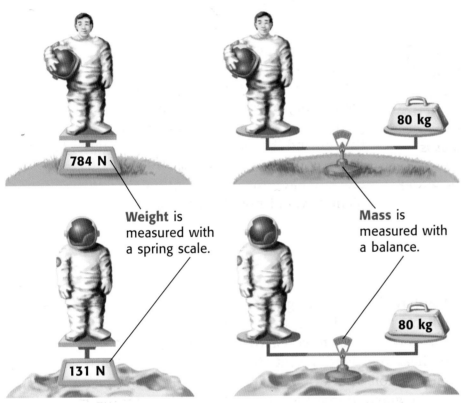

784 N

80 kg

Weight is measured with a spring scale.

Mass is measured with a balance.

131 N

80 kg

Figure 22 *The astronaut's weight on the moon is about one-sixth of his weight on Earth, but his mass remains constant.*

REVIEW

1. How does the mass of an object relate to the gravitational force the object exerts on other objects?

2. How does the distance between objects affect the gravity between them?

3. **Comparing Concepts** Explain why your weight would change if you orbited Earth in the space shuttle but your mass would not.

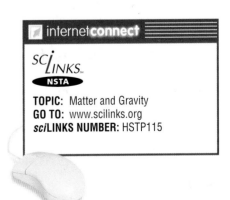

internet connect

SC_i_**LINKS**
NSTA

TOPIC: Matter and Gravity
GO TO: www.scilinks.org
sciLINKS NUMBER: HSTP115

Chapter Highlights

Vocabulary

motion (p. 108)

speed (p. 109)

velocity (p. 110)

acceleration (p. 112)

Section Notes

- An object is in motion if it changes position over time when compared with a reference point.

- The speed of a moving object depends on the distance traveled by the object and the time taken to travel that distance.

- Speed and velocity are not the same thing. Velocity is speed in a given direction.

- Acceleration is the rate at which velocity changes.

- An object can accelerate by changing speed, changing direction, or both.

- Acceleration is calculated by subtracting starting velocity from final velocity, then dividing by the time required to change velocity.

Labs

Built for Speed (p. 646)

Detecting Acceleration (p. 647)

Vocabulary

force (p. 115)

newton (p. 115)

net force (p. 116)

Section Notes

- A force is a push or a pull.

- Forces are expressed in newtons.

- Force is always exerted by one object on another object.

- Net force is determined by combining forces.

- Unbalanced forces produce a change in motion. Balanced forces produce no change in motion.

☑ Skills Check

Math Concepts

ACCELERATION An object's acceleration can be determined using the following equation:

$$\text{Acceleration} = \frac{\text{final velocity} - \text{starting velocity}}{\text{time it takes to change velocity}}$$

For example, suppose a cheetah running at a velocity of 27 m/s east slows down. After 15 seconds, the cheetah has stopped.

$$\frac{0 \text{ m/s} - 27 \text{ m/s}}{15 \text{ s}} = -1.8 \text{ m/s/s east}$$

Visual Understanding

THE SOURCE OF FRICTION Even surfaces that look or feel very smooth are actually rough at the microscopic level. To understand how this roughness causes friction, review Figure 11 on page 119.

THE LAW OF UNIVERSAL GRAVITATION This law explains that the gravity between objects depends on their masses and the distance between them. Review the effects of this law by looking at Figure 20 on page 127.

SECTION 3

Vocabulary

friction (p. 119)

Section Notes

- Friction is a force that opposes motion.

- Friction is caused by "hills and valleys" touching on the surfaces of two objects.

- The amount of friction depends on factors such as the roughness of the surfaces and the force pushing the surfaces together.

- Four kinds of friction that affect your life are sliding friction, rolling friction, fluid friction, and static friction.

- Friction can be harmful or helpful.

Labs

Science Friction (p. 650)

SECTION 4

Vocabulary

gravity (p. 125)
weight (p. 128)
mass (p. 129)

Section Notes

- Gravity is a force of attraction between objects that is due to their masses.

- The law of universal gravitation states that all objects in the universe attract each other through gravitational force. The size of the force depends on the masses of the objects and the distance between them.

- Weight and mass are not the same. Mass is the amount of matter in an object; weight is a measure of the gravitational force on an object.

Labs

Relating Mass and Weight (p. 651)

---

internetconnect

go.hrw.com

GO TO: go.hrw.com

Visit the **HRW** Web site for a variety of learning tools related to this chapter. Just type in the keyword:

KEYWORD: HSTMOT

SCiLINKSsm
NSTA

GO TO: www.scilinks.org

Visit the **National Science Teachers Association** on-line Web site for Internet resources related to this chapter. Just type in the *sci*LINKS number for more information about the topic:

TOPIC:	*sci*LINKS NUMBER:
TOPIC: Measuring Motion	*sci*LINKS NUMBER: HSTP105
TOPIC: Forces	*sci*LINKS NUMBER: HSTP107
TOPIC: Force and Friction	*sci*LINKS NUMBER: HSTP110
TOPIC: Matter and Gravity	*sci*LINKS NUMBER: HSTP115
TOPIC: The Science of Bridges	*sci*LINKS NUMBER: HSTP125

Chapter Review

USING VOCABULARY

To complete the following sentences, choose the correct term from each pair of terms listed below:

1. ___?___ opposes motion between surfaces that are touching. (*Friction* or *Gravity*)

2. Forces are expressed in ___?___. (*newtons* or *mass*)

3. A ___?___ is determined by combining forces. (*net force* or *newton*)

4. ___?___ is the rate at which ___?___ changes. (*Velocity* or *Acceleration*/*velocity* or *acceleration*)

UNDERSTANDING CONCEPTS

Multiple Choice

5. A student riding her bicycle on a straight, flat road covers one block every 7 seconds. If each block is 100 m long, she is traveling at
   a. constant speed.
   b. constant velocity.
   c. 10 m/s.
   d. Both (a) and (b)

6. Friction is a force that
   a. opposes an object's motion.
   b. does not exist when surfaces are very smooth.
   c. decreases with larger mass.
   d. All of the above

7. Rolling friction
   a. is usually less than sliding friction.
   b. makes it difficult to move objects on wheels.
   c. is usually greater than sliding friction.
   d. is the same as fluid friction.

8. If Earth's mass doubled, your weight would
   a. increase because gravity increases.
   b. decrease because gravity increases.
   c. increase because gravity decreases.
   d. not change because you are still on Earth.

9. A force
   a. is expressed in newtons.
   b. can cause an object to speed up, slow down, or change direction.
   c. is a push or a pull.
   d. All of the above

10. The amount of gravity between 1 kg of lead and Earth is _____ the amount of gravity between 1 kg of marshmallows and Earth.
    a. greater than   c. the same as
    b. less than   d. none of the above

Short Answer

11. Describe the relationship between motion and a reference point.

12. How is it possible to be accelerating and traveling at a constant speed?

13. Explain the difference between mass and weight.

Concept Mapping

14. Use the following terms to create a concept map: speed, velocity, acceleration, force, direction, motion.

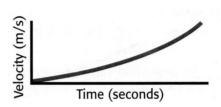

19. Is this a graph of positive or negative acceleration? How can you tell?

CRITICAL THINKING AND PROBLEM SOLVING

15. Your family is moving, and you are asked to help move some boxes. One box is so heavy that you must push it across the room rather than lift it. What are some ways you could reduce friction to make moving the box easier?

16. Explain how using the term *accelerator* when talking about a car's gas pedal can lead to confusion, considering the scientific meaning of the word *acceleration*.

17. Explain why it is important for airplane pilots to know wind velocity, not just wind speed, during a flight.

20. You know how to combine two forces that act in one or two directions. The same method you learned can be used to combine several forces acting in several directions. Examine the diagrams below, and predict with how much force and in what direction the object will move.

MATH IN SCIENCE

18. A kangaroo hops 60 m to the east in 5 seconds.
   a. What is the kangaroo's speed?
   b. What is the kangaroo's velocity?
   c. The kangaroo stops at a lake for a drink of water, then starts hopping again to the south. Every second, the kangaroo's velocity increases 2.5 m/s. What is the kangaroo's acceleration after 5 seconds?

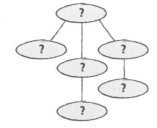

Reading Check-up

Take a minute to review your answers to the Pre-Reading Questions found at the bottom of page 106. Have your answers changed? If necessary, revise your answers based on what you have learned since you began this chapter.

Science, Technology, and Society

Is It Real . . . or Is It Virtual?

You stand in the center of a darkened room and put on a helmet. The helmet covers your head and face, making it impossible for you to see or hear anything from outside. Wires run from the helmet to a series of computers, carrying information about how your head is positioned and where you are looking. Other wires carry back to you the sights and sounds the computer wants you to "see" and "hear." All of a sudden you find yourself driving a race car around a tricky course at 300 km/h. Then in another instant, you are in the middle of a rain forest staring at a live snake!

It's All an Illusion

Such simulated-reality experiences were once thought the stuff of science fiction alone. But today devices called motion simulators can stimulate the senses of sight and sound to create illusions of movement.

Virtual-reality devices, as these motion simulators are called, were first used during World War II to train pilots. Mock-ups of fighter-plane cockpits, films of simulated terrain, and a joystick that manipulated large hydraulic arms simulated the plane in "virtual flight." Today's jet pilots train with similar equipment, except the simulators use extremely sophisticated computer graphics instead of films.

Fooled You!

Virtual-reality hoods and gloves take people into a variety of "realities." Inside the hood, two small television cameras or computer-graphic images fool the wearer's sense of vision. The brain perceives the image as three-dimensional because one image is placed in front of each eye. As the images change, the computer adjusts the scene's perspective so that it appears to the viewer as though he or she is moving through the scene. When the position of the head changes, the computer adjusts the scene to account for the movement. All the while, sounds coming through the headphones trick the wearer's ears into thinking he or she is moving too.

In addition to hoods, gloves, and images, virtual-reality devices may have other types of sensors. Driving simulators, for instance, often have a steering wheel, a gas pedal, and a brake so that the participant has the sensation of driving. So whether you want spine-tingling excitement or on-the-job training, virtual reality could very well take *you* places!

▲ *Wearing a virtual-reality helmet helps to lessen the pain this burn patient feels while his dressings are changed.*

Explore New Realities

▶ What other activities or skills could be learned or practiced with virtual reality? What are some problems with relying on this technology? Record your ideas in your ScienceLog.

The Golden Gate Bridge

Have you ever relaxed in a hammock? If so, you may have noticed how tense the strings got when the hammock supported your weight. Now imagine a hammock 1,965 m long supporting a 20-ton roadway with more than 100,000 cars traveling along its length each day. That describes the Golden Gate Bridge! Because of the way the bridge is built, it is very much like a giant hammock.

Tug of War

The bridge's roadway is suspended from main cables 2.33 km long that sweep from one end of the bridge to the other and that are anchored at each end. Smaller cables called *hangers* connect the main cables to the roadway. Tension, the force of being pulled apart, is created as the cables are pulled down by the weight of the roadway while being pulled up by their attachment to the top of each tower.

▲ *The Golden Gate Bridge spans the San Francisco Bay.*

Towering Above

Towers 227 m tall support the cables over the long distance across San Francisco Bay, making the Golden Gate the tallest bridge in the world. The towers receive a force that is the exact opposite of tension—compression. Compression is the force of being pushed together. The main cables holding the weight of the roadway push down on the top of the towers while Earth pushes up on the bottom.

Stretching the Limits

Tension and compression are elastic forces, which means they are dependent on elasticity, the ability of an object to return to its original shape after being stretched or compressed. If an object is not very elastic, it breaks easily or becomes permanently deformed when subjected to an elastic force. The cables and towers of the Golden Gate Bridge are made of steel, a material with great elastic strength. A single steel wire 2.54 mm thick can support over half a ton without breaking!

On the Road

The roadway of the Golden Gate Bridge is subjected to multiple forces at the same time, including friction, gravity, and elastic forces. Rolling friction is caused by the wheels of each vehicle moving across the roadway's surface. Gravity pulls down on the roadway but is counteracted by the support of the towers and cables. This causes each roadway span to bend slightly and experience both tension and compression. The bottom of each span is under tension because the cables and towers pull up along the road's sides, while gravity pulls down at its center. These same forces cause compression of the top of each span. Did you ever imagine that so many forces were at work on a bridge?

Bridge the Gap

▶ Find out more about another type of bridge, such as an arch, a beam, or a cable-stayed bridge. How do forces such as friction, gravity, tension, and compression affect these types of bridges?

Forces in Motion

Pre-Reading
Questions

1. How does the force of gravity affect falling objects?

2. What is projectile motion?

3. What are Newton's laws of motion?

4. What is momentum?

VOMIT COMET

Have you ever wondered what it would be like to move around without gravity? To help train astronauts for space flight, scientists have designed a special airplane called the KC-135 that simulates what it feels like to move with reduced gravity. The KC-135 first flies upward at a steep angle. When the airplane flies downward at a 45° angle, the effect of reduced gravity is produced inside. Then, the astronaut trainees in the plane can "float." Because the floating often makes passengers queasy, the KC-135 has earned a nickname—the Vomit Comet. In this chapter, you will learn how gravity affects the motion of objects and how the laws of motion apply to your life.

FALLING WATER

Gravity is one of the most important forces in your life. In this activity, you will observe the effect of gravity on a falling object.

Procedure

1. Place a **wide plastic tub** on the floor. Punch a small hole in the side of a **paper cup,** near the bottom.

2. Hold your finger over the hole, and fill the cup with **water.** Keeping your finger over the hole, hold the cup about waist high above the tub.

3. Uncover the hole. Describe your observations in your ScienceLog.

4. Next, predict what will happen to the water if you drop the cup at the same time you uncover the hole. Write your prediction in your ScienceLog.

5. Cover the hole with your finger again, and refill the cup.

6. Uncover the hole, and drop the cup at the same time. Record your observations.

7. Clean up any spilled water with **paper towels.**

Analysis

8. What differences did you observe in the behavior of the water during the two trials?

9. In the second trial, how fast did the cup fall compared with the water?

What You'll Do

- ◆ Explain how gravity and air resistance affect the acceleration of falling objects.
- ◆ Explain why objects in orbit appear to be weightless.
- ◆ Describe how an orbit is formed.
- ◆ Describe projectile motion.

Gravity and Motion

Suppose you drop a baseball and a marble at the same time from the same height. Which do you think would land first? In ancient Greece around 400 B.C., an important philosopher named Aristotle (ER is TAWT uhl) believed that the rate at which an object falls depends on the object's mass. Imagine that you could ask Aristotle which object would land first. He would predict that the baseball would land first.

All Objects Fall with the Same Acceleration

In the late 1500s, a young Italian scientist named Galileo questioned Aristotle's idea about falling objects. Galileo proved that the mass of an object does not affect the rate at which it falls. According to one story, Galileo did this by dropping two cannonballs of different masses from the top of the Leaning Tower of Pisa. The crowd watching from the ground was amazed to see the two cannonballs land at the same time. Whether or not this story is true, Galileo's idea changed people's understanding of gravity and falling objects.

Acceleration Due to Gravity Objects fall to the ground at the same rate because the acceleration due to gravity is the same for all objects. Does that seem odd? The force of gravity is greater between Earth and an object with a large mass than between Earth and a less massive object, so you may think that the acceleration due to gravity should be greater too. But a greater force must be applied to a large mass than to a small mass to produce the same acceleration. Thus, the difference in force is canceled by the difference in mass. **Figure 1** shows objects with different masses falling with the same acceleration.

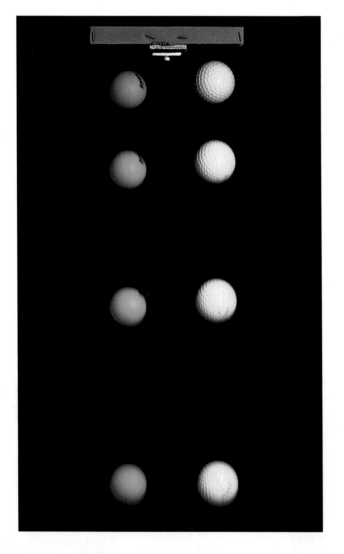

Figure 1 *A table tennis ball and a golf ball fall with the same acceleration even though they have different masses.*

Accelerating at a Constant Rate All objects accelerate toward Earth at a rate of 9.8 meters per second per second, which is expressed as 9.8 m/s/s. This means that for every second that an object falls, the object's downward velocity increases by 9.8 m/s, as shown in **Figure 2**. Remember, this acceleration is the same for all objects regardless of their mass. Do the MathBreak at right to learn how to calculate the velocity of a falling object.

1st s
4.9 m

v = 0 m/s downward

v = 9.8 m/s downward

2nd s
14.7 m

v = 19.6 m/s downward

3rd s
24.5 m

Figure 2 *A falling object accelerates at a constant rate. Each second, the object falls faster and farther than it did the second before.*

v = 29.4 m/s downward

MATH BREAK

Velocity of Falling Objects

To find the change in velocity (Δv) of a falling object, multiply the acceleration due to gravity (g) by the time it takes for the object to fall in seconds (t):

$$\Delta v = g \times t$$

For example, a stone at rest is dropped from a cliff, and it takes 3 seconds to hit the ground. Its downward velocity when it hits the ground is as follows:

$$\Delta v = 9.8 \,\frac{m/s}{\cancel{s}} \times 3 \,\cancel{s}$$
$$= 29.4 \text{ m/s}$$

Now It's Your Turn

A penny at rest is dropped from the top of a tall stairwell.

1. What is the penny's velocity after it has fallen for 2 seconds?

2. The penny hits the ground in 4.5 seconds. What is its final velocity?

Air Resistance Slows Down Acceleration

Try this simple experiment. Drop two sheets of paper—one crumpled in a tight ball and the other kept flat. Did your results contradict what you just learned about falling objects? The flat paper fell more slowly because of fluid friction that opposes the motion of objects through air. This fluid friction is also known as *air resistance*. Air resistance occurs between the surface of the falling object and the air that surrounds it.

Gravity helps make roller coasters thrilling to ride. Read about a roller coaster designer on page 159.

Self-Check

Which is more affected by air resistance—a leaf or an acorn? (See page 724 to check your answer.)

Air Resistance Affects Some Objects More than Others

The amount of air resistance acting on an object depends on the size and shape of the object. Air resistance affects the flat sheet of paper more than the crumpled one, causing the flat sheet to fall more slowly than the crumpled one. Because air is all around you, any falling object you see is affected by air resistance. **Figure 3** shows the effect of air resistance on the downward acceleration of a falling object.

Figure 3 *The force of gravity pulls the object downward as the force of air resistance pushes it upward.*

This arrow represents **the force of air resistance** pushing up on the object. This force is subtracted from the force of gravity to produce the net force.

This arrow represents **the net force** on the object. Because the net force is not zero, the object still accelerates downward, but not as fast as it would without air resistance.

This arrow represents **the force of gravity** on the object. If this were the only force acting on the object, it would accelerate at a rate of 9.8 m/s/s.

Acceleration Stops at the Terminal Velocity

As long as the net force on a falling object is not zero, the object accelerates downward. But the amount of air resistance on an object increases as the speed of the object increases. As an object falls, the upward force of air resistance continues to increase until it exactly matches the downward force of gravity. When this happens, the net force is zero, and the object stops accelerating. The object then falls at a constant velocity, which is called the **terminal velocity.**

Sometimes the fact that falling objects have a terminal velocity is a good thing. The terminal velocity of hailstones is between 5 and 40 m/s, depending on the size of the stones. Every year cars, buildings, and vegetation are all severely damaged in hail storms. Imagine how much more destructive hail would be if there were no air resistance—hailstones would hit the Earth at velocities near 350 m/s! **Figure 4** shows another situation in which terminal velocity is helpful.

Figure 4
The parachute increases the air resistance of this sky diver, slowing him to a safe terminal velocity.

Free Fall Occurs When There Is No Air Resistance Sky divers are often described as being in free fall before they open their parachutes. However, that is an incorrect description, because air resistance is always acting on the sky diver.

An object is in **free fall** only if gravity is pulling it down and no other forces are acting on it. Because air resistance is a force (fluid friction), free fall can occur only where there is no air—in a vacuum (a place in which there is no matter) or in space. **Figure 5** shows objects falling in a vacuum. Because there is no air resistance, the two objects are in free fall.

Figure 5 *Air resistance normally causes a feather to fall more slowly than an apple. But in a vacuum, the feather and the apple fall with the same acceleration because both are in free fall.*

Orbiting Objects Are in Free Fall

Look at the astronaut in **Figure 6.** Why is the astronaut floating inside the space shuttle? It might be tempting to say it is because she is "weightless" in space. In fact, you may have read or heard that objects are weightless in space. However, it is impossible to be weightless anywhere in the universe.

Weight is a measure of gravitational force. The size of the force depends on the masses of objects and the distances between them. If you traveled in space far away from all the stars and planets, the gravitational force acting on you would be almost undetectable because the distance between you and other objects would be great. But you would still have mass, and so would all the other objects in the universe. Therefore, gravity would still attract you to other objects—even if just slightly—so you would still have weight.

Astronauts "float" in orbiting spaceships because of free fall. To understand this better, you need to understand what *orbiting* means and then consider the astronauts inside the ship.

Figure 6 *Astronauts appear to be weightless while floating inside the space shuttle—but they're not!*

Two Motions Combine to Cause Orbiting An object is said to be orbiting when it is traveling in a circular or nearly circular path around another object. When a spaceship orbits Earth, it is moving forward, but it is also in free fall toward Earth. **Figure 7** shows how these two motions occur together to cause orbiting.

Figure 7 How an Orbit Is Formed

a The shuttle moves forward at a constant speed. This would be its path if there were no gravity.

b The shuttle is in free fall because gravity pulls it down toward Earth. This would be its path if it were not traveling forward.

c The actual path of the shuttle follows the curve of Earth's surface. This is known as orbiting.

As you can see in the illustration above, the space shuttle is always falling while it is in orbit. So why don't astronauts hit their heads on the ceiling of the falling shuttle? Because they are also in free fall—they are always falling, too. Because the astronaut in Figure 6 is in free fall, she appears to be floating.

The Role of Gravity in Orbiting Besides spaceships and satellites, many other objects in the universe are in orbit. The moon orbits the Earth, Earth and the other planets orbit the sun, and many stars orbit large masses in the center of galaxies. All of these objects are traveling in a circular or nearly circular path. Remember, any object in circular motion is constantly changing direction. Because an unbalanced force is necessary to change the motion of any object, there must be an unbalanced force working on any object in circular motion.

The unbalanced force that causes objects to move in a circular path is called a *centripetal force*. Gravity provides the centripetal force that keeps objects in orbit. The word *centripetal* means "toward the center." As you can see in **Figure 8,** the centripetal force on the moon points toward the center of the circle traced by the moon's orbit.

Path of moon

Centripetal force on the moon

Figure 8 *The moon stays in orbit around the Earth because Earth's gravitational force provides a centripetal force on the moon.*

Projectile Motion and Gravity

The orbit of the space shuttle around the Earth is an example of projectile (proh JEK tuhl) motion. **Projectile motion** is the curved path an object follows when thrown or propelled near the surface of the Earth. The motions of leaping dancers, thrown balls, hopping grasshoppers, and arrows shot from a bow are all examples of projectile motion. Projectile motion has two components—horizontal and vertical. The two components are independent; that is, they have no effect on each other. When the two motions are combined, they form a curved path, as shown in **Figure 9.**

Figure 9 *Two motions combine to form projectile motion.*

a After the ball leaves the pitcher's hand, its **horizontal** velocity is constant.

b The ball's **vertical** velocity increases because gravity causes it to accelerate downward.

c The two motions combine to form a **curved path.**

Examples of Objects in Projectile Motion

- A football being passed
- Balls being juggled
- An athlete doing a high jump
- Water sprayed by a sprinkler
- A swimmer diving into water
- A leaping frog

Horizontal Motion   When you throw a ball, your hand exerts a force on the ball that makes the ball move forward. This force gives the ball its horizontal motion. Horizontal motion is motion that is parallel to the ground.

After you let go of the ball, there are no horizontal forces acting on the ball (if you ignore air resistance). Therefore, there are no forces to change the ball's horizontal motion. Thus, the horizontal velocity of the ball is constant after the ball leaves your hand, as shown in Figure 9.

Penny Projectile Motion

1. Position a **flat ruler** and **two pennies** on a desk or table as shown below.

2. Hold the ruler by the end that is on the desk. Move the ruler quickly in the direction shown so that the ruler knocks the penny off the table and so that the other penny also drops. Repeat several times.

3. Which penny travels with projectile motion? In what order do the pennies hit the ground? Record and explain your answers in your ScienceLog.

Vertical Motion   After you throw a ball, gravity pulls it downward, giving the ball vertical motion. Vertical motion is motion that is perpendicular to the ground. Because objects in projectile motion accelerate downward, you always have to aim above a target if you want to hit it with a thrown or propelled object. That's why when you aim an arrow directly at a bull's-eye, your arrow strikes the bottom of the target rather than the middle.

Gravity pulls objects in projectile motion down with an acceleration of 9.8 m/s/s (if air resistance is ignored), just as it does all falling objects. **Figure 10** shows that the downward acceleration of a thrown object and a falling object are the same.

Figure 10 Projectile Motion and Acceleration Due to Gravity

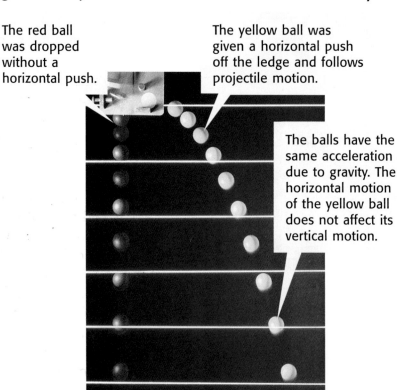

The red ball was dropped without a horizontal push.

The yellow ball was given a horizontal push off the ledge and follows projectile motion.

The balls have the same acceleration due to gravity. The horizontal motion of the yellow ball does not affect its vertical motion.

REVIEW

1. How does air resistance affect the acceleration of falling objects?

2. Explain why an astronaut in an orbiting spaceship floats.

3. How is an orbit formed?

4. **Applying Concepts**   Think about a sport you play that involves a ball. Identify at least four different instances in which an object is in projectile motion.

Newton's Laws of Motion

Terms to Learn

inertia   momentum

What You'll Do

♦ State and apply Newton's laws of motion.
♦ Compare the momentum of different objects.
♦ State and apply the law of conservation of momentum.

In 1686, Sir Isaac Newton published his book *Principia*. In it, he described three laws that relate forces to the motion of objects. Although he did not discover all three of the laws, he explained them in a way that helped many people understand them. Thus, the three laws are commonly known as Newton's laws of motion. In this section, you will learn about these laws and how they influence the motion of objects.

Newton's First Law of Motion

> *An object at rest remains at rest and an object in motion remains in motion at constant speed and in a straight line unless acted on by an unbalanced force.*

Newton's first law of motion describes the motion of an object that has a net force of zero acting on it. This law may seem complicated when you first read it, but it's easy to understand when you consider its two parts separately.

Part 1: Objects at Rest What does it mean for an object to be at rest? Objects don't get tired! An object that is not moving is said to be at rest. Objects are at rest all around you. A plane parked on a runway, a chair on the floor, and a golf ball balanced on a tee are all examples of objects at rest.

Newton's first law says that objects at rest will remain at rest unless they are acted on by an unbalanced force. That means that objects will not start moving until a push or a pull is exerted on them. A plane won't soar in the air unless it is pushed by the exhaust from its jet engines, a chair won't slide across the room unless you push it, and a golf ball won't move off the tee unless struck by a golf club, as shown in **Figure 11.**

Figure 11 *A golf ball will remain at rest on a tee until it is acted on by the unbalanced force of a moving club.*

Unbalanced force

Object at rest

Object in motion

a An unbalanced force from another car acts on your car, changing its motion.

b The collision changes your car's motion, but not yours. Your motion continues with the same velocity.

c Another unbalanced force, from your seat belt, changes your motion.

Figure 12 *Bumper cars let you have fun with Newton's first law.*

Part 2: Objects in Motion

Think about riding in a bumper car at an amusement park. Your ride is pleasant as long as you are driving in an open space. But the name of the game is bumper cars, so sooner or later you are likely to run into another car, as shown in **Figure 12.**

The second part of Newton's first law explains that an object moving at a certain velocity will continue to move *forever* at the same speed and in the same direction unless some unbalanced force acts on it. Thus, your bumper car stops, but you continue to move forward until your seat belt stops you.

Friction and Newton's First Law Because an object in motion will stay in motion forever unless it is acted on by an unbalanced force, you should be able to give your desk a small push and send it sailing across the floor. If you try it, you will find that the desk quickly comes to a stop. What does this tell you?

There must be an unbalanced force that acts on the desk to stop its motion. That unbalanced force is friction. The friction between the desk and the floor works against the motion of the desk. Because of friction, it is often difficult to observe the effects of Newton's first law on the motion of everyday objects. For example, friction will cause a ball rolling on grass to slow down and stop. Friction will also make a car decelerate on a flat surface if the driver lets up on the gas pedal. Because of friction, the motion of these objects changes.

Stopping Motion

The dummy in this crash test is wearing a seat belt, but the car does not have an air bag. Explain why Newton's first law of motion could lead to serious injuries in accidents involving cars without air bags.

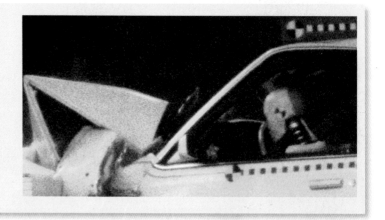

Inertia Is Related to Mass Newton's first law of motion is sometimes called the law of inertia. **Inertia** (in UHR shuh) is the tendency of all objects to resist any change in motion. Due to inertia, an object at rest will remain at rest until something makes it move. Likewise, inertia is why a moving object stays in motion with the same velocity unless a force acts on it to change its speed or direction. Inertia causes you to slide toward the side of a car when the driver makes a sharp turn. Inertia is also why it is impossible for a plane, car, or bicycle to stop instantaneously.

Mass Is a Measure of Inertia An object with a small mass has less inertia than an object with a large mass. Therefore, it is easier to start and to change the motion of an object with a small mass. For example, a softball has less mass and therefore less inertia than a bowling ball. Because the softball has a small amount of inertia, it is easy to pitch a softball and to change its motion by hitting it with a bat. Imagine how difficult it would be to play softball with a bowling ball! **Figure 13** further illustrates the relationship between mass and inertia. Try the QuickLab at right to test the relationship yourself.

Figure 13 *Inertia makes it harder to push a car than to push a bicycle. Inertia also makes it easier to stop a moving bicycle than a car moving at the same speed.*

First-Law Magic

1. On a table or desk, place a **large, empty plastic cup** on top of a **paper towel.**

2. Without touching the cup or tipping it over, remove the paper towel from under the cup. What did you do to accomplish this?

3. Repeat the first two steps a few times until you are comfortable with the procedure.

4. Fill the cup half full with **water,** and place the cup on the paper towel.

5. Once again, remove the paper towel from under the cup. Was it easier or harder to do this? Explain your answer in terms of mass and inertia.

✔ Self-Check

When you stand while riding a bus, why do you tend to fall backward when the bus starts moving?
(See page 724 to check your answer.)

Newton's Second Law of Motion

The acceleration of an object depends on the mass of the object and the amount of force applied.

Newton's second law describes the motion of an object when an unbalanced force is acting on it. As with Newton's first law, it is easier to consider the parts of this law separately.

Part 1: Acceleration Depends on Mass Suppose you are pushing a shopping cart at the grocery store. At the beginning of your shopping trip, you have to exert only a small force on the cart to accelerate it. But when the cart is full, the same amount of force will not accelerate the cart as much as before, as shown in **Figure 14.** This example illustrates that for the same force, an object's acceleration *decreases* as its mass *increases* and its acceleration *increases* as its mass *decreases*.

Environment

C O N N E C T I O N

Modern cars pollute the air less than older cars. One reason for this is that modern cars are less massive than older models and have considerably smaller engines. According to Newton's second law, a less massive object requires less force to achieve the same acceleration as a more massive object. This is why a smaller car can have a smaller engine and still have acceptable acceleration. And because smaller engines use less fuel, they pollute less.

Figure 14 *If the force applied is the same, the acceleration of the empty cart is greater than the acceleration of the full cart.*

Part 2: Acceleration Depends on Force Now suppose you give the shopping cart a hard push, as shown in **Figure 15.** The cart will start moving faster than if you only gave it a soft push. This illustrates that an object's acceleration *increases* as the force on it *increases*. Conversely, an object's acceleration *decreases* as the force on it *decreases*.

The acceleration of an object is always in the same direction as the force applied. The shopping cart moved forward because the push was in the forward direction. To change the direction of an object, you must exert a force in the direction you want the object to go.

Figure 15 *Acceleration will increase when a larger force is exerted.*

Expressing Newton's Second Law Mathematically The relationship of acceleration (*a*) to mass (*m*) and force (*F*) can be expressed mathematically with the following equation:

$$a = \frac{F}{m}$$

This equation is often rearranged to the following form:

$$F = m \times a$$

Both forms of the equation can be used to solve problems. Try the MathBreak at right to practice using the equations. Newton's second law explains why objects fall to Earth with the same acceleration. In **Figure 16,** you can see how the larger weight of the watermelon is offset by its greater inertia. Thus, the accelerations of the watermelon and the apple are the same when you put the numbers into the equation for acceleration.

MATH BREAK

Second-Law Problems

You can rearrange the equation $F = m \times a$ to find acceleration and mass as shown below.

$$a = \frac{F}{m} \qquad m = \frac{F}{a}$$

1. What is the acceleration of a 7 kg mass if a force of 68.6 N is used to move it toward Earth? (Hint: 1 N is equal to 1 kg•m/s/s.)

2. What force is necessary to accelerate a 1,250 kg car at a rate of 40 m/s/s?

3. What is the mass of an object if a force of 34 N produces an acceleration of 4 m/s/s?

Figure 16 Newton's Second Law and Acceleration Due to Gravity

The **apple** has less mass, so the gravitational force on it is smaller. However, the apple also has less inertia and is easier to move.

The **watermelon** has more mass and therefore more inertia, so it is harder to move.

$m = 0.102$ kg

$F = 1$ N

1 N = 1 kg•m/s/s

$m = 1.02$ kg

$F = 10$ N

10 N = 10 kg•m/s/s

$$a = \frac{1 \text{ kg•m/s/s}}{0.102 \text{ kg}} = 9.8 \text{ m/s/s}$$

$$a = \frac{10 \text{ kg•m/s/s}}{1.02 \text{ kg}} = 9.8 \text{ m/s/s}$$

REVIEW

1. How is inertia related to Newton's first law of motion?

2. Name two ways to increase the acceleration of an object.

3. **Making Predictions** If the acceleration due to gravity were somehow doubled to 19.6 m/s/s, what would happen to your weight?

internet connect

SC*i*LINKS
NSTA

TOPIC: Newton's Laws of Motion
GO TO: www.scilinks.org
*sci*LINKS NUMBER: HSTP145

Newton's Third Law of Motion

Whenever one object exerts a force on a second object, the second object exerts an equal and opposite force on the first.

Newton's third law can be simply stated as follows: All forces act in pairs. If a force is exerted, another force occurs that is equal in size and opposite in direction. The law itself addresses only forces. But the way that force pairs interact affects the motion of objects.

What is meant by "forces act in pairs"? Study **Figure 17** to learn how one force pair helps propel a swimmer through water.

Figure 17 *The action force and reaction force are a pair. The two forces are equal in size but opposite in direction.*

The **action force** is the swimmer's hands and feet pushing on the water.

The **reaction force** is the water pushing on the hands and feet. The reaction force moves the swimmer forward.

Action and reaction force pairs occur even when there is no motion. For example, you exert a force on a chair when you sit on it. Your weight pushing down on the chair is the action force. The reaction force is the force exerted by the chair that pushes up on your body and is equal to your weight.

Force Pairs Do Not Act on the Same Object You know that a force is always exerted by one object on another object. This is true for all forces, including action and reaction forces. However, it is important to remember that action and reaction forces in a pair do not act on the same object. If they did, the net force would always be zero and nothing would ever move! To understand this better, look back at Figure 17. In this example, the action force was exerted on the water by the swimmer's hands and feet. But the reaction force was exerted on the swimmer's hands and feet by the water. The forces did not act on the same object.

Activity

Choose a sport that you enjoy playing or watching. In your ScienceLog, list five ways that Newton's laws of motion are involved in the game you selected.

TRY at HOME

The Effect of a Reaction Can Be Difficult to See Another example of a force pair is shown in **Figure 18.** Remember, gravity is a force of attraction between objects that is due to their masses. If you drop a ball off a ledge, the force of gravity pulls the ball toward Earth. This is the action force exerted by Earth on the ball. But the force of gravity also pulls Earth toward the ball. That is the reaction force exerted by the ball on Earth.

It's easy to see the effect of the action force—the ball falls to Earth. Why don't you notice the effect of the reaction force—Earth being pulled upward? To find the answer to this question, think back to Newton's second law. It states that the acceleration of an object depends on the force applied to it and on the mass of the object. The force on Earth is equal to the force on the ball, but the mass of Earth is much *larger* than the mass of the ball. Therefore, the acceleration of Earth is much *smaller* than the acceleration of the ball. The acceleration is so small that you can't even see it or feel it. Thus, it is difficult to observe the effect of Newton's third law on falling objects.

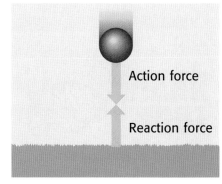

Figure 18 *The force of gravity between Earth and a falling object is a force pair.*

More Examples of Action and Reaction Force Pairs The examples below illustrate a variety of action and reaction force pairs. In each example, notice which object exerts the action force and which object exerts the reaction force.

The rabbit's legs exert a force on Earth. Earth exerts an equal force on the rabbit's legs, causing the rabbit to accelerate upward.

The bat exerts a force on the ball, sending the ball into the outfield. The ball exerts an equal force on the bat, but the bat does not fly toward the catcher because the batter is exerting another force on the bat.

The shuttle's thrusters push the exhaust gases downward as the gases push the shuttle upward with an equal force.

When you hit a table with your hand, your hand will hurt. This is because the table meets your hand with a force equal in size to the force you exerted.

Momentum Is a Property of Moving Objects

If a compact car and a large truck are traveling with the same velocity, it takes longer for the truck to stop than it does for the car if the same braking force is applied. Likewise, it takes longer for a fast moving car to stop than it does for a slow moving car with the same mass. The truck and the fast moving car have more momentum than the compact car and the slow moving car.

Momentum is a property of a moving object that depends on the object's mass and velocity. The more momentum an object has, the harder it is to stop the object or change its direction. Although the compact car and the truck are traveling with the same velocity, the truck has more mass and therefore more momentum, so it is harder to stop than the car. Similarly, the fast moving car has a greater velocity and thus more momentum than the slow moving car.

Momentum Is Conserved When a moving object hits another object, some or all of the momentum of the first object is transferred to the other object. If only some of the momentum is transferred, the rest of the momentum stays with the first object.

Imagine you hit a billiard ball with a cue ball so that the billiard ball starts moving and the cue ball stops, as shown in **Figure 19.** The cue ball had a certain amount of momentum before the collision. During the collision, all of the cue ball's momentum was transferred to the billiard ball. After the collision, the billiard ball moved away with the same amount of momentum the cue ball had. This example illustrates the *law of conservation of momentum.* Any time two or more objects interact, they may exchange momentum, but the total amount of momentum stays the same.

Figure 19 *The momentum before a collision is equal to the momentum after the collision.*

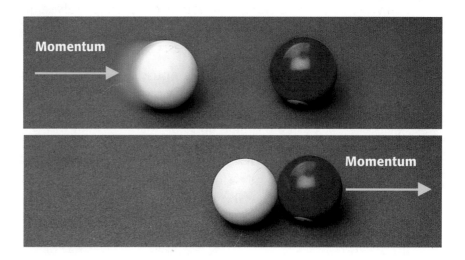

Bowling is another example of how conservation of momentum is used in a game. The bowling ball rolls down the lane with a certain amount of momentum. When the ball hits the pins, some of the ball's momentum is transferred to the pins and the pins move off in different directions. Furthermore, some of the pins that were hit by the ball go on to hit other pins, transferring the momentum again.

Conservation of Momentum and Newton's Third Law
Conservation of momentum can be explained by Newton's third law. In the example with the billiard ball, the cue ball hit the billiard ball with a certain amount of force. This was the action force. The reaction force was the equal but opposite force exerted by the billiard ball on the cue ball. The action force made the billiard ball start moving, and the reaction force made the cue ball stop moving, as shown in **Figure 20.** Because the action and reaction forces are equal and opposite, momentum is conserved.

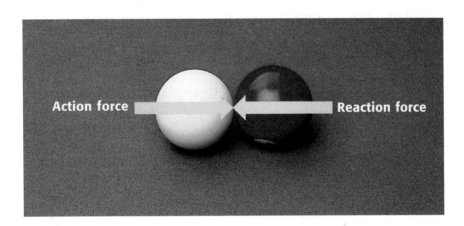

Action force → ← Reaction force

Figure 20 *The action force makes the billiard ball begin moving, and the reaction force stops the cue ball's motion.*

REVIEW

1. Name three action and reaction force pairs involved in doing your homework. Name what object is exerting and what object is receiving the forces.

2. Which has more momentum, a mouse running at 1 m/s north or an elephant walking at 3 m/s east? Explain your answer.

3. **Applying Concepts**   When a truck pulls a trailer, the trailer and truck accelerate forward even though the action and reaction forces are the same size but in opposite directions. Why don't these forces balance each other out?

Catapult forward! Or is it backward? Find out on page 656 of the LabBook.

Chapter Highlights

Vocabulary

terminal velocity *(p. 140)*

free fall *(p. 141)*

projectile motion *(p. 143)*

Section Notes

- All objects accelerate toward Earth at 9.8 m/s/s.

- Air resistance slows the acceleration of falling objects.

- An object is in free fall if gravity is the only force acting on it.

- An orbit is formed by combining forward motion and free fall.

- Objects in orbit appear to be weightless because they are in free fall.

- A centripetal force is needed to keep objects in circular motion. Gravity acts as a centripetal force to keep objects in orbit.

- Projectile motion is the curved path an object follows when thrown or propelled near the surface of Earth.

- Projectile motion has two components—horizontal and vertical. Gravity affects only the vertical motion of projectile motion.

Labs

A Marshmallow Catapult *(p. 652)*

☑ Skills Check

Math Concepts

NEWTON'S SECOND LAW The equation $a = F/m$ on page 149 summarizes Newton's second law of motion. The equation shows the relationship between the acceleration of an object, the force causing the acceleration, and the object's mass. For example, if you apply a force of 18 N to a 6 kg object, the object's acceleration is

$$a = \frac{F}{m} = \frac{18\,\text{N}}{6\,\text{kg}} = \frac{18\,\cancel{\text{kg}}\cdot\text{m/s/s}}{6\,\cancel{\text{kg}}} = 3\ \text{m/s/s}$$

Visual Understanding

HOW AN ORBIT IS FORMED An orbit is a combination of two motions—forward motion and free fall. Figure 7 on page 142 shows how the two motions combine to form an orbit.

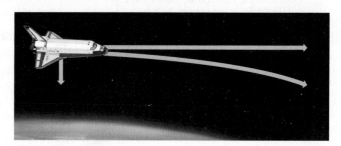

Vocabulary

inertia *(p. 147)*

momentum *(p. 152)*

Section Notes

- Newton's first law of motion states that the motion of an object will not change if no unbalanced forces act on it.

- Inertia is the tendency of matter to resist a change in motion. Mass is a measure of inertia.

- Newton's second law of motion states that the acceleration of an object depends on its mass and on the force exerted on it.

- Newton's third law of motion states that whenever one object exerts a force on a second object, the second object exerts an equal and opposite force on the first.

- Momentum is the property of a moving object that depends on its mass and velocity.

- When two or more objects interact, momentum may be exchanged, but the total amount of momentum does not change. This is the law of conservation of momentum.

Labs

Blast Off! *(p. 653)*

Inertia-Rama! *(p. 654)*

Quite a Reaction *(p. 656)*

 internetconnect

 GO TO: go.hrw.com

SCILINKS sm

N S T A

GO TO: www.scilinks.org

Visit the **HRW** Web site for a variety of learning tools related to this chapter. Just type in the keyword:

KEYWORD: HSTFOR

Visit the **National Science Teachers Association** on-line Web site for Internet resources related to this chapter. Just type in the *sci*LINKS number for more information about the topic:

TOPIC: The Force of Gravity	*sci***LINKS NUMBER:** HSTP130
TOPIC: Gravity and Orbiting Objects	*sci***LINKS NUMBER:** HSTP135
TOPIC: Projectile Motion	*sci***LINKS NUMBER:** HSTP140
TOPIC: Newton's Laws of Motion	*sci***LINKS NUMBER:** HSTP145

Chapter Review

To complete the following sentences, choose the correct term from each pair of terms listed below:

1. An object in motion tends to stay in motion because it has ___?___. (*inertia* or *terminal velocity*)

2. Falling objects stop accelerating at ___?___. (*free fall* or *terminal velocity*)

3. ___?___ is the path that a thrown object follows. (*Free fall* or *Projectile motion*)

4. A property of moving objects that depends on mass and velocity is ___?___. (*inertia* or *momentum*)

5. ___?___ only occurs when there is no air resistance. (*Momentum* or *Free fall*)

UNDERSTANDING CONCEPTS

Multiple Choice

6. A feather and a rock dropped at the same time from the same height would land at the same time when dropped by
   a. Galileo in Italy.
   b. Newton in England.
   c. an astronaut on the moon.
   d. an astronaut on the space shuttle.

7. When a soccer ball is kicked, the action and reaction forces do not cancel each other out because
   a. the force of the foot on the ball is bigger than the force of the ball on the foot.
   b. the forces act on two different objects.
   c. the forces act at different times.
   d. All of the above

8. An object is in projectile motion if
   a. it is thrown with a horizontal push.
   b. it is accelerated downward by gravity.
   c. it does not accelerate horizontally.
   d. All of the above

9. Newton's first law of motion applies
   a. to moving objects.
   b. to objects that are not moving.
   c. to objects that are accelerating.
   d. Both (a) and (b)

10. Acceleration of an object
    a. decreases as the mass of the object increases.
    b. increases as the force on the object increases.
    c. is in the same direction as the force on the object.
    d. All of the above

11. A golf ball and a bowling ball are moving at the same velocity. Which has more momentum?
    a. the golf ball, because it has less mass
    b. the bowling ball, because it has more mass
    c. They both have the same momentum because they have the same velocity.
    d. There is no way to know without additional information.

Short Answer

12. Explain how an orbit is formed.

13. Describe how gravity and air resistance combine when an object reaches terminal velocity.

14. Explain why friction can make observing Newton's first law of motion difficult.

Concept Mapping

15. Use the following terms to create a concept map: gravity, free fall, terminal velocity, projectile motion, air resistance.

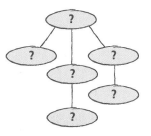

19. A 12 kg rock falls from rest off a cliff and hits the ground in 1.5 seconds.

   a. Ignoring air resistance, what is the rock's velocity just before it hits the ground?

   b. What is the rock's weight after it hits the ground? (Hint: Weight is a measure of the gravitational force on an object.)

CRITICAL THINKING AND PROBLEM SOLVING

16. During a shuttle launch, about 830,000 kg of fuel is burned in 8 minutes. The fuel provides the shuttle with a constant thrust, or push off the ground. How does Newton's second law of motion explain why the shuttle's acceleration increases during takeoff?

INTERPRETING GRAPHICS

20. The picture below shows a common desk toy. If you pull one ball up and release it, it hits the balls at the bottom and comes to a stop. In the same instant, the ball on the other side swings up and repeats the cycle. How does conservation of momentum explain how this toy works?

17. When using a hammer to drive a nail into wood, you have to swing the hammer through the air with a certain velocity. Because the hammer has both mass and velocity, it has momentum. Describe what happens to the hammer's momentum after the hammer hits the nail.

18. Suppose you are standing on a skateboard or on in-line skates and you toss a backpack full of heavy books toward your friend. What do you think will happen to you and why? Explain your answer in terms of Newton's third law of motion.

Reading Check-up

Take a minute to review your answers to the Pre-Reading Questions found at the bottom of page 136. Have your answers changed? If necessary, revise your answers based on what you have learned since you began this chapter.

Eureka!

A Bat with Dimples

Wouldn't it be nice to hit a home run every time? Jeff DiTullio, a teacher at MIT, in Cambridge, Massachusetts, has found a way for you to get more bang from your bat. Would you believe *dimples?*

Building a Better Bat

If you look closely at the surface of a golf ball, you'll see dozens of tiny craterlike dimples. When air flows past these dimples, it gets stirred up. By keeping air moving near the surface of the ball, the dimples help the golf ball move faster and farther through the air.

DiTullio decided to apply this same idea to a baseball bat. His hypothesis was that dimples would allow a bat to move more easily through the air. This would help batters swing the bat faster and hit the ball harder. To test his hypothesis, DiTullio pressed hundreds of little dimples about 1 mm deep and 2 mm across into the surface of a bat.

When DiTullio tested his dimpled bat in a wind tunnel, he found that it could be swung 3 to 5 percent faster. That may not sound like much, but it could add about 5 m to a fly ball!

Safe . . . or Out?

As you might imagine, many baseball players would love to have a bat that could turn a long fly ball into a home run. But are dimpled baseball bats legal?

The size and shape of every piece of equipment used in Major League Baseball games are regulated. A baseball bat, for instance, must be no more than 107 cm long and no more than 7 cm across at its widest point. When DiTullio

Drag

Reduced drag

▲ *By reducing the amount of drag behind the bat, dimples help the bat move faster through the air.*

designed his dimpled bat, there was no rule stating that bats had to be smooth. But when Major League Baseball found out about the new bat, they changed the rules! Today official rules require that all bats be smooth, and they prohibit any type of "experimental" bat. Someday the rules may be revised to allow DiTullio's dimpled bat. When that happens, fans of the dimpled baseball bat will all shout, "Play ball!"

Dimple Madness

▶ Now that you know how dimples can improve baseball bats, think of other uses for dimples. How might dimples improve the way other objects move through the air? Draw a sketch of a dimpled object, and describe how the dimples improve the design.

▶ *Jeff DiTullio, pictured with his dimpled baseball bat, is an aeronautical engineer— someone who studies both the way air moves and the way things move through air.*

CAREERS

ROLLER COASTER DESIGNER

Roller coasters have fascinated **Steve Okamoto** ever since his first ride on one. "I remember going to Disneyland as a kid. My mother was always upset with me because I kept looking over the sides of the rides, trying to figure out how they worked," he laughs. To satisfy his curiosity, Okamoto became a mechanical engineer. Today he uses his scientific knowledge to design and build machines, systems, and buildings. But his specialty is roller coasters.

His West Coaster, which sits on the Santa Monica pier in Santa Monica, California, towers five stories above the Pacific Ocean. The cars on the Steel Force, at Dorney Park, in Pennsylvania, reach speeds of over 120 km/h and drop more than 60 m to disappear into a 37 m long tunnel. The Mamba, at Worlds of Fun, in Missouri, sends cars flying along as high and as fast as the Steel Force does, but it also has two giant back-to-back hills, a fast spiral, and five "camelback" humps. The camelbacks are designed to pull riders' seats out from under them, giving the riders "air time."

Coaster Motion

Roller-coaster cars really do coast along the track. A motor pulls the cars up a high hill to start the ride. After that, the cars are powered by gravity alone. As the cars roll downhill, they pick up enough speed to whiz through the rest of the curves, loops, twists, and bumps in the track.

Designing a successful coaster is no simple task. Steve Okamoto has to calculate the cars' speed and acceleration on each part of the track. "The coaster has to go fast enough to make it up the next hill," he explains. Okamoto uses his knowledge of geometry and physics to create safe but scary curves, loops, humps, and dips. Okamoto must also keep in mind that the ride's towers and structures need to be strong enough to support both the track and

the speeding cars full of people. The cars themselves need special wheels to keep them locked onto the track and seat belts or bars to keep passengers safely inside. "It's like putting together a puzzle, except the pieces haven't been cut out yet," says Okamoto.

Take the Challenge

▶ Step outside for a moment. Gather some rope and a medium-sized plastic bucket half-full of water. Can you get the bucket over your head and upside down without any water escaping? How does this relate to roller coasters?

▲ *The Wild Thing, in Shakopee, Minnesota, was designed by Steve Okamoto.*

Forces in Fluids

Sections

Pre-Reading
Questions

1. What is a fluid?
2. How is fluid pressure
   exerted?
3. Do moving fluids exert
   different forces than
   nonmoving fluids?

A NEED FOR SPEED

Even when you are racing downhill on your bicycle, a fluid force slows you down. "What a drag!" you say. Well, actually, it is a drag. When designing bicycle gear and clothing, manufacturers consider more than just looks and comfort. They also try to decrease drag, a fluid force that opposes motion. Here a cyclist rides a bike in a wind tunnel in a study of how a fluid—air—affects his ride. In this chapter, you'll learn more about forces that fluids exert on objects in your everyday life.

TAKING FLIGHT

In this activity, you will build a model airplane to help you identify how wing size affects flight.

Procedure

1. Fold a **sheet of paper** in half lengthwise. Then open it. Fold the top corners toward the center crease. Then fold the entire sheet in half along the center crease.

2. With the plane on its side, fold the top front edge down so that it meets the bottom edge. Fold the top edge down again so that it meets the bottom edge.

3. Turn the plane over. Repeat step 2.

4. Raise both wings so that they are perpendicular to the body.

5. Point the plane slightly upward, and gently throw it. Repeat several times. Describe what you see.

6. Make the wings smaller by folding them one more time. Gently throw the plane. Repeat several times. Describe what you see.

7. Try to achieve the same flight path you saw when the wings were bigger. Record your technique.

Analysis

8. What happened to the plane's flight when you reduced the size of its wings? Explain.

9. What gave your plane its forward motion?

Fluids and Pressure

Terms to Learn

fluid
pressure
pascal
atmospheric pressure
density
Pascal's principle

What You'll Do

- ◆ Describe how fluids exert pressure.
- ◆ Analyze how fluid depth affects pressure.
- ◆ Give examples of fluids flowing from high to low pressure.
- ◆ State and apply Pascal's principle.

What does a dolphin have in common with a sea gull? What does a dog have in common with a fly? What do you have in common with all these living things? The answer is that you and all these other living things spend a lifetime moving through and even breathing fluids. A **fluid** is any material that can flow and that takes the shape of its container. Fluids include liquids (such as water and oil) and gases (such as oxygen and carbon dioxide). Fluids are able to flow because the particles in fluids, unlike the particles in solids, can move easily past each other. As you will find out, the remarkable properties of fluids allow huge ships to float, divers to explore the ocean depths, and jumbo jets to soar across the skies.

All Fluids Exert Pressure

You probably have heard the terms *air pressure, water pressure,* and *blood pressure.* Air, water, and blood are all fluids, and all fluids exert pressure. So what's pressure? Well, think about this example. When you pump up a bicycle tire, you push air into the tire. And like all matter, air is made of tiny particles that are constantly moving. Inside the tire, the air particles push against each other and against the walls of the tire, as shown in **Figure 1.** The more air you pump into the tire, the more the air particles push against the inside of your tire. Together, these pushes create a force against the tire. The amount of force exerted on a given area is **pressure.** Pressure can be calculated by dividing the force that a fluid exerts by the area over which the force is exerted:

$$\text{Pressure} = \frac{\text{Force}}{\text{Area}}$$

The SI unit for pressure is the **pascal.** One pascal (1 Pa) is the force of one newton exerted over an area of one square meter (1 N/m^2). Try the MathBreak at left to practice calculating pressure.

Figure 1 *The force of the air particles hitting the inner surface of the tire creates pressure, which keeps the tire inflated.*

$$\div \ 5 \div \ \overset{\Omega}{\leq} \ \overset{\infty}{\leq} \ +\Omega \ \overset{\vee}{\underset{\infty}{9}} \ \overset{\leq}{\Sigma} \ 2$$

MATH BREAK

Pressure, Force, and Area

The equation on this page can be used to find pressure or rearranged to find force or area.

$$\text{Force} = \text{Pressure} \times \text{Area}$$
$$\text{Area} = \frac{\text{Force}}{\text{Pressure}}$$

1. Find the pressure exerted by a 3,000 N crate with an area of 2 m^2.

2. Find the weight of a rock with an area of 10 m^2 that exerts a pressure of 250 Pa.

(Be sure to express your answers in the correct SI unit.)

Why Are Bubbles Round?   When you blow a soap bubble, you blow in only one direction. So why doesn't the bubble get longer and longer as you blow instead of rounder and rounder? The shape of the bubble is due in part to an important property of fluids: Fluids exert pressure evenly in all directions. The air you blow into the bubble exerts pressure evenly in every direction, so the bubble expands in every direction, helping to create a sphere, as shown in **Figure 2.** This property also explains why tires inflate evenly (unless there is a weak spot in the tire).

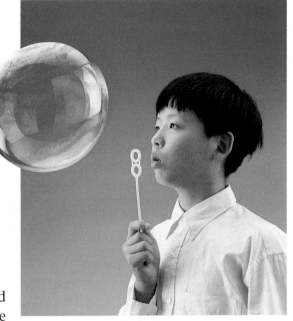

Figure 2 *You can't blow a square bubble, because fluids exert pressure equally in every direction.*

Atmospheric Pressure

The *atmosphere* is the layer of nitrogen, oxygen, and other gases that surrounds the Earth. The atmosphere stretches about 150 km above us. If you could stack 500 Eiffel Towers on top of each other, they would come close to reaching the top of the atmosphere. However, approximately 80 percent of the gases in the atmosphere are found within 10 km of the Earth's surface. Earth's atmosphere is held in place by gravity, which pulls the gases toward Earth. The pressure caused by the weight of the atmosphere is called **atmospheric pressure.**

Atmospheric pressure is exerted on everything on Earth, including you. The atmosphere exerts a pressure of approximately 101,300 N on every square meter, or 101,300 Pa. This means that there is a weight of about 10 N (roughly the weight of a pineapple) on every square centimeter (roughly the area of the tip of your little finger) of your body. Ouch!

Why don't you feel this crushing pressure? The fluids inside your body also exert pressure, just like the air inside a balloon exerts pressure. **Figure 3** can help you understand.

Figure 3 *The pressure exerted by the air inside a balloon keeps the balloon inflated against atmospheric pressure. Similarly, the pressure exerted by the fluid (mostly water) inside your body works against atmospheric pressure.*

Forces in Fluids   **163**

Figure 4 Differences in Atmospheric Pressure

At 150,000 m above sea level, atmospheric pressure is almost zero. Humans cannot travel this high without protection. The space shuttle travels past this point on its way into orbit.

The atmospheric pressure at 12,000 m is about 20 kPa. Airplane cabins must be pressurized for passenger safety.

At the top of Mount Everest (8,847 m above sea level), atmospheric pressure is about a third that at sea level.

Atmospheric pressure at La Paz, Bolivia (the world's highest capital city at 4,000 m) is about 51 kPa.

At sea level (0 m), the full pressure of the atmosphere—101 kPa—is exerted on you.

Atmospheric Pressure Varies At the top of the atmosphere, pressure is almost non-existent because there is no atmosphere pressing down. At the top of Mount Everest in south-central Asia (which is the highest point on Earth), atmospheric pressure is about 33,000 Pa, or 33 kilopascals (kPa). At sea level, atmospheric pressure is about 101 kPa.

Pressure Depends on Depth As shown in **Figure 4,** pressure increases as you descend through the atmosphere. In other words, the pressure increases as the atmosphere gets "deeper." This is an important point about fluids: Pressure depends on the depth of the fluid. At lower levels of the atmosphere, there is more fluid above you being pulled by Earth's gravitational force, so there is more pressure.

If you travel to higher or lower points in the atmosphere, the fluids in your body have to adjust to maintain equal pressure. You may have experienced this if your ears have "popped" when you were in a plane taking off or a car traveling down a steep mountain road. Small pockets of air behind your eardrums contract or expand as atmospheric pressure increases or decreases. The "pop" occurs when air is released due to these pressure changes.

REVIEW

1. How do particles in a fluid exert pressure on a container?

2. Why are you not crushed by atmospheric pressure?

3. **Applying Concepts** Explain why dams on deep lakes should be thicker at the bottom than near the top.

Water Pressure

Water is a fluid; therefore, it exerts pressure, just like the atmosphere does. Water pressure also increases with depth because of gravity. Take a look at **Figure 5.** The deeper a diver goes in the water, the greater the pressure becomes because more water above the diver is being pulled by Earth's gravitational force. In addition, the atmosphere presses down on the water, so the total pressure on the diver includes water pressure as well as atmospheric pressure.

But pressure does not depend on the total amount of fluid present, only on the depth of the fluid. A swimmer would feel the same pressure swimming at 5 m below the surface of a small pond as at 5 m below the surface of an ocean, even though there is more water in the ocean.

Density Makes a Difference Water is about 1,000 times more dense than air. (Remember, **density** is the amount of matter in a certain volume, or mass per unit volume.) Because water is more dense than air, a certain volume of water has more mass—and therefore weighs more—than the same volume of air. Therefore, water exerts greater pressure than air.

For example, if you climb a 10 m tree, the decrease in atmospheric pressure is too small to notice. But if you dive 10 m underwater, the pressure on you increases to 201 kPa, which is almost twice the atmospheric pressure at the surface!

Figure 5 **Differences in Water Pressure**

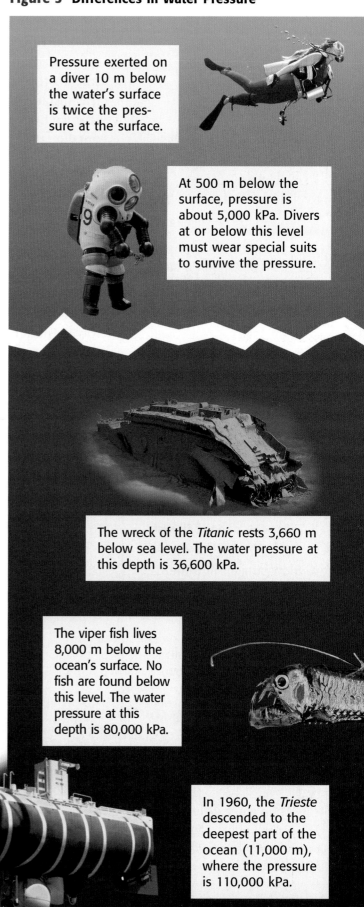

Pressure exerted on a diver 10 m below the water's surface is twice the pressure at the surface.

At 500 m below the surface, pressure is about 5,000 kPa. Divers at or below this level must wear special suits to survive the pressure.

The wreck of the *Titanic* rests 3,660 m below sea level. The water pressure at this depth is 36,600 kPa.

The viper fish lives 8,000 m below the ocean's surface. No fish are found below this level. The water pressure at this depth is 80,000 kPa.

In 1960, the *Trieste* descended to the deepest part of the ocean (11,000 m), where the pressure is 110,000 kPa.

Fluids Flow from High Pressure to Low Pressure

Look at **Figure 6.** When you drink through a straw, you remove some of the air in the straw. Because there is less air, the pressure in the straw is reduced. But the atmospheric pressure on the surface of the liquid remains the same. This creates a difference between the pressure inside the straw and the pressure outside the straw. The outside pressure forces the liquid up into the straw and into your mouth. So just by sipping your drink through a straw, you can observe another important property of fluids: Fluids flow from regions of high pressure to regions of low pressure.

Go with the Flow   Take a deep breath—that's fluid flowing from high to low pressure! When you inhale, a muscle increases the space in your chest, giving your lungs room to expand. This expansion lowers the pressure in your lungs so that it becomes lower than the outside air pressure. Air then flows into your lungs—from higher to lower pressure. This air carries oxygen that you need to live. **Figure 7** shows how exhaling also causes fluids to flow from higher to lower pressure. You can see this same exchange when you open a carbonated beverage or squeeze toothpaste onto your toothbrush.

Figure 6 *Atmospheric pressure helps you sip through a straw!*

Quick Lab

Blown Away

1. Lay an **empty plastic soda bottle** on its side.
2. Wad **a small piece of paper** (about 4 × 4 cm) into a ball.
3. Place the paper ball just inside the bottle's opening.
4. Blow straight into the opening.
5. Record your observations in your ScienceLog.
6. Explain your results in terms of high and low fluid pressures.

TRY at HOME

Figure 7   *Just as when you inhale, fluids flow from high to low pressure when you exhale.*

c Exhaled air carries carbon dioxide out of the lungs.

b The decrease in space causes the pressure in your lungs to increase. The air in your lungs flows from a region of higher pressure (your chest) to a region of lower pressure (outside of your body).

a When you exhale, a muscle in your chest moves upward, decreasing the space in your chest.

Pascal's Principle

Imagine that the water-pumping station in your town can now increase the water pressure by 20 Pa. Will the water pressure be increased more at a supermarket two blocks away or at a home 2 km away?

Believe it or not, the increase in water pressure will be transmitted through all of the water and will be the same—20 Pa—at both locations. This is explained by Pascal's principle, named for Blaise Pascal, the seventeenth-century French scientist who discovered it. **Pascal's principle** states that a change in pressure at any point in an enclosed fluid will be transmitted equally to all parts of that fluid.

Figure 8 *Thanks to Pascal's principle, the touch of a foot can stop tons of moving metal.*

Putting Pascal's Principle to Work

Devices that use liquids to transmit pressure from one point to another are called *hydraulic* (hie DRAW lik) devices. Hydraulic devices use liquids because they cannot be compressed, or squeezed, into a smaller space very much. This property allows liquids to transmit pressure more efficiently than gases, which can be compressed a great deal.

Hydraulic devices can multiply forces. The brakes of a typical car are a good example. In **Figure 8,** a driver's foot exerts pressure on a cylinder of liquid. Pascal's principle tells you that this pressure is transmitted equally to all parts of the liquid-filled brake system. This liquid presses a brake pad against each wheel, and friction brings the car to a stop. The force is multiplied because the pistons that push the brake pads on each wheel are much larger than the piston that is pushed by the brake pedal.

REVIEW

1. Explain how atmospheric pressure helps you drink through a straw.

2. What does Pascal's principle state?

3. **Making Predictions** When you squeeze a balloon, where is the pressure inside the balloon increased the most? Explain your answer in terms of Pascal's principle.

internet connect

SC*i*LINKS
NSTA

TOPIC: Fluids and Pressure
GO TO: www.scilinks.org
*sci*LINKS **NUMBER:** HSTP160

What You'll Do

◆ Explain the relationship between fluid pressure and buoyant force.
◆ Predict whether an object will float or sink in a fluid.
◆ Analyze the role of density in an object's ability to float.

Buoyant Force

Why does a rubber duck float on water? Why doesn't it sink to the bottom of your bathtub? Even if you pushed the rubber duck to the bottom, it would pop back to the surface when you released it. Some force pushes the rubber duck to the top of the water. That force is **buoyant force,** the upward force that fluids exert on all matter.

Air is a fluid, so it exerts a buoyant force. But why don't you ever see rubber ducks floating in air? Read on to find out!

Buoyant Force Is Caused by Differences in Fluid Pressure

Look at **Figure 9.** Water exerts fluid pressure on all sides of an object. The pressure exerted horizontally on one side of the object is equal to the pressure exerted horizontally on the opposite side. These equal pressures cancel one another. Thus, the only fluid pressures affecting the object are at the top and at the bottom. Because pressure increases with depth, the pressure on the bottom of the object is greater than the pressure at the top, as shown by the width of the arrows. Therefore, the water exerts a net upward force on the object. This upward force is buoyant force.

Determining Buoyant Force Archimedes (ahr kuh MEE deez), a Greek mathematician who lived in the third century B.C., discovered how to determine buoyant force. **Archimedes' principle** states that the buoyant force on an object in a fluid is an upward force equal to the weight of the volume of fluid that the object displaces. (*Displace* means "to take the place of.") For example, suppose the object in Figure 9 displaces 250 mL of water. The weight of that volume of displaced water is about 2.5 N. Therefore, the buoyant force on the object is 2.5 N. Notice that the weight of the object has nothing to do with the buoyant force. Only the weight of the displaced fluid determines the buoyant force on an object.

Figure 9 *There is more fluid pressure on the bottom of an object because pressure increases with depth. This results in an upward force on the object—buoyant force.*

Weight Vs. Buoyant Force

An object in a fluid will sink if it has a weight greater than the weight of the fluid that is displaced. In other words, an object will sink if its weight is greater than the buoyant force acting on it. An object floats only when it displaces a volume of fluid that has a weight equal to the object's weight—that is, if the buoyant force on the object is equal to the object's weight.

Sinking The lake scene in **Figure 10** looks quite peaceful, but there are forces being exerted! The rock weighs 75 N. It displaces 5 L of water. According to Archimedes' principle, the buoyant force is equal to the weight of the displaced water—about 50 N. Because the rock's weight is greater than the buoyant force, the rock sinks.

Floating The fish weighs 12 N. It displaces a volume of water that has a weight of 12 N. Because the fish's weight is equal to the buoyant force, the fish floats in the water. Now look at the duck. The duck weighs 9 N. The duck does not sink. What does that tell you? The buoyant force on the duck must be equal to the duck's weight. But the duck isn't even all the way underwater! Only the duck's feet, legs, and stomach have to be underwater in order to displace enough water to equal 9 N. Thus, the duck floats.

Buoying Up If the duck dove underwater, it would then displace more water, and the buoyant force would therefore be greater. When the buoyant force on an object is greater than the object's weight, the object is *buoyed up* (pushed up) out of the water until what's left underwater displaces an amount of water that equals the object's entire weight. That's why a rubber duck pops to the surface when it is pushed to the bottom of a filled bathtub.

Figure 10 *Will an object sink or float? It depends on whether the buoyant force is less than or equal to the object's weight.*

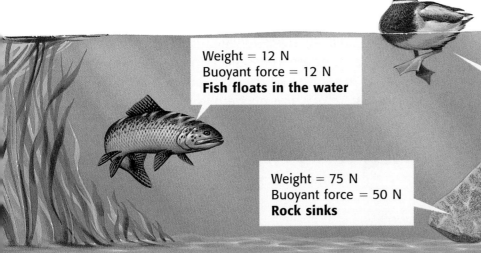

Weight = 12 N
Buoyant force = 12 N
Fish floats in the water

Weight = 9 N
Buoyant force = 9 N
Duck floats on the surface

Weight = 75 N
Buoyant force = 50 N
Rock sinks

MATH **BREAK**

How to Calculate Density

The volume of any sample of matter, no matter what state or shape, can be calculated using this equation:

$$\text{Density} = \frac{\text{Mass}}{\text{Volume}}$$

1. What is the density of a 20 cm³ sample of liquid with a mass of 25 g?
2. A 546 g fish displaces 420 cm³ of water. What is the density of the fish?

An Object Will Float or Sink Based on Its Density

Think again about the rock at the bottom of the lake. The rock displaces 5 L of water, which means that the volume of the rock is 5,000 cm³. (Remember that liters are used only for fluid volumes.) But 5,000 cm³ of rock weighs more than an equal volume of water. This is why the rock sinks. Because mass is proportional to weight on Earth, you can say that the rock has more mass per volume than water. Remember, mass per unit volume is *density*. The rock sinks because it is more dense than water. The duck floats because it is less dense than water. In Figure 10, the density of the fish is exactly equal to the density of the water.

More Dense Than Air Think back to the question about the rubber duck: "Why does it float on water but not in air?" The rubber duck floats because it is less dense than water. However, most substances are *more* dense than air. Therefore, there are few substances that float in air. The plastic that makes up the rubber duck is more dense than air, so the rubber duck doesn't float in air.

Less Dense Than Air One substance that is less dense than air is helium, a gas. In fact, helium is over 70 times less dense than air. A volume of helium displaces a volume of air that is much heavier than itself, so helium floats. That's why helium is used in airships and parade balloons, like the one shown in **Figure 11.**

Figure 11 *Helium in a balloon floats in air for the same reason a duck floats in water—it is less dense than the surrounding fluid.*

The Mystery of Floating Steel

Steel is almost eight times more dense than water. And yet huge steel ships cruise the oceans with ease, even while carrying enormous loads. But hold on! Didn't you just learn that substances that are more dense than water will sink in water? You bet! So how does a steel ship float?

The secret is in the shape of the ship. What if a ship were just a big block of steel, as shown in **Figure 12**? If you put that steel block into water, the block would sink because it is more dense than water. For this reason, ships are built with a hollow shape, as shown below. The amount of steel in the ship is the same as in the block, but the hollow shape increases the volume of the ship. Because density is mass per volume, an increase in the ship's volume leads to a decrease in its density. Therefore, ships made of steel float because their *overall density* is less than the density of water. This is true of boats of any size, made of any material. Most ships are actually built to displace even more water than is necessary for the ship to float so that the ship won't sink when people and cargo are loaded onboard.

BRAIN FOOD

The *Seawise Giant* is the largest ship in the world. It is so large that crew members often use bicycles to travel around the ship.

Figure 12 A Ship's Shape Makes the Difference

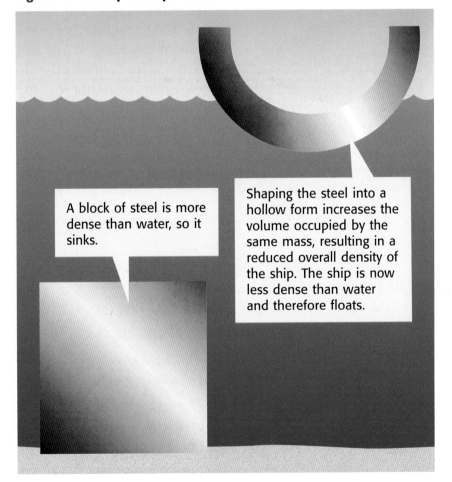

A block of steel is more dense than water, so it sinks.

Shaping the steel into a hollow form increases the volume occupied by the same mass, resulting in a reduced overall density of the ship. The ship is now less dense than water and therefore floats.

QuickLab

Ship-Shape

1. Roll a **piece of clay** into a ball the size of a golf ball, and drop it into a **container of water**. Record your observations in your ScienceLog.

2. With your hands, flatten the ball of clay until it is a bit thinner than your little finger, and press it into the shape of a bowl or canoe.

3. Place the clay boat gently in the water. How does the change of shape affect the buoyant force on the clay? How is that change related to the average density of the clay boat? Record your answers in your ScienceLog.

Density on the Move   A submarine is a special kind of ship that can travel on the surface of the water and underwater. Submarines have special tanks that can be opened to allow sea water to flow in. This water adds mass, thus increasing the submarine's overall density so it can descend into the ocean. Crew members can control the amount of water taken in, thereby controlling the submarine's change in density and thus its depth in the ocean. Compressed air is used to blow the water out of the tanks so the submarine can rise through the water. Most submarines are built of high-strength metals that withstand water pressure. Still, most submarines can go no deeper than 400 m below the surface of the ocean.

How Is a Fish Like a Submarine?   No, this is not a trick question! Like a submarine, some fish adjust their overall density in order to stay at a certain depth in the water. Most bony fish have an organ called a *swim bladder,* shown in **Figure 13.** This swim bladder is filled with gases produced in the fish's blood. The inflated swim bladder increases the fish's volume, thereby decreasing the fish's overall density and keeping it from sinking in the water. The fish's nervous system controls the amount of gas in the bladder according to the fish's depth in the water. Some fish, such as sharks, do not have a swim bladder. These fish must swim constantly to keep from sinking to the bottom of the water.

Figure 13 *Most bony fish have an organ called a swim bladder that allows the fish to adjust its overall density.*

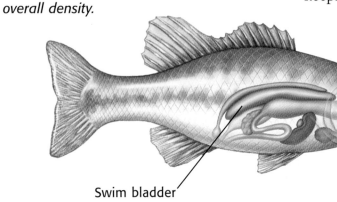

Swim bladder

REVIEW

1. Explain how differences in fluid pressure create buoyant force on an object.

2. An object weighs 20 N. It displaces a volume of water that weighs 15 N.

   a. What is the buoyant force on the object?

   b. Will this object float or sink? Explain your answer.

3. Iron has a density of 7.9 g/cm^3. Mercury has a density of 13.6 g/cm^3. Will iron float or sink in mercury? Explain your answer.

4. **Applying Concepts**   Why is it inaccurate to say that all heavy objects will sink in water?

Bernoulli's Principle

Has this ever happened to you? You've just turned on the shower. Upon stepping into the water stream, you decide that the water pressure is not strong enough. You turn the faucet to provide more water, and all of a sudden the bottom edge of the shower curtain starts swirling around your legs. What's going on? It might surprise you that the explanation for this unusual occurrence also explains how wings help birds and planes fly and how pitchers throw curve balls.

Fluid Pressure Decreases as Speed Increases

The strange reaction of the shower curtain is caused by a property of moving fluids that was first described in the eighteenth century by Daniel Bernoulli (buhr NOO lee), a Swiss mathematician. **Bernoulli's principle** states that as the speed of a moving fluid increases, its pressure decreases. In the case of the shower curtain, the faster the water moves, the less pressure it exerts. This creates an imbalance between the pressure inside the shower curtain and the pressure outside it. Because the pressure outside is now greater than the pressure inside, the shower curtain is pushed toward the water stream.

Science in a Sink You can see Bernoulli's principle at work in **Figure 14.** A table-tennis ball is attached to a string and swung gently into a moving stream of water. Instead of being pushed back out, the ball is actually held in the moving water when the string is given a tug. Why does the ball do that? The water is moving, so it has a lower pressure than the surrounding air. The higher air pressure then pushes the ball into the area of lower pressure—the water stream. Try this at home to see for yourself!

Figure 14 *This ball is pushed by the higher pressure of the air into an area of reduced pressure—the water stream.*

QuickLab

Breathing Bernoulli-Style

1. Hold **two pieces of paper** by their top edges, one in each hand, so that they hang next to one another about 5 cm apart.

2. Blow a steady stream of air between the two sheets of paper.

3. Record your observations in your ScienceLog. Explain the results according to Bernoulli's principle.

TRY at HOME

It's a Bird! It's a Plane! It's Bernoulli's Principle!

The most common commercial airplane in the skies today is the Boeing 737 jet. A 737 jet is almost 37 m long and has a wingspan of 30 m. Even without passengers, the plane weighs 350,000 N. That's more than 35 times heavier than an average car! How can something so big and heavy get off the ground, much less fly 10,000 m into the sky? Wing shape plays a role in helping these big planes—as well as smaller planes and even birds—achieve flight, as shown in **Figure 15.**

According to Bernoulli's principle, the faster-moving air above the wing exerts less pressure than the slower-moving air below the wing. The increased pressure that results below the wing exerts an upward force. This upward force, known as **lift,** pushes the wings (and the rest of the airplane or bird) upward against the downward pull of gravity.

Figure 15 Wing Shape Creates Differences in Air Speed

a The curved top of the wing forces air passing above the wing to travel a longer distance than the air passing below the wing.

c The air above must speed up to converge with the air below at the tail end of the wing. Therefore, the air moving above the wing must move faster than the air below it.

b As the wing moves through the sky, air passing below the wing travels in a fairly straight path.

Thrust and Wing Size Determine Lift

The amount of lift created by a plane's wing is determined in part by the size of the wing and the speed at which air travels around the wing. The speed of an airplane is in large part determined by its **thrust**—the forward force produced by the plane's engine. In general, a plane with a greater amount of thrust moves faster than a plane with less thrust. This faster speed means air travels around the wing at a greater speed, which increases lift.

You can understand the relationship between wing size, thrust, and speed by thinking about a jet plane, like the one in **Figure 16.** This plane is able to fly with a relatively small wing size because its engine creates an enormous amount of thrust. This thrust pushes the plane through the sky at tremendous speeds. Therefore, the jet generates sufficient lift with small wings by moving very quickly through the air. Smaller wings keep a plane's weight low, which also contributes to speed.

Compared with the jet, a glider, like the one in **Figure 17,** has a large wing area. A glider is an engineless plane that rides rising air currents to stay in flight. Without engines, gliders produce no thrust and move more slowly than many other kinds of planes. Thus, a glider must have large wings to create the lift necessary to keep it in the air.

Figure 16 *The engine of this jet creates a great deal of thrust, so the wings don't have to be very big.*

Figure 17 *The wings of this glider are very large in order to maximize the amount of lift achieved.*

✔ Self-Check

Does air travel faster or slower over the top of a wing? *(See page 724 to check your answer.)*

Bernoulli's Principle Is for the Birds Birds don't have engines, of course, so they must flap their wings to push themselves through the air. The hawk shown at left uses its large wing size to fly with a minimum of effort. By extending its large wings to their full length and gliding on wind currents, a hawk can achieve enough lift to stay in the air while flapping only occasionally. Smaller birds must flap their wings more often to stay in the air.

LabBook

Soaring science! See how wing shape affects the flight of your own airplane on page 661 of the LabBook.

Lift and Spoilers

At high speeds, air moving around the body of this race car could lift the car just as it lifts a plane's wing. This could cause the wheels to lose contact with the ground, sending the car out of control. To prevent this situation, an upside-down wing, or spoiler, is mounted on the rear of the car. How do spoilers help reduce the danger of accidents?

Drag Opposes Motion in Fluids

Have you ever walked into a strong wind and noticed that the wind seemed to slow you down? Fluids exert a force that opposes motion. The force that opposes or restricts motion in a fluid is called **drag.** In a strong wind, air "drags" on your clothes and body, making it difficult for you to move forward. Drag forces in flight work against the forward motion of a plane or bird and are usually caused by an irregular flow of air around the wings. An irregular or unpredictable flow of fluids is known as *turbulence.*

Lift is often reduced when turbulence causes drag. At faster speeds, drag can become a serious problem, so airplanes are equipped with ways to reduce turbulence as much as possible when in flight. For example, flaps like those shown in **Figure 18** can be used to change the shape or area of a wing, thereby reducing drag and increasing lift. Similarly, birds can adjust their wing feathers in response to turbulence to achieve greater lift.

Figure 18 *During flight, the pilot of this airplane can adjust these flaps to help increase lift.*

Wings Are Not Always Required

You don't have to look up at a bird or a plane flying through the sky to see Bernoulli's principle in your world. In fact, you've already learned how Bernoulli's principle can affect such things as shower curtains and race cars. Any time fluids are moving, Bernoulli's principle is at work. In **Figure 19,** you can see how Bernoulli's principle can mean the difference between a home run and a strike during a baseball game.

Bernoulli's principle at play—read how Frisbees® were invented on page 182.

Figure 19 *A pitcher can take advantage of Bernoulli's principle to produce a confusing curveball that is difficult for the batter to hit.*

a Air speed on the left side of the ball is decreased because air being dragged around the ball moves in the opposite direction of the airflow. This results in a region of increased pressure on the left side of the ball.

Direction of airflow

Direction of spin

b Air speed on the right side of the ball is increased because air being dragged around the ball moves in the same direction as the airflow. This results in a region of decreased pressure on the right side of the ball.

c Because air pressure on the left side is greater than that on the right side, the ball is pushed toward the right in a curved path.

REVIEW

1. Does fluid pressure increase or decrease as fluid speed increases?

2. Explain how wing shape can contribute to lift during flight.

3. What force opposes motion through a fluid?

4. **Interpreting Graphics** When the space through which a fluid flows becomes narrow, fluid speed increases. Explain how this could lead to a collision for the two boats shown at right.

Chapter **Highlights**

SECTION 1

Vocabulary
  fluid *(p. 162)*
  pressure *(p. 162)*
  pascal *(p. 162)*
  atmospheric pressure *(p. 163)*
  density *(p. 165)*
  Pascal's principle *(p. 167)*

Section Notes

• A fluid is any material that flows and that takes the shape of its container.

• Pressure is force exerted on a given area.

• Moving particles of matter create pressure by colliding with one another and with the walls of their container.

• Fluids exert pressure equally in all directions.

• The pressure caused by the weight of Earth's atmosphere is called atmospheric pressure.

• Fluid pressure increases as depth increases.

• Fluids flow from areas of high pressure to areas of low pressure.

• Pascal's principle states that a change in pressure at any point in an enclosed fluid will be transmitted equally to all parts of the fluid.

• Hydraulic devices transmit changes of pressure through liquids.

SECTION 2

Vocabulary
  buoyant force *(p. 168)*
  Archimedes' principle *(p. 168)*

Section Notes

• All fluids exert an upward force called buoyant force.

• Buoyant force is caused by differences in fluid pressure.

• Archimedes' principle states that the buoyant force on an object is equal to the weight of the fluid displaced by the object.

☑ **Skills Check**

Math Concepts

PRESSURE If an object exerts a force of 10 N over an area of 2 m^2, the pressure exerted can be calculated as follows:

$$\text{Pressure} = \frac{\text{Force}}{\text{Area}}$$
$$= \frac{10 \text{ N}}{2 \text{ m}^2}$$
$$= \frac{5 \text{ N}}{1 \text{ m}^2} \text{, or 5 Pa}$$

Visual Understanding

ATMOSPHERIC PRESSURE Why aren't you crushed by atmospheric pressure? Figure 3 on page 163 can help you understand.

BUOYANT FORCE To understand how differences in fluid pressure cause buoyant force, review Figure 9 on page 168.

BERNOULLI'S PRINCIPLE AND WING SHAPE Turn to page 174 to review how a wing is often shaped to take advantage of Bernoulli's principle in creating lift.

SECTION 2

- Any object that is more dense than the surrounding fluid will sink; any object that is less dense than the surrounding fluid will float.

Labs

Fluids, Force, and Floating *(p. 658)*

Density Diver *(p. 660)*

SECTION 3

Vocabulary

Bernoulli's principle *(p. 173)*

lift *(p. 174)*

thrust *(p. 175)*

drag *(p. 176)*

Section Notes

- Bernoulli's principle states that fluid pressure decreases as the speed of a moving fluid increases.

- Wings are often shaped to allow airplanes to take advantage of decreased pressure in moving air in order to achieve flight.

- Lift is an upward force that acts against gravity.

- Lift on an airplane is determined by wing size and thrust (the forward force produced by the engine).

- Drag opposes motion through fluids.

Labs

Taking Flight *(p. 661)*

internetconnect

GO TO: go.hrw.com

Visit the **HRW** Web site for a variety of learning tools related to this chapter. Just type in the keyword:

KEYWORD: HSTFLU

*SCiLINKS*ₛₘ

N S T A

GO TO: www.scilinks.org

Visit the **National Science Teachers Association** on-line Web site for Internet resources related to this chapter. Just type in the *sci*LINKS number for more information about the topic:

TOPIC: Submarines and Undersea Technology	*sci*LINKS NUMBER: HSTP155
TOPIC: Fluids and Pressure	*sci*LINKS NUMBER: HSTP160
TOPIC: The Buoyant Force	*sci*LINKS NUMBER: HSTP165
TOPIC: Bernoulli's Principle	*sci*LINKS NUMBER: HSTP170

Chapter Review

To complete the following sentences, choose the correct term from each of the pair of terms listed below:

1. __?__ increases with the depth of a fluid. (*Pressure* or *Lift*)

2. A plane's engine produces __?__ to push the plane forward. (*thrust* or *drag*)

3. Force divided by area is known as __?__. (*density* or *pressure*)

4. The hydraulic brakes of a car transmit pressure through fluid. This is an example of __?__. (*Archimedes' principle* or *Pascal's principle*)

5. Bernoulli's principle states that the pressure exerted by a moving fluid is __?__ (*greater than* or *less than*) the pressure of the fluid when it is not moving.

UNDERSTANDING CONCEPTS

Multiple Choice

6. The curve on the top of a wing
   a. causes air to travel farther in the same amount of time as the air below the wing.
   b. helps create lift.
   c. creates a low-pressure zone above the wing.
   d. All of the above

7. An object displaces a volume of fluid that
   a. is equal to its own volume.
   b. is less than its own volume.
   c. is greater than its own volume.
   d. is more dense than itself.

8. Fluid pressure is always directed
   a. up.   c. sideways.
   b. down.   d. in all directions.

9. If an object weighing 50 N displaces a volume of water with a weight of 10 N, what is the buoyant force on the object?
   a. 60 N
   b. 50 N
   c. 40 N
   d. 10 N

10. A helium-filled balloon will float in air because
    a. there is more air than helium.
    b. helium is less dense than air.
    c. helium is as dense as air.
    d. helium is more dense than air.

11. Materials that can flow to fit their containers include
    a. gases.
    b. liquids.
    c. both gases and liquids.
    d. neither gases nor liquids.

Short Answer

12. What two factors determine the amount of lift achieved by an airplane?

13. Where is water pressure greater, at a depth of 1 m in a large lake or at a depth of 2 m in a small pond? Explain.

14. Is there buoyant force on an object at the bottom of an ocean? Explain your reasoning.

15. Why are liquids used in hydraulic brakes instead of gases?

Concept Mapping

16. Use the following terms to create a concept map: fluid, pressure, depth, buoyant force, density.

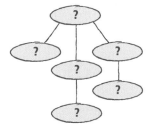

CRITICAL THINKING AND PROBLEM SOLVING

17. Compared with an empty ship, will a ship loaded with plastic-foam balls float higher or lower in the water? Explain your reasoning.

18. Inside all vacuum cleaners is a high-speed fan. Explain how this fan causes dirt to be picked up by the vacuum cleaner.

19. A 600 N clown on stilts says to two 600 N clowns sitting on the ground, "I am exerting twice as much pressure as the two of you together!" Could this statement be true? Explain your reasoning.

MATH IN SCIENCE

20. Calculate the area of a 1,500 N object that exerts a pressure of 500 Pa (N/m²). Then calculate the pressure exerted by the same object over twice that area. Be sure to express your answers in the correct SI unit.

INTERPRETING GRAPHICS

Examine the illustration of an iceberg below, and answer the questions that follow.

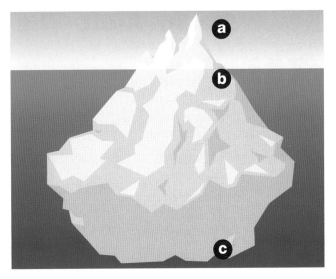

21. At what point (*a*, *b*, or *c*) is water pressure greatest on the iceberg?

22. How much of the iceberg has a weight equal to the buoyant force?
    a. all of it
    b. the section from *a* to *b*
    c. the section from *b* to *c*

23. How does the density of ice compare with the density of water?

24. Why do you think icebergs are so dangerous to passing ships?

Reading Check-up

Take a minute to review your answers to the Pre-Reading Questions found at the bottom of page 160. Have your answers changed? If necessary, revise your answers based on what you have learned since you began this chapter.

Eureka!

Stayin' Aloft—The Story of the Frisbee®

Whoa! Nice catch! Your friend 30 m away just sent a disk spinning toward you. As you reached for it, a gust of wind floated it up over your head. With a quick jump, you snagged it. A snap of your wrist sends the disk soaring back. You are "Frisbee-ing," a game more than 100 years old. But back then, there were no plastic disks, only pie plates.

From Pie Plate...

In the late 1800s, ready-made pies baked in tin plates began to appear in stores and restaurants. A bakery near Yale University, in New Haven, Connecticut, embossed its name, Frisbie's Pies, on its pie plates. When a few fun-loving college students tossed empty pie plates, they found that the metal plates had a marvelous ability to stay in the air. Soon the students began alerting their companions of an incoming pie plate by shouting "Frisbie!" So tossing pie plates became known as Frisbie-ing. By the late 1940s, the game was played across the country.

...to Plastic

In 1947, California businessmen Fred Morrison and Warren Franscioni needed to make a little extra money. They were familiar with pie-plate tossing, and they knew the plates often cracked when they landed and developed sharp edges that caused injuries.

At the time, plastic was becoming widely available. Plastic is more durable and flexible than metal, and it isn't as likely to injure fingers. Why not make a "pie plate" out of plastic, thought Morrison and Franscioni? They did, and their idea was a huge success.

Years later, a toy company bought the rights to make the toy. One day the president of the company heard someone yelling "Frisbie!" while tossing a disk and decided to use that name, changing the spelling to "Frisbee."

Saucer Science

It looks simple, but Frisbee flight is quite complicated. It involves *thrust,* the force you give the disk to move it through the air; *angle of attack,* the slight upward tilt you give the disk when you throw it; and *lift,* the upward forces (explained by Bernoulli's principle) acting on the Frisbee to counteract gravity. But perhaps the most important aspect of Frisbee physics is *spin,* which gives the Frisbee stability as it flies. The faster a Frisbee spins, the more stable it is and the farther it can fly.

What Do You Think?

▶ From what you've learned in class, why do you think the Frisbee has a curved lip? Would a completely flat Frisbee fly as well? Why or why not? Find out more about the interesting aerodynamics of Frisbee flight. Fly a Frisbee for the class, and explain what you've learned.

Science Fiction

"Wet Behind the Ears"

by Jack C. Haldeman II

Willie Joe Thomas is a college student who lied to get into college and cheated to get a swimming scholarship. Now he is faced with a major swim meet, and his coach has told him that he has to swim or be kicked off the team. Willie Joe could lose his scholarship. What's worse, he would have to get a *job.*

"Wet Behind the Ears" is Willie Joe's story. It's the story of someone who has always taken the easy way (even if it takes more work), of someone who lies and cheats as easily as he breathes. Willie Joe could probably do things the right way, but it never even occurred to him to try it!

So when Willie Joe's roommate, Frank Emerson, announces that he has made an amazing discovery in the chemistry lab, Willie Joe doesn't much care. Frank works too hard. Frank follows the rules. Willie Joe isn't impressed.

But when he is running late for the all-important swim meet, Willie Joe remembers what Frank's new compound does. Frank said it was a "sliding compound." Willie Joe may not know chemistry, but "slippery" he understands. And Frank also said something about selling the stuff to the Navy to make its ships go faster. Hey, if it works for ships . . .

See what happens when Willie Joe tries to save his scholarship. Go to the *Holt Anthology of Science Fiction,* and read "Wet Behind the Ears," by Jack C. Haldeman II.

UNIT

3

Work, Machines, and Energy

C an you imagine living in a world with no machines? In this unit, you will explore the scientific meaning of *work* and learn how machines make work easier. You will find out how energy allows you to do work and how different forms of energy can be converted into other forms of energy. You will also learn about heat and how heating and cooling systems work. This timeline shows some of the inventions and discoveries made throughout history as people have advanced their understanding of work, machines, and energy.

Around 3000 B.C.

The sail is used in Egypt. Sails use the wind rather than human power to move boats through the water.

Around 200 B.C.

Under the Han dynasty, the Chinese become one of the first civilizations to use coal as fuel.

1926

American scientist Robert Goddard launches the first rocket powered by liquid fuel. It reaches a height of 56 m and a speed of 97 km/h.

1948

Maria Telkes, a Hungarian-born physicist, designs the heating system for the first solar-heated house.

1972

The first American self-service gas station opens.

1656

Dutch scientist Christiaan Huygens invents the pendulum clock.

1776

The American colonies declare their independence from Great Britain.

1818

The first two-wheeled, rider-propelled machine is invented by German Baron Karl von Drais de Sauerbrun. Made of wood, this early machine paves the way for the invention of the bicycle.

1893

The zipper is patented.

1908

The automobile age begins with the mass production of the Ford Model T.

1988

The world's most powerful wind-powered generator begins generating electrical energy in Scotland's Orkney Islands.

2000

The 2000 Olympic Summer Games are held in Sydney, Australia.

Work and Machines

Pre-Reading Questions

1. What does it mean to do work?

2. How are machines helpful when doing work?

3. What are some examples of simple machines?

"ONE, TWO, STROKE!" . . .

. . . shouts the coach as the team races to the finish line. This paddling team is competing in Hong Kong's annual Dragon Boat Races. The Dragon Boat Festival is a 2,000-year-old Chinese tradition that commemorates the death of the national hero, Qu Yuan. The paddlers you see here are using the paddles to move the boat forward. Even though they are celebrating by racing their dragon boat, in scientific terms this team is doing *work*. How is this possible? Read on to find out!

C'MON, LEVER A LITTLE!

In this activity, you will use a simple machine, a lever, to make your task a little easier.

Procedure

1. Gather a few **books** and stack them on a table, one on top of the other.

2. Slide your index finger underneath the edge of the bottom book. Using only the force of your finger, try to lift one side of the books 2 or 3 cm off the table. Is it difficult? Write your observations in your ScienceLog.

3. Slide the end of a **wooden ruler** underneath the edge of the bottom book. Then slip a **large pencil eraser** under the ruler.

4. Again using only your index finger, push down on the edge of the ruler and try to lift the books. Record your observations.

   Caution: Push down slowly to keep the ruler and eraser from flipping.

Analysis

5. Which was easier, lifting the books with your finger or with the ruler? Explain.

6. What was different about the direction of the force your finger applied on the books compared with the direction of the force you applied on the ruler?

What You'll Do

- ◆ Determine when work is being done on an object.
- ◆ Calculate the amount of work done on an object.
- ◆ Explain the difference between work and power.

Work and Power

Suppose your science teacher has just given you a homework assignment. You have to read an entire chapter by tomorrow! Wow, that's a lot of work, isn't it? Actually, in the scientific sense, you won't be doing any work at all! How can that be?

The Scientific Meaning of *Work*

In science, **work** occurs when a force causes an object to move in the direction of the force. In the example above, you may put a lot of mental effort into doing your homework, but you won't be using a force to move an object. Therefore, in the scientific sense, you will not be doing work.

Now think about the example shown in **Figure 1.** This student is having a lot of fun, isn't she? But she is doing work, even though she is having fun. That's because she's applying a force to the bowling ball to make it move through a distance. However, it's important to understand that she is doing work on the ball only as long as she is touching it. The ball will continue to move away from her after she releases it, but she will no longer be doing work on the ball because she will no longer be applying a force to it.

Figure 1 *You might be surprised to find out that bowling is doing work!*

Working Hard or Hardly Working? You should understand that applying a force doesn't always result in work being done. Suppose your neighbor asks you to help push his stalled car. You push and push, but the car doesn't budge. Even though you may be exhausted and sweaty, you haven't done any work on the car. Why? Because the car hasn't moved. Remember, work is done on an object only when a force makes that object move. In this case, your pushing doesn't make the car move. You only do work on the car if it starts to move.

Force and Motion in the Same Direction Suppose you're in the airport and you're late for a flight. You have to run through the airport carrying a heavy suitcase. Because you're making the suitcase move, you're doing work on it, right? Wrong! For work to be done, the object must move in the same direction as the force. In this case, the motion is in a different direction than the force, as shown in **Figure 2.** So no work is done on the suitcase. However, work *is* done on the suitcase when you lift it off the ground.

You'll know that work is done on an object if two things occur: (1) the object moves as a force is applied and (2) the direction of the object's motion is the same as the direction of the force applied. The pictures and the arrows in the chart below will help you understand how to determine when work is being done on an object.

Direction of force

Direction of motion

Figure 2 *You exert an upward force on the suitcase. But the motion of the suitcase is forward. Therefore, you are not doing work on the suitcase.*

Work or Not Work?

Example	Direction of force	Direction of motion	Doing work?
	→	→	Yes
	↑	→	No
	↑	↑	Yes
	↑	→	No

✓ Self-Check

If you pulled a wheeled suitcase instead of carrying it, would you be doing work on the suitcase? Why or why not? *(See page 724 to check your answer.)*

MATH BREAK

Working It Out

Use the equation for work shown on this page to solve the following problems:

1. A man applies a force of 500 N to push a truck 100 m down the street. How much work does he do?

2. In which situation do you do more work?
   a. You lift a 75 N bowling ball 2 m off the floor.
   b. You lift two 50 N bowling balls 1 m off the floor.

Calculating Work

Do you do more work when you lift an 80 N barbell or a 160 N barbell? It would be tempting to say that you do more work when you lift the 160 N barbell because it weighs more. But actually, you can't answer this question with the information given. You also need to know how high each barbell is being lifted. Remember, work is a force applied through a distance. The greater the distance through which you exert a given force, the more work you do. Similarly, the greater the force you exert through a given distance, the more work you do.

The amount of work (W) done in moving an object can be calculated by multiplying the force (F) applied to the object by the distance (d) through which the force is applied, as shown in the following equation:

$$W = F \times d$$

Recall that force is expressed in newtons, and the meter is the basic SI unit for length or distance. Therefore, the unit used to express work is the newton-meter (N•m), which is more simply called the **joule (J).** Look at **Figure 3** to learn more about calculating work. You can also practice calculating work yourself by doing the MathBreak on this page.

Figure 3 Work Depends on Force and Distance

$W = 80\ N \times 1\ m = 80\ J$

The force needed to lift an object is equal to the gravitational force on the object—in other words, the object's weight.

$W = 160\ N \times 1\ m = 160\ J$

Increasing the amount of force increases the amount of work done.

$W = 80\ N \times 2\ m = 160\ J$

Increasing the distance also increases the amount of work done.

Power—How Fast Work Is Done

Like *work,* the term *power* is used a lot in everyday language but has a very specific meaning in science. **Power** is the rate at which work is done. To calculate power (*P*), you divide the amount of work done (*W*) by the time (*t*) it takes to do that work, as shown in the following equation:

$$P = \frac{W}{t}$$

You just learned that the unit for work is the joule, and the basic unit for time is the second. Therefore, the unit used to express power is joules per second (J/s), which is more simply called the **watt (W).** So if you do 50 J of work in 5 seconds, your power is 10 J/s, or 10 W. You can calculate your own power in the QuickLab at right.

Increasing Power Power is how fast work happens. Power is increased when more work is done in a given amount of time. Power is also increased when the time it takes to do a certain amount of work is decreased, as shown in **Figure 4.**

Figure 4 *No matter how fast you can sand with sandpaper, an electric sander can do the same amount of work faster. Therefore, the electric sander has more power.*

QuickLab

More Power to You

1. Use a loop of **string** to attach a **spring scale** to a **book.**

2. Slowly pull the book across a table by the spring scale. Use a **stopwatch** to determine the time this takes. In your ScienceLog, record the amount of time it took and the force used as the book reached the edge of the table.

3. With a **metric ruler,** measure the distance you pulled the book.

4. Now quickly pull the book across the same distance. Again record the time and force.

5. Calculate work and power for both trials.

6. How were the amounts of work and power affected by your pulling the book faster? Record your answers in your ScienceLog.

REVIEW

1. Work is done on a ball when a pitcher throws it. Is the pitcher still doing work on the ball as it flies through the air? Explain.

2. Explain the difference between work and power.

3. **Doing Calculations** You lift a chair that weighs 50 N to a height of 0.5 m and carry it 10 m across the room. How much work do you do on the chair?

internetconnect

SC*i*LINKS.
NSTA

TOPIC: Work and Power
GO TO: www.scilinks.org
*sci*LINKS NUMBER: HSTP180

What Is a Machine?

Imagine you're in the car with your mom on the way to a party when suddenly—*KABLOOM hissss*—a tire blows out. "Now I'm going to be late!" you think as your mom pulls over to the side of the road. You watch as she opens the trunk and gets out a jack and a tire iron. She places the jack under the car at the proper location and turns the handle until the car just starts to lift off the ground. Using the tire iron, she pries off the hubcap and loosens the lug nuts that hold the wheel. Next, she turns the handle on the jack until the car is no longer touching the ground and carefully removes the lug nuts and then the wheel. After exchanging the flat tire with the spare and replacing and tightening the lug nuts, she lowers and removes the jack, tightens the lug nuts once again, and puts the hubcap back on the wheel. "Wow!" you think, "That wasn't as hard as I thought it would be." As your mom drops you off at the party, you think how lucky it was that she had the right equipment to change the tire.

Terms to Learn

machine
work input
work output
mechanical advantage
mechanical efficiency

What You'll Do

- Explain how a machine makes work easier.
- Describe and give examples of the force-distance trade-off that occurs when a machine is used.
- Calculate mechanical advantage.
- Explain why machines are not 100 percent efficient.

Machines—Making Work Easier

Now imagine changing a tire without the jack and the tire iron. Would it have been so easy? No, you would have needed several people just to hold up the car! Sometimes you need a little help to do work. That's where machines come in. A **machine** is a device that helps make work easier by changing the size or direction of a force.

When you think of machines, you might think of things like cars, big construction equipment, or even computers. But not all machines are complicated or even have moving parts. In fact, the tire iron, jack, and lug nut shown above are all machines. Even the items shown in **Figure 5** are machines.

Figure 5 *You might be surprised to find out that all of these common objects are machines.*

Work In, Work Out Suppose you need to get the lid off a can of paint. What do you do? Well, one way to pry the lid off is to use the flat end of a common machine known as a screwdriver, as shown in **Figure 6.** You place the tip of the screwdriver under the edge of the lid and then push down on the handle. The other end of the screwdriver lifts the lid as you push down. In other words, you do work on the screwdriver, and the screwdriver does work on the lid. This example illustrates that two kinds of work are always involved when a machine is used— the work done on the machine and the work the machine does on another object.

Output force

Input force

The width of the arrows representing **input force** and **output force** indicates the relative size of the forces. The length of the arrows indicates the distance through which they are exerted.

Figure 6 *When you use a machine, you do work on the machine, and the machine does work on something else.*

Remember that work is a force applied through a distance. Look again at Figure 6. The work you do on a machine is called **work input.** You apply a force, called the *input force,* to the machine and move it through a distance. The work done by the machine is called **work output.** The machine applies a force, called the *output force,* through a distance. The output force opposes the forces you and the machine are working against—in this case, the weight of the lid and the friction between the can and the lid.

How Machines Help You might think that machines help you because they increase the amount of work done. But that's not true. If you multiplied the forces by the distances through which they are applied in Figure 6 (remember, $W = F \times d$), you would find that the screwdriver does *not* do more work on the lid than you do on the screwdriver. Work output can *never* be greater than work input.

Machines Do Not Save Work Machines make work easier because they change the size or direction of the input force. And using a screwdriver to open a paint can changes *both* the size and direction of the input force. Just remember that using a machine does not mean that you do less work. As you can see in **Figure 7,** the same amount of work is involved with or without the ramp. The ramp decreases the amount of input force necessary to do the work of lifting the box. But the distance over which the force is exerted increases. In other words, the machine allows a smaller force to be applied over a longer distance.

Figure 7 *A simple plank of wood acts as a machine when it is used to help raise a load.*

Force: 450 N	**Distance: 1 m**

$$W = 450 \text{ N} \times 1 \text{ m} = 450 \text{ J}$$

Lifting this box straight up requires an input force equal to the weight of the box.

Force: 150 N	**Distance: 3 m**

$$W = 150 \text{ N} \times 3 \text{ m} = 450 \text{ J}$$

Using a ramp to lift the box requires an input force less than the weight of the box, but the input force must be exerted over a greater distance.

The Force-Distance Trade-off When a machine changes the size of the force, the distance through which the force is exerted must also change. Force or distance can increase, but not together. When one increases, the other must decrease. This is because the work output is never greater than the work input.

The diagram on the next page will help you better understand this force-distance trade-off. It also shows that some machines affect only the direction of the force, not the size of the force or the distance through which it is exerted.

Machines Change the Size or Direction (or Both) of a Force

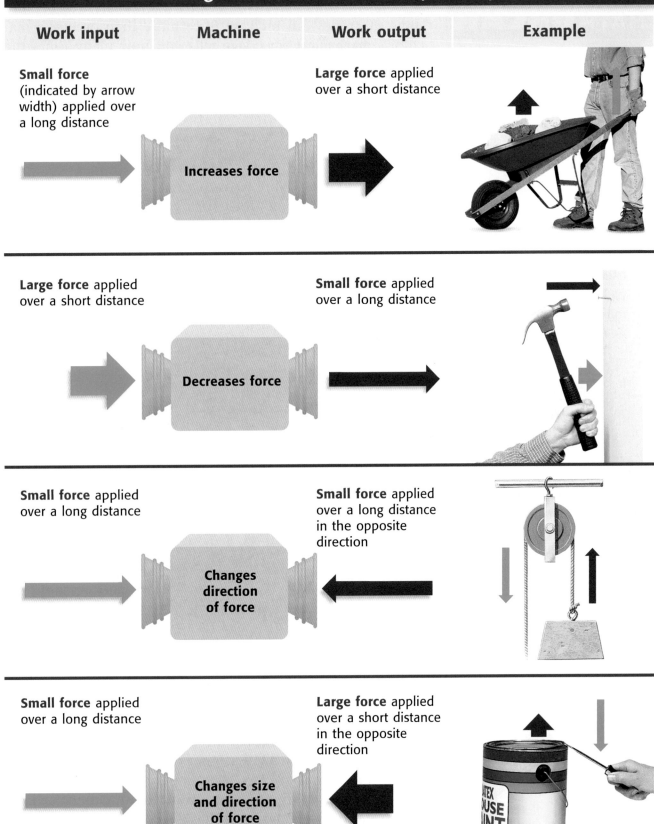

Work input	Machine	Work output	Example
Small force (indicated by arrow width) applied over a long distance	**Increases force**	**Large force** applied over a short distance	
Large force applied over a short distance	**Decreases force**	**Small force** applied over a long distance	
Small force applied over a long distance	**Changes direction of force**	**Small force** applied over a long distance in the opposite direction	
Small force applied over a long distance	**Changes size and direction of force**	**Large force** applied over a short distance in the opposite direction	

MATH BREAK

Mechanical Advantage

Do some machines make work easier than others? Yes, because some machines can increase force more than others. A machine's **mechanical advantage** tells you how many times the machine multiplies force. In other words, it compares the input force with the output force. You can find mechanical advantage by using the following equation:

$$\text{Mechanical advantage } (MA) = \frac{\text{output force}}{\text{input force}}$$

Take a look at **Figure 8.** In this example, the output force is greater than the input force. Using the equation above, you can find the mechanical advantage of the handcart:

$$MA = \frac{500 \text{ N}}{50 \text{ N}} = 10$$

Input force = 50 N

Output force = 500 N

Figure 8 *A machine that has a large mechanical advantage can make lifting a heavy load a whole lot easier.*

Because the mechanical advantage of the handcart is 10, the output force is 10 times bigger than the input force. The larger the mechanical advantage, the easier a machine makes your work. But as mechanical advantage increases, the distance that the output force moves the object decreases.

Remember that some machines only change the direction of the force. In such cases, the output force is equal to the input force, and the mechanical advantage is 1. Other machines have a mechanical advantage that is less than 1. That means that the input force is greater than the output force. Although such a machine actually decreases your force, it does allow you to exert the force over a longer distance, as shown in **Figure 9.**

Figure 9 *With chopsticks you can pick up a big bite of food with just a little wiggle of your fingers.*

Mechanical Efficiency

As mentioned earlier, the work output of a machine can never be greater than the work input. In fact, the work output of a machine is always *less* than the work input. Why? Because some of the work done by the machine is used to overcome the friction created by the use of the machine. But keep in mind that no work is *lost*. The work output plus the work done to overcome friction equals the work input.

The less work a machine has to do to overcome friction, the more *efficient* it is. **Mechanical efficiency** (e FISH uhn see) is a comparison of a machine's work output with the work input. A machine's mechanical efficiency is calculated using the following equation:

$$\text{Mechanical efficiency} = \frac{\text{work output}}{\text{work input}} \times 100$$

The 100 in this equation means that mechanical efficiency is expressed as a percentage. Mechanical efficiency tells you what percentage of the work input gets converted into work output. No machine is 100 percent efficient, but reducing the amount of friction in a machine is a way to increase its mechanical efficiency. Inventors have tried for many years to create a machine that has no friction to overcome, but so far they have been unsuccessful. If a machine could be made that had 100 percent mechanical efficiency, it would be called an *ideal machine*.

Oil Improves Efficiency

Car manufacturers recommend regular oil changes. That's because over time, motor oil in a car's engine starts to get dark and thick and doesn't flow as well as fresh motor oil. Why do you think a car engine needs motor oil? How does getting regular oil changes improve the mechanical efficiency of a car's engine?

REVIEW

1. Explain how using a ramp makes work easier.

2. Why can't a machine be 100 percent efficient?

3. Suppose you exert 15 N on a machine, and the machine exerts 300 N on another object. What is the machine's mechanical advantage?

4. **Comparing Concepts**   For the machine described in question 3, how does the distance through which the output force is exerted differ from the distance through which the input force is exerted?

internet**connect**

SC*L*INKS.
NSTA

TOPIC: Mechanical Efficiency
GO TO: www.scilinks.org
*sci*LINKS NUMBER: HSTP185

Terms to Learn

lever	wheel and axle
inclined plane	pulley
wedge	compound
screw	machine

What You'll Do

- Identify and give examples of the six types of simple machines.
- Analyze the mechanical advantage provided by each simple machine.
- Identify the simple machines that make up a compound machine.

Types of Machines

All machines are constructed from these six simple machines: *lever, inclined plane, wedge, screw, wheel and axle,* and *pulley.* You've seen a couple of these machines already—a screwdriver can be used as a lever, and a ramp is an inclined plane. In the next few pages, each of the six simple machines will be discussed separately. Then you'll learn how compound machines are formed from combining simple machines.

Levers

Have you ever used the claw end of a hammer to remove a nail from a piece of wood? If so, you were using the hammer as a lever. A **lever** is a simple machine consisting of a bar that pivots at a fixed point, called a *fulcrum.* Levers are used to apply a force to a load. There are three classes of levers, based on the locations of the fulcrum, the load, and the input force.

First Class Levers With a first class lever, the fulcrum is between the input force and the load, as shown in **Figure 10.** First class levers always change the direction of the input force. And depending on the location of the fulcrum, first class levers can be used to increase force or to increase distance. Some examples of first class levers are shown below.

Figure 10 A First Class Lever

Input force   Output force

Load

Fulcrum

Examples of First Class Levers

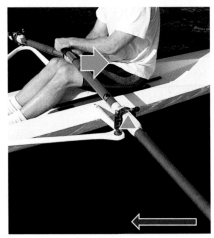

When the fulcrum is closer to the load than to the input force, a **mechanical advantage of greater than 1 results.** The output force is increased because it is exerted over a shorter distance.

When the fulcrum is exactly in the middle, a **mechanical advantage of 1 results.** The output force is not increased because the input force's distance is not increased.

When the fulcrum is closer to the input force than to the load, a **mechanical advantage of less than 1 results.** Although the output force is less than the input force, a gain in distance occurs.

Second Class Levers With a second class lever, the load is between the fulcrum and the input force, as shown in **Figure 11.** Second class levers do not change the direction of the input force, but they allow you to apply less force than the force exerted by the load. Because the output force is greater than the input force, you must exert the input force over a greater distance. Some examples of second class levers are shown at right.

Examples of Second Class Levers

Figure 11 A Second Class Lever

Input force
Output force
Load
Fulcrum

Using a second class lever results in a **mechanical advantage of greater than 1.** The closer the load is to the fulcrum, the more the force is increased and the greater the mechanical advantage.

Third Class Levers With a third class lever, the input force is between the fulcrum and the load, as shown in **Figure 12.** Third class levers do not change the direction of the input force. In addition, they do *not* increase the input force. Therefore, the output force is always less than the input force. Some examples of third class levers are shown at right.

Examples of Third Class Levers

Figure 12 A Third Class Lever

Output force
Input force
Load
Fulcrum

Using a third class lever results in a **mechanical advantage of less than 1** because force is decreased. But third class levers are helpful because they increase the distance through which the output force is exerted.

Inclined Planes

Do you remember the story about how the Egyptians built the Great Pyramid? One of the machines they used was the *inclined plane*. An **inclined plane** is a simple machine that is a straight, slanted surface. A ramp is an example of an inclined plane.

Inclined planes can make work easier. Look at **Figure 13.** Using an inclined plane to load an upright piano into the back of a truck is easier than just lifting it into the truck. Rolling the piano into the truck along an inclined plane requires a smaller input force than is required to lift the piano into the truck. But remember that machines do not save work—therefore, the input force must be exerted over a longer distance.

Figure 13 *The work you do on the piano to roll it up the ramp is the same as the work you would do to lift it straight up. An inclined plane simply allows you to apply a smaller force over a greater distance.*

Compare work done with and without an inclined plane on page 664 of the LabBook.

Mechanical Advantage of Inclined Planes The longer the inclined plane is compared with its height, the greater the mechanical advantage. The mechanical advantage (*MA*) of an inclined plane can be calculated by dividing the *length* of the inclined plane by the *height* to which the load is lifted, as shown below:

3 m

0.6 m

$$MA = \frac{3 \text{ m}}{0.6 \text{ m}} = 5$$

Wedges

Imagine trying to cut a watermelon in half with a spoon. It wouldn't be easy, would it? A knife is a much more useful utensil for cutting because it's a *wedge*. A **wedge** is a double inclined plane that moves. When you move a wedge through a distance, it applies a force on an object. A wedge applies an output force that is greater than your input force, but you apply the input force over a greater distance. The greater the distance you move the wedge, the greater the force it applies on the object. For example, the deeper you move a knife into a watermelon, as shown in **Figure 14,** the more force the knife applies to the two halves. Eventually, it pushes them apart. Other useful wedges include doorstops, plows, axe heads, and chisels.

Figure 14 *Wedges, which are often used to cut materials, allow you to exert your force over an increased distance.*

Mechanical Advantage of Wedges   The longer and thinner the wedge is, the greater the mechanical advantage. That's why axes and knives cut better when you sharpen them—you are making the wedge thinner. Therefore, less input force is required. The mechanical advantage of a wedge can be determined by dividing the *length* of the wedge by its greatest *thickness,* as shown below.

$$MA = \frac{8 \text{ cm}}{2 \text{ cm}} = 4$$

Screws

A **screw** is an inclined plane that is wrapped in a spiral. When a screw is rotated, a small force is applied over the long distance along the inclined plane of the screw. Meanwhile, the screw applies a large force through the short distance it is pushed. In other words, you apply a small input force over a large distance, while the screw exerts a large output force over a small distance. Screws are used most commonly as fasteners. Some examples of screws are shown in **Figure 15.**

Figure 15 *When you turn a screw, you exert a small input force over a large turning distance, but the screw itself doesn't move very far.*

Figure 16 *The threads on the top screw are closer together and wrap more times around, so that screw has a greater mechanical advantage than the one below it.*

Mechanical Advantage of Screws If you could "unwind" the inclined plane of a screw, you would see that it is very long and has a gentle slope. Recall that the longer an inclined plane is compared with its height, the greater its mechanical advantage. Similarly, the longer the spiral on a screw is and the closer together the threads, the greater the screw's mechanical advantage, as shown in **Figure 16.**

REVIEW

1. Give an example of each of the following simple machines: first class lever, second class lever, third class lever, inclined plane, wedge, and screw.

2. A third class lever has a mechanical advantage of less than 1. Explain why it is useful for some tasks.

3. **Interpreting Graphics** Look back at Figures 6, 7, and 8 in Section 2. Identify the type of simple machine shown in each case. (If a lever is shown, identify its class.)

Figure 17
How a Wheel and Axle Works

ⓐ When a small input force is applied to the wheel, it rotates through a circular distance.

Wheel and Axle

Did you know that when you turn a doorknob you are using a machine? A doorknob is an example of a **wheel and axle,** a simple machine consisting of two circular objects of different sizes. A wheel can be a crank, such as the handle on a fishing reel, or it can be a knob, such as a volume knob on a radio. The axle is the smaller of the two circular objects. Doorknobs, wrenches, ferris wheels, screwdrivers, and steering wheels all use a wheel and axle. **Figure 17** shows how a wheel and axle works.

Wheel

Input force

Axle

Output force

ⓑ As the wheel turns, so does the axle. But because the axle is smaller than the wheel, it rotates through a smaller distance, which makes the output force larger than the input force.

Mechanical Advantage of a Wheel and Axle The mechanical advantage of a wheel and axle can be determined by dividing the *radius* (the distance from the center to the edge) of the wheel by the radius of the axle, as shown at right. Turning the wheel results in a mechanical advantage of greater than 1 because the radius of the wheel is larger than the radius of the axle.

Radius of axle
3 cm

Radius of wheel
15 cm

$$MA = \frac{15 \text{ cm}}{3 \text{ cm}} = 5$$

Pulleys

When you open window blinds by pulling on a cord, you're using a pulley. A **pulley** is a simple machine consisting of a grooved wheel that holds a rope or a cable. A load is attached to one end of the rope, and an input force is applied to the other end. There are two kinds of pulleys—*fixed* and *movable*. Fixed and movable pulleys can be combined to form a *block and tackle*.

Fixed Pulleys Some pulleys only change the direction of a force. This kind of pulley is called a fixed pulley. Fixed pulleys do not increase force. A fixed pulley is attached to something that does not move. By using a fixed pulley, you can pull down on the rope in order to lift the load up. This is usually easier than trying to lift the load straight up. Elevators make use of fixed pulleys.

Input force

Output force

A **fixed pulley** only spins. So the distance through which the input force and the output force are exerted—and thus the forces themselves—are the same. Therefore, a fixed pulley provides a mechanical advantage of 1.

Movable Pulleys Unlike fixed pulleys, movable pulleys are attached to the object being moved. A movable pulley does not change a force's direction. Movable pulleys do increase force, but you must exert the input force over a greater distance than the load is moved. This is because you must make *both* sides of the rope move in order to lift the load.

Input force

Output force

A **movable pulley** moves up with the load as it is lifted. Force is multiplied because the combined input force is exerted over twice the distance of the output force. The mechanical advantage of a movable pulley is the number of rope segments that support the load. In this example, the mechanical advantage is 2.

Block and Tackles When a fixed pulley and a movable pulley are used together, the pulley system is called a *block and tackle*. A block and tackle can have a large mechanical advantage if several pulleys are used. A block and tackle used within a larger pulley system is shown in **Figure 18.**

Input force

Output force

The mechanical advantage of this **block and tackle** is 4 because there are four rope segments that support the load. This block and tackle multiplies your input force four times, but you have to pull the rope 4 m just to lift the load 1 m.

Figure 18 *The combination of pulleys used by this crane allows it to lift heavy pieces of scrap metal.*

Compound Machines

You are surrounded by machines. As you saw earlier, you even have machines in your body! But most of the machines in your world are **compound machines,** machines that are made of two or more simple machines. You've already seen one example of a compound machine: a block and tackle. A block and tackle consists of two or more pulleys. On this page and the next, you'll see some other examples of compound machines.

Activity

List five machines that you have encountered today and indicate what type of machine each is. Try to include at least one compound machine and one machine that is part of your body.

TRY at HOME

Can Opener

The axle has gear teeth on it that grip the can and act as tiny levers to push the can along when the axle turns.

Wheel and axle

Wedge

Second class lever

Each arm of the scissors is a first class lever.

Each sharpened edge of the scissors is a wedge.

Wheelchair

Wheel and axle

Zipper

Inside the metal clasp of this zipper are three wedges. One wedge opens the zipper by splitting the teeth apart. Two other wedges close the zipper by pushing the teeth together.

Mechanical Efficiency of Compound Machines In general, the more moving parts a machine has, the lower its mechanical efficiency. Thus the mechanical efficiency of compound machines is often quite low. For compound machines that involve many simple machines, such as automobiles and airplanes, it is very important that friction be reduced as much as possible through the use of lubrication and other techniques. Too much friction could cause heating and damage the simple machines involved, which could create safety problems and could be expensive to repair.

REVIEW

1. Give an example of a wheel and axle.

2. Identify the simple machines that make up tweezers and nail clippers.

3. **Doing Calculations** The radius of the wheel of a wheel and axle is four times greater than the radius of the axle. What is the mechanical advantage of this machine?

internet**connect**

SC*i*LINKS.
NSTA

TOPIC: Simple Machines, Compound Machines
GO TO: www.scilinks.org
*sci***LINKS NUMBER:** HSTP190, HSTP195

Chapter Highlights

SECTION 1

Vocabulary

work *(p. 188)*
joule *(p. 190)*
power *(p. 191)*
watt *(p. 191)*

Section Notes

- Work occurs when a force causes an object to move in the direction of the force. The unit for work is the joule (J).

- Work is done on an object only when a force makes an object move and only while that force is applied.

- For work to be done on an object, the direction of the object's motion must be in the same direction as the force applied.

- Work can be calculated by multiplying force by distance.

- Power is the rate at which work is done. The unit for power is the watt (W).

- Power can be calculated by dividing the amount of work by the time taken to do that work.

Labs

A Powerful Workout *(p. 662)*

SECTION 2

Vocabulary

machine *(p. 192)*
work input *(p. 193)*
work output *(p. 193)*
mechanical advantage *(p. 196)*
mechanical efficiency *(p. 197)*

Section Notes

- A machine makes work easier by changing the size or direction (or both) of a force.

- When a machine changes the size of a force, the distance through which the force is exerted must also change. Force or distance can increase, but not together.

☑ Skills Check

Math Concepts

WORK AND POWER Suppose a woman raises a 65 N object 1.6 m in 4 s. The work done and her power can be calculated as follows:

$$W = F \times d \qquad\qquad P = \frac{W}{t}$$

$$= 65 \text{ N} \times 1.6 \text{ m} \qquad = \frac{104 \text{ J}}{4 \text{ s}}$$

$$= 104 \text{ J} \qquad\qquad\qquad = 26 \text{ W}$$

Visual Understanding

MACHINES MAKE WORK EASIER A machine can change the size or direction (or both) of a force. Review the table on page 195 to learn more about how machines make work easier.

COMPOUND MACHINES A compound machine is made of two or more simple machines. Review the examples on pages 204 and 205.

- Mechanical advantage tells how many times a machine multiplies force. It can be calculated by dividing the output force by the input force.

- Mechanical efficiency is a comparison of a machine's work output with work input. Mechanical efficiency is calculated by dividing work output by work input and is expressed as a percentage.

- Machines are not 100 percent efficient because some of the work done by a machine is used to overcome friction. So work output is always less than work input.

Vocabulary

lever *(p. 198)*
inclined plane *(p. 200)*
wedge *(p. 201)*
screw *(p. 201)*
wheel and axle *(p. 202)*
pulley *(p. 203)*
compound machine *(p. 204)*

Section Notes

- All machines are constructed from these six simple machines: lever, inclined plane, wedge, screw, wheel and axle, and pulley.

- Compound machines consist of two or more simple machines.

- Compound machines have low mechanical efficiencies because they have more moving parts and thus more friction to overcome.

Labs

Inclined to Move *(p. 664)*
Building Machines *(p. 665)*
Wheeling and Dealing *(p. 666)*

---

 internetconnect

GO TO: go.hrw.com

Visit the **HRW** Web site for a variety of learning tools related to this chapter. Just type in the keyword:

KEYWORD: HSTWRK

 SCiLINKS ₛₘ
N S T A

GO TO: www.scilinks.org

Visit the **National Science Teachers Association** on-line Web site for Internet resources related to this chapter. Just type in the *sci*LINKS number for more information about the topic:

TOPIC: Work and Power   *sci*LINKS NUMBER: HSTP180
TOPIC: Mechanical Efficiency   *sci*LINKS NUMBER: HSTP185
TOPIC: Simple Machines   *sci*LINKS NUMBER: HSTP190
TOPIC: Compound Machines   *sci*LINKS NUMBER: HSTP195

Chapter Review

USING VOCABULARY

For each pair of terms, explain the difference in their meanings.

1. joule/watt

2. work output/work input

3. mechanical efficiency/mechanical advantage

4. screw/inclined plane

5. simple machine/compound machine

UNDERSTANDING CONCEPTS

Multiple Choice

6. Work is being done when
   a. you apply a force to an object.
   b. an object is moving after you apply a force to it.
   c. you exert a force that moves an object in the direction of the force.
   d. you do something that is difficult.

7. The work output for a machine is always less than the work input because
   a. all machines have a mechanical advantage.
   b. some of the work done is used to overcome friction.
   c. some of the work done is used to overcome distance.
   d. power is the rate at which work is done.

8. The unit for work is the
   a. joule.   c. newton.
   b. joule per second.   d. watt.

9. Which of the following is not a simple machine?
   a. a faucet handle
   b. a jar lid
   c. a can opener
   d. a seesaw

10. Power is
    a. how strong someone or something is.
    b. how much force is being used.
    c. how much work is being done.
    d. how fast work is being done.

11. The unit for power is the
    a. newton.   c. watt.
    b. kilogram.   d. joule.

12. A machine can increase
    a. distance at the expense of force.
    b. force at the expense of distance.
    c. neither distance nor force.
    d. Both (a) and (b)

Short Answer

13. Identify the simple machines that make up a pair of scissors.

14. In two or three sentences, explain the force-distance trade-off that occurs when a machine is used to make work easier.

15. Explain why you do work on a bag of groceries when you pick it up but not when you are carrying it.

Concept Mapping

16. Create a concept map using the following terms: work, force, distance, machine, mechanical advantage.

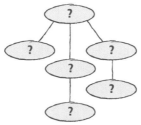

CRITICAL THINKING AND PROBLEM SOLVING

17. Why do you think levers usually have a greater mechanical efficiency than other simple machines do?

18. The winding road shown below is actually a series of inclined planes. Describe how a winding road makes it easier for vehicles to travel up a hill.

19. Why do you think you would not want to reduce the friction involved in using a winding road?

MATH IN SCIENCE

20. You and a friend together apply a force of 1,000 N to a 3,000 N automobile to make it roll 10 m in 1 minute and 40 seconds.
    a. How much work did you and your friend do together?
    b. What was your combined power?

INTERPRETING GRAPHICS

For each of the images below, identify the class of lever used and calculate the mechanical advantage.

21.

22.

Reading Check-up

Take a minute to review your answers to the Pre-Reading Questions found at the bottom of page 186. Have your answers changed? If necessary, revise your answers based on what you have learned since you began this chapter.

Science, Technology, and Society

Micromachines

The technology of making things smaller and smaller keeps growing and growing. Powerful computers can now be held in the palm of your hand. But what about motors smaller than a grain of pepper? Or gnat-sized robots that can swim through the bloodstream? These are just a couple of the possibilities for micromachines.

Microscopic Motors

Researchers have already built gears, motors, and other devices so small that you could accidentally inhale one! For example, one engineer devised a motor so small that five of the motors would fit on the period at the end of this sentence. This micromotor is powered by static electricity instead of electric current, and the motor spins at 15,000 revolutions per minute. This is about twice as fast as most automobile engines running at top speed.

Small Sensors

So far micromachines have been most useful as sensing devices. Micromechanical sensors can be used in places too small for ordinary instruments. For example, blood-pressure sensors can fit inside blood vessels and can detect minute changes in a person's blood pressure. Each sensor has a patch so thin that it bends when the pressure changes.

Cell-Sized Robots

Some scientists are investigating the possibility of creating cell-sized machines called nanobots. These tiny robots may have many uses in medicine. For instance, if nanobots could be injected

▲ *The earliest working micromachine had a turning central rotor.*

into a person's bloodstream, they might be used to destroy disease-causing organisms such as viruses and bacteria. Nanobots might also be used to count blood cells or to deliver medicine.

The ultimate in micromachines would be machines created from individual atoms and molecules. Although these machines do not currently exist, scientists are already able to manipulate single atoms and molecules. For example, the "molecular man" shown below is made of individual molecules. These molecules are moved by using a scanning tunneling microscope.

A Nanobot's "Life"

▶ Imagine that you are a nanobot traveling through a person's body. What types of things do you think you would see? What type of work could you do? Write a story that describes what your experiences as a nanobot might be like.

▶ *"Molecular man" is composed of 28 carbon monoxide molecules.*

Eureka!

Wheelchair Innovators

Two recent inventions have dramatically improved the technology of wheelchairs. With these new inventions, some wheelchair riders can now control their chairs with voice commands and others can take a cruise over a sandy beach.

Voice-Command Wheelchair

At age 27, Martine Kemph invented a voice-recognition system that enables people without arms or legs to use spoken commands to operate their motorized wheelchairs. Here's how it works: The voice-recognition computer translates spoken words into digital commands, which are then directed to electric motors. These commands completely control the operating speed and direction of the motors, giving the operator total control over the chair's movement.

Kemph's system can execute spoken commands almost instantly. In addition, the system is easy to program, so each user can tailor the computer's list of commands to his or her needs.

Kemph named the computer Katalvox, using the root words *katal*, which is Greek for "to understand," and *vox*, which is Latin for "voice."

The Surf Chair

Mike Hensler was a lifeguard at Daytona Beach, Florida, when he realized that it was next to impossible for someone in a wheelchair to come onto the beach. Although he had never invented a machine before, Hensler decided to build a wheelchair that could be maneuvered across sand without getting stuck. He began spending many evenings in his driveway with a pile of lawn-chair parts, designing the chair by trial and error.

The result of Hensler's efforts looks very different from a conventional wheelchair. With huge rubber wheels and a thick frame of white PVC pipe, the Surf Chair not only moves easily over sandy terrain but also is weather resistant and easy to clean. The newest models of the Surf Chair come with optional attachments, such as a variety of umbrellas, detachable armrests and footrests, and even places to attach fishing rods.

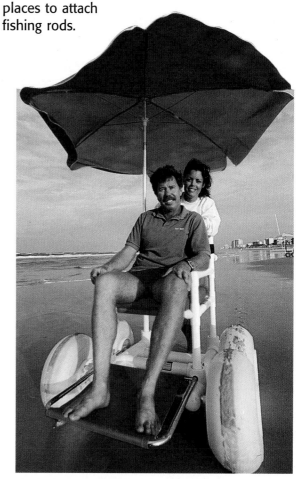

▲ *Mike Hensler tries out his Surf Chair.*

Design One Yourself

▶ Can you think of any other ways to improve wheelchairs? Think about it, and put your ideas down on paper. To inspire creative thinking, consider how a wheelchair could be made lighter, faster, safer, or easier to maneuver.

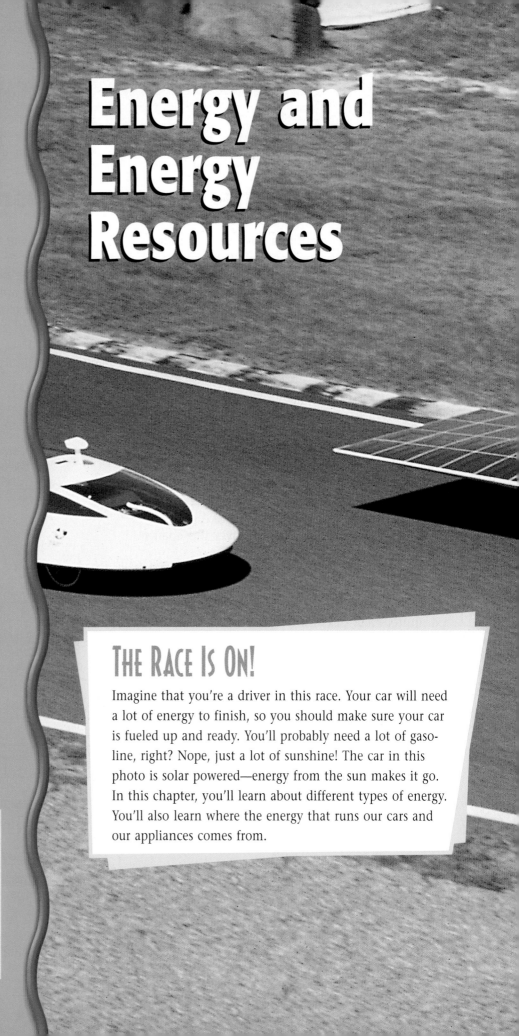

Energy and Energy Resources

Pre-Reading
Questions

1. What is energy?
2. How is energy converted
   from one form to
   another?
3. What is an energy
   resource?

The Race Is On!

Imagine that you're a driver in this race. Your car will need
a lot of energy to finish, so you should make sure your car
is fueled up and ready. You'll probably need a lot of gasoline, right? Nope, just a lot of sunshine! The car in this
photo is solar powered—energy from the sun makes it go.
In this chapter, you'll learn about different types of energy.
You'll also learn where the energy that runs our cars and
our appliances comes from.

Activity

ENERGY SWINGS!

All matter has energy. But what is energy? In this activity, you'll observe a moving pendulum to learn about energy.

Procedure

1. Make a pendulum by tying a **15 cm long string** around the hook of the **100 g hooked mass.**

2. Hold the string with one hand. Pull the mass slightly to the side, and let go of the mass without pushing it. Watch at least 10 swings of the pendulum.

3. In your ScienceLog, record your observations. Be sure to note how fast and how high the pendulum swings.

4. Repeat step 2, but pull the mass farther to the side.

5. Record your observations, noting how fast and how high the pendulum swings.

Analysis

6. Do you think the pendulum has energy? Explain your answer.

7. What causes the pendulum to move?

8. Do you think the pendulum has energy before you let go of the mass? Explain your answer.

What Is Energy?

Terms to Learn

energy
kinetic energy
potential energy
mechanical energy

What You'll Do

◆ Explain the relationship between energy and work.
◆ Compare kinetic and potential energy.
◆ Summarize the different forms of energy.

It's match point. The crowd is dead silent. The tennis player steps up to serve. With a look of determination, she bounces the tennis ball several times. Next, in one fluid movement, she tosses the ball into the air and then slams it with her racket. The ball flies toward her opponent, who steps up and swings her racket at the ball. Suddenly, *THWOOSH!!* The ball goes into the net, and the net wiggles from the impact. Game, set, and match!!

Energy and Work—Working Together

Energy is around you all the time. So what is it exactly? In science, you can think of **energy** as the ability to do work. Work occurs when a force causes an object to move in the direction of the force. How are energy and work involved in playing tennis? In this example, the tennis player does work on her racket, the racket does work on the ball, and the ball does work on the net. Each time work is done, something is given by one object to another that allows it to do work. That "something" is energy. As you can see in **Figure 1,** work is a transfer of energy.

Because work and energy are so closely related, they are expressed in the same units—joules (J). When a given amount of work is done, the same amount of energy is involved.

Figure 1 *When one object does work on another, energy is transferred.*

a The tennis player can do work on her racket because she has energy.

b When she does work on the racket, the racket gains the ability to do work on the ball. Energy is transferred from the tennis player to the racket.

c When the racket does work on the ball, the ball gains the ability to do work on something else. Energy is transferred from the racket to the ball.

Kinetic Energy Is Energy of Motion

From the tennis example on the previous page, you learned that energy is transferred from the racket to the ball. As the ball flies over the net, it has **kinetic** (ki NET ik) **energy,** the energy of motion. All moving objects have kinetic energy. Does the tennis player have kinetic energy? Definitely! She has kinetic energy when she steps up to serve and when she swings the racket. When she's standing still, she doesn't have any kinetic energy. However, the parts of her body that are moving—her eyes, her heart, and her lungs—do have some kinetic energy.

Objects with kinetic energy can do work. If you've ever gone bowling, you've done work using kinetic energy. When you throw the ball down the lane, you do work on it, transferring your kinetic energy to the ball. As a result, the bowling ball can do work on the pins. Another example of doing work with kinetic energy is shown in **Figure 2.**

Figure 2 *When you swing a hammer, you give it kinetic energy, which it uses to do work on the nail.*

Kinetic Energy Depends on Speed and Mass An object's kinetic energy can be determined with the following equation:

$$\text{Kinetic energy} = \frac{mv^2}{2}$$

In this equation, *m* stands for an object's mass, and *v* stands for an object's speed. The faster something is moving, the more kinetic energy it has. In addition, the more massive a moving object is, the more kinetic energy it has. But which do you think has more of an effect on an object's kinetic energy, its mass or its speed? As you can see from the equation, speed is squared, so speed has a greater effect on kinetic energy than does mass. You can see an example of how kinetic energy depends on speed and mass in **Figure 3.**

Figure 3 *The red car has more kinetic energy than the green car because the red car is moving faster. But the truck has more kinetic energy than the red car because the truck is more massive.*

25 m/s

20 m/s

25 m/s

Figure 4 *The stored potential energy of the bow and string allows them to do work on the arrow when the string is released.*

Potential Energy Is Energy of Position

Not all energy involves motion. **Potential energy** is the energy an object has because of its position or shape. For example, the stretched bow shown in **Figure 4** has potential energy. The bow is not moving, but it has energy because work has been done to change its shape. A similar example of potential energy is in a stretched rubber band.

Gravitational Potential Energy Depends on Weight and Height When you lift an object, you do work on it by using a force that opposes gravitational force. As a result, you give that object *gravitational potential energy*. Books on a bookshelf have gravitational potential energy, as does your backpack after you lift it onto your back. As you can see in **Figure 5,** the amount of gravitational potential energy an object has depends on its weight and its distance above Earth's surface.

Figure 5 Weight and Height Affect Gravitational Potential Energy

a The diver on the left weighs less and therefore has less gravitational potential energy than the diver on the right. The diver on the left did less work to climb up the platform.

b The diver on the higher platform has more gravitational potential energy than the diver on the lower platform. The diver on the higher platform did more work to climb up to the platform.

Calculating Gravitational Potential Energy You can calculate gravitational potential energy by using the following equation:

Gravitational potential energy = weight × height

Because weight is expressed in newtons and height is expressed in meters, gravitational potential energy is expressed in newton-meters (N•m), or joules (J). So a 25 N object at a height of 3 m has 25 N × 3 m = 75 J of gravitational potential energy.

Recall that work = force × distance. Weight is the amount of force you must exert on an object in order to lift it, and height is a distance. So calculating an object's gravitational potential energy is done by calculating the amount of work done on the object to lift it to a given height. You can practice calculating gravitational potential energy as well as kinetic energy in the MathBreak at right.

÷ 5 ÷ Ω ∞ +Ω √ 9 ∞ Σ 2
+ ≤ ≤

MATH BREAK

Calculating Energy

1. What is the kinetic energy of a 4,000 kg elephant running at 3 m/s? at 4 m/s?

2. If you lift a 50 N watermelon to the top of a 2 m refrigerator, how much gravitational potential energy do you give the watermelon?

Mechanical Energy Sums It All Up

How would you describe the energy of the juggler's pins in **Figure 6**? Well, to describe their total energy, you would describe their mechanical energy. **Mechanical energy** is the total energy of motion and position of an object. Mechanical energy can be all potential energy, all kinetic energy, or some of both. The following equation defines mechanical energy as the sum of kinetic and potential energy:

Mechanical energy = potential energy + kinetic energy

When potential energy increases (or decreases), kinetic energy has to decrease (or increase) in order for mechanical energy to remain constant. So the amount of an object's kinetic or potential energy may change, but its mechanical energy remains the same. You'll learn more about these changes in the next section.

Figure 6 As a pin is juggled, its mechanical energy is the sum of its potential energy and its kinetic energy at any point.

REVIEW

1. How are energy and work related?

2. What is the difference between kinetic and potential energy?

3. **Applying Concepts** Explain why a high-speed collision might cause more damage to vehicles than a low-speed collision.

Forms of Energy

All energy involves either motion or position. But energy takes different forms. These forms of energy include thermal, chemical, electrical, sound, light, and nuclear energy. In the next few pages, you will learn how the different forms of energy relate to kinetic and potential energy.

Thermal Energy All matter is made of particles that are constantly in motion. Because the particles are in motion, they have kinetic energy. The particles also have energy because of how they are arranged. *Thermal energy* is the total energy of the particles that make up an object. At higher temperatures, particles move faster. The faster the particles move, the more kinetic energy they have and the greater the object's thermal energy is. In addition, particles of a substance that are farther apart have more energy than particles of the same substance that are closer together. Look at **Figure 7.** Thermal energy also depends on the number of particles in a substance.

Figure 7 *The particles in steam have more energy than the particles in ice or ocean water. But the ocean has the most thermal energy because it has the most particles.*

The particles in an **ice cube** vibrate in fixed positions and therefore do not have a lot of energy.

The particles in **ocean water** are not in fixed positions and can move around. They have more energy than the particles in an ice cube.

The particles in **steam** are far apart. They move rapidly, so they have more energy than the particles in ocean water.

Chemical Energy What is the source of the energy in food? Food consists of chemical compounds. When compounds, such as the sugar in some foods, are formed, work is done to join, or bond, the different atoms together to form molecules. *Chemical energy* is the energy of a compound that changes as its atoms are rearranged to form new compounds. Chemical energy is a form of potential energy. Some molecules that have many atoms bonded together, such as gasoline, have a lot of chemical energy. In **Figure 8** on the next page, you can see an example of chemical energy.

Figure 8 Examples of Chemical Energy

When wood is burned, the chemical energy stored in the wood is used to toast your marshmallows.

Chemical energy is stored in the marshmallow's sugar molecules.

When you eat a marshmallow, chemical energy stored in the sugar becomes available for you to use.

Electrical Energy The electrical outlets in your home allow you to use electrical energy. *Electrical energy* is the energy of moving electrons. Electrons are the negatively charged particles of atoms. An atom is the smallest particle into which an element can be divided.

Suppose you plug an electrical device, such as the portable stereo shown in **Figure 9,** into an outlet and turn it on. The electrons in the wires will move back and forth, changing directions 120 times per second. As they do, energy is transferred to different parts within the stereo. The electrical energy created by moving electrons is used to do work. The work of a stereo is to produce sound.

The electrical energy available to your home is produced at power plants. Huge generators rotate magnets within coils of wire to produce electrical energy. Because the electrical energy results from the changing position of the magnet, electrical energy can be considered a form of potential energy. As soon as a device is plugged into an outlet and turned on, electrons move back and forth within the wires of the cord and within parts of the device. So electrical energy can also be considered a form of kinetic energy.

Figure 9 *The movement of electrons produces the electrical energy that a stereo uses to produce sound.*

Figure 10 *As the guitar strings vibrate, they cause particles in the air to vibrate. These vibrations transmit energy.*

Sound Energy You probably know that your vocal cords determine the sound of your voice. When you speak, air passes through your vocal cords, making them vibrate, or move back and forth. *Sound energy* is caused by an object's vibrations. **Figure 10** describes how a vibrating object transmits energy through the air around it.

Sound energy is a form of potential and kinetic energy. To make an object vibrate, work must be done to change its position. For example, when you pluck a guitar string, you stretch it and release it. The stretching changes the string's position. As a result, the string stores potential energy. In the release, the string uses its potential energy to move back to its original position. The moving guitar string has kinetic energy, which the string uses to do work on the air particles around it. The air particles vibrate and transmit this kinetic energy from particle to particle. When the vibrating air particles cause your eardrum to vibrate, you hear the sound of the guitar.

Light Energy Light allows us to see, but did you know that not all light can be seen? **Figure 11** shows a type of light that we use but can't see. *Light energy* is produced by the vibrations of electrically charged particles. Like sound vibrations, light vibrations cause energy to be transmitted. But unlike sound, the vibrations that transmit light energy don't cause other particles to vibrate. In fact, light energy can be transmitted through a vacuum (the absence of matter).

Hear That Energy!

1. Make a simple drum by covering the open end of an **empty coffee can** with **wax paper.** Secure the wax paper with a **rubber band.**

2. Using the eraser end of a **pencil,** tap lightly on the wax paper. In your ScienceLog, describe how the paper responds. What do you hear?

3. Repeat step 2, but tap the paper a bit harder. In your ScienceLog, compare your results with those of step 2.

4. Cover half of the wax paper with one hand. Now tap the paper. What happened? How can you describe sound energy as a form of mechanical energy?

TRY at HOME

Figure 11 *The energy used to cook food in a microwave is a form of light energy.*

Nuclear Energy What form of energy can come from a tiny amount of matter, can be used to generate electrical energy, and gives the sun its energy? It's *nuclear* (NOO klee uhr) *energy,* the energy associated with changes in the nucleus (NOO klee uhs) of an atom. Nuclear energy is produced in two ways—when two or more nuclei (NOO klee IE) join together or when the nucleus of an atom splits apart.

In the sun, shown in **Figure 12,** hydrogen nuclei join together to make a larger helium nucleus. This reaction releases a huge amount of energy, which allows the sun to light and heat the Earth.

The nuclei of some atoms, such as uranium, store a lot of potential energy. When work is done to split these nuclei apart, that energy is released. This type of nuclear energy is used to generate electrical energy at nuclear power plants, such as the one shown in **Figure 13.**

Figure 12 *Without the nuclear energy from the sun, life on Earth would not be possible.*

Figure 13 *In a nuclear power plant, small amounts of matter can produce large amounts of nuclear energy.*

REVIEW

1. What determines an object's thermal energy?

2. Describe why chemical energy is a form of potential energy.

3. Explain how sound energy is produced when you beat a drum.

4. **Analyzing Relationships** When you hit a nail into a board using a hammer, the head of the nail gets warm. In terms of kinetic and thermal energy, describe why you think this happens.

internetconnect

SC*LINKS*
NSTA

TOPIC: What Is Energy?, Forms of Energy
GO TO: www.scilinks.org
*sci*LINKS NUMBER: HSTP205, HSTP210

Energy Conversions

When you use a hammer to pound a nail into a board, you transfer your kinetic energy to the hammer, and the hammer transfers that kinetic energy to the nail. But energy is involved in other ways too. For example, sound energy is produced when you hit the nail. An energy transfer often leads to an **energy conversion,** a change from one form of energy into another. Any form of energy can be converted into any other form of energy, and often one form of energy is converted into more than one other form. In this section, you'll learn how energy conversions make your daily activities possible.

From Kinetic to Potential and Back

Take a look at **Figure 14.** Have you ever jumped on a trampoline? What types of energy are involved in this bouncing activity? Because you're moving when you jump, you have kinetic energy. And each time you jump into the air, you change your position with respect to the ground, so you also have gravitational potential energy. Another kind of potential energy is involved too—that of the trampoline stretching when you jump on it.

Figure 14 *Kinetic and potential energy are converted back and forth as you jump up and down on a trampoline.*

1 When you jump down, your kinetic energy is converted into the potential energy of the stretched trampoline.

2 The trampoline's potential energy is converted into kinetic energy, which is transferred to you, making you bounce up.

3 At the top of your jump, all of your kinetic energy has been converted into potential energy.

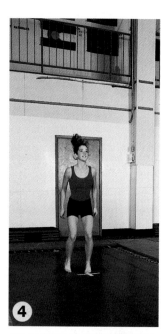

4 Right before you hit the trampoline, all of your potential energy has been converted back into kinetic energy.

Another example of the energy conversions between kinetic and potential energy is the motion of a pendulum (PEN dyoo luhm). Shown in **Figure 15,** a pendulum is a mass hung from a fixed point so that it can swing freely. When you lift the pendulum to one side, you do work on it, and the energy used to do that work is stored by the pendulum as potential energy. As soon as you let the pendulum go, it swings because the Earth exerts a force on it. The work the Earth does converts the pendulum's potential energy into kinetic energy.

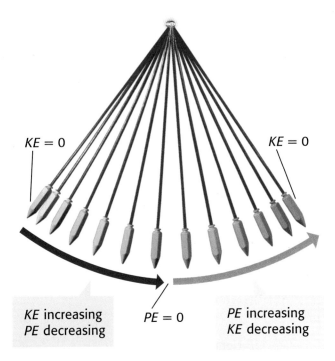

$KE = 0$

$KE = 0$

KE increasing
PE decreasing

$PE = 0$

PE increasing
KE decreasing

Figure 15 *A pendulum's mechanical energy is all kinetic (KE) at the bottom of its swing and all potential (PE) at the top of its swing.*

Self-Check

At what point does a roller coaster have the greatest potential energy? the greatest kinetic energy? *(See page 724 to check your answer.)*

Conversions Involving Chemical Energy

You've probably heard the expression "Breakfast is the most important meal of the day." What does this statement mean? Why does eating breakfast help you start the day? As your body digests food, chemical energy is released and is available to you, as discussed in **Figure 16.**

Figure 16 *Your body performs energy conversions.*

Chemical energy of food is converted into . . .

. . . kinetic energy when you are active and thermal energy to maintain body temperature.

Would you believe that the chemical energy in the food you eat is a result of the sun's energy? It's true! When you eat fruits, vegetables, grains, or meat from animals that ate fruits, vegetables, or grains, you are taking in chemical energy that resulted from a chemical change involving the sun's energy. As shown in **Figure 17,** photosynthesis (FOHT oh SIN thuh sis) uses light energy to produce new substances with chemical energy. In this way light energy is converted into chemical energy.

Figure 17 *Green plants use chlorophyll and light energy from the sun to produce the chemical energy in the food you eat.*

Photosynthesis

$$\text{carbon dioxide} + \text{water} \xrightarrow[\text{chlorophyll}]{\text{light energy}} \text{sugar} + \text{oxygen}$$

Light energy

Chlorophyll in green leaves

Carbon dioxide in the air

Water in the soil

Sugar in food

APPLY

Camping with Energy

If you go camping, you probably use a stove, such as the one shown here, to prepare meals. Describe some of the energy conversions that take place when lighting the stove, cooking the food, eating the prepared meal, and then setting out on a long hike.

Conversions Involving Electrical Energy

You use electrical energy all the time—when you listen to the radio, when you make toast, and when you take a picture with a camera. Electrical energy can be easily converted into other forms of energy. **Figure 18** shows how electrical energy is converted in a hair dryer.

Figure 18 Energy Conversions in a Hair Dryer

1 Electrical energy enters the hair dryer and is converted into kinetic energy as a small electric motor spins a fan blade.

2 Electrical energy is also converted into thermal energy in a grid of wires that heats up.

3 The fan forces air across the hot wires, and hot air blows out the nozzle of the hair dryer. You can hear the sound energy that is also produced.

Examples of Conversions Involving Electrical Energy

Alarm clock	electrical energy ⟶	light energy and sound energy
Battery	chemical energy ⟶	electrical energy
Light bulb	electrical energy ⟶	light energy and thermal energy
Blender	electrical energy ⟶	kinetic energy and sound energy

REVIEW

1. What is an energy conversion?

2. Describe an example in which electrical energy is converted into thermal energy.

3. Describe an energy conversion involving chemical energy.

4. **Applying Concepts** Describe the kinetic-potential energy conversions that occur when you bounce a basketball.

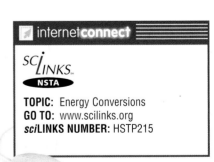

internet**connect**

*sci*LINKS
NSTA

TOPIC: Energy Conversions
GO TO: www.scilinks.org
*sci*LINKS **NUMBER:** HSTP215

Energy and Machines

You've been learning about energy, its different forms, and how it can undergo conversions. Another way to learn about energy is to look at how machines use energy. A machine can make work easier by changing the size or direction (or both) of the force required to do the work. Suppose you want to crack open a walnut. Using a nutcracker, like the one shown in **Figure 19**, would be much easier (and less painful) than using your fingers. You transfer your energy to the nutcracker, and it transfers energy to the nut. But the nutcracker will not transfer more energy to the nut than you transfer to the nutcracker. In addition, some of the energy you transfer to a machine can be converted by the machine into other forms of energy. Another example of how energy is used by a machine is shown in **Figure 20**.

Figure 19 *Some of the kinetic energy you transfer to a nutcracker is converted into sound energy as the nutcracker transfers energy to the nut.*

Figure 20 *To start and keep your bike moving, energy must be converted and transferred.*

1 Chemical energy in your body is converted into kinetic energy when your muscle fibers contract and relax.

2 Your legs transfer this kinetic energy to the pedals, pushing them around in a circle.

4 The chain moves and transfers energy to the back wheel, which gets you moving!

3 The pedals transfer this kinetic energy to the gear wheel, which transfers kinetic energy to the chain.

Machines Are Energy Converters As you saw in the examples on the previous page, when machines transfer energy, energy conversions can often result. For example, you can hear the sounds that your bike makes when you pedal it, change gears, or brake swiftly. That means that some of the kinetic energy being transferred gets converted into sound energy as the bike moves. Some machines are especially useful because they are energy converters. **Figure 21** shows an example of a machine specifically designed to convert energy from one form to another. In addition, the chart at right lists other machines that perform useful energy conversions.

Some Machines that Convert Energy	
▪ electric motor	▪ microphone
▪ windmill	▪ toaster
▪ doorbell	▪ dishwasher
▪ gas heater	▪ lawn mower
▪ telephone	▪ clock

Figure 21 *The continuous conversion of chemical energy into thermal energy and kinetic energy in a car's engine is necessary to make a car move.*

1 A mixture of gasoline and air enters the engine as the piston moves downward.

Piston

2 The kinetic energy of the crankshaft raises the piston, and the gasoline mixture is forced up toward the spark plug, which uses electrical energy to ignite the gasoline mixture.

Spark plug

Crankshaft

3 As the gasoline mixture burns, chemical energy is converted into thermal energy and kinetic energy, forcing the piston back down.

4 The kinetic energy of the crankshaft forces the piston up again, pushing exhaust gases out. Then the cycle repeats.

Figure 22 *In a wind turbine, the kinetic energy of the wind can be collected and converted into electrical energy.*

Science
CONNECTION

Turn to page 242 to find out about buildings that are energy efficient as well as environmentally friendly.

Why Energy Conversions Are Important

Everything we do is related to energy conversions. Heating our homes, obtaining energy from a meal, growing plants, and many other activities all require energy conversions.

Making Energy Useful You can think of energy conversions as a way of getting energy in the form that you need. Machines help harness existing energy and make that energy work for you. Did you know that the wind could help you cook a meal? A wind turbine, shown in **Figure 22,** can perform an energy conversion that would allow you to use an electric stove to do just that.

Making Conversions Efficient You may have heard that a car may be considered energy efficient if it gets good gas mileage, and your home may be energy efficient if it is well insulated. In terms of energy conversions, *energy efficiency* (e FISH uhn see) is a comparison of the amount of energy before a conversion with the amount of useful energy after a conversion. For example, the energy efficiency of a light bulb would be a comparison of the electrical energy going into it with the light energy coming out of it. The less electrical energy that is converted into thermal energy instead of into light energy, the more efficient the bulb.

Not all of the energy in a conversion becomes useful energy. Just as work input is always greater than work output, energy input is also always greater than energy output. But the closer the energy output is to the energy input, the more efficient the conversion is. Making energy conversions more efficient is important because greater efficiency means less waste.

REVIEW

1. What is the role of machines in energy conversions?

2. Give an example of a machine that is an energy converter, and explain how the machine converts one form of energy to another.

3. **Applying Concepts** A car that brakes suddenly comes to a screeching halt. Is the sound energy produced in this conversion a useful form of energy? Explain your answer.

Conservation of Energy

Many roller coasters have a mechanism that pulls the cars up to the top of the first hill, but the cars are on their own the rest of the ride. As the cars go up and down the hills on the track, their potential energy is converted into kinetic energy and back again. But the cars never return to the same height they started from. Does that mean that energy gets *lost* somewhere along the way? Nope—it just gets converted into other forms of energy.

Where Does the Energy Go?

In order to find out where a roller coaster's original potential energy goes, you have to consider more than just the hills of the roller coaster. You have to consider friction too. **Friction** is a force that opposes motion between two surfaces that are touching. For the roller coaster to move, work must be done to overcome the friction between the cars' wheels and the coaster track and between the cars and the surrounding air. The energy used to do this work comes from the original amount of potential energy that the cars have on the top of the first hill. The need to overcome friction affects the design of a roller coaster track. In **Figure 23,** you can see that the second hill will always be shorter than the first.

When energy is used to overcome friction, some of the energy is converted into thermal energy. Some of the cars' potential energy is converted into thermal energy on the way down the first hill, and then some of their kinetic energy is converted into thermal energy on the way up the second hill. So energy isn't lost at all—it just undergoes a conversion.

Figure 23 *Due to friction, not all of the cars' potential energy (PE) is converted into kinetic energy (KE) as the cars go down the first hill. In addition, not all of the cars' kinetic energy is converted into potential energy as the cars go up the second hill.*

a *PE is greatest at the top of the first hill.*

b *KE at the bottom of the first hill is less than the PE was at the top.*

c *PE on top of the second hill is less than KE and PE from the first hill.*

Try to keep an egg from breaking while learning more about the law of conservation of energy on page 671 in the LabBook.

Energy Is Conserved Within a Closed System

A *closed system* is a well-defined group of objects that transfer energy between one another. For example, a closed system that involves a roller coaster consists of the track, the cars, and the surrounding air. On a roller coaster, some mechanical energy (the sum of kinetic and potential energy) is always converted into thermal energy because of friction. Sound energy is also a result of the energy conversions in a roller coaster. You can understand that energy is not lost on a roller coaster only when you consider all of the factors involved in a closed system. If you add together the cars' kinetic energy at the bottom of the first hill, the thermal energy due to overcoming friction, and the sound energy produced, you end up with the same total amount of energy as the original amount of potential energy. In other words, energy is conserved.

Law of Conservation of Energy No situation has been found where energy is not conserved. Because this phenomenon is always observed during energy conversions, it is described as a law. According to the **law of conservation of energy,** energy can be neither created nor destroyed. The total amount of energy in a closed system is always the same. Energy can be changed from one form to another, but all the different forms of energy in a system always add up to the same total amount of energy, no matter how many energy conversions occur.

Consider the energy conversions in a light bulb, shown in **Figure 24.** You can define the closed system to include the outlet, the wires, and the parts of the bulb. While not all of the original electrical energy is converted into light energy, no energy is lost. At any point during its use, the total amount of electrical energy entering the light bulb is equal to the total amount of light and thermal energy that leaves the bulb. Energy is conserved.

Figure 24 Energy Conservation in a Light Bulb

Some energy is converted to thermal energy, which makes the bulb feel warm.

Some electrical energy is converted into light energy.

Some electrical energy is converted into thermal energy because of friction in the wire.

No Conversion Without Thermal Energy

Any time one form of energy is converted into another form, some of the original energy always gets converted into thermal energy. The thermal energy due to friction that results from energy conversions is not useful energy. That is, this thermal energy is not used to do work. Think about a car. You put gas into a car, but not all of the gasoline's chemical energy makes the car move. Some waste thermal energy will always result from the energy conversions. Much of this waste thermal energy exits a car engine through the radiator and the exhaust pipe.

Perpetual Motion? No Way! People have dreamed of constructing a machine that runs forever without any additional energy—a *perpetual* (puhr PECH oo uhl) *motion machine*. Such a machine would put out exactly as much energy as it takes in. But because some waste thermal energy always results from energy conversions, perpetual motion is impossible. The only way a machine can keep moving is to have a continuous supply of energy. For example, the "drinking bird" shown in **Figure 25** continually uses thermal energy from the air to evaporate the water from its head. So it is *not* a perpetual motion machine.

Biology CONNECTION

Whenever you do work, you use chemical energy stored in your body that comes from food you've eaten. As you do work, some of that chemical energy is always converted into thermal energy. That's why your body heats up after performing a task, such as raking leaves, for several minutes.

Figure 25 The "Drinking Bird"

a When the bird "drinks," the felt covering its head gets wet.

b When the bird is upright, water evaporates from the felt, decreasing the temperature and pressure in the head. Fluid is drawn up from the tail, where pressure is higher, and the bird tips.

c After the bird "drinks," fluid returns to the tail, the bird flips upright, and the cycle repeats.

REVIEW

1. Describe the energy conversions that take place in a pendulum, and explain how energy is conserved.

2. Why is perpetual motion impossible?

3. **Analyzing Viewpoints** Imagine that you drop a ball. It bounces a few times, but then it stops. Your friend says that the ball has lost all of its energy. Using what you know about the law of conservation of energy, respond to your friend's statement.

internetconnect

*sci*LINKS
NSTA

TOPIC: Law of Conservation of Energy
GO TO: www.scilinks.org
*sci*LINKS **NUMBER:** HSTP217

Terms to Learn

energy resource
nonrenewable resources
fossil fuels
renewable resources

What You'll Do

◆ Name several energy resources.
◆ Explain how the sun is the source of most energy on Earth.
◆ Evaluate the advantages and disadvantages of using various energy resources.

Energy Resources

Energy is used to light and warm our homes; to produce food, clothing, and other products; and to transport people and products from place to place. Where does all this energy come from? An **energy resource** is a natural resource that can be converted by humans into other forms of energy in order to do useful work. In this section, you will learn about several energy resources, including the resource responsible for most other energy resources—the sun.

Nonrenewable Resources

Some energy resources, called **nonrenewable resources,** cannot be replaced after they are used or can be replaced only over thousands or millions of years. Fossil fuels are the most important nonrenewable resources.

Fossil Fuels Coal, petroleum, and natural gas, shown in **Figure 26,** are the most common fossil fuels. **Fossil fuels** are energy resources that formed from the buried remains of plants and animals that lived millions of years ago. These plants stored energy from the sun by photosynthesis. Animals used and stored this energy by eating the plants or by eating animals that ate plants. So fossil fuels are concentrated forms of the sun's energy.

This piece of coal containing a fern fossil shows that coal formed from plants that lived millions of years ago.

Figure 26 Formation of Fossil Fuels

Natural gas was formed much in the same way that petroleum was formed, and it is often found along with petroleum deposits.

Petroleum, or oil, was formed from organisms that lived in prehistoric lakes and seas. Crushed by layers of sediment and heated by the Earth, the remains were slowly changed into petroleum.

Now, millions of years later, energy from the sun is released when fossil fuels are burned. Any fossil fuel contains stored energy from the sun that can be converted into other types of energy. The information below shows how important fossil fuels are to our society.

Coal

Most coal used in the United States is burned to produce steam to run electric generators.

Coal Use (U.S.)

Heating

Coal used in the making of steel

Electric power

Industrial uses

Coal exports

Petroleum

Petroleum supplies us with gasoline, kerosene, and wax as well as petrochemicals, which are used to make synthetic fibers, such as rayon.

Annual Oil Production—Past & Predicted

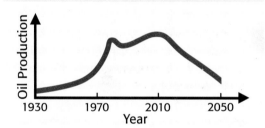

Oil Production

1930   1970   2010   2050
Year

Finding alternative energy resources will become more important in years to come.

Natural Gas

Natural gas is used in heating systems, in stoves and ovens, and in vehicles as an alternative to gasoline.

Natural gas is the cleanest burning fossil fuel.

Comparing Fossil Fuel Emissions

■ Nitrogen oxides
■ Carbon dioxide
■ Particulates

Natural gas   Petroleum   Coal

Turn to page 243 to read about a day in the life of a power-plant manager.

Electrical Energy from Fossil Fuels One way to generate electrical energy is to burn fossil fuels. In fact, fossil fuels are the primary source of electrical energy generated in the United States. Earlier in this chapter, you learned that electrical energy can result from energy conversions. Kinetic energy is converted into electrical energy by an *electric generator*. This energy conversion is part of a larger process, shown in **Figure 27,** of converting the chemical energy in fossil fuels into the electrical energy you use every day.

Figure 27
Converting Fossil Fuels into Electrical Energy

❶ Water is pumped into a boiler.

❷ Coal, oil, or natural gas is burned in a combustion chamber in order to boil water. In this way, the chemical energy of the fossil fuels is converted into thermal energy.

❸ Thermal energy is used to boil water and turn it to steam.

❹ Thermal energy is converted into kinetic energy as the steam pushes against the blades of a turbine, causing the central shaft to spin.

❺ An electric generator converts kinetic energy into electrical energy. The central shaft from the turbine spins a large magnet within a ring of wire coils. As the magnet spins, electric current is generated in the wire coils.

❻ The electrical energy can be distributed to a community through electrical wires.

Nuclear Energy Another way to generate electrical energy is to use nuclear energy. Like fossil-fuel power plants, a nuclear power plant generates thermal energy that boils water to produce steam. The steam then turns a turbine, which rotates a generator that converts kinetic energy into electrical energy. However, the fuels used in nuclear power plants are different from fossil fuels. Nuclear energy is generated from radioactive elements, such as uranium, shown in **Figure 28.** In a process called *nuclear fission* (FISH uhn), the nucleus of a uranium atom is split into two smaller nuclei, releasing nuclear energy. Because the supply of these elements is limited, nuclear energy can be thought of as a nonrenewable resource.

Renewable Resources

Some energy resources, called **renewable resources,** can be used and replaced in nature over a relatively short period of time. Some renewable resources, such as solar energy and wind energy, are considered practically limitless.

Figure 28 *A single uranium fuel pellet contains the energy equivalent of about 1 metric ton of coal.*

Solar Energy

Sunlight can be converted into electrical energy through solar cells, which can be used in devices such as calculators or installed in a home to provide electrical energy.

Some houses allow sunlight into the house through large windows. The sunlight is converted into thermal energy that heats the house naturally.

Energy from Water

The sun causes water to evaporate and fall again as rain that flows through rivers. The potential energy of water in a reservoir is converted into kinetic energy as the water flows downhill through a dam.

Falling water turns a turbine in a dam, which is connected to a generator that converts kinetic energy into electrical energy. Electrical energy produced from falling water is called *hydroelectricity.*

Wind Energy

Wind is caused by the sun's uneven heating of the Earth's surface, which creates currents of air. The kinetic energy of wind can turn the blades of a windmill. Windmills are often used to pump water from the ground.

A wind turbine converts kinetic energy into electrical energy by rotating a generator.

Geothermal Energy

Thermal energy resulting from the heating of Earth's crust is called *geothermal energy.* Ground water that seeps into hot spots near the surface of the Earth can form geysers.

Some geothermal power plants pump water underground into areas of hot rock. The water returns to the surface as steam, which can then be used to turn a generator to produce electrical energy.

Biomass

Plants capture and store energy from the sun. Organic matter, such as plants, wood, and waste, that can be burned to release energy is called *biomass.* Nonindustrialized countries rely heavily on biomass for energy.

Certain plants can also be converted into liquid fuel. For example, corn can be used to make ethanol, which is often mixed with gasoline to make a cleaner-burning fuel for cars.

The Two Sides to Energy Resources

The table below compares several energy resources. Depending on where you live, what you need energy for, and how much you need, sometimes one energy resource is a better choice than another.

Energy resource	Advantages	Disadvantages
Fossil fuels	■ provide a large amount of thermal energy per unit of mass ■ easy to get and easy to transport ■ can be used to generate electrical energy and make products, such as plastic	■ nonrenewable ■ burning produces smog ■ burning coal releases substances that can cause acid precipitation ■ risk of oil spills
Nuclear	■ very concentrated form of energy ■ power plants do not produce smog	■ produces radioactive waste ■ radioactive elements are nonrenewable
Solar	■ almost limitless source of energy ■ does not produce pollution	■ expensive to use for large-scale energy production ■ only practical in sunny areas
Water	■ renewable ■ does not produce air pollution	■ dams disrupt a river's ecosystem ■ available only in areas that have rivers
Wind	■ renewable ■ relatively inexpensive to generate ■ does not produce air pollution	■ only practical in windy areas
Geothermal	■ almost limitless source of energy ■ power plants require little land	■ only practical in locations near hot spots ■ waste water can damage soil
Biomass	■ renewable	■ requires large areas of farmland ■ produces smoke

REVIEW

1. Compare fossil fuels and biomass.

2. Why is nuclear energy a nonrenewable resource?

3. Trace electrical energy back to the sun.

4. **Interpreting Graphics** Use the pie chart at right to explain why renewable resources will become more important in years to come.

U.S. Energy Sources

Chapter Highlights

SECTION 1

Vocabulary

energy (*p. 214*)
kinetic energy (*p. 215*)
potential energy (*p. 216*)
mechanical energy (*p. 217*)

Section Notes

- Energy is the ability to do work, and work is the transfer of energy. Both energy and work are expressed in joules.

- Kinetic energy is energy of motion and depends on speed and mass.

- Potential energy is energy of position or shape. Gravitational potential energy depends on weight and height.

- Mechanical energy is the sum of kinetic energy and potential energy.

- Thermal energy, sound energy, electrical energy, and light energy can all be forms of kinetic energy.

- Chemical energy, electrical energy, sound energy, and nuclear energy can all be forms of potential energy.

SECTION 2

Vocabulary

energy conversion (*p. 222*)

Section Notes

- An energy conversion is a change from one form of energy to another. Any form of energy can be converted into any other form of energy.

- Machines can transfer energy and convert energy into a more useful form.

- Energy conversions help to make energy useful by changing energy into the form you need.

Labs

Finding Energy (*p. 668*)
Energy of a Pendulum (*p. 670*)

☑ Skills Check

Math Concepts

GRAVITATIONAL POTENTIAL ENERGY To calculate an object's gravitational potential energy, multiply the weight of the object by its height above the Earth's surface. For example, the gravitational potential energy (*GPE*) of a box that weighs 100 N and that is sitting in a moving truck 1.5 m above the ground is calculated as follows:

$$GPE = \text{weight} \times \text{height}$$

$$GPE = 100 \text{ N} \times 1.5 \text{ m} = 150 \text{ J}$$

Visual Understanding

POTENTIAL-KINETIC ENERGY CONVERSIONS
When you jump up and down on a trampoline, potential and kinetic energy are converted back and forth. Review the picture of the pendulum on page 223 for another example of potential-kinetic energy conversions.

ENERGY RESOURCES Look back at the diagram on page 234. Converting fossil fuels into electrical energy requires several energy conversions.

SECTION 3

Vocabulary

friction *(p. 229)*

law of conservation of energy *(p. 230)*

Section Notes

- Because of friction, some energy is always converted into thermal energy during an energy conversion.

- Energy is conserved within a closed system. According to the law of conservation of energy, energy can be neither created nor destroyed.

- Perpetual motion is impossible because some of the energy put into a machine will be converted into thermal energy due to friction.

Labs

Eggstremely Fragile *(p. 671)*

SECTION 4

Vocabulary

energy resource *(p. 232)*

nonrenewable resources *(p. 232)*

fossil fuels *(p. 232)*

renewable resources *(p. 235)*

Section Notes

- An energy resource is a natural resource that can be converted into other forms of energy in order to do useful work.

- Nonrenewable resources cannot be replaced after they are used or can only be replaced after long periods of time. They include fossil fuels and nuclear energy.

- Fossil fuels are nonrenewable resources formed from the remains of ancient organisms. Coal, petroleum, and natural gas are fossil fuels.

- Renewable resources can be used and replaced in nature over a relatively short period of time. They include solar energy, wind energy, energy from water, geothermal energy, and biomass.

- The sun is the source of most energy on Earth.

- Depending on where you live and what you need energy for, one energy resource can be a better choice than another.

Chapter Review

USING VOCABULARY

For each pair of terms, explain the difference in their meanings.

1. potential energy/kinetic energy

2. friction/energy conversion

3. energy conversion/law of conservation of energy

4. energy resources/fossil fuels

5. renewable resources/nonrenewable resources

UNDERSTANDING CONCEPTS

Multiple Choice

6. Kinetic energy depends on
   a. mass and volume.
   b. speed and weight.
   c. weight and height.
   d. speed and mass.

7. Gravitational potential energy depends on
   a. mass and speed.
   b. weight and height.
   c. mass and weight.
   d. height and distance.

8. Which of the following is not a renewable resource?
   a. wind energy
   b. nuclear energy
   c. solar energy
   d. geothermal energy

9. Which of the following is a conversion from chemical energy to thermal energy?
   a. Food is digested and used to regulate body temperature.
   b. Charcoal is burned in a barbecue pit.
   c. Coal is burned to boil water.
   d. all of the above

10. Machines can
    a. increase energy.
    b. transfer energy.
    c. convert energy.
    d. Both (b) and (c)

11. In every energy conversion, some energy is always converted into
    a. kinetic energy.
    b. potential energy.
    c. thermal energy.
    d. mechanical energy.

12. An object that has kinetic energy must be
    a. at rest.
    b. lifted above the Earth's surface.
    c. in motion.
    d. None of the above

13. Which of the following is *not* a fossil fuel?
    a. gasoline   c. firewood
    b. coal   d. natural gas

Short Answer

14. Name two forms of energy, and relate them to kinetic or potential energy.

15. Give three specific examples of energy conversions.

16. Explain how energy is conserved within a closed system.

17. How are fossil fuels formed?

Concept Mapping

18. Use the following terms to create a concept map: energy, machines, energy conversions, thermal energy, friction.

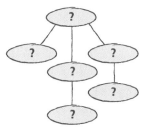

CRITICAL THINKING AND PROBLEM SOLVING

19. What happens when you blow up a balloon and release it? Describe what you would see in terms of energy.

20. After you coast down a hill on your bike, you eventually come to a complete stop unless you keep pedaling. Relate this to the reason why perpetual motion is impossible.

21. Look at the photo of the pole-vaulter below. Trace the energy conversions involved in this event, beginning with the pole-vaulter's breakfast of an orange-banana smoothie.

22. If the sun were exhausted of its nuclear energy, what would happen to our energy resources on Earth?

MATH IN SCIENCE

23. A box has 400 J of gravitational potential energy.
  a. How much work had to be done to give the box that energy?
  b. If the box weighs 100 N, how far was it lifted?

INTERPRETING GRAPHICS

24. Look at the illustration below, and answer the questions that follow.

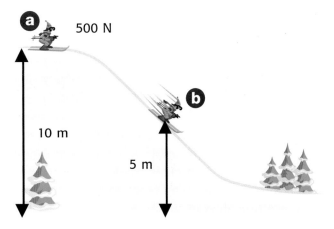

500 N

10 m

5 m

  a. What is the skier's gravitational potential energy at point *A*?
  b. What is the skier's gravitational potential energy at point *B*?
  c. What is the skier's kinetic energy at point *B*? (Hint: mechanical energy = potential energy + kinetic energy.)

Reading Check-up

Take a minute to review your answers to the Pre-Reading Questions found at the bottom of page 212. Have your answers changed? If necessary, revise your answers based on what you have learned since you began this chapter.

Green Buildings

How do you make a building green without painting it? You make sure it does as little damage to the environment as possible. *Green,* in this case, does not refer to the color of pine trees or grass. Instead, *green* means "environmentally safe." And the "green movement" is growing quickly.

Green Methods and Materials

One strategy that architects employ to turn a building green is to minimize its energy consumption. They also reduce water use wherever possible. One way to do this would be to create landscapes that use only native plants that require little watering. Green builders also use recycled building materials whenever possible. For example, crushed light bulbs can be recycled into floor tiles, and recycled cotton can replace fiberglass as insulation.

Seeing Green

Although green buildings cost more than conventional buildings to construct, they save a lot of money in the long run. For example, the Audubon Building, in Manhattan, saves $100,000 in maintenance costs every year—that is $60,000 in electricity bills alone! The building uses more than 60 percent less energy and electricity than a conventional building does. Inside, the workers enjoy natural lighting, cleaner air, and an environment that is free of unnecessary chemicals.

Some designers want to create buildings that are even more environmentally friendly than the Audubon Building. Walls can be made of straw bales or packed dirt, and landscapes can be maintained with rainwater collected from rooftops. By conserving, recycling, and reducing waste, green builders are doing a great deal to help the environment.

Design It Yourself!

▶ Design a building, a home, or even a doghouse that is made of only recycled materials. Be inventive! When you think you have the perfect design, create a scale model. Describe how your green structure saves resources.

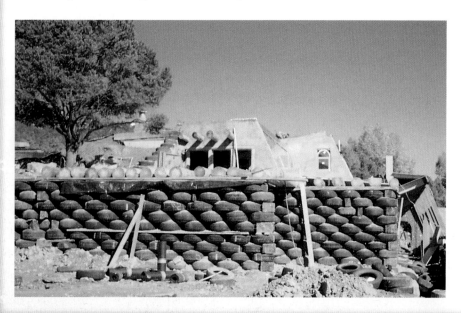

◀ *The walls of this building are being made out of worn-out tires packed with soil. The walls will later be covered with stucco.*

CAREERS

POWER-PLANT MANAGER

As a power-plant manager, **Cheryl Mele** is responsible for almost a billion watts of electric power generation at the Decker Power Plant in Austin, Texas. More than 700 MW are produced using a steam-driven turbine system with natural gas fuel and oil as a backup fuel. Another 200 MW are generated by gas turbines. The steam-driven turbine system and gas turbines together provide enough electrical energy for many homes and businesses.

*A*ccording to Cheryl Mele, her job as plant manager includes "anything that needs doing." Her training as a mechanical engineer allows her to conduct routine testing and to diagnose problems successfully. A firm believer in protecting our environment, Mele operates the plant responsibly. Mele states, "It is very important to keep the plant running properly and burning as efficiently as possible." Her previous job helping to design more-efficient gas turbines helped make her a top candidate for the job of plant manager.

The Team Approach

Mele uses the team approach to maintain the power plant. She says, "We think better as a team. We all have areas of expertise and interest, and we maximize our effectiveness." Mele observes that working together makes everyone's job easier.

Advice to Young People

Mele believes that mechanical engineering and managing a power plant are interesting careers because you get to work with many exciting new technologies. These professions are excellent choices for both men and women. In these careers you interact with creative people as you try to improve mechanical equipment to make it more efficient and reduce harm to the environment. Her advice for young people is to pursue what interests you. "Be sure to connect the math you learn to the science you are doing," she says. "This will help you to understand both."

A Challenge

▶ With the help of an adult, find out how much electrical energy your home uses each month. How many homes like yours could Mele's billion-watt power plant supply energy to each month?

▶ *Cheryl Mele manages the Decker Power Plant in Austin, Texas.*

Heat and Heat Technology

Pre-Reading
Questions

1. How do you measure how hot or cold an object is?

2. What makes an object hot or cold?

3. How can heat be used in your home?

UP, UP, AND AWAY

A hot-air balloon race is fun to watch. The balloons start out flat, but as they fill with hot air, the balloons grow larger until they are ready to take off. Balloons don't need engines or wings. They rely on heat and thermal expansion to get them off the ground and into the sky. In this chapter, you will learn more about heat and its place in your daily life.

Activity

SOME LIKE IT HOT

Sometimes you can tell the relative temperature of something by touching it with your hand. In this activity, you will find out how well your hand works as a thermometer!

Procedure

1. Gather small pieces of the following materials from your teacher: **metal, wood, plastic foam, rock, plastic,** and **cardboard.**

2. Allow the materials to sit untouched on a table for several minutes.

3. Put your hands palms down on each of the various materials. Observe how warm or cool each one feels.

4. In your ScienceLog, list the materials in order from coolest to warmest.

5. Place a **thermometer strip** on the surface of each material. In your ScienceLog, record the temperature of each material.

Analysis

6. Which material felt the warmest?

7. Which material had the highest temperature? Was it the same material as in question 6?

8. Why do you think some materials felt warmer than others?

9. Was your hand a good thermometer? Why or why not?

Temperature

You probably put on a sweater or a jacket when it's cold outside. Likewise, you probably wear shorts in the summer when it gets hot. But how hot is hot, and how cold is cold? Think about how the knobs on a water faucet are labeled "H" for hot and "C" for cold. But does only hot water come out when the hot water knob is on? You may have noticed that when you first turn on the water, it is warm or even cool. Are you being misled by the label on the knob? The terms *hot* and *cold* are not very scientific terms. If you really want to specify how hot or cold something is, you must use temperature.

What Is Temperature?

You probably think of temperature as a measure of how hot or cold something is. But scientifically, **temperature** is a measure of the average kinetic energy of the particles in an object. Using *temperature* instead of words like *hot* or *cold* reduces confusion. The scenario below emphasizes the importance of communicating about temperature. You can learn more about hot and cold comparisons by doing the QuickLab on the next page.

Temperature Depends on the Kinetic Energy of Particles

All matter is made of particles—atoms or molecules—that are in constant motion. Because the particles are in motion, they have kinetic energy. The faster the particles are moving, the more kinetic energy they have. What does temperature have to do with kinetic energy? Well, as described in **Figure 1,** the more kinetic energy the particles of an object have, the higher the temperature of the object.

Figure 1 *The gas particles on the right have more kinetic energy than those on the left. So, the gas on the right is at a higher temperature.*

Temperature Is an Average Measure Particles of matter are constantly moving, but they don't all move at the same speed and in the same direction all the time. Look back at Figure 1. As you can see, the motion of the particles is random. The particles of matter in an object move in different directions, and some particles move faster than others. As a result, some particles have more kinetic energy than others. So what determines an object's temperature? An object's temperature is the best approximation of the kinetic energy of the particles. When you measure an object's temperature, you measure the average kinetic energy of the particles in the object.

The temperature of a substance is not determined by how much of the substance you have. As shown in **Figure 2,** different amounts of the same substance can have the same temperature. However, the total kinetic energy of the particles in each amount is different. You will learn more about total kinetic energy in the next section.

Figure 2 *Even though there is more tea in the teapot than in the mug, the temperature of the tea in the mug is the same as the temperature of the tea in the teapot.*

Hot or Cold?

1. Put both your hands into a **bucket of warm water,** and note how it feels.

2. Now put one hand into a **bucket of cold water** and the other into a **bucket of hot water.**

3. After a minute, take your hands out of the hot and cold water and put them back in the warm water.

4. Can you rely on your hands to determine temperature? In your ScienceLog, explain your observations.

Measuring Temperature

How would you measure the temperature of a steaming cup of hot chocolate? Would you take a sip of it or stick your finger into it? Probably not—you would use a thermometer.

Using a Thermometer Many thermometers are a thin glass tube filled with a liquid. Mercury and alcohol are often used in thermometers because they remain liquids over a large temperature range. Thermometers can measure temperature because of thermal expansion. **Thermal expansion** is the increase in volume of a substance due to an increase in temperature. As a substance gets hotter, its particles move faster. The particles themselves do not expand; they just spread out so that the entire substance expands. Different substances expand by different amounts for a given temperature change. When you insert a thermometer into a hot substance, the liquid inside the thermometer expands and rises. You measure the temperature of a substance by measuring the expansion of the liquid in the thermometer.

Temperature Scales Temperature can be expressed according to different scales. Notice how the same temperatures have different readings on the three temperature scales shown below.

Three Temperature Scales

	Fahrenheit	Celsius	Kelvin
Water boils	212°	100°	373
Body temperature	98.6°	37°	310
Room temperature	68°	20°	293
Water freezes	32°	0°	273

When you hear a weather report that gives the current temperature as 65°, chances are that you are given the temperature in degrees Fahrenheit (°F). In science, the Celsius scale is used more often than the Fahrenheit scale. The Celsius scale is divided into 100 equal parts, called degrees Celsius (°C), between the freezing point and boiling point of water. A third scale, called the Kelvin (or absolute) scale, is the official SI temperature scale. The Kelvin scale is divided into units called kelvins (K)—not degrees kelvin. The lowest temperature on the Kelvin scale is 0 K, which is called **absolute zero.** It is not possible to reach a temperature lower than absolute zero. In fact, temperatures within a few billionths of a kelvin above absolute zero have been achieved in laboratories, but absolute zero itself has never been reached.

Temperature Conversion As shown by the thermometers illustrated on the previous page, a given temperature is represented by different numbers on the three temperature scales. For example, the freezing point of water is 32°F, 0°C, or 273 K. As you can see, 0°C is actually a much higher temperature than 0 K, but a change of 1 K is equal to a change of one Celsius degree. In addition, 0°C is a higher temperature than 0°F, but a change of one Fahrenheit degree is *not* equal to a change of one Celsius degree. You can convert from one scale to another using the simple equations shown below. After reading the examples given, try the MathBreak on this page.

What can you do at temperatures near absolute zero? Turn to page 274 to find out!

To convert	Use this equation:	Example
Celsius to Fahrenheit °C ⟶ °F	$°F = \left(\dfrac{9}{5} \times °C\right) + 32$	Convert 45°C to °F. $°F = \left(\dfrac{9}{5} \times 45°C\right) + 32 = 113°F$
Fahrenheit to Celsius °F ⟶ °C	$°C = \dfrac{5}{9} \times (°F - 32)$	Convert 68°F to °C. $°C = \dfrac{5}{9} \times (68°F - 32) = 20°C$
Celsius to Kelvin °C ⟶ K	$K = °C + 273$	Convert 45°C to K. $K = 45°C + 273 = 318 K$
Kelvin to Celsius K ⟶ °C	$°C = K - 273$	Convert 32 K to °C. $°C = 32 K - 273 = -241°C$

MATH BREAK

Converting Temperatures
Use the equations at left to answer the following questions:

1. What temperature on the Celsius scale is equivalent to 373 K?

2. Absolute zero is 0 K. What is the equivalent temperature on the Celsius scale? on the Fahrenheit scale?

3. Which temperature is colder, 0°F or 200 K?

More About Thermal Expansion

Have you ever gone across a highway bridge in a car? You probably heard and felt a *"thuh-thunk"* every couple of seconds as you went over the bridge. That sound occurs when the car goes over small gaps called expansion joints, shown in **Figure 3.** These joints keep the bridge from buckling as a result of thermal expansion. Recall that thermal expansion is the increase in volume of a substance due to an increase in temperature.

Thermal expansion also occurs in a thermostat, the device that controls the heater in your home. Inside a thermostat is a bimetallic strip. A *bimetallic strip* is made of two different metals stacked in a thin strip. Because different materials expand at different rates, one of the metals expands more than the other when the strip gets hot. This makes the strip coil and uncoil in response to changes in temperature. This coiling and uncoiling closes and opens an electric circuit that turns the heater on and off in your home, as shown in **Figure 4.**

Figure 3 *The concrete segments of a bridge can expand on hot days. When the temperature drops, the segments contract.*

Figure 4   How a Thermostat Works

Electrical contacts

a As the room temperature drops below the desired level, the bimetallic strip coils up and the glass tube tilts. A drop of mercury closes an electric circuit that turns the heater on.

b As the room temperature rises above the desired level, the bimetallic strip uncoils. The drop of mercury rolls back in the tube, opening the electric circuit, and the heater turns off.

REVIEW

1. What is temperature?

2. What is the coldest temperature possible?

3. Convert 35°C to degrees Fahrenheit.

4. **Inferring Conclusions**   Why do you think heating a full pot of soup on the stove could cause the soup to overflow?

What Is Heat?

What You'll Do

◆ Define *heat* as the transfer of energy between objects at different temperatures.

◆ Compare conduction, convection, and radiation.

◆ Use specific heat capacity to calculate heat.

◆ Explain the differences between temperature, thermal energy, and heat.

It's time for your annual physical. The doctor comes in and begins her exam by looking down your throat using a wooden tongue depressor. Next she listens to your heart and lungs. But when she places a metal stethoscope on your back, as shown in **Figure 5,** you jump a little and say, "Whoa! That's cold!" The doctor apologizes and continues with your checkup.

Why did the metal stethoscope feel cold? After all, it was at the same temperature as the tongue depressor, which didn't make you jump. What is it about the stethoscope that made it feel cold? The answer has to do with how energy is transferred between the metal and your skin. In this section, you'll learn about this kind of energy transfer.

Heat Is a Transfer of Energy

You might think of the word *heat* as having to do with things that feel hot. But heat also has to do with things that feel cold—like the stethoscope. In fact, heat is what causes objects to feel hot or cold or to get hot or cold under the right conditions. You probably use the word *heat* every day to mean different things. However, in this chapter, you will learn a specific meaning for it. **Heat** is the transfer of energy between objects that are at different temperatures.

Why do some things feel hot, while others feel cold? When two objects at different temperatures come in contact, energy is always transferred from the object with the higher temperature to the object with the lower temperature. When the doctor's stethoscope touches your back, energy is transferred from your back to the stethoscope because your back has a higher temperature (37°C) than the stethoscope (probably room temperature, 20°C). So to you, the stethoscope is cold, but compared to the stethoscope, you are hot! You'll learn why the tongue depressor didn't feel cold to you a little later in this section.

Figure 5 *The reason the metal stethoscope feels cold is actually because of heat!*

Heat and Thermal Energy If heat is a transfer of energy, what form of energy is being transferred? The answer is thermal energy. **Thermal energy** is the total energy of the particles that make up a substance. Thermal energy, which is expressed in joules (J), depends partly on temperature. An object at a high temperature has more thermal energy than it would at a lower temperature. Thermal energy also depends on how much of a substance you have. As described in **Figure 6,** the more moving particles there are in a substance at a given temperature, the greater the thermal energy of the substance.

When you hold an ice cube, thermal energy is transferred from your hand to the ice cube. The ice cube's thermal energy increases, and it starts to melt. But your hand's thermal energy decreases. The particles in the surface of your skin move more slowly, and the surface temperature of your skin drops slightly. So your hand feels cold!

Figure 6 *Although both soups are at the same temperature, the soup in the pan has more thermal energy than the soup in the bowl.*

Reaching the Same Temperature Take a look at **Figure 7.** When objects at different temperatures come in contact, energy will always be transferred from the higher-temperature object to the lower-temperature object until both objects reach the same temperature. This point is called *thermal equilibrium* (EE kwi LIB ree uhm). When objects are at thermal equilibrium, no net change in either object's thermal energy occurs. Although one object may have more thermal energy, both objects have the same temperature.

Figure 7
Reaching Thermal Equilibrium

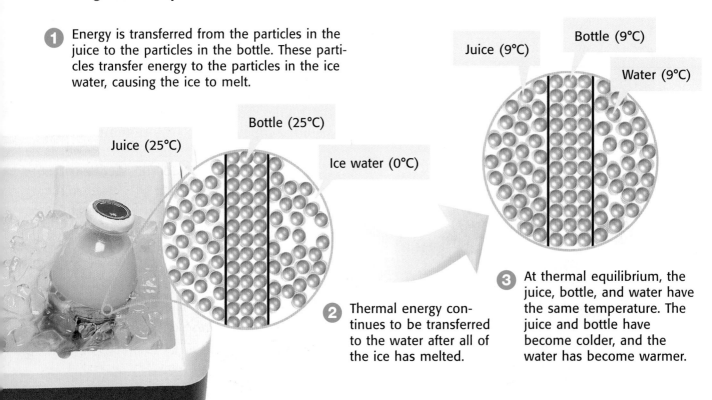

1 Energy is transferred from the particles in the juice to the particles in the bottle. These particles transfer energy to the particles in the ice water, causing the ice to melt.

Juice (25°C)

Bottle (25°C)

Ice water (0°C)

Juice (9°C)

Bottle (9°C)

Water (9°C)

2 Thermal energy continues to be transferred to the water after all of the ice has melted.

3 At thermal equilibrium, the juice, bottle, and water have the same temperature. The juice and bottle have become colder, and the water has become warmer.

Conduction, Convection, and Radiation

So far you've read about several examples of energy transfer: stoves transfer energy to substances in pots and pans; you can adjust the temperature of your bath water by adding cold or hot water to the tub; and the sun warms your skin. In the next couple of pages you'll learn about three processes involving this type of energy transfer: *conduction, convection,* and *radiation.*

Conduction   Imagine that you put a cold metal spoon in a bowl of hot soup, as shown in **Figure 8.** Soon the handle of the spoon warms up—even though it is not in the soup! The entire spoon gets warm because of conduction. **Conduction** is the transfer of thermal energy from one substance to another through direct contact. Conduction can also occur within a substance, such as the spoon in Figure 8.

How does conduction work? As substances come in contact, particles collide and thermal energy is transferred from the higher-temperature substance to the lower-temperature substance. Remember that particles of substances at different temperatures have different average kinetic energy. So when particles collide, higher-kinetic-energy particles transfer kinetic energy to lower-kinetic-energy particles. This makes some particles slow down and other particles speed up until all particles have the same average kinetic energy. As a result, the substances have the same temperature.

Figure 8 *The end of this spoon will warm up because conduction, the transfer of energy through direct contact, occurs all the way up the handle.*

Conductors	Insulators
Curling iron	Flannel shirt
Iron skillet	Oven mitt
Cookie sheet	Plastic spatula
Copper pipes	Fiberglass insulation
Stove coils	Ceramic bowl

Conductors and Insulators Substances that conduct thermal energy very well are called **conductors.** For example, the metal in a doctor's stethoscope is a conductor. Energy is transferred rapidly from your higher-temperature skin to the room-temperature stethoscope. That's why the stethoscope feels cold. Substances that do not conduct thermal energy very well are called **insulators.** For example, the doctor's wooden tongue depressor is an insulator. It has the same temperature as the stethoscope, but the tongue depressor doesn't feel cold. That's because thermal energy is transferred very slowly from your tongue to the wood. Compare some typical conductors and insulators in the chart at left.

APPLY

Keepin' It Cool

The drink holder shown here is made from a foamlike material that helps keep your can of soda cold. How is this drink holder an insulator?

Figure 9 *The repeated rising and sinking of water during boiling is due to convection.*

Convection When you boil a pot of water, like the one shown in **Figure 9,** the water moves in roughly circular patterns because of convection. **Convection** is the transfer of thermal energy by the movement of a liquid or a gas. The water at the bottom of a pot on a stove burner gets hot because of contact with the pot itself (conduction). As a result, the hot water becomes less dense because its higher-energy particles have spread apart. The warmer water rises through the denser, cooler water above it. At the surface, the warm water begins to cool, and the lower-energy particles move closer together, making the water denser. The denser, cooler water sinks back to the bottom, where it will be heated again. This circular motion of liquids or gases due to density differences that result from temperature differences is called a *convection current.*

Radiation Unlike conduction and convection, radiation can involve either an energy transfer between particles of matter or an energy transfer across empty space. **Radiation** is the transfer of energy through matter or space as electromagnetic waves, such as visible light and infrared waves.

All objects, including the heater in **Figure 10,** radiate electromagnetic waves. The sun emits mostly visible light, which you can see and your body can absorb, making you feel warmer. The Earth emits mostly infrared waves, which you cannot see but can still make you feel warmer.

Figure 10 *The coils of this portable heater warm a room by radiating visible light and infrared waves.*

Radiation and the Greenhouse Effect Earth's atmosphere, like the windows of a greenhouse, allows the sun's visible light to pass through it. But like the windows of a greenhouse keep energy inside the greenhouse, the atmosphere traps some reradiated energy. This process, called the *greenhouse effect,* is illustrated in **Figure 11.** Some scientists are concerned that high levels of greenhouse gases (water vapor, carbon dioxide, and methane) in the atmosphere may trap too much energy and make Earth too warm. However, if not for the greenhouse effect, the Earth would be a cold, lifeless planet.

Figure 11 The Greenhouse Effect

b The Earth radiates infrared waves, some of which escape into space.

c Greenhouse gases trap some of the reradiated energy near the Earth's surface.

a Visible light passes through the atmosphere and heats the Earth.

REVIEW

1. What is heat?

2. Explain how radiation is different from conduction and convection.

3. **Applying Concepts** Why do many metal cooking utensils have wooden handles?

internet**connect**

SCi LINKS.
NSTA

TOPIC: What Is Heat?; Conduction, Convection, and Radiation
GO TO: www.scilinks.org
*sci*LINKS NUMBER: HSTP240, HSTP245

Heat and Temperature Change

On a hot summer day, have you ever fastened your seat belt in a car, as shown in **Figure 12**? If so, you may have noticed that the metal buckle felt hotter than the cloth belt. Why? Keep reading to learn more.

Figure 12 *On a hot summer day, the metal part of a seat belt feels hotter than the cloth part.*

Thermal Conductivity Different substances have different thermal conductivities. *Thermal conductivity* is the rate at which a substance conducts thermal energy. Conductors, such as the metal buckle, have higher thermal conductivities than do insulators, such as the cloth belt. Because of the metal's higher thermal conductivity, it transfers energy more rapidly to your hand when you touch it than the cloth does. So even when the cloth and metal are the same temperature, the metal feels hotter.

Specific Heat Capacity Another difference between the metal and the cloth is how easily they change temperature when they absorb or lose energy. When equal amounts of energy are transferred to or from equal masses of different substances, the change in temperature for each substance will differ. **Specific heat capacity** is the amount of energy needed to change the temperature of 1 kg of a substance by 1°C.

Look at the table below. Notice that the specific heat capacity of the cloth of a seat belt is more than twice that of the metal seat belt buckle. This means that for equal masses of metal and cloth, less energy is required to change the temperature of the metal. So the metal buckle gets hot (and cools off) more quickly than an equal mass of the cloth belt.

Different substances have different specific heat capacities. Check out the specific heat capacities for various substances in the table below.

Meteorology

CONNECTION

Water has a higher specific heat capacity than land. This difference affects the climate of different areas on Earth. Climates in coastal areas are moderated by the ocean. Because of water's high specific heat capacity, the ocean retains a lot of thermal energy. So even in the winter, when inland temperatures drop, coastal areas stay moderately warm. Because water does not heat up as easily as land does, oceans can help to keep coastal areas cool during the summer when inland temperatures soar.

Specific Heat Capacities of Some Common Substances			
Substance	**Specific heat capacity (J/kg•°C)**	**Substance**	**Specific heat capacity (J/kg•°C)**
Lead	128	Glass	837
Gold	129	Aluminum	899
Mercury	138	Cloth of seat belt	1,340
Silver	234	Wood	1,760
Copper	387	Steam	2,010
Iron	448	Ice	2,090
Metal of seat belt	500	Water	4,184

Heat—The Amount of Energy Transferred

Unlike temperature, energy transferred between objects cannot be measured directly—it must be calculated. When calculating energy transferred between objects, it is helpful to define *heat* as the amount of energy that is transferred between two objects that are at different temperatures. Heat can then be expressed in joules (J).

How much energy is required to heat a cup of water to make tea? To answer this question, you have to consider the water's mass, its change in temperature, and its specific heat capacity. In general, if you know an object's mass, its change in temperature, and its specific heat capacity, you can use the equation below to calculate heat (the amount of energy transferred).

Heat (J) = specific heat capacity (J/kg•°C) × mass (kg) × change in temperature (°C)

Mass of water = 0.2 kg
Temperature (before) = 25°C
Temperature (after) = 80°C
Specific heat capacity of water = 4,184 J/kg•°C

Figure 13 *Information used to calculate heat, the amount of energy transferred to the water, is shown above.*

Calculating Heat Using the equation above and the data in **Figure 13,** you can follow the steps below to calculate the heat added to the water. Because the water's temperature increases, the value of heat is positive. You can also use this equation to calculate the heat removed from an object when it cools down. The value for heat would then be negative because the temperature decreases.

1 Write down what you know.

Specific heat capacity of water = 4,184 J/kg•°C
Mass of water = 0.2 kg
Change in temperature = 80°C – 25°C = 55°C

2 Substitute the values into the equation.

Heat = specific heat capacity × mass × change in temperature
= 4,184 J/kg•°C × 0.2 kg × 55°C

3 Solve and cancel units.

Heat = 4,184 J/kg•°C × 0.2 kg × 55°C
= 4,184 J × 0.2 × 55
= 46,024 J

Build your own calorimeter! Try the lab on page 675 of the LabBook.

Calorimeters When one object transfers thermal energy to another object, the energy lost by one object is gained by the other object. This is the key to how a *calorimeter* (KAL uh RIM uh ter) works. Inside a calorimeter, shown in **Figure 14,** thermal energy is transferred from a known mass of a test substance to a known mass of another substance, usually water.

Using a Calorimeter If a hot test substance is placed inside the calorimeter's inner container of water, the substance transfers energy to the water until thermal equilibrium is reached. By measuring the temperature change of the water and using water's specific heat capacity, you can determine the exact amount of energy transferred by the test substance to the water. You can then use this amount of energy (heat), the change in the test substance's temperature, and the mass of the test substance to calculate that substance's specific heat capacity.

Figure 14 *A calorimeter is used to find the specific heat capacity of a substance.*

Thermometer

Lid

Stirrer

Water

Inner container

Test substance

Insulated outer container

Figure 15 *A serving of this fruit contains 120 Cal (502,080 J) of energy that becomes available when it is eaten and digested.*

Calories and Kilocalories Heat can also be expressed in units called calories. A *calorie (cal)* is the amount of energy needed to change the temperature of 0.001 kg of water by 1°C. Therefore, 1,000 calories are required to change the temperature of 1 kg of water by 1°C. One calorie is equivalent to 4.184 J. Another unit used to express heat is the *kilocalorie (kcal),* which is equivalent to 1,000 calories. The kilocalorie is also known as a *Calorie* (with a capital C). These are the Calories listed on food labels, such as the label shown in **Figure 15.**

The Differences Between Temperature, Thermal Energy, and Heat

So far in this chapter, you have been learning about some concepts that are closely related: temperature, heat, and thermal energy. But the differences between these concepts are very important.

Temperature Versus Thermal Energy Temperature is a measure of the average kinetic energy of an object's particles, and thermal energy is the total energy of an object's particles. While thermal energy varies with the mass of an object, temperature does not. A drop of boiling water has the same temperature as a pot of boiling water, but the pot has more thermal energy because there are more particles.

Thermal Energy Versus Heat Heat and thermal energy are not the same thing; heat is a transfer of thermal energy. In addition, heat can refer to the amount of energy transferred from one object to another. Objects contain thermal energy, but they do not contain heat. The table below summarizes the differences between temperature, thermal energy, and heat.

Self-Check

How can two substances have the same temperature but different amounts of thermal energy? *(See page 724 to check your answer.)*

Temperature	Thermal energy	Heat
A measure of the average kinetic energy of the particles in a substance	The total energy of the particles in a substance	The transfer of energy between objects that are at different temperatures
Expressed in degrees Fahrenheit, degrees Celsius, or kelvins	Expressed in joules	Amount of energy transferred expressed in joules or calories
Does not vary with the mass of a substance	Varies with the mass and temperature of a substance	Varies with the mass, specific heat capacity, and temperature change of a substance

REVIEW

1. Some objects get hot more quickly than others. Why?

2. How are temperature and heat different?

3. **Applying Concepts** Examine the photo at right. How do you think the specific heat capacities for water and air influence the temperature of a swimming pool and the area around it?

What You'll Do

◆ Identify three states of matter.
◆ Explain how heat affects matter during a change of state.
◆ Describe how heat affects matter during a chemical change.

Matter and Heat

Have you ever eaten a frozen juice bar outside on a hot summer day? It's pretty hard to finish the entire thing before it starts to drip and make a big mess! The juice bar melts because the sun radiates energy to the air, which transfers energy to the frozen juice bar. The energy absorbed by the juice bar increases the kinetic energy of the molecules in the juice bar, which starts to turn to a liquid. In this section, you'll learn more about how heat affects matter.

States of Matter

The matter that makes up a frozen juice bar has the same identity whether the juice bar is frozen or has melted. The matter is just in a different form, or state. The **states of matter** are the physical forms in which a substance can exist. Recall that matter consists of particles—atoms or molecules—that can move around at different speeds. The state a substance is in depends on the speed of its particles and the attraction between them. Three familiar states of matter are solid, liquid, and gas, represented in **Figure 16.** You may recall that thermal energy is the total energy of the particles that make up a substance. Suppose you have equal masses of a substance in its three states, each at a different temperature. The substance will have the most thermal energy as a gas and the least thermal energy as a solid. That's because the particles move around fastest in a gas.

Figure 16 Models of a Solid, a Liquid, and a Gas

Particles of a solid do not move fast enough to overcome the strong attraction between them, so they are held tightly together. The particles vibrate in place.

Particles of a liquid move fast enough to overcome some of the attraction between them. The particles are able to slide past one another.

Particles of a gas move fast enough to overcome nearly all of the attraction between them. The particles move independently of one another.

Changes of State

When you melt cheese to make a cheese dip, like that shown in **Figure 17,** the cheese changes from a solid to a thick, gooey liquid. A **change of state** is the conversion of a substance from one physical form to another. A change of state is a *physical change* that affects one or more physical properties of a substance without changing the substance's identity. Changes of state include *freezing* (liquid to solid), *melting* (solid to liquid), *boiling* (liquid to gas), and *condensing* (gas to liquid).

Graphing Changes of State Suppose you put an ice cube in a pan and set the pan on a stove burner. Soon the ice will turn to water and then to steam. If you made a graph of the energy involved versus the temperature of the ice during this process, it would look something like the graph below.

As the ice is heated, its temperature increases from –25°C to 0°C. At 0°C, the ice begins to melt. Notice that the temperature of the ice remains 0°C even as more energy is added. This added energy changes the arrangement of the particles, or molecules, in the ice. The temperature of the ice remains constant until all of the ice has become liquid water. At that point, the water's temperature will start to increase from 0°C to 100°C. At 100°C, the water will begin to turn into steam. Even as more energy is added, the water's temperature stays at 100°C. The energy added at the boiling point changes the arrangement of the particles until the water has entirely changed to a gaseous state. When all of the water has become steam, the temperature again increases.

Figure 17 *When you melt cheese, you change the state of the cheese but not its identity.*

✓ **Self-Check**

Why do you think you can get a more severe burn from steam than from boiling water? *(See page 724 to check your answer.)*

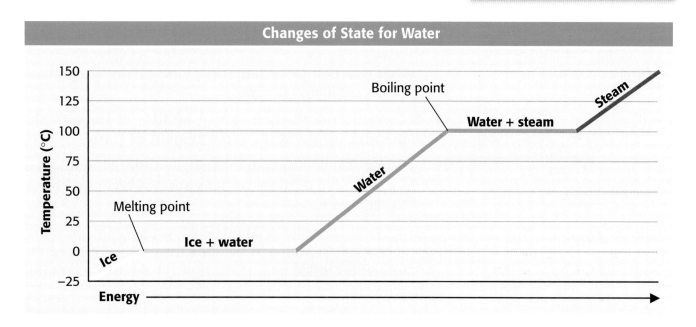

Changes of State for Water

Biology
CONNECTION

The substances your body needs to survive and grow come from food. Carbohydrates, proteins, and fats are major sources of energy for the body. The energy content of food can be found by burning a dry food sample in a special calorimeter. Both carbohydrates and proteins provide 4 Cal of energy per gram, while fats provide 9 Cal of energy per gram.

Figure 18 *In a natural-gas fireplace, the methane in natural gas and the oxygen in air change into carbon dioxide and water. As a result of the change, energy is given off, making a room feel warmer.*

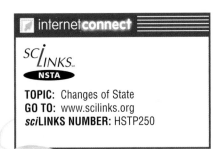

internet**connect**

SCI**LINKS**
NSTA

TOPIC: Changes of State
GO TO: www.scilinks.org
*sci*LINKS NUMBER: HSTP250

Heat and Chemical Changes

Heat is involved not only in changes of state, which are physical changes, but also in *chemical changes*—changes that occur when one or more substances are changed into entirely new substances with different properties. During a chemical change, new substances are formed. For a new substance to form, old bonds between particles must be broken and new bonds must be created. The breaking and creating of bonds between particles involves energy. Sometimes a chemical change requires that thermal energy be absorbed. For example, photosynthesis is a chemical change in which carbon dioxide and water combine to form sugar and oxygen. In order for this change to occur, energy must be absorbed. That energy is radiated by the sun. Other times, a chemical change, such as the one shown in **Figure 18,** will result in energy being released.

REVIEW

1. During a change of state, why doesn't the temperature of the substance change?

2. Compare the thermal energy of 10 g of ice with the thermal energy of the same amount of water.

3. When water evaporates (changes from a liquid to a gas), the air near the water's surface becomes cooler. Explain why.

4. **Applying Concepts**   Many cold packs used for sports injuries are activated by bending the package, causing the substances inside to interact. How is heat involved in this process?

Heat Technology

What You'll Do

- ◆ Analyze several kinds of heating systems.
- ◆ Describe how a heat engine works.
- ◆ Explain how a refrigerator keeps food cold.
- ◆ Give examples of some effects of heat technology on the environment.

You probably wouldn't be surprised to learn that the heater in your home is an example of heat technology. But did you know that automobiles, refrigerators, and air conditioners are also examples of heat technology? It's true! You can travel long distances, you can keep your food cold, and you can feel comfortable indoors during the summer—all because of heat technology.

Heating Systems

Many homes and buildings have a central heating system that controls the temperature in every room. On the next few pages, you will see some different central heating systems.

Hot-Water Heating The high specific heat capacity of water makes it useful for heating systems. In a hot-water heating system, shown in **Figure 19,** water is heated by burning fuel (usually natural gas or fuel oil) in a hot-water heater. The hot water is pumped through pipes that lead to radiators in each room. The hot water heats the radiators, and the radiators then heat the colder air surrounding them. The water returns to the hot-water heater to be heated again. A *steam-heating system* is similar, except that steam is used in place of water.

Figure 19
A Hot-Water Heating System

Smoke outlet

Air heated by the radiators circulates in the room by convection currents.

Radiators

An expansion tank handles the increased volume of the heated water.

Pump

Hot-water heater

Warm-Air Heating Although air has a lower specific heat capacity than water, warm-air heating systems are used in many homes and offices in the United States. In a warm-air heating system, shown in **Figure 20,** air is heated in a separate chamber by burning fuel (usually natural gas) in a furnace. The warm air travels through ducts to different rooms, which it enters through vents. The warm air heats air in the rooms. Cooler air sinks below the warm air and enters a vent near the floor. Then a fan forces the cooler air into the furnace, where the air will be heated and returned to the ducts. An air filter cleans the air as it circulates through the system.

Figure 20
A Warm-Air Heating System

Warm air is circulated in the rooms by convection currents.

Smoke outlet

Vent

Filter

Fan

Duct

Furnace

Heating and Insulation Thermal energy may be transferred out of a house during cold weather and into a house during hot weather. To keep the house comfortable, a heating system must run almost continuously during the winter, and air conditioners often do the same during the summer. This can be wasteful. That's where insulation comes in. **Insulation** is a substance that reduces the transfer of thermal energy. Insulation, such as the fiberglass insulation shown in **Figure 21,** is made of insulators—materials that do not conduct thermal energy very well. Insulation that is used in walls, ceilings, and floors helps a house stay warm in the winter and cool in the summer.

Do you remember the Earthships described at the beginning of this chapter? The tightly packed aluminum cans in the walls of an Earthship have spaces between them. Air filling these spaces insulates the Earthship. These homes also rely on a solar heating system, which you will learn about on the next page.

Figure 21 *Millions of tiny air pockets in this insulation help prevent thermal energy from flowing into or out of a building.*

Solar Heating The sun radiates an enormous amount of energy. Solar heating systems use this energy to heat houses and buildings. *Passive solar heating* systems do not have moving parts. They rely on a building's structural design and materials to use energy from the sun as a means of heating. *Active solar heating* systems do have moving parts. They use pumps and fans to distribute the sun's energy throughout a building.

Look at the house in **Figure 22.** The large windows on the south side of the house are part of the passive solar heating system. These windows receive maximum sunlight, and energy is radiated through the windows into the rooms. Thick, well-insulated concrete walls absorb energy and heat the house at night or when it is cloudy. In the active solar heating system, water is pumped to the solar collector, where it is heated. The hot water is pumped through pipes and transfers its energy to them. A fan blowing over the pipes helps the pipes transfer their thermal energy to the air. Warm air is then sent into rooms through vents. Cooler water returns to the water storage tank to be pumped back through the solar collector.

Figure 22 *Passive and active solar heating systems work together to use the sun's energy to heat an entire house.*

Solar energy collector

Active solar heating systems often consist of solar collectors, a network of pipes, a fan, and a water storage tank.

Water storage tank

Fan

Passive solar heating systems utilize thick walls and large windows that face south.

Pumps

Oceanography
C O N N E C T I O N

Ocean engineers are developing a new technology known as Ocean Thermal Energy Conversion, or OTEC. OTEC uses temperature differences between surface water and deep water in the ocean to do work like a heat engine does. Warm surface water vaporizes a fluid, such as ammonia, causing it to expand. Then cool water from ocean depths causes the fluid to condense and contract. The continuous cycle of vaporizing and condensing converts thermal energy into kinetic energy that can be used to generate electrical energy.

Heat Engines

Did you know that automobiles work because of heat? A car has a **heat engine,** a machine that uses heat to do work. In a heat engine, fuel combines with oxygen in a chemical change that produces thermal energy. This process, called *combustion,* is how engines burn fuel. Heat engines that burn fuel outside the engine are called *external combustion engines.* Heat engines that burn fuel inside the engine are called *internal combustion engines.* In both types of engines, fuel is burned to produce thermal energy that can be used to do work.

External Combustion Engine A simple steam engine, shown in **Figure 23,** is an example of an external combustion engine. Coal is burned to heat water in a boiler and change the water to steam. When water changes to steam, it expands. The expanding steam is used to drive a piston, which can be attached to other mechanisms that do work, such as a flywheel. Modern steam engines, such as those used to generate electrical energy at a power plant, drive turbines instead of pistons.

Figure 23 An External Combustion Engine

Steam enters through the open valve.

Used steam exits the cylinder through an exhaust outlet.

Flywheel

Cylinder   Piston

a The expanding steam enters the cylinder from one side. The steam does work on the piston, forcing the piston to move.

b As the piston moves to the other side, a second valve opens and steam enters. The steam does work on the piston and moves it back. The motion of the piston turns a flywheel.

Internal Combustion Engine In the six-cylinder car engine shown in **Figure 24,** fuel is burned inside the engine. During the intake stroke, a mixture of gasoline and air enters each cylinder as the piston moves down. Next the crankshaft turns and pushes the piston up, compressing the fuel mixture. This is called the compression stroke. Next comes the power stroke, in which the spark plug uses electrical energy to ignite the compressed fuel mixture, causing the mixture to expand and force the piston down. Finally, during the exhaust stroke, the crankshaft turns and the piston is forced back up, pushing exhaust gases out of the cylinder.

Wire to spark plug

Cylinder

Piston

Crankshaft

Figure 24 *The continuous cycling of the four strokes in the cylinders converts thermal energy into the kinetic energy required to make a car move.*

Cooling Systems

When it gets hot in the summer, an air-conditioned room can feel very refreshing. Cooling systems are used to transfer thermal energy out of a particular area so that it feels cooler. An air conditioner, shown in **Figure 25,** is a cooling system that transfers thermal energy from a warm area inside a building or car to an area outside, where it is often even warmer. But wait a minute—doesn't that go against the natural direction of heat—from higher temperatures to lower temperatures? Well, yes. A cooling system moves thermal energy from cooler temperatures to warmer temperatures. But in order to do that, the cooling system must do work.

Figure 25 *This air conditioning unit keeps a building cool by moving thermal energy from inside the building to the outside.*

Cooling Takes Energy Most cooling systems require electrical energy to do the work of cooling. The electrical energy is used by a device called a compressor. The compressor does the work of compressing the refrigerant, a gas that has a boiling point below room temperature. This property of the refrigerant allows it to condense easily.

To keep many foods fresh, you store them in a refrigerator. A refrigerator is another example of a cooling system. **Figure 26** shows how a refrigerator continuously transfers thermal energy from inside the refrigerator to the condenser coils on the outside of the refrigerator. That's why the area near the back of a refrigerator feels warm.

Figure 26 How a Refrigerator Works

3 When the liquid passes through the expansion valve, it goes from a high-pressure area to a low-pressure area. As a result, the temperature of the liquid decreases.

High pressure

Low pressure

4 As the cold liquid refrigerant moves through the evaporating coils, it absorbs thermal energy from the refrigerator compartment, making the inside of the refrigerator cold. As a result, the temperature of the refrigerant increases, and it changes into a gas.

5 The gas is then returned to the compressor, and the cycle repeats.

2 The hot gas flows through the condenser coils on the outside of the refrigerator. The gas condenses into a liquid, transferring some of its thermal energy to the coils.

1 The compressor uses electrical energy to compress the refrigerant gas; this compression increases the pressure and temperature of the gas.

Heat Technology and Thermal Pollution

Heating systems, car engines, and cooling systems all transfer thermal energy to the environment. Unfortunately, too much thermal energy can have a negative effect on the environment.

One of the negative effects of excess thermal energy is **thermal pollution,** the excessive heating of a body of water. Thermal pollution can occur near large power plants, which are often located near a body of water. Electric power plants burn fuel to produce thermal energy that is used to generate electrical energy. Unfortunately, it is not possible for all of that thermal energy to do work, so some waste thermal energy results. **Figure 27** shows how a cooling tower helps remove this waste thermal energy in order to keep the power plants operating smoothly. In extreme cases, the increase in temperature downstream from a power plant can adversely affect the ecosystem of the river or lake. Some power plants reduce thermal pollution by reducing the temperature of the water before it is returned to the river.

Environment
C O N N E C T I O N

Large cities can exhibit something called a heat island effect when excessive amounts of waste thermal energy are added to the urban environment. This thermal energy comes from automobiles, factories, home heating and cooling, lighting, and even just the number of people living in a relatively small area. The heat island effect can make the temperature of the air in a city higher than that of the air in the surrounding countryside.

Figure 27 *Cool water is circulated through a power plant to absorb waste thermal energy.*

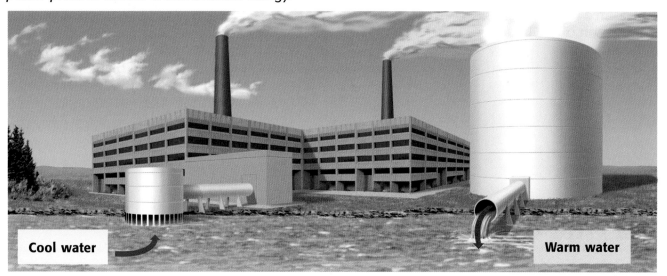

Cool water

Warm water

REVIEW

1. Compare a hot-water heating system with a warm-air heating system.

2. What is the difference between an external combustion engine and an internal combustion engine?

3. **Analyzing Relationships** How are changes of state an important part of the way a refrigerator works?

internet**connect**

*sci*LINKS.
NSTA

TOPIC: Heating Systems
GO TO: www.scilinks.org
*sci*LINKS NUMBER: HSTP252

Chapter Highlights

SECTION 1

Vocabulary

temperature (p. 246)
thermal expansion (p. 248)
absolute zero (p. 249)

Section Notes

- Temperature is a measure of the average kinetic energy of the particles of a substance. It is a specific measurement of how hot or cold a substance is.

- Thermal expansion is the increase in volume of a substance due to an increase in temperature. Temperature is measured according to the expansion of the liquid in a thermometer.

- Fahrenheit, Celsius, and Kelvin are three temperature scales.

- Absolute zero—0 K, or –273°C— is the lowest possible temperature.

- A thermostat works according to the thermal expansion of a bimetallic strip.

SECTION 2

Vocabulary

heat (p. 251)
thermal energy (p. 252)
conduction (p. 253)
conductor (p. 254)
insulator (p. 254)
convection (p. 254)
radiation (p. 255)
specific heat capacity (p. 256)

Section Notes

- Heat is the transfer of energy between objects that are at different temperatures.

- Thermal energy is the total energy of the particles that make up a substance.

- Energy transfer will always occur from higher temperatures to lower temperatures until thermal equilibrium is reached.

☑ Skills Check

Math Concepts

TEMPERATURE CONVERSION To convert between different temperature scales, you can use the equations found on page 249. The example below shows you how to convert a Fahrenheit temperature to a Celsius temperature.

Convert 41°F to °C.

$$°C = \frac{5}{9} \times (°F - 32)$$

$$°C = \frac{5}{9} \times (41°F - 32)$$

$$°C = \frac{5}{9} \times 9 = 5°C$$

Visual Understanding

HEAT—A TRANSFER OF ENERGY
Remember that thermal energy is transferred between objects at different temperatures until both objects reach the same temperature. Look back at Figure 7, on page 252, to review what you've learned about heat.

SECTION 2

- Conduction, convection, and radiation are three methods of energy transfer.

- Specific heat capacity is the amount of energy needed to change the temperature of 1 kg of a substance by 1°C. Different substances have different specific heat capacities.

- Energy transferred by heat cannot be measured directly. It must be calculated using specific heat capacity, mass, and change in temperature.

- A calorimeter is used to determine the specific heat capacity of a substance.

Labs

Feel the Heat (*p. 672*)
Save the Cube! (*p. 674*)
Counting Calories (*p. 675*)

SECTION 3

Vocabulary

states of matter (*p. 260*)
change of state (*p. 261*)

Section Notes

- A substance's state is determined by the speed of its particles and the attraction between them.

- Thermal energy transferred during a change of state does not change a substance's temperature. Rather, it causes a substance's particles to be rearranged.

- Chemical changes can cause thermal energy to be absorbed or released.

SECTION 4

Vocabulary

insulation (*p. 264*)
heat engine (*p. 266*)
thermal pollution (*p. 269*)

Section Notes

- Central heating systems include hot-water heating systems and warm-air heating systems.

- Solar heating systems can be passive or active.

- Heat engines use heat to do work. External combustion engines burn fuel outside the engine. Internal combustion engines burn fuel inside the engine.

- A cooling system transfers thermal energy from cooler temperatures to warmer temperatures by doing work.

- Transferring excess thermal energy to lakes and rivers can result in thermal pollution.

---

internetconnect

GO TO: go.hrw.com

Visit the **HRW** Web site for a variety of learning tools related to this chapter. Just type in the keyword:

KEYWORD: HSTHOT

GO TO: www.scilinks.org

Visit the **National Science Teachers Association** on-line Web site for Internet resources related to this chapter. Just type in the *sci*LINKS number for more information about the topic:

TOPIC:	*sci*LINKS NUMBER:
TOPIC: What Is Temperature?	*sci*LINKS NUMBER: HSTP230
TOPIC: What Is Heat?	*sci*LINKS NUMBER: HSTP240
TOPIC: Conduction, Convection, and Radiation	*sci*LINKS NUMBER: HSTP245
TOPIC: Changes of State	*sci*LINKS NUMBER: HSTP250
TOPIC: Heating Systems	*sci*LINKS NUMBER: HSTP252

Chapter Review

USING VOCABULARY

For each pair of terms, explain the difference in their meanings.

1. temperature/thermal energy

2. heat/thermal energy

3. conductor/insulator

4. conduction/convection

5. states of matter/change of state

UNDERSTANDING CONCEPTS

Multiple Choice

6. Which of the following temperatures is the lowest?
   a. 100°C
   b. 100°F
   c. 100 K
   d. They are the same.

7. Compared with the Pacific Ocean, a cup of hot chocolate has
   a. more thermal energy and a higher temperature.
   b. less thermal energy and a higher temperature.
   c. more thermal energy and a lower temperature.
   d. less thermal energy and a lower temperature.

8. The energy units on a food label are
   a. degrees.
   b. Calories.
   c. calories.
   d. joules.

9. Which of the following materials would not be a good insulator?
   a. wood
   b. cloth
   c. metal
   d. rubber

10. The engine in a car is a(n)
    a. heat engine.
    b. external combustion engine.
    c. internal combustion engine.
    d. Both (a) and (c)

11. Materials that warm up or cool down very quickly have a
    a. low specific heat capacity.
    b. high specific heat capacity.
    c. low temperature.
    d. high temperature.

12. In an air conditioner, thermal energy is
    a. transferred from higher to lower temperatures.
    b. transferred from lower to higher temperatures.
    c. used to do work.
    d. taken from air outside a building and transferred to air inside the building.

Short Answer

13. How does temperature relate to kinetic energy?

14. What is specific heat capacity?

15. Explain how heat affects matter during a change of state.

16. Describe how a bimetallic strip works in a thermostat.

Concept Mapping

17. Use the following terms to create a concept map: thermal energy, temperature, radiation, heat, conduction, convection.

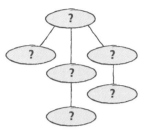

CRITICAL THINKING AND PROBLEM SOLVING

18. Why does placing a jar under warm running water help loosen the lid on the jar?

19. Why do you think a down-filled jacket keeps you so warm? (Hint: Think about what insulation does.)

20. Would opening the refrigerator cool a room in a house? Why or why not?

21. In a hot-air balloon, air is heated by a flame. Explain how this enables the balloon to float in the air.

MATH IN SCIENCE

22. The weather forecast calls for a temperature of 86°F. What is the corresponding temperature in degrees Celsius? in kelvins?

23. Suppose 1,300 mL of water are heated from 20°C to 100°C. How much energy was transferred to the water? (Hint: Water's specific heat capacity is 4,184 J/kg•°C.)

INTERPRETING GRAPHICS

Examine the graph below, and then answer the questions that follow.

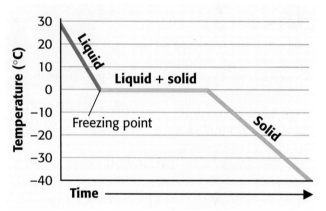

24. What physical change does this graph illustrate?

25. What is the freezing point of this liquid?

26. What is happening at the point where the line is horizontal?

Reading Check-up

Take a minute to review your answers to the Pre-Reading Questions found at the bottom of page 244. Have your answers changed? If necessary, revise your answers based on what you have learned since you began this chapter.

Science, Technology, and Society

The Deep Freeze

In the dark reaches of outer space, temperatures can drop below −270°C. Perhaps the only place colder is a laboratory here on Earth!

The Quest for Zero

All matter is made up of tiny, constantly vibrating particles. Temperature is a measure of the average kinetic energy of these particles. The colder a substance gets, the less kinetic energy its particles have and the slower the particles move. In theory, at absolute zero (−273°C), all movement of matter should stop. Scientists are working in laboratories to slow down matter so much that the temperature approaches absolute zero.

How Low Can They Go?

Using lasers, along with magnets, mirrors, and supercold chemicals, scientists have cooled matter to within a few billionths of a degree of absolute zero. In one method, scientists aim lasers at tiny gas particles inside a special chamber. The lasers hold the particles so still that their temperature approaches −272.999998°C.

To get an idea of what takes place, imagine turning on several garden hoses as high as they can go. Then direct the streams of water at a soccer ball so that each stream pushes the ball from a different angle. If the hoses are aimed properly, the ball won't roll in any direction. That's similar to what happens to the particles in the scientists' experiment.

▲ *This laser device is used to cool matter to nearly absolute zero.*

Cryogenics—Cold Temperature Technology

Supercold temperatures have led to some super-cool technology. Cryosurgery, which is surgery that uses extremely low temperatures, allows doctors to seal off tiny blood vessels during an operation or to freeze diseased cells and destroy them.

Cooling materials to near absolute zero has also led to the discovery of superconductors. Superconductors are materials that lose all of their electrical resistance when they are cooled to a low enough temperature. Imagine the possibilities for materials that could conduct electricity indefinitely without any energy loss. Unfortunately, it takes a great deal of energy to cool such materials. Right now, applications for superconductors are still just the stuff of dreams.

Freezing Fun on Your Own

▶ You can try your hand at cryoinvestigation. Place 50 mL of tap water, 50 mL of salt water (50 mL of water plus 15 g of salt), and 50 mL of rubbing alcohol (isopropanol) in three separate plastic containers. Then put all three containers in your freezer at the same time. Check the containers every 5 minutes for 40 minutes. Which liquid freezes first? How can you explain any differences?

DiAPLEX®: The Intelligent Fabric

Wouldn't it be great if you had a winter coat that could automatically adjust to keep you cozy regardless of the outside temperature? Well, scientists have developed a new fabric, called DiAPLEX, that can be used to make such a coat!

With Pores or Without?

Winter adventurers usually wear nylon fabrics to keep warm. These nylon fabrics are laminated with a thin coating that contains thousands of tiny pores, or openings. The pores allow moisture, such as sweat from your body, and excess thermal energy to escape. You might think the pores would let moisture and cold air into the fabric, but that's not the case. Because the pores are so small, the nylon fabric is windproof and waterproof.

DiAPLEX is also made from laminated nylon, but the coating is different. DiAPLEX doesn't have pores; it is a solid film. This film makes DiAPLEX even more waterproof and breathable than other laminated nylon fabrics. So how does it work?

Moving Particles

DiAPLEX keeps you warm by taking advantage of how particles move. When the air outside is cold, the particles of DiAPLEX arrange themselves into a solid sheet, forming an insulator and preventing the transfer of thermal energy from your body to colder surroundings. As your body gets warm, such as after exercising, the fabric's particles respond to your body's increased thermal energy. Their kinetic energy increases, and they rearrange to create millions of tiny openings that allow excess thermal energy and moisture to escape.

Donning DiAPLEX

DiAPLEX has a number of important advantages over traditional nylon fabrics. Salts in perspiration and ice can clog the pores of traditional nylon fabrics, decreasing their ability to keep you warm and dry. But DiAPLEX does not have this problem because it contains no pores. Because DiAPLEX is unaffected by UV light and is machine washable, it is also a durable fabric that is easy to care for.

Anatomy Connection

▶ Do some research to find out how your skin lets thermal energy and moisture escape.

▶ *When your body is cold, the DiAPLEX garment adjusts to prevent the transfer of thermal energy from your body to its surroundings, and you feel warmer.*

▶ *When your body gets too warm, the DiAPLEX garment adjusts to allow your body to transfer excess thermal energy and moisture to your surroundings, and you feel cooler.*

Thermal energy

Moisture

UNIT 4

The Atom

Thousands of years ago, people began asking the question, "What is matter made of?" This unit follows the discoveries and ideas that have led to our current theories about what makes up matter. You will learn about the atom—the building block of all matter—and its structure. You will also learn how the periodic table is used to classify and organize elements according to patterns in atomic structure and other properties. This timeline illustrates some of the events that have brought us to our current understanding of atoms and of the periodic table in which they are organized.

Around 400 B.C.

The Greek philosopher Democritus proposes that small particles called atoms make up all matter.

1911

Ernest Rutherford, a physicist from New Zealand, discovers the positively charged nucleus of the atom.

1932

The neutron, one of the particles in the nucleus of an atom, is discovered by British physicist James Chadwick.

1945

The United Nations is formed. Its purpose is to maintain world peace and develop friendly relations between countries.

1964

Scientists propose the idea that smaller particles make up protons and neutrons. The particles are named quarks after a word used by James Joyce in his book *Finnegans Wake*.

1803

British scientist and school teacher John Dalton reintroduces the concept of atoms with evidence to support his ideas.

1848

James Marshall finds gold while building Sutter's Mill, starting the California gold rush.

1898

British scientists Sir William Ramsay and Morris W. Travers discover three elements—krypton, neon, and xenon—in three months. The periodic table developed by Mendeleev helps guide their research.

1897

British scientist J. J. Thomson identifies electrons as particles that are present in every atom.

1869

Russian chemist Dmitri Mendeleev develops a periodic table that organizes the elements known at the time.

1981

Scientists in Switzerland develop a scanning tunneling microscope, which is used to see atoms for the first time.

1989

Germans celebrate when the Berlin Wall ceases to function as a barrier between East and West Germany.

1996

Another element is added to the periodic table after a team of German scientists synthesize an atom containing 112 protons in its nucleus.

Introduction to Atoms

Pre-Reading Questions

1. What are some ways that scientists have described the atom?

2. What are the parts of the atom, and how are they arranged?

3. How are atoms of all elements alike?

ATOMIC BUBBLES

You probably have made bubbles with a plastic wand and a soapy liquid. To trace the paths of atoms, some scientists also made bubbles, but they did not use a wand. They used a bubble chamber. A bubble chamber is filled with a hot, pressurized liquid that forms bubbles when a charged particle moves through it. Why are scientists interested in bubbles? The bubbles give them information about particles called atoms that make up all objects. In this chapter, you will learn about atoms and experiments that led to the modern atomic theory. You will also learn about the parts and structure of an atom.

WHERE IS IT?

Some theories about the internal structure of atoms were formed by observing the effects of aiming very small moving particles at atoms. In this activity, you will form an idea about the location and size of a hidden object by rolling marbles at it.

Procedure

1. Place a **rectangular piece of cardboard** on **four books or blocks** so that each corner of the cardboard rests on a book or block.

2. Ask your teacher to place the **unknown object** under the cardboard. Be sure that you do not see the object.

3. Place a **large piece of paper** on top of the cardboard.

4. Carefully roll a **marble** under the cardboard. Record on the paper the position where the marble enters and exits. Also record the direction it travels.

5. Keep rolling the marble from different directions to collect data about the shape and location of the object.

6. Write down all your observations in your ScienceLog.

Analysis

7. Form a conclusion about the object's shape, size, and location. Record your conclusion in your ScienceLog.

What You'll Do

◆ Describe some of the experiments that led to the current atomic theory.
◆ Compare the different models of the atom.
◆ Explain how the atomic theory has changed as scientists have discovered new information about the atom.

Development of the Atomic Theory

The photo at right shows uranium atoms magnified 3.5 million times by a scanning tunneling microscope. An **atom** is the smallest particle into which an element can be divided and still be the same substance. Atoms make up elements; elements combine to form compounds. Because all matter is made of elements or compounds, atoms are often called the building blocks of matter.

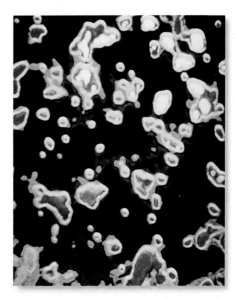

Before the scanning tunneling microscope was invented, in 1981, no one had ever seen an atom. But the existence of atoms is not a new idea. In fact, atomic theory has been around for more than 2,000 years. A **theory** is a unifying explanation for a broad range of hypotheses and observations that have been supported by testing. In this section, you will travel through history to see how our understanding of atoms has developed. Your first stop—ancient Greece.

Democritus Proposes the Atom

Imagine that you cut the silver coin shown in **Figure 1** in half, then cut those halves in half, and so on. Could you keep cutting the pieces in half forever? Around 440 B.C., a Greek philosopher named Democritus (di MAHK ruh tuhs) proposed that you would eventually end up with an "uncuttable" particle. He called this particle an *atom* (from the Greek word *atomos*, meaning "indivisible"). Democritus proposed that all atoms are small, hard particles made of a single material formed into different shapes and sizes. He also claimed that atoms are always moving and that they form different materials by joining together.

Figure 1 *This coin was in use during Democritus's time. Democritus thought the smallest particle in an object like this silver coin was an atom.*

Aristotle Disagrees Aristotle (ER is TAHT uhl), a Greek philosopher who lived from 384 to 322 B.C., disagreed with Democritus's ideas. He believed that you would never end up with an indivisible particle. Although Aristotle's ideas were eventually proved incorrect, he had such a strong influence on popular belief that Democritus's ideas were largely ignored for centuries.

Dalton Creates an Atomic Theory Based on Experiments

By the late 1700s, scientists had learned that elements combine in specific proportions based on mass to form compounds. For example, hydrogen and oxygen always combine in the same proportion to form water. John Dalton, a British chemist and school teacher, wanted to know why. He performed experiments with different substances. His results demonstrated that elements combine in specific proportions because they are made of individual atoms. Dalton, shown in **Figure 2,** published his own atomic theory in 1803. His theory stated the following:

In 342 or 343 B.C., King Phillip II of Macedon appointed Aristotle to be a tutor for his son, Alexander. Alexander later conquered Greece and the Persian Empire (in what is now Iran) and became known as Alexander the Great.

- All substances are made of atoms. Atoms are small particles that cannot be created, divided, or destroyed.

- Atoms of the same element are exactly alike, and atoms of different elements are different.

- Atoms join with other atoms to make new substances.

Figure 2 John Dalton developed his atomic theory from observations gathered from many experiments.

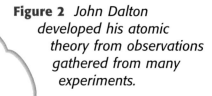

Not Quite Correct Toward the end of the nineteenth century scientists agreed that Dalton's theory explained many of their observations. However, as new information was discovered that could not be explained by Dalton's ideas, the atomic theory was revised to more correctly describe the atom. As you read on, you will learn how Dalton's theory has changed, step by step, into the current atomic theory.

Thomson Finds Electrons in the Atom

In 1897, a British scientist named J. J. Thomson made a discovery that identified an error in Dalton's theory. Using simple equipment (compared with modern equipment), Thomson discovered that there are small particles *inside* the atom. Therefore, atoms *can* be divided into even smaller parts.

Thomson experimented with a cathode-ray tube, as shown in **Figure 3.** He discovered that a positively charged plate (marked with a positive sign in the illustration) attracts the beam. Thomson concluded that the beam was made of particles with a negative electric charge.

Figure 3 Thomson's Cathode-Ray Tube Experiment

a Almost all gas was removed from the glass tube.

d When the plates were not charged, the beam produced a glowing spot here.

b An invisible beam was produced when the tube was connected to a source of electrical energy.

c Metal plates could be charged to change the path of the beam.

e When the plates were charged, the beam produced a glowing spot here after being pulled toward the positively charged plate.

Just What Is Electric Charge?

Have you ever rubbed a balloon on your hair? The properties of your hair and the balloon seem to change, making them attract one another. To describe these observations, scientists say that the balloon and your hair become "charged." There are two types of electric charges—positive and negative. Objects with opposite charges attract each other, while objects with the same charge push each other away.

Negative Corpuscles Thomson repeated his experiment several times and found that the particle beam behaved in exactly the same way each time. He called the particles in the beam corpuscles (KOR PUHS uhls). His results led him to conclude that corpuscles are present in every type of atom and that all corpuscles are identical. The negatively charged particles found in all atoms are now called **electrons.**

Like Plums in a Pudding Thomson revised the atomic theory to account for the presence of electrons. Because Thomson knew that atoms have no overall charge, he realized that positive charges must be present to balance the negative charges of the electrons. But Thomson didn't know the location of the electrons or of the positive charges. So he proposed a model to describe a possible structure of the atom. A **model** is a representation of an object or system. A model is different from a theory in that a model presents a picture of what the theory explains.

Thomson's model, illustrated in **Figure 4,** came to be known as the plum-pudding model, named for an English dessert that was popular at the time. Today you might call Thomson's model the chocolate-chip-ice-cream model; electrons in the atom could be compared to the chocolate chips found throughout the ice cream!

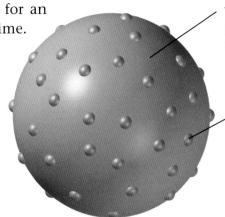

The atom is mostly positively charged material.

Electrons are small, negatively charged particles located throughout the positive material.

Figure 4 *Thomson's plum-pudding model of the atom is shown above. A modern version of Thomson's model might be chocolate-chip ice cream.*

REVIEW

1. What discovery demonstrated that atoms are not the smallest particles?

2. What did Dalton do in developing his theory that Democritus did not do?

3. **Analyzing Methods** Why was it important for Thomson to repeat his experiment?

internet connect

SC*i*LINKS
NSTA

TOPIC: Development of the Atomic Theory
GO TO: www.scilinks.org
***sci*LINKS NUMBER:** HSTP255

Rutherford Opens an Atomic "Shooting Gallery"

Find out about Melissa Franklin, a modern atom explorer, on page 299.

In 1909, a former student of Thomson's named Ernest Rutherford decided to test Thomson's theory. He designed an experiment to investigate the structure of the atom. He aimed a beam of small, positively charged particles at a thin sheet of gold foil. These particles were larger than *protons*, even smaller positive particles identified in 1902. **Figure 5** shows a diagram of Rutherford's experiment. To find out where the particles went after being "shot" at the gold foil, Rutherford surrounded the foil with a screen coated with zinc sulfide, a substance that glowed when struck by the particles.

Figure 5 Rutherford's Gold Foil Experiment

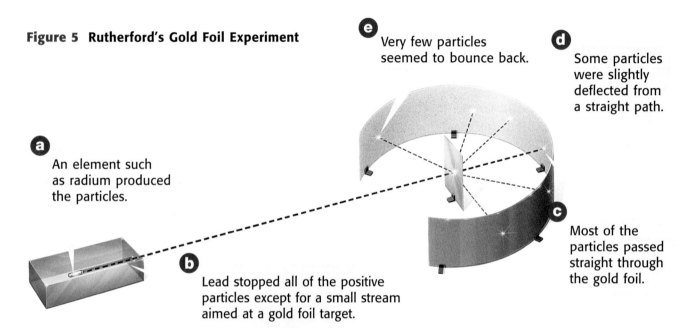

e Very few particles seemed to bounce back.

d Some particles were slightly deflected from a straight path.

a An element such as radium produced the particles.

b Lead stopped all of the positive particles except for a small stream aimed at a gold foil target.

c Most of the particles passed straight through the gold foil.

Rutherford Gets Surprising Results Rutherford thought that if atoms were soft "blobs" of material, as suggested by Thomson, then the particles would pass through the gold and continue in a straight line. Most of the particles did just that. But to Rutherford's great surprise, some of the particles were deflected (turned to one side) a little, some were deflected a great deal, and some particles seemed to bounce back. Rutherford reportedly said,

"It was quite the most incredible event that has ever happened to me in my life. It was almost as if you fired a fifteen-inch shell into a piece of tissue paper and it came back and hit you."

Rutherford Presents a New Atomic Model Rutherford realized that the plum-pudding model of the atom did not explain his results. In 1911, he revised the atomic theory and developed a new model of the atom, as shown in **Figure 6.** To explain the deflection of the particles, Rutherford proposed that in the center of the atom is a tiny, extremely dense, positively charged region called the **nucleus** (NOO klee uhs). Most of the atom's mass is concentrated here. Rutherford reasoned that positively charged particles that passed close by the nucleus were pushed away by the positive charges in the nucleus. A particle that headed straight for a nucleus would be pushed almost straight back in the direction from which it came. From his results, Rutherford calculated that the diameter of the nucleus was 100,000 times smaller than the diameter of the gold atom. To imagine how small this is, look at **Figure 7.**

Figure 6
Rutherford's Model of the Atom

The atom has a small, dense, positively charged **nucleus.**

The atom is mostly **empty space** through which electrons travel.

Electrons travel around the nucleus like planets around the sun, but their exact arrangement could not be described.

Figure 7 *The diameter of this pinhead is 100,000 times smaller than the diameter of the stadium.*

 Self-Check

Why did Thomson think the atom contains positive charges? *(See page 724 to check your answer.)*

Figure 8 Bohr's Model of the Atom

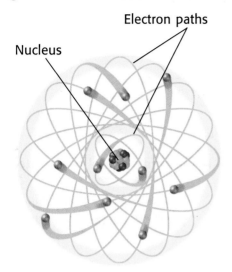

Electron paths

Nucleus

Bohr States That Electrons Can Jump Between Levels

In 1913, Niels Bohr, a Danish scientist who worked with Rutherford, suggested that electrons travel around the nucleus in definite paths. These paths are located in levels at certain distances from the nucleus, as illustrated in **Figure 8.** Bohr proposed that no paths are located between the levels, but electrons can jump from a path in one level to a path in another level. Think of the levels as rungs on a ladder. You can stand *on* the rungs of a ladder but not *between* the rungs. Bohr's model was a valuable tool in predicting some atomic behavior, but the atomic theory still had room for improvement.

The Modern Theory: Electron Clouds Surround the Nucleus

Many twentieth-century scientists have contributed to our current understanding of the atom. An Austrian physicist named Erwin Schrödinger and a German physicist named Werner Heisenberg made particularly important contributions. Their work further explained the nature of electrons in the atom. For example, electrons do not travel in definite paths as Bohr suggested. In fact, the exact path of a moving electron cannot be predicted. According to the current theory, there are regions inside the atom where electrons are *likely* to be found—these regions are called **electron clouds.** Electron clouds are related to the paths described in Bohr's model. The electron-cloud model of the atom is illustrated in **Figure 9.**

Figure 9 The Current Model of the Atom

Electron clouds

Nucleus

internetconnect

SC*i*LINKS.
NSTA

TOPIC: Modern Atomic Theory
GO TO: www.scilinks.org
*sci*LINKS NUMBER: HSTP260

REVIEW

1. In what part of an atom is most of its mass located?

2. What are two differences between the atomic theory described by Thomson and that described by Rutherford?

3. **Comparing Concepts** Identify the difference in how Bohr's theory and the modern theory describe the location of electrons.

The Atom

In the last section, you learned how the atomic theory developed through centuries of observation and experimentation. Now it's time to learn about the atom itself. In this section, you'll learn about the particles inside the atom, and you'll learn about the forces that act on those particles. But first you'll find out just how small an atom really is.

How Small Is an Atom?

The photograph below shows the pattern that forms when a beam of electrons is directed at a sample of aluminum. By analyzing this pattern, scientists can determine the size of an atom. Analysis of similar patterns for many elements has shown that aluminum atoms, which are average-sized atoms, have a diameter of about 0.00000003 cm. That's three hundred-millionths of a centimeter. That is so small that it would take a stack of 50,000 aluminum atoms to equal the thickness of a sheet of aluminum foil from your kitchen!

As another example, consider an ordinary penny. Believe it or not, a penny contains about 2×10^{22} atoms, which can be written as 20,000,000,000,000,000,000,000 atoms, of copper and zinc. That's twenty thousand billion billion atoms—over 3,000,000,000,000 times more atoms than there are people on Earth! So if there are that many atoms in a penny, each atom must be very small. You can get a better idea of just how small an atom is in **Figure 10.**

BRAIN FOOD

The size of atoms varies widely. Helium atoms have the smallest diameter, and francium atoms have the largest diameter. In fact, about 600 atoms of helium would fit in the space occupied by a single francium atom!

Figure 10 *If you could enlarge a penny until it was as wide as the continental United States, each of its atoms would be only about 3 cm in diameter—about the size of this table-tennis ball.*

What's Inside an Atom?

As tiny as an atom is, it consists of even smaller particles—protons, neutrons, and electrons—as shown in the model in **Figure 11.** (The particles represented in the figures are not shown in their correct proportions because the electrons would be too small to see.)

Figure 11 Parts of an Atom

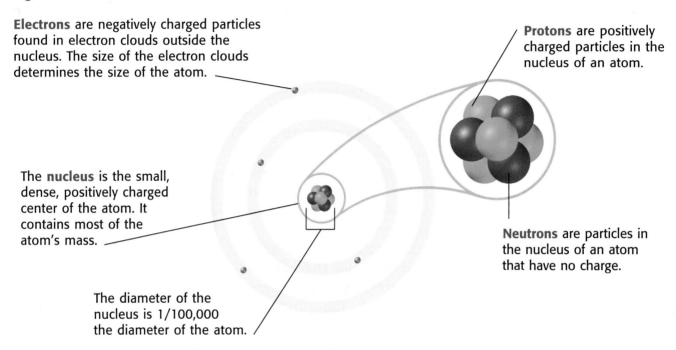

Electrons are negatively charged particles found in electron clouds outside the nucleus. The size of the electron clouds determines the size of the atom.

Protons are positively charged particles in the nucleus of an atom.

The **nucleus** is the small, dense, positively charged center of the atom. It contains most of the atom's mass.

Neutrons are particles in the nucleus of an atom that have no charge.

The diameter of the nucleus is 1/100,000 the diameter of the atom.

Proton Profile

Charge: positive

Mass: 1 amu

Location: nucleus

Neutron Profile

Charge: none

Mass: 1 amu

Location: nucleus

The Nucleus Protons are the positively charged particles of the nucleus. It was these particles that repelled Rutherford's "bullets." All protons are identical. The mass of a proton is approximately 1.7×10^{-24} g, which can also be written as 0.0000000000000000000000017 g. Because the masses of particles in atoms are so small, scientists developed a new unit for them. The SI unit used to express the masses of particles in atoms is the **atomic mass unit (amu).** Scientists assign each proton a mass of 1 amu.

Neutrons are the particles of the nucleus that have no charge. All neutrons are identical. Neutrons are slightly more massive than protons, but the difference in mass is so small that neutrons are also given a mass of 1 amu.

Protons and neutrons are the most massive particles in an atom, yet the nucleus has a very small volume. So the nucleus is very dense. If it were possible to have a nucleus the volume of an average grape, that nucleus would have a mass greater than 9 million metric tons!

Outside of the Nucleus *Electrons* are the negatively charged particles in atoms. Electrons are likely to be found around the nucleus within electron clouds. The charges of protons and electrons are opposite but equal in size. An atom is neutral (has no overall charge) because there are equal numbers of protons and electrons, so their charges cancel out. If the numbers of electrons and protons are not equal, the atom becomes a charged particle called an *ion* (IE ahn). Ions are positively charged if the protons outnumber the electrons, and they are negatively charged if the electrons outnumber the protons.

Electrons are very small in mass compared with protons and neutrons. It takes more than 1,800 electrons to equal the mass of 1 proton. In fact, the mass of an electron is so small that it is usually considered to be zero.

Electron Profile

Charge: negative

Mass: almost zero

Location: electron clouds

REVIEW

1. What particles form the nucleus?

2. Explain why atoms are neutral.

3. **Summarizing Data** Why do scientists say that most of the mass of an atom is located in the nucleus?

LabBook

Help wanted! Elements-4-U needs qualified nucleus builders. Report to page 676 of the LabBook.

How Do Atoms of Different Elements Differ?

There are over 110 different elements, each of which is made of different atoms. What makes atoms different from each other? To find out, imagine that it's possible to "build" an atom by putting together protons, neutrons, and electrons.

Starting Simply It's easiest to start with the simplest atom. Protons and electrons are found in all atoms, and the simplest atom consists of just one of each. It's so simple it doesn't even have a neutron. Put just one proton in the center of the atom for the nucleus. Then put one electron in the electron cloud, as shown in the model in **Figure 12.** Congratulations! You have just made the simplest atom—a hydrogen atom.

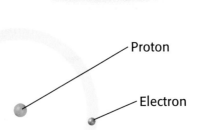

Proton

Electron

Figure 12 *The simplest atom has one proton and one electron.*

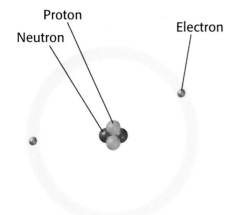

Figure 13 *A helium nucleus must have neutrons in it to keep the protons from moving apart.*

Proton

Neutron

Electron

Astronomy

C O N N E C T I O N

Hydrogen is the most abundant element in the universe. It is the fuel for the sun and other stars. It is currently believed that there are roughly 2,000 times more hydrogen atoms than oxygen atoms and 10,000 times more hydrogen atoms than carbon atoms.

Now for Some Neutrons Now build an atom containing two protons. Both of the protons are positively charged, so they repel one another. You cannot form a nucleus with them unless you add some neutrons. For this atom, two neutrons will do. Your new atom will also need two electrons outside the nucleus, as shown in the model in **Figure 13.** This is an atom of the element helium.

Building Bigger Atoms You could build a carbon atom using 6 protons, 6 neutrons, and 6 electrons; or you could build an oxygen atom using 8 protons, 9 neutrons, and 8 electrons. You could even build a gold atom with 79 protons, 118 neutrons, and 79 electrons! As you can see, an atom does not have to have equal numbers of protons and neutrons.

The Number of Protons Determines the Element How can you tell which elements these atoms represent? The key is the number of protons. The number of protons in the nucleus of an atom is the **atomic number** of that atom. All atoms of an element have the same atomic number. Every hydrogen atom has only one proton in its nucleus, so hydrogen has an atomic number of 1. Every carbon atom has six protons in its nucleus, so carbon has an atomic number of 6.

Are All Atoms of an Element the Same?

Back in the atom-building workshop, you make an atom that has one proton, one electron, and one neutron, as shown in **Figure 14.** The atomic number of this new atom is 1, so the atom is hydrogen. However, this hydrogen atom's nucleus has two particles; therefore, this atom has a greater mass than the first hydrogen atom you made. What you have is another isotope (IE suh TOHP) of hydrogen. **Isotopes** are atoms that have the same number of protons but have different numbers of neutrons. Atoms that are isotopes of each other are always the same element because the number of protons in each atom is the same.

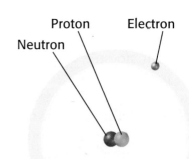

Proton   Electron

Neutron

Figure 14 *The atom in this model and the one in Figure 12 are isotopes because each has one proton but a different number of neutrons.*

Properties of Isotopes Each element has a limited number of isotopes that occur naturally. Some isotopes of an element have unique properties because they are unstable. An unstable atom is an atom whose nucleus can change its composition. This type of isotope is *radioactive*. However, isotopes of an element share most of the same chemical and physical properties. For example, the most common oxygen isotope has 8 neutrons in the nucleus, but other isotopes have 9 or 10 neutrons. All three isotopes are colorless, odorless gases at room temperature. Each isotope has the chemical property of combining with a substance as it burns and even behaves the same in chemical changes in your body.

How Can You Tell One Isotope from Another?

You can identify each isotope of an element by its mass number. The **mass number** is the sum of the protons and neutrons in an atom. Electrons are not included in an atom's mass number because their mass is so small that they have very little effect on the atom's total mass. Look at the boron isotope models shown in **Figure 15** to see how to calculate an atom's mass number.

Isotopes and Light Bulbs

Oxygen reacts, or undergoes a chemical change, with the hot filament in a light bulb, quickly burning out the bulb. Argon does not react with the filament, so a light bulb filled with argon burns out more slowly than one filled with oxygen. Do all three naturally-occurring isotopes of argon have the same effect in light bulbs? Explain your reasoning.

Figure 15 *Each of these boron isotopes has five protons. But because each has a different number of neutrons, each has a different mass number.*

Protons: 5
Neutrons: 5
Electrons: 5
Mass number = protons + neutrons = 10

Protons: 5
Neutrons: 6
Electrons: 5
Mass number = protons + neutrons = 11

Naming Isotopes   To identify a specific isotope of an element, write the name of the element followed by a hyphen and the mass number of the isotope. A hydrogen atom with one proton and no neutrons has a mass number of 1. Its name is hydrogen-1. Hydrogen-2 has one proton and one neutron. The carbon isotope with a mass number of 12 is called carbon-12. If you know that the atomic number for carbon is 6, you can calculate the number of neutrons in carbon-12 by subtracting the atomic number from the mass number. For carbon-12, the number of neutrons is $12 - 6$, or 6.

12	Mass number
-6	Number of protons (atomic number)
6	Number of neutrons

Calculating the Mass of an Element

Most elements found in nature contain a mixture of two or more stable (nonradioactive) isotopes. For example, all copper is composed of copper-63 atoms and copper-65 atoms. The term *atomic mass* describes the mass of a mixture of isotopes. **Atomic mass** is the weighted average of the masses of all the naturally occurring isotopes of an element. A weighted average accounts for the percentages of each isotope that are present. Copper, including the copper in the Statue of Liberty (shown in **Figure 16**), is 69 percent copper-63 and 31 percent copper-65. The atomic mass of copper is 63.6 amu. You can try your hand at calculating atomic mass by doing the MathBreak at left.

Figure 16 *The copper used to make the Statue of Liberty includes both copper-63 and copper-65. Copper's atomic mass is 63.6 amu.*

What Forces Are at Work in Atoms?

You have seen how atoms are composed of protons, neutrons, and electrons. But what are the *forces* (the pushes or pulls between two objects) acting between these particles? Four basic forces are at work everywhere, including within the atom—gravity, the electromagnetic force, the strong force, and the weak force. These forces are discussed below.

Forces in the Atom

Gravity Probably the most familiar of the four forces is *gravity.* Gravity acts between all objects all the time. The amount of gravity between objects depends on their masses and the distance between them. Gravity pulls objects, such as the sun, Earth, cars, and books, toward one another. However, because the masses of particles in atoms are so small, the force of gravity within atoms is very small.

Electromagnetic Force As mentioned earlier, objects that have the same charge repel each other, while objects with opposite charge attract each other. This is due to the *electromagnetic force.* Protons and electrons are attracted to each other because they have opposite charges. The electromagnetic force holds the electrons around the nucleus.

Particles with the same charges repel each other.

Particles with opposite charges attract each other.

Strong Force Protons push away from one another because of the electromagnetic force. A nucleus containing two or more protons would fly apart if it were not for the *strong force.* At the close distances between protons in the nucleus, the strong force is greater than the electromagnetic force, so the nucleus stays together.

Weak Force The *weak force* is an important force in radioactive atoms. In certain unstable atoms, a neutron can change into a proton and an electron. The weak force plays a key role in this change.

REVIEW

1. List the charge, location, and mass of a proton, a neutron, and an electron.

2. Determine the number of protons, neutrons, and electrons in an atom of aluminum-27.

3. **Doing Calculations** The metal thallium occurs naturally as 30 percent thallium-203 and 70 percent thallium-205. Calculate the atomic mass of thallium.

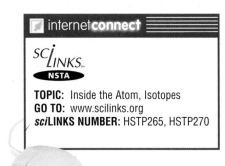

internet**connect**

SC*i*LINKS
NSTA

TOPIC: Inside the Atom, Isotopes
GO TO: www.scilinks.org
*sci*LINKS **NUMBER:** HSTP265, HSTP270

Chapter Highlights

Vocabulary

atom *(p. 280)*

theory *(p. 280)*

electrons *(p. 283)*

model *(p. 283)*

nucleus *(p. 285)*

electron clouds *(p. 286)*

Section Notes

- Atoms are the smallest particles of an element that retain the properties of the element

- In ancient Greece, Democritus argued that atoms were the smallest particles in all matter.

- Dalton proposed an atomic theory that stated the following: Atoms are small particles that make up all matter; atoms cannot be created, divided, or destroyed; atoms of an element are exactly alike; atoms of different elements are different; and atoms join together to make new substances.

- Thomson discovered electrons. His plum-pudding model described the atom as a lump of positively charged material with negative electrons scattered throughout.

- Rutherford discovered that atoms contain a small, dense, positively charged center called the nucleus.

- Bohr suggested that electrons move around the nucleus at only certain distances.

- According to the current atomic theory, electron clouds are where electrons are most likely to be in the space around the nucleus.

☑ Skills Check

Math Concepts

ATOMIC MASS The atomic mass of an element takes into account the mass of each isotope and the percentage of the element that exists as that isotope. For example, magnesium occurs naturally as 79 percent magnesium-24, 10 percent magnesium-25, and 11 percent magnesium-26. The atomic mass is calculated as follows:

$$
\begin{aligned}
(24 \times 0.79) &= 19.0 \\
(25 \times 0.10) &= 2.5 \\
(26 \times 0.11) &= \underline{+2.8} \\
&24.3 \ \text{amu}
\end{aligned}
$$

Visual Understanding

ATOMIC MODELS
The atomic theory has changed over the past several hundred years. To understand the different models of the atom, look over Figures 2, 4, 6, 8, and 9.

PARTS OF THE ATOM Atoms are composed of protons, neutrons, and electrons. To review the particles and their placement in the atom, study Figure 11 on page 288.

Vocabulary

protons *(p. 288)*

atomic mass unit *(p. 288)*

neutrons *(p. 288)*

atomic number *(p. 290)*

isotopes *(p. 290)*

mass number *(p. 291)*

atomic mass *(p. 292)*

Section Notes

- A proton is a positively charged particle with a mass of 1 amu.

- A neutron is a particle with no charge that has a mass of 1 amu.

- An electron is a negatively charged particle with an extremely small mass.

- Protons and neutrons make up the nucleus. Electrons are found in electron clouds outside the nucleus.

- The number of protons in the nucleus of an atom is the atomic number. The atomic number identifies the atoms of a particular element.

- Isotopes of an atom have the same number of protons but have different numbers of neutrons. Isotopes share most of the same chemical and physical properties.

- The mass number of an atom is the sum of the atom's neutrons and protons.

- The atomic mass is an average of the masses of all naturally occurring isotopes of an element.

- The four forces at work in an atom are gravity, the electromagnetic force, the strong force, and the weak force.

Labs

Made to Order *(p. 676)*

internetconnect

GO TO: go.hrw.com

Visit the **HRW** Web site for a variety of learning tools related to this chapter. Just type in the keyword:

KEYWORD: HSTATS

SCiLINKS

N S T A

GO TO: www.scilinks.org

Visit the **National Science Teachers Association** on-line Web site for Internet resources related to this chapter. Just type in the *sci*LINKS number for more information about the topic:

TOPIC: Development of the Atomic Theory   *sci*LINKS NUMBER: HSTP255

TOPIC: Modern Atomic Theory   *sci*LINKS NUMBER: HSTP260

TOPIC: Inside the Atom   *sci*LINKS NUMBER: HSTP265

TOPIC: Isotopes   *sci*LINKS NUMBER: HSTP270

Chapter Review

The statements below are false. For each statement, replace the underlined word to make a true statement.

1. Electrons are found in the <u>nucleus</u> of an atom.

2. All atoms of the same element contain the same number of <u>neutrons</u>.

3. <u>Protons</u> have no electric charge.

4. The <u>atomic number</u> of an element is the number of protons and neutrons in the nucleus.

5. The <u>mass number</u> is an average of the masses of all naturally occurring isotopes of an element.

UNDERSTANDING CONCEPTS

Multiple Choice

6. The discovery of which particle proved that the atom is not indivisible?
   a. proton
   b. neutron
   c. electron
   d. nucleus

7. In his gold foil experiment, Rutherford concluded that the atom is mostly empty space with a small, massive, positively charged center because
   a. most of the particles passed straight through the foil.
   b. some particles were slightly deflected.
   c. a few particles bounced back.
   d. All of the above

8. How many protons does an atom with an atomic number of 23 and a mass number of 51 have?
   a. 23
   b. 28
   c. 51
   d. 74

9. An atom has no overall charge if it contains equal numbers of
   a. electrons and protons.
   b. neutrons and protons.
   c. neutrons and electrons.
   d. None of the above

10. Which statement about protons is true?
   a. Protons have a mass of 1/1,840 amu.
   b. Protons have no charge.
   c. Protons are part of the nucleus of an atom.
   d. Protons circle the nucleus of an atom.

11. Which statement about neutrons is true?
   a. Neutrons have a mass of 1 amu.
   b. Neutrons circle the nucleus of an atom.
   c. Neutrons are the only particles that make up the nucleus.
   d. Neutrons have a negative charge.

12. Which of the following determines the identity of an element?
   a. atomic number
   b. mass number
   c. atomic mass
   d. overall charge

13. Isotopes exist because atoms of the same element can have different numbers of
   a. protons.
   b. neutrons.
   c. electrons.
   d. None of the above

Short Answer

14. Why do scientific theories change?

15. What force holds electrons in atoms?

16. In two or three sentences, describe the plum-pudding model of the atom.

Concept Mapping

17. Use the following terms to create a concept map: atom, nucleus, protons, neutrons, electrons, isotopes, atomic number, mass number.

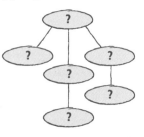

CRITICAL THINKING AND PROBLEM SOLVING

18. Particle accelerators, like the one shown below, are devices that speed up charged particles in order to smash them together. Sometimes the result of the collision is a new nucleus. How can scientists determine whether the nucleus formed is that of a new element or that of a new isotope of a known element?

19. John Dalton made a number of statements about atoms that are now known to be incorrect. Why do you think his atomic theory is still found in science textbooks?

MATH IN SCIENCE

20. Calculate the atomic mass of gallium consisting of 60 percent gallium-69 and 40 percent gallium-71.

21. Calculate the number of protons, neutrons, and electrons in an atom of zirconium-90, which has an atomic number of 40.

INTERPRETING GRAPHICS

22. Study the models below, and answer the questions that follow:

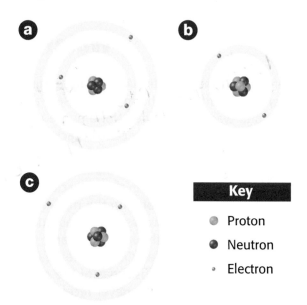

Key

- Proton
- Neutron
- Electron

a. Which models represent isotopes of the same element?

b. What is the atomic number for (a)?

c. What is the mass number for (b)?

23. Predict how the direction of the moving particle in the figure below will change, and explain what causes the change to occur.

Reading Check-up

Take a minute to review your answers to the Pre-Reading Questions found at the bottom of page 278. Have your answers changed? If necessary, revise your answers based on what you have learned since you began this chapter.

Water on the Moon?

When the astronauts of the Apollo space mission explored the surface of the moon in 1969, all they found was rock powder. None of the many samples of moon rocks they carried back to Earth contained any hint of water. Because the astronauts didn't see water on the moon and scientists didn't detect any in the lab, scientists believed there was no water on the moon.

Then in 1994, radio waves suggested another possibility. On a 4-month lunar jaunt, an American spacecraft called *Clementine* beamed radio waves toward various areas of the moon, including a few craters that never receive sunlight. Mostly, the radio waves were reflected by what appeared to be ground-up rock. However, in part of one huge, dark crater, the radio waves were reflected as if by . . . *ice.*

Hunting for Hydrogen Atoms

Scientists were intrigued by *Clementine's* evidence. Two years later, another spacecraft, *Lunar Prospector,* traveled to the moon. Instead of trying to detect water with radio waves, *Prospector* scanned the moon's surface with a device called a *neutron spectrometer* (NS). A neutron spectrometer counts the number of slow neutrons bouncing off a surface. When a neutron hits something about the same mass as itself, it slows down. As it turns out, the only thing close to the mass of a neutron is an *atom* of the lightest of all elements, hydrogen. So when the NS located high concentrations of slow-moving neutrons on the moon, it indicated to scientists that the neutrons were crashing into hydrogen atoms.

As you know, water consists of two atoms of hydrogen and one atom of oxygen. The presence of hydrogen atoms on the moon is more evidence that water may exist there.

▲ *The* Lunar Prospector *spacecraft may have found water on the moon.*

How Did It Get There?

Some scientists speculate that the water molecules came from comets (which are 90 percent water) that hit the moon more than 4 billion years ago. Water from comets may have landed in the frigid, shadowed craters of the moon, where it mixed with the soil and froze. The Aitken Basin, at the south pole of the moon, where much of the ice was detected, is more than 12 km deep in places. Sunlight never touches most of the crater. And it is very cold—temperatures there may fall to −229°C. The conditions seem right to lock water into place for a very long time.

Think About Lunar Life

▶ Do some research on conditions on the moon. What conditions would humans have to overcome before we could establish a colony there?

CAREERS

EXPERIMENTAL PHYSICIST

In the course of a single day, you could find **Melissa Franklin** operating a huge drill, giving a tour of her lab to a 10-year-old, putting together a gigantic piece of electronic equipment, or even telling a joke. Then you'd see her really get down to business—studying the smallest particles of matter in the universe.

Melissa Franklin is an experimental physicist. "I am trying to understand the forces that describe how everything in the world moves—especially the smallest things," she explains. "I want to find the things that make up all matter in the universe and then try to understand the forces between them."

Other scientists rely on her to test some of the most important hypotheses in physics. For instance, Franklin and her team recently contributed to the discovery of a particle called the top quark. (Quarks are the tiny particles that make up protons and neutrons.)

Physicists had theorized that the top quark might exist but had no evidence. Franklin and more than 450 other scientists worked together to prove the existence of the top quark. Finding it required the use of a massive machine called a particle accelerator. Basically, a particle accelerator smashes particles together, and then scientists look for the remains of the collision. The physicists had to build some very complicated machines to detect the top quark, but the discovery was worth the effort. Franklin and the other researchers have earned the praise of scientists all over the world.

Getting Her Start

"I didn't always want to be a scientist, but what happens is that when you get hooked, you really get hooked. The next thing you know, you're driving forklifts and using overhead cranes while at the same time working on really tiny, incredibly complicated electronics. What I do is a combination of exciting things. It's better than watching TV."

It isn't just the best students who grow up to be scientists. "You can understand the ideas without having to be a math genius," Franklin says. Anyone can have good ideas, she says, absolutely anyone.

Don't Be Shy!

▶ Franklin also has some good advice for young people interested in physics. "Go and bug people at the local university. Just call up a physics person and say, 'Can I come visit you for a couple of hours?' Kids do that with me, and it's really fun." Why don't you give it a try? Prepare for the visit by making a list of questions you would like answered.

▲ *This particle accelerator was used in the discovery of the top quark.*

The Periodic Table

Pre-Reading Questions

1. How are elements organized in the periodic table?
2. Why is the table of the elements called "periodic"?
3. What one property is shared by elements in a group?

A BUILDING AS A PIECE OF ART!

Would you believe that this strange-looking building is an art museum? It is! It's the Guggenheim Museum in Bilbao, Spain. The building is made of limestone blocks, glass, and the element titanium. Titanium was chosen because it is strong, lightweight, and very resistant to corrosion and rust. In fact, the half-millimeter-thick fish-scale titanium panels covering most of the building are guaranteed to last 100 years! In this chapter, you will learn about some other elements on the periodic table and their properties.

PLACEMENT PATTERN

In this activity, you will determine the pattern behind a new seating chart your teacher has created.

Procedure

1. In your ScienceLog, draw a seating chart for the classroom arrangement given to you by your teacher. Write the name of each of your classmates in the correct place on the chart.

2. Write information about yourself, such as your name, date of birth, hair color, and height, in the space that represents you on the chart.

3. Starting with the people around you, gather the same information about them. Write each person's information in the proper space on the seating chart.

Analysis

4. In your ScienceLog, identify a pattern to the information you gathered that might explain the order of the people in the seating chart. If you cannot find a pattern, collect more information and look again.

5. Test your pattern by gathering information from a person you did not talk to before.

6. If the new information does not support your pattern, reanalyze your data and collect more information to determine another pattern.

Arranging the Elements

Terms to Learn

periodic   period
periodic law   group

What You'll Do

◆ Describe how elements are arranged in the periodic table.

◆ Compare metals, nonmetals, and metalloids based on their properties and on their location in the periodic table.

◆ Describe the difference between a period and a group.

Imagine you go to a new grocery store to buy a box of cereal. You are surprised by what you find. None of the aisles are labeled, and there is no pattern to the products on the shelves! You think it might take you days to find your cereal.

Some scientists probably felt a similar frustration before 1869. By that time, more than 60 elements had been discovered and described. However, it was not until 1869 that the elements were organized in any special way.

Discovering a Pattern

In the 1860s, a Russian chemist named Dmitri Mendeleev began looking for patterns among the properties of the elements. He wrote the names and properties of the elements on pieces of paper. He included density, appearance, atomic mass, melting point, and information about the compounds formed from the element. He then arranged and rearranged the pieces of paper, as shown in **Figure 1.** After much thought and work, he determined that there was a repeating pattern to the properties of the elements when the elements were arranged in order of increasing atomic mass.

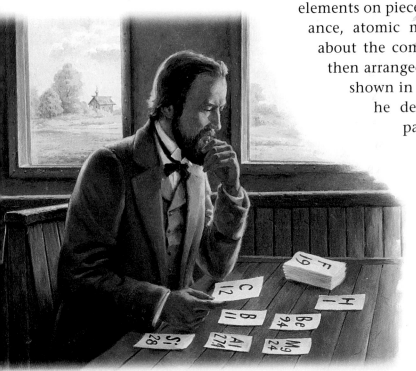

Figure 1 *By playing "chemical solitaire" on long train rides, Mendeleev organized the elements according to their properties.*

The Properties of Elements Are Periodic Mendeleev saw that the properties of the elements were **periodic,** meaning they had a regular, repeating pattern. Many things that are familiar to you are periodic. For example, the days of the week are periodic because they repeat in the same order every 7 days.

When the elements were arranged in order of increasing atomic mass, similar chemical and physical properties were observed in every eighth element. Mendeleev's arrangement of the elements came to be known as a periodic table because the properties of the elements change in a periodic way.

Predicting Properties of Missing Elements Look at the section of Mendeleev's periodic table shown in **Figure 2**. Notice the question marks. Mendeleev recognized that there were elements missing and boldly predicted that elements yet to be discovered would fill the gaps. He also predicted the properties of the missing elements by using the pattern of properties in the periodic table. When one of the missing elements, gallium, was discovered a few years later, its properties matched Mendeleev's predictions very well. Since that time, all of the missing elements on Mendeleev's periodic table have been discovered. In the chart below, you can see Mendeleev's predictions for another missing element—germanium—and the actual properties of that element.

	Ni=Co=59
H=1	Cu=63,4
Be=9,4 Mg=24	Zn=65,2
B=11 Al=27,4	?=68
C=12 Si=28	?=70
N=14 P=31	As=75
O=16 S=32	Se=79,4
F=19 Cl=35,5	Br=80
Li=7 Na=23 K=39	Rb=85,4
Ca=40	Sr=87,6
?=45	Ce=92
?Er=56	La=94
?Yt=60	Di=95
?In=75,6	Th=118?

Figure 2 *Mendeleev used question marks to indicate some elements that he believed would later be identified.*

Properties of Germanium		
	Mendeleev's predictions	**Actual properties**
Atomic mass	72	72.6
Density	5.5 g/cm^3	5.3 g/cm^3
Appearance	dark gray metal	gray metal
Melting point	high melting point	937°C

Changing the Arrangement

Mendeleev noticed that a few elements in the table were not in the correct place according to their properties. He thought that the calculated atomic masses were incorrect and that more accurate atomic masses would eventually be determined. However, new measurements of the atomic masses showed that the masses were in fact correct.

The mystery was solved in 1914 by a British scientist named Henry Moseley (MOHZ lee). From the results of his experiments, Moseley was able to determine the number of protons—the atomic number—in an atom. When he rearranged the elements by atomic number, every element fell into its proper place in an improved periodic table.

Since 1914, more elements have been discovered. Each discovery has supported the periodic law, considered to be the basis of the periodic table. The **periodic law** states that the chemical and physical properties of elements are periodic functions of their atomic numbers. The modern version of the periodic table is shown on the following pages.

BRAIN FOOD

Moseley was 26 when he made his discovery. His work allowed him to predict that only three elements were yet to be found between aluminum and gold. The following year, as he fought for the British in World War I, he was killed in action at Gallipoli, Turkey. The British government no longer assigns scientists to combat duty.

Periodic Table of the Elements

Each square on the table includes an element's name, chemical symbol, atomic number, and atomic mass.

Atomic number ——— 6
Chemical symbol ——— **C**
Element name ——— Carbon
Atomic mass ——— 12.0

The background color indicates the type of element. Carbon is a nonmetal.

Background
Metals
Metalloids
Nonmetals

The color of the chemical symbol indicates the physical state at room temperature. Carbon is a solid.

Chemical symbol
Solid
Liquid
Gas

	Group 1	Group 2	Group 3	Group 4	Group 5	Group 6	Group 7	Group 8	Group 9
Period 1	1 **H** Hydrogen 1.0								
Period 2	3 **Li** Lithium 6.9	4 **Be** Beryllium 9.0							
Period 3	11 **Na** Sodium 23.0	12 **Mg** Magnesium 24.3							
Period 4	19 **K** Potassium 39.1	20 **Ca** Calcium 40.1	21 **Sc** Scandium 45.0	22 **Ti** Titanium 47.9	23 **V** Vanadium 50.9	24 **Cr** Chromium 52.0	25 **Mn** Manganese 54.9	26 **Fe** Iron 55.8	27 **Co** Cobalt 58.9
Period 5	37 **Rb** Rubidium 85.5	38 **Sr** Strontium 87.6	39 **Y** Yttrium 88.9	40 **Zr** Zirconium 91.2	41 **Nb** Niobium 92.9	42 **Mo** Molybdenum 95.9	43 **Tc** Technetium (97.9)	44 **Ru** Ruthenium 101.1	45 **Rh** Rhodium 102.9
Period 6	55 **Cs** Cesium 132.9	56 **Ba** Barium 137.3	57 **La** Lanthanum 138.9	72 **Hf** Hafnium 178.5	73 **Ta** Tantalum 180.9	74 **W** Tungsten 183.8	75 **Re** Rhenium 186.2	76 **Os** Osmium 190.2	77 **Ir** Iridium 192.2
Period 7	87 **Fr** Francium (223.0)	88 **Ra** Radium (226.0)	89 **Ac** Actinium (227.0)	104 **Rf** Rutherfordium (261.1)	105 **Db** Dubnium (262.1)	106 **Sg** Seaborgium (263.1)	107 **Bh** Bohrium (262.1)	108 **Hs** Hassium (265)	109 **Mt** Meitnerium (266)

A row of elements is called a period.

A column of elements is called a group or family.

Lanthanides	58 **Ce** Cerium 140.1	59 **Pr** Praseodymium 140.9	60 **Nd** Neodymium 144.2	61 **Pm** Promethium (144.9)	62 **Sm** Samarium 150.4
Actinides	90 **Th** Thorium 232.0	91 **Pa** Protactinium 231.0	92 **U** Uranium 238.0	93 **Np** Neptunium (237.0)	94 **Pu** Plutonium 244.1

These elements are placed below the table to allow the table to be narrower.

This zigzag line reminds you where the metals, nonmetals, and metalloids are.

Group 18

| 2 **He** Helium 4.0 |

Group 13 | **Group 14** | **Group 15** | **Group 16** | **Group 17**

| 5 **B** Boron 10.8 | 6 **C** Carbon 12.0 | 7 **N** Nitrogen 14.0 | 8 **O** Oxygen 16.0 | 9 **F** Fluorine 19.0 | 10 **Ne** Neon 20.2 |

| 13 **Al** Aluminum 27.0 | 14 **Si** Silicon 28.1 | 15 **P** Phosphorus 31.0 | 16 **S** Sulfur 32.1 | 17 **Cl** Chlorine 35.5 | 18 **Ar** Argon 39.9 |

Group 10 | **Group 11** | **Group 12**

| 28 **Ni** Nickel 58.7 | 29 **Cu** Copper 63.5 | 30 **Zn** Zinc 65.4 | 31 **Ga** Gallium 69.7 | 32 **Ge** Germanium 72.6 | 33 **As** Arsenic 74.9 | 34 **Se** Selenium 79.0 | 35 **Br** Bromine 79.9 | 36 **Kr** Krypton 83.8 |

| 46 **Pd** Palladium 106.4 | 47 **Ag** Silver 107.9 | 48 **Cd** Cadmium 112.4 | 49 **In** Indium 114.8 | 50 **Sn** Tin 118.7 | 51 **Sb** Antimony 121.8 | 52 **Te** Tellurium 127.6 | 53 **I** Iodine 126.9 | 54 **Xe** Xenon 131.3 |

| 78 **Pt** Platinum 195.1 | 79 **Au** Gold 197.0 | 80 **Hg** Mercury 200.6 | 81 **Tl** Thallium 204.4 | 82 **Pb** Lead 207.2 | 83 **Bi** Bismuth 209.0 | 84 **Po** Polonium (209.0) | 85 **At** Astatine (210.0) | 86 **Rn** Radon (222.0) |

| 110 **Uun** Ununnilium (271) | 111 **Uuu** Unununium (272) | 112 **Uub** Ununbium (277) |

The names and symbols of elements 110–112 are temporary. They are based on the atomic number of the element. The official name and symbol will be approved by an international committee of scientists.

| 63 **Eu** Europium 152.0 | 64 **Gd** Gadolinium 157.3 | 65 **Tb** Terbium 158.9 | 66 **Dy** Dysprosium 162.5 | 67 **Ho** Holmium 164.9 | 68 **Er** Erbium 167.3 | 69 **Tm** Thulium 168.9 | 70 **Yb** Ytterbium 173.0 | 71 **Lu** Lutetium 175.0 |

| 95 **Am** Americium (243.1) | 96 **Cm** Curium (247.1) | 97 **Bk** Berkelium (247.1) | 98 **Cf** Californium (251.1) | 99 **Es** Einsteinium (252.1) | 100 **Fm** Fermium (257.1) | 101 **Md** Mendelevium (258.1) | 102 **No** Nobelium (259.1) | 103 **Lr** Lawrencium (262.1) |

A number in parentheses is the mass number of the most stable isotope of that element.

Finding Your Way Around the Periodic Table

At first glance, you might think studying the periodic table is like trying to explore a thick jungle without a guide—it would be easy to get lost! However, the table itself contains a lot of information that will help you along the way.

Classes of Elements   Elements are classified as metals, nonmetals, and metalloids, according to their properties. The number of electrons in the outer energy level of an atom also helps determine which category an element belongs in. The zigzag line on the periodic table can help you recognize which elements are metals, which are nonmetals, and which are metalloids.

Metals

Most elements are metals. Metals are found to the left of the zigzag line on the periodic table. Atoms of most metals have few electrons in their outer energy level, as shown at right.

Most metals are solid at room temperature. Mercury, however, is a liquid. Some additional information on properties shared by most metals is shown below.

A model of a magnesium atom

Most metals are **good conductors** of thermal energy. This iron griddle conducts thermal energy from a stovetop to cook your favorite foods.

Most metals are **malleable,** meaning that they can be flattened with a hammer without shattering. Aluminum is flattened into sheets to make cans and foil.

Most metals are **ductile,** which means that they can be drawn into thin wires. All metals are good conductors of electric current. The wires in the electrical devices in your home are made from the metal copper.

Metals tend to be **shiny.** You can see a reflection in a mirror because light reflects off the shiny surface of a thin layer of silver behind the glass.

Nonmetals

Nonmetals are found to the right of the zigzag line on the periodic table. Atoms of most nonmetals have an almost complete set of electrons in their outer level, as shown at right. (Atoms of one group of nonmetals, the noble gases, have a complete set of electrons, with most having eight electrons in their outer energy level.)

More than half of the nonmetals are gases at room temperature. The properties of nonmetals are the opposite of the properties of metals, as shown below.

A model of a chlorine atom

Conduction Connection

1. Fill a **plastic-foam cup** with **hot water.**
2. Stand a piece of **copper wire** and a **graphite lead** from a mechanical pencil in the water.
3. After 1 minute, touch the top of each object. Record your observations.
4. Which material conducted thermal energy the best? Why?

Sulfur, like most nonmetals, is **not shiny.**

Nonmetals are **not malleable or ductile.** In fact, solid nonmetals, like carbon (shown here in the graphite of the pencil lead), are brittle and will break or shatter when hit with a hammer.

Nonmetals are **poor conductors** of thermal energy and electric current. If the gap in a spark plug is too wide, the nonmetals nitrogen and oxygen in the air will stop the spark, and a car's engine will not run.

Metalloids

Metalloids, also called semiconductors, are the elements that border the zigzag line on the periodic table. Atoms of metalloids have about a half-complete set of electrons in their outer energy level, as shown at right.

Metalloids have some properties of metals and some properties of nonmetals, as shown below.

A model of a silicon atom

Boron is almost as **hard** as diamond, but it is also **very brittle.** At high temperatures, boron is a good conductor of electric current.

Tellurium is **shiny,** but it is also **brittle** and is easily smashed into a powder.

Draw a line down a sheet of paper to divide it into two columns. Look at the elements with atomic numbers 1 through 10 on the periodic table. Write all the chemical symbols and names that follow one pattern in one column on your paper and all chemical symbols and names that follow a second pattern in the second column. Write a sentence describing each pattern you found.

TRY at HOME

Each Element Is Identified by a Chemical Symbol Each square on the periodic table contains information about an element, including its atomic number, atomic mass, name, and chemical symbol. An international committee of scientists is responsible for approving the names and chemical symbols of the elements. The names of the elements come from many sources. For example, some elements are named after important scientists (mendelevium, einsteinium), and others are named for geographical regions (germanium, californium).

The chemical symbol for each element usually consists of one or two letters. The first letter in the symbol is always capitalized, and the second letter, if there is one, is always written in lowercase. The chart below lists the patterns that the chemical symbols follow, and the Activity will help you investigate two of those patterns further.

Writing the Chemical Symbols

Pattern of chemical symbols	Examples
first letter of the name	S—sulfur
first two letters of the name	Ca—calcium
first letter and third or later letter of the name	Mg—magnesium
letter(s) of a word other than the English name	Pb—lead (from the Latin *plumbum*, meaning "lead")
first letter of root words that stand for the atomic number (used for elements whose official names have not yet been chosen)	Uun—ununnilium (uhn uhn NIL ee uhm) (for atomic number 110)

You can create your own well-rounded periodic table using coins, washers, and buttons on page 678 of the LabBook.

One Set of Symbols

Look at the periodic table shown here. How is it the same as the periodic table you saw earlier? How is it different? Explain why it is important for scientific communication that the chemical symbols used are the same around the world.

元素の周期表

	1 H 1.0079 水素	
1		
2	3 Li 6.941 リチウム	4 Be 9.01218 ベリリウム
3	11 Na 22.98977 ナトリウム	12 Mg 24.305 マグネシウム
4	19 K	20

Rows Are Called Periods   Each horizontal row of elements (from left to right) on the periodic table is called a **period**. For example, the row from lithium (Li) to neon (Ne) is Period 2. A row is called a period because the properties of elements in a row follow a repeating, or periodic, pattern as you move across each period. The physical and chemical properties of elements, such as conductivity and the number of electrons in the outer level of atoms, change gradually from those of a metal to those of a nonmetal in each period, as shown in **Figure 3**.

Figure 3   *The elements in a row become less metallic from left to right.*

19	20	21	22	23	24	25	26	27	28	29	30	31	32	33	34	35	36
K	Ca	Sc	Ti	V	Cr	Mn	Fe	Co	Ni	Cu	Zn	Ga	Ge	As	Se	Br	Kr

| 22 |
| Ti |
| Titanium |
| 47.9 |

| 32 |
| Ge |
| Germanium |
| 72.6 |

| 35 |
| Br |
| Bromine |
| 79.9 |

Elements at the left end of a period, such as titanium, are very metallic in their properties.

Elements farther to the right, like germanium, are less metallic in their properties.

Elements at the far right end of a period, such as bromine, are nonmetallic in their properties.

Columns Are Called Groups   Each column of elements (from top to bottom) on the periodic table is called a **group**. Elements in the same group often have similar chemical and physical properties. For this reason, sometimes a group is also called a family. You will learn more about each group in the next section.

REVIEW

1. Compare a period and a group on the periodic table.

2. How are the elements arranged in the modern periodic table?

3. **Comparing Concepts**   Compare metals, nonmetals, and metalloids in terms of their electrical conductivity.

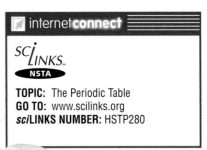

internetconnect

SCLINKS
NSTA

TOPIC: The Periodic Table
GO TO: www.scilinks.org
*sci*LINKS **NUMBER:** HSTP280

Grouping the Elements

You probably know a family with several members that look a lot alike. Or you may have a friend whose little brother or sister acts just like your friend. Members of a family often—but not always—have a similar appearance or behavior. Likewise, the elements in a family or group in the periodic table often—but not always—share similar properties. The properties are similar because the atoms of the elements have the same number of electrons in their outer energy level.

Groups 1 and 2: Very Reactive Metals

The most reactive metals are the elements in Groups 1 and 2. What makes an element reactive? The answer has to do with electrons in the outer energy level of atoms. Atoms will often take, give, or share electrons with other atoms in order to have a complete set of electrons in their outer energy level. Elements whose atoms undergo such processes are *reactive* and combine to form compounds. Elements whose atoms need to take, give, or share only one or two electrons to have a filled outer level tend to be very reactive.

The elements in Groups 1 and 2 are so reactive that they are only found combined with other elements in nature. To study the elements separately, the naturally occurring compounds must first be broken apart through chemical changes.

Group 1: Alkali Metals

Although the element hydrogen appears above the alkali metals on the periodic table, it is not considered a member of Group 1. It will be described separately at the end of this section.

| 3
Li
Lithium |
| 11
Na
Sodium |
| 19
K
Potassium |
| 37
Rb
Rubidium |
| 55
Cs
Cesium |
| 87
Fr
Francium |

Group contains: Metals
Electrons in the outer level: 1
Reactivity: Very reactive
Other shared properties: Soft; silver-colored; shiny; low density

Alkali (AL kuh LIE) **metals** are soft enough to be cut with a knife, as shown in **Figure 4.** The densities of the alkali metals are so low that lithium, sodium, and potassium are actually less dense than water.

Figure 4 *Metals so soft that they can be cut with a knife? Welcome to the alkali metals.*

Alkali metals are the most reactive of the metals. This is because their atoms can easily give away the single electron in their outer level. For example, alkali metals react violently with water, as shown in **Figure 5.** Alkali metals are usually stored in oil to prevent them from reacting with water and oxygen in the atmosphere.

The compounds formed from alkali metals have many uses. Sodium chloride (table salt) can be used to add flavor to your food. Sodium hydroxide can be used to unclog your drains. Potassium bromide is one of several potassium compounds used in photography.

Lithium

Sodium

Potassium

Figure 5 *As alkali metals react with water, they form hydrogen gas.*

Group 2: Alkaline-earth Metals

4
Be
Beryllium

12
Mg
Magnesium

20
Ca
Calcium

38
Sr
Strontium

56
Ba
Barium

88
Ra
Radium

Group contains: Metals
Electrons in the outer level: 2
Reactivity: Very reactive, but less reactive than alkali metals
Other shared properties: Silver-colored; more dense than alkali metals

Alkaline-earth metals are not as reactive as alkali metals because it is more difficult for atoms to give away two electrons than to give away only one when joining with other atoms.

The alkaline-earth metal magnesium is often mixed with other metals to make low-density materials used in airplanes. Compounds of alkaline-earth metals also have many uses. For example, compounds of calcium are found in cement, plaster, chalk, and even you, as shown in **Figure 6.**

Figure 6 *Smile! Calcium, an alkaline-earth metal, is an important component of a compound that makes your bones and teeth healthy.*

Groups 3–12: Transition Metals

Groups 3–12 do not have individual names. Instead, these groups are described together under the name *transition metals*.

> **Group contains:** Metals
> **Electrons in the outer level:** 1 or 2
> **Reactivity:** Less reactive than alkaline-earth metals
> **Other shared properties:** Shiny; good conductors of thermal energy and electric current; higher densities and melting points (except for mercury) than elements in Groups 1 and 2

21 **Sc** Scandium	22 **Ti** Titanium	23 **V** Vanadium	24 **Cr** Chromium	25 **Mn** Manganese	26 **Fe** Iron	27 **Co** Cobalt	28 **Ni** Nickel	29 **Cu** Copper	30 **Zn** Zinc
39 **Y** Yttrium	40 **Zr** Zirconium	41 **Nb** Niobium	42 **Mo** Molybdenum	43 **Tc** Technetium	44 **Ru** Ruthenium	45 **Rh** Rhodium	46 **Pd** Palladium	47 **Ag** Silver	48 **Cd** Cadmium
57 **La** Lanthanum	72 **Hf** Hafnium	73 **Ta** Tantalum	74 **W** Tungsten	75 **Re** Rhenium	76 **Os** Osmium	77 **Ir** Iridium	78 **Pt** Platinum	79 **Au** Gold	80 **Hg** Mercury
89 **Ac** Actinium	104 **Rf** Rutherfordium	105 **Db** Dubnium	106 **Sg** Seaborgium	107 **Bh** Bohrium	108 **Hs** Hassium	109 **Mt** Meitnerium	110 **Uun** Ununnilium	111 **Uuu** Unununium	112 **Uub** Ununbium

The atoms of transition metals do not give away their electrons as easily as atoms of the Group 1 and Group 2 metals do, making transition metals less reactive than the alkali metals and the alkaline-earth metals. The properties of the transition metals vary widely, as shown in **Figure 7.**

Figure 7 *Transition metals have a wide range of physical and chemical properties.*

Mercury is used in thermometers because, unlike the other transition metals, it is in the liquid state at room temperature.

Some transition metals, including the **titanium** in the artificial hip at right, are not very reactive. But others, such as **iron**, are reactive. The iron in the steel trowel above has reacted with oxygen to form rust.

Many transition metals are silver-colored—but not all! This **gold** ring proves it!

✓ Self-Check

Why are alkali metals more reactive than alkaline-earth metals? *(See page 724 to check your answer.)*

57
La
Lanthanum
138.9

89
Ac
Actinium
(227.0)

Lanthanides and Actinides Some transition metals from Periods 6 and 7 are placed at the bottom of the periodic table to keep the table from being too wide. The properties of the elements in each row tend to be very similar.

Lanthanides	58 Ce	59 Pr	60 Nd	61 Pm	62 Sm	63 Eu	64 Gd	65 Tb	66 Dy	67 Ho	68 Er	69 Tm	70 Yb	71 Lu
Actinides	90 Th	91 Pa	92 U	93 Np	94 Pu	95 Am	96 Cm	97 Bk	98 Cf	99 Es	100 Fm	101 Md	102 No	103 Lr

Elements in the first row are called *lanthanides* because they follow the transition metal lanthanum. The lanthanides are shiny, reactive metals. Some of these elements are used to make different types of steel. An important use of a compound of one lanthanide element is shown in **Figure 8.**

Elements in the second row are called *actinides* because they follow the transition metal actinium. All atoms of actinides are radioactive, which means they are unstable. The atoms of a radioactive element can change into atoms of a different element. Elements listed after plutonium, element 94, do not occur in nature but are instead produced in laboratories. You might have one of these elements in your home. Very small amounts of americium (AM uhr ISH ee uhm), element 95, are used in some smoke detectors.

Figure 8 *Seeing red? The color red appears on a computer monitor because of a compound formed from europium that coats the back of the screen.*

REVIEW

1. What are two properties of the alkali metals?

2. What causes the properties of elements in a group to be similar?

3. **Applying Concepts** Why are neither the alkali metals nor the alkaline-earth metals found uncombined in nature?

internet**connect**

*SCI*LINKS
NSTA

TOPIC: Metals
GO TO: www.scilinks.org
*sci*LINKS NUMBER: HSTP285

The Periodic Table **313**

Groups 13–16: Groups with Metalloids

Moving from Group 13 across to Group 16, the elements shift from metals to nonmetals. Along the way, you find the metalloids. These elements have some properties of metals and some properties of nonmetals.

Group 13: Boron Group

5 **B** Boron
13 **Al** Aluminum
31 **Ga** Gallium
49 **In** Indium
81 **Tl** Thallium

Group contains: One metalloid and four metals
Electrons in the outer level: 3
Reactivity: Reactive
Other shared properties: Solid at room temperature

The most common element from Group 13 is aluminum. In fact, aluminum is the most abundant metal in Earth's crust. Until the 1880s, it was considered a precious metal because the process used to produce pure aluminum was very expensive. In fact, aluminum was even more valuable than gold, as shown in **Figure 9.**

Today, the process is not as difficult or expensive. Aluminum is now an important metal used in making lightweight automobile parts and aircraft, as well as foil, cans, and wires.

Figure 9 *During the 1850s and 1860s, Emperor Napoleon III of France used aluminum dinnerware because aluminum was more valuable than gold!*

Group 14: Carbon Group

6 **C** Carbon
14 **Si** Silicon
32 **Ge** Germanium
50 **Sn** Tin
82 **Pb** Lead

Group contains: One nonmetal, two metalloids, and two metals
Electrons in the outer level: 4
Reactivity: Varies among the elements
Other shared properties: Solid at room temperature

The metalloids silicon and germanium are used to make computer chips. The metal tin is useful because it is not very reactive. A tin can is really made of steel coated with tin. The tin is less reactive than the steel, and it keeps the steel from rusting.

Environment

CONNECTION

Recycling aluminum uses less energy than obtaining aluminum in the first place. Aluminum must be separated from bauxite, a mixture containing naturally occurring compounds of aluminum. Twenty times more electrical energy is required to separate aluminum from bauxite than to recycle used aluminum.

The nonmetal carbon can be found uncombined in nature, as shown in **Figure 10.** Carbon forms a wide variety of compounds. Some of these compounds, including proteins, fats, and carbohydrates, are essential to life on Earth.

Figure 10 *Diamonds and soot have very different properties, yet both are natural forms of carbon.*

Diamond is the hardest material known. It is used as a jewel and on cutting tools such as saws, drills, and files.

Soot—formed from burning oil, coal, and wood—is used as a pigment in paints and crayons.

Group 15: Nitrogen Group

7 **N** Nitrogen
15 **P** Phosphorus
33 **As** Arsenic
51 **Sb** Antimony
83 **Bi** Bismuth

Group contains: Two nonmetals, two metalloids, and one metal
Electrons in the outer level: 5
Reactivity: Varies among the elements
Other shared properties: All but nitrogen are solid at room temperature.

Nitrogen, which is a gas at room temperature, makes up about 80 percent of the air you breathe. Nitrogen removed from air is reacted with hydrogen to make ammonia for fertilizers.

Although nitrogen is unreactive, phosphorus is extremely reactive, as shown in **Figure 11.** In fact, phosphorus is only found combined with other elements in nature.

Figure 11
Simply striking a match on the side of this box causes chemicals on the match to react with phosphorus on the box and begin to burn.

Group 16: Oxygen Group

8 **O** Oxygen
16 **S** Sulfur
34 **Se** Selenium
52 **Te** Tellurium
84 **Po** Polonium

Group contains: Three nonmetals, one metalloid, and one metal
Electrons in the outer level: 6
Reactivity: Reactive
Other shared properties: All but oxygen are solid at room temperature.

Oxygen makes up about 20 percent of air. Oxygen is necessary for substances to burn, such as the chemicals on the match in Figure 11. Sulfur, another common member of Group 16, can be found as a yellow solid in nature. The principal use of sulfur is to make sulfuric acid, the most widely used compound in the chemical industry.

FIRES
32 Strike-o
SAFETY MA
Keep Away From
Acme Match Co. Au

Groups 17 and 18: Nonmetals Only

The elements in Groups 17 and 18 are nonmetals. The elements in Group 17 are the most reactive nonmetals, but the elements in Group 18 are the least reactive nonmetals. In fact, the elements in Group 18 normally won't react at all with other elements.

Group 17: Halogens

Chlorine is a yellowish green gas.

Bromine is a dark red liquid.

Iodine is a dark gray solid.

Figure 12 *Physical properties of some halogens at room temperature are shown here.*

| 9 F Fluorine |
| 17 Cl Chlorine |
| 35 Br Bromine |
| 53 I Iodine |
| 85 At Astatine |

Group contains: Nonmetals
Electrons in the outer level: 7
Reactivity: Very reactive
Other shared properties: Poor conductors of electric current; react violently with alkali metals to form salts; never found uncombined in nature

Halogens are very reactive nonmetals because their atoms need to gain only one electron to have a complete outer level. The atoms of halogens combine readily with other atoms, especially metals, to gain that missing electron.

Although the chemical properties of the halogens are similar, the physical properties are quite different, as shown in **Figure 12.**

Both chlorine and iodine are used as disinfectants. Chlorine is used to treat water, while iodine mixed with alcohol is used in hospitals.

Group 18: Noble Gases

| 2 He Helium |
| 10 Ne Neon |
| 18 Ar Argon |
| 36 Kr Krypton |
| 54 Xe Xenon |
| 86 Rn Radon |

Group contains: Nonmetals
Electrons in the outer level: 8 (2 for helium)
Reactivity: Unreactive
Other shared properties: Colorless, odorless gases at room temperature

Noble gases are unreactive nonmetals. Because the atoms of the elements in this group have a complete set of electrons in their outer level, they do not need to lose or gain any electrons. Therefore, they do not react with other elements under normal conditions.

All of the noble gases are found in Earth's atmosphere in small amounts. Argon, the most abundant noble gas in the atmosphere, makes up almost 1 percent of the atmosphere.

BRAIN FOOD

The term *noble gases* describes the nonreactivity of these elements. Just as nobles, such as kings and queens, did not often mix with common people, the noble gases do not normally react with other elements.

The nonreactivity of the noble gases makes them useful. Ordinary light bulbs last longer when filled with argon than they would if filled with a reactive gas. Because argon is unreactive, it does not react with the metal filament in the light bulb even when the filament gets hot. The low density of helium causes blimps and weather balloons to float, and its nonreactivity makes helium safer to use than hydrogen. One popular use of noble gases that does *not* rely on their nonreactivity is shown in **Figure 13.**

Argon produces a lavender color.

Xenon produces a blue color.

Neon produces an orange-red color.

Figure 13 *Besides neon, other noble gases are often used in "neon" lights.*

Hydrogen Stands Apart

H
Hydrogen

Electrons in the outer level: 1
Reactivity: Reactive
Other properties: Colorless, odorless gas at room temperature; low density; reacts explosively with oxygen

The properties of hydrogen do not match the properties of any single group, so hydrogen is set apart from the other elements in the table.

Hydrogen is placed above Group 1 in the periodic table because atoms of the alkali metals also have only one electron in their outer level. Atoms of hydrogen, like atoms of alkali metals, can give away one electron when joining with other atoms. However, hydrogen's physical properties are more like the properties of nonmetals than of metals. As you can see, hydrogen really is in a group of its own.

Hydrogen is the most abundant element in the universe. Hydrogen's reactive nature makes it useful as a fuel in rockets, as shown in **Figure 14.**

Figure 14 *Hydrogen reacts violently with oxygen. The hot water vapor that forms as a result pushes the space shuttle into orbit.*

REVIEW

1. In which group are the unreactive nonmetals found?

2. What are two properties of the halogens?

3. **Making Predictions** In the future, a new halogen may be synthesized. Predict its atomic number and properties.

4. **Comparing Concepts** Compare the element hydrogen with the alkali metal sodium.

Chapter Highlights

Vocabulary

periodic *(p. 302)*

periodic law *(p. 303)*

period *(p. 309)*

group *(p. 309)*

Section Notes

- Mendeleev developed the first periodic table. He arranged elements in order of increasing atomic mass. The properties of elements repeated in an orderly pattern, allowing Mendeleev to predict properties for elements that had not yet been discovered.

- Moseley rearranged the elements in order of increasing atomic number.

- The periodic law states that the chemical and physical properties of elements are periodic functions of their atomic numbers.

- Elements in the periodic table are divided into metals, metalloids, and nonmetals.

- Each element has a chemical symbol that is recognized around the world.

- A horizontal row of elements is called a period. The elements gradually change from metallic to nonmetallic from left to right across each period.

- A vertical column of elements is called a group or family. Elements in a group usually have similar properties.

Labs

Create a Periodic Table *(p. 678)*

☑ Skills Check

Visual Understanding

PERIODIC TABLE OF THE ELEMENTS Scientists rely on the periodic table as a resource for a large amount of information. Review the periodic table on pages 304–305. Pay close attention to the labels and the key; they will help you understand the information presented in the table.

CLASSES OF ELEMENTS Identifying an element as a metal, nonmetal, or metalloid gives you a better idea of the properties of that element. Review the figures on pages 306–307 to understand how to use the zigzag line on the periodic table to identify the classes of elements and to review the properties of elements in each category.

Vocabulary

alkali metals *(p. 310)*

alkaline-earth metals *(p. 311)*

halogens *(p. 316)*

noble gases *(p. 316)*

Section Notes

- The alkali metals (Group 1) are the most reactive metals. Atoms of the alkali metals have one electron in their outer level.

- The alkaline-earth metals (Group 2) are less reactive than the alkali metals. Atoms of the alkaline-earth metals have two electrons in their outer level.

- The transition metals (Groups 3–12) include most of the well-known metals as well as the lanthanides and actinides located below the periodic table.

- Groups 13–16 contain the metalloids along with some metals and nonmetals. The atoms of the elements in each of these groups have the same number of electrons in their outer level.

- The halogens (Group 17) are very reactive nonmetals. Atoms of the halogens have seven electrons in their outer level.

- The noble gases (Group 18) are unreactive nonmetals. Atoms of the noble gases have a complete set of electrons in their outer level.

- Hydrogen is set off by itself because its properties do not match the properties of any one group.

 internetconnect

GO TO: go.hrw.com

Visit the **HRW** Web site for a variety of learning tools related to this chapter. Just type in the keyword:

KEYWORD: HSTPRT

GO TO: www.scilinks.org

Visit the **National Science Teachers Association** on-line Web site for Internet resources related to this chapter. Just type in the *sci*LINKS number for more information about the topic:

TOPIC: The Periodic Table	*sci*LINKS NUMBER: HSTP280
TOPIC: Metals	*sci*LINKS NUMBER: HSTP285
TOPIC: Metalloids	*sci*LINKS NUMBER: HSTP290
TOPIC: Nonmetals	*sci*LINKS NUMBER: HSTP295
TOPIC: Buckminster Fuller and the Buckyball	*sci*LINKS NUMBER: HSTP300

Chapter Review

Complete the following sentences by choosing the appropriate term from each pair of terms listed below.

1. Elements in the same vertical column in the periodic table belong to the same __?__. (*group* or *period*)

2. Elements in the same horizontal row in the periodic table belong to the same __?__. (*group* or *period*)

3. The most reactive metals are __?__. (*alkali metals* or *alkaline-earth metals*)

4. Elements that are unreactive are called __?__. (*noble gases* or *halogens*)

UNDERSTANDING CONCEPTS

Multiple Choice

5. An element that is a very reactive gas is most likely a member of the
   a. noble gases.   c. halogens.
   b. alkali metals.   d. actinides.

6. Which statement is true?
   a. Alkali metals are generally found in their uncombined form.
   b. Alkali metals are Group 1 elements.
   c. Alkali metals should be stored under water.
   d. Alkali metals are unreactive.

7. Which statement about the periodic table is false?
   a. There are more metals than nonmetals.
   b. The metalloids are located in Groups 13 through 16.
   c. The elements at the far left of the table are nonmetals.
   d. Elements are arranged by increasing atomic number.

8. One property of most nonmetals is that they are
   a. shiny.
   b. poor conductors of electric current.
   c. flattened when hit with a hammer.
   d. solids at room temperature.

9. Which is a true statement about elements?
   a. Every element occurs naturally.
   b. All elements are found in their uncombined form in nature.
   c. Each element has a unique atomic number.
   d. All of the elements exist in approximately equal quantities.

10. Which is NOT found on the periodic table?
    a. the atomic number of each element
    b. the symbol of each element
    c. the density of each element
    d. the atomic mass of each element

Short Answer

11. Why was Mendeleev's periodic table useful?

12. How is Moseley's basis for arranging the elements different from Mendeleev's?

13. How is the periodic table like a calendar?

14. Describe the location of metals, metalloids, and nonmetals on the periodic table.

Concept Mapping

15. Use the following terms to create a concept map: periodic table, elements, groups, periods, metals, nonmetals, metalloids.

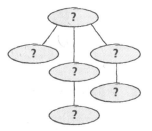

CRITICAL THINKING AND PROBLEM SOLVING

16. When an element with 115 protons in its nucleus is synthesized, will it be a metal, a nonmetal, or a metalloid? Explain.

17. Look at Mendeleev's periodic table in Figure 2. Why was Mendeleev not able to make any predictions about the noble gas elements?

18. Your classmate offers to give you a piece of sodium he found while hiking. What is your response? Explain.

19. Determine the identity of each element described below:
   a. This metal is very reactive, has properties similar to magnesium, and is in the same period as bromine.
   b. This nonmetal is in the same group as lead.
   c. This metal is the most reactive metal in its period and cannot be found uncombined in nature. Each atom of the element contains 19 protons.

MATH IN SCIENCE

20. The chart below shows the percentages of elements in the Earth's crust.

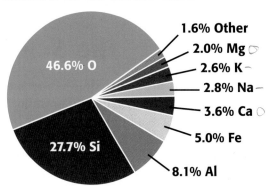

46.6% O
27.7% Si
1.6% Other
2.0% Mg
2.6% K
2.8% Na
3.6% Ca
5.0% Fe
8.1% Al

Excluding the "Other" category, what percentage of the Earth's crust is
   a. alkali metals?
   b. alkaline-earth metals?

INTERPRETING GRAPHICS

21. Study the diagram below to determine the pattern of the images. Predict the missing image, and draw it. Identify which properties are periodic and which properties are shared within a group.

Reading Check-up

Take a minute to review your answers to the Pre-Reading Questions found at the bottom of page 300. Have your answers changed? If necessary, revise your answers based on what you have learned since you began this chapter.

The Periodic Table   **321**

Science, Technology, and Society

The Science of Fireworks

What do the space shuttle and the Fourth of July have in common? The same scientific principles that help scientists launch a space shuttle also help pyrotechnicians create spectacular fireworks shows. The word *pyrotechnics* comes from the Greek words for "fire art." Explosive and dazzling, a fireworks display is both a science and an art.

An Ancient History

More than 1,000 years ago, Chinese civilizations made black powder, the original gunpowder used in pyrotechnics. They used the powder to set off firecrackers and primitive missiles. Black powder is still used today to launch fireworks into the air and to give fireworks an explosive charge. Even the ingredients—saltpeter (potassium nitrate), charcoal, and sulfur—haven't changed since ancient times.

Quick-burning fuse

Time-delay fuse

Light-burst mixture

Fuse

Sound-burst mixture

Black-powder propellant

▲ *Cutaway view of a typical firework. Each shell creates a different type of display.*

Snap, Crackle, Pop!

The shells of fireworks contain the ingredients that create the explosions. Inside the shells, black powder and other chemicals are packed in layers. When ignited, one layer may cause a bright burst of light while a second layer produces a loud booming sound. The shell's shape affects the shape of the explosion. Cylindrical shells produce a trail of lights that looks like an umbrella. Round shells produce a star-burst pattern of lights.

The color and sound of fireworks depend on the chemicals used. To create colors, chemicals like strontium (for red), magnesium (for white), and copper (for blue) can be mixed with the gunpowder.

Explosion in the Sky

Fireworks are launched from metal, plastic, or cardboard tubes. Black powder at the bottom of the shell explodes and shoots the shell into the sky. A fuse begins to burn when the shell is launched. Seconds later, when the explosive chemicals are high in the air, the burning fuse lights another charge of black powder. This ignites the rest of the ingredients in the shell, causing an explosion that lights up the sky!

Bang for Your Buck

▶ The fireworks used during New Year's Eve and Fourth of July celebrations can cost anywhere from $200 to $2,000 apiece. Count the number of explosions at the next fireworks show you see. If each of the fireworks cost just $200 to produce, how much would the fireworks for the entire show cost?

BUCKYBALLS

Researchers are scrambling for the ball—the buckyball, that is. This special form of carbon has 60 carbon atoms linked together in a shape much like a soccer ball. Scientists are having a field day trying to find new uses for this unusual molecule.

Potassium atom trapped inside buckyball

Carbon atoms

Bond

▲ *The buckyball, short for buckminster-fullerene, was named after architect Buckminster Fuller.*

The Starting Lineup

Named for architect Buckminster Fuller, bucky-balls resemble the geodesic domes that are characteristic of the architect's work. Excitement over buckyballs began in 1985 when scientists projected light from a laser onto a piece of graphite. In the soot that remained, researchers found a completely new kind of molecule! Buckyballs are also found in the soot from a candle flame. Some scientists claim to have detected buckyballs in outer space. In fact, one hypothesis suggests that buckyballs might be at the center of the condensing clouds of gas, dust, and debris that form galaxies.

The Game Plan

Ever since buckyballs were discovered, chemists have been busy trying to identify the molecules' properties. One interesting property is that sub-stances can be trapped inside a buckyball. A buckyball can act like a cage that surrounds smaller substances, such as individual atoms. Buckyballs also appear to be both slippery and strong. They can be opened to insert materials, and they can even link together in tubes.

How can buckyballs be used? They may have a variety of uses, from carrying messages through atom-sized wires in computer chips to delivering medicines right where the body needs them. Making tough plastics and cutting tools are uses that are also under investigation. With so many possibilities, scientists expect to get a kick out of bucky-balls for some time!

The Kickoff

▶ A soccer ball is a great model for a buckyball. On the model, the places where three seams meet correspond to the carbon atoms on a buckyball. What represents the bonds between carbon atoms? Does your soccer-ball model have space for all 60 carbon atoms? You'll have to count and see for yourself.

UNIT

5

Interactions of Matter

In this unit you will study the inter-actions through which matter can change its identity. You will learn how atoms bond with one another to form compounds and how atoms join in different combinations to form new substances through chemical reactions. You will also learn about the prop-erties of several cate-gories of compounds. Finally, you will learn how nuclear interac-tions can actually change the identity of an atom. This timeline includes some of the events leading to the current understanding of these interactions of matter.

1828

Urea, a compound found in urine, is produced in a laboratory. Until this time, chemists had believed that compounds created by living organisms could not be produced in the laboratory.

➤ 1858

German chemist Friedrich August Kekulé suggests that carbon forms four chemical bonds and can form long chains of car-bon bonded to itself.

1964 ◀

Dr. Martin Luther King, Jr., American civil rights leader, is awarded the Nobel Peace Prize.

1969 ◀

The *Nimbus III* weather satellite is launched by the United States, representing the first civilian use of nuclear batteries.

➤ 1979

Public fear about nuclear power grows after an accident occurs at the Three Mile Island nuclear power station, in Pennsylvania.

1867

Swedish chemist Alfred Nobel develops dynamite. Dynamite's explosive power is a result of the decomposition reaction of nitroglycerin.

1898

The United States defeats Spain in the Spanish-American War.

1942

The first nuclear chain reaction is carried out in a squash court under the football stadium at the University of Chicago.

1903

Marie Curie, Pierre Curie, and Henri Becquerel are awarded the Nobel Prize in Physics for the discovery of radioactivity.

1996

Evidence of organic compounds in a meteorite leads scientists to speculate that life may have existed on Mars more than 3.6 billion years ago.

2001

The first total solar eclipse of the millenium occurs on June 21.

Chemical Bonding

Pre-Reading
Questions

1. What is a chemical bond?
2. How are ionic bonds different from covalent bonds?
3. How are the properties of metals related to the type of bonds in them?

BONDED FOR LIFE

Look at the photo. What looks like a fantastic modern art "sculpture" is actually a model of DNA, one of the longest and most complex molecules in living things. In DNA, two very long spiral strands of atoms bond together, forming a double spiral. The DNA in living cells contains all the coding for passing on the traits of that cell and that organism to each new cell as it is formed. In this chapter, you will learn how atoms bond in different ways during chemical reactions.

FROM GLUE TO GOOP

Particles of glue can bond to other particles and hold objects together. Different types of bonds create differences in the properties of substances. In this activity, you will see how the formation of bonds causes an interesting change in the properties of white glue.

Procedure

1. Fill a **small paper cup** $\frac{1}{4}$ full of **white glue.** Observe the properties of the glue, and record your observations.

2. Fill a **second small paper cup** $\frac{1}{4}$ full of **borax solution.**

3. Pour the borax solution into the cup containing the white glue, and stir well using a **plastic spoon.**

4. When it becomes too thick to stir, remove the material from the cup and knead it with your fingers. Observe the properties of the material, and record your observations.

Analysis

5. Compare the properties of the glue with those of the new material.

6. The properties of the new material resulted from the bonds between the borax and the particles of the glue. If too little borax were used, in what way would the properties of the material have been different?

Electrons and Chemical Bonding

Terms to Learn

chemical bonding
chemical bond
valence electrons

What You'll Do

◆ Describe chemical bonding.
◆ Identify the number of valence electrons in an atom.
◆ Predict whether an atom is likely to form bonds.

Have you ever stopped to consider that by using just the 26 letters of the alphabet, you make all of the words you use every day? Even though the number of letters is limited, their ability to be combined in different ways allows you to make an enormous number of words.

Now look around the room. Everything around you—desks, chalk, paper, even your friends—is made of atoms of elements. How can so many substances be formed from about 100 elements? In the same way that words can be formed by combining letters, different substances can be formed by combining atoms.

 Science
CONNECTION

Why are the amino acids that are chemically bonded together to form your proteins all left-handed? Read about one cosmic explanation on page 346.

Atoms Combine Through Chemical Bonding

The atoms of just three elements—carbon, hydrogen, and oxygen—combine in different patterns to form the substances sugar, alcohol, and citric acid. **Chemical bonding** is the joining of atoms to form new substances. The properties of these new substances are different from those of the original elements. A force of attraction that holds two atoms together is called a **chemical bond.** As you will see, chemical bonds involve the electrons in the atoms.

Atoms and the chemical bonds that connect them cannot be observed with your eyes. During the past 150 years, scientists have performed many experiments that have led to the development of a theory of chemical bonding. Remember that a *theory* is a unifying explanation for a broad range of hypotheses and observations that have been supported by testing. The use of models helps people to discuss the theory of how and why atoms form chemical bonds.

Electron Number and Organization

To understand how atoms form chemical bonds, you first need to know how many electrons are in a particular atom and how the electrons in an atom are organized. The number of electrons in an atom can be determined from the atomic number of the element. The atomic number is the number of protons in an atom. However, atoms have no charge, so the atomic number also represents the number of electrons in the atom.

The electrons in an atom are organized in energy levels. The levels farther from the nucleus contain electrons that have more energy than levels closer to the nucleus. The arrangement of electrons in a chlorine atom is shown in **Figure 1.**

Figure 1 Electron Arrangement in an Atom

ⓐ The **first energy level** is closest to the nucleus and can hold up to 2 electrons.

ⓑ Electrons will enter the **second energy level** only after the first level is full. The second energy level can hold up to 8 electrons.

ⓒ The **third energy level** in this model of a chlorine atom contains only 7 electrons, for a total of 17 electrons in the atom. This outer level of the atom is not full.

Outer-Level Electrons Are the Key to Bonding As you just saw in Figure 1, a chlorine atom has a total of 17 electrons. When a chlorine atom bonds to another atom, not all of these electrons are used to create the bond. Most atoms form bonds using only the electrons in their outermost energy level. The electrons in the outermost energy level of an atom are called **valence** (VAY luhns) **electrons.** Thus, a chlorine atom has 7 valence electrons. You can see the valence electrons for atoms of some other elements in **Figure 2.**

Figure 2 *Valence electrons are the electrons in the outermost energy level of an atom.*

Oxygen
Electron total: 8
First level: 2 electrons
Second level: 6 electrons

The second energy level is the outermost level, so an oxygen atom has 6 valence electrons.

Sodium
Electron total: 11
First level: 2 electrons
Second level: 8 electrons
Third level: 1 electron

The third energy level is the outermost level, so a sodium atom has 1 valence electron.

Valence Electrons and the Periodic Table You can determine the number of valence electrons in Figure 2 because you have a model to look at. But what if you didn't have a model? You have a tool that helps you determine the number of valence electrons for some elements—the periodic table!

Remember that elements in a group often have similar properties, including the number of electrons in the outermost energy level of their atoms. The number of valence electrons for many elements is related to the group number, as shown in **Figure 3.**

Figure 3 Determining the Number of Valence Electrons

Atoms of elements in **Groups 1 and 2** have the same number of valence electrons as their group number.

Atoms of elements in **Groups 13–18** have 10 fewer valence electrons than their group number. However, helium atoms have only 2 valence electrons.

Atoms of elements in **Groups 3–12** do not have a general rule relating their valence electrons to their group number.

H																	18
1	2											13	14	15	16	17	He
Li	Be											B	C	N	O	F	Ne
Na	Mg	3	4	5	6	7	8	9	10	11	12	Al	Si	P	S	Cl	Ar
K	Ca	Sc	Ti	V	Cr	Mn	Fe	Co	Ni	Cu	Zn	Ga	Ge	As	Se	Br	Kr
Rb	Sr	Y	Zr	Nb	Mo	Tc	Ru	Rh	Pd	Ag	Cd	In	Sn	Sb	Te	I	Xe
Cs	Ba	La	Hf	Ta	W	Re	Os	Ir	Pt	Au	Hg	Tl	Pb	Bi	Po	At	Rn
Fr	Ra	Ac	Rf	Db	Sg	Bh	Hs	Mt	Uun	Uuu	Uub						

Activity

Determine the number of valence electrons in each of the following atoms: lithium (Li), beryllium (Be), aluminum (Al), carbon (C), nitrogen (N), sulfur (S), bromine (Br), and krypton (Kr).

TRY at HOME

To Bond or Not to Bond

Atoms do not all bond in the same manner. In fact, some atoms rarely bond at all! The number of electrons in the outermost energy level of an atom determines whether an atom will form bonds.

Atoms of the noble, or inert, gases (Group 18) do not normally form chemical bonds. As you just learned, atoms of Group 18 elements (except helium) have 8 valence electrons. Therefore, having 8 valence electrons must be a special condition. In fact, atoms that have 8 electrons in their outermost energy level do not normally form new bonds. The outermost energy level of an atom is considered to be full if it contains 8 electrons.

Atoms Bond to Have a Filled Outermost Level An atom that has fewer than 8 valence electrons is more reactive, or more likely to form bonds, than an atom with 8 valence electrons. Atoms bond by gaining, losing, or sharing electrons in order to have a filled outermost energy level with 8 valence electrons. **Figure 4** describes the ways in which atoms can achieve a filled outermost energy level.

Figure 4 *These atoms achieve a full set of valence electrons in different ways.*

Sulfur

An atom of sulfur has 6 valence electrons. It can have 8 valence electrons by sharing 2 electrons with or gaining 2 electrons from other atoms to fill its outermost energy level.

Magnesium

An atom of magnesium has 2 valence electrons. It can have a full outer level by losing 2 electrons. The second energy level becomes the outermost energy level and contains a full set of 8 electrons.

A Full Set—with Two? Not all atoms need 8 valence electrons for a filled outermost energy level. Helium atoms need only 2 valence electrons. With only 2 electrons in the entire atom, the first energy level (which is also the outermost energy level) is full. Atoms of hydrogen and lithium form bonds with other atoms in order to have 2 electrons.

internet connect

*sci*LINKS
NSTA

TOPIC: The Electron, The Periodic Table
GO TO: www.scilinks.org
*sci*LINKS **NUMBER:** HSTP305, HSTP310

REVIEW

1. What is a chemical bond?

2. What are valence electrons?

3. How many valence electrons does a silicon atom have?

4. Predict how atoms with 5 valence electrons will achieve a full set of valence electrons.

5. **Interpreting Graphics** At right is a diagram of a fluorine atom. Will fluorine form bonds? Explain.

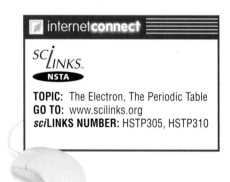

Fluorine

Types of Chemical Bonds

Terms to Learn

ionic bond   covalent bond
ions   molecule
crystal lattice   metallic bond

What You'll Do

◆ Describe ionic, covalent, and metallic bonding.
◆ Describe the properties associated with substances containing each type of bond.

Atoms bond by gaining, losing, or sharing electrons to have a filled outermost energy level containing eight valence electrons. The way in which atoms interact through their valence electrons determines the type of bond that forms. The three types of bonds are ionic (ie AHN ik), covalent (koн VAY luhnt), and metallic.

Ionic Bonds

The materials shown in **Figure 5** have much in common. They are all hard, brittle solids at room temperature, they all have high melting points, and they all contain ionic bonds. An **ionic bond** is the force of attraction between oppositely charged ions. **Ions** are charged particles that form during chemical changes when one or more valence electrons transfer from one atom to another.

A Transfer of Electrons An atom is neutral because the number of electrons equals the number of protons. So their charges cancel each other. A transfer of electrons between atoms changes the number of electrons in each atom, while the number of protons stays the same. The negative charges and positive charges no longer cancel out, and the atoms become ions. Although an atom cannot gain (or lose) electrons without another atom nearby to lose (or gain) electrons, it is easier to study the formation of ions one at a time.

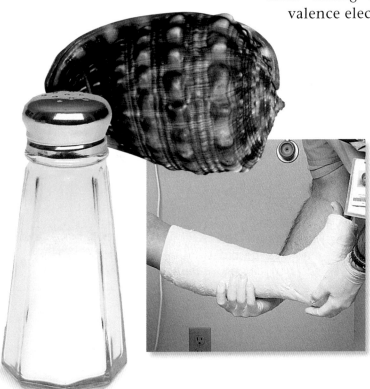

Figure 5 *Calcium carbonate in seashells, sodium chloride in table salt, and calcium sulfate used to make plaster of Paris casts all contain ionic bonds.*

Atoms That Lose Electrons Form Positive Ions Ionic bonds form during chemical changes when atoms pull electrons away from other atoms. The atoms that lose electrons form ions that have fewer electrons than protons. Because the positive charges outnumber the negative charges, these ions have an overall positive charge.

Metal Atoms Lose Electrons Atoms of most metals have few electrons in their outer energy level. When metal atoms bond with other atoms, the metal atoms tend to lose these valence electrons and form positive ions. For example, look at the model in **Figure 6.** An atom of sodium has one valence electron. When a sodium atom loses this electron to another atom, it becomes a sodium ion. A sodium ion has a charge of 1+ because it contains 1 more proton than electrons. To show the difference between a sodium atom and a sodium ion, the chemical symbol for the ion is written as Na^+. Notice that the charge is written to the upper right of the chemical symbol. Figure 6 also shows a model for the formation of an aluminum ion.

Figure 6 Forming Positive Ions

Sodium atom (Na)
11+ protons
11− electrons
  0   charge

Sodium ion (Na^+)
11+ protons
10− electrons
  1+ charge

Here's How It Works: During chemical changes, a sodium atom can lose its 1 electron in the third energy level to another atom. The filled second level becomes the outermost level, so the resulting sodium ion has 8 valence electrons.

Aluminum atom (Al)
13+ protons
13− electrons
  0   charge

Aluminum ion (Al^{3+})
13+ protons
10− electrons
  3+ charge

Here's How It Works: During chemical changes, an aluminum atom can lose its 3 electrons in the third energy level to another atom. The filled second level becomes the outermost level, so the resulting aluminum ion has 8 valence electrons.

The Energy of Losing Electrons When an atom loses electrons, energy is needed to overcome the attraction between the electrons and the protons in the atom's nucleus. Removing electrons from atoms of metals requires only a small amount of energy, so metal atoms lose electrons easily. In fact, the energy needed to remove electrons from atoms of elements in Groups 1 and 2 is so low that these elements react very easily and can be found only as ions in nature. On the other hand, removing electrons from atoms of nonmetals requires a large amount of energy. Rather than give up electrons, these atoms gain electrons when they form ionic bonds.

Self-Check

Look at the periodic table, and determine which noble gas has the same electron arrangement as a sodium ion. *(See page 724 to check your answer.)*

MATH BREAK

Charge!

Calculating the charge of an ion is the same as adding integers (positive or negative whole numbers or zero) with opposite signs. You write the number of protons as a positive integer and the number of electrons as a negative integer and then add the integers. Calculate the charge of an ion that contains 16 protons and 18 electrons. Write the ion's symbol and name.

Atoms That Gain Electrons Form Negative Ions Atoms that gain electrons from other atoms during chemical changes form ions that have more electrons than protons. The negative charges outnumber the positive charges, giving each of these ions an overall negative charge.

The outermost energy level of nonmetal atoms is almost full. Only a few electrons are needed to fill the outer level, so atoms of nonmetals tend to gain electrons from other atoms. For example, look at the model in **Figure 7.** An atom of chlorine has 7 valence electrons. When a chlorine atom gains 1 electron to complete its outer level, it becomes an ion with a 1– charge called a chloride ion. The symbol for the chloride ion is Cl⁻. Notice that the name of the negative ion formed from chlorine has the ending *-ide*. This ending is used for the names of the negative ions formed when atoms gain electrons. Figure 7 also shows a model of how an oxide ion is formed.

Figure 7 Forming Negative Ions

Chlorine atom (Cl)	Chloride ion (Cl⁻)	Oxygen atom (O)	Oxide ion (O²⁻)
17+ protons	17+ protons	8+ protons	8+ protons
17– electrons	18– electrons	8– electrons	10– electrons
0 charge	1– charge	0 charge	2– charge

Here's How It Works: During chemical changes, a chlorine atom gains 1 electron in the third energy level from another atom. A chloride ion is formed with 8 valence electrons. Thus, its outermost energy level is filled.

Here's How It Works: During chemical changes, an oxygen atom gains 2 electrons in the second energy level from another atom. An oxide ion is formed with 8 valence electrons. Thus, its outermost energy level is filled.

The Energy of Gaining Electrons Atoms of most nonmetals fill their outermost energy level by gaining electrons. Energy is given off by most nonmetal atoms during this process. The more easily an atom gains an electron, the more energy an atom gives off. Atoms of the Group 17 elements (the halogens) give off the most energy when they gain an electron. The halogens, such as fluorine and chlorine, are extremely reactive nonmetals because they release a large amount of energy.

Charged Ions Form a Neutral Compound When a metal reacts with a nonmetal, the same number of electrons is lost by the metal atoms as is gained by the nonmetal atoms. Even though the ions that bond are charged, the compound formed is neutral because the charges of the ions cancel each other through ionic bonding. An ionic bond is an example of electrostatic attraction in which opposite electric charges stick together. Another example is static cling, illustrated in **Figure 8.**

Figure 8 *Like ionic bonds, static cling is the result of the attraction between opposite charges.*

Ions Bond to Form a Crystal Lattice The ions that make up an ionic compound are bonded in a repeating three-dimensional pattern called a **crystal lattice** (KRI stuhl LAT is). In ionic compounds, such as table salt, the ions in the crystal lattice are arranged as alternating positive and negative ions, forming a solid. The model in **Figure 9** shows a small part of a crystal lattice. The arrangement of bonded ions in a crystal lattice determines the shape of the crystals of an ionic compound.

The strong force of attraction between bonded ions in a crystal lattice gives ionic compounds certain properties, including a high melting point and boiling point. Ionic compounds tend to be brittle solids at room temperature and usually break apart when hit with a hammer.

Figure 9 *This model of the crystal lattice of sodium chloride, or table salt, shows a three-dimensional view of the bonded ions.*

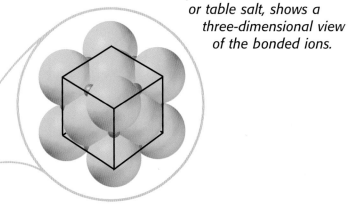

REVIEW

1. How does an atom become a negative ion?

2. What are two properties of ionic compounds?

3. **Applying Concepts** Which group of elements lose 2 valence electrons when their atoms form ionic bonds? What charge would the ions formed have?

Covalent Bonds

Most materials you encounter every day, such as water, sugar, and carbon dioxide, are held together by bonds that do not involve ions. These substances tend to have low melting and boiling points, and some of these substances are brittle in the solid state. The type of bonds found in these substances, including the substances shown in **Figure 10,** are covalent bonds.

A **covalent bond** is the force of attraction between the nuclei of atoms and the electrons shared by the atoms. When two atoms of nonmetals bond, a large amount of energy is required for either atom to lose an electron, so no ions are formed. Rather than transferring electrons to complete their outermost energy levels, two nonmetal atoms bond by sharing electrons with one another, as shown in the model in **Figure 11.**

Figure 10 *Covalent bonds are found in this plastic ball, the paddle's rubber covering, the cotton fibers in clothes, and even many of the substances that make up the human body!*

Figure 11 *By sharing electrons in a covalent bond, each hydrogen atom (the smallest atom known) has a full outermost energy level containing two electrons.*

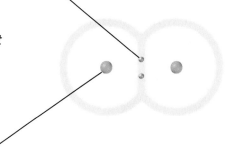

The shared electrons spend most of their time between the nuclei of the atoms.

The protons and the shared electrons attract one another. This attraction is the basis of the covalent bond that holds the atoms together.

Make models of molecules out of marshmallows on page 680 of the LabBook.

Covalently Bonded Atoms Make Up Molecules The particles of substances containing covalent bonds differ from those containing ionic bonds. Ionic compounds consist of ions organized in a crystal. Covalent compounds consist of individual particles called molecules (MAHL i ĸʏooʟz). A **molecule** is a neutral group of atoms held together by covalent bonds. In Figure 11, you saw a model of a hydrogen molecule, which is composed of two hydrogen atoms covalently bonded. However, most molecules are composed of atoms of two or more elements. The models in **Figure 12** show two ways to represent the covalent bonds in a molecule.

Figure 12 Covalent Bonds in a Water Molecule

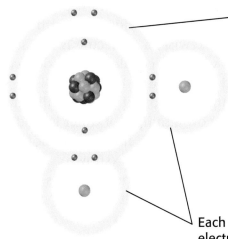

Through covalent bonding, the oxygen atom shares one of its electrons with each of the two hydrogen atoms. As a result, it has a filled outermost energy level with 8 electrons.

Each hydrogen atom shares its 1 electron with the oxygen atom. This allows each hydrogen to have a filled outer level with 2 electrons.

Another way to show covalent bonds is to draw an electron-dot diagram. An electron-dot diagram shows only the outermost level of electrons for each atom. But you can still see how electrons are shared between the atoms.

Making Electron-Dot Diagrams

An electron-dot diagram is a model that shows only the valence electrons in an atom. Electron-dot diagrams are helpful when predicting how atoms might bond. You draw an electron-dot diagram by writing the symbol of the element and placing the correct number of dots around it. This type of model can help you to better understand bonding by showing the number of valence electrons and how atoms share electrons to fill their outermost energy levels, as shown below.

Carbon atoms have 4 valence electrons, so 4 dots are placed around the symbol. A carbon atom needs 4 more electrons for a filled outermost energy level.

Oxygen atoms have 6 valence electrons, so 6 dots are placed around the symbol. An oxygen atom needs only 2 more electrons for a filled outermost energy level.

: Kr :

The noble gas krypton has a full set of 8 valence electrons in its atoms. Thus, krypton is nonreactive because its atoms do not need any more electrons.

H : H

This electron-dot diagram represents hydrogen gas, the same substance shown in the model in Figure 11.

 Self-Check

1. How many dots does the electron-dot diagram of a sulfur atom have?
2. How is a covalent bond different from an ionic bond?
   (See page 724 to check your answers.)

Figure 13 *The water in this fishbowl is made up of many tiny water molecules. Each molecule is the smallest particle that still has the chemical properties of water.*

A Molecule Is the Smallest Particle of a Covalent Compound An atom is the smallest particle into which an element can be divided and still be the same substance. Likewise, a molecule is the smallest particle into which a covalently bonded compound can be divided and still be the same compound. **Figure 13** illustrates how a sample of water is made up of many individual molecules of water (shown as three-dimensional models). If you could divide water over and over, you would eventually end up with a single molecule of water. However, if you separated the hydrogen and oxygen atoms that make up a water molecule, you would no longer have water.

Activity

Try your hand at drawing electron-dot diagrams for a molecule of chlorine (a diatomic molecule) and a molecule of ammonia (one nitrogen atom bonded with three hydrogen atoms).

TRY at HOME

The Simplest Molecules All molecules are composed of at least two covalently bonded atoms. The simplest molecules, known as *diatomic molecules,* consist of two atoms bonded together. Some elements are called diatomic elements because they are found in nature as diatomic molecules composed of two atoms of the element. Hydrogen is a diatomic element, as you saw in Figure 11. Oxygen, nitrogen, and the halogens fluorine, chlorine, bromine, and iodine are also diatomic. By sharing electrons, both atoms of a diatomic molecule can fill their outer energy level, as shown in **Figure 14.**

Figure 14 Models of a Diatomic Fluorine Molecule

Two covalently bonded fluorine atoms have filled outermost energy levels. The pair of electrons shared by the atoms are counted as valence electrons for each atom.

This is a three-dimensional model of a fluorine molecule.

More-Complex Molecules Diatomic molecules are the simplest—and some of the most important—of all molecules. You could not live without diatomic oxygen molecules. But other important molecules are much more complex. Gasoline, plastic, and even proteins in the cells of your body are examples of complex molecules. Carbon atoms are the basis of many of these complex molecules. Each carbon atom needs to make 4 covalent bonds to have 8 valence electrons. These bonds can be with atoms of other elements or with other carbon atoms, as shown in the model in **Figure 15.**

Biology
CONNECTION

Proteins perform many functions throughout your body, such as digesting your food, building components of your cells, and transporting nutrients to each cell. A single protein can have a chain of 7,000 atoms of carbon and nitrogen with atoms of other elements covalently bonded to it.

Figure 15 *A granola bar contains sucrose, or table sugar. A molecule of sucrose is composed of carbon atoms, hydrogen atoms, and oxygen atoms joined by covalent bonds.*

Hydrogen

Carbon

Oxygen

Metallic Bonds

Look at the unusual metal sculpture shown in **Figure 16.** Notice that some metal pieces have been flattened, while other metal pieces have been shaped into wires. How could the artist change the shape of the metal into all of these different forms without breaking the metal into pieces? A metal can be shaped because of the presence of a special type of bond called a metallic bond. A **metallic bond** is the force of attraction between a positively charged metal ion and the electrons in a metal. (Remember that metal atoms tend to lose electrons and form positively charged ions.)

Figure 16 *The different shapes of metal in this sculpture are possible because of the bonds that hold the metal together.*

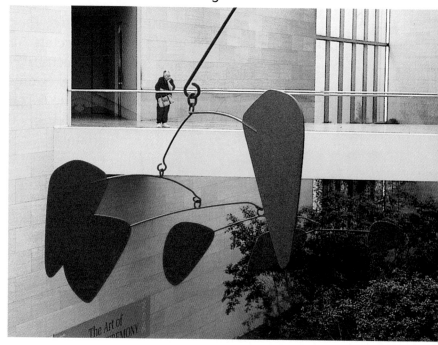

The Art of

Electrons Move Throughout a Metal The scientific understanding of the bonding in metals is that the metal atoms get so close to one another that their outermost energy levels overlap. This allows their valence electrons to move throughout the metal from the energy level of one atom to the energy levels of the atoms nearby. The atoms form a crystal much like the ions associated with ionic bonding. However, the negative charges (electrons) in the metal are free to move about. You can think of a metal as being made up of positive metal ions with enough valence electrons "swimming" about to keep the ions together and to cancel the positive charge of the ions, as shown in **Figure 17.** The ions are held together because metallic bonds extend throughout the metal in all directions.

Figure 17 *The moving electrons are attracted to the metal ions, forming metallic bonds.*

The positive metal ions are in fixed positions in the metal.

Negative electrons are free to move about.

Metals Conduct Electric Current Metallic bonding is the reason why metals have particular properties. One of these properties is electrical conductivity—the ability to conduct electric current. For example, when you turn on a lamp, electrons move within the copper wire that connects the lamp with the outlet. The electrons that move are the valence electrons in the copper atoms. These electrons are free to move because of metallic bonds—they are not connected to any one atom.

Metals Can Be Reshaped Metallic bonds allow atoms in metals to be rearranged. As a result, metals can be reshaped. The properties of *ductility* (the ability to be drawn into wires) and *malleability* (the ability to be hammered into sheets) describe a metal's ability to be reshaped. For example, copper is made into wires for use in electrical cords. Aluminum can be pounded into thin sheets and made into aluminum foil and cans.

BRAIN FOOD

Gold can be pounded out to make a foil only a few atoms thick. A piece of gold the size of the head of a pin can be beaten into a thin "leaf" that would cover this page!

How Metals Can Bend Without Breaking When a piece of metal is bent, some of the metal ions are forced closer together. You might expect the metal to break because the positive ions repel one another. However, even in their new positions, the positive ions are surrounded by and attracted to the electrons, as shown in **Figure 18.** (Ionic compounds do break when hit because neither the positive ions nor the negative ions are free to move.)

Figure 18 *The shape of a metal can be changed without breaking because metallic bonds occur in many directions.*

The repulsion between the positively charged metal ions increases as the ions are pushed closer to one another.

The moving electrons maintain the metallic bonds no matter how the shape of the metal changes.

APPLY

Metallic Bonding in Staples

Although they are not very glamorous, metal staples are very useful in holding things such as sheets of paper together. Explain how the metallic bonds in a staple allow it to change shape so that it can function properly.

REVIEW

1. What happens to electrons in covalent bonding?

2. What type of element is most likely to form covalent bonds?

3. What is a metallic bond?

4. **Interpreting Graphics** This electron-dot diagram is not yet complete. Which atom needs to form another covalent bond? How do you know?

internet**connect**

*sci*LINKS.
NSTA

TOPIC: Types of Chemical Bonds, Properties of Metals
GO TO: www.scilinks.org
*sci*LINKS NUMBER: HSTP315, HSTP320

Chapter Highlights

Vocabulary

chemical bonding *(p. 328)*

chemical bond *(p. 328)*

valence electrons *(p. 329)*

Section Notes

• Chemical bonding is the joining of atoms to form new substances. A chemical bond is a force of attraction that holds two atoms together.

• Valence electrons are the electrons in the outermost energy level of an atom. These electrons are used to form bonds.

• Most atoms form bonds by gaining, losing, or sharing electrons until they have 8 valence electrons. Atoms of hydrogen, lithium, and helium need only 2 electrons to fill their outermost level.

Vocabulary

ionic bond *(p. 332)*

ions *(p. 332)*

crystal lattice *(p. 335)*

covalent bond *(p. 336)*

molecule *(p. 336)*

metallic bond *(p. 339)*

Section Notes

• In ionic bonding, electrons are transferred between two atoms. The atom that loses electrons becomes a positive ion. The atom that gains electrons becomes a negative ion. The force of attraction between these oppositely charged ions is an ionic bond.

• Ionic bonding usually occurs between atoms of metals and atoms of nonmetals.

☑ Skills Check

Math Concepts

CALCULATING CHARGE To calculate the charge of an ion, you must add integers with opposite signs. The total positive charge of the ion (the number of protons) is written as a positive integer. The total negative charge of the ion (the number of electrons) is written as a negative integer. For example, the charge of an ion containing 11 protons and 10 electrons would be calculated as follows:

$$(11+) + (10-) = 1+$$

Visual Understanding

DETERMINING VALENCE ELECTRONS Knowing the number of valence electrons in an atom is important in predicting how it will bond with other atoms. Review Figure 3 on page 330 to learn how an element's location on the periodic table helps you determine the number of valence electrons in an atom.

FORMING IONS Turn back to Figures 6 and 7 on pages 333–334 to review how ions are formed when atoms lose or gain electrons.

- Energy is needed to remove electrons from metal atoms to form positive ions. Energy is released when most non-metal atoms gain electrons to form negative ions.

- In covalent bonding, electrons are shared by two atoms. The force of attraction between the nuclei of the atoms and the shared electrons is a covalent bond.

- Covalent bonding usually occurs between atoms of nonmetals.

- Electron-dot diagrams are a simple way to represent the valence electrons in an atom.

- Covalently bonded atoms form a particle called a molecule. A molecule is the smallest particle of a compound with the chemical properties of the compound.

- Diatomic elements are the only elements found in nature as diatomic molecules consisting of two atoms of the same element covalently bonded together.

- In metallic bonding, the outermost energy levels of metal atoms overlap, allowing the valence electrons to move throughout the metal. The force of attraction between a positive metal ion and the electrons in the metal is a metallic bond.

- Many properties of metals, such as conductivity, ductility, and malleability, result from the freely moving electrons in the metal.

Labs
Covalent Marshmallows (*p. 680*)

internetconnect

GO TO: go.hrw.com

Visit the **HRW** Web site for a variety of learning tools related to this chapter. Just type in the keyword:

KEYWORD: HSTBND

GO TO: www.scilinks.org

Visit the **National Science Teachers Association** on-line Web site for Internet resources related to this chapter. Just type in the *sci*LINKS number for more information about the topic:

TOPIC:	The Electron	*sci*LINKS NUMBER: HSTP305
TOPIC:	The Periodic Table	*sci*LINKS NUMBER: HSTP310
TOPIC:	Types of Chemical Bonds	*sci*LINKS NUMBER: HSTP315
TOPIC:	Properties of Metals	*sci*LINKS NUMBER: HSTP320

Chapter Review

USING VOCABULARY

To complete the following sentences, choose the correct term from each pair of terms listed below.

1. The force of attraction that holds two atoms together is a ____. (*crystal lattice* or *chemical bond*)

2. Charged particles that form when atoms transfer electrons are ____. (*molecules* or *ions*)

3. The force of attraction between the nuclei of atoms and shared electrons is a(n) ____. (*ionic bond* or *covalent bond*)

4. Electrons free to move throughout a material are associated with a(n) ____. (*ionic bond* or *metallic bond*)

5. Shared electrons are associated with a ____. (*covalent bond* or *metallic bond*)

UNDERSTANDING CONCEPTS

Multiple Choice

6. Which element has a full outermost energy level containing only two electrons?
   a. oxygen (O)   c. fluorine (F)
   b. hydrogen (H)   d. helium (He)

7. Which of the following describes what happens when an atom becomes an ion with a 2– charge?
   a. The atom gains 2 protons.
   b. The atom loses 2 protons.
   c. The atom gains 2 electrons.
   d. The atom loses 2 electrons.

8. The properties of ductility and malleability are associated with which type of bonds?
   a. ionic
   b. covalent
   c. metallic
   d. none of the above

9. In which area of the periodic table do you find elements whose atoms easily gain electrons?
   a. across the top two rows
   b. across the bottom row
   c. on the right side
   d. on the left side

10. What type of element tends to lose electrons when it forms bonds?
   a. metal
   b. metalloid
   c. nonmetal
   d. noble gas

11. Which pair of atoms can form an ionic bond?
   a. sodium (Na) and potassium (K)
   b. potassium (K) and fluorine (F)
   c. fluorine (F) and chlorine (Cl)
   d. sodium (Na) and neon (Ne)

Short Answer

12. List two properties of covalent compounds.

13. Explain why an iron ion is attracted to a sulfide ion but not to a zinc ion.

14. Using your knowledge of valence electrons, explain the main reason so many different molecules are made from carbon atoms.

15. Compare the three types of bonds based on what happens to the valence electrons of the atoms.

Concept Mapping

16. Use the following terms to create a concept map: chemical bonds, ionic bonds, covalent bonds, metallic bonds, molecule, ions.

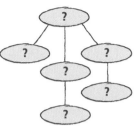

CRITICAL THINKING AND PROBLEM SOLVING

17. Predict the type of bond each of the following pairs of atoms would form:
    a. zinc (Zn) and zinc (Zn)
    b. oxygen (O) and nitrogen (N)
    c. phosphorus (P) and oxygen (O)
    d. magnesium (Mg) and chlorine (Cl)

18. Draw electron-dot diagrams for each of the following atoms, and state how many bonds it will have to make to fill its outer energy level.
    a. sulfur (S)
    b. nitrogen (N)
    c. neon (Ne)
    d. iodine (I)
    e. silicon (Si)

19. Does the substance being hit in the photo below contain ionic or metallic bonds? Explain.

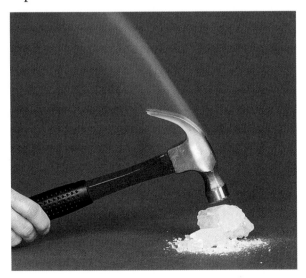

20. For each atom below, write the number of electrons it must gain or lose to have 8 valence electrons. Then calculate the charge of the ion that would form.
    a. calcium (Ca)   c. bromine (Br)
    b. phosphorus (P)   d. sulfur (S)

Look at the picture of the wooden pencil below, and answer the following questions.

21. In which part of the pencil are metallic bonds found?

22. List three materials composed of molecules with covalent bonds.

23. Identify two differences between the properties of the metallically bonded material and one of the covalently bonded materials.

Reading Check-up

Take a minute to review your answers to the Pre-Reading Questions found at the bottom of page 326. Have your answers changed? If necessary, revise your answers based on what you have learned since you began this chapter.

Left-Handed Molecules

Some researchers think that light from a newly forming star 1,500 light-years away (1 light-year is equal to about 9.6 trillion kilometers) may hold the answer to an Earthly riddle that has been puzzling scientists for over 100 years!

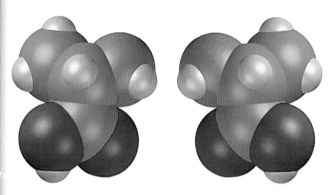

▲ *Molecules, such as the carbon molecules shown above, often come in two mirror-image forms, just as hands do.*

We Are All Lefties!

In 1848, Louis Pasteur discovered that carbon-containing molecules come in left-handed and right-handed forms. Each of the molecules is an exact mirror image of the other, just as each of your hands is a mirror image of the other. These molecules are made of the same elements, but they differ in the elements' arrangement in space.

Shortly after Pasteur's discovery, researchers stumbled across an interesting but unexplained phenomenon—all organisms, including humans, are made almost entirely of left-handed molecules! Chemists were puzzled by this observation because when they made amino acids in the laboratory, the amino acids came out in equal numbers of right- and left-handed forms. Scientists also found that organisms cannot even use the right-handed form of the amino acids to make proteins! For years, scientists have tried to explain this. Why are biological molecules usually left-handed and not right-handed?

Cosmic Explanation

Astronomers recently discovered that a newly forming star in the constellation Orion emits a unique type of infrared light. Infrared light has a wavelength longer than the wavelenth of visible light. The wave particles of this light spiral through space like a corkscrew. This light spirals in only one direction. Researchers suspect that this light might give clues to why all organisms are lefties.

Laboratory experiments show that depending on the direction of the ultraviolet light spirals, either left-handed or right-handed molecules are destroyed. Scientists wonder if a similar type of light may have been present when life was beginning on Earth. Such light may have destroyed most right-handed molecules, which explains why life's molecules are left-handed.

Skeptics argue that the infrared light has less energy than the ultraviolet light used in the laboratory experiments and thus is not a valid comparison. Some researchers, however, hypothesize that both infrared and ultraviolet light may be emitted from the newly forming star that is 1,500 light-years away.

Find Out More

▶ The French chemist Pasteur discovered left-handed and right-handed molecules in tartaric acid. Do some research to find out more about Pasteur and his discovery. Share your findings with the class.

Eureka!

Here's Looking At Ya'!

To some people, just the thought of putting small pieces of plastic in their eyes is uncomfortable. But for millions of others, those little pieces of plastic, known as contact lenses, are a part of daily life. So what would you think about putting a piece of glass in your eye instead? Strangely enough, the humble beginning of the contact lens began with doing just that—inserting a glass lens right in the eye! Ouch!

Molded Glass

Early developers of contact lenses had only glass to use until plastics were discovered. In 1929, a Hungarian physician named Joseph Dallos came up with a way to make a mold of the human eye. This was a critical step in the development of contact lenses. He used these molds to make a glass lens that followed the shape of the eye rather than laying flat against it. In combination with the eye's natural lens, light was refocused to improve a person's eyesight. As you can probably guess, glass lenses weren't very comfortable.

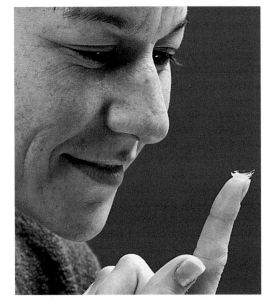

▲ *Does the thought of putting something in your eye make you squirm?*

Still Too Hard

Seven years later, an American optometrist, William Feinbloom, introduced contact lenses made of hard plastic. Plastic was a newly developed material made from long, stable chains of carbon, hydrogen, and oxygen molecules called polymers. But polymers required a lot of work to make. Chemists heated short chains, forcing them to chemically bond to form a longer, more-stable polymer. The whole process was also expensive. To make matters worse, the hard-plastic lenses made from polymers weren't much more comfortable than the glass lenses.

How About Spinning Plastic Gel?

In an effort to solve the comfort problem, Czech chemists Otto Wichterle and Drahoslav Lim invented a water-absorbing plastic gel. The lenses made from this gel were soft and pliable, and they allowed air to pass through the lens to the eye. These characteristics made the lenses much more comfortable to wear than the glass lenses.

Wichterle solved the cost problem by developing a simple and inexpensive process to make the plastic-gel lenses. In this process, called spin casting, liquid plastic is added to a spinning mold of an eye. When the plastic forms the correct shape, it is treated with ultraviolet and infrared light, which hardens the plastic. Both plastic gel and spin casting were patented in 1963, becoming the foundation for the contact lenses people wear today.

Look Toward the Future

▶ What do you think contact lenses might be like in 20 years? Let your imagination run wild. Sometimes the strangest ideas are the best seeds of new inventions!

Chemical Reactions

Pre-Reading Questions

1. What clues can help you identify a chemical reaction?

2. What are some types of chemical reactions?

3. How can you change the rate of a chemical reaction?

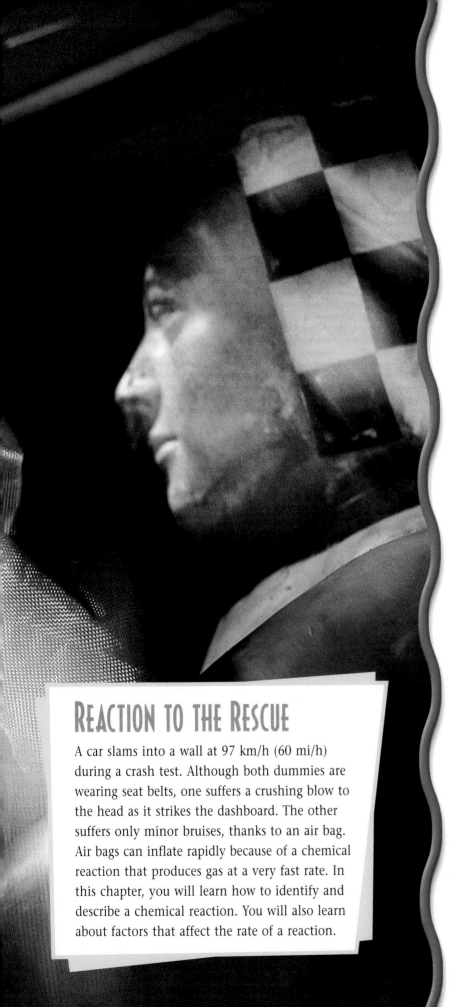

REACTION TO THE RESCUE

A car slams into a wall at 97 km/h (60 mi/h) during a crash test. Although both dummies are wearing seat belts, one suffers a crushing blow to the head as it strikes the dashboard. The other suffers only minor bruises, thanks to an air bag. Air bags can inflate rapidly because of a chemical reaction that produces gas at a very fast rate. In this chapter, you will learn how to identify and describe a chemical reaction. You will also learn about factors that affect the rate of a reaction.

START-UP Activity

A MODEL FORMULA

Chemicals react in very precise ways. In this activity, you will model a chemical reaction and predict how chemicals react.

Procedure

1. You will receive **several models** that are made from marshmallows stuck together with toothpicks. Each of these models is a Model A.

2. Your teacher will show you Model B and Model C. Take apart one or more Model A's to make copies of model B and Model C.

3. Do you have any pieces left over? If so, use them to make more Model B's and/or Model C's. Do you need more parts to complete Model B or Model C? If so, take apart another Model A.

4. If necessary, repeat step 3 until you have no parts left over.

Analysis

5. How many Model A's did you use to make copies of Model B and Model C?

6. How many Model B's did you make? How many Model C's did you make?

7. Suppose you needed to make six Model B's. How many Model A's would you need? How many Model C's could you make with the leftover parts?

Forming New Substances

Terms to Learn

chemical reaction
chemical formula
chemical equation
reactants
products
law of conservation of mass

What You'll Do

◆ Identify the clues that indicate a chemical reaction might be taking place.
◆ Interpret and write simple chemical formulas.
◆ Interpret and write simple balanced chemical equations.
◆ Explain how a balanced equation illustrates the law of conservation of mass.

Each fall, an amazing transformation takes place. Leaves change color, as shown in **Figure 1.** Vibrant reds, oranges, and yellows that had been hidden by green all year are seen as the temperatures get cooler and the hours of sunlight become fewer. What is happening to cause this change? Leaves have a green color as a result of a compound called chlorophyll (KLOR uh FIL). Each fall, the chlorophyll undergoes a chemical change and forms simpler substances that have no color. You can see the red, orange, and yellow colors in the leaves because the green color of the chlorophyll no longer hides them.

Figure 1 *The change of color in the fall is a result of chemical changes in the leaves.*

Chemical Reactions

The chemical change that occurs as chlorophyll breaks down into simpler substances is one example of a chemical reaction. A **chemical reaction** is the process by which one or more substances undergo change to produce one or more different substances. These new substances have different chemical and physical properties from the original substances. Many of the changes you are familiar with are chemical reactions, including the ones shown in **Figure 2.**

Figure 2 Examples of Chemical Reactions

The substances that make up baking powder undergo a chemical reaction when mixed with water. One new substance that forms is carbon dioxide gas, which causes the bubbles in this muffin.

Once ignited, gasoline reacts with oxygen gas in the air. The new substances that form, carbon dioxide and water, push against the pistons in the engine to keep the car moving.

Clues to Chemical Reactions How can you tell when a chemical reaction is taking place? There are several clues that indicate when a reaction might be occurring. The more of these clues you observe, the more likely it is that the change is a chemical reaction. Several of these clues are described below.

Some Clues to Chemical Reactions

Gas Formation
The formation of gas bubbles is a clue that a chemical reaction might be taking place. For example, bubbles of carbon dioxide are produced when hydrochloric acid is placed on a piece of limestone.

Solid Formation
A solid formed in a solution as a result of a chemical reaction is called a *precipitate* (pruh SIP uh TAYT). Here you see potassium chromate solution being added to a silver nitrate solution. The dark red solid is a precipitate of silver chromate.

Color Change
Chlorine bleach is great for removing the color from stains on white clothes. But don't spill it on your jeans. The bleach reacts with the blue dye on the fabric, causing the color of the material to change.

Energy Change
Energy is released during some chemical reactions. A fire heats a room and provides light. Electrical energy is released when chemicals in a battery react. During some other chemical reactions, energy is absorbed. Chemicals on photographic film react when they absorb energy from light shining on the film.

Breaking and Making Bonds New substances are formed in a chemical reaction because chemical bonds in the starting substances break, atoms rearrange, and new bonds form to make the new substances. Look at the model in **Figure 3** to understand how this process occurs.

Figure 3
Reaction of Hydrogen and Chlorine

Breaking Bonds The elements hydrogen and chlorine are diatomic, meaning they are composed of molecules that consist of two atoms bonded together. For these molecules to react, the bonds joining the atoms must break.

Making Bonds Molecules of the new substance, hydrogen chloride, are formed as new bonds are made between hydrogen atoms and chlorine atoms.

Chemical Formulas

Remember that a chemical symbol is a shorthand method of identifying an element. A **chemical formula** is a shorthand notation for a compound or a diatomic element using chemical symbols and numbers. A chemical formula indicates the chemical makeup by showing how many of each kind of atom is present in a molecule.

The chemical formula for water, H_2O, tells you that a water molecule is composed of two atoms of hydrogen and one atom of oxygen. The small number 2 in the formula is a subscript. A *subscript* is a number written below and to the right of a chemical symbol in a formula. When no subscript is written after a symbol, as with the oxygen in water's formula, only one atom of that element is present. **Figure 4** shows two more chemical formulas and what they mean.

Figure 4 *A chemical formula shows the number of atoms of each element present.*

$$O_2$$

$$C_6H_{12}O_6$$

Oxygen is a diatomic element. Each molecule of oxygen gas is composed of two atoms of oxygen bonded together.

Every molecule of **glucose** (the sugar formed by plants during photosynthesis) is composed of six atoms of carbon, twelve atoms of hydrogen, and six atoms of oxygen.

Writing Formulas for Covalent Compounds You can often write a chemical formula if you know the name of the substance. Remember that covalent compounds are usually composed of two nonmetals. The names of covalent compounds use prefixes to tell you how many atoms of each element are in the formula. A *prefix* is a syllable or syllables joined to the beginning of a word. Each prefix used in a chemical name represents a number, as shown in the table at right. **Figure 5** demonstrates how to write a chemical formula from the name of a covalent compound.

Prefixes Used in Chemical Names			
mono-	1	hexa-	6
di-	2	hepta-	7
tri-	3	octa-	8
tetra-	4	nona-	9
penta-	5	deca-	10

Carbon dioxide

$$CO_2$$

The *lack of a prefix* indicates 1 carbon atom.

The prefix *di-* indicates 2 oxygen atoms.

Dinitrogen monoxide

$$N_2O$$

The prefix *di-* indicates 2 nitrogen atoms.

The prefix *mono-* indicates 1 oxygen atom.

Figure 5 *The formulas of these covalent compounds can be written using the prefixes in their names.*

Self-Check

How many atoms of each element make up Na_2SO_4?
(See page 724 to check your answer.)

Writing Formulas for Ionic Compounds If the name of a compound contains the name of a metal and a nonmetal, the compound is probably ionic. To write the formula for an ionic compound, you must make sure the compound's overall charge is zero. In other words, the formula must have subscripts that cause the charges of the ions to cancel out. (Remember that the charge of many ions can be determined by looking at the periodic table.) **Figure 6** demonstrates how to write a chemical formula from the name of an ionic compound.

Figure 6 *The formula of an ionic compound is written by using enough of each ion so the overall charge is zero.*

Sodium chloride

$$NaCl$$

A sodium ion has a 1+ **charge**.
A chloride ion has a 1− **charge**.

One sodium ion and one chloride ion have an overall **charge of $(1+) + (1-) = 0$**

Magnesium chloride

$$MgCl_2$$

A magnesium ion has a 2+ **charge**.
A chloride ion has a 1− **charge**.

One magnesium ion and two chloride ions have an overall **charge of $(2+) + 2(1-) = 0$**

Chemical Equations

A composer writing a piece of music, like the one in **Figure 7,** must communicate to the musician what notes to play, how long to play each note, and in what style each note should be played. The composer does not use words to describe what must happen. Instead, he or she uses musical symbols to communicate in a way that can be easily understood by anyone in the world who can read music.

Similarly, people who work with chemical reactions need to communicate information about reactions clearly to other people throughout the world. Describing reactions using long descriptive sentences would require translations into other languages. Chemists have developed a method of describing reactions that is short and easily understood by anyone in the world who understands chemical formulas. A **chemical equation** is a shorthand description of a chemical reaction using chemical formulas and symbols. Because each element's chemical symbol is understood around the world, a chemical equation needs no translation.

Figure 7 *The symbols on this music are understood around the world—just like chemical symbols!*

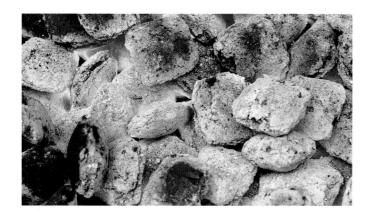

Figure 8 *Charcoal is used to cook food on a barbecue. When carbon in charcoal reacts with oxygen in the air, the primary product is carbon dioxide.*

Reactants Yield Products Consider the example of carbon reacting with oxygen to yield carbon dioxide, as shown in **Figure 8.** The starting materials in a chemical reaction are **reactants** (ree AKT uhnts). The substances formed from a reaction are **products.** In this example, carbon and oxygen are reactants, and carbon dioxide is the product formed. The parts of the chemical equation for this reaction are described in **Figure 9.**

Figure 9 The Parts of a Chemical Equation

The formulas of the **reactants** are written before the arrow.

The formulas of the **products** are written after the arrow.

$$C + O_2 \rightarrow CO_2$$

A **plus sign** separates the formulas of two or more reactants or products from one another.

The **arrow,** also called the yields sign, separates the formulas of the reactants from the formulas of the products.

Accuracy Is Important The symbol or formula for each substance in the reaction must be written correctly. For a compound, determine if it is covalent or ionic, and write the appropriate formula. For an element, use the proper chemical symbol, and be sure to use a subscript of 2 for the diatomic elements. (The seven diatomic elements are hydrogen, nitrogen, oxygen, fluorine, chlorine, bromine, and iodine.) An equation with an incorrect chemical symbol or formula will not accurately describe the reaction. In fact, even a simple mistake can make a huge difference, as shown in **Figure 10.**

Figure 10 *The symbols and formulas shown here are similar, but don't confuse them while writing an equation!*

The chemical formula for the compound carbon dioxide is **CO_2.** Carbon dioxide is a colorless, odorless gas that you exhale.

The chemical formula for the compound carbon monoxide is **CO.** Carbon monoxide is a colorless, odorless, poisonous gas.

The chemical symbol for the element cobalt is **Co.** Cobalt is a hard, bluish gray metal.

✓ Self-Check

When calcium bromide reacts with chlorine, bromine and calcium chloride are produced. Write an equation to describe this reaction. Identify each substance as either a reactant or a product. *(See page 724 to check your answers.)*

An Equation Must Be Balanced In a chemical reaction, every atom in the reactants becomes part of the products. Atoms are never lost or gained in a chemical reaction. When writing a chemical equation, you must show that the number of atoms of each element in the reactants equals the number of atoms of those elements in the products by writing a balanced equation.

MATH BREAK

Balancing Act

When balancing a chemical equation, you must place coefficients in front of an entire chemical formula, never in the middle of a formula. Notice where the coefficients are in the balanced equation below:

$$F_2 + 2KCl \longrightarrow 2KF + Cl_2$$

Now It's Your Turn

Write balanced equations for the following:

$$HCl + Na_2S \longrightarrow H_2S + NaCl$$
$$Al + Cl_2 \longrightarrow AlCl_3$$

Become a better balancer of chemical equations on page 682 of the LabBook.

How to Balance an Equation Writing a balanced equation requires the use of coefficients (кон uh FISH uhnts). A *coefficient* is a number placed in front of a chemical symbol or formula. When counting atoms, you multiply a coefficient by the subscript of each of the elements in the formula that follows it. Thus, $2CO_2$ represents 2 carbon dioxide molecules. Together the two molecules contain a total of 2 carbon atoms and 4 oxygen atoms. Coefficients are used when balancing equations because the subscripts in the formulas cannot be changed. Changing a subscript changes the formula so that it no longer represents the correct substance. Study **Figure 11** to see how to use coefficients to balance an equation. Then you can practice balancing equations by doing the MathBreak at left.

Figure 11 *Follow these steps to write a balanced equation for $H_2 + O_2 \longrightarrow H_2O$.*

1 **Count the atoms** of each element in the reactants and in the products. You can see that there are fewer oxygen atoms in the products than in the reactants.

$$H_2 + O_2 \longrightarrow H_2O$$

Reactants   **Products**

H = 2   O = 2   H = 2
                                 O = 1

2 **To balance the oxygen atoms,** place the coefficient *2* in front of water's formula. This gives you 2 oxygen atoms in both the reactants and the products. But now there are too few hydrogen atoms in the reactants.

$$H_2 + O_2 \longrightarrow 2H_2O$$

Reactants   **Products**

H = 2   O = 2   H = 4
                                 O = 2

3 **To balance the hydrogen atoms,** place the coefficient *2* in front of hydrogen's formula. But just to be sure your answer is correct, always double-check your work!

$$2H_2 + O_2 \longrightarrow 2H_2O$$

Reactants   **Products**

H = 4   O = 2   H = 4
                                 O = 2

Mass Is Conserved—It's a Law! The practice of balancing equations is a result of the work of a French chemist, Antoine Lavoisier (luh vwa ZYAY). In the 1700s, Lavoisier performed experiments in which he carefully measured and compared the masses of the substances involved in chemical reactions. He determined that the total mass of the reactants equaled the total mass of the products. Lavoisier's work led to the **law of conservation of mass,** which states that mass is neither created nor destroyed in ordinary chemical and physical changes. Thus, a chemical equation must show the same number and kind of atom on both sides of the arrow. The law of conservation of mass is demonstrated in **Figure 12.** You can explore this law for yourself in the QuickLab at right.

Figure 12 *In this demonstration, magnesium in the flash-bulb of a camera reacts with oxygen. Notice that the mass is the same before and after the reaction takes place.*

REVIEW

1. List four clues that a chemical reaction is occurring.

2. How many atoms of each element make up $2Na_3PO_4$?

3. Write the chemical formulas for carbon tetrachloride and calcium bromide.

4. Explain how a balanced chemical equation illustrates that mass is never lost or gained in a chemical reaction.

5. **Applying Concepts** Write the balanced chemical equation for methane, CH_4, reacting with oxygen gas to produce water and carbon dioxide.

Types of Chemical Reactions

Imagine having to learn 50 chemical reactions. Sound tough? Well, there are thousands of known chemical reactions. It would be impossible to remember them all. But there is help! Remember that the elements are divided into categories based on their properties. In a similar way, reactions can be classified according to their similarities.

Many reactions can be grouped into one of four categories: synthesis (SIN thuh sis), decomposition, single replacement, and double replacement. By dividing reactions into these categories, you can better understand the patterns of how reactants become products. As you learn about each type of reaction, study the models provided to help you recognize each type of reaction.

Synthesis Reactions

A **synthesis reaction** is a reaction in which two or more substances combine to form a single compound. For example, the synthesis reaction in which the compound magnesium oxide is produced is seen in **Figure 13.** (This is the same reaction that occurs in the flashbulb in Figure 12.) One way to remember what happens in each type of reaction is to imagine people at a dance. A synthesis reaction would be modeled by two people joining to form a dancing couple, as shown in **Figure 14.**

Figure 13 *The synthesis reaction that occurs when magnesium reacts with oxygen in the air forms the compound magnesium oxide.*

Figure 14 *A model for the synthesis reaction of sodium reacting with chlorine to form sodium chloride is shown below.*

$$2Na + Cl_2 \longrightarrow 2NaCl$$

Decomposition Reactions

A **decomposition reaction** is a reaction in which a single compound breaks down to form two or more simpler substances. The decomposition of water is shown in **Figure 15.** Decomposition is the reverse of synthesis. The dance model would represent a decomposition reaction as a dancing couple splitting up, as shown in **Figure 16.**

Figure 15 *Water can be decomposed into the elements hydrogen and oxygen through electrolysis.*

Figure 16 *A model for the decomposition reaction of carbonic acid to form water and carbon dioxide is shown below.*

$$H_2CO_3 \longrightarrow H_2O + CO_2$$

Single-Replacement Reactions

A **single-replacement reaction** is a reaction in which an element takes the place of another element that is part of a compound. The products of single-replacement reactions are a new compound and a different element. The dance model for single-replacement reactions is a person who cuts in on a couple dancing. A new couple is formed and a different person is left alone, as shown in **Figure 17.**

Figure 17 *A model for a single-replacement reaction of zinc reacting with hydrochloric acid to form zinc chloride and hydrogen is shown below.*

$$Zn + 2HCl \longrightarrow ZnCl_2 + H_2$$

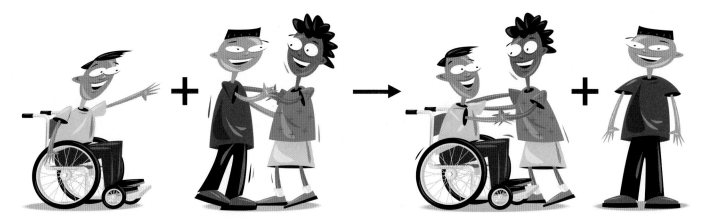

Some Elements Are More Reactive Than Others In a single-replacement reaction, a more-reactive element can replace a less-reactive one from a compound. However, the opposite reaction does not occur, as shown in **Figure 18.**

Figure 18 *More-reactive elements replace less-reactive elements in single-replacement reactions.*

$$Cu + 2AgNO_3 \rightarrow 2Ag + Cu(NO_3)_2$$
Copper is more reactive than silver.

$$Ag + Cu(NO_3)_2 \rightarrow \text{No reaction}$$
Silver is less reactive than copper.

Double-Replacement Reactions

A **double-replacement reaction** is a reaction in which ions in two compounds switch places. One of the products of this reaction is often a gas or a precipitate. A double-replacement reaction in the dance model would be two couples dancing and switching partners, as shown in **Figure 19.**

Figure 19 *A model for the double-replacement reaction of sodium chloride reacting with silver fluoride to form sodium fluoride and the precipitate silver chloride is shown below.*

$$NaCl + AgF \longrightarrow NaF + AgCl$$

REVIEW

1. What type of reaction does each of the following equations represent?

   a. $FeS + 2HCl \longrightarrow FeCl_2 + H_2S$

   b. $NH_4OH \longrightarrow NH_3 + H_2O$

2. Which type of reaction always has an element and a compound as reactants?

3. **Comparing Concepts** Compare synthesis and decomposition reactions.

Terms to Learn

exothermic
endothermic
law of conservation of energy
activation energy
catalyst
inhibitor

What You'll Do

◆ Compare exothermic and endothermic reactions.
◆ Explain activation energy.
◆ Interpret an energy diagram.
◆ Describe the factors that affect the rate of a reaction.

Energy and Rates of Chemical Reactions

You just learned one method of classifying chemical reactions. In this section, you will learn how to classify reactions in terms of the energy associated with the reaction and learn how to change the rate at which the reaction occurs.

Every Reaction Involves Energy

All chemical reactions involve chemical energy. Remember that during a reaction, chemical bonds in the reactants break as they absorb energy. As new bonds form in the products, energy is released. Energy is released or absorbed in the overall reaction depending on how the chemical energy of the reactants compares with the chemical energy of the products.

Energy Is Released in Exothermic Reactions If the chemical energy of the reactants is greater than the chemical energy of the products, the difference in energy is released during the reaction. A chemical reaction in which energy is released or removed is called **exothermic.** *Exo* means "go out" or "exit," and *thermic* means "heat" or "energy." The energy can be released in several different forms, as shown in **Figure 20.** The energy released in an exothermic reaction is often written as a product in a chemical equation, as in this equation:

$$2Na + Cl_2 \longrightarrow 2NaCl + energy$$

Figure 20 Types of Energy Released in Reactions

Light energy is released in the exothermic reaction taking place in these light sticks.

Electrical energy is released in the exothermic reaction taking place in the dry cells in this flashlight.

Light and thermal energy are released in the exothermic reaction taking place in this campfire.

Photosynthesis is an endothermic process in which light energy from the sun is used to produce glucose, a simple sugar. The equation that describes photosynthesis is as follows:

$6CO_2 + 6H_2O + \text{energy} \longrightarrow$
$C_6H_{12}O_6 + 6O_2$

The cells in your body use glucose to get the energy they need through cellular respiration, an exothermic process described by the reverse of the above reaction:

$C_6H_{12}O_6 + 6O_2 \longrightarrow$
$6CO_2 + 6H_2O + \text{energy}$

Energy Is Absorbed in Endothermic Reactions If the chemical energy of the reactants is less than the chemical energy of the products, the difference in energy is absorbed during the reaction. A chemical reaction in which energy is absorbed is called **endothermic.** *Endo* means "go in," and *thermic* means "heat" or "energy." The energy absorbed in an endothermic reaction is often written as a reactant in a chemical equation, as in this equation:

$$2H_2O + \text{energy} \longrightarrow 2H_2 + O_2$$

Energy Is Conserved—It's a Law! You learned that mass is never created or destroyed in chemical reactions. The same holds true for energy. The **law of conservation of energy** states that energy can be neither created nor destroyed. The energy released in exothermic reactions was originally stored in the reactants. And the energy absorbed in endothermic reactions does not just vanish. It is stored in the products that form. If you could carefully measure all the energy in a reaction, you would find that the total amount of energy (of all types) is the same before and after the reaction.

Activation Energy Gets a Reaction Started A match can be used to light a campfire—but only if the match is lit! A strike-anywhere match, like the one shown in **Figure 21,** has all the reactants it needs to be able to burn. And though the chemicals on a match are intended to react and burn, they will not ignite by themselves. Energy is needed to start the reaction. The minimum amount of energy needed for substances to react is called **activation energy.**

Figure 21 *Rubbing the tip of this strike-anywhere match on a rough surface provides the energy needed to get the chemicals to react.*

Matches rubbing together in a box could provide the activation energy to light a strike-anywhere match. Safety matches, which must be struck on a strike plate on the box, were developed to prevent such accidents.

The friction of striking a match heats the substances on the match, breaking bonds in the reactants and allowing the new bonds in the products to form. Chemical reactions require some energy to get started. An electric spark in a car's engine provides activation energy to begin the burning of gasoline. Light can also provide the activation energy for a reaction. You can better understand activation energy and the differences between exothermic reactions and endothermic reactions by studying the diagrams in **Figure 22.**

Figure 22 Energy Diagrams

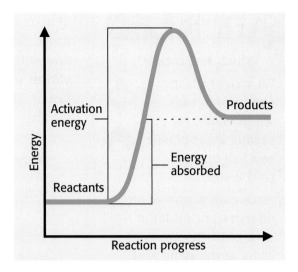

Exothermic Reaction Once begun, an exothermic reaction can continue to occur, as in a fire. The energy released as the product forms continues to supply the activation energy needed for the substances to react.

Endothermic Reaction An endothermic reaction requires a continuous supply of energy. Energy must be absorbed to provide the activation energy needed for the substances to react.

Fresh Hydrogen Peroxide

Hydrogen peroxide is used as a disinfectant for minor scrapes and cuts because it decomposes to produce oxygen gas and water, which help cleanse the wound. The decomposition of hydrogen peroxide is an exothermic reaction. Explain why hydrogen peroxide must be stored in a dark bottle to maintain its freshness. (HINT: What type of energy would be blocked by this type of container?

Factors Affecting Rates of Reactions

You can think of a reaction as occurring only if the particles of reactants collide when they have enough energy to break the appropriate bonds. The rate of a reaction is a measure of how rapidly the reaction takes place. Four factors that affect the rate of a reaction are temperature, concentration, surface area, and the presence of a catalyst or inhibitor.

Fighting fires with slime? Read more about it on page 370.

QuickLab

Which Is Quicker?

1. Fill a **clear plastic cup** half-full with **warm water.** Fill a **second clear plastic cup** half-full with **cold water.**

2. Place one-quarter of an **effervescent tablet** in each of the two cups of water at the same time.

3. Observe the reaction, and record your observations in your ScienceLog.

4. In which cup did the reaction occur at a greater rate? What evidence supports your answer?

Do you feel as though you are not up to speed on controlling the rate of a reaction? Then hurry over to page 686 of the LabBook.

Temperature An increase in temperature increases the rate of a reaction. At higher temperatures, particles of reactants move faster, so they collide with each other more frequently and with more energy. More particles therefore have the activation energy needed to react and can change into products faster. Thus, more particles react in a shorter time. You can see this effect in **Figure 23** and by doing the QuickLab at left.

Figure 23 *The light stick on the right glows brighter than the one on the left because the higher temperature causes the rate of the reaction to increase.*

Concentration Generally, increasing the concentration of reactants increases the rate of a reaction, as shown in **Figure 24.** *Concentration* is a measure of the amount of one substance dissolved in another. Increasing the concentration increases the number of reactant particles present and decreases the distance between them. The reactant particles collide more often, so more particles react each second. Increasing the concentration is similar to having more people in a room. The more people that are in the room, the more frequently they will collide and interact.

Figure 24 *The reaction on the right produces bubbles of hydrogen gas at a faster rate because the concentration of hydrochloric acid used is higher.*

Surface Area Increasing the surface area, or the amount of exposed surface, of solid reactants increases the rate of a reaction. Grinding a solid into a powder exposes more particles of the reactant to other reactant particles. The number of collisions between reactant particles increases, increasing the rate of the reaction. You can see the effect of increasing the surface area in the QuickLab at right.

Catalysts and Inhibitors Some reactions would be too slow to be useful without a catalyst (KAT uh LIST). A **catalyst** is a substance that speeds up a reaction without being permanently changed. A catalyst lowers the activation energy of a reaction, which allows the reaction to occur more rapidly. Most reactions in your body are sped up using catalysts called enzymes. Catalysts are even found in cars, as seen in **Figure 25.**

An **inhibitor** is a substance that slows down or stops a chemical reaction. Preservatives added to foods are inhibitors that slow down reactions in the bacteria or fungus that can spoil food. Many poisons are also inhibitors.

Figure 25 *This catalytic converter contains platinum and palladium—two catalysts that increase the rate of reactions that make the car's exhaust less polluting.*

Quick Lab

I'm Crushed!

1. Fill **two clear plastic cups** half-full with **room-temperature water.**

2. Fold a **sheet of paper** around one-quarter of an **effervescent tablet.** Carefully crush the tablet.

3. Get another one-quarter of an effervescent tablet. Carefully pour the crushed tablet into one cup, and place the uncrushed tablet in the second cup.

4. Observe the reaction, and record your observations in your ScienceLog.

5. In which cup did the reaction occur at a greater rate? What evidence supports your answer?

6. Explain why the water in each cup must have the same temperature.

REVIEW

1. What is activation energy?

2. List four ways to increase the rate of a reaction.

3. **Comparing Concepts** Compare exothermic and endothermic reactions.

4. **Interpreting Graphics** Does this energy diagram show an exothermic or an endothermic reaction? How can you tell?

internet connect

SC*LINKS*
NSTA

TOPIC: Exothermic and Endothermic Reactions
GO TO: www.scilinks.org
*sci*LINKS NUMBER: HSTP345

Chapter Highlights

SECTION 1

Vocabulary

chemical reaction (*p. 350*)

chemical formula (*p. 352*)

chemical equation (*p. 354*)

reactants (*p. 354*)

products (*p. 354*)

law of conservation of mass (*p. 357*)

Section Notes

- Chemical reactions form new substances with different properties than the starting substances.

- Clues that a chemical reaction is taking place include formation of a gas or solid, a color change, and an energy change.

- A chemical formula tells the composition of a compound using chemical symbols and subscripts. Subscripts are small numbers written below and to the right of a symbol in a formula.

- Chemical formulas can sometimes be written from the names of covalent compounds and ionic compounds.

- A chemical equation describes a reaction using formulas, symbols, and coefficients.

- A balanced equation uses coefficients to illustrate the law of conservation of mass, that mass is neither created nor destroyed during a chemical reaction.

Labs

Finding a Balance (*p. 682*)

SECTION 2

Vocabulary

synthesis reaction (*p. 358*)

decomposition reaction (*p. 359*)

single-replacement reaction (*p. 359*)

double-replacement reaction (*p. 360*)

Section Notes

- Many chemical reactions can be classified as one of four types by comparing reactants with products.

- In synthesis reactions, the reactants form a single product.

- In decomposition reactions, a single reactant breaks apart into two or more simpler products.

☑ Skills Check

Math Concepts

SUBSCRIPTS AND COEFFICIENTS   A subscript is a number written below and to the right of a chemical symbol when writing the chemical formula of a compound. A coefficient is a number written in front of a chemical formula in a chemical equation. When you balance a chemical equation, you cannot change the subscripts in a formula; you can only add coefficients, as seen in the equation $2H_2 + O_2 \longrightarrow 2H_2O$.

Visual Understanding

REACTION TYPES   It can be challenging to identify which type of reaction a particular chemical equation represents. Review four reaction types by studying Figures 14, 16, 17, and 19.

- In single-replacement reactions, a more-reactive element takes the place of a less-reactive element in a compound. No reaction will occur if a less-reactive element is placed with a compound containing a more-reactive element.

- In double-replacement reactions, ions in two compounds switch places. A gas or precipitate is often formed.

Labs

Putting Elements Together *(p. 684)*

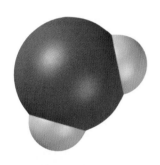

Vocabulary

exothermic *(p. 361)*

endothermic *(p. 362)*

law of conservation of energy *(p. 362)*

activation energy *(p. 362)*

catalyst *(p. 365)*

inhibitor *(p. 365)*

Section Notes

- Energy is released in exothermic reactions. The energy released can be written as a product in a chemical equation.

- Energy is absorbed in endothermic reactions. The energy absorbed can be written as a reactant in a chemical equation.

- The law of conservation of energy states that energy is neither created nor destroyed.

- Activation energy is the energy needed to start a chemical reaction.

- Energy diagrams indicate whether a reaction is exothermic or endothermic by showing whether energy is given off or absorbed during the reaction.

- The rate of a chemical reaction is affected by temperature, concentration, surface area, and the presence of a catalyst or inhibitor.

- Raising the temperature, increasing the concentration, increasing the surface area, and adding a catalyst can increase the rate of a reaction.

Labs

Cata-what? Catalyst! *(p. 683)*

Speed Control *(p. 686)*

---

internetconnect

GO TO: go.hrw.com

Visit the **HRW** Web site for a variety of learning tools related to this chapter. Just type in the keyword:

KEYWORD: HSTREA

GO TO: www.scilinks.org

Visit the **National Science Teachers Association** on-line Web site for Internet resources related to this chapter. Just type in the *sci*LINKS number for more information about the topic:

TOPIC: Chemical Reactions	*sci*LINKS NUMBER: HSTP330
TOPIC: Chemical Formulas	*sci*LINKS NUMBER: HSTP335
TOPIC: Chemical Equations	*sci*LINKS NUMBER: HSTP340
TOPIC: Reaction Types	*sci*LINKS NUMBER: HSTP343
TOPIC: Exothermic and Endothermic Reactions	*sci*LINKS NUMBER: HSTP345

Chapter Review

Concept Mapping

14. Use the following terms to create a concept map: chemical reaction, chemical equation, chemical formulas, reactants, products, coefficients, subscripts.

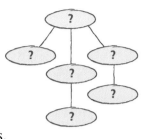

CRITICAL THINKING AND PROBLEM SOLVING

15. Your friend is very worried by rumors he has heard about a substance called dihydrogen monoxide. What could you say to your friend to calm his fears? (Be sure to write the formula of the substance.)

16. As long as proper safety precautions have been taken, why can explosives be transported long distances without exploding?

MATH IN SCIENCE

17. Calculate the number of atoms of each element shown in each of the following:
    a. $CaSO_4$
    b. $4NaOCl$
    c. $Fe(NO_3)_2$
    d. $2Al_2(CO_3)_3$

18. Write balanced equations for the following:
    a. $Fe + O_2 \longrightarrow Fe_2O_3$
    b. $Al + CuSO_4 \longrightarrow Al_2(SO_4)_3 + Cu$
    c. $Ba(CN)_2 + H_2SO_4 \longrightarrow BaSO_4 + HCN$

19. Write and balance chemical equations from each of the following descriptions:
    a. Bromine reacts with sodium iodide to form iodine and sodium bromide.
    b. Phosphorus reacts with oxygen gas to form diphosphorus pentoxide.
    c. Lithium oxide decomposes to form lithium and oxygen.

INTERPRETING GRAPHICS

20. What evidence in the photo supports the claim that a chemical reaction is taking place?

21. Use the energy diagram below to answer the questions that follow.

a. Which letter represents the energy of the products?
b. Which letter represents the activation energy of the reaction?
c. Is energy given off or absorbed by this reaction?

Reading Check-up

Take a minute to review your answers to the Pre-Reading Questions found at the bottom of page 348. Have your answers changed? If necessary, revise your answers based on what you have learned since you began this chapter.

EYE ON THE ENVIRONMENT

Slime That Fire!

Once a fire starts in the hard-to-reach mountains of the western United States, it is difficult to stop. Trees, grasses, and brush can provide an overwhelming supply of fuel. In order to stop a fire, firefighters make a fire line. This is an area where all the burnable materials are removed from the ground. How would you slow down a fire to give a ground crew more time to build a fire line? Would you suggest dropping water from a plane? That is not a bad idea, but what if you had something even better than water—like some slimy red goop?

Red Goop Goes the Distance

The slimy red goop is actually a powerful fire retardant. The goop is a mixture of a powder and water that is loaded directly onto an old military plane. Carrying between 4,500 and 11,000 L of the slime, the plane drops it all in front of the raging flames when the pilot presses the button.

The amount of water added to the powder depends on the location of the fire. If a fire is burning over shrubs and grasses, more water is needed. In this form the goop actually rains down to the ground through the treetops. But if a fire is burning in tall trees, less water is used so the slime will glob onto the branches and ooze down very slowly.

Failed Flames

The burning of trees, grass, and brush is an exothermic reaction. A fire retardant slows or stops this self-feeding reaction. A fire retardant increases the activation energy for the materials it is applied to. Although a lot depends on how hot the fire is when it hits the area treated with the retardant and how much of the retardant

▲ *This plane is dropping fire retardant on a forest fire.*

is applied, firefighters on the ground can gain valuable time when a fire is slowed with a fire retardant. This extra time allows them to create a fire line that will ultimately stop the fire.

Neon Isn't Necessary

Once a fire is put out, the slimy red streaks left on the blackened ground can be an eyesore. To solve the problem, scientists have created special dyes for the retardant. These dyes make the goop neon colors when it is first applied, but after a few days in the sun, the goop turns a natural brown shade!

What Do They Study?

▶ Do some research to learn about a firefighter's training. What classes and exams are firefighters required to pass? How do they maintain their certifications once they become firefighters?

CAREERS

ARSON INVESTIGATOR

Once a fire dies down, you might see arson investigator **Lt. Larry McKee** on the scene. "After the fire is out, I can investigate the fire scene to determine where the fire started and how it started. If it was intentionally set and I'm successful at putting the arson case together, I can get a conviction. That's very satisfying," says Lt. McKee.

During a fire, fuel and oxygen combine in a chemical reaction called combustion. On the scene, Lt. Larry McKee questions witnesses and firefighters about what they saw. He knows, for example, that the color of the smoke can indicate certain chemicals.

McKee explains that fires usually burn "up and out, in a V shape." To find where the V begins, he says, "We work from the area with the least amount of damage to the one with the most damage. This normally leads us to the point of origin." Once the origin has been determined, it's time to call in the dogs!

An Accelerant-Sniffing Canine

"We have what we call an accelerant-sniffing canine. Our canine, Nikki, has been trained to detect approximately 11 different chemicals." When Nikki arrives on the scene, she sniffs for traces of chemicals, called accelerants, that may have been used to start the fire. When she finds one, she immediately starts to dig at it. At that point, McKee takes a sample from the area and sends it to the lab for analysis.

At the Lab

Once at the laboratory, the sample is treated so that any accelerants in it are dissolved in a liquid. A small amount of the liquid is then injected into an instrument called a *gas chromatograph.* The instrument heats the liquid, forming a mixture of gases. The gases then are passed through a flame. As each gas passes through the flame, it "causes a fluctuation in an electronic signal, which creates our graphs."

Solving the Case

If the laboratory report indicates that a suspicious accelerant has been found, McKee begins to search for arson suspects. By combining detective work with scientific evidence, fire investigators can successfully catch and convict arsonists.

Fascinating Fire Facts

▶ The temperature of a house fire can reach 980°C! At that temperature, aluminum window frames melt, and furniture goes up in flames. Do some research to discover three more facts about fires. Create a display with two or more classmates to illustrate some of your facts.

▲ *Nikki searches for traces of gasoline, kerosene, and other accelerants.*

Chemical Compounds

SOMETHING'S FISHY

Some people keep saltwater aquariums as a hobby. The living organisms in these aquariums—fish, coral, and algae—must have the correct environment, or they might die. Many things must be controlled in the aquarium. For example, the pH of the water must stay within a certain range. The amount of salt and other compounds in the water also must be within a certain range. In this chapter, you will learn about pH. You will also learn about salts and other chemical compounds.

Pre-Reading Questions

1. What is the difference between ionic compounds and covalent compounds?

2. What is an acid?

3. What is a hydrocarbon?

STICKING TOGETHER

In this activity you will demonstrate the force that keeps particles together in some compounds.

Procedure

1. Blow up **two balloons.** Rub them with a piece of **wool cloth.**

2. Hold the balloons by their necks. Move the balloons near each other. Describe in your ScienceLog what you see.

3. Put one of the balloons against a wall. Record your observations in your ScienceLog.

Analysis

4. The balloons are charged by rubbing them with the wool cloth. Like charges repel each other. Opposite charges attract each other. Infer whether the balloons have like or opposite charges. Explain your answer.

5. The two types of charge are negative and positive. The balloon in step 3 has a negative charge. Infer what the charge is on the wall where you put the balloon. Explain.

6. The particles that make up some compounds are attracted to each other in the same way that the balloon is attracted to the wall. What can you infer about the particles that make up such compounds?

Ionic and Covalent Compounds

Terms to Learn

ionic compounds
covalent compounds

What You'll Do

◆ Describe the properties of ionic and covalent compounds.
◆ Classify compounds as ionic or covalent based on their properties.

The world around you is made up of chemical compounds. Chemical compounds are pure substances composed of ions or molecules. There are millions of different kinds of compounds, so you can imagine how classifying them might be helpful. One simple way to classify compounds is by grouping them according to the type of bond they contain.

Ionic Compounds

Compounds that contain ionic bonds are called **ionic compounds.** Remember that an ionic bond is the force of attraction between two oppositely charged ions. Ionic compounds can be formed by the reaction of a metal with a nonmetal. Electrons are transferred from the metal atoms (which become positively charged ions) to the nonmetal atoms (which become negatively charged ions). For example, when sodium reacts with chlorine, as shown in **Figure 1,** the ionic compound sodium chloride, or ordinary table salt, is formed.

Figure 1 *An ionic compound is formed when the metal sodium reacts with the nonmetal chlorine. Sodium chloride is formed in the reaction, and energy is released as light and thermal energy.*

Brittleness The forces acting between the ions that make up ionic compounds give these compounds certain properties. Ionic compounds tend to be brittle, as shown in **Figure 2.** The ions that make up an ionic compound are arranged in a repeating three-dimensional pattern called a crystal lattice. The ions that make up the crystal lattice are arranged as alternating positive and negative ions. Each ion in the lattice is surrounded by ions of the opposite charge, and each ion is bonded to the ions around it. When an ionic compound is struck with a hammer, the pattern of ions in the crystal lattice is shifted. Ions with the same charge line up and repel one another, causing the crystal to shatter.

Figure 2 *Ionic compounds will shatter when hit with a hammer.*

High Melting Points Ionic compounds are almost always solid at room temperature, as shown in **Figure 3.** An ionic compound will melt only at temperatures high enough to overcome the strong ionic bonds between the ions. Sodium chloride, for instance, must be heated to 801°C before it will melt. This temperature is much higher than you can produce in your kitchen or even your school laboratory.

Magnesium oxide melts at 2,800°C.

Potassium dichromate melts at 398°C.

Nickel(II) oxide melts at 1,984°C.

Figure 3 *Each of these ionic compounds has a high melting point and is solid at room temperature.*

Solubility and Electrical Conductivity Many ionic compounds dissolve easily in water. Molecules of water attract each of the ions of an ionic compound and pull them away from one another. The solution created when an ionic compound dissolves in water can conduct an electric current, as shown in **Figure 4.** The ions are able to move past one another and conduct the electric current in the solution. Keep in mind that an undissolved crystal of an ionic compound does not conduct an electric current.

Pure water

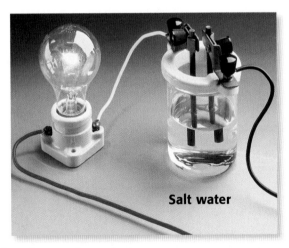

Salt water

Figure 4 *The pure water in the left beaker does not conduct an electric current. The solution of salt water in the right beaker conducts an electric current, and the bulb lights up.*

Covalent Compounds

Compounds composed of elements that are covalently bonded are called **covalent compounds.** Remember that covalent bonds form when atoms share electrons. Gasoline, carbon dioxide, water, and sugar are well-known examples of covalent compounds.

Low Melting Points Covalent compounds exist as independent particles called molecules. The forces of attraction between molecules of covalent compounds are much weaker than the bonds between ions in a crystal lattice. Thus, covalent compounds have lower melting points than ionic compounds.

Solubility and Electrical Conductivity You have probably heard the phrase "oil and water don't mix." Oil, such as that used in salad dressing, is composed of covalent compounds. Many covalent compounds do not dissolve well in water. Water molecules have a stronger attraction for one another than they have for the molecules of most other covalent compounds. Thus, the molecules of the covalent compound get squeezed out as the water molecules pull together. Some covalent compounds do dissolve in water. Most of these solutions contain uncharged molecules dissolved in water and do not conduct an electric current, as shown in **Figure 5.** Some covalent compounds form ions when they dissolve in water. Solutions of these compounds, including compounds called acids, do conduct an electric current. You will learn more about acids in the next section.

Figure 5 *This solution of sugar, a covalent compound, in water does not conduct an electric current because the individual molecules of sugar are not charged.*

Sugar water

REVIEW

1. List two properties of ionic compounds.

2. List two properties of covalent compounds.

3. Methane is a gas at room temperature. What type of compound is this most likely to be?

4. **Comparing Concepts** Compare ionic and covalent compounds based on the type of particle that makes up each.

Acids, Bases, and Salts

What You'll Do

- Describe the properties and uses of acids and bases.
- Explain the difference between strong acids and bases and weak acids and bases.
- Identify acids and bases using the pH scale.
- Describe the properties and uses of salts.

Have you ever noticed that when you squeeze lemon juice into tea, the color of the tea becomes lighter? Shown in **Figure 6,** lemon juice contains a substance called an acid that changes the color of a substance in the tea. The ability to change the color of certain chemicals is one property used to classify substances as acids or bases. A third category of substances, called salts, are formed by the reaction of an acid with a base.

Figure 6 *Acids, like those found in lemon juice, can change the color of tea.*

NEVER touch or taste a concentrated solution of a strong acid.

Acids

An **acid** is any compound that increases the number of hydrogen ions when dissolved in water, and whose solution tastes sour and can change the color of certain compounds.

Properties of Acids If you have ever had orange juice, you have experienced the sour taste of an acid. The taste of lemons, limes, and other citrus fruits is a result of citric acid. Taste, however, should NEVER be used as a test to identify an unknown chemical. Many acids are *corrosive,* meaning they destroy body tissue and clothing, and many are also poisonous.

Acids react with some metals to produce hydrogen gas, as shown in **Figure 7.** Adding an acid to baking soda or limestone produces a different gas, carbon dioxide.

Solutions of acids conduct an electric current because acids break apart to form ions in water. Acids increase the number of hydrogen ions, H^+, in a solution. However, the hydrogen ion does not normally exist alone. In a water solution, each hydrogen ion bonds to a water molecule, H_2O, to form a hydronium ion, H_3O^+.

Figure 7 *Bubbles of hydrogen gas are produced when zinc metal reacts with hydrochloric acid.*

Detecting Acids As mentioned earlier, a property of acids is their ability to change the color of a substance. An *indicator* is a substance that changes color in the presence of an acid or base. An indicator commonly used is litmus. Paper strips containing litmus are available in both blue and red. When an acid is added to blue litmus paper, the color of the litmus changes to red, as shown in **Figure 8.** (Red litmus paper is used to detect bases, as will be discussed shortly.) Many plant materials, such as red cabbage, contain compounds that are indicators.

Figure 8 *Vinegar turns blue litmus paper red because it contains acetic acid.*

Figure 9 *The label on this car battery warns you that sulfuric acid is found in the battery.*

Uses of Acids Acids are used in many areas of industry as well as in your home. Sulfuric acid is the most widely produced industrial chemical in the world. It is used in the production of metals, paper, paint, detergents, and fertilizers. It is also used in car batteries, as shown in **Figure 9.** Nitric acid is used to make fertilizers, rubber, and plastics. Hydrochloric acid is used in the production of metals and to help keep swimming pools free of algae. It is also found in your stomach, where it aids in digestion. Citric acid and ascorbic acid (vitamin C) are found in orange juice, while carbonic acid and phosphoric acid help give extra "bite" to soft drinks.

Strong Versus Weak As an acid dissolves in water, its molecules break apart and produce hydrogen ions. When all the molecules of an acid break apart in water to produce hydrogen ions, the acid is considered a strong acid. Strong acids include sulfuric acid, nitric acid, and hydrochloric acid.

When few molecules of an acid break apart in water to produce hydrogen ions, the acid is considered a weak acid. Acetic acid, citric acid, carbonic acid, and phosphoric acid are all weak acids.

Bases

A **base** is any compound that increases the number of hydroxide ions when dissolved in water, and whose solution tastes bitter, feels slippery, and can change the color of certain compounds.

Properties of Bases   If you have ever accidentally tasted soap, then you know the bitter taste of a base. Soap also demonstrates that a base feels slippery. However, NEVER use taste or touch as a test to identify an unknown chemical. Like acids, many bases are corrosive. If your fingers feel slippery when you are using a base in an experiment, you might have gotten the base on your hands. You should immediately rinse your hands with large amounts of water.

Solutions of bases conduct an electric current because bases increase the number of hydroxide ions, OH^-, in a solution. A hydroxide ion is actually a hydrogen atom and an oxygen atom bonded together. An extra electron gives the ion a negative charge.

Detecting Bases   Like acids, bases change the color of an indicator. Most indicators turn a different color for bases than they do for acids. For example, bases will change the color of red litmus paper to blue, as shown in **Figure 10.**

To determine how acidic or basic a solution is, just use your head—of cabbage! Try it for yourself on page 688 of the LabBook.

NEVER touch or taste a concentrated solution of a strong base.

Figure 10 *Sodium hydroxide, a base, turns red litmus paper blue.*

Uses of Bases   Like acids, bases have many uses. Sodium hydroxide is used to make soap and paper. It is also in oven cleaners and in products that unclog drains, as shown in **Figure 11.** Remember, bases can harm your skin, so carefully follow the safety instructions when using these products. Calcium hydroxide is used to make cement, mortar, and plaster. Ammonia is found in many household cleaners and is also used in the production of fertilizers. Magnesium hydroxide and aluminum hydroxide are used in antacids to treat heartburn.

Figure 11 *This drain cleaner contains sodium hydroxide to help dissolve grease that can clog the drain.*

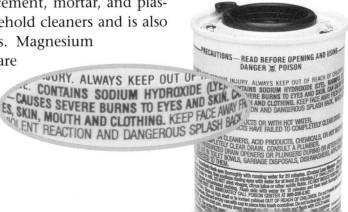

Strong Versus Weak When all the molecules of a base break apart in water to produce hydroxide ions, the base is called a strong base. Strong bases include sodium hydroxide, calcium hydroxide, and potassium hydroxide.

When only a few of the molecules of a base produce hydroxide ions in water, the base is called a weak base. Ammonia, magnesium hydroxide, and aluminum hydroxide are all weak bases.

Acids and Bases Neutralize One Another

If you have ever suffered from an acid stomach, or heartburn, as shown in **Figure 12,** you might have taken an antacid. Antacids contain weak bases that soothe your heartburn by reacting with and neutralizing the acid in your stomach. Acids and bases neutralize one another because the H^+ of the acid and the OH^- of the base react to form water, H_2O. Other ions from the acid and base are also dissolved in the water. If the water is evaporated, these ions join to form a compound called a salt. You'll learn more about salts later in this section.

The pH Scale Indicators such as litmus can identify whether a solution contains an acid or base. To describe how acidic or basic a solution is, the pH scale is used. The **pH** of a solution is a measure of the hydronium ion concentration in the solution. By measuring the hydronium ion concentration, the pH is also a measure of the hydrogen ion concentration. On the scale, a solution that has a pH of 7 is neutral, meaning that it is neither acidic nor basic. Pure water has a pH of 7. Basic solutions have a pH greater than 7, and acidic solutions have a pH less than 7. Look at **Figure 13** to see the pH values for many common materials.

Figure 12 *Have heartburn? Take an antacid! Antacid tablets contain a base that neutralizes the acid in your stomach.*

QuickLab

pHast Relief!

1. Fill a **small plastic cup** halfway with **vinegar.** Test the vinegar with **red** and **blue litmus paper.** Record your results in your ScienceLog.

2. Carefully crush an **antacid tablet,** and mix it with the vinegar. Test the mixture with litmus paper. Record your results in your ScienceLog.

3. Compare the acidity of the solution before and after the reaction.

Figure 13 pH Values of Common Materials

Using Indicators to Determine pH A single indicator allows you to determine if a solution is acidic or basic, but a mixture of different indicators can be used to determine the pH of a solution. After determining the colors for this mixture at different pH values, the indicators can be used to determine the pH of an unknown solution, as shown in **Figure 14.** Indicators can be used as paper strips or solutions, and they are often used to test the pH of soil and of water in pools and aquariums. Another way to determine the acidity of a solution is to use an instrument called a pH meter, which can detect and measure hydrogen ions electronically.

Figure 14 *The paper strip contains several indicators. The pH of a solution is determined by comparing the color of the strip to the scale provided.*

Self-Check

Which is more acidic, a soft drink or milk? (Hint: Refer to Figure 13 to find the pH values of these drinks.) *(See page 724 to check your answer.)*

Biology
CONNECTION

Human blood has a pH of between 7.38 and 7.42. If the pH is above 7.8 or below 7, the body cannot function properly. Sudden changes in blood pH that are not quickly corrected can be fatal.

pH and the Environment Living things depend on having a steady pH in their environment. Plants are known to have certain preferred growing conditions. Some plants, such as pine trees, prefer acidic soil with a pH between 4 and 6. Other plants, such as lettuce, require basic soil with a pH between 8 and 9. Fish require water near pH 7. As you can see in Figure 13, rainwater can have a pH as low as 3. This occurs in areas where compounds found in pollution react with water to make the strong acids sulfuric acid and nitric acid. As this acid precipitation collects in lakes, it can lower the pH to levels that may kill the fish and other organisms in the lake. To neutralize the acid and bring the pH closer to 7, a base can be added to the lakes, as shown in **Figure 15.**

Figure 15 *This helicopter is adding a base to an acidic lake. Neutralizing the acid in the lake might help protect the organisms living in the lake.*

Salts

When you hear the word *salt,* you probably think of the table salt you use to season your food. But the sodium chloride found in your salt shaker is only one example of a large group of compounds called salts. A **salt** is an ionic compound formed from the positive ion of a base and the negative ion of an acid. You may remember that a salt and water are produced when an acid neutralizes a base. However, salts can also be produced in other reactions, as shown in **Figure 16.**

Neutralization of an acid and a base:
$$HCl + KOH \longrightarrow H_2O + KCl$$

Reaction of a metal with an acid:
$$2K + 2HCl \longrightarrow 2KCl + H_2$$

Reaction of a metal and a nonmetal:
$$2K + Cl_2 \longrightarrow 2KCl$$

Figure 16 *The salt potassium chloride can be formed from several different reactions.*

Uses of Salts Salts have many uses in industry and in your home. You already know that sodium chloride is used to season foods. It is also used in the production of other compounds, including lye (sodium hydroxide), hydrochloric acid, and baking soda. The salt calcium sulfate is made into wallboard, or plasterboard, which is used in construction. Sodium nitrate is one of many salts used as a preservative in foods. Calcium carbonate is a salt that makes up limestone, chalk, and seashells. Another use of salts is shown in **Figure 17.**

Figure 17 *Salts are used to help keep roads free of ice.*

internetconnect

SCI**LINKS**
NSTA

TOPIC: Acids and Bases, Salts
GO TO: www.scilinks.org
*sci***LINKS NUMBER:** HSTP365, HSTP370

REVIEW

1. What ion is present in all acid solutions?

2. What are two ways scientists can measure pH?

3. What products are formed when an acid and base react?

4. **Comparing Concepts**   Compare the properties of acids and bases.

5. **Applying Concepts**   Would you expect the pH of a solution of soap to be 4 or 9?

Organic Compounds

Of all the known compounds, more than 90 percent are members of a group of compounds called organic compounds. **Organic compounds** are covalent compounds composed of carbon-based molecules. Sugar, starch, oil, protein, nucleic acid, and even cotton and plastic are organic compounds. How can there be so many different kinds of organic compounds? The huge variety of organic compounds is explained by examining the carbon atom.

Each Carbon Atom Forms Four Bonds

Carbon atoms form the backbone of organic compounds. Because each carbon atom has four valence electrons (electrons in the outermost energy level of an atom), each atom can make four bonds. Thus, a carbon atom can bond to one, two, or even three other carbon atoms and still have electrons remaining to bond to other atoms. Three types of carbon backbones on which many organic compounds are based are shown in the models in **Figure 18.**

Some organic compounds have hundreds or even thousands of carbon atoms making up their backbone! Although the elements hydrogen and oxygen, along with carbon, make up many of the organic compounds, sulfur, nitrogen, and phosphorus are also important—especially in forming the molecules that make up all living things.

What You'll Do

◆ Explain why so many organic compounds are possible.
◆ Describe the characteristics of carbohydrates, lipids, proteins, and nucleic acids and their functions in the body.
◆ Describe and identify saturated, unsaturated, and aromatic hydrocarbons.

Figure 18 *These models, called structural formulas, are used to show how atoms in a molecule are connected. Each line represents a pair of electrons shared in a covalent bond.*

Straight Chain All carbon atoms are connected one after another in a line.

Branched Chain The chain of carbon atoms continues in more than one direction where a carbon atom bonds to three or more other carbon atoms.

Ring The chain of carbon atoms forms a ring.

Chemical Compounds **383**

Biochemicals: The Compounds of Life

Organic compounds made by living things are called **biochemicals.** The molecules of most biochemicals are very large. Biochemicals can be divided into four categories: carbohydrates, lipids, proteins, and nucleic acids. Each type of biochemical has important functions in living organisms.

Carbohydrates   Starch and cellulose are examples of carbohydrates. **Carbohydrates** are biochemicals that are composed of one or more simple sugars bonded together; they are used as a source of energy and for energy storage. There are two types of carbohydrates: simple carbohydrates and complex carbohydrates. A single sugar molecule, represented using a hexagon, or a few sugar molecules bonded together are examples of simple carbohydrates, as illustrated in **Figure 19.** Glucose is a simple carbohydrate produced by plants through photosynthesis.

Figure 19 *The sugar molecules in the left image are simple carbohydrates. The starch in the right image is a complex carbohydrate because it is composed of many sugar molecules bonded together.*

Sugar Storage System   When an organism has more sugar than it needs, its extra sugar may be stored for later use in the form of complex carbohydrates, as shown in Figure 19. Molecules of complex carbohydrates are composed of hundreds or even thousands of sugar molecules bonded together. Because carbohydrates provide the energy you need each day, you should include sources of carbohydrates in your diet, such as the foods shown in **Figure 20.**

Figure 20 *Simple carbohydrates include sugars found in fruits and honey. Complex carbohydrates, such as starches, are found in bread, cereal, and pasta.*

Lipids   Fats, oils, waxes, and steroids are examples of lipids. **Lipids** are biochemicals that do not dissolve in water and have many different functions, including storing energy and making up cell membranes. Although too much fat in your diet can be unhealthy, some fat is extremely important to good health. The foods in **Figure 21** are sources of lipids.

Lipids store excess energy in the body. Animals tend to store lipids primarily as fats, while plants store lipids as oils. When an organism has used up most of its carbohydrates, it can obtain energy by breaking down lipids. Lipids are also used to store vitamins that dissolve in fat but not in water.

Figure 21 *Vegetable oil, meat, cheese, nuts, and milk are sources of lipids in your diet.*

Lipids Make Up Cell Membranes   Each cell is surrounded by a cell membrane. Much of the cell membrane is formed from molecules of phospholipids. The structure of these molecules plays an important part in the phospholipid's role in the cell membrane. The tail of a phospholipid molecule is a long, straight-chain carbon backbone composed only of carbon and hydrogen atoms. The tail is not attracted to water. The head of a phospholipid molecule is attracted to water because it is composed of phosphorus, oxygen, and nitrogen atoms in addition to carbon and hydrogen atoms. This results in the double layer of phospholipid molecules shown in the model in **Figure 22.** This arrangement of phospholipid molecules creates a barrier to help control the flow of chemicals into and out of the cell.

Deposits of the lipid cholesterol in the body have been linked to health problems such as heart disease. However, cholesterol is needed in nerve and brain tissue as well as to make certain hormones that regulate body processes such as growth.

Figure 22 *A cell membrane is composed primarily of two layers of phospholipid molecules.*

The **head** of each phospholipid molecule is attracted to water either inside or outside of the cell.

The **tail** of each phospholipid molecule is pushed against other tails because they are not attracted to water.

Figure 23 *Meat, fish, cheese, and beans contain proteins, which are broken down into amino acids as they are digested.*

Biology
C O N N E C T I O N

All the proteins in your body are made from just 20 amino acids. Nine of these amino acids are called essential amino acids because your body cannot make them. You must get them from the food you eat.

Proteins Most of the biochemicals found in living things are proteins. In fact, after water, proteins are the most abundant molecules in your cells. **Proteins** are biochemicals that are composed of amino acids; they have many different functions, including regulating chemical activities, transporting and storing materials, and providing structural support.

Every protein is composed of small "building blocks" called *amino acids*. Amino acids are smaller molecules composed of carbon, hydrogen, oxygen, and nitrogen atoms. Some amino acids also include sulfur atoms. Amino acids chemically bond to form proteins of many different shapes and sizes. The function of a protein depends on the shape that the bonded amino acids adopt. If even a single amino acid is missing or out of place, the protein may not function correctly or at all. The foods shown in **Figure 23** provide amino acids that your body needs to make new proteins.

Examples of Proteins Enzymes are proteins that regulate chemical reactions in the body by acting as catalysts to increase the rate at which the reactions occur. Some hormones are proteins. Insulin is a hormone that helps regulate the level of sugar in your blood. Oxygen is carried by the protein hemoglobin, allowing red blood cells to deliver oxygen throughout your body. There are also large proteins that extend through cell membranes and help control the transport of materials into and out of cells. Proteins that provide structural support often form structures that are easy to see, like those in **Figure 24.**

Figure 24 *Hair and spider webs are made up of proteins that are shaped like long fibers.*

Nucleic Acids The largest molecules made by living organisms are nucleic acids. **Nucleic acids** are biochemicals that store information and help to build proteins and other nucleic acids. Nucleic acids are sometimes called the "blueprints of life" because they contain all the information needed for the cell to make all of its proteins.

Like proteins, nucleic acids are long chains of smaller molecules joined together. These smaller molecules are composed of carbon, hydrogen, oxygen, nitrogen, and phosphorus atoms. Nucleic acids are much larger than proteins even though nucleic acids are composed of only five building blocks.

DNA and RNA There are two types of nucleic acids: DNA and RNA. DNA (**d**eoxyribo**n**ucleic **a**cid), like that shown in **Figure 25,** is the genetic material of the cell. DNA molecules can store an enormous amount of information because of their length. The DNA molecules in a single human cell have an overall length of about 2 m—that's over 6 ft long! When a cell needs to make a certain protein, it copies the important part of the DNA. The information copied from the DNA directs the order in which amino acids are bonded together to make that protein. DNA also contains information used to build the second type of nucleic acid, RNA (**r**ibo**n**ucleic **a**cid). RNA is involved in the actual building of proteins.

Science CONNECTION

Nucleic acids store information—even about ancient peoples. Read more about these incredible biochemicals on page 394.

Figure 25 *The DNA from a fruit fly contains all of the instructions for making proteins, nucleic acids . . . in fact, for making everything in the organism!*

REVIEW

1. What are organic compounds?

2. What are the four categories of biochemicals?

3. What are two functions of proteins?

4. What biochemicals are used to provide energy?

5. **Inferring Relationships** Sickle-cell anemia is a condition that results from a change of one amino acid in the protein hemoglobin. Why is this condition a genetic disorder?

Hydrocarbons

Organic compounds that are composed of only carbon and hydrogen are called **hydrocarbons.** Hydrocarbons are an important group of organic compounds. Many fuels, including gasoline, methane, and propane, are hydrocarbons. Hydrocarbons can be divided into three categories: saturated, unsaturated, and aromatic.

Saturated Hydrocarbons   Propane, like that used in the stove in **Figure 26,** is an example of a saturated hydrocarbon. A *saturated hydrocarbon* is a hydrocarbon in which each carbon atom in the molecule shares a single bond with each of four other atoms. A single bond is a covalent bond that consists of one pair of shared electrons. Hydrocarbons that contain carbon atoms connected only by single bonds are called saturated because no other atoms can be added without replacing an atom that is part of the molecule. Saturated hydrocarbons are also called *alkanes.*

Figure 26 *The propane in this camping stove is a saturated hydrocarbon.*

Unsaturated Hydrocarbons   Each carbon atom forms four bonds. However, these bonds do not always have to be single bonds. An *unsaturated hydrocarbon* is a hydrocarbon in which at least two carbon atoms share a double bond or a triple bond. A double bond is a covalent bond that consists of two pairs of shared electrons. Compounds that contain two carbon atoms connected by a double bond are called *alkenes.*

A triple bond is a covalent bond that consists of three pairs of shared electrons. Hydrocarbons that contain two carbon atoms connected by a triple bond are called *alkynes.*

Hydrocarbons that contain double or triple bonds are called unsaturated because the double or triple bond can be broken to allow more atoms to be added to the molecule. Examples of unsaturated hydrocarbons are shown in **Figure 27.**

Figure 27 *Fruits produce ethene, which helps ripen the fruit. Ethyne, better known as acetylene, is burned in this miner's lamp and is also used in welding.*

Aromatic Hydrocarbons Most aromatic compounds are based on benzene, the compound represented by the model in **Figure 28.** Look for this structure to help identify an aromatic hydrocarbon. As the name implies, aromatic hydrocarbons often have strong odors and are therefore used in such products as air fresheners and moth balls.

Figure 28 *Benzene has a ring of six carbons with alternating double and single bonds. Benzene is the starting material for manufacturing many products, including medicines.*

Other Organic Compounds

Many other types of organic compounds exist that have atoms of halogens, oxygen, sulfur, and phosphorus in their molecules. A few of these types of compounds and their uses are described in the chart below.

Types and Uses of Organic Compounds		
Type of compound	**Uses**	**Examples**
Alkyl halides	starting material for Teflon refrigerant (freon)	chloromethane (CH_3Cl) bromoethane (C_2H_5Br)
Alcohols	rubbing alcohol gasoline additive antifreeze	methanol (CH_3OH) ethanol (C_2H_5OH)
Organic acids	food preservatives flavorings	ethanoic acid (CH_3COOH) propanoic acid (C_2H_5COOH)
Esters	flavorings fragrances clothing (polyester)	methyl ethanoate (CH_3COOCH_3) ethyl propanoate ($C_2H_5COOC_2H_5$)

REVIEW

1. What is a hydrocarbon?

2. How many electrons are shared in a double bond? a triple bond?

3. **Comparing Concepts** Compare saturated and unsaturated hydrocarbons.

Chapter Highlights

SECTION 1

Vocabulary
ionic compounds (p. 374)
covalent compounds (p. 375)

Section Notes
- Ionic compounds contain ionic bonds and are composed of oppositely charged ions arranged in a repeating pattern called a crystal lattice.
- Ionic compounds tend to be brittle, have high melting points, and dissolve in water to form solutions that conduct an electric current.
- Covalent compounds are composed of elements that are covalently bonded and consist of independent particles called molecules.
- Covalent compounds tend to have low melting points. Most do not dissolve well in water and do not form solutions that conduct an electric current.

SECTION 2

Vocabulary
acid (p. 377)
base (p. 379)
pH (p. 380)
salt (p. 382)

Section Notes
- An acid is a compound that increases the number of hydrogen ions in solution. Acids taste sour, turn blue litmus paper red, react with metals to produce hydrogen gas, and react with limestone or baking soda to produce carbon dioxide gas.
- A base is a compound that increases the number of hydroxide ions in solution. Bases taste bitter, feel slippery, and turn red litmus paper blue.
- When dissolved in water, every molecule of a strong acid or base breaks apart to form ions. Few molecules of weak acids and bases break apart to form ions.
- When combined, an acid and a base neutralize one another to produce water and a salt.
- pH is a measure of hydronium ion concentration in a solution. A pH of 7 indicates a neutral substance. A pH of less than 7 indicates an acidic substance. A pH of greater than 7 indicates a basic substance.
- A salt is an ionic compound formed from the positive ion of a base and the negative ion of an acid.

Labs
Cabbage Patch Indicators (p. 688)
Making Salt (p. 690)

☑ Skills Check

Visual Understanding

LITMUS PAPER You can use the ability of acids and bases to change the color of indicators to identify a chemical as an acid or base. Litmus is an indicator commonly used in schools. Review Figures 8 and 10, which show how the color of litmus paper is changed by an acid and by a base.

pH SCALE Knowing whether a substance is an acid or a base can help explain some of the properties of the substance. The pH scale shown in Figure 13 illustrates the pH ranges for many common substances.

SECTION 3

Vocabulary

organic compounds *(p. 383)*

biochemicals *(p. 384)*

carbohydrates *(p. 384)*

lipids *(p. 385)*

proteins *(p. 386)*

nucleic acids *(p. 387)*

hydrocarbons *(p. 388)*

Section Notes

- Organic compounds are covalent compounds composed of carbon-based molecules.

- Each carbon atom forms four bonds with other carbon atoms or with atoms of other elements to form straight chains, branched chains, or rings.

- Biochemicals are organic compounds made by living things.

- Carbohydrates are biochemicals that are composed of one or more simple sugars bonded together; they are used as a source of energy and for energy storage.

- Lipids are biochemicals that do not dissolve in water and have many functions, including storing energy and making up cell membranes.

- Proteins are biochemicals that are composed of amino acids and have many functions, including regulating chemical activities, transporting and storing materials, and providing structural support.

- Nucleic acids are biochemicals that store information and help to build proteins and other nucleic acids.

- Hydrocarbons are organic compounds composed of only carbon and hydrogen.

- In a saturated hydrocarbon, each carbon atom in the molecule shares a single bond with each of four other atoms.

- In an unsaturated hydrocarbon, at least two carbon atoms share a double bond or a triple bond.

- Many aromatic hydrocarbons are based on the six-carbon ring of benzene.

- Other organic compounds, including alkyl halides, alcohols, organic acids, and esters, are formed by adding atoms of other elements.

---

internet connect

GO TO: go.hrw.com

Visit the **HRW** Web site for a variety of learning tools related to this chapter. Just type in the keyword:

KEYWORD: HSTCMP

N S T A

GO TO: www.scilinks.org

Visit the **National Science Teachers Association** on-line Web site for Internet resources related to this chapter. Just type in the *sci*LINKS number for more information about the topic:

TOPIC: Ionic Compounds	*sci***LINKS NUMBER:** HSTP355
TOPIC: Covalent Compounds	*sci***LINKS NUMBER:** HSTP360
TOPIC: Acids and Bases	*sci***LINKS NUMBER:** HSTP365
TOPIC: Salts	*sci***LINKS NUMBER:** HSTP370
TOPIC: Organic Compounds	*sci***LINKS NUMBER:** HSTP375

Chapter Review

USING VOCABULARY

To complete the following sentences, choose the correct term from each pair of terms listed below:

1. Compounds that have low melting points and do not usually dissolve well in water are __?__. (*ionic compounds* or *covalent compounds*)

2. A(n) __?__ turns red litmus paper blue. (*acid* or *base*)

3. __?__ are composed of only carbon and hydrogen. (*Ionic compounds* or *Hydrocarbons*)

4. A biochemical composed of amino acids is a __?__. (*lipid* or *protein*)

5. A source of energy for living things can be found in __?__. (*nucleic acids* or *carbohydrates*)

UNDERSTANDING CONCEPTS

Multiple Choice

6. Which of the following describes lipids?
   a. used to store energy
   b. do not dissolve in water
   c. make up most of the cell membrane
   d. all of the above

7. An acid reacts to produce carbon dioxide when the acid is added to
   a. water.
   b. limestone.
   c. salt.
   d. sodium hydroxide.

8. Which of the following does NOT describe ionic compounds?
   a. high melting point
   b. brittle
   c. do not conduct electric currents in water
   d. dissolve easily in water

9. An increase in the concentration of hydronium ions in solution __?__ the pH.
   a. raises
   b. lowers
   c. does not affect
   d. doubles

10. Which of the following compounds makes up the majority of cell membranes?
    a. lipids
    b. ionic compounds
    c. acids
    d. nucleic acids

11. The compounds that store information for building proteins are
    a. lipids.
    b. hydrocarbons.
    c. nucleic acids.
    d. carbohydrates.

Short Answer

12. What type of compound would you use to neutralize a solution of potassium hydroxide?

13. Explain why the reaction of an acid with a base is called *neutralization*.

14. What characteristic of carbon atoms helps to explain the wide variety of organic compounds?

15. Compare acids and bases based on the ion produced when each compound is dissolved in water.

Concept Mapping

16. Use the following terms to create a concept map: acid, base, salt, neutral, pH.

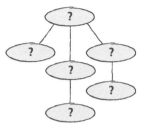

CRITICAL THINKING AND PROBLEM SOLVING

17. Fish give off the base ammonia, NH_3, as waste. How does the release of ammonia affect the pH of the water in the aquarium? What can be done to correct the problem?

18. Many insects, such as fire ants, inject formic acid, a weak acid, when they bite or sting. Describe the type of compound that should be used to treat the bite.

19. Organic compounds are also covalent compounds. What properties would you expect organic compounds to have as a result?

20. Farmers often can taste their soil to determine whether the soil has the correct acidity for their plants. How would taste help the farmer determine the acidity of the soil?

21. A diet that includes a high level of lipids is unhealthy. Why is a diet containing no lipids also unhealthy?

INTERPRETING GRAPHICS

Study the structural formulas below, and then answer the questions that follow.

a

b

c

d

22. A saturated hydrocarbon is represented by which structural formula(s)?

23. An unsaturated hydrocarbon is represented by which structural formula(s)?

24. An aromatic hydrocarbon is represented by which structural formula(s)?

Reading Check-up

Take a minute to review your answers to the Pre-Reading Questions found at the bottom of page 372. Have your answers changed? If necessary, revise your answers based on what you have learned since you began this chapter.

Unique Compounds

What makes you unique? Would you believe it's a complex pattern of information found on the deoxyribonucleic acid (DNA) in your cells? Well it is! And by analyzing how this information is arranged, scientists are finding clues about human ancestry.

Mummy Knows Best

If you compare the DNA from an older species and a more recent species, you can tell which traits were passed on. To consider the question of human evolution, scientists must use DNA from older humans—like mummies. Molecular archeologists study DNA from mummies in order to understand human evolution at a molecular level. Since well-preserved DNA fragments from mummies are scarce, you might be wondering why some ancient DNA fragments have been preserved better than others.

Neutralizing Acids

The condition of preserved DNA fragments depends on how the mummy was preserved. The tannic acid—commonly found in peat bogs—that is responsible for preserving mummies destroys DNA. But if there are limestone rocks nearby, the calcium carbonate from these rocks neutralizes the tannic acid, thereby preserving the DNA.

Molecular Photocopying

When scientists find well-preserved DNA, they make copies of it by using a technique called polymerase chain reaction (PCR). PCR takes advantage of *polymerases* to generate copies of DNA fragments. Polymerases are found in all living things, and their job is to make strands of genetic material using existing strands as templates. That is why PCR is also called molecular photocopying. But researchers who use this technique risk contaminating the ancient DNA with their own DNA. If even one skin cell falls into the PCR mixture, the results are ruined.

Mysteries Solved?

PCR has been used to research ancient civilizations and peoples. For example, scientists found an 8,000-year-old human brain in Florida. This brain was preserved well enough for scientists to analyze the DNA and to conclude that today's Native Americans are not direct descendants of this group of people.

PCR has also been used to analyze the culture of ancient peoples. When archeologists tested the pigments used in 4,000-year-old paintings on rocks along the Pecos River, in Texas, they found DNA that was probably from bison. This was an unexpected discovery because there were no bison along the Pecos River when the paintings were made. The archeologists have concluded, therefore, that the artists must have tried very hard to find this specific pigment for their paint. This leads the archeologists to believe that the paintings must have had some spiritual meaning.

On Your Own

▶ Research ways PCR is being used to detect diseases and infections in humans and animals.

▲ *DNA from mummies like this one provides scientists with valuable information.*

THE SECRETS OF SPIDER SILK

What is as strong as steel, more elastic than a rubber band, and able to stop a speeding bullet? Spider silk! Spiders make this silk to weave their delicate but deadly webs.

▲ *A golden orb-weaving spider on its web*

The Tangled Web We Weave

If you've seen a spider web, you've probably noticed that it resembles a bicycle wheel. The "spokes" of the web are made of a silk thread called *dragline silk.* The sticky, stretchy part of the web is called *capture silk* because that's what spiders use to capture their prey. Spider silk is made of proteins, and these proteins are made of blocks of amino acids.

There are 20 naturally occurring amino acids, but spider silk has only seven of them. Until recently, scientists knew what the silk is made of, but they didn't know how these amino acids were distributed throughout the protein chains.

Scientists used a technique called nuclear magnetic resonance (NMR) to see the structure of dragline silk. The silk fiber is made of two tough strands of alanine–rich protein embedded in a glycine–rich substance. If you look at this protein even closer, it looks like tangled spaghetti. Scientists believe that this tangled part makes the silk springy and a repeating sequence of five amino acids makes the protein stretchy.

Spinning Tails

Scientists think they have identified the piece of DNA needed to make spider silk. Synthetic silk can be made by copying a small part of this DNA and inserting it into the bacterium *Escherichia coli.* The bacteria read the gene and make liquid silk protein. Biologists at the University of Wyoming, in Laramie, have come up with a way to spin spider silk into threads by pushing the liquid protein through fine tubes.

What Do You Think?

▶ Scientists seem to think that there are many uses for synthetic spider silk. Make a list in your ScienceLog of as many things as you can think of that this material would be good for.

▲ *Spiders use organs called spinnerets to spin their webs. This image of spinnerets was taken with a scanning electron microscope.*

Atomic Energy

Pre-Reading
Questions

1. What is nuclear radiation?

2. How are radioactive
   materials used?

3. What are two concerns
   about energy obtained
   from nuclear reactions?

NUCLEAR DETECTIVE AGENTS

Look closely at the blood vessel pathways that show up so clearly in this image of a human hand. Medical scientists sometimes inject radioactive substances into the body to help locate tumors and measure the activity of certain organs. After radioactive emissions from the substance are measured using a scanning device, computers turn this data into an image. In this chapter, you will learn about the radioactive energy of some atoms, about nuclear energy as a power source, and about other uses of radioactive materials.

WATCH YOUR HEADSIUM!

The nuclei of radioactive atoms are unstable. Therefore, they decay and change into different nuclei. In this activity, you will model the decay of unstable nuclei into stable nuclei.

Procedure

1. Place **100 pennies** heads-up in a **box with a lid.** The pennies represent radioactive "headsium" nuclei. Record the 100 headsium nuclei present as Trial 0 in your ScienceLog.

2. Close the box, and shake it vigorously up and down for 5 seconds.

3. Open the box, and remove all of the "tailsium" nuclei, pennies that are tails-up. These pennies represent stable nuclei that result from decay. Count the number of headsium nuclei remaining, and record it in your ScienceLog as Trial 1.

4. Continue performing trials until you have no more pennies in the box or you have finished five trials, whichever comes first. Record all your results.

Analysis

5. On a piece of **graph paper,** graph your data by plotting "Number of headsium nuclei" on the y-axis and "Trial number" on the x-axis.

6. What trend do you see in the number of headsium nuclei over time?

7. Compare your graph with the graphs of other students in your class.

Atomic Energy **397**

What You'll Do

◆ Compare alpha, beta, and gamma decay.
◆ Describe the penetrating power of the three types of nuclear radiation.
◆ Calculate ages of objects using half-life.
◆ Identify uses of radioactive materials.

Radioactivity

When scientists perform experiments, they don't always get the results they expect. In 1896, a French scientist named Henri Becquerel did not get the results he expected, but he did discover a fascinating new area of science.

Discovering Radioactivity

Becquerel's hypothesis was that fluorescent minerals could give off X rays. (*Fluorescent* materials glow when exposed to light, as shown in **Figure 1.**) To test his hypothesis, Becquerel placed a fluorescent mineral on top of a photographic plate wrapped in paper. He placed the setup in bright sunlight.

Becquerel predicted that an image of the mineral would appear on the plate. After developing the plate, he saw the image he expected.

Figure 1 *The brightly colored portions of this sample are fluorescent in ultraviolet light.*

An Unexpected Result Becquerel tried to confirm his results, but cloudy weather delayed his plans. He placed his materials in a drawer. After several days, he developed the plate anyway. He was amazed to see a strong image, shown in **Figure 2.**

Becquerel's results showed that even without light, the mineral gave off energy that passed through paper and made an image on the plate. After more tests, Becquerel concluded that this energy comes from uranium, an element in the mineral.

Naming the Unexpected Scientists call this energy **nuclear radiation,** high-energy particles and rays that are emitted by the nuclei of some atoms. Marie Curie, a scientist working with Becquerel, named the ability of some elements to give off nuclear radiation **radioactivity.**

Figure 2 *The blurry image on this photographic plate surprised Becquerel.*

Nuclear Radiation Is Produced Through Decay

Radioactive decay is the process in which the nucleus of a radioactive atom releases nuclear radiation. Three types of radioactive decay are alpha decay, beta decay, and gamma decay.

Alpha Decay   The release of an alpha particle from a nucleus is called **alpha decay.** An *alpha particle* consists of two protons and two neutrons, so it has a mass number of 4 and a charge of 2+. An alpha particle is identical to the nucleus of a helium atom. Many large radioactive nuclei give off alpha particles to become nuclei of atoms of different elements. One example is radium-226. (Remember that the number that follows the name of an element indicates the **mass number**—the sum of the protons and neutrons in an atom.)

Conservation in Decay   Look at the model of alpha decay in **Figure 3.** This model illustrates two important features of all types of radioactive decay. First, the mass number is conserved. The sum of the mass numbers of the starting materials is always equal to the sum of the mass numbers of the products. Second, charge is conserved. The sum of the charges of the starting materials is always equal to the sum of the charges of the products.

Geology
CONNECTION

Alpha particles emitted during alpha decay eventually gain two electrons from nearby atoms and become helium atoms. Almost all of the helium in Earth's atmosphere formed from alpha particles emitted by nuclei of radioactive atoms.

Figure 3 Alpha Decay of Radium-226

Radium-226

Radon-222

Energy

Charge: 86+

Alpha particle (helium-4)

Charge: 88+

Charge: 2+

Mass number is conserved.
226 = 222 + 4

Charge is conserved.
(88+) = (86+) + (2+)

Beta Decay The release of a beta particle from a nucleus is called **beta decay.** A *beta particle* can be either an electron (having a charge of 1− and a mass of almost 0) or a *positron* (having a charge of 1+ and a mass of almost 0). Because electrons and positrons do not contain protons or neutrons, the mass number of a beta particle is 0.

Two Types of Beta Decay A carbon-14 nucleus undergoes beta decay as shown in the model in **Figure 4.** During this decay, a neutron breaks into a proton and an electron. Notice that the nucleus becomes a nucleus of a different element, and mass number and charge are conserved, similar to alpha decay.

Not all isotopes of an element decay in the same way. (Remember that **isotopes** are atoms that have the same number of protons but different numbers of neutrons.) A carbon-11 nucleus undergoes beta decay when a proton breaks into a positron and a neutron. However, the beta decay of carbon-11 still changes the nucleus into a nucleus of a different element while conserving both mass number and charge.

Figure 4 Beta Decay of Carbon-14

Carbon-14

Nitrogen-14

Energy

Mass number is conserved.
14 = 14 + 0

Charge is conserved.
(6+) = (7+) + (1−)

Charge: 7+

Beta particle (electron)

Charge: 6+

Charge: 1−

Gamma Decay Did you notice in Figures 3 and 4 that energy is released during alpha decay and beta decay? Some of this energy is in the form of *gamma rays,* a form of light with very high energy. The release of gamma rays from a nucleus is called **gamma decay.** Gamma decay occurs after alpha or beta decay as the particles in the nucleus shift to a more stable arrangement. Because gamma rays have no mass or charge, gamma decay alone does not cause one element to change into another as do alpha decay and beta decay.

✔ Self-Check

Which type of nuclear radiation has the largest mass number?

(See page 724 to check your answer.)

The Penetrating Power of Radiation

The three forms of nuclear radiation differ in their ability to penetrate (go through) matter. This difference is due to the mass and charge associated with each type of radiation, as you can see in **Figure 5.**

Figure 5 The Penetrating Abilities of Nuclear Radiation

Alpha particles have the greatest charge and mass. They travel about 7 cm through air and are stopped by paper or clothing.

Beta particles have a 1– or 1+ charge and almost no mass. They are more penetrating than alpha particles. They travel about 1 m through air, but are stopped by 3 mm of aluminum.

Gamma rays have no charge or mass and are the most penetrating. They are blocked by very dense, thick materials, such as a few centimeters of lead or a few meters of concrete.

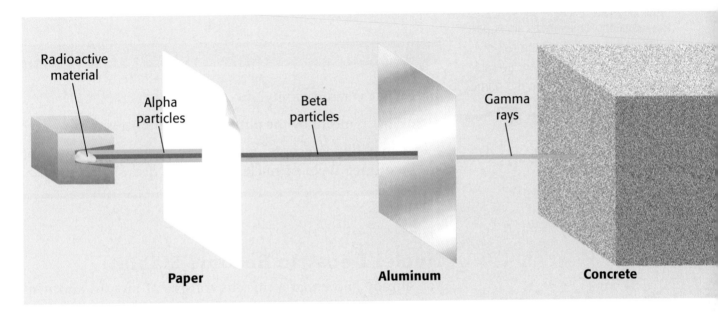

Radioactive material

Alpha particles

Beta particles

Gamma rays

Paper

Aluminum

Concrete

Effects of Radiation on Matter Nuclear radiation can "knock" electrons out of atoms and break chemical bonds between atoms. Both of these actions can cause damage to living and nonliving matter.

Damage to Living Matter When an organism absorbs radiation, its cells can be damaged, causing burns similar to those caused by touching a hot object. A single large exposure to radiation can lead to *radiation sickness.* Symptoms of this condition range from fatigue and loss of appetite to hair loss, destruction of blood cells, and even death. Exposure to radiation can also increase the risk of cancer because of the damage done to cells.

BRAIN FOOD

Marie and Irene Curie died of leukemia, a type of cancer in which abnormal white blood cells multiply and interfere with the body's immune system. It is thought that exposure to radiation caused their leukemia.

Damage to Nonliving Matter Radiation can also damage nonliving matter. When radiation knocks electrons out of metal atoms, the metal is weakened. The metal structures of buildings, such as nuclear power plants, can become unsafe. High levels of radiation, such as gamma rays from the sun, can damage space vehicles.

Damage at Different Depths Because gamma rays are the most penetrating nuclear radiation, they can cause damage deep within an object. Beta particles cause damage closer to the surface, while alpha particles cause damage very near the surface. However, if a source of alpha particles enters an organism, alpha particles cause the most damage because they are the largest and most massive radiation.

> **REVIEW**
>
> 1. What is radioactivity?
>
> 2. What is meant by the phrase "mass number is conserved"?
>
> 3. **Comparing Concepts** Compare the penetrating power of the three types of nuclear radiation discussed.

Nuclei Decay to Become Stable

You already know that a nucleus consists of protons and neutrons together in a very small space. Protons have a positive charge, so they repel one another. (Remember, opposite charges attract, but like charges repel.) Why don't the protons fly apart? Because of the *strong force*, an attractive force that holds the protons and neutrons together in the nucleus.

Polonium
atomic number 84

Too Many Protons The strong force acts only at extremely short distances. As a result, a large nucleus, as modeled in **Figure 6,** is often radioactive. In fact, all nuclei composed of more than 83 protons are radioactive. There are simply too many protons. Although some of these nuclei can exist for billions of years before they decay, they do eventually decay and are therefore called *unstable*.

Figure 6 *This nucleus is unstable, or radioactive, because the repulsion between the protons overcomes the strong force.*

Ratio of Neutrons to Protons A nucleus can also be unstable if it contains too many or too few neutrons compared with protons. Nuclei with more than 60 protons are stable when the ratio of neutrons to protons is about 3 to 2. Nuclei with fewer than 20 protons only need a ratio of about 1 to 1 for stability. This explains the existence of small radioactive isotopes, like the ones modeled in **Figure 7.**

Hydrogen-3

2 neutrons
1 proton

Beryllium-10

6 neutrons
4 protons

Figure 7 *The ratio of neutrons to protons in hydrogen-3 and beryllium-10 is greater than 1 to 1. Therefore, the nuclei of these isotopes are unstable.*

How Does a Nucleus Become Stable? An unstable nucleus will emit (give off) nuclear radiation until it has a stable number of neutrons and protons. An unstable nucleus doesn't always achieve stability through one decay. In fact, some nuclei are just the first in a series of radioactive isotopes formed as a result of alpha and beta decays. Eventually, a nonradioactive nucleus is formed. The nuclei of the most common isotope of uranium, uranium-238, forms the nonradioactive nuclei of lead-206 after a series of 14 decays.

Finding a Date by Decay

Finding a date for someone can be challenging—especially if they are several thousand years old! When hikers in the Italian Alps found the remains shown in **Figure 8** in 1991, scientists were able to estimate the time of death—about 5,300 years ago! How did they do this? The decay of radioactive carbon was the key.

Figure 8 *The remains of the Iceman, a 5,300-year-old mummy, are the best preserved of a human from that time.*

Carbon-14—It's in You! Carbon atoms are found in all living things. A small percentage of these atoms are radioactive carbon-14 atoms. During an organism's life, the percentage of carbon-14 in the organism stays about the same because the atoms that decay are replaced by atoms taken in from the atmosphere by plants or from food by animals. But when an organism dies, the carbon-14 is no longer replaced. Over time, the level of carbon-14 in the remains drops through decay.

Decay Occurs at a Steady Rate Scientists have determined that every 5,730 years, half of the carbon-14 in a sample decays. The rate of decay is constant and is not affected by other conditions, such as temperature or pressure. Each radioactive isotope has its own rate of decay, called half-life. A **half-life** is the amount of time it takes for one-half of the nuclei of a radioactive isotope to decay. **Figure 9** is a model of this process. The table below lists some radioactive isotopes with a wide range of half-lives.

Figure 9 *Half of any radioactive sample decays during each half-life.*

The **original sample** contains a certain amount of radioactive isotope.

After **one half-life,** one-half of the original sample has decayed, leaving half unchanged.

After **two half-lives,** one-fourth of the original sample remains unchanged.

After **three half-lives,** only one-eighth of the original sample remains unchanged.

MATH BREAK

How Old Is It?

An antler has one-fourth of its original carbon-14 unchanged. As shown in Figure 9, two half-lives have occurred. To determine the age of the antler, multiply the number of half-lives that have passed by the length of a half-life. The antler's age is two times the half-life of carbon-14:

2 × 5,730 years = 11,460 years

Now It's Your Turn

Determine the age of a spear containing one-eighth its original amount of carbon-14.

Examples of Half-lives			
Isotope	**Half-life**	**Isotope**	**Half-life**
Uranium-238	4.5 billion years	Polonium-210	138 days
Oxygen-21	3.14 seconds	Nitrogen-13	10 minutes
Hydrogen-3	12.3 years	Calcium-36	0.1 second

Determining Age By measuring the number of decays each minute, scientists determined that a little less than half of the carbon-14 in the Iceman's body had decayed. This means that not quite one complete half-life (5,730 years) had passed since he died. You can try your hand at determining ages with the MathBreak at left.

Carbon-14 can be used to determine the age of objects up to 50,000 years old. To calculate the age of older objects, other elements must be used. For example, potassium-40, with a half-life of 1.3 billion years, is used to date dinosaur fossils.

Radioactivity and Your World

Although radioactivity can be dangerous, it also has positive uses. Most medical and industrial uses involve small amounts of nuclei with very short half-lives, so human exposure is low. Keep in mind that there are risks involved, but often, the benefits outweigh the risks.

Uses of Radioactivity You have learned how radioactive isotopes are used to determine the age of objects. Some isotopes can be used as *tracers*— radioactive elements whose paths can be followed through a process or reaction. Tracers help farmers determine how well plants take in elements from fertilizers. Tracers also help doctors diagnose medical problems, as shown in **Figure 10.** Radiation detectors are needed to locate the radioactive material in the organism.

Radioactive isotopes can also help detect defects in structures. For example, radiation is used to test the thickness of metal sheets as they are made. Another structure-testing use of radioactive isotopes is shown in **Figure 11.** More uses of radioactive isotopes are listed in the chart below.

Figure 10
This scan of a thyroid was made using radioactive iodine-131. The dark area shows the location of a tumor.

Figure 11 *Engineers can find weak spots in materials and leaks in pipes by detecting a tracer using a Geiger counter.*

More Uses of Radioactive Isotopes

- Killing cancer cells
- Sterilizing food and health-care products
- Detecting smoke
- Powering space probes

REVIEW

1. What is a half-life?

2. Give two examples each of how radioactivity is useful and how it is harmful.

3. How many half-lives have passed if a sample contains one-eighth of its original amount of radioactive material?

4. **Doing Calculations** A rock contains one-fourth of its original amount of potassium-40. Calculate the rock's age if the half-life of potassium-40 is 1.3 billion years.

Energy from the Nucleus

Terms to Learn

nuclear fission
nuclear chain reaction
nuclear fusion

What You'll Do

- ◆ Describe the process of nuclear fission.
- ◆ Describe the process of nuclear fusion.
- ◆ Identify advantages and disadvantages of energy from the nucleus.

From an early age, you were probably told not to play with fire. But fire itself is neither good nor bad, it simply has benefits and hazards. Likewise, getting energy from the nucleus has benefits and hazards. In this section you will learn about two methods used to get energy from the nucleus—fission and fusion. Gaining an understanding of their advantages and disadvantages is important for people who will make decisions regarding the use of this energy—people like you!

Nuclear Fission

Not all unstable nuclei decay by releasing an alpha or beta particle or gamma rays. The nuclei of some atoms decay by breaking into two smaller, more stable nuclei during a process called nuclear fission. **Nuclear fission** is the process in which a large nucleus splits into two smaller nuclei with the release of energy.

The nuclei of uranium atoms, as well as the nuclei of other large atoms, can undergo nuclear fission naturally. They can also be made to undergo fission by hitting them with neutrons, as shown by the model in **Figure 12.**

Figure 12 Fission of a Uranium-235 Nucleus

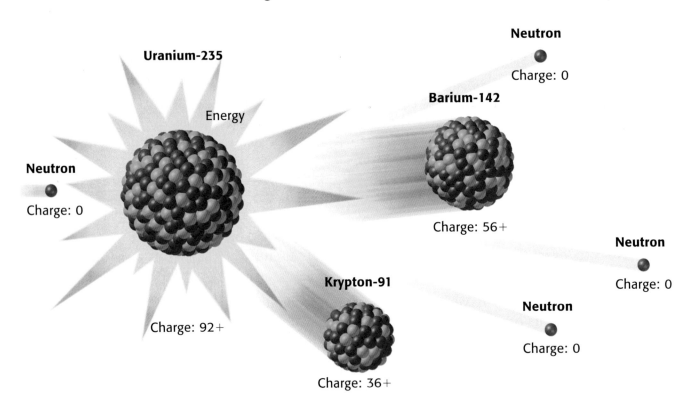

Uranium-235

Energy

Neutron
Charge: 0

Charge: 92+

Neutron
Charge: 0

Barium-142
Charge: 56+

Neutron
Charge: 0

Neutron
Charge: 0

Krypton-91
Charge: 36+

Energy from Matter Did you know that matter can be changed into energy? It's true! If you could determine the total mass of the products in Figure 12 and compare it with the total mass of the reactants, you would find something strange. The products have a tiny bit less mass than the reactants. Why are the masses different? Some of the matter was converted into energy.

The amount of energy released when a single uranium nucleus splits is not very great. But, keep in mind that this energy comes from an incredibly tiny amount of matter—about one-fifth of the mass of a hydrogen atom, the smallest atom that exists. In **Figure 13** you'll see an example of how small amounts of matter can yield large amounts of energy through nuclear fission.

Nuclear Chain Reactions Look at Figure 12 again. Suppose that two or three of the neutrons produced split other uranium-235 nuclei, which released energy and some neutrons. And then suppose that two or three of *those* neutrons split other nuclei, and so on. This situation is one type of **nuclear chain reaction**—a continuous series of nuclear fission reactions. A model of an uncontrolled chain reaction is shown in **Figure 14.**

Figure 13 *The nuclear fission of the uranium nuclei in one fuel pellet releases as much energy as the chemical change of burning about 1,000 kg of coal!*

Figure 14 *A chain reaction results in the release of an enormous amount of energy.*

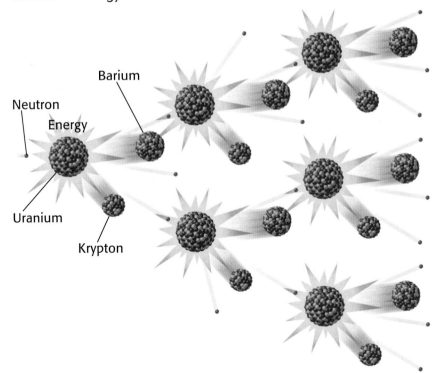

Barium

Neutron

Energy

Uranium

Krypton

Gone Fission

1. Make two paper balls from a **sheet of paper.**

2. Stand in a group, arm's length apart, with your classmates.

3. Your teacher will gently toss one paper ball into the group. If you are touched by a ball, gently toss your paper balls into the group.

4. Explain how this activity is a model of a chain reaction. Be sure to explain what the students and the paper balls represent.

LabBook

They all fall down—but not at the same rate. Experiment with models of nuclear chain reactions on page 692 of the LabBook.

Energy from a Chain Reaction In an uncontrolled chain reaction, huge amounts of energy are released very quickly. In fact, the tremendous energy of an atomic bomb is the result of an uncontrolled chain reaction. In contrast, nuclear power plants use controlled chain reactions. The energy released from the nuclei in the uranium fuel is used to generate electrical energy. **Figure 15** shows how a nuclear power plant works.

Nuclear Versus Fossil Fuel Although nuclear power plants are more expensive to build than power plants using fossil fuels, they are often less expensive to operate because less fuel is needed. Also, nuclear power plants do not release gases, such as carbon dioxide, into the atmosphere. The use of fission extends our supply of fossil fuels. However, the supply of uranium is limited. Many nations rely on nuclear power to supply their energy needs. Nuclear power plants provide about 20 percent of the electrical energy used in the United States.

Figure 15 How a Nuclear Power Plant Works

1 Uranium-235 nuclei in the fuel rods (blue) undergo a nuclear chain reaction. Control rods (gray) absorb neutrons to keep the chain reaction at a safe level.

2 Energy from the chain reaction is absorbed by a coolant, often water.

3 Water turns to steam as it absorbs energy from the hot coolant.

To cooling tower

4 The steam turns a turbine attached to a generator.

5 The generator converts the kinetic energy of the spinning turbine into electrical energy.

Accidents Can Happen With the advantages described, why is fission not more widely used? Well, there are risks involved with generating electrical energy from fission. Probably the most immediate concern is the possibility of an accident. This fear was realized in Chernobyl, Ukraine, on April 26, 1986, as shown in **Figure 16.** An explosion released large amounts of radioactive uranium fuel and waste products into the atmosphere. The cloud of radioactive material spread over most of Europe and Asia and even reached as far as North America.

Figure 16 *During a test at the Chernobyl nuclear power plant, the emergency protection system was turned off. The reactor overheated, resulting in an explosion.*

What Waste! Another concern is nuclear waste, including used fuel rods, chemicals used to process uranium, and even shoe covers and overalls worn by workers. Although artificial fission has been carried out for only about 50 years, the waste will give off high levels of radiation for thousands of years. The rate of radioactive decay cannot be changed, so the waste must be stored until it becomes less radioactive. Most of the used fuel rods are stored in huge vats of water. Some of the liquid wastes are stored in underground tanks. However, scientists continue to look for more long-term storage solutions.

What would you say if a nuclear waste storage facility was planned near your town? Read about the debate over Yucca Mountain on page 416.

Storage Site Selection

A law that passed in 1987 requires the United States government to build a large underground storage facility to store nuclear waste. Imagine that you are a scientist in charge of finding a location for the site. Describe the characteristics of a good location. Keep in mind that the waste will need to be stored for a very long time without escaping into the environment.

Atomic Energy **409**

Nuclear Fusion

Astronomy
C O N N E C T I O N

Hydrogen is not the only fuel stars use for fusion. As a star gets older, its supply of hydrogen runs low and it begins to fuse larger atoms, such as helium, carbon, and silicon.

Fusion is another nuclear reaction in which matter is converted into energy. In the process of **nuclear fusion,** two or more nuclei with small masses join together, or *fuse,* to form a larger, more massive nucleus.

In order for fusion to occur, the repulsion between positively charged nuclei must be overcome. That requires unbelievably high temperatures—over 100,000,000°C! But you already know a place where such temperatures are reached—the sun. In the sun's core, hydrogen nuclei fuse to form a helium nucleus, as shown in the model in **Figure 17.**

Figure 17 *The energy that sustains life on Earth is produced from fusion.*

Hydrogen-1 Charge: 1+
Hydrogen-1 Charge: 1+
Hydrogen-1 Charge: 1+
Hydrogen-1 Charge: 1+
Helium-4 Charge: 2+
Beta particle (positron) Charge: 1+
Beta particle (positron) Charge: 1+
Energy

Figure 18 *Electric current in large coils of wire produces a strong magnetic field that can contain plasma.*

Energy from Fusion? Energy for your home cannot yet be generated using nuclear fusion. First, incredibly high temperatures are needed. At these temperatures, hydrogen is a plasma, the state of matter in which electrons have been removed from atoms. No material on Earth can hold this plasma—imagine trying to bottle up plasma from the sun! **Figure 18** shows equipment used by researchers to try to contain plasma. Second, more energy is needed to create and contain the plasma than is produced by fusion. In spite of these problems, scientists predict that fusion will be used to provide electrical energy—possibly in your lifetime!

Oceans of Fuel Unlike nuclear fission, there is little concern about running out of fuel for nuclear fusion. Although the hydrogen-2 and hydrogen-3 isotopes used as fuel are much less common than hydrogen-1, there is still enough hydrogen in the waters of oceans and lakes to provide fuel for millions of years. In addition, a fusion reaction releases more energy than a fission reaction per gram of fuel, allowing for even greater savings of other resources, as shown in **Figure 19.**

Figure 19 *The energy generated by the fusion of the hydrogen-2 in 3.8 L (1 gal) of water would be about the same amount of energy generated by the chemical change of burning 1,140 L (300 gal) of gasoline!*

Less Accident Prone The concern over an accident such as the one at Chernobyl is much lower for fusion reactors. If an explosion occurred, there would be very little release of radioactive materials. The radioactive hydrogen-3 used for fuel in experimental fusion reactors is much less radioactive than the uranium fuel used in fission reactors.

Less Waste In addition to the advantages mentioned above, the products of fusion reactions are not radioactive, so there would be much less radioactive waste to worry about. This would make fusion an even "cleaner" source of energy than fission. While fusion has many benefits over fission as an energy source, large amounts of money will be required to pay for the research to make fusion possible.

REVIEW

1. Which nuclear reaction is currently used to generate electrical energy?

2. Which nuclear reaction is the source of the sun's energy?

3. What particle is needed to begin a nuclear chain reaction?

4. In both fission and fusion, what is converted into energy?

5. **Comparing Concepts** Compare the processes of nuclear fission and nuclear fusion.

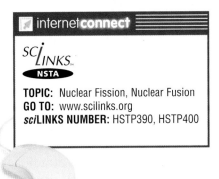

internet connect

SC*LINKS*
NSTA

TOPIC: Nuclear Fission, Nuclear Fusion
GO TO: www.scilinks.org
*sci*LINKS NUMBER: HSTP390, HSTP400

Chapter Highlights

Vocabulary

nuclear radiation *(p. 398)*

radioactivity *(p. 398)*

radioactive decay *(p. 399)*

alpha decay *(p. 399)*

mass number *(p. 399)*

beta decay *(p. 400)*

isotopes *(p. 400)*

gamma decay *(p. 400)*

half-life *(p. 404)*

Section Notes

- Radioactive nuclei give off nuclear radiation in the form of alpha particles, beta particles, and gamma rays through a process called radioactive decay.

- During alpha decay, an alpha particle is released from the nucleus. An alpha particle is composed of two protons and two neutrons.

- During beta decay, a beta particle is released from the nucleus. A beta particle can be an electron or a positron.

- Gamma decay occurs with alpha decay and beta decay when particles in the nucleus rearrange and emit energy in the form of gamma rays.

- Gamma rays penetrate matter better than alpha or beta particles. Beta particles penetrate matter better than alpha particles.

- Nuclear radiation can damage living and nonliving matter.

- Half-life is the amount of time it takes for one-half of the nuclei of a radioactive isotope to decay. The age of some objects can be determined using half-lives.

- Uses of radioactive materials include detecting defects in materials, sterilizing products, tracing a plant's or animal's use of an element, diagnosing illness, and producing electrical energy.

☑ Skills Check

Math Concepts

HALF-LIFE Radioactive decay occurs at a steady rate. To calculate the time that has passed, multiply the number of half-lives by the length of a half-life. For example, a radioactive isotope has a half-life of 10 days. If one-eighth of the original sample remains, then three half-lives have passed. The time that has passed is:

$$3 \times 10 \text{ days} = 30 \text{ days}$$

Visual Understanding

FISSION VERSUS FUSION The changes that occur in nuclear fission and nuclear fusion are very different. Review Figure 12 on page 406 and Figure 17 on page 410 to better understand the starting materials, products, and process involved in fission and fusion.

Vocabulary

nuclear fission *(p. 406)*

nuclear chain reaction *(p. 407)*

nuclear fusion *(p. 410)*

Section Notes

- Nuclear fission occurs when a massive, unstable nucleus breaks into two less massive nuclei. Nuclear fission is used in power plants to generate electrical energy.

- Nuclear fusion occurs when two or more nuclei combine to form a larger nucleus. The sun's energy comes from the fusion of hydrogen to form helium.

- The energy released by nuclear fission and nuclear fusion is produced when matter is converted into energy.

- Nuclear power plants use nuclear fission to supply many homes with electrical energy without releasing carbon dioxide or other gases into the atmosphere. A limited fuel supply, radioactive waste products, and the possible release of radioactive material are disadvantages of fission.

- Fuel for nuclear fusion is plentiful, and only small amounts of radioactive waste products are produced. Fusion is not currently a practical energy source because of the large amount of energy needed to heat and contain the hydrogen plasma.

Labs

Domino Chain Reactions *(p. 692)*

---

internet connect

go.hrw.com

GO TO: go.hrw.com

Visit the **HRW** Web site for a variety of learning tools related to this chapter. Just type in the keyword:

KEYWORD: HSTRAD

SCiLINKS SM

NSTA

GO TO: www.scilinks.org

Visit the **National Science Teachers Association** on-line Web site for Internet resources related to this chapter. Just type in the *sci*LINKS number for more information about the topic:

TOPIC: Discovering Radioactivity	***sci*LINKS NUMBER:** HSTP380
TOPIC: Radioactive Isotopes	***sci*LINKS NUMBER:** HSTP385
TOPIC: Nuclear Fission	***sci*LINKS NUMBER:** HSTP390
TOPIC: Nuclear Reactors	***sci*LINKS NUMBER:** HSTP395
TOPIC: Nuclear Fusion	***sci*LINKS NUMBER:** HSTP400

Chapter Review

USING VOCABULARY

The statements below are false. For each statement, replace the underlined term to make a true statement.

1. Nuclear fusion involves splitting a nucleus.

2. During one beta decay, half of a radioactive sample will decay.

3. Nuclear fission includes the particles and rays released by radioactive nuclei.

4. Alpha decay occurs during the rearrangement of protons and neutrons in the nucleus.

UNDERSTANDING CONCEPTS

Multiple Choice

5. Which of the following is a use of radioactive material?
   a. detecting smoke
   b. locating defects in materials
   c. generating electrical energy
   d. all of the above

6. Which particle both begins and is produced by a nuclear chain reaction?
   a. positron
   b. neutron
   c. alpha particle
   d. beta particle

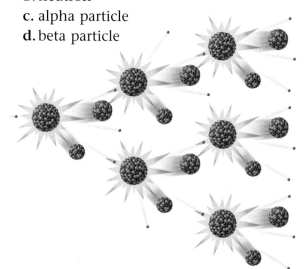

7. Nuclear radiation that can be stopped by paper is called
   a. alpha particles.   c. gamma rays.
   b. beta particles.   d. None of the above

8. The half-life of a radioactive atom is 2 months. If you start with 1 g of the element, how much will remain after 6 months?
   a. One-half of a gram will remain.
   b. One-fourth of a gram will remain.
   c. One-eighth of a gram will remain.
   d. None will remain.

9. The waste products of nuclear fission
   a. are harmless.
   b. are safe after 20 years.
   c. can be destroyed by burning them.
   d. remain radioactive for thousands of years.

10. Which statement about nuclear fusion is false?
    a. Nuclear fusion occurs in the sun.
    b. Nuclear fusion is the joining of the nuclei of atoms.
    c. Nuclear fusion is currently used to generate electrical energy.
    d. Nuclear fusion uses hydrogen as fuel.

Short Answer

11. What conditions could cause a nucleus to be unstable?

12. What are two dangers associated with nuclear fission?

13. What are two of the problems that need to be solved in order to make nuclear fusion a practical energy source?

14. In fission, the products have less mass than the starting materials. Explain what happened.

Concept Mapping

15. Use the following terms to create a concept map: radioactive decay, alpha particle, beta particle, gamma ray, nuclear radiation.

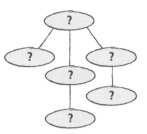

CRITICAL THINKING AND PROBLEM SOLVING

16. Smoke detectors often use americium-243 to detect smoke particles in the air. Americium-243 undergoes alpha decay. Do you think that these smoke detectors are safe to have in your home if used properly? Explain. (Hint: How penetrating are alpha particles?)

17. Explain how radiation can cause cancer.

18. Explain why nuclei of carbon, oxygen, and even iron can be found in stars.

19. If you could block all radiation from sources outside your body, explain why you would still be exposed to some radiation.

MATH IN SCIENCE

20. A scientist used 10 g of phosphorus-32 in a test on plant growth but forgot to record the date. When he measured the phosphorus-32 some time later, he found only 2.5 g remaining. If the half-life is 14 days, how many days ago did he start the experiment?

INTERPRETING GRAPHICS

21. Use the graph to answer the questions below:

a. What is the half-life of fermium-256? of fermium-251?

b. Which of these isotopes is more stable? Explain.

22. The image of a small purse, shown below, was made in a similar manner as Becquerel's original experiment. What conclusions can be drawn about the penetrating power of radiation from this image?

Reading Check-up

Take a minute to review your answers to the Pre-Reading Questions found at the bottom of page 396. Have your answers changed? If necessary, revise your answers based on what you have learned since you began this chapter.

Wasting Yucca Mountain?

Isolated, unspoiled, quiet . . . a small mountain in Nevada called Yucca Mountain seems like a perfect spot for a long hike—or perhaps a nuclear waste site! Yucca Mountain has been chosen as the nation's first storage site for high-level radioactive waste. The plan is to seal 77,000 tons of radioactive waste in steel canisters and store them in a maze of underground tunnels.

Construction of the facility has already begun—Yucca Mountain is scheduled to receive its first shipment of nuclear waste by 2010. But the debate continues about

▲ *Supporters of the Yucca Mountain storage facility think that this isolated spot in Nevada is a suitable place for permanent nuclear-waste disposal. Opponents of the site disagree.*

whether it would be safer to store radioactive waste at Yucca Mountain or to keep it where it is now—in temporary storage facilities at various nuclear power plants.

▲ *Spent fuel rods are stored underwater at a nuclear power plant.*

Pros and Cons

Those who support construction of the Yucca Mountain facility point out that there are two major advantages to the plan. First, Yucca Mountain is far from any densely populated areas. Second, the climate is extremely dry. A dry climate means that rainfall is unlikely to cause the water table to rise and come in contact with the stored radioactive waste.

Many opponents fear that the highly toxic waste could eventually leak and contaminate the water in wells, springs, and streams. In time, the

contamination could spread farther from the site and into the biosphere. The biosphere is the layer above and below the surface of the earth that supports life.

In addition, some scientific reports suggest that it is possible that the current dry climate could change over thousands of years into a rainy one, and the water table could rise dramatically.

Nevada residents argue that their economy is booming and they don't particularly need the construction jobs the facility would bring. Also their economy depends heavily on tourism, and residents worry that fears about Nevada being a dangerous place could cause the tourists to stay away.

Today construction at the Yucca Mountain facility continues. And existing storage sites expand with the waste generated by nuclear power plants. So, where should the waste go?

Have Waste, Will Travel

▶ What do you think? Jot down your initial thoughts. Then do research to find out whether any of the proposed routes from nuclear power plants to Yucca Mountain are near your town. Do your findings change your opinion? Why or why not?

CAREERS

MATERIALS SCIENTIST

Have you noticed that your forks, knives, and spoons don't tarnish easily? Most metal flatware is made of stainless steel. Because it doesn't tarnish easily, stainless steel is also used in nuclear reactors. **Dr. Michael Atzmon** studies radiation's effects on metals and other substances. He has a special interest in radiation's effect on stainless steel. He hopes that by understanding the changes that occur, scientists can prevent future radiation defects.

*T*he damage to stainless steel is caused mainly by neutron and heavy ion radiation inside nuclear reactors. The radiation causes stress in the metal, which leads to corrosion and finally to cracking. Clearly this is not a desirable feature in parts of a nuclear reactor! Atzmon's goal is to try to understand how to make the metal more corrosion resistant. He also hopes that by studying the way radiation affects the atoms of metals, he can find a way to use the incoming radiation to make the surface stronger.

Training the Team

A large part of Atzmon's job is to train graduate students to assist him with his research. He happily reports that these creative new scientists "absolutely contribute" to the development of novel approaches. One interesting proposal is to use radiation effects to create crystal structures different from those that exist in nature. This could lead to the invention of new types of semiconductors, which are useful in modern electronic devices.

Always an Explorer

Atzmon spends time sharing ideas with other materials scientists. He also teaches at the University of Michigan. This very busy man recalls that as a young boy he became interested in experimenting with things to see how they work. He chose to play with toys that encouraged his exploration. This curiosity has remained with him and has been helpful in his profession.

▶ *Understanding material structures can help in the development of better semiconductors for microchips.*

Advice to Young People

Atzmon believes that students should choose to study a field that gives them the deepest background. This opens up many career opportunities and allows students to pursue what they eventually find interesting. Most important, he adds, "People should do what they love doing!"

UNIT 6

Electricity

Can you imagine a world without computers, motors, or even light bulbs? Your life would be very different indeed without electricity and the devices that depend on it. In this unit, you will learn how electricity results from tiny charged particles, how electricity and magnetism interact, and how electronic technology has revolutionized the world in a relatively short amount of time. This timeline includes some of the events leading to our current understanding of electricity, electromagnetism, and electronic technology.

1752 Benjamin Franklin flies a kite with a key attached to it in a thunderstorm to demonstrate that lightning is a form of electricity.

1911 Superconductivity is discovered. Superconductivity is the ability that some metals and alloys have under certain conditions to carry electric current without resistance.

1945 Grace Murray Hopper, a pioneer in computers and computer languages, coins the term "debugging the computer" after removing from the wiring of her computer a moth that caused the computer to fail.

1948 The transistor is invented.

1961 The invention of the integrated circuit, which uses millions of transistors, revolutionizes electronic technology.

1773

American colonists hold the "Boston Tea Party" and dump 342 chests of British tea into Boston Harbor.

1831

British scientist Michael Faraday and American physicist Joseph Henry separately demonstrate the principle of electromagnetic induction (using magnetism to generate electricity).

1876

The telephone is officially invented by Alexander Graham Bell, who beats Elisha Gray to the patent office by only a few hours.

1902

Dutch physician Willem Einthoven develops the first electrocardiograph machine to record the tiny electric currents that pass through the body's tissues.

1985

The first portable CD player is introduced.

1974

The first commercially successful microprocessor chip is introduced.

1997

Garry Kasparov, reigning world chess champion, loses a historic match to a computer named Deep Blue.

Introduction to Electricity

Pre-Reading
Questions

1. What is static electricity, and how is it formed?
2. How is electrical energy produced?
3. What is a circuit, and what parts make up a circuit?

It's shocking!

This eighth-grader is having fun learning firsthand about static electricity. She is touching a Van de Graaf generator, a device that produces positive electrical charges on the metal globe. These positive charges move through her body to the strands of hair on her head. Like charges repel each other, so each strand of her hair repels all the other hairs. In this chapter, you'll learn more about static electricity and how you use electrical energy in your everyday life.

CHARGE OVER MATTER

In this activity, you will make an electrically charged object and use it to pick up other objects.

Procedure

1. Cut **6–8 small squares of tissue paper.** Each square should be about 2 cm × 2 cm. Place the squares on your desk.

2. Hold a **plastic comb** close to the paper squares. Record what, if anything, happens.

3. Now rub the comb with a **piece of silk cloth** for about 30 seconds.

4. Hold the comb close to the tissue-paper squares, but don't touch them. Record your observations. If nothing happens, rub the comb for a little while longer and try again.

Analysis

5. When you rubbed the comb with the cloth, you gave the comb a negative electric charge. Why do you think this charge allowed you to pick up tissue-paper squares?

6. What other objects do you think you can use to pick up tissue-paper squares?

TRY at HOME

What You'll Do

- ◆ State and give examples of the law of electric charges.
- ◆ Describe three ways an object can become charged.
- ◆ Compare conductors with insulators.
- ◆ Give examples of static electricity and electric discharge.

Electric Charge and Static Electricity

Have you ever reached out to open a door and received a shock from the knob? You may have been surprised, and your finger or hand probably felt tingly afterward. On dry days, you can easily produce shocks by shuffling your feet on a carpet and then lightly touching a metal object. These shocks are a result of a buildup of static electricity. But what is static electricity, and how is it formed? To answer these questions, you need to learn about charge.

Atoms and Charge

To investigate charge, you must know a little about the nature of matter. All matter is composed of very small particles called atoms. Atoms are made of even smaller particles called protons, neutrons, and electrons, as shown in **Figure 1.** One important difference between protons, neutrons, and electrons is that protons and electrons are charged particles and neutrons are not.

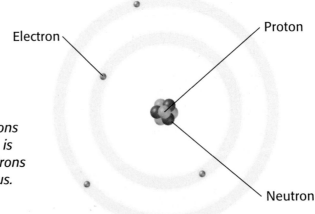

Figure 1 *Protons and neutrons make up the nucleus, which is the center of the atom. Electrons are found outside the nucleus.*

Electron

Proton

Neutron

Charges Can Exert Forces Charge is a physical property that is best understood by describing how charged objects interact with each other. A charged object exerts a force—a push or a pull—on other charged objects. There are two types of charge— positive and negative. The force between two charged objects varies depending on whether the objects have the same type of charge or opposite charges, as shown in **Figure 2.** The charged balls in Figure 2 illustrate the **law of electric charges,** which states that like charges repel and opposite charges attract.

Protons are positively charged, and electrons are negatively charged. Because protons and electrons are oppositely charged, protons and electrons are attracted to each other. If this attraction didn't exist, electrons would fly away from the nucleus of an atom.

Figure 2 *The law of electric charges states that like charges repel and opposite charges attract.*

Objects that have opposite charges are attracted to each other, and the force between the objects pulls them together.

Objects that have the same charge are repelled, and the force between the objects pushes them apart.

The Electric Force and the Electric Field The force between charged objects is an **electric force.** The strength of the electric force is determined by two factors. One factor is the size of the charges. The greater the charges are, the greater the electric force. The other factor that determines the strength of the electric force is the distance between the charges. The closer together the charges are, the greater the electric force.

The electric force exists because charged particles have electric fields around them. An *electric field* is a region around a charged particle that can exert a force on another charged particle. If a charged particle is in the electric field of another charged particle, the first particle is attracted or repelled by the electric force exerted on it.

Charge It!

Although an atom contains charged particles, the atom itself does not have a charge. Atoms contain an equal number of protons and electrons. Therefore, the positive and negative charges cancel each other out, and the atom has no overall charge. If the atoms of an object have no charge, how can the object become charged? Objects become charged because the atoms in the objects can gain or lose electrons. If the atoms of an object lose electrons, the object becomes positively charged. If the atoms gain electrons, the object becomes negatively charged. There are three common ways for an object to become charged—friction, conduction, and induction. When an object is charged by any method, no charges are created or destroyed. The charge on any object can be detected by a device called an electroscope.

Friction Rubbing two objects together can cause electrons to be "wiped" from one object and transferred to the other. If you rub a plastic ruler with a cloth, electrons are transferred from the cloth to the ruler. Because the ruler gains electrons, the ruler becomes negatively charged. Conversely, because the cloth loses electrons, the cloth becomes positively charged. **Figure 3** shows a fun example of objects becoming charged by friction.

Figure 3 *When you rub a balloon against your hair, electrons from your hair are transferred to the balloon.*

After the electrons are transferred, the balloon is negatively charged and your hair is positively charged.

Your hair and the balloon are attracted to each other because they are oppositely charged.

Conduction Charging by **conduction** occurs when electrons are transferred from one object to another by direct contact. For example, if you touch an uncharged piece of metal with a positively charged glass rod, electrons from the metal will move to the glass rod. Because the metal loses electrons, it becomes positively charged. **Figure 4** shows what happens when you touch a negatively charged object to an uncharged object.

Figure 4 *Touching a negatively charged plastic ruler to an uncharged metal rod causes the electrons in the ruler to travel to the rod. The rod becomes negatively charged by conduction.*

Induction Charging by **induction** occurs when charges in an uncharged object are rearranged without direct contact with a charged object. For example, when a positively charged object is near a neutral object, the electrons in the neutral object are attracted to the positively charged object and move toward it. This movement produces a region of negative charge on the neutral object. **Figure 5** shows what happens when you hold a negatively charged balloon close to a neutral wall.

Figure 5 *A negatively charged balloon induces a positive charge on a small section of a wall because the electrons in the wall are repelled and move away from the balloon.*

Conservation of Charge When you charge objects by any method, no charges are created or destroyed. Electrons simply move from one atom to another, producing objects or regions with different charges. If you could count all the protons and all the electrons of all the atoms before and after charging an object, you would find that the numbers of protons and electrons do not change. Because charges are not created or destroyed, charge is said to be conserved.

✓ Self-Check

Plastic wrap clings to food containers because the wrap has a charge. Explain how plastic wrap becomes charged. (*See page 724 to check your answer.*)

Detecting Charge To determine if an object has a charge, you can use a device called an *electroscope*. An electroscope is a glass flask that contains a metal rod inserted through a rubber stopper. There are two metal leaves at the bottom of the rod. The leaves hang straight down when the electroscope is not charged but spread apart when it is charged, as shown in **Figure 6**.

Figure 6 *When an electroscope is charged, the metal leaves have the same charge and repel each other.*

Electrons from a negatively charged plastic ruler move to the electroscope and travel down the rod. The metal leaves become negatively charged and spread apart.

A positively charged glass rod attracts the electrons in the metal rod, causing the electrons to travel up the rod. The metal leaves become positively charged and spread apart.

REVIEW

1. Describe how an object is charged by friction.

2. Compare charging by conduction and induction.

3. **Inferring Conclusions** Suppose you are conducting experiments using an electroscope. You touch an object to the top of the electroscope, the metal leaves spread apart, and you determine that the object has a charge. However, you cannot determine the type of charge (positive or negative) the object has. Explain why not.

Moving Charges

Have you ever noticed that the cords that connect electrical devices to outlets are always covered in plastic, while the prongs that fit into the socket are always metal? Both plastic and metal are used to make electrical cords because they differ in their ability to transmit charges. In fact, most materials can be divided into two groups based on how easily charges travel through the material. The two groups are conductors and insulators.

Conductors A **conductor** is a material in which charges can move easily. Most metals are good conductors because some of the electrons in metals are free to move about. Copper, silver, aluminum, and mercury are good conductors.

Conductors are used to make wires and other objects that transmit charges. For example, the prongs on a lamp's cord are made of metal so that charges can move in the cord and transfer energy to light the lamp.

Figure 7 *Because tap water is a conductor, this hair dryer has a label that warns people not to use it near water.*

Not all conductors are metal. Household, or "tap," water conducts charges very well. Because tap water is a conductor, you can receive an electric shock from charges traveling in it. Therefore, you should avoid using electrical devices (such as the one in **Figure 7**) near water unless they are specially designed to be waterproof.

Insulators An **insulator** is a material in which charges cannot easily move. Insulators do not conduct charges very well because electrons are tightly bound to the atoms of the insulator and cannot flow freely. Plastic, rubber, glass, wood, and air are all good insulators.

Wires used to conduct electric charges are usually covered with an insulating material. The insulator prevents charges from leaving the wire and protects you from electric shock.

Static Electricity

After taking your clothes out of the dryer, you sometimes find clothing stuck together. When this happens, you might say that the clothes stick together because of static electricity. **Static electricity** is the buildup of electric charges on an object.

When something is *static*, it is not moving. The charges that create static electricity do not move away from the object they are stuck to. Therefore, the object remains charged. For example, your clothes are charged by friction as they rub against each other inside a dryer. Positive charges build up on some clothes, and negative charges build up on other clothes. Because clothing is an insulator, the charges stay on each piece of clothing, creating static electricity. You can see the result of static electricity in **Figure 8**.

Figure 8 *Opposite charges on pieces of clothing are caused by static electricity. The clothes stick together because their charges attract each other.*

Electric Discharge Charges that build up as static electricity on an object eventually leave the object. The loss of static electricity as charges move off an object is called **electric discharge.** Sometimes electric discharge occurs slowly. For example, clothes stuck together by static electricity will eventually separate on their own because their electric charges are transferred to water molecules in the air over time.

Sometimes electric discharge occurs quickly and may be accompanied by a flash of light, a shock, or a cracking noise. For example, when you walk on a carpet with rubber-soled shoes, negative charges build up in your body. When you touch a metal doorknob, the negative charges in your body move quickly to the doorknob. Because the electric discharge happens quickly, you feel a shock.

Lightning

One of the most dramatic examples of electric discharge is lightning. Benjamin Franklin was the first to discover that lightning is a form of electricity. During a thunderstorm, Franklin flew a kite connected to a wire and successfully stored charge from a bolt of lightning. How does lightning form from a buildup of static electricity? **Figure 9** shows the answer.

Figure 9 How Lightning Forms

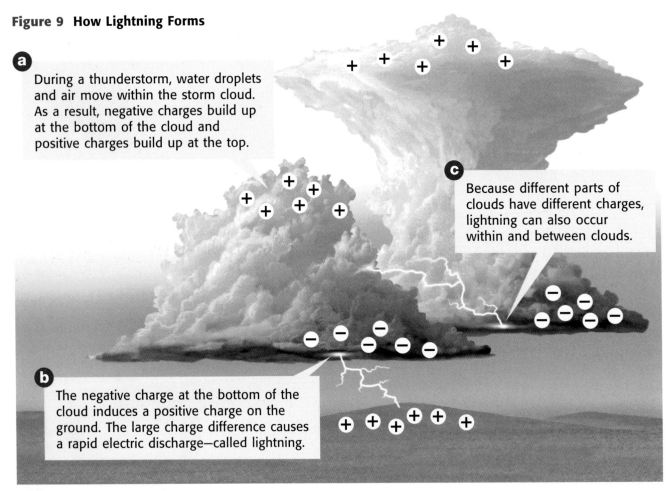

a During a thunderstorm, water droplets and air move within the storm cloud. As a result, negative charges build up at the bottom of the cloud and positive charges build up at the top.

c Because different parts of clouds have different charges, lightning can also occur within and between clouds.

b The negative charge at the bottom of the cloud induces a positive charge on the ground. The large charge difference causes a rapid electric discharge—called lightning.

Lightning Rods Benjamin Franklin also invented the lightning rod. A *lightning rod* is a pointed rod connected to the ground by a wire. Lightning usually strikes the highest point in a charged area because that point provides the easiest path for the charges to reach the ground. Therefore, lightning rods are always mounted so that they "stick out" and are the tallest point on a building, as shown in **Figure 10.**

Objects, such as a lightning rod, that are in contact with the Earth are *grounded*. Any object that is grounded provides a path for electric charges to travel to the Earth. Because the Earth is so large, it can give up or absorb electric charges without being damaged. When lightning strikes a lightning rod, the electric charges are carried safely to the Earth through the rod's wire. By directing the lightning's charge to the Earth, lightning rods prevent lightning damage to buildings.

Lightning Dangers Anything that sticks out in an area can provide a path for lightning. Trees and people in open areas are at risk of being struck by lightning. This is why it is particularly dangerous to be at the beach or on a golf course during a lightning storm. And standing under a tree during a storm is dangerous because the charge from lightning striking a tree can jump to your body.

Science
CONNECTION

Sprites and elves aren't just creatures in fairy tales! Read about how they are related to lightning on page 451.

Figure 10 *Lightning strikes the lightning rod rather than the building because the lightning rod is the tallest point on the building.*

REVIEW

1. What is static electricity? Give an example of static electricity.

2. How is the shock you receive from a metal doorknob similar to a bolt of lightning?

3. **Applying Concepts** When you use an electroscope, you touch a charged object to a metal rod that is held in place by a rubber stopper. Why is it important to touch the object to the metal rod and not to the rubber stopper?

internet**connect**

SC*i*LINKS
NSTA

TOPIC: Static Electricity
GO TO: www.scilinks.org
*sci*LINKS NUMBER: HSTP405

Electrical Energy

Imagine living without electrical energy. You could not watch television or listen to a portable radio, and you could not even turn on a light bulb to help you see in the dark! *Electrical energy*—the energy of electric charges—provides people with many comforts and conveniences. A flow of charges is called an *electric current*. Electric currents can be produced in many ways. One common way to produce electric current is through chemical reactions in a battery.

What You'll Do

- Explain how a cell produces an electric current.
- Describe how the potential difference is related to electric current.
- Describe how photocells and thermocouples produce electrical energy.

Batteries Are Included

In science, energy is defined as the ability to do work. Energy cannot be created or destroyed; it can only be converted into other types of energy. A **cell** is a device that produces an electric current by converting chemical energy into electrical energy. A **battery** also converts chemical energy into electrical energy and is made of several cells.

Parts of a Cell Every cell contains a mixture of chemicals that conducts a current; the mixture is called an *electrolyte* (ee LEK troh LIET). Chemical reactions in the electrolyte convert chemical energy into electrical energy. Every cell also contains a pair of electrodes made from two different conducting materials that are in contact with the electrolyte. An *electrode* (ee LEK TROHD) is the part of a cell through which charges enter or exit. **Figure 11** shows how a cell produces an electric current.

Figure 11 *This cell has a zinc electrode and a copper electrode dipped in a liquid electrolyte.*

Flow

a A chemical reaction leaves extra electrons on the zinc electrode. Therefore, the zinc electrode has a negative charge.

b A different chemical reaction causes electrons to be pulled off the copper electrode, making the copper electrode positively charged.

c If the electrodes are connected by a wire, charges will flow from the negative zinc electrode through the wire to the positive copper electrode, producing an electric current.

Types of Cells Cells are divided into two groups—wet cells and dry cells. Wet cells, such as the cell shown in Figure 11, contain liquid electrolytes. A car battery is made of several wet cells that use sulfuric acid as the electrolyte.

Dry cells work in a similar way, but dry cells contain electrolytes that are solid or pastelike. The cells used in portable radios and flashlights are examples of dry cells.

You can make your own cell by inserting strips of zinc and copper into a lemon. The electric current produced when the metal strips are connected is strong enough to power a small clock, as shown in **Figure 12.**

Potatoes aren't just for eating anymore! Learn how to use a potato to produce an electric current on page 695 of the LabBook.

Figure 12 *This cell uses the juice of a lemon as an electrolyte and uses strips of zinc and copper as electrodes.*

Bring On the Potential

So far you have learned that cells and batteries can produce electric currents. But why does the electric current exist between the two electrodes? The electric current exists because a chemical reaction causes a difference in charge between the two electrodes. The difference in charge means that an electric current—a flow of electric charges—can be produced by the cell to provide energy. The energy per unit charge is called the **potential difference** and is expressed in volts (V).

As long as there is a potential difference between the electrodes of a cell and there is a wire connecting them, charges will flow through the cell and the wire, creating an electric current. The current depends on the potential difference. The greater the potential difference is, the greater the current. **Figure 13** shows batteries and cells with different potential differences.

12 V battery

6 V battery

9 V battery

1.5 V cells

Figure 13 *Batteries are made with different potential differences. The potential difference of a battery depends on the number of cells it contains.*

Solar panel

Other Ways of Producing Electrical Energy

The conversion of chemical energy to electrical energy in batteries is not the only way electrical energy can be generated. Several technological devices have been developed to convert different types of energy into electrical energy for use every day. For example, generators convert kinetic energy into electrical energy. Two other devices that produce electrical energy are photocells and thermocouples.

Photocells Have you ever wondered how a solar-powered calculator works? If you look above the display of the calculator, you will see a dark strip called a solar panel. This panel is made of several photocells. A **photocell** is the part of a solar panel that converts light into electrical energy.

Photocells contain silicon atoms. When light strikes the photocell, electrons are ejected from the silicon atoms. If light continues to shine on the photocell, electrons will be steadily emitted. The ejected electrons are gathered into a wire to create an electric current.

Thermocouples Thermal energy can be converted to electrical energy by a **thermocouple.** A simple thermocouple is made by joining wires made of two different metals into a loop, as shown in **Figure 14.** The temperature difference within the loop causes charges to flow through the loop. Thermocouples are used to monitor the temperature of car engines, furnaces, and ovens.

Figure 14 A Simple Thermocouple

One section of the loop is heated.

Burner

Iron wire

Copper wire

Ice water

One section of the loop is cooled.

The greater the temperature difference is, the greater the current.

Meter

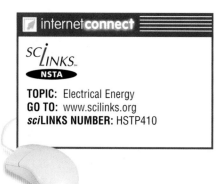

internet connect

SC*i*LINKS

NSTA

TOPIC: Electrical Energy
GO TO: www.scilinks.org
*sci***LINKS NUMBER:** HSTP410

REVIEW

1. Name the parts of a cell, and explain how they work together to produce an electric current.

2. How do the currents produced by a 1.5 V flashlight cell and a 12 V car battery compare?

3. **Inferring Conclusions** Why do you think some solar calculators contain batteries?

Electric Current

Terms to Learn

current   resistance
voltage   electric power

What You'll Do

◆ Describe electric current.
◆ Identify the four factors that determine the resistance of an object.
◆ Explain how current, voltage, and resistance are related by Ohm's law.
◆ Describe how electric power is related to electrical energy.

So far you have read how electrical energy can be generated by a variety of methods. A battery produces electrical energy very effectively, but electric power plants provide most of the electrical energy used every day. In this section, you will learn more about electric current and about the electrical energy you use at home.

Current Revisited

In the previous section, you learned that electric current is a continuous flow of charge. **Current** is more precisely defined as the rate at which charge passes a given point. The higher the current is, the more charge passes the point each second. The unit for current is the *ampere* (A), which is sometimes called amp for short. In equations, the symbol for current is the letter *I*.

Charge Ahead! When you flip a light switch, the light comes on instantly. Many people think that happens because electrons travel through the wire at the speed of light. In fact, it's because an electric field is created at close to the speed of light.

Flipping the light switch sets up an electric field in the wire that connects to the light bulb. The electric field causes the free electrons in the wire to move, as illustrated in **Figure 15.** Because the electric field is created so quickly, the electrons start moving through the wire at practically the same instant. You can think of the electric field as a kind of command to the electrons to "Charge ahead!" The light comes on instantly because the electrons simultaneously obey this command. So the current that causes the bulb to light up is established very quickly, even though individual electrons move quite slowly. In fact, it may take a single electron over an hour to travel 1 m through a wire.

Figure 15 *Electrons moving in a wire make up current, a continuous flow of charge.*

Let's See, AC/DC . . . There are two different types of electric current—direct current (DC) and alternating current (AC). In *direct current* the charges always flow in the same direction. In *alternating current* the charges continually switch from flowing in one direction to flowing in the reverse direction. **Figure 16** illustrates the difference between DC and AC.

The electric current produced by batteries and cells is DC, but the electric current from outlets in your home is AC. Both types of electric current can be used to provide electrical energy. For example, if you connect a flashlight bulb to a battery, the light bulb will light. You can light a household light bulb by attaching it to a lamp and turning the lamp switch on.

Alternating current is used in homes because it is more practical for transferring electrical energy. In the United States, the alternating current provided to households changes directions 120 times each second.

Figure 16 *Unlike DC, charges continually change direction in AC.*

Direct current has one direction.

Alternating current continually changes direction.

Voltage

The current in a wire is determined by voltage. **Voltage** is the difference in energy per unit charge as a charge moves between two points in the path of a current. Voltage is another word for potential difference. Because voltage is the same as potential difference, voltage is expressed in volts. The symbol for voltage is the letter *V*. You can think of voltage as the amount of energy released as a charge moves between two points in the path of a current. The higher the voltage is, the more energy is released per charge. The current depends on the voltage. The greater the voltage is, the greater the current.

Voltage May Vary In the United States, electrical outlets usually supply a voltage of 120 V. Therefore, most electrical devices, such as televisions, toasters, lamps, and alarm clocks, are designed to run on 120 V. Devices that run on batteries or cells usually need a lower voltage. For example, a portable radio needs only 3 V. Compare this with the voltage created by the eel in **Figure 17.**

Biology
C O N N E C T I O N

Pacemaker cells in the heart produce low electric currents at regular intervals to make the heart beat. During a heart attack, pacemaker cells do not work together and the heart beats irregularly. To correct this, doctors sometimes "jump start" the heart by creating a high voltage across a person's chest, which forces the pacemaker cells to act together, restoring a regular heartbeat.

Figure 17 *An electric eel can create a voltage of more than 600 V!*

Resistance

In addition to voltage, resistance also determines the current in a wire. **Resistance** is the opposition to the flow of electric charge. Resistance is expressed in ohms (Ω, the Greek letter *omega*). In equations, the symbol for resistance is the letter *R*.

You can think of resistance as "electrical friction." The higher the resistance of a material is, the lower the current is in it. Therefore, as resistance increases, current decreases if the voltage is kept the same. An object's resistance varies depending on the object's material, thickness, length, and temperature.

Material Good conductors, such as copper, have low resistance. Poorer conductors, such as iron, have higher resistance. The resistance of insulators is so high that electric charges cannot flow in them.

Materials with low resistance are used to make wires and other objects that are used to transfer electrical energy from place to place. For example, most of the electrical cords in your house contain copper wires. However, it is sometimes helpful to use a material with high resistance, as shown in **Figure 18.**

Figure 18 *Tungsten light bulb filaments have a high resistance. This property causes electrical energy to be converted to light and thermal energy.*

Thickness and Length To understand how the thickness and length of a wire affect the wire's resistance, consider the model in **Figure 19.** The pipe filled with gravel represents a wire, and the water flowing through the pipe represents electric charges. This analogy illustrates that thick wires have less resistance than thin wires and that long wires have more resistance than short wires.

Figure 19 *Gravel in a pipe is like resistance in a wire. Just as gravel makes it more difficult for water to flow through the pipe, resistance makes it more difficult for electric charges to flow in a wire.*

A thick pipe has less resistance than a thin pipe because there are more spaces between pieces of gravel in a thick pipe for water to flow through.

A short pipe has less resistance than a long pipe because the water in a short pipe does not have to work its way around as many pieces of gravel.

Temperature Resistance also depends somewhat on temperature. In general, the resistance of metals increases as temperature increases. This happens because atoms move faster at higher temperatures and get in the way of the flowing electric charges.

If you cool certain materials to an extremely low temperature, resistance will drop to nearly 0 Ω. Materials in this state are called *superconductors*. A small superconductor is shown in **Figure 20.** Superconductors can be useful because very little energy is wasted when electric charges travel in them. However, so much energy is necessary to cool them that superconductors are not practical for everyday use.

Figure 20 *One interesting property of super-conductors is that they repel magnets. The superconductor in this photo is repelling the magnet so strongly that the magnet is floating.*

Ohm's Law: Putting It All Together

So far, you have learned about current, voltage, and resistance. But how are they related? A German school teacher named Georg Ohm asked this very question. He determined that the relationship between current (*I*), voltage (*V*), and resistance (*R*) could be expressed with the equation shown at right. This equation, which is known as *Ohm's law*, shows that the units of current, voltage, and resistance are related in the following way:

$$\text{amperes (A)} = \frac{\text{volts (V)}}{\text{ohms (Ω)}}$$

$$I = \frac{V}{R}$$

You can use Ohm's law to find the current in a wire if you know the voltage applied and the resistance of the wire. For example, if a voltage of 30 V is applied to a wire with a resistance of 60 Ω, the current is as follows:

$$I = \frac{V}{R} = \frac{30\ V}{60\ \Omega} = 0.5\ A$$

Electric Power

You probably hear the word *power* used in different ways. Power can be used to mean force, strength, or energy. In science, power is the rate at which work is done. **Electric power** is the rate at which electrical energy is used to do work. The unit for power is the watt (W), and the symbol for power is the letter *P*. Electric power is calculated with the following equation:

$$\text{power} = \text{voltage} \times \text{current,} \quad \text{or} \quad P = V \times I$$

For the units:

$$\text{watts (W)} = \text{volts (V)} \times \text{amperes (A)}$$

÷ 5 ÷ Ω $\leq$ ∞ + Ω $\vee$ 9 ∞ $\leq$ Σ 2

MATH BREAK

Using Ohm's Law

You can use Ohm's law to find voltage or resistance:

$$V = I \times R \qquad R = \frac{V}{I}$$

If a 2 A current flows through a resistance of 12 Ω, the voltage is calculated as follows.

$$V = I \times R$$
$$V = 2\ A \times 12\ \Omega$$
$$V = 24\ V$$

Now It's Your Turn

1. Find the resistance of an object if a voltage of 10 V produces a current of 0.5 A.

2. Find the current produced if a voltage of 36 V is applied to a resistance of 4 Ω.

Watt Is a Power Rating?! If you have ever changed a light bulb, you are probably familiar with watts. Light bulbs have labels such as "60 W," "75 W," or "120 W." As electrical energy is supplied to a light bulb, the light bulb glows. As power increases, the bulb burns brighter because more electrical energy is converted to light energy. That is why a 120 W bulb burns brighter than a 60 W bulb.

Another common unit of power is the kilowatt (kW). One kilowatt is equal to 1,000 W. Kilowatts are used to express high values of power, such as the power needed to heat a house. The table shows the power ratings of some appliances you use every day.

Power Ratings of Household Appliances	
Appliance	**Power (W)**
Clothes dryer	4,000
Toaster	1,100
Hair dryer	1,000
Refrigerator/freezer	600
Color television	200
Radio	100
Clock	3

✓ Self-Check

How much electrical energy is used by a color television that stays on for 2 hours? *(See page 724 to check your answer.)*

Measuring Electrical Energy

Electric power companies sell electrical energy to homes and businesses. Such companies determine how much a household or business has to pay based on power and time. For example, the amount of electrical energy used by a household depends on the power of the electrical devices in the house and how long those devices are on. The equation for electrical energy is as follows:

$$\text{electrical energy} = \text{power} \times \text{time}, \quad \text{or} \quad E = P \times t$$

Measuring Household Energy Use Households use varying amounts of electrical energy during a day. Electric companies usually calculate electric energy by multiplying the power in kilowatts by the time in hours. The unit of electrical energy is usually kilowatt-hours (kWh). If a household used 2,000 W (2 kW) of power for 3 hours, it used 6 kWh of energy.

Electric power companies use electric meters such as the one shown at right to determine the number of kilowatt-hours of energy used by a household. Meters are often located outside houses and apartment buildings so someone from the power company can read them.

How to Save Energy

The amount of electrical energy used by an appliance depends on the power rating of the appliance and how long it is on. For example, a clock has a power rating of 3 W, and it is on 24 hours a day. Therefore, the clock uses 72 Wh (3 W × 24 hours), or 0.072 kWh, of energy a day. Using the information in the table on the previous page and an estimate of how long each appliance is on during a day, determine which appliances use the most energy and which use the least. Based on your findings, describe what you can do to use less energy.

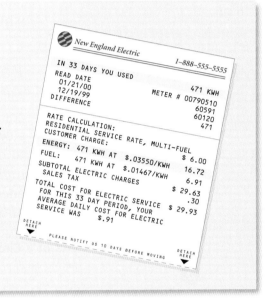

REVIEW

1. What is electric current?

2. How does increasing the voltage affect the current?

3. How does an electric power company calculate electrical energy from electric power?

4. **Making Predictions** Which wire would have the lowest resistance: a long, thin iron wire at a high temperature or a short, thick copper wire at a low temperature?

5. **Doing Calculations** Use Ohm's law to find the voltage needed to produce a current of 3 A in a device with a resistance of 9 Ω.

internet connect

SC*LINKS*
NSTA

TOPIC: Electric Current
GO TO: www.scilinks.org
*sci*LINKS NUMBER: HSTP415

Electric Circuits

What You'll Do

◆ Name the three essential parts of a circuit.

◆ Compare series circuits with parallel circuits.

◆ Explain how fuses and circuit breakers protect your home against short circuits and circuit overloads.

Imagine that you are lost in a forest. You need to find your way back to camp, where your friends are waiting for you. Unfortunately, there are no trails to follow, so you don't know which way to go. Just as you need a trail to follow in order to return to camp, electric charges need a path to follow in order to travel from an outlet or a battery to the device it provides energy to. A path that charges follow is called a circuit.

A circuit, however, is not exactly the same as a trail in a forest. A trail may begin in one place and end in another. But a circuit always begins and ends in the same place, forming a loop. Because a circuit forms a loop, it is said to be a closed path. So an electric **circuit** is a complete, closed path through which electric charges flow.

Parts of a Circuit

All circuits consist of an energy source, a load, and wires to connect the other parts together. A **load** is a device that uses electrical energy to do work. All loads offer some resistance to electric currents and cause the electrical energy to change into other forms of energy such as light energy or kinetic energy. **Figure 21** shows some examples of the different parts of a circuit.

Figure 21 Parts of a Circuit

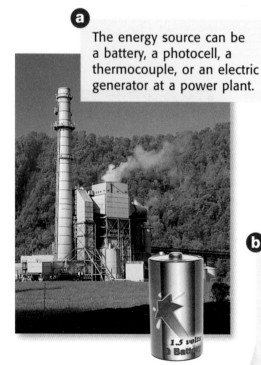

a The energy source can be a battery, a photocell, a thermocouple, or an electric generator at a power plant.

b Wires connect the other parts of a circuit together. Wires are usually made of conducting materials with low resistance, such as copper.

c Examples of loads are light bulbs, appliances, televisions, and motors.

Opening and Closing a Circuit Sometimes a circuit also contains a switch. A switch is used to open and close a circuit. Usually a switch is made of two pieces of conducting material, one of which can be moved, as shown in **Figure 22.** For charges to flow through a circuit, the switch must be closed, or "turned on." If a switch is open, or "off," the loop of the circuit is broken and no charges can flow through the circuit. Light switches, power buttons on radios, and even the keys on calculators and computers work this way.

Biology
C O N N E C T I O N

Believe it or not, your body is controlled by a large electric circuit. Electrical impulses from your brain control all the muscles and organs in your body. The food you eat is the energy source for your body's circuit, your nerves are the wires, and your muscles and organs are the loads.

Figure 22 *You can turn a light bulb on and off by using a switch to close and open a circuit.*

When the switch is **closed,** the two pieces of conducting material touch, allowing the electric charges to flow through the circuit.

When the switch is **open,** the gap between the two pieces of conducting material prevents the electric charges from traveling through the circuit.

 Self-Check

Is a microwave oven an example of a load? Why or why not? *(See page 724 to check your answer.)*

Types of Circuits

Look around the room for a moment, and count the number of objects that use electrical energy. You probably found several objects, such as lights, a clock, and maybe a computer. All of the objects you counted are loads in a large circuit that may include several rooms in the building. In fact, most circuits contain more than one load. The loads in a circuit can be connected in two different ways—in series or in parallel.

Series Circuits A **series circuit** is a circuit in which all parts are connected in a single loop. The charges traveling through a series circuit must flow through each part and can only follow one path. **Figure 23** shows an example of a series circuit.

Figure 23 *The charges flow from the battery through each light bulb (load) and finally back to the battery.*

Quick Lab

A Series of Circuits

1. Connect a **6 V battery** and **two flashlight bulbs** in a series circuit. Draw a picture of your circuit in your ScienceLog.

2. Add another **flashlight bulb** in series with the other two bulbs. How does the brightness of the light bulbs change?

3. Replace one of the light bulbs with a **burned-out light bulb.** What happens to the other lights in the circuit?

All the loads in a series circuit share the same current. Because the current in all the light bulbs in Figure 23 is the same, the light bulbs glow with the same brightness. However, if you add more light bulbs, the resistance of the entire circuit would increase and the current would decrease. Therefore, all the bulbs would be dimmer.

Uses for Series Circuits Some series circuits use a load as a switch. For example, the automatic door at the grocery store is operated by a series circuit with a motor that opens the door and a photoelectric device—an "electric eye"—that acts as an on-off switch. When no light hits the device, charges flow to the motor and the door opens.

For charges to flow in a series circuit, all the loads must be turned on and working. Charges pass through one load after another, in order, around the circuit. If one load is broken or missing, the other loads will not work. For example, if a television and a table lamp were connected in series and the lamp broke, your television would go off. This would be a problem at home, but it is useful in wiring bank alarms, some types of street lights, and certain computer circuits.

Parallel Circuits Think about what would happen if all the lights in your home were connected in series. If you needed a light on in your room, all the other lights in the house would have to be turned on too! Luckily, circuits in buildings are wired in parallel rather than in series. A **parallel circuit** is a circuit in which different loads are located on separate branches. Because there are separate branches, the charges travel through more than one path. **Figure 24** shows a parallel circuit.

Figure 24 *The electric charges flow from the battery to each of the bulbs separately and then flow back to the battery.*

Unlike a series circuit, the loads in a parallel circuit do not have the same current in them. Instead, each load in a parallel circuit uses the same voltage. For example, the full voltage of the battery is applied to each bulb in Figure 24. As a result, each light bulb glows at full brightness, no matter how many bulbs are connected in parallel. You can connect loads that require different currents to the same parallel circuit. For example, you can connect a hair dryer, which requires a high current to operate, to the same circuit as a lamp, which requires less current.

Uses for Parallel Circuits In a parallel circuit, each branch of the circuit can function by itself. If one load is broken or missing, charges will still run through the other branches, and the loads on those branches will continue to work. In your home, each electrical outlet is usually on its own branch, with its own on-off switch. It would be inconvenient if each time a light bulb went out, your television or stereo stopped working. With parallel circuits, you can use one light or appliance at a time, even if another branch fails.

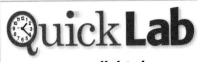

Quick Lab

A Parallel Lab

1. Connect a **6 V battery** and **two flashlight bulbs** in a parallel circuit. Draw a picture of your circuit in your ScienceLog.

2. Add another **flashlight bulb** in parallel with the other two bulbs. How does the brightness of the light bulbs change?

3. Replace one of the light bulbs with a **burned-out light bulb.** What happens to the other lights in the circuit?

Household Circuits

In every home, several circuits connect lights, major appliances, and outlets throughout the building. Most household circuits are parallel circuits that can have several loads attached to them. The circuits branch out from a breaker box or a fuse box that acts as the "electrical headquarters" for the building. Each branch receives a standard voltage, which is 120 V in the United States.

Mayday! Circuit Failure! Broken wires or water can cause electrical appliances to short-circuit. A short circuit occurs when charges bypass the loads in the circuit. When the loads are bypassed, the resistance of the circuit drops, and the current in the circuit increases. If the current increases too much, it can produce enough thermal energy to start a fire. **Figure 25** shows how a short circuit might occur.

Figure 25 *If the insulating plastic around a cord is broken, the two wires inside can touch. The charges can then bypass the load and travel from one wire to the other.*

Circuits also may fail if they are overloaded. A circuit is overloaded when too many loads, or electrical devices, are attached to it. Each time you add a load to a parallel circuit, the entire circuit draws more current. If too many loads are attached to one circuit, the current increases to an unsafe level that can cause the temperature of the wires to increase and cause a fire. **Figure 26** shows a situation that can cause a circuit overload.

Figure 26 *Plugging too many devices into one outlet can cause a circuit to overload.*

Circuit Safety

Because short circuits and circuit overloads can be so dangerous, safety features are built into the circuits in your home. The two most commonly used safety devices are fuses and circuit breakers, which are located in a fuse box or a breaker box.

Fuses A fuse contains a thin strip of metal through which the charges for a circuit flow. If the current in the circuit is too high, the metal in the fuse warms up and melts, as shown in **Figure 27.** A break or gap in the circuit is produced, and the charges stop flowing. This is referred to as blowing a fuse. After a fuse is blown, you must replace it with a new fuse in order for the charges to flow through the circuit again.

Figure 27 *The blown fuse on the left must be replaced with a new fuse, such as the one on the right.*

Circuit Breakers A circuit breaker is a switch that automatically opens if the current in the circuit is too high. If the current in a circuit is too high, a strip of metal in the circuit breaker warms up and bends away from the wires in the circuit. A break in the circuit results. Open circuit breakers can be closed easily by flipping a switch inside the breaker box once the problem has been corrected.

A device that acts like a miniature circuit breaker is a ground fault circuit interrupter (GFCI). A GFCI, like the one shown in **Figure 28,** provides protection by comparing the current in one side of an outlet with the current in the other side. If there is even a small difference, the GFCI opens the circuit. To close the circuit, you must push the RESET button.

Figure 28 *GFCI devices are usually found on outlets in bathrooms and kitchens to protect you from electric shock.*

REVIEW

1. Name and describe the three essential parts of a circuit.

2. Why are switches useful in a circuit?

3. What is the difference between series and parallel circuits?

4. How do fuses and circuit breakers protect your home against electrical fires?

5. **Developing Hypotheses** Whenever you turn on the portable heater in your room, the circuit breaker for the circuit in your room opens and all the lights go out. Propose two possible reasons for why this occurs.

internetconnect

SC*i*LINKS
NSTA

TOPIC: Electric Circuits
GO TO: www.scilinks.org
*sci*LINKS NUMBER: HSTP420

Chapter Highlights

SECTION 1

Vocabulary

law of electric charges (*p. 423*)

electric force (*p. 423*)

conduction (*p. 425*)

induction (*p. 425*)

conductor (*p. 427*)

insulator (*p. 427*)

static electricity (*p. 427*)

electric discharge (*p. 428*)

Section Notes

• The law of electric charges states that like charges repel and opposite charges attract.

• The electric force varies depending on the size of the charges exerting the force and the distance between them.

• Objects become charged when they gain or lose electrons. Objects may become charged by friction, conduction, or induction.

• Charges are not created or destroyed and are said to be conserved.

• An electroscope can be used to detect charges.

• Charges move easily in conductors but do not move easily in insulators.

• Static electricity is the buildup of electric charges on an object. Static electricity is lost through electric discharge. Lightning is a form of electric discharge.

• Lightning rods work by directing the electric charge carried by lightning safely to the Earth.

Labs

Stop the Static Electricity! (*p. 694*)

SECTION 2

Vocabulary

cell (*p. 430*)

battery (*p. 430*)

potential difference (*p. 431*)

photocell (*p. 432*)

thermocouple (*p. 432*)

Section Notes

• Batteries are made of cells that convert chemical energy to electrical energy.

• Electric currents can be produced when there is a potential difference.

• Photocells and thermocouples are devices used to produce electrical energy.

Labs

Potato Power (*p. 695*)

☑ Skills Check

Math Concepts

OHM'S LAW Ohm's law, shown on page 437, describes the relationship between current, voltage, and resistance. If you know two of the values, you can always calculate the third. For example, the current in a wire with a resistance of 4 Ω produced by a voltage of 12 V is calculated as follows:

$$I = \frac{V}{R} = \frac{12\ \text{V}}{4\ \Omega} = 3\ \text{A}$$

Visual Understanding

SERIES AND PARALLEL CIRCUITS There are two types of circuits—series and parallel. The charges in a series circuit follow only one path, but the charges in a parallel circuit follow more than one path. Look at Figures 23 and 24 on pages 442–443 to review series and parallel circuits.

SECTION 3

Vocabulary

current *(p. 433)*

voltage *(p. 434)*

resistance *(p. 435)*

electric power *(p. 437)*

Section Notes

- Electric current is a continuous flow of charge caused by the motion of electrons.

- Voltage is the same as potential difference. As voltage increases, current increases.

- An object's resistance varies depending on the object's material, thickness, length, and temperature. As resistance increases, current decreases.

- Ohm's law describes the relationship between current, resistance, and voltage.

- Electric power is the rate at which electrical energy does work. It is expressed in watts or kilowatts.

- Electrical energy is electric power multiplied by time. It is usually expressed in kilowatt-hours.

SECTION 4

Vocabulary

circuit *(p. 440)*

load *(p. 440)*

series circuit *(p. 442)*

parallel circuit *(p. 443)*

Section Notes

- Circuits consist of an energy source, a load, wires, and sometimes a switch.

- All parts of a series circuit are connected in a single loop.

- The loads in a parallel circuit are on separate branches.

- Circuits can fail because of a short circuit or circuit overload.

- Fuses or circuit breakers protect your home against circuit failure.

Labs

Circuitry 101 *(p. 696)*

---

internet connect

GO TO: go.hrw.com

Visit the **HRW** Web site for a variety of learning tools related to this chapter. Just type in the keyword:

KEYWORD: HSTELE

GO TO: www.scilinks.org

Visit the **National Science Teachers Association** on-line Web site for Internet resources related to this chapter. Just type in the *sci***LINKS** number for more information about the topic:

TOPIC: Static Electricity	*sci***LINKS NUMBER:** HSTP405
TOPIC: Electrical Energy	*sci***LINKS NUMBER:** HSTP410
TOPIC: Electric Current	*sci***LINKS NUMBER:** HSTP415
TOPIC: Electric Circuits	*sci***LINKS NUMBER:** HSTP420

Chapter Review

USING VOCABULARY

To complete the following sentences, choose the correct term from each pair of terms listed below:

1. A __?__ converts chemical energy into electrical energy. *(battery or photocell)*

2. Charges flow easily in a(n) __?__. *(insulator or conductor)*

3. __?__ is the opposition to the flow of electric charge. *(Resistance or Electric power)*

4. A __?__ is a complete, closed path through which charges flow. *(load or circuit)*

5. Lightning is a form of __?__. *(static electricity or electric discharge)*

UNDERSTANDING CONCEPTS

Multiple Choice

6. If two charges repel each other, the two charges must be
   a. positive and positive.
   b. positive and negative.
   c. negative and negative.
   d. Either (a) or (c)

7. A device that can convert chemical energy to electrical energy is a
   a. lightning rod.
   b. cell.
   c. light bulb.
   d. All of the above

8. Which of the following wires has the lowest resistance?
   a. a short, thick copper wire at 25°C
   b. a long, thick copper wire at 35°C
   c. a long, thin copper wire at 35°C
   d. a short, thick iron wire at 25°C

9. An object becomes charged when the atoms in the object gain or lose
   a. protons.   c. electrons.
   b. neutrons.   d. All of the above

10. A device used to protect buildings from electrical fires is a(n)
   a. electric meter.   c. fuse.
   b. circuit breaker.   d. Both (b) and (c)

11. In order to produce a current from a cell, the electrodes of the cell must
   a. have a potential difference.
   b. be in a liquid.
   c. be exposed to light.
   d. be at two different temperatures.

12. What type of current comes from the outlets in your home?
   a. direct current   c. electric discharge
   b. alternating current   d. static electricity

Short Answer

13. List and describe the three essential parts of a circuit.

14. Name the two factors that affect the strength of electric force, and explain how they affect electric force.

15. Describe how direct current differs from alternating current.

Concept Mapping

16. Use the following terms to create a concept map: electric current, battery, charges, photocell, thermocouple, circuit, parallel circuit, series circuit.

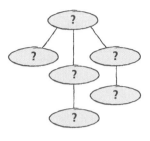

Use Ohm's law to solve the following problems:

20. What voltage is needed to produce a 6 A current through a resistance of 3 Ω?

21. Find the current produced when a voltage of 60 V is applied to a resistance of 15 Ω.

22. What is the resistance of an object if a voltage of 40 V produces a current of 5 A?

CRITICAL THINKING AND PROBLEM SOLVING

17. Your science classroom was rewired over the weekend. On Monday, you notice that the electrician may have made a mistake. In order for the fish-tank bubbler to work, the lights in the room must be on. And if you want to use the computer, you must turn on the overhead projector. Describe what mistake the electrician made with the circuits in your classroom.

18. You can make a cell using an apple, a strip of copper, and a strip of silver. Explain how you would construct the cell, and identify the parts of the cell. What type of cell is formed? Explain your answer.

19. Your friend shows you a magic trick. She rubs a plastic comb with a piece of silk and holds the comb close to a stream of water. When the comb is close to the water, the water bends toward the comb. Explain how this trick works. (Hint: Think about how objects become charged.)

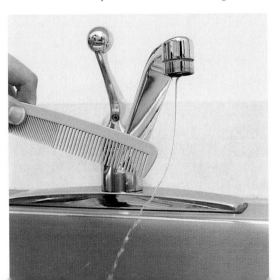

INTERPRETING GRAPHICS

23. Classify the objects in the photograph below as conductors or insulators.

Reading Check-up

Take a minute to review your answers to the Pre-Reading Questions found at the bottom of page 420. Have your answers changed? If necessary, revise your answers based on what you have learned since you began this chapter.

Science, Technology, and Society

Riding the Electric Rails

For more than 100 years, the trolley, or streetcar, was a popular way to travel around a city. Then, beginning in the 1950s, most cities ripped up their trolley tracks to make way for automobiles. Today, trolleys are making a comeback around the world.

From Horse Power to Electric Power

In 1832, the first trolleys, called *horsecars,* were pulled by horses through the streets of New York. Soon horsecars were used in most large cities in the United States. However, using horses for power presented several problems. Among other things, the horses were slow and required special attention and constant care. So inventors began looking for other sources of power.

In 1888, Frank J. Sprague developed a way to operate trolleys with electrical energy. These electric trolleys ran on a metal track and were connected by a pole to an overhead power line. Electric charges flowed down the pole to motors in the trolley. A wheel at the top of the pole, called a *shoe,* rolled along the power line, allowing the trolley to move along its track without losing contact with its power source. The charges passed through the motor and then returned to a power generator by way of the metal track.

Taking It to the Streets

By World War I, more than 40,000 km of electric-trolley tracks were in use in the United States. The trolley's popularity helped shape American cities because businesses were built along the trolley lines. But competition from cars and buses grew over the next decade, and many trolley lines were abandoned.

By the 1980s, nearly all of the trolley lines had been shut down. But by then, people were looking for new ways to cut down on the pollution, noise, and traffic problems caused by auto-

▲ *The horsecar was a popular mode of travel in many cities during the early 1900s.*

mobiles and buses. Trolleys provided one possible solution. Because they run on electrical energy, they create little pollution, and because many people can ride on a single trolley, they cut down on traffic.

Today, a new form of trolley is being used in a number of major cities. These light-rail transit vehicles are quieter, faster, and more economical than the older trolleys. They usually run on rails alongside the road and contain new systems, such as automated brakes and speed controls.

Think About It!

▶ Because trolleys operate on electrical energy, does this mean that they don't create any pollution? Explain your answer.

▲ *Many cities across the country now use light-rail systems for public transportation.*

Sprites and Elves

Imagine you are a pilot flying a plane on a moonless night. About 80 km away, you notice a powerful thunderstorm and see the lightning move *between* the clouds and the Earth. This makes sense because you know that all weather activity takes place in the lowest layer of Earth's atmosphere, which is called the troposphere. But all of a sudden, a ghostly red glow stretches many kilometers *above* the storm clouds and *into* the stratosphere!

Capturing Sprites

In 1989, scientists at the University of Minnesota followed the trail of many such reports. They captured the first image of this strange, red-glowing lightning using a video camera. Since then, photographs from space shuttles, airplanes, telescopes, and observers on the ground have identified several types of wispy electrical glows. Two of these types were named sprites and elves because, like the mythical creatures, they last only a few thousandths of a second and disappear just as the eye begins to see them.

Photographs show that sprites and elves occur only when ordinary lightning is discharged from a cloud. Sprites are very large, extending from the cloud tops at an altitude of about 15 km to as high as 95 km. They are up to 50 km wide. Elves are expanding disks of red light, probably caused by an electromagnetic pulse from lightning or sprites. Elves can be 200 km across, and they appear at altitudes above 90 km.

What Took So Long?

It is likely that sprites and elves have been occurring for thousands of years but went unrecorded. This is because they are produced with only about 1 percent of lightning flashes. They also last for a short period of time and are very faint. Since they occur above thunderclouds, where few people can see, observers are more often distracted by the brighter lightning below.

▲ *Sprites (left) and elves (right) are strange electric discharges in the atmosphere.*

Still, scientists are not surprised to learn that electric discharges extend up from clouds. There is a large potential difference between thunderclouds and the ionosphere, an atmospheric level above the clouds. The ionosphere is electrically conductive and provides a path for these electric discharges.

Search and Find

► Would you like to find sprites on your own? (Elves disappear too quickly.) Go with an adult, avoid being out in a thunderstorm, and remember:

- It must be completely dark, and your eyes must adjust to the total darkness.
- Viewing is best when a large thunderstorm is 48 to 97 km away, with no clouds in between.
- Block out the lightning below the clouds with dark paper so that you can still see above the clouds.
- Be patient.

Report sightings to a university geophysical department. Scientists need more information to fully understand how these discharges affect the chemical and electrical workings of our atmosphere.

Electromagnetism

Pre-Reading Questions

1. What are the properties of magnets?
2. How does electricity produce magnetism?
3. How does magnetism produce electricity?

Electric High Speed Trains

Meet the Eurostar, an electric passenger train that runs at speeds up to 298 kilometers per hour (186 mph). The Eurostar railway connects France, England, and Belgium, traveling through the "Chunnel," a 50-kilometer (30-mile)-long tunnel under the English Channel. The train gets its electrical power either through a third rail beneath the train or through overhead wires. In this chapter, you will learn how electricity and magnetic force are related, how electric motors work, and how electrical power is generated.

MAGNETIC ATTRACTION

In this activity, you will investigate ways you can use a magnet to lift steel.

Procedure

1. Place **5 steel paper clips** on your desk. Touch the clips with an **unmagnetized iron nail.** Lift the nail and record the number of clips that stick to the nail.

2. Touch the clips with the end of a **strong bar magnet.** Record the number of clips that stick to it.

3. While holding the magnet against the head of the nail, touch the tip of the nail to the paper clips. Count the number of paper clips that stick to the nail.

4. Remove the magnet from the end of the nail, and observe what happens. Record the number of paper clips you counted in step 3 and your observations from step 4.

5. Drag one end of the bar magnet 50 times down the nail. Drag the magnet in only one direction.

6. Set the magnet aside. Touch the nail to the clips. Record the number of clips that stick to it.

Analysis

7. What caused the difference between the number of paper clips you picked up in step 1 and step 3?

8. What effect did the magnet have on the nail in step 5?

Magnets and Magnetism

Terms to Learn

magnet
poles
magnetic force

What You'll Do

- Describe the force between two magnetic poles.
- Explain why some materials are magnetic and some are not.
- Describe four different categories of magnets.
- Give two examples of the effect of Earth's magnetic field.

You've probably seen magnets like the ones at right and below, stuck to a refrigerator door. These magnets might have been used to hold up notes or pictures or might have been used just for decoration. If you have ever played with magnets, you know that they stick to each other and to some types of metals. You also know that magnets can stick to objects without directly touching them—like when one is used to hold a piece of paper to a refrigerator door. How do magnets work? Read on to find out.

BREAD
MILK
EGGS
CHEESE
APPLES

Properties of Magnets

More than 2,000 years ago, the Greeks discovered a mineral that attracted objects containing iron. Because this mineral was found in a part of Turkey called Magnesia, the Greeks called it magnetite. Today any material that attracts iron or materials containing iron is called a **magnet.** All magnets have certain properties. For example, all magnets have two poles, exert forces, and are surrounded by a magnetic field.

Magnetic Poles The magnetic effects of a magnet are not evenly distributed throughout the magnet. For example, if you dip a bar magnet into a box of paper clips, you will find that most of the paper clips stick to the ends of the bar, as shown in **Figure 1.** As you can see, the magnetic effects are strongest near the ends of the bar magnet. The parts of a magnet where the magnetic effects are strongest are called **poles.**

Figure 1 More paper clips stick to the ends, or poles, of a magnet because that's where the magnetic effects are strongest.

North and South If you attach a magnet to a string so that the magnet is free to rotate, you will see that one end of the magnet always ends up pointing to the north, as shown in **Figure 2.** The pole of a magnet that points to the north is called the magnet's north pole. The opposite end of the magnet points to the south and is therefore called the magnet's south pole. Magnetic poles always occur in pairs; you will never find a magnet with only a north pole or only a south pole.

Figure 2 *The needle in a compass is a magnet that is free to rotate.*

Magnetic Forces When you bring two magnets close together, the magnets each exert a force that can either push the magnets apart or pull them together. The force of repulsion or attraction between the poles of magnets is called the **magnetic force.** The magnetic force between a pair of magnets depends on how the poles of the magnets line up, as shown in **Figure 3.** As you can see, magnetic poles are similar to electric charges in that like poles repel and opposite poles attract.

Figure 3 Magnetic Force Between Magnets

If you hold the north poles of two magnets close together, the magnetic force will push the magnets apart. The same is true if you hold the south poles close together.

If you hold the north pole of one magnet close to the south pole of another magnet, the magnetic force will pull the magnets together.

Magnetic Fields A *magnetic field* exists in the region around a magnet in which magnetic forces can act. The shape of a magnetic field can be shown with lines drawn from the north pole of a magnet to the south pole, as shown in **Figure 4.** These lines map the strength of magnetic force and are called magnetic field lines. The closer together the field lines are, the stronger the magnetic field is. Magnetic field lines around a magnet are closest together at the poles, showing that the magnetic force is strongest at these two places.

Figure 4 *Magnetic field lines show the shape of a magnetic field around a magnet. You can model magnetic field lines by sprinkling iron filings around a magnet.*

What Makes Materials Magnetic?

Some materials are magnetic, and some are not. For example, a magnet can pick up objects such as paper clips and iron nails, but it cannot pick up paper, plastic, pennies, or aluminum foil. What causes the difference? Whether a material is magnetic depends on the atoms in the material.

Atoms and Domains All matter is composed of atoms. In the atoms, electrons are the negatively charged particles that move around the nucleus. Moving electrons produce magnetic fields that can give an atom a north and a south pole. In most materials, such as copper and aluminum, the magnetic fields of the individual atoms cancel each other out, so the materials aren't magnetic. However, in materials like iron, nickel, and cobalt, the atoms group together in tiny regions called *domains*. The atoms in a domain are arranged so that the north and south poles of all the atoms line up and create a strong magnetic field. Domains are like tiny magnets of different sizes within an object. **Figure 5,** on the next page, shows how domains affect the magnetic properties of an object.

BRAIN FOOD

Grazing cows sometimes eat pieces of metal that have fallen on the ground. To protect their cows, ranchers have them swallow special cow magnets. These magnets stay in one of the cow's stomachs and attract any metal objects containing iron that the cow eats. This keeps the metal from traveling through the rest of the cow's digestive system.

Figure 5 *The arrangement of domains in an object determines whether the object is magnetic.*

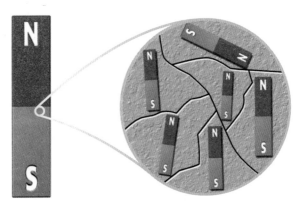

If the domains in an object are randomly arranged, the magnetic fields of the individual domains cancel each other out, and the object overall has no magnetic properties.

If most of the domains in an object are aligned, the magnetic fields of the individual domains combine to make the whole object magnetic.

Losing Alignment The domains of a magnet may not always stay aligned. Dropping a magnet or striking it too hard can jostle the domains out of alignment, causing the magnet to lose its magnetic properties. Increasing the temperature of a magnet can also demagnetize it. At higher temperatures, atoms in the magnet vibrate faster and lose their alignment within the domains.

Making Magnets A magnet can be made from an unmagnetized object made of iron, cobalt, or nickel by aligning the domains in the object. For example, you can magnetize an iron nail if you rub it in one direction with one pole of a magnet. The magnetic field of the magnet will cause the domains in the nail to rotate and align with the domains in the magnet. As more domains become aligned, the overall magnetic field of the nail will strengthen, and the nail will become a magnet, as shown in **Figure 6.**

The process of making a magnet also explains how a magnet can pick up an unmagnetized object, such as a paper clip. When you hold a magnet close to a paper clip, the magnetic field of the magnet causes the domains in the paper clip to align slightly, creating a temporary magnet. The domains align such that the north pole of the paper clip points toward the south pole of the magnet. The paper clip is therefore attracted to the magnet. The domains of the paper clip return to a random arrangement after the magnet is removed.

Figure 6 *This nail was magnetized by rubbing it with a magnet.*

Half a Magnet? What do you think would happen if you cut a magnet in half? You might predict that you would end up with one north-pole piece and one south-pole piece. But that's not what happens. When you cut a magnet in half, you end up with two magnets, each with its own north pole and south pole, as shown in **Figure 7.** Each domain within a magnet is like a tiny magnet with a north and south pole, so even the smallest pieces of a magnet have two poles.

Figure 7 *If you cut a magnet into pieces, each piece will still be a magnet with two poles.*

REVIEW

1. Name three properties of magnets.

2. Why are some iron objects magnetic and others not magnetic?

3. **Applying Concepts** Suppose you have two bar magnets. One has its north and south poles marked, but the other one does not. Describe how you could use the first magnet to identify the poles of the second magnet.

Figure 8 *Magnetite attracts objects containing iron and is a ferromagnet.*

Types of Magnets

There are different ways to describe magnets. The magnets you may be most familiar with are those made of iron, nickel, cobalt, or alloys of those metals. Magnets made with these metals have strong magnetic properties and are called *ferromagnets.* The mineral magnetite, which you read about at the beginning of this section and which is shown in **Figure 8,** is an example of a naturally occurring ferromagnet. Another type of magnet is the *electromagnet.* An electromagnet is a magnet, usually with an iron core, produced by an electric current. You will learn more about electromagnets in the next section.

Temporary and Permanent Magnets Magnets can also be described as temporary magnets or permanent magnets. *Temporary magnets* are made from materials that are easy to magnetize but tend to lose their magnetization easily. Soft iron (iron that is not mixed with any other materials) can be made into temporary magnets. *Permanent magnets,* on the other hand, are difficult to magnetize but tend to retain their magnetic properties better. Strong permanent magnets are made with alnico (AL ni кон)—an alloy of aluminum, nickel, and cobalt.

Earth as a Magnet

Recall that one end of every magnet points to the north if the magnet is allowed to rotate freely. For more than 2,000 years, travelers and explorers have relied on this to help them navigate. In fact, you take advantage of this property any time you use a compass, because a compass contains a freely rotating magnet. But why do magnets point to the north? Read on to find out.

One Giant Magnet In 1600, an English physician named William Gilbert suggested that magnets point to the north because Earth itself is one giant magnet. In fact, Earth behaves as if it has a bar magnet running through its center. The poles of this imaginary magnet are located near Earth's geographic poles, as shown in **Figure 9.**

QuickLab

Model of Earth's Magnetic Field

1. On a **sheet of butcher paper,** draw a circle with a diameter larger than a bar magnet. This represents the surface of the Earth. Label Earth's North and South Poles.

2. Place a **bar magnet** under the butcher paper and line it up with the poles.

3. Sprinkle some **iron filings** lightly around the perimeter of the circle. In your ScienceLog, describe and sketch the pattern you see.

Figure 9 *The magnetic poles of Earth are close to—but not the same as—the geographic poles.*

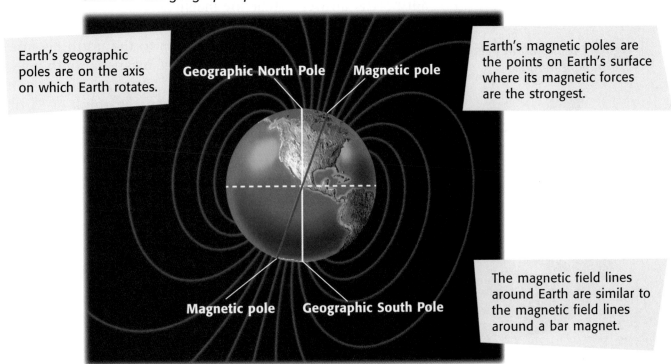

Earth's geographic poles are on the axis on which Earth rotates.

Geographic North Pole

Magnetic pole

Earth's magnetic poles are the points on Earth's surface where its magnetic forces are the strongest.

Magnetic pole

Geographic South Pole

The magnetic field lines around Earth are similar to the magnetic field lines around a bar magnet.

North or South? Try this simple experiment. Place a compass on a bar magnet that has its north and south poles marked. Which pole of the magnet did the marked end of the needle of the compass point to? If your compass is working properly, the marked end should have pointed to the south pole of the magnet, as shown in **Figure 10.** Does that surprise you? Think about what you have already learned about magnets.

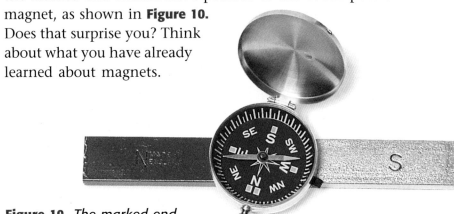

Figure 10 *The marked end of a compass needle always points to the south pole of a magnet.*

One property of magnets is that opposite poles attract each other. That means that the north pole of one magnet is attracted to the south pole of another magnet. A compass needle is a small magnet, and the tip that points to the north is the needle's north pole. Therefore, the point of a compass needle will be attracted to the south pole of a bar magnet.

North Is South! So why does the needle of a compass point north? The answer is that the magnetic pole of Earth that is closest to the geographic North Pole is actually a magnetic *south* pole! So a compass needle points to the north because its north pole is attracted to a very large magnetic south pole.

Figure 11 *The Earth acts like a giant magnet.*

The Core of the Matter Although you can think of Earth as having a giant bar magnet in its center, as shown in **Figure 11,** there isn't really a magnet there. The temperature of Earth's core (or center) is so high that atoms in it move too violently to remain aligned in domains. Scientists think that the Earth's magnetic field is produced by the movement of electric charges in the Earth's core. The Earth's core is made mostly of iron and nickel. The inner core is solid because it is under such great pressure. In the outer core, the pressure is less and the metals are in a liquid state. As Earth rotates, the liquid in the core flows and causes electric charges to move, creating a magnetic field.

A Magnetic Light Show One of the most spectacular effects caused by the Earth's magnetic field is a curtain of light called an *aurora,* like the one shown in **Figure 12.** An aurora is formed when charged particles from the sun interact with oxygen and nitrogen atoms in Earth's atmosphere. When charged particles from the sun strike these atoms, the atoms emit light of different colors.

Figure 12 *The photo at left shows what an aurora looks like from the ground.*

Earth's magnetic field acts like a barrier to most charged particles from the sun, so the particles cannot strike the atmosphere in most places. But because Earth's magnetic field bends inward at the magnetic poles, the charged particles can crash into the atmosphere at and near the poles. Therefore, auroras are most often seen in areas near the north and south magnetic poles. Auroras seen near the north magnetic pole are called aurora borealis (ah ROHR uh BOHR ee AL is), the northern lights, and auroras seen near the south magnetic pole are called aurora australis (ah ROHR uh ah STRAY lis), the southern lights.

Science
C O N N E C T I O N

Auroras are a result of geomagnetic storms. Read more about these storms on page 478.

REVIEW

1. Name the metals used to make ferromagnets.

2. How are temporary magnets different from permanent magnets?

3. **Applying Concepts** Why are auroras more commonly seen in places like Alaska and Australia than in places like Florida and Mexico?

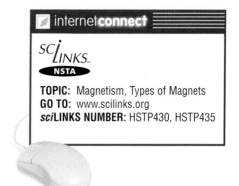

internet**connect**

*sci*LINKS
NSTA

TOPIC: Magnetism, Types of Magnets
GO TO: www.scilinks.org
*sci*LINKS NUMBER: HSTP430, HSTP435

Magnetism from Electricity

Terms to Learn

electromagnetism
solenoid
electromagnet
electric motor

What You'll Do

- Identify the relationship between an electric current and a magnetic field.
- Compare solenoids, electromagnets, and magnets.
- Describe how electromagnetism is involved in the operation of doorbells, electric motors, and galvanometers.

Most of the trains you see roll on wheels on top of a track. But engineers have developed trains that have no wheels and actually float above the track. These trains are able to levitate because of magnetic forces between the track and the train cars. Such trains are called maglev trains. The name *maglev* is short for magnetic levitation. To levitate, maglev trains use a type of magnet called an electromagnet, which can produce a strong magnetic field. In this section you will learn how electricity and magnetism are related and how electromagnets are made.

The Discovery of Electromagnetism

Danish physicist Hans Christian Oersted discovered the relationship between electricity and magnetism in 1820. During a lecture, he held a compass near a wire carrying an electric current. Oersted noticed that when the compass was close to the wire, the compass needle no longer pointed to the north. This result surprised Oersted because a compass needle is a magnet and only moves from its usual north-south orientation when it is in a magnetic field different from Earth's magnetic field. Oersted tried a few experiments with the compass and the wire and found the results shown in **Figure 13.**

Figure 13 *Oersted's experiments show that an electric current can move a compass needle.*

a If no electric current exists in the wire, the compass needles point in the same direction.

b Electric current in one direction in the wire causes the compass needles to deflect in a clockwise direction.

c Electric current in the opposite direction makes the compass needles deflect in a counter-clockwise direction.

More Research From his experiments, Oersted concluded that an electric current produces a magnetic field and that the direction of the magnetic field depends on the direction of the current. The French scientist André-Marie Ampère heard about Oersted's findings and did more research with electricity and magnetism. Together, their work was the first research conducted on electromagnetism. **Electromagnetism** is the interaction between electricity and magnetism.

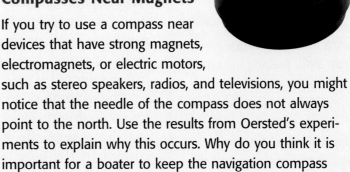

Compasses Near Magnets

If you try to use a compass near devices that have strong magnets, electromagnets, or electric motors, such as stereo speakers, radios, and televisions, you might notice that the needle of the compass does not always point to the north. Use the results from Oersted's experiments to explain why this occurs. Why do you think it is important for a boater to keep the navigation compass away from the boat's radio?

Using Electromagnetism

Although the magnetic field created by an electric current in a wire may deflect a compass needle, it is not strong enough to be very useful. However, two devices, the solenoid and the electromagnet, strengthen the magnetic field created by a current-carrying wire. Both devices make electromagnetism more useful for practical applications.

Solenoids The scientists mentioned at the beginning of this chapter used a solenoid to levitate a frog. A **solenoid** is a coil of wire that produces a magnetic field when carrying an electric current. A single loop of wire carrying a current does not have a very strong magnetic field. However, if many loops are used to form a coil, the magnetic fields of the individual loops can combine to produce a much stronger magnetic field. In fact, the magnetic field around a solenoid is very similar to the magnetic field of a bar magnet, as shown in **Figure 14.** The strength of the magnetic field produced by a solenoid increases as more loops are added and as the current in the wire is increased.

Figure 14 *The ends of the solenoid are like the poles of a magnet.*

Electromagnets An **electromagnet** is a magnet that consists of a solenoid wrapped around an iron core. The magnetic field produced by the solenoid causes the domains inside the iron core to become better aligned. The magnetic field for the entire electromagnet is the field produced by the solenoid plus the field produced by the magnetized iron core. As a result, the magnetic field produced by an electromagnet may be hundreds of times stronger than the magnetic field produced by just a solenoid with the same number of loops.

The strength of an electromagnet can be made even stronger by increasing the number of loops in the solenoid, by increasing the size of the iron core, and by increasing the electric current in the wire. Some electromagnets are strong enough to lift a car or levitate a train!

Heavy Lifting Do you remember the maglev trains discussed at the beginning of this section? Those trains levitate because there are strong magnets on the cars that are repelled by powerful electromagnets in the rails. Electromagnets are particularly useful because they can be turned on and off as needed. Electromagnets attract objects containing iron only when a current exists in the wire. When there is no current in the wire, the electromagnet is turned off. **Figure 15** shows an example of how this property can be useful.

Figure 15 *The electromagnets used in salvage yards can lift heavy scrap metal when turned on. To put the metal back down, the electromagnet is turned off.*

✔ Self-Check

Can you make an electromagnet by wrapping a coil of wire around a wooden core? Explain your answer.
(See page 724 to check your answer.)

Magnetic Force and Electric Current

At the beginning of this section you learned that an electric current can cause a compass needle to move. The needle, a small magnet, moves because the electric current in a wire creates a magnetic field that exerts a force on the needle. If a current-carrying wire causes a magnet to move, can a magnet cause a current-carrying wire to move? **Figure 16** shows that the answer is yes.

Figure 16 *A magnet exerts a force on a current-carrying wire.*

a When a current-carrying wire is placed between two poles of a magnet, the wire will jump up.

b If the direction of the electric current in the wire is reversed, the wire is pushed down instead of up.

Applications of Electromagnetism

Electromagnetism is useful in your everyday life. You already know that electromagnets can be used to lift heavy objects containing iron. But did you know that you use a solenoid whenever you ring a doorbell or that there are electromagnets in motors? Keep reading to learn how electromagnetism makes these devices work.

Doorbells Many doorbells contain a solenoid with an iron rod inserted part way in it. The electric current in the solenoid is controlled by the doorbell button. When you press the button, a switch in the solenoid circuit closes, creating an electric current in the solenoid. What happens next is shown in **Figure 17.**

Figure 17 *An electric current in the solenoid of a doorbell produces a magnetic field. This field pulls the iron rod through the solenoid, and the rod strikes the bell.*

Electric Motors An **electric motor** is a device that changes electrical energy into kinetic energy. All electric motors have an *armature*—a loop or coil of wire that can rotate. The armature is mounted between the poles of a permanent magnet or electromagnet.

In electric motors that use direct current, a device called a *commutator* is attached to the armature to reverse the direction of the electric current in the wire. A commutator is a ring that is split in half and connected to the ends of the armature. Electric current enters the armature through brushes that touch the commutator. Every time the armature and the commutator make a half-turn, the direction of the current is reversed. **Figure 18** shows how a direct-current motor works.

Figure 18 A Direct-Current Electric Motor

Getting Started An electric current in the armature causes the magnet to exert a force on the armature. Because of the direction of the current on either side of the armature, the magnet pulls up on one side and down on the other. This makes the armature rotate.

Permanent magnet

Brushes

N

S

Source of electrical energy

Armature

Running the Motor As the armature rotates, the commutator causes the electric current in the coil to change directions. When the electric current is reversed, the side of the coil that was pulled up is pulled down, and the side that was pulled down is pulled up. This keeps the armature rotating.

Commutator

Direction of rotation

N

S

Galvanometers A galvanometer is a device used to measure current through the interaction of an electromagnet and a permanent magnet. Galvanometers are sometimes found in equipment used by electricians, such as ammeters and voltmeters. Galvanometers contain an electromagnet placed between the poles of a permanent magnet. The electromagnet is free to rotate and is attached to a pointer. The pointer moves along a scale that shows the size and direction of the current. When there is a current in the coil of the electromagnet, the poles of the electromagnet are repelled by the poles of the permanent magnet. **Figure 19** shows how the parts of a galvanometer work.

Figure 19 *The pointer will move farther when there is a large current in the electromagnet than when there is a small current.*

REVIEW

1. Describe what happens when you hold a compass close to a wire carrying a current.

2. How is a solenoid like a bar magnet?

3. What makes the armature in an electric motor rotate?

4. Explain how a solenoid works to make a doorbell ring.

5. **Applying Concepts** What do Hans Christian Oersted's experiments have to do with a galvanometer? Explain your answer.

internet connect

SC*LINKS*
NSTA

TOPIC: Electromagnetism
GO TO: www.scilinks.org
*sci*LINKS NUMBER: HSTP440

Terms to Learn

electromagnetic induction
generator
transformer

What You'll Do

◆ Explain how a magnetic field can produce an electric current.
◆ Explain how electromagnetic induction is used in a generator.
◆ Compare step-up and step-down transformers.

Electricity from Magnetism

When you use an electric appliance or turn on a light in your home, you probably don't think about where the electrical energy comes from. For most people, an electric power company supplies their home with electrical energy. In this section, you'll learn how a magnetic field can produce an electric current and how power companies use this process to supply electrical energy.

Electric Current from a Magnetic Field

After Oersted discovered that an electric current could produce a magnetic field, scientists began to wonder if a magnetic field could produce an electric current. In 1831, two scientists—Michael Faraday, from Great Britain, and Joseph Henry, from the United States—independently solved this problem. Although Henry was the first to make the discovery, Faraday's results are better known because Faraday published his results first and reported them in greater detail.

Faraday's Failure? In his experiments, Faraday used a setup similar to the one shown in **Figure 20.** Faraday hoped that the magnetic field created by the electromagnet would create—or induce—an electric current in the second wire. But no matter how strong the electromagnet was, no electric current could be produced in the second wire.

Figure 20 Faraday's Setup

One wire was wound around one half of an iron ring.

A second wire was wound around the other half of the iron ring.

A battery supplied an electric current to the wire, making an electromagnet.

A galvanometer measured any current produced in the second wire by the magnetic field.

Success for an Instant As Faraday experimented with this electromagnetic ring, he noticed something interesting. At the instant he connected the wires of the electromagnet to the battery, the galvanometer pointer moved, indicating that an electric current was present. The pointer moved again at the instant he disconnected the electromagnet. But as long as the electromagnet was fully connected to the battery, the galvanometer measured no electric current.

Faraday realized that electric current in the second wire was produced only when the magnetic field was changing—in this case, when the magnetic field was turned on and off as the battery was connected and disconnected. The process by which an electric current is produced by a changing magnetic field is called **electromagnetic induction.** Faraday did many more experiments on electromagnetic induction. Some of his results are summarized in **Figure 21.**

You too can have instant success with the activity on page 699 of the LabBook.

Figure 21 *The size and direction of the electric current induced by a changing magnetic field depends on several factors.*

a An electric current is induced when you move a magnet through a coil of wire.

b A greater electric current is induced if you move the magnet faster through the coil because the magnetic field is changing faster.

c A greater electric current is induced if you add more loops of wire. This magnet is moving at the same speed as the magnet in (b).

d The induced electric current reverses direction if the magnet is pulled out rather than pushed in.

Figure 22 *As the wire moves between the poles of the magnet, it cuts through magnetic field lines, and an electric current is induced.*

Inducing Electric Current Faraday's experiments also showed that the magnetic field around a wire can be changed by moving either the magnet or the wire. Therefore, an electric current could be induced by moving a magnet in a coil of wire or by moving a wire between the poles of a magnet.

One way to remember when an electric current is produced by electromagnetic induction is to consider the magnetic field lines between the poles of the magnet. An electric current is induced only when a wire cuts through, or crosses, the magnetic field lines, as shown in **Figure 22.** This is because the magnetic force causes electric charges to move through the wire as the wire moves through the magnetic field.

Applications of Electromagnetic Induction

Electromagnetic induction is very important for the production of electrical energy at an electric power plant, and it is important for the transmission of energy from the plant to your home. Generators and transformers work on the principle of electromagnetic induction and are used by power plants to provide the electrical energy that you need every day.

Generators A **generator** is a device that uses electromagnetic induction to convert kinetic energy into electrical energy. **Figure 23** shows the parts of a simple generator, and **Figure 24,** on the next page, explains how the generator works.

Figure 23
Parts of a Simple Generator

Generators contain a **coil of wire** attached to a rod that is free to rotate. This generator has a crank that is used to turn the coil.

Slip rings are attached to the ends of the wire in the coil.

Electric current leaves the generator when the slip rings touch a pair of **brushes.**

The coil is placed between the poles of a **permanent magnet** or electromagnet.

Figure 24 How a Generator Works

1 As the crank is turned, the rotating coil cuts through the magnetic field lines of the magnet, and an electric current is induced in the wire.

2 When the coil is not cutting through the magnetic field lines, no electric current is induced.

3 As the coil continues to rotate, the magnetic field lines are cut from a different direction, and an electric current is induced in the opposite direction.

Alternating Current The electric current produced by the generator shown in Figure 24 changes direction each time the coil makes a half-turn. Because the electric current continually changes direction, the electric current is an alternating current. Generators in power plants also produce alternating current. But generators in power plants are much larger and contain many coils of wire instead of just one. In most large generators, the magnet is turned instead of the coils.

Generating Electrical Energy The energy that generators convert to electrical energy comes from different sources. In nuclear power plants, thermal energy from a nuclear reaction boils water to produce steam, which turns a turbine. The turbine turns the magnet of the generator, inducing an electric current and generating electrical energy. **Figure 25** shows a similar process in a hydroelectric power plant.

Figure 25 *As water flows down a chute, it turns a turbine. The turbine spins the magnet of the generator, inducing an electric current.*

Transformers Another device that relies on electromagnetic induction is a transformer. A **transformer** increases or decreases the voltage of an alternating current. A simple transformer consists of two coils of wire wrapped around an iron ring.

Alternating current from an electrical energy source is supplied to one coil, called the primary coil. The electric current makes the ring an electromagnet. But the electric current in the primary coil is alternating, so the magnetic field of the electromagnet changes with every change in electric current direction. The changing magnetic field in the iron ring induces an electric current in the other coil, called the secondary coil.

Step-Up, Step-Down The number of loops in the primary and secondary coils of a transformer determines whether it increases or decreases the voltage. If a transformer increases voltage, it is a step-up transformer. If a transformer decreases voltage, it is a step-down transformer. Both kinds of transformers are shown in **Figure 26.**

Figure 26 *Transformers can either increase or decrease voltage.*

The primary coil of a **step-up transformer** has fewer loops than the secondary coil. So the voltage of the electric current in the secondary coil is higher than the voltage of the electric current in the primary coil. Therefore, voltage is increased.

Primary coil   Secondary coil

The primary coil of a **step-down transformer** has more loops than the secondary coil. So the voltage of the electric current in the secondary coil is lower than the voltage of the electric current in the primary coil. Therefore, voltage is decreased.

Electrical Energy for Your Home The electric current that provides your home with electrical energy is usually transformed three times before it reaches your home. Generators at the power plants produce electric current with high voltage. To decrease the loss of power that occurs during transmission over long distance, the voltage is increased thousands of times with a step-up transformer. Of course, the voltage must be decreased before it is distributed to households. Two different step-down transformers are used before the electric current reaches consumers. **Figure 27** shows how electric current is transformed on its way to your home.

Figure 27 *Electric current is transformed three times before reaching your home.*

Home-supply (120 V) step-down transformer

Local power lines, lower voltage

Distribution station step-down transformer

Power plant, high voltage

Step-up transformer

Transmission lines, very high voltage

REVIEW

1. How does a generator produce an electric current?

2. Explain why rotating either the coil or the magnet induces an electric current in a generator.

3. **Inferring Conclusions** One reason why electric power plants do not distribute electrical energy as direct current is that direct current cannot be transformed. Explain why not.

internet**connect**

SC*I*INKS.
NSTA

TOPIC: Electromagnetic Induction
GO TO: www.scilinks.org
*sci*LINKS **NUMBER:** HSTP445

Chapter Highlights

SECTION 1

Vocabulary

magnet *(p. 454)*
poles *(p. 454)*
magnetic force *(p. 455)*

Section Notes

- All magnets have two poles. One pole will always point to the north if allowed to rotate freely, and it is called the north pole. The other pole is called the south pole.

- Like magnetic poles repel each other; opposite magnetic poles attract.

- All magnets are surrounded by a magnetic field. The shape of that magnetic field can be shown with magnetic field lines.

- A material is magnetic if its domains are aligned. Iron, nickel, and cobalt atoms group together in domains.

- Magnets can be classified as ferromagnets, electromagnets, temporary magnets, and permanent magnets. A magnet can belong to more than one group.

- Earth acts as if it has a big bar magnet in its core.

- Compass needles and the north pole of magnets point to Earth's magnetic south pole—which is close to Earth's geographic North Pole.

- Auroras are most commonly seen near Earth's magnetic poles because Earth's magnetic fields bend inward at the poles.

Labs

Magnetic Mystery *(p. 698)*

SECTION 2

Vocabulary

electromagnetism *(p. 463)*
solenoid *(p. 463)*
electromagnet *(p. 464)*
electric motor *(p. 466)*

Section Notes

- Oersted discovered that a wire carrying an electric current produces a magnetic field.

- Electromagnetism is the interaction between electricity and magnetism.

- A solenoid is a coil of current-carrying wire that produces a magnetic field.

- An electromagnet is a solenoid with an iron core. The electromagnet has a stronger magnetic field than a solenoid of the same size does.

- Increasing the current in a solenoid or an electromagnet increases the magnetic field.

☑ Skills Check

Visual Understanding

ELECTROMAGNETISM The two important concepts in electromagnetism were discovered by Oersted and Faraday. Figure 13 on page 462 summarizes Oersted's work, which showed that an electric current can produce a magnetic field.

ELECTROMAGNETIC INDUCTION Faraday's work showed that a changing magnetic field can induce an electric current in a wire. His results are summarized in Figure 21 on page 469.

SECTION 2

- Increasing the number of loops on a solenoid or an electromagnet increases the magnetic field.

- A magnet can exert a force on a wire carrying a current.

- In a doorbell, the magnetic field of a solenoid pulls an iron rod, and the iron rod strikes the bell.

- The magnetic force between a magnet and wires carrying an electric current makes an electric motor turn.

- An electric motor converts electrical energy into kinetic energy.

- A galvanometer measures current by using the magnetic force between an electromagnet and a permanent magnet.

Labs

Build a DC Motor *(p. 700)*

SECTION 3

Vocabulary

electromagnetic induction *(p. 469)*

generator *(p. 470)*

transformer *(p. 472)*

Section Notes

- Faraday discovered that a changing magnetic field can create an electric current in a wire. This is called electromagnetic induction.

- Generators use electromagnetic induction to convert kinetic energy into electrical energy.

- Kinetic energy can be supplied to a generator in different ways.

- Transformers increase or decrease the voltage of an alternating current using electromagnetic induction.

- A step-up transformer increases the voltage of an alternating current. Its primary coil has fewer loops than its secondary coil.

- A step-down transformer decreases the voltage of an alternating current. Its primary coil has more loops than its secondary coil.

Labs

Electricity from Magnetism *(p. 699)*

Chapter Review

USING VOCABULARY

To complete the following sentences, choose the correct term from each pair of terms listed below:

1. All magnets have two __?__. (*magnetic forces* or *poles*)

2. A(n) __?__ converts kinetic energy into electrical energy. (*electric motor* or *generator*)

3. __?__ occurs when an electric current is produced by a changing magnetic field. (*Electromagnetic induction* or *Magnetic force*)

4. The interaction between electricity and magnetism is called __?__. (*electromagnetism* or *electromagnetic induction*)

UNDERSTANDING CONCEPTS

Multiple Choice

5. The region around a magnet in which magnetic forces can act is called the
   a. magnetic field.
   b. domain.
   c. pole.
   d. solenoid.

6. An electric fan has an electric motor inside to change
   a. kinetic energy into electrical energy.
   b. thermal energy into electrical energy.
   c. electrical energy into thermal energy.
   d. electrical energy into kinetic energy.

7. The marked end of a compass needle always points directly to
   a. Earth's geographic South Pole.
   b. Earth's geographic North Pole.
   c. a magnet's south pole.
   d. a magnet's north pole.

8. A device that increases the voltage of an alternating current is called a(n)
   a. electric motor.
   b. galvanometer.
   c. step-up transformer.
   d. step-down transformer.

9. The magnetic field of a solenoid can be increased by
   a. adding more loops.
   b. increasing the current.
   c. putting an iron core inside the coil to make an electromagnet.
   d. All of the above

10. What do you end up with if you cut a magnet in half?
    a. one north-pole piece and one south-pole piece
    b. two unmagnetized pieces
    c. two pieces, each with a north pole and a south pole
    d. two north-pole pieces

Short Answer

11. Explain why auroras are seen mostly near the North and South Poles.

12. Compare the function of a generator with the function of an electric motor.

13. Explain why some pieces of iron are more magnetic than others.

Concept Mapping

14. Use the following terms to create a concept map: electromagnetism, electricity, magnetism, electromagnetic induction, generator, transformer.

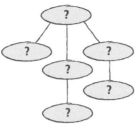

15. You win a hand-powered flashlight as a prize in your school science fair. The flashlight has a clear plastic case so you can look inside to see how it works. When you press the handle, a gray ring spins between two coils of wire. The ends of the wire are connected to the light bulb. So when you press the handle, the light bulb glows. Explain how an electric current is produced to light the bulb. (Hint: Paper clips are attracted to the gray ring.)

16. Fire doors are doors that can slow the spread of fire from room to room when they are closed. In some buildings, fire doors are held open by electromagnets. The electromagnets are controlled by the building's fire alarm system. If a fire is detected, the doors automatically shut. Explain why electromagnets are used instead of permanent magnets.

17. Study the solenoids and electromagnets shown below. Rank them in order of strongest magnetic field to weakest magnetic field. Explain your ranking.

a

Current = 2 A

b

Current = 2 A

c

Current = 4 A

d

Current = 4 A

Reading Check-up

Take a minute to review your answers to the Pre-Reading Questions found at the bottom of page 452. Have your answers changed? If necessary, revise your answers based on what you have learned since you began this chapter.

Geomagnetic Storms

On March 13, 1989, a storm hit Montreal, Quebec. But this wasn't an ordinary storm. This was a geomagnetic storm that caused an electrical blackout. About 6 million people went without electricity for 9 hours.

What Is a Geomagnetic Storm?

To understand a geomagnetic storm, you must first know a few things about the sun. By looking closely at the surface of the sun, scientists have discovered that it has cycles of very violent activity. Powerful eruptions called solar flares occur periodically, sending charged particles outward at almost the speed of light and with the energy of millions of hydrogen bombs. As particles explode away from the solar surface, they create a solar wind of charged particles that travels several million kilometers per hour through space between the sun and the Earth. A geomagnetic storm occurs when the solar wind sweeps across Earth's atmosphere, causing a variety of disturbances.

Grids and Pipelines

Geomagnetic storms happen frequently, especially in the north. As the people of Quebec found out in 1989, such storms can interfere with systems used to operate power grids. They can also cause heavy static in long-distance radio reception and can affect the orbit of satellites. Geomagnetic storms can even cause corrosion in the metal of petroleum pipelines. In fact, scientists are not sure that they know of all the systems and materials that are affected by geomagnetic storms.

Knowledge Is the First Line of Defense

Solar flares are not well understood and are difficult to predict. There may be nothing that can be done to stop geomagnetic storms, but understanding them better is the first step toward protecting valuable systems from an eruption's effects. Scientists prepared several satellites to study the sun's activity and solar flares in 2000 and 2001. By studying solar eruptions, scientists think they can predict a geomagnetic storm 50 to 70 hours in advance. This could give industries affected by these storms time to protect their systems.

Solar Sails for Solar Wind

▶ Do research on solar flares and geomagnetic storms. Government agencies and universities have a number of programs, including satellites, to study and predict solar events. Create a model or a poster to explain something you learned from your research.

◀ *Solar flares on the sun can result in geomagnetic storms here on Earth.*

Health

Magnets in Medicine

Think about what it would be like to peer inside the human body to locate a tumor, find tiny blockages in blood vessels, or even identify damage to the brain. Medical technology known as magnetic resonance imaging (MRI) gives doctors a quick and painless way to see and diagnose these problems and more.

▲ *This color-enhanced MRI image of a brain shows a tumor (tinted yellow). The tumor was removed, and the patient resumed a healthy life.*

Magnetic Images

Like X rays, MRI creates pictures of a person's internal organs and skeleton. But MRI produces clearer pictures than X rays do, and MRI does not expose the body to the potentially harmful radiation of X rays. Instead, MRI uses powerful electromagnets and radio waves to create images.

The patient is placed in a large machine. An electric current in the electromagnet creates a powerful magnetic field around the patient. Because the human body is composed mostly of fat and water, there are many hydrogen atoms in the body. The magnetic field causes the nuclei of the hydrogen atoms to align in the direction of the magnetic field. Then another, weaker magnetic signal is sent out to the cells. The energy in this signal causes some hydrogen nuclei to change their position. As the signal's energy is absorbed and then released by the hydrogen nuclei, the MRI machine collects the signals and its computer converts the information into an image.

A Diagnostic Device

MRI is particularly useful for locating small tumors, revealing subtle changes in the brain, pinpointing blockages in blood vessels, and showing damage to the spinal cord. This technology also allows doctors to observe the function of specific body parts, such as the ears, heart, muscles, tendons, and blood vessels.

Researchers are experimenting with more-powerful magnets that work on other types of atoms. This technology is known as magnetic resonance spectroscopy (MRS). One current use of MRS is to monitor the effectiveness of chemotherapy in cancer patients. Doctors analyze MRS images to find chemical changes that might indicate whether the therapy is successful.

Picture This

▶ You may be familiar with X rays, but procedures like CAT or CT scans and MRI may be new to you. Research the different imaging tools—including X-ray tomography, CT or CAT scans, and MRI—that doctors can use to diagnose and treat injuries and disease. Select one of the imaging processes and make a model of how it works to demonstrate to the class. Be sure to include the procedure's advantages and disadvantages and the types of injuries or diseases for which it is used.

Electronic Technology

Pre-Reading
Questions

1. What is an electronic
   device?
2. What are some electronic
   devices used for communication?
3. What are the parts of a
   computer?

ELECTRONIC TRAFFIC CONTROL

Is this a photo of a futuristic town, seen from high in the
air? Look more closely. Those pathways are not streets and
highways. They are tiny, complex electrical pathways on a
microchip, a device that controls the flow of electric current. Microchips are the basic building blocks of computers
and other high-tech devices. In this chapter, you will learn
how electronic devices, such as computers, radios, and
televisions, work and how circuit boards are made and
electronic signals are produced.

START-UP Activity

TALKING LONG DISTANCE

Using a telephone allows you to communicate with someone from a distance. In this activity, you'll construct a model of a telephone.

Procedure

1. Thread one end of a **piece of string** through the hole in the bottom of one **empty coffee can.**

2. Tie a knot in the end of the string inside the can. The knot should be large enough to keep the string in place. The rest of the string should be coming out of the bottom of the can.

3. Repeat steps 1 and 2 with **another can** and the other end of the string.

4. Hold one can and have a classmate hold the other. Walk away from each other until the string is pulled fairly taut.

5. Speak into your can while your classmate holds the other can at his or her ear. Switch roles.

Analysis

6. In your ScienceLog, describe what you heard.

7. How is your apparatus similar to a real telephone? How is it different?

8. How are signals sent back and forth along the string?

9. Why do you think it was important to pull the string taut?

Electronic Components

What You'll Do

◆ Describe semiconductors and how their conductivity can be modified.

◆ Identify diodes, transistors, and integrated circuits as electronic components.

◆ Explain how integrated circuits have influenced electronic technology.

◆ Compare vacuum tubes and transistors.

Electronic devices rely on electrical energy, but not in the same way that appliances and machines do. Some machines can convert electrical energy into light, thermal, and mechanical energy in order to do work. Electronic devices use electrical energy to transmit information.

Inside an Electronic Device

A TV remote control is an example of an electronic device. It transmits information to a TV about volume levels and what channel to display. Have you ever looked inside of a TV remote control? If so, you would have seen something similar to **Figure 1.** A remote control contains a **circuit board,** a collection of hundreds of tiny circuits that supply electric current to the various parts of an electronic device.

To change channels or adjust the volume on the TV, you push buttons on the remote control. When you push a button, a tiny bulb called a light-emitting diode (DIE OHD), or LED, sends information to the TV in the form of infrared light. The components of the circuit board you see in Figure 1 control the electric current within the remote control in order to send the correct information to the TV. In this section you'll learn about some components of electronic devices and how they control electric current.

Figure 1 *Each part of a remote control has a role in transmitting information.*

Semiconductors

Many electronic components are made from semiconductors (SEM i kuhn DUHK tuhrz). A **semiconductor** is a substance that conducts an electric current better than an insulator but not as well as a conductor. The use of semiconductors has resulted in some incredible advances in electronic technology.

How Do Semiconductors Work? The way a semiconductor conducts electric current is based on how its electrons are arranged. Silicon (Si) is a widely used semiconductor in electronic technology. When silicon atoms bond, they share their valence electrons, as shown in **Figure 2.** Because all the valence electrons are shared, there are no electrons free to create much electric current in the semiconductor. So why are semiconductors like silicon used in electronic devices? Because their conductivity can be modified.

Doping In order to modify the conductivity of a semiconductor, its arrangement of electrons must be altered. This is done through **doping** (DOHP eeng), the process of replacing a few atoms of a semiconductor with a few atoms of another substance that have a different number of valence electrons. Two types of doped semiconductors are shown in **Figure 3.**

Figure 2 *Each silicon atom shares its four valence electrons with other silicon atoms.*

Figure 3 Types of Doped Semiconductors

N-type semiconductor An atom of arsenic (As) has five electrons in its outermost energy level. Replacing a silicon atom with an arsenic atom results in an "extra" electron.

P-type semiconductor An atom of gallium (Ga) has three electrons in its outermost energy level. Replacing a silicon atom with a gallium atom results in a "hole" where an electron could be.

Figure 4 *This diode is shown over four times actual size.*

Diodes

Layers of semiconductors can be put together like sandwiches to make electronic components. For example, joining one layer of an n-type semiconductor and one layer of a p-type semiconductor creates a semiconductor diode, like the one shown in **Figure 4**. A **diode** is an electronic component that allows electric current in only one direction.

Diodes in Circuits The way in which a diode works has to do with its semiconductor layers. Where the p-type and n-type layers meet, some "extra" electrons move from the n-type layer to fill some "holes" in the p-type layer. This gives the p-type layer a negative charge and the n-type layer a positive charge. If a diode is connected to a source of electrical energy so that the positive terminal is closest to the p-type layer, a current is established. However, if the terminals are reversed so that the negative terminal is closest to the p-type layer, there will be no current. **Figure 5** illustrates how a diode works.

Figure 5 How a Diode Works

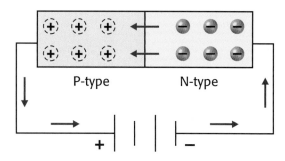

a Electrons move from the negatively charged p-type layer toward the positive terminal. As a result, electrons from the n-type layer can move to fill the newly created "holes" in the p-type layer, and a current is established.

b Electrons in the negatively charged p-type layer are repelled by the negative terminal. No new "holes" are created, so no electrons can move from the n-type layer to the p-type layer. As a result, there is no current.

Using Diodes to Change AC to DC

Power plants supply electrical energy to homes by means of AC (alternating current). Many electronic systems, however, such as radios, require DC (direct current). Because diodes allow current in only one direction, they can convert AC to pulses of DC. An AC adapter contains a diode.

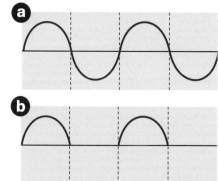

a Alternating current, which periodically changes direction, is supplied to the diode.

b The diode blocks the current in one direction, resulting in pulsed direct current.

Transistors

What do you get when you sandwich three layers of semi-conductors together? A transistor! A **transistor** is an electronic component that can be used as an amplifier or as a switch. Transistors, such as the one shown in **Figure 6,** can be NPN or PNP transistors. An NPN transistor consists of one layer of a p-type semiconductor between two layers of an n-type semiconductor. A PNP transistor consists of one layer of an n-type semiconductor between two layers of a p-type semiconductor. When connected in a circuit, the transistor's "legs" conduct electric current into and out of the transistor's layers.

Figure 6 *This transistor is smaller than a pencil eraser!*

Transistors as Amplifiers To see how a transistor is used as an amplifier, look at the circuit shown in **Figure 7.** A microphone does not supply a large enough current to operate a loudspeaker. But if a transistor is used, the small electric current in the microphone side of the circuit can trigger a larger electric current in the loudspeaker side of the circuit. The electric current can be larger because of the large source of electrical energy in the loudspeaker side of the circuit.

Figure 7 A Transistor as an Amplifier

❶ Sound waves from your voice enter the microphone. As a result, a small electric current is produced in the microphone side of the circuit.

❷ A transistor allows the small electric current to trigger a larger electric current that operates the loudspeaker.

❸ The current in the loudspeaker is identical to the current produced by the microphone, except that it has a larger amplitude.

Transistors as Switches A transistor can also be used as an electronic on-off switch in a circuit. When the manual switch in **Figure 8** is closed, a small current is established in the left side of the circuit. The small current causes the transistor to close the right side of the circuit. As a result, a larger current, which operates a small motor, is established in the right side of the circuit. Basically, you switch on a small current, and the transistor switches on a larger current. If the manual switch is opened, there will no longer be a current in the left side of the circuit. As a result, the transistor will switch off the current that operates the motor. Circuits similar to the one in Figure 8 can be found in remote-controlled toy cars and in windshield wipers.

Figure 8 A Transistor as a Switch

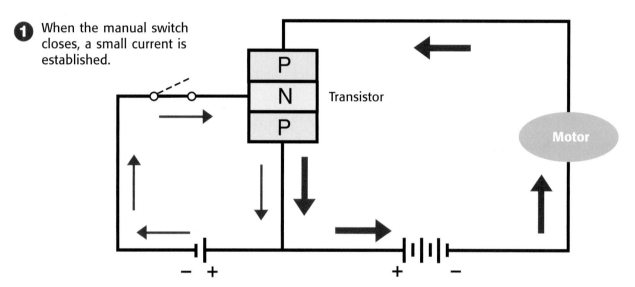

① When the manual switch closes, a small current is established.

② The transistor acts as a switch because a small current in the transistor closes the right side of the circuit. A larger current can therefore operate the motor.

Integrated Circuits Look at the electronic device shown in **Figure 9.** This is an **integrated** (IN tuh GRAYT ed) **circuit,** an entire circuit containing many transistors and other electronic components formed on a single silicon chip. The components of the circuit are constructed on the silicon layer by doping the silicon at specific places.

Integrated circuits and circuit boards, such as the one in the TV remote control at the beginning of this section, have helped shrink electronic systems. Because several complete circuits can fit into one integrated circuit, complicated electronic systems can be made very small. In addition, integrated circuit devices can operate at high speeds because the electric charges traveling through them do not have to travel very far.

Figure 9 *This integrated circuit contains thousands of electronic components, yet its dimensions are only about 1 × 3 cm!*

Electronic Technology of Yesterday . . .

Before the invention of transistors and semiconductor diodes, electronic devices used vacuum tubes, like the one shown here. Vacuum tubes can amplify electric current and convert AC to DC. However, vacuum tubes are much larger, give off more thermal energy, and don't last as long as transistors and semiconductor diodes. Early radios were very bulky because they were made with vacuum tubes. Another reason the radios had to be so big was so that the vacuum tubes had space to give off thermal energy.

. . . and Today

Modern radios are built with transistors and semiconductor diodes. Frequently, a radio comes with other features, such as a clock or a tape deck, all packaged in less space than a radio made with vacuum tubes. Modern electronic components have enabled electronic devices to become much smaller and perform more functions.

REVIEW

1. Describe how p-type and n-type semiconductors are made.

2. Explain how a diode changes AC to DC.

3. What two purposes do transistors serve?

4. **Comparing Concepts** How might an electronic system that uses vacuum tubes be different from one that uses integrated circuits?

internet**connect**

SC*i*LINKS.
NSTA

TOPIC: Transistors
GO TO: www.scilinks.org
*sci*LINKS NUMBER: HSTP455

Communication Technology

One of the first electronic communication devices was the telegraph, which was invented in the 1830s. **Figure 10** shows the telegraph key invented by Samuel Morse. The telegraph used an electric current to send messages between two devices connected by wires. Telegraph operators sent messages in Morse code by tapping the telegraph key to close an electric circuit, causing "clicks" at the receiving end of the telegraph. Although telegraphs are not used much today, they served as the first example of **telecommunication,** the sending of information across long distances by electronic means. In this section you'll learn about some electronic devices that are used for communication.

International Morse Code

A	•—	G	——•	Q	——•—	1	•————
B	—•••	H	••••	R	•—•	2	••———
C	—•—•	I	••	S	•••	3	•••——
D	—••	J	•———	T	—	4	••••—
E	•	K	—•—	U	••—	5	•••••
F	••—•	L	•—••	V	•••—	6	—••••
		M	——	W	•——	7	——•••
		N	—•	X	—••—	8	———••
		O	———	Y	—•——	9	————•
		P	•——•	Z	——••	0	—————

Figure 10 *Combinations of short taps (dots) and longer taps (dashes) represent numbers and letters.*

Communicating with Signals

Electronic communication devices transmit information by using signals. A **signal** is something that represents information. A signal can be a command, a sound, or a series of numbers and letters. Often a signal travels better when contained in another form of energy, called a *carrier*. For example, in a telegraph, electric current is the carrier of the signals created by tapping the telegraph key. Two types of signals that carry information in electronic communication devices are analog signals and digital signals.

Analog Signals

The signals that carry the information through telephone lines are analog signals. An **analog** (AN uh LAHG) **signal** is a signal whose properties, such as amplitude and frequency, can change continuously according to changes in the original information. For example, when you talk on the phone, the sound of your voice is converted into changing electric current in the form of a wave. This wave is an analog signal that is similar in frequency and amplitude to the original sound wave. Just remember that the analog signal is not a sound wave—it is a wave of electric current.

Talking on the Phone Look at the telephone in **Figure 11.** The part you talk into is called the transmitter, and the part you listen to is called the receiver. The transmitter converts the sound waves produced when you speak into the analog signal that travels through phone wires to the receiver of another phone. The receiver converts the analog signal back into the sound of your voice.

Geology
CONNECTION

A seismograph is a device geologists use to record earthquakes. A seismograph produces a seismogram—wavy lines on paper that represent earthquake waves. A seismogram is an example of an analog signal. The waves on a seismogram are similar in amplitude and frequency to the waves produced by an earthquake. As the earthquake changes in magnitude, the lines change accordingly.

Figure 11 How a Telephone Works

ⓐ Sound waves in the transmitter cause a metal disk to vibrate. The vibrations are converted into a changing electric current that is carried by the telephone wires.

ⓒ The electric current is converted back into a sound wave by the receiver. The sound heard is almost the same as the sound that was generated on the other end of the line.

ⓑ The analog signal, a changing electric current, is sent over the phone wires.

Electric current

Electromagnet

Stylus

Figure 12 *As the stylus rides in the record's grooves, it causes an electromagnet to vibrate.*

Analog Recording One way to reproduce sound is by storing an analog signal of the sound wave. In vinyl records, the analog signal is carved into a grooved plastic disk. The frequency and loudness of the sound are represented by the number and depth of the contours carved into the grooved disk.

Playing a Record **Figure 12** shows how a record player's needle, called a stylus (STIE luhs), creates vibrations in an electromagnet. The vibrating electromagnet creates an electric current that is used to produce sound. Although analog recording produces sound that is very similar to the original sound, it has some drawbacks. First, undesirable sounds are sometimes recorded and are difficult to filter out. Also, because the stylus physically touches the record to play it, records can wear out, so the sound can be changed over time.

Digital Signals

A **digital signal** is a series of electric pulses that represents the digits of binary (BIE neh ree) numbers. *Binary* means two. A series of digits, which are composed of only two numbers—1 and 0—represent binary numbers. Each pulse in a digital signal stands for a 1, and each missing pulse is a 0.

Digital Storage on a CD You've probably listened to the digital sound from a compact disc, or CD. Sound is recorded onto a CD by means of a digital signal. A CD stores digital signals in a thin layer of aluminum. As shown in **Figure 13,** the aluminum layer has a series of pits. Each pit is a 0, and each nonpitted region, called a land, is a 1.

Figure 13 *Pits and lands form a tight spiral from the center to the outer edge on a CD. They store information that can be converted by a CD player into sound.*

Label   Protective coating   Aluminum   Plastic

Land   Pit

Digital Recording In a digital recording, the amplitude of the sound wave is sampled many times per second. From the samples, numbers are generated that are equal to the amplitude of the sound at each instant. **Figure 14** shows how these sample values represent the original sound signal. These numbers are then represented in binary as 1s and 0s and stored as pits and lands on a CD. Undesirable sample values can be filtered out, resulting in a cleaner sound.

The drawback to digital recording is that the sample values don't exactly match the original sound wave. To improve the reproduction of sound, a higher sampling rate can be used. A higher sampling rate means that there will be more sample values taken each second (narrower bars), and the resulting digital sound will be closer to the original sound.

Playing a CD In a CD player, the CD spins around while a laser scans it from underneath. As shown in **Figure 15,** the detector in a CD player receives light reflected from the surface of the CD. The detector converts the pattern of reflected light into a digital signal. The digital signal is changed into an analog signal, which is used to generate a sound wave. Because only light touches the CD, the CD doesn't wear out even after it has been played many times.

Figure 14 *Each bar represents a digital sample of the sound wave.*

Figure 15 *Different sequences and sizes of pits and lands will register different patterns of numbers that are converted into different sounds.*

a A laser beam shines on the disc.

Laser

b The patterns of reflected light are treated as a code using 1s and 0s.

c The pattern of 1s and 0s is converted into a sound wave.

Detector

Get tuned in! Turn to page 702 in the LabBook, and build your own radio-wave receiver.

Radio and Television

When you turn on your radio or television, you can hear or see programs broadcast from a radio or TV station that may be many kilometers away. Radio and television use electromagnetic waves. An *electromagnetic wave* is a wave that consists of changing electric and magnetic fields.

Radio Radio waves are one type of electromagnetic wave. The basic operation of a radio involves using radio waves to carry signals that represent sound. As shown in **Figure 16,** radio waves are transmitted by a radio tower, travel through the air, and are picked up by a radio antenna.

Figure 16 How Radio Works

1 A microphone creates an electric current that is an analog signal of the original sound wave.

2 A modulator combines the amplified analog signal with radio waves that have a specific frequency.

3 A radio tower transmits modulated radio waves through the air.

4 The antenna in a radio "tuned in" to the correct frequency receives the modulated radio waves. The receiver removes the radio waves from the analog signal.

5 The radio's speakers convert the analog signal, the electric current, into sound.

Television   The images you see on your television are produced by beams of electrons projected onto a screen. Three beams of electrons are produced within a cathode-ray tube, or CRT. The screen is coated with special fluorescent (FLOO uh RES uhnt) materials that glow when hit by electrons. Video signals, which contain the information that produces an image, are carried by electromagnetic waves. Electromagnetic waves also carry the audio signals that produce sound from the speakers. **Figure 17** illustrates how a color television works.

Figure 17   Images on a Color Television

1 Video signals transmitted from a TV station are received by the antenna of a TV receiver.

2 Electronic circuits separate the video signal into separate signals for each of three electron beams. The beams, one for each primary color of light (red, green, and blue), strike the screen in varying strengths determined by the video signal.

3 Three fluorescent materials (each corresponding to an electron beam) are arranged in stripes or dots on the screen. The electron beams sweep the screen to activate the flourescent materials. These materials then emit colored light that is viewed as a picture.

REVIEW

1. How are analog signals different from digital signals?

2. Compare how a telephone and a radio tower transmit information.

3. **Making Predictions**   How could a digital signal be corrupted?

Terms to Learn

computer
microprocessor
hardware
software
Internet

What You'll Do

◆ List the basic functions of a computer.
◆ Identify the main components of computer hardware.
◆ Describe what computer software allows a computer to do.
◆ Describe how the Internet works.

Computers

Did you use a computer to wake up this morning? You might think of a computer as something you use to send e-mail or surf the Net, but computers are around you all the time. Computers are in automobiles, VCRs, and telephones. Even an alarm clock is a computer! An alarm clock, like the one in **Figure 18,** lets you program the time you want to wake up, and will wake you up at that time.

Figure 18 *Believe it or not, this alarm clock is a computer!*

What Is a Computer?

A **computer** is an electronic device that performs tasks by processing and storing information. A computer performs a task when it is given a command and has the instructions necessary to carry out that command. Computers do not operate by themselves, or "think."

Basic Functions The basic functions a computer performs are shown in **Figure 19.** The information you give to a computer is called *input.* Setting your alarm clock is a type of input. To perform a task, a computer *processes* the input, changing it to a desirable form. Processing could mean adding a list of numbers, executing a drawing, or even moving a piece of equipment. Input doesn't have to be processed immediately; it can also be stored until it is needed. Computers store information in their *memory.* For example, your alarm clock stores the time you want to wake up. It can then process this stored information by going off when it is the programmed time. *Output* is the final result of the task performed by the computer. What's the output of an alarm clock? The sound that wakes you up!

Figure 19
The Functions of a Computer

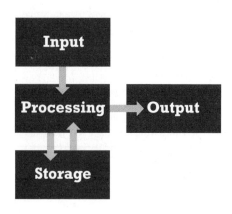

Historic Developments

Your pocket calculator is a simple example of a computer. But computers weren't always so small and efficient. The first computers were massive systems consisting of large pieces of electronic equipment that could fill up an entire room.

The First Computers The first general-purpose computer is shown in **Figure 20.** This monstrous collection of equipment is the ENIAC (Electronic Numerical Integrator and Computer), developed in 1946 by the U.S. Army. The ENIAC consisted of thousands of vacuum tubes and, as a result, produced a lot of excess thermal energy. It was also extremely expensive to build and maintain.

When the ENIAC was built, transistors and integrated circuits did not exist. Instead, it used 18,000 vacuum tubes, filled a 10×15.25 m room, had a mass of more than 23,500 kg, and used as much electrical energy as 150 ordinary light bulbs!

Figure 20 *Fast for its time, the ENIAC could add 5,000 numbers per second.*

Modern Computers With the invention of transistors and integrated circuits, the size of computers could be greatly reduced. Computers today use microprocessors, like the one shown in **Figure 21.** A **microprocessor** is an integrated circuit that contains many of a computer's capabilities on a single silicon chip. The first commercially available microprocessor contained only 4,800 transistors, but microprocessors made today may contain more than 3 million transistors. As a result, computers can now be made so small and lightweight that we can carry them around like a notebook!

Figure 21 *This microprocessor is about 4×4 cm.*

Computer Hardware

For each function of a computer, there is a corresponding part of the computer where each function occurs. **Hardware** refers to the parts or equipment that make up a computer. As you read about each piece of hardware, refer to **Figure 22.**

Input Devices Instructions given to a computer are called input. An *input device* is the piece of hardware that feeds information to the computer. You can enter information into a computer using a keyboard, a mouse, a scanner, a digitizing pad and pen—even your own voice!

Central Processing Unit A computer performs tasks within an area called the *central processing unit,* or CPU. In a personal computer, the CPU is a microprocessor. Input goes through the CPU for immediate processing or for storage in memory. The CPU is where the computer does calculations, solves problems, and executes the instructions given to it.

Figure 22 Computer Hardware

Memory Information can be stored in the computer's memory until it is needed. Hard disks inside a computer and floppy disks or CD-ROMs inserted into a computer have memory to store information. Two other types of memory are *ROM* (read-only memory) and *RAM* (random-access memory).

ROM is permanent. It handles functions such as computer start-up, maintenance, and hardware management. ROM normally cannot be added to or changed, and it cannot be lost when the computer is turned off. On the other hand, RAM is temporary. It stores information only while that information is being used. RAM is sometimes called working memory. Large amounts of RAM allow more information to be input, which makes for a more powerful computer.

Output Devices Once a computer performs a task, it shows the results on an *output device*. Monitors, printers, and speaker systems are all examples of output devices.

Modems One piece of computer hardware that serves as an input device as well as an output device is a *modem*. Modems allow computers to communicate. One computer can input information into another computer over a telephone line, as long as each computer has its own modem. As a result, modems permit computers to "talk" with other computers.

Printer

Scanner

Digitizing pad and pen

CD-ROM

Floppy disk

Computer Software

Computers need a set of instructions before they can perform any given task. **Software** is a set of instructions, or commands, that tells a computer what to do. A computer program is an example of software.

Kinds of Software Software can be classified into two categories: operating system software and application software. Operating system software manages basic operations required by the computer and supervises all interactions between software and hardware. It interprets commands from the input device, such as locating programming instructions on a hard disk to be loaded into memory.

Application software contains instructions ordering the computer to operate a utility, such as a word processor, spreadsheet, or even a computer game. The pages in this book were created using a variety of application software! Some examples of application software are shown in **Figure 23**.

Figure 23 *Computer software allows a computer to perform all kinds of tasks, such as word processing, video games, interactive tutoring, and graphics.*

The Internet—A Global Network

Thanks to modems and computer software, it is possible to connect many computers and allow them to communicate with one another. That's what the **Internet** is—a huge computer network consisting of millions of computers that can all share information with one another.

How the Internet Works Computers can connect to one another on the Internet by using modems to dial into an Internet Service Provider, or ISP. A home computer connects to an ISP over a normal phone line. A school, business, or other group can have a Local Area Network (LAN) that connects to an ISP using one phone line. As depicted in **Figure 24,** ISPs are connected globally by satellite. And that's how computers go global!

Figure 24 *Through a series of connections like this, every computer on the Internet can share information.*

REVIEW

1. Using the terms *input, output, processing,* and *memory,* explain how you use a pocket calculator to add numbers.

2. What is the difference between hardware and software?

3. **Analyzing Relationships** Could something like the Internet exist without modems and telephone lines? Explain.

internet**connect**

SC*i*LINKS
NSTA

TOPIC: Computer Technology, Internet
GO TO: www.scilinks.org
*sci***LINKS NUMBER:** HSTP470, HSTP475

Chapter Highlights

Vocabulary

circuit board (p. 482)

semiconductor (p. 483)

doping (p. 483)

diode (p. 484)

transistor (p. 485)

integrated circuit (p. 486)

Section Notes

• Electronic devices use electrical energy to transmit information.

• Many electronic components are made of semiconductors. Two types of semiconductors result from a process called doping. They are n-type and p-type semiconductors.

• The two types of semiconductors can be sandwiched together to produce diodes and transistors.

• Diodes allow electric current in only one direction.

• Transistors can be used as amplifiers or as switches.

• Integrated circuits can contain many electronic components. They allow electronic systems to be smaller.

Vocabulary

telecommunication (p. 488)

signal (p. 488)

analog signal (p. 489)

digital signal (p. 490)

Section Notes

• Electronic devices use signals to transmit information. The signals are usually contained in another form of energy, such as radio waves or electric current.

• The properties of analog signals change continuously according to changes in the original signal. Telephones use analog signals.

• A digital signal is a series of electrical pulses that represents the digits of binary numbers. CD players use digital signals.

☑ Skills Check

Visual Understanding

DIODES Sandwiching an n-type semiconductor and a p-type semiconductor together produces a diode. Charges can pass through a diode in only one direction.

TRANSMITTING SIGNALS BY RADIO Electronic devices transmit information through signals. Look at Figure 16 on page 492 to see how electromagnetic waves can transmit radio signals.

COMPUTERS In order for a computer to perform a task, it must be given information. Look at the diagram on page 494 to learn about the steps a computer takes to perform various tasks.

SECTION 2

- Sound can be recorded digitally or as an analog signal.

- Radio and television rely on electromagnetic waves.

- In radio, signals that represent sound are combined with radio waves and sent through the air. Radios can pick up the radio waves and convert them back to sound waves.

- A color television image is produced by three electron beams that scan the screen of a cathode-ray tube, or CRT. Fluorescent materials on the screen glow to create the picture.

Labs

Tune In! *(p. 702)*

SECTION 3

Vocabulary

computer *(p. 494)*

microprocessor *(p. 495)*

hardware *(p. 496)*

software *(p. 498)*

Internet *(p. 499)*

Section Notes

- The basic functions of a computer involve input, processing, memory, and output. A computer cannot perform a task without a set of commands.

- The first computers were very large and could not perform many tasks.

- Because microprocessors contain many computer capabilities on a single chip, computers have been reduced in size.

- Computer hardware refers to the parts or the equipment that make up a computer.

- Computer software is a set of instructions or commands that tells a computer what to do.

- Modems allow millions of computers to connect with one another and share information on the Internet.

---

internet connect

GO TO: go.hrw.com

Visit the **HRW** Web site for a variety of learning tools related to this chapter. Just type in the keyword:

KEYWORD: HSTELT

SCILINKSSM

NSTA

GO TO: www.scilinks.org

Visit the **National Science Teachers Association** on-line Web site for Internet resources related to this chapter. Just type in the *sci*LINKS number for more information about the topic:

TOPIC: Transistors	*sci*LINKS NUMBER: HSTP455
TOPIC: Telephone Technology	*sci*LINKS NUMBER: HSTP460
TOPIC: Television Technology	*sci*LINKS NUMBER: HSTP465
TOPIC: Computer Technology	*sci*LINKS NUMBER: HSTP470
TOPIC: Internet	*sci*LINKS NUMBER: HSTP475

Chapter Review

USING VOCABULARY

For each pair of terms, explain the difference in their meanings.

1. semiconductor/doping

2. transistor/diode

3. signal/telecommunication

4. analog signal/digital signal

5. computer/microprocessor

6. hardware/software

UNDERSTANDING CONCEPTS

Multiple Choice

7. All electronic devices transmit information using
   a. signals.
   b. electromagnetic waves.
   c. radio waves.
   d. modems.

8. Semiconductors are used to make
   a. transistors.
   b. integrated circuits.
   c. diodes.
   d. All of the above

9. Which of the following is an example of a telecommunication device?
   a. vacuum tube
   b. telephone
   c. radio
   d. Both (b) and (c)

10. A monitor, printer, and speaker are examples of
    a. input devices.   c. computers.
    b. memory.   d. output devices.

11. Record players play sounds that were recorded in the form of
    a. digital signals.
    b. electric current.
    c. analog signals.
    d. radio waves.

12. Memory in a computer that is permanent and cannot be added to is called
    a. RAM.
    b. ROM.
    c. CPU.
    d. None of the above

13. Cathode-ray tubes are used in
    a. telephones.
    b. telegraphs.
    c. televisions.
    d. radios.

Short Answer

14. How is an electronic device different from a machine that uses electrical energy?

15. How does a diode allow current to flow in one direction?

16. In one or two sentences, describe how a TV works.

17. Give three examples of how computers are used in your everyday life.

18. Explain the advantages that transistors have over vacuum tubes.

Concept Mapping

19. Use the following terms to create a concept map: electronic devices, radio waves, electric current, signals, information.

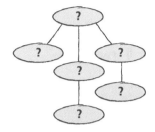

CRITICAL THINKING AND PROBLEM SOLVING

20. Your friend is preparing an oral report on the history of radio and finds the photograph shown below. "Why is this radio so huge?" he asks you. Using what you know about electronic devices, how do you explain the size of this vintage radio?

21. Using what you know about the differences between analog and digital signals, explain how the sound from a record player is different from the sound from a CD player.

22. What do Morse code and digital signals have in common?

23. Computers can process a lot of information, but they cannot think. Explain why this is true.

24. Based on what you learned in the chapter, how do you think an automatic garage door opener works?

INTERPRETING GRAPHICS

Look at the diagram below, and answer the questions that follow.

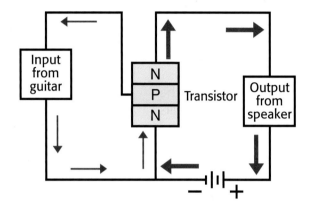

25. What purpose does the transistor serve in this situation?

26. How does the current in the left side of the circuit compare with the current in the right side of the circuit?

27. How does the sound from the speaker compare with the sound from the guitar?

Reading Check-up

Take a minute to review your answers to the Pre-Reading Questions found at the bottom of page 480. Have your answers changed? If necessary, revise your answers based on what you have learned since you began this chapter.

Listening Lower

Do you ever listen to your favorite music on headphones? Many people like to use headphones while they exercise. Terrific! But doctors believe that this habit may be putting people's hearing at risk.

The Blood Brain Drain

Aerobic exercise, including walking, jogging, skating, dancing, and competitive sports, is an important part of a healthy lifestyle. However, when you exercise, more blood is sent to your arms and legs than is sent to your ears. The inner ear is more easily damaged when the blood flow is lowered. Once the cells of the inner ear are damaged, they cannot be replaced. A study in Sweden showed that hearing loss doubles when loud noise and aerobic exercise are combined!

How Loud Is Too Loud?

The federal Occupational Safety and Health Administration (OSHA) requires hearing protection for workers exposed to 95 decibels for 4 hours. A lawn mower emits 95 decibels. If workers are exposed to 100 decibels for 3 hours, they must wear hearing protection. People generally listen to headphones at levels between 90 and 115 decibels.

Why So Loud?

Most people turn the volume up as they continue to listen to music because their ears adapt to the volume. However, permanent hearing

▲ *How high should the volume be when listening to music on headphones?*

loss can occur at well below painful or even uncomfortable levels. Another concern is that hearing loss is often gradual, starting at high frequencies. The loss goes unnoticed until the damage is quite extensive. Generally, more problems occur when noise is louder, lasts longer, or occurs frequently.

What to Do

How can you protect your hearing and still use those headphones? Keep the volume of your headphones as low as possible, and try not to raise the volume once it is set. Then always remember this: If a person 1 m away has to shout in order for you to hear, the volume is too high. However, this test does not work for headphones with muffs that fit around the ear. The volume is probably too high if your hearing is dulled after you remove your headphones. This usually goes away quickly, but it may become permanent if you keep the volume high.

Sound It Out

▶ Obtain a sound meter, and survey the sound levels around your school. Measure the levels at dances and other noisy locations. Report your findings to your class, and discuss ways to lower your exposure to loud sounds. You may just save someone's hearing!

Science Fiction

"There Will Come Soft Rains"

by Ray Bradbury

Ticktock, seven o'clock, time to get up, time to get up, seven o'clock. The voice clock in the living room sends out the wake-up message, gently calling to the family to get up and begin their new day.

It is August 4, 2026, in Allandale, California. The house is attractive, in an attractive neighborhood, just right for a mother, father, two children, and a dog. And it is state of the art: automatic kitchen, extremely sensitive fire-detection and fire-protection systems, walls that look like walls but become video display screens—everything a family could want.

A few minutes after the wake-up call, the automatic stove in the kitchen begins the family breakfast—toast, eggs (sunny side up), and bacon. While the breakfast is cooking, the voice in the kitchen ceiling lists the reminders for the day: a birthday, an anniversary, the bills that are due.

About an hour after the wake-up message, the ceiling voice speaks again, this time to remind anyone listening that it is time to go to school. A soft rain is falling outside, so the weather box by the front door suggests that raincoats are necessary today.

But something has happened. No family sounds come from the house. The house goes on talking to itself and carrying on its routine as if it were keeping itself company. Why doesn't anyone answer? Find out when you read Ray Bradbury's "There Will Come Soft Rains" in the *Holt Anthology of Science Fiction*.

UNIT

7

Waves, Sound, and Light

When you hear the word *waves,* you probably think of waves in the ocean. But waves that you encounter every day have a much bigger effect on your life than do water waves! In this unit, you will learn about different types of waves, how waves behave and interact, and how sound energy and light energy travel in waves. This timeline shows some events and discoveries that have occurred throughout history as scientists have sought to learn more about the energy of waves.

Around 1600

Italian astronomer and physicist Galileo Galilei attempts to calculate the speed of light by using lanterns and shutters. He writes that the speed is "extraordinarily rapid."

1929

American astronomer Edwin Hubble uses the Doppler effect of light to determine that the universe is expanding.

1947

The *Diary of Anne Frank* is published. The book is an edited version of the diary kept by a Jewish teenager while in hiding during World War II.

1971

Hungarian physicist Dennis Gabor wins the Nobel Prize in Physics for his invention of holography, the method used to make holograms.

1960

The first working laser is demonstrated.

1704

Sir Isaac Newton publishes his book *Optiks,* which contains his theories about light and color.

1711

The tuning fork—an instrument that produces a single-frequency note—is invented by English trumpeter John Shore.

1801

British scientist Thomas Young is the first to provide experimental data showing that light behaves as a wave.

1905

Physicist Albert Einstein suggests that light sometimes behaves as a particle.

1903

The popularity of an early movie called *The Great Train Robbery* leads to the establishment of permanent movie theaters.

1984

A "mouse" is first used on personal computers.

1983

The exact speed of light is determined to be 299,792,458 m/s.

1997

British pilot Andy Green drives a jet-powered car at 341 m/s, making him the first person to travel faster than the speed of sound on land.

The Energy of Waves

Pre-Reading
Questions

1. What is a wave?
2. What properties do all
   waves have?
3. What can happen when
   waves interact?

ENERGETIC WAVES

In this activity, you will observe the movement of a wave. Then you will determine the source of the wave's energy.

Procedure

1. Tie one end of a **piece of rope** to the back of a **chair.**

2. Hold the other end in one hand, and stand away from the chair so that the rope is almost straight but is not pulled tight.

3. Move the rope up and down quickly to create a single wave. Repeat this step several times. Record your observations in your ScienceLog.

Analysis

4. Which direction does the wave move?

5. How does the movement of the rope compare with the movement of the wave?

6. Where does the energy of the wave come from? Make an inference using direct evidence.

TRY at HOME

CATCH THE WAVE!

A surfer takes advantage of a wave's energy to catch an exciting ride. The ocean wave that this surfer is riding is just one type of wave that you may encounter. You probably are very familiar with water waves, but did you know that waves are also responsible for light, sound, and even earthquakes? From music to television, waves play an important role in your life every day. In this chapter, you will learn about the properties of waves and how waves interact with each other and everything around them.

The Nature of Waves

Terms to Learn

wave   transverse wave
medium   longitudinal wave

What You'll Do

◆ Describe how waves transfer energy without transferring matter.
◆ Distinguish between waves that require a medium and waves that do not.
◆ Explain the difference between transverse and longitudinal waves.

Imagine that your family has just returned home from a day at the beach. You had fun, but you are hungry from playing in the ocean under a hot sun. You put some leftover pizza in the microwave for dinner, and you turn on the radio. Just then, the phone rings. It's your best friend calling to find out if you've done your math homework yet.

In the events described above, how many different waves were present? Believe it or not, at least five can be identified! Can you name them? Here's a hint: A **wave** is any disturbance that transmits energy through matter or space. Okay, here are the answers: water waves in the ocean; microwaves inside the microwave oven; light waves from the sun; radio waves transmitted to the radio; and sound waves from the radio, telephone, and voices. Don't worry if you didn't get very many. You will be able to name them all after you read this section.

Waves Carry Energy

Energy can be carried away from its source by a wave. However, the material through which the wave travels does not move with the energy. For example, sound waves often travel through air, but the air does not travel with the sound. If air were to travel with sound, you would feel a rush of air every time you heard the phone ring! **Figure 1** illustrates how waves carry energy but not matter.

Wave motion

Figure 1 *Waves on a pond move toward the shore, but the water and the leaf floating on the surface do not move with the wave.*

As a wave travels, it uses its energy to do work on everything in its path. For example, the waves in a pond do work on the water to make it move up and down. The waves also do work on anything floating on the water's surface—for example, boats and ducks bob up and down with waves.

Energy Transfer Through a Medium Some waves transfer energy by the vibration of particles in a medium. A **medium** is a substance through which a wave can travel. A medium can be a solid, a liquid, or a gas. The plural of *medium* is *media*.

When a particle vibrates (moves back and forth, as in **Figure 2**), it can pass its energy to a particle next to it. As a result, the second particle will vibrate in a way similar to the first particle. In this way, energy is transmitted through a medium.

Sound waves require a medium. Sound energy travels by the vibration of particles in liquids, solids, and gases. If there are no particles to vibrate, no sound is possible. For example, if you put an alarm clock inside a jar and remove all the air from the jar to create a vacuum, you will not be able to hear the alarm.

Other waves that require a medium include ocean waves, which travel through water, and waves on guitar and cello strings. Waves that require a medium are called *mechanical waves*. **Figure 3** shows the effect of another mechanical wave.

Figure 2 *A vibration is one complete back-and-forth motion of an object.*

Figure 3 *Seismic waves travel through the ground. The 1964 earthquake in Alaska changed the features of this area.*

You can see distant objects in space using electromagnetic waves. Turn to page 530 to learn how.

Energy Transfer Without a Medium Some waves can transfer energy without traveling through a medium. Visible light is an example of a wave that doesn't require a medium. Other examples include microwaves produced by microwave ovens, TV and radio signals, and X rays used by dentists and doctors. Waves that do not require a medium are called *electromagnetic waves.*

Although electromagnetic waves do not require a medium, they can travel through substances such as air, water, and glass. However, they travel fastest through empty space. Light from the sun is a type of electromagnetic wave. **Figure 4** shows that light waves from the sun can travel through both space and matter to support life on Earth.

Astronomy

C O N N E C T I O N

Light waves from some stars and galaxies travel distances so great that they can be expressed only in light-years. A light-year is the distance that light travels in a year. Some of the light waves from these stars have traveled billions of light-years before reaching Earth. This means that the light that we see today from some distant stars left the star's surface before the Earth was formed.

Figure 4 *Light waves from the sun travel more than 100 million kilometers through nearly empty space, then more than 300 km through the atmosphere, and then another 10 m through water to support life in and around a coral reef.*

 Self-Check

How do mechanical waves differ from electromagnetic waves? *(See page 724 to check your answer.)*

Types of Waves

Waves can be classified based on the direction in which the particles of the medium vibrate compared with the direction in which the waves travel. The two main types of waves are transverse waves and longitudinal (LAHN juh TOOD nuhl) waves. In certain conditions, a transverse wave and a longitudinal wave can combine to form another type of wave, called a surface wave.

Transverse Waves   Waves in which the particles vibrate with an up-and-down motion are called **transverse waves.** *Transverse* means "moving across." The particles in a transverse wave move across, or perpendicular to, the direction that the wave is traveling. To be *perpendicular* means to be "at right angles." Try the MathBreak to practice identifying perpendicular lines.

A wave moving on a rope is an example of a transverse wave. In **Figure 5,** you can see that the points along the rope vibrate perpendicular to the direction the wave is traveling. The highest point of a transverse wave is called a *crest,* and the lowest point between each crest is called a *trough.* Although electromagnetic waves do not travel by vibrating particles in a medium, all electromagnetic waves are classified as transverse waves.

MATH BREAK

Perpendicular Lines

If the angle between two lines is 90°, the lines are said to be perpendicular. The figure below shows a set of perpendicular lines.

Look at the objects around you. Identify five objects with perpendicular lines or edges and five objects that do not have perpendicular lines. Sketch these objects in your ScienceLog.

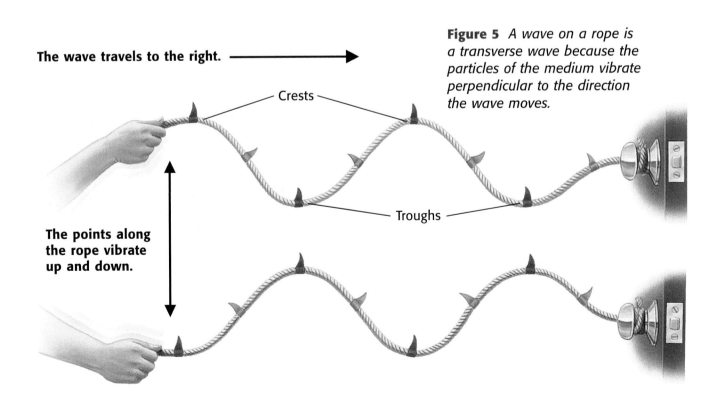

The wave travels to the right. ⟶

Crests

Troughs

The points along the rope vibrate up and down.

Figure 5 *A wave on a rope is a transverse wave because the particles of the medium vibrate perpendicular to the direction the wave moves.*

Longitudinal Waves In a **longitudinal wave,** the particles of the medium vibrate back and forth along the path that the wave travels. You can create a longitudinal wave on a spring, as shown in **Figure 6.**

When you push on the end of the spring, the coils of the spring are crowded together. A section of a longitudinal wave where the particles are crowded together is called a *compression.* When you pull back on the end of the spring, the coils are less crowded than normal. A section where the particles are less crowded than normal is called a *rarefaction* (RER uh FAK shuhn).

Compressions and rarefactions travel along a longitudinal wave much in the way the crests and troughs of a transverse wave move from one end to the other, as shown in **Figure 7.**

Figure 6 *Pushing a spring back and forth creates a longitudinal wave.*

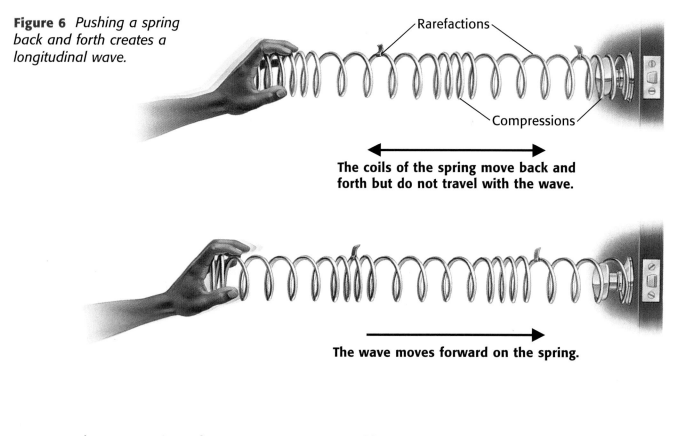

Rarefactions

Compressions

The coils of the spring move back and forth but do not travel with the wave.

The wave moves forward on the spring.

Figure 7 *The compressions of a longitudinal wave are like the crests of a transverse wave, and the rarefactions are like troughs.*

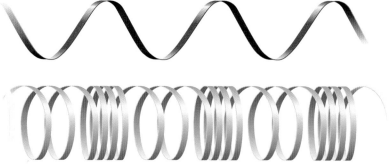

A sound wave is an example of a longitudinal wave. Sound waves travel by compressions and rarefactions of air particles. **Figure 8** shows how a vibrating drumhead creates these compressions and rarefactions.

When the drumhead moves out after being hit, a compression is created in the air particles.

When the drumhead moves back in, a rarefaction is created.

Figure 8 *Sound energy is carried away from a drum in a longitudinal wave.*

Combinations of Waves When waves occur at or near the boundary between two media, a transverse wave and a longitudinal wave can combine to form a *surface wave.* An example is shown in **Figure 9.** Surface waves look like transverse waves, but the particles of the medium in a surface wave move in circles rather than up and down. The particles move forward at the crest of each wave and move backward at the trough. The arrows in Figure 9 show the movement of particles in a surface wave.

Figure 9 *Ocean waves are surface waves because they travel at the water's surface, where the water meets the air. A floating bottle shows the motion of particles in a surface wave.*

Wave motion

REVIEW

1. Describe how transverse waves differ from longitudinal waves.

2. Why can't you cause a floating leaf to move to the edge of a pond by throwing stones behind it?

3. Explain why supernova explosions in space can be seen but not heard on Earth.

4. **Applying Concepts** Sometimes people at a sports event do "the wave." Do you think this is a real example of a wave? Why or why not?

internet connect

*SCI*LINKS
NSTA

TOPIC: The Nature of Waves, Types of Waves
GO TO: www.scilinks.org
*sci*LINKS NUMBER: HSTP480, HSTP490

Properties of Waves

Imagine that you are canoeing on a lake. You decide to stop paddling for a while and relax in the sunshine. The breeze makes small waves on the water. These waves are short and close together, and they have little effect on the canoe. Then a speedboat roars past you. The speedboat creates tall, widely spaced waves that cause your canoe to rock wildly. So much for relaxation!

Waves have properties that are useful for description and comparison. In this example, you could compare properties such as the height of the waves and the distance between the waves. In this section, you will learn about the properties of waves and how to measure them.

Amplitude

If you tie one end of a rope to the back of a chair, you can create waves by moving the other end up and down. If you move the rope a small distance, you will make a short wave. If you move the rope a greater distance, you will make a tall wave.

The property of waves that is related to the height of a wave is known as amplitude. The **amplitude** of a wave is the maximum distance the wave vibrates from its rest position. The rest position is where the particles of a medium stay when there are no disturbances. The larger the amplitude is, the taller the wave is. **Figure 10** shows how the amplitude of a transverse wave is measured.

Figure 10 *The amplitude of a transverse wave is measured from the rest position to the crest or to the trough of the wave.*

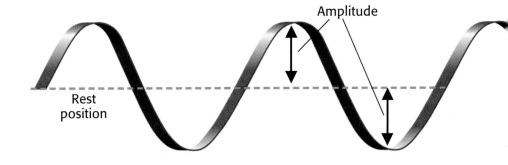

Larger Amplitude Means More Energy When using a rope to make waves, you have to work harder to create a wave with a large amplitude than to create one with a small amplitude. This is because it takes more energy to move the rope farther from its rest position. Therefore, a wave with a large amplitude carries more energy than a wave with a small amplitude, as shown in **Figure 11.**

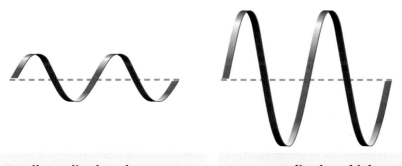

Small amplitude = low energy   **Large amplitude = high energy**

Figure 11 *The amplitude of a wave depends on the amount of energy.*

Wavelength

Another property of waves is wavelength. A **wavelength** is the distance between any two adjacent crests or compressions in a series of waves. The distance between two adjacent troughs or rarefactions is also a wavelength. In fact, the wavelength can be measured from any point on one wave to the corresponding point on the next wave. All of the measurements will be equal, as shown in **Figure 12.**

Wavelength

Wavelength

Longitudinal wave

Figure 12 *Wavelengths measured from any two corresponding points are the same for a given wave.*

Wavelength

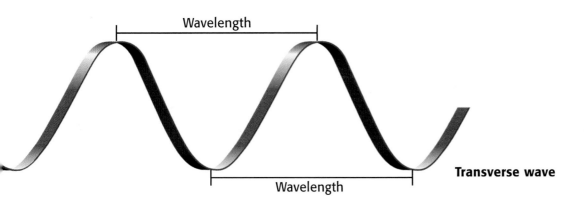

Wavelength

Transverse wave

Quick Lab

Springy Waves

1. Hold a **coiled spring toy** on the floor between you and a classmate so that the spring is straight. This is the rest position.

2. Move one end of the spring from side to side at a constant rate. The number of times you move it in a complete cycle (back and forth) each second is the frequency.

3. Keeping the frequency the same, increase the amplitude. What did you have to do? How did the change in amplitude affect the wavelength?

4. Now shake the spring back and forth about twice as fast (to double the frequency). What happens to the wavelength?

5. Record your observations and answers in your ScienceLog.

Spring into action! Find the speed of waves on a spring toy. Turn to page 708 of the LabBook.

Frequency

Think about making rope waves again. The number of waves that you can make in 1 second depends on how quickly you move the rope. If you move the rope slowly, you make only a small number of waves each second. If you move it quickly, you make a large number of waves. The number of waves produced in a given amount of time is the **frequency** of the wave.

Measuring Frequency   You can measure frequency by counting either the number of crests or the number of troughs that pass a point in a certain amount of time. If you were measuring the frequency of a longitudinal wave, you would count the number of compressions or rarefactions. Frequency is usually expressed in *hertz* (Hz). For waves, one hertz equals one wave per second (1 Hz = 1/s). The frequency of a wave is related to its wavelength, as shown in **Figure 13.**

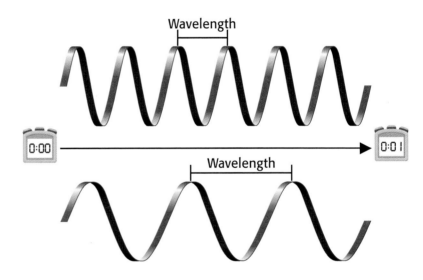

Figure 13 *At a given speed, the higher the frequency is, the shorter the wavelength.*

Higher Frequency Means More Energy   It takes more energy to vibrate a rope quickly than to vibrate a rope slowly. If the amplitudes are equal, high-frequency waves carry more energy than low-frequency waves. In Figure 13, the top wave carries more energy than the bottom wave.

Because frequency and wavelength are so closely related, you can also relate the amount of energy carried by a wave to the wavelength. In general, a wave with a short wavelength carries more energy than a wave with a long wavelength.

518   Chapter 20

Wave Speed

Another property of waves is **wave speed**—the speed at which a wave travels. Speed is the distance traveled over time, so wave speed can be found by measuring the distance a single crest or compression travels in a given amount of time.

The speed of a wave depends on the medium in which the wave is traveling. For example, the wave speed of sound in air is about 340 m/s, but the wave speed of sound in steel is about 5,200 m/s.

Calculating Wave Speed   Wave speed can be calculated using wavelength and frequency. The relationship between wave speed (v), wavelength (λ, the Greek letter lambda), and frequency (f) is expressed in the following equation:

$$v = \lambda \times f$$

You can see in **Figure 14** how this equation can be used to determine wave speed. Try the MathBreak to practice using this equation.

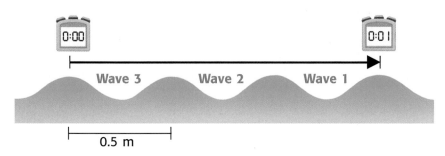

$\lambda = 0.5 \text{ m}$ $f = 3 \text{ Hz (3/s)}$
$v = 0.5 \text{ m} \times 3 \text{ Hz} = 1.5 \text{ m/s}$

Figure 14 *To calculate wave speed, multiply the wavelength by the number of waves that pass in 1 second (frequency).*

REVIEW

1. Draw a transverse wave, and identify its amplitude and wavelength.

2. What is the speed (v) of a wave that has a wavelength (λ) of 2 m and a frequency (f) of 6 Hz?

3. **Inferring Conclusions**   Compare the amplitudes and frequencies of the two types of waves discussed at the beginning of this section, and infer which type of wave carried the most energy. Explain your answer.

■ internet**connect** ≡≡≡

*SC/*INKS.
NSTA

TOPIC: Properties of Waves
GO TO: www.scilinks.org
*sci*LINKS NUMBER: HSTP485

Wave Interactions

What You'll Do

◆ Describe reflection, refraction, diffraction, and interference.
◆ Compare destructive interference with constructive interference.
◆ Describe resonance, and give examples.

Imagine that you wake up early one morning before the sun has risen and go outside. You look up and notice that a full moon is high in the sky, and the stars are twinkling brilliantly, as shown in **Figure 15.** The sky is so clear you can find constellations (groupings of stars), such as the Big Dipper and Cassiopeia, and planets, such as Venus and Mars.

All stars, including the sun, produce light. But planets and the moon do not produce light. So why do they shine so brightly? Light from the sun *reflects* off the planets and the moon. Reflection is one of the wave interactions that you will learn about in this section.

Figure 15 *A wave interaction is responsible for this beautiful morning scene.*

Figure 16 *These water waves are reflecting off the side of the container.*

Reflection

Reflection occurs when a wave bounces back after striking a barrier. All waves—including water, sound, and light waves—can be reflected. The reflection of water waves is shown in **Figure 16.** Reflected sound waves are called *echoes,* and light waves reflecting off an object allow you to see that object. For example, light waves from the sun are reflected when they strike the surface of the moon. These reflected waves allow us to enjoy moonlit nights.

Refraction

Try this simple experiment: place a pencil in a half-filled glass of water. Now look at the pencil from the side. The pencil appears to be broken into two pieces! But when you take the pencil out of the water, it is perfectly fine.

What you observed in this experiment was the result of the refraction of light waves. **Refraction** is the bending of a wave as it passes at an angle from one medium to another.

Remember that the speed of a wave varies depending on the medium in which the wave is traveling. So when a wave moves from one medium to another, the wave's speed changes. When a wave enters a new medium at an angle, the part of the wave that enters first begins traveling at a different speed from the rest of the wave. This causes the wave to bend, as shown in **Figure 17.**

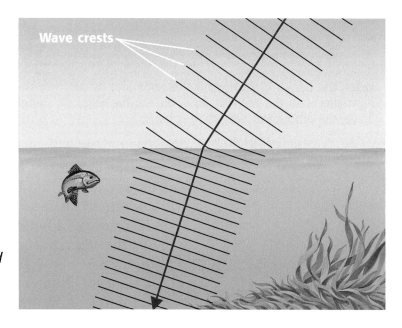

Figure 17 *Light waves passing at an angle into a new medium—such as water—are refracted because the speed of the waves changes.*

Self-Check

Will a light wave refract if it enters a new medium perpendicular to the surface? Explain. *(See page 724 to check your answer.)*

Diffraction

Suppose you are walking down a city street and you hear music. The sound seems to be coming from around the corner, but you cannot see who is playing the music because the building on the corner blocks your view. Why is it that sound waves travel around a corner better than light waves do?

Most of the time, waves travel in straight lines. For example, a beam of light from a flashlight is fairly straight. But in some circumstances, waves curve or bend when they reach the edge of an object. The bending of waves around a barrier or through an opening is known as **diffraction.**

Activity

Light waves diffract around corners of buildings much less than sound waves. Imagine what would happen if light waves diffracted around corners much more than sound waves. Write a paragraph describing how this would change what you see and hear as you walk around your neighborhood.

TRY at HOME

Figure 18 Diffraction of Waves

(a)

(b)

When the barrier or opening is the same size as or is smaller than the wavelength of an approaching wave, the amount of diffraction is large.

If the barrier or opening is larger than the wavelength of the wave, there is only a small amount of diffraction.

The amount of diffraction a wave experiences depends on its wavelength and the size of the barrier or opening the wave encounters, as shown in **Figure 18.** You can hear music around the corner of a building because sound waves have long wavelengths and are able to diffract around corners. However, you cannot see who is playing the music because the wavelengths of light waves are much smaller than the building, so light is not diffracted very much.

Interference

You know that all matter has volume. Therefore, objects cannot occupy the same space at the same time. But because waves are energy and not matter, more than one wave can exist in the same place at the same time. In fact, two waves can meet, share the same space, and pass through each other! When two or more waves share the same space, they overlap. The result of two or more waves overlapping is called **interference. Figure 19** shows one situation where waves occupy the same space.

Figure 19 *When sound waves from several instruments combine through interference, the result is a wave with a larger amplitude, which means a louder sound.*

Constructive Interference Increases Amplitude *Constructive interference* occurs when the crests of one wave overlap the crests of another wave or waves. The troughs of the waves also overlap. An example of constructive interference is shown in **Figure 20.** When waves combine in this way, the result is a new wave with higher crests and deeper troughs than the original waves. In other words, the resulting wave has a larger amplitude than the original waves had.

Figure 20 *When waves combine by constructive interference, the resulting wave has an amplitude that is larger than those of the original waves. After the waves interfere, they continue traveling in their original directions.*

Waves approaching   **Waves overlapping**   **Waves continuing**

Destructive Interference Decreases Amplitude *Destructive interference* occurs when the crests of one wave and the troughs of another wave overlap. The resulting wave has a smaller amplitude than the original waves had. What do you think happens when the waves involved in destructive interference have the same amplitude? Find out in **Figure 21.**

Figure 21 *When two waves with the same amplitude combine by destructive interference, they cancel each other out. This is called total destructive interference.*

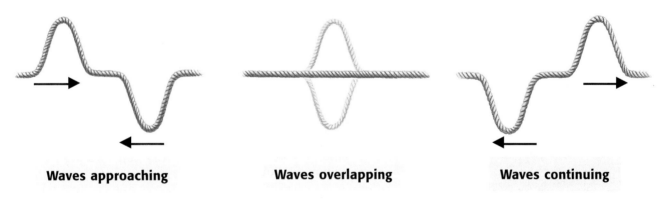

Waves approaching   **Waves overlapping**   **Waves continuing**

Sound Waves in Movie Theaters

Movie theaters use large screens and several speakers to make your moviegoing experience exciting. Theater designers know that increasing the amplitude of sound waves increases the volume of the sound. In terms of interference, how do you think the positioning of the speakers adds to the excitement?

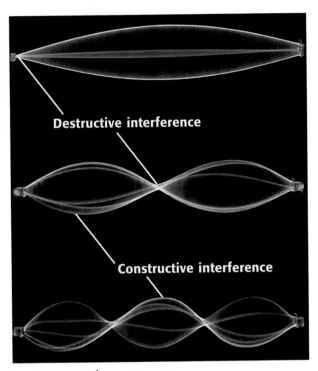

Figure 22 *When you move a rope at certain frequencies, you can create different standing waves.*

Interference Can Create Standing Waves

If you tie one end of a rope to the back of a chair and move the other end up and down, the waves you create travel down the rope and are reflected back. If you move the rope at certain frequencies, the rope appears to vibrate in loops, as shown in **Figure 22.** The loops result from the interference between the wave you created and the reflected wave. The resulting wave is called a standing wave. A **standing wave** is a wave that forms a stationary pattern in which portions of the wave are at the rest position due to total destructive interference and other portions have a large amplitude due to constructive interference. However, it only *looks* as if the wave is standing still. In reality, waves are traveling in both directions. Standing waves can be formed with transverse waves, as shown here, as well as with longitudinal waves.

One Object Causes Another to Vibrate During Resonance

As shown above, standing waves can occur at more than one frequency. The frequencies at which standing waves are produced are called *resonant frequencies.* When an object vibrating at or near the resonant frequency of a second object causes the second object to vibrate, **resonance** occurs. A resonating object absorbs energy from the vibrating object and therefore vibrates, too. An example of resonance is shown in **Figure 23.**

a The marimba bars are struck with a mallet, causing the bars to vibrate.

b The vibrating bars cause the air in the columns to vibrate.

Figure 23 *A marimba produces notes through the resonance of air columns.*

c The lengths of the columns have been adjusted so that the resonant frequency of the air column matches the frequency of the bar.

d The air column resonates with the bar, increasing the amplitude of the vibrations to produce a loud note.

The Tacoma Narrows Bridge Resonance was partially responsible for the destruction of the Tacoma Narrows Bridge, in Washington. The bridge opened in July 1940 and soon earned the nickname Galloping Gertie because of its wavelike motions. These motions were created by wind that blew across the bridge. The wind caused vibrations that were close to a resonant frequency of the bridge. Because the bridge was in resonance, it absorbed a large amount of energy from the wind, which caused it to vibrate with a large amplitude.

On November 7, 1940, a supporting cable slipped, and the bridge began to twist. The twisting of the bridge, combined with high winds, further increased the amplitude of the bridge's motion. Within hours, the amplitude became so great that the bridge collapsed, as shown in **Figure 24.** Luckily, all the people on the bridge that day were able to escape before it crashed into the river below.

Figure 24 *The twisting motion that led to the destruction of the bridge was partially caused by resonance.*

REVIEW

1. Name two wave interactions that can occur when a wave encounters a barrier.

2. Describe what happens when a wave is refracted.

3. **Inferring Relationships** Sometimes when music is played loudly, you can feel your body shake. Explain what is happening in terms of resonance.

internet**connect**

SC*i*LINKS
NSTA

TOPIC: Interactions of Waves
GO TO: www.scilinks.org
***sci*LINKS NUMBER:** HSTP495

The Energy of Waves **525**

Chapter Highlights

Vocabulary

wave *(p. 510)*

medium *(p. 511)*

transverse wave *(p. 513)*

longitudinal wave *(p. 514)*

Section Notes

- A wave is a disturbance that transmits energy.

- A medium is a substance through which a wave can travel. The particles of a medium do not travel with the wave.

- Waves that require a medium are called mechanical waves. Waves that do not require a medium are called electromagnetic waves.

- Particles in a transverse wave vibrate perpendicular to the direction the wave travels.

- Particles in a longitudinal wave vibrate back and forth in the same direction that the wave travels.

- Transverse and longitudinal waves can combine to form surface waves.

Vocabulary

amplitude *(p. 516)*

wavelength *(p. 517)*

frequency *(p. 518)*

wave speed *(p. 519)*

Section Notes

- Amplitude is the maximum distance the particles in a wave vibrate from their rest position. Large-amplitude waves carry more energy than small-amplitude waves.

- Wavelength is the distance between two adjacent crests (or compressions) of a wave.

- Frequency is the number of waves that pass a given point in a given amount of time. High-frequency waves carry more energy than low-frequency waves.

☑ Skills Check

Math Concepts

WAVE-SPEED CALCULATIONS The relationship between wave speed (v), wavelength (λ), and frequency (f) is expressed by the equation:

$$v = \lambda \times f$$

For example, if a wave has a wavelength of 1 m and a frequency of 6 Hz (6/s), the wave speed is calculated as follows:

$$v = 1 \text{ m} \times 6 \text{ Hz} = 1 \text{ m} \times 6/\text{s}$$
$$v = 6 \text{ m/s}$$

Visual Understanding

TRANSVERSE AND LONGITUDINAL WAVES
Two common types of waves are transverse waves (shown below) and longitudinal waves. Study Figure 5 on page 513 and Figure 6 on page 514 to review the differences between these two types of waves.

SECTION 2

- Wave speed is the speed at which a wave travels. Wave speed can be calculated by multiplying the wavelength by the wave's frequency.

Labs

Wave Energy and Speed (p. 706)

Wave Speed, Frequency, and Wavelength (p. 708)

SECTION 3

Vocabulary

reflection (p. 520)

refraction (p. 521)

diffraction (p. 521)

interference (p. 522)

standing wave (p. 524)

resonance (p. 524)

Section Notes

- Waves bounce back after striking a barrier during reflection.

- Refraction is the bending of a wave when it passes at an angle from one medium to another.

- Waves bend around barriers or through openings during diffraction. The amount of diffraction depends on the wavelength of the waves and the size of the barrier or opening.

- The result of two or more waves overlapping is called interference.

- Amplitude increases during constructive interference and decreases during destructive interference.

- Standing waves are waves in which portions of the wave do not move and other portions move with a large amplitude.

- Resonance occurs when a vibrating object causes another object to vibrate at one of its resonant frequencies.

---

internetconnect

GO TO: go.hrw.com

Visit the **HRW** Web site for a variety of learning tools related to this chapter. Just type in the keyword:

KEYWORD: HSTWAV

SCiLINKS NSTA

GO TO: www.scilinks.org

Visit the **National Science Teachers Association** on-line Web site for Internet resources related to this chapter. Just type in the *sci*LINKS number for more information about the topic:

TOPIC: The Nature of Waves   *sci*LINKS NUMBER: HSTP480

TOPIC: Properties of Waves   *sci*LINKS NUMBER: HSTP485

TOPIC: Types of Waves   *sci*LINKS NUMBER: HSTP490

TOPIC: Interactions of Waves   *sci*LINKS NUMBER: HSTP495

Chapter Review

For each pair of terms, explain the difference in their meanings.

1. longitudinal wave/transverse wave

2. frequency/wave speed

3. wavelength/amplitude

4. reflection/refraction

5. constructive interference/destructive interference

UNDERSTANDING CONCEPTS

Multiple Choice

6. As the wavelength increases, the frequency
   a. decreases.
   b. increases.
   c. remains the same.
   d. increases, then decreases.

7. Which wave interaction explains why sound waves can be heard around corners?
   a. reflection
   b. refraction
   c. diffraction
   d. interference

8. Refraction occurs when a wave enters a new medium at an angle because
   a. the frequency changes.
   b. the amplitude changes.
   c. the wave speed changes.
   d. None of the above

9. The speed of a wave with a frequency of 2 Hz (2/s), an amplitude of 3 m, and a wavelength of 10 m is
   a. 0.2 m/s.   c. 12 m/s.
   b. 5 m/s.   d. 20 m/s.

10. Waves transfer
    a. matter.   c. particles.
    b. energy.   d. water.

11. A wave that is a combination of longitudinal and transverse waves is a
    a. sound wave.   c. rope wave.
    b. light wave.   d. surface wave.

12. The wave property that is related to the height of a wave is the
    a. wavelength.   c. frequency.
    b. amplitude.   d. wave speed.

13. During constructive interference,
    a. the amplitude increases.
    b. the frequency decreases.
    c. the wave speed increases.
    d. All of the above

14. Waves that don't require a medium are
    a. longitudinal waves.
    b. electromagnetic waves.
    c. surface waves.
    d. mechanical waves.

Short Answer

15. Draw a transverse and a longitudinal wave. Label a crest, a trough, a compression, a rarefaction, and wavelengths. Also label the amplitude on the transverse wave.

16. What is the relationship between frequency, wave speed, and wavelength?

17. Explain how two waves can cancel each other out.

Concept Mapping

18. Use the following terms to create a concept map: wave, refraction, transverse wave, longitudinal wave, wavelength, wave speed, diffraction.

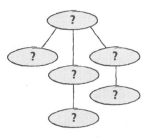

CRITICAL THINKING AND PROBLEM SOLVING

19. After you set up stereo speakers in your school's music room, you notice that in certain areas of the room the sound from the speakers is very loud and in other areas the sound is very soft. Explain how interference causes this.

20. You have lost the paddles for the canoe you rented, and the canoe has drifted to the center of the pond. You need to get the canoe back to shore, but you do not want to get wet by swimming in the pond. Your friend on the shore wants to throw rocks behind the canoe to create waves that will push the canoe toward shore. Will this solution work? Why or why not?

21. Some opera singers have voices so power-ful they can break crystal glasses! To do this, they sing one note very loudly and hold it for a long time. The walls of the glass move back and forth until the glass shatters. Explain how this happens in terms of resonance.

MATH IN SCIENCE

22. A fisherman in a rowboat notices that one wave crest passes his fishing line every 5 seconds. He estimates the distance between the crests to be 2 m and esti-mates the crests of the waves to be 0.4 m above the troughs. Using these data, determine the amplitude and wave speed of the waves. Remember that wave speed is calculated with the formula $v = \lambda \times f$.

INTERPRETING GRAPHICS

23. Rank the waves below from highest energy to lowest energy, and explain your reasoning.

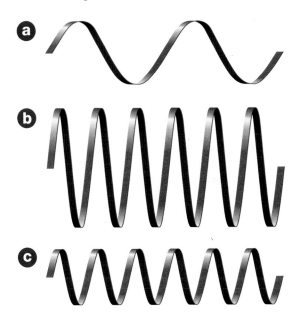

Reading Check-up

Take a minute to review your answers to the Pre-Reading Questions found at the bottom of page 508. Have your answers changed? If necessary, revise your answers based on what you have learned since you began this chapter.

Science, Technology, and Society

The Ultimate Telescope

The largest telescopes in the world don't depend on visible light, lenses, or mirrors. Instead, they collect radio waves from the far reaches of outer space. One radio telescope, called the Very Large Array (VLA), is located in a remote desert in New Mexico.

From Radio Waves to Computer Images

Objects in space give off radio waves that radio telescopes collect. A bowl-shaped dish called a reflector focuses the radio waves onto a small radio antenna hung over the center of the dish. The antenna converts the waves into electric signals. The signals are relayed to a radio receiver, where they are amplified and recorded on tape that can be read by a computer. The computer combines the signals to create an image of the source of the radio waves.

A Marvel at "Seeing"

Radio telescopes have some distinct advantages over optical telescopes. They can "see" objects that are as far as 13 billion light-years away. They can even detect objects that don't release any light at all. Radio telescopes can be used in any kind of weather, can receive signals through atmospheric pollution, and can even penetrate the cosmic dust and gas clouds that occupy vast areas of space. However, radio telescopes must be large in order to be accurate.

Telescope Teamwork

The VLA is an array of 27 separate radio telescopes mounted on railroad tracks and electronically linked by computers. Each of the

▲ *Only a few of the 27 radio telescopes of the VLA, near Datil, New Mexico, can be seen in this photograph.*

27 reflectors is 25 m in diameter. When they operate together, they work like a single telescope with a diameter of 47 km! Using the VLA, astronomers have been able to explore distant galaxies, pulsars, quasars, and possible black holes.

A system of telescopes even larger than the VLA has been used. In the Very Long Baseline Array (VLBA), radio telescopes in different parts of the world all work together. The result is a telescope that is almost as large as the Earth itself!

What Do They See?

▶ Find out about some of the objects "seen" by the VLA, such as pulsars, quasars, and possible black holes. Prepare a report or create a model of one of the objects, and make a presentation to your class. Use diagrams and photographs to make your presentation more interesting.

Sounds of Silence

It's morning on the African savanna. Suddenly, without a sound, a family of elephants stops eating and begins to move off. At the same moment, about 6 km away, other members of the same family move off in a direction that will reunite them with the first group. How did the groups know when it was time to go?

Do You Hear What I Hear?

Elephants do much of their communicating by infrasound. This is sound energy with a frequency too low to be heard by humans. These infrasonic conversations take place through deep, soft rumblings produced by the animals. Though humans can't hear the sounds, elephants as far as 10 km away respond quickly to the messages.

Because scientists couldn't hear the elephant "conversations," they couldn't understand how the animals coordinated their activities. Of course, the elephants, which have superb low-frequency hearing, heard the messages clearly. It turns out that much elephant behavior is affected by infrasonic messages. For instance, one kind of rumble from a mother to her calf tells the calf it is all right to nurse. Another rumble, from the group's leader, is the "time to move on" message. Still another infrasonic message may be sent to other elephant groups in the area, warning them of danger.

Radio Collars

Once scientists learned about elephants' infrasonic abilities, they devised ways to study the sounds. Researchers developed radio collars for individual animals to wear. The collars are connected to a computer that helps researchers identify which elephant sent the message. The collars also record the messages. This information helps scientists understand both the messages and the social organization of the group.

Let's Talk

Elephants have developed several ways to "talk" to each other. For example, they greet each other by touching trunks and tusks. And elephants have as many as 25 vocal calls, including the familiar bellowing trumpet call (a sign of great excitement). In other situations, they use chemical signals.

▲ *Two elephants greeting each other*

Recently, researchers recording elephant communications found that when elephants vocalize their low-frequency sounds, they create seismic waves. Elephant messages sent by these underground energy waves may be felt more than 8 km away. Clearly, there is a lot more to elephant conversations than meets the ear!

On Your Own

▶ Elephants are very intelligent and highly sociable. Find out more about the complex social structure of elephant groups. Why is it important for scientists to understand how elephants communicate with each other? How can that understanding help elephants?

The Nature of Sound

Pre-Reading
Questions

1. How does sound travel
   from one place to
   another?

2. What determines a sound's
   pitch and loudness?

3. What can happen when
   sound waves interact with
   each other?

SOUND UNDER THE SEA

Look at these dolphins swimming swiftly and silently
through their watery world. Wait a minute—swiftly? Yes.
Silently? No way! Dolphins use sound to communicate.
In fact, each dolphin has a special whistle that it uses to
identify itself. Dolphins also use sound to locate their food
and find their way through murky water. In this chapter,
you'll learn more about the properties and the interactions
of sound waves. You'll also learn how sound is used to
locate objects.

A HOMEMADE GUITAR

In this chapter, you will learn about sound. You can start by making your own guitar. It won't sound as good as a real guitar, but it will help you explore the nature of sound.

Procedure

1. Stretch a **rubber band** lengthwise around an empty **shoe box.** Gently pluck the rubber band. In your ScienceLog, describe what you hear.

2. Stretch **another rubber band of a different thickness** around the box. Pluck both rubber bands. Describe the difference in the sounds.

3. Put a **pencil** across the center of the box and under the rubber bands, and pluck again. Compare this sound with the sound you heard before the pencil was used.

4. Move the pencil closer to one end of the shoe box. Pluck on both sides of the pencil. Describe the differences in the sounds you hear.

Analysis

5. How did the thicknesses of the rubber bands affect the sound?

6. In steps 3 and 4, you changed the length of the rubber bands. What is the relationship between the length of the rubber band and the sound that you hear?

What Is Sound?

Think about all the sounds you hear every day. Indoors, you might hear people talking, the radio blaring, or dishes clattering in the kitchen sink. Outdoors, you might hear birds singing, cars driving by, or a mosquito buzzing in your ear. That's a lot of different sounds! In this section, you'll explore some common characteristics of the different sounds you hear.

Sound Is Produced by Vibrations

As different as they are, all sounds have some things in common. One characteristic of sound is that it is created by vibrations. A *vibration* is the complete back-and-forth motion of an object. **Figure 1** shows an example of how sound is created by vibrations.

Figure 1 Sounds from a Stereo Speaker

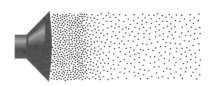

a As the speaker cone moves forward, it pushes the air particles in front of it closer together, creating a region of higher density and pressure called a *compression.*

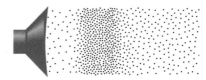

b As the speaker cone moves backward, air particles close to the cone become less crowded, creating a region of lower density and pressure called a *rarefaction.*

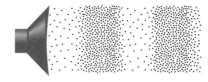

c Every time the cone vibrates, compression and rarefaction are formed. As the compressions and rarefactions travel away from the speaker, sound is transmitted through the air.

Terms to Learn

wave
medium
outer ear
middle ear
inner ear

What You'll Do

◆ Describe how sound is caused by vibrations.
◆ Explain how sound is transmitted through a medium.
◆ Explain how the human ear works, and identify its parts.

QuickLab

Good Vibrations

1. Gently strike a **tuning fork** on a **rubber eraser.** Watch the prongs, and listen for a sound. Describe what you see and hear.

2. Lightly touch the fork with your fingers. What do you feel?

3. Grasp the prongs of the fork firmly with your hand. What happens to the sound?

4. Strike the tuning fork on the stopper again, and dip the prongs in a **cup of water.** Describe what happens to the water.

5. Record your observations in your ScienceLog.

Sound Travels as Longitudinal Waves A **wave** is a disturbance that transmits energy through matter or space. In a longitudinal wave, particles vibrate back and forth along the path that the wave travels. Longitudinal (LAHN juh TOOD nuhl) waves consist of compressions and rarefactions. Sound is transmitted through the vibrations and collisions of particles of matter, such as air particles. Because the particles vibrate back and forth along the paths that sound travels, sound travels as longitudinal waves.

Sound waves travel in all directions away from their source as illustrated in **Figure 2.** However, air or other matter does not travel with the sound waves. The particles of air only vibrate back and forth in place. If air did travel with sound, wind gusts from music speakers would blow you over at a school dance!

Biology CONNECTION

The vibrations that produce your voice are made inside your throat. When you speak, laugh, or sing, your lungs force air up your windpipe, causing your vocal cords to vibrate.

Compression

Rarefaction

Figure 2 *You can't actually see sound waves, but they can be represented by spheres that spread out in all directions.*

Creating Sound Vs. Detecting Sound

Have you heard this riddle before?
If a tree falls in the forest and no one is around
to hear it, does the tree make a sound?

Think about this situation for a minute. When a tree falls and hits the ground, the tree and the ground vibrate. These vibrations create compressions and rarefactions in the surrounding air. So, yes, there would be a sound!

Making sound is separate from detecting sound. The fact that no one heard the tree fall doesn't mean that there wasn't a sound. A sound was created—it just wasn't detected.

Figure 3 *You can still hear traffic sounds when you are in a car because sound waves can travel through the glass windows and metal body of the car.*

Sound Waves Require a Medium

Another characteristic of sound is that all sound waves require a medium. A **medium** is a substance through which a wave can travel. In the example of a falling tree on the previous page, the medium is air. Most of the sounds that you hear travel through air at least part of the time. But sound waves can also travel through other materials, such as water, glass, and metal, as shown in **Figure 3.**

What would happen if a tree fell in a vacuum? No sound would be created because in a vacuum, there are no air particles to vibrate. Sound cannot travel in a vacuum. This helps to explain the effect described in **Figure 4.** Sound must travel through air or some other medium to reach your ears and be detected.

Figure 4 *Tubing is connected to a pump that is removing air from the jar. As the air is removed, the ringing alarm clock gets quieter and quieter.*

Astronomy
CONNECTION

The moon has no atmosphere, so there is no air through which sound can travel. The astronauts who walked on the moon had to use radios to talk to each other even when they were standing side by side. Radio waves could travel between the astronauts because they are electromagnetic waves, which don't require a medium. The radio speakers were inside the astronauts' helmets, which were filled with air for the astronauts to breathe.

How You Detect Sound

Imagine you are watching a suspenseful movie. Just before a door is opened, the background music becomes louder. You know that there is something scary behind that door! Now imagine watching the same scene without the sound. It's hard to figure out what's going on without sound to help you understand what you see. Your ears play an important role in this understanding. On the next page, you will see how your ears convert sound waves into electrical signals, which are then sent to your brain for interpretation.

How the Human Ear Works

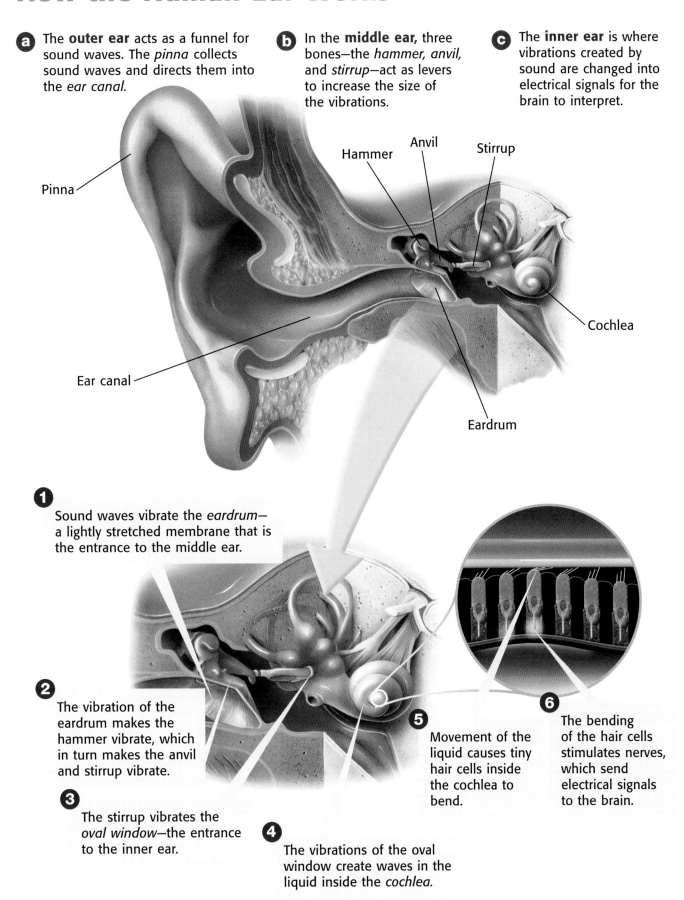

a The **outer ear** acts as a funnel for sound waves. The *pinna* collects sound waves and directs them into the *ear canal.*

b In the **middle ear,** three bones—the *hammer, anvil,* and *stirrup*—act as levers to increase the size of the vibrations.

c The **inner ear** is where vibrations created by sound are changed into electrical signals for the brain to interpret.

Pinna

Hammer

Anvil

Stirrup

Cochlea

Ear canal

Eardrum

1 Sound waves vibrate the *eardrum*—a lightly stretched membrane that is the entrance to the middle ear.

2 The vibration of the eardrum makes the hammer vibrate, which in turn makes the anvil and stirrup vibrate.

3 The stirrup vibrates the *oval window*—the entrance to the inner ear.

4 The vibrations of the oval window create waves in the liquid inside the *cochlea.*

5 Movement of the liquid causes tiny hair cells inside the cochlea to bend.

6 The bending of the hair cells stimulates nerves, which send electrical signals to the brain.

Could a dinosaur have played a horn? Check it out on page 560.

Hearing Loss and Deafness The many parts of the ear must work together for you to hear sounds. If any part of the ear is damaged or does not work properly, hearing loss or deafness may result.

One of the most common types of hearing loss is called *tinnitus* (ti NIE tuhs), which results from long-term exposure to loud sounds. Loud sounds can cause damage to the hair cells and nerve endings in the cochlea. Damage to the cochlea or any part of the inner ear usually results in permanent hearing loss.

People who have tinnitus often complain about hearing a ringing in their ears. They also have difficulties understanding other people and hearing the difference between words that sound very similar. Tinnitus can affect people of any age. Fortunately, tinnitus can be prevented. **Figure 5** shows some ways that you can protect yourself from hearing loss.

Figure 5 *Reducing exposure to loud sounds will protect your ears.*

Wearing ear protection while working with machinery blocks out some of the sounds that can injure your ears.

Turning your radio down will prevent hearing loss, especially when you use headphones.

REVIEW

1. Describe how a bell produces sound.

2. Explain why a person at a rock concert will not feel gusts of wind coming out of the speakers.

3. Name the three main parts of the ear, and briefly explain the function of each part.

4. **Inferring Conclusions** If a meteorite crashed on the moon, would you be able to hear it on Earth? Why or why not?

Terms to Learn

pitch   Doppler effect
infrasonic   loudness
ultrasonic   decibel

What You'll Do

◆ Compare the speed of sound in different media.
◆ Explain how frequency and pitch are related.
◆ Describe the Doppler effect, and give examples of it.
◆ Explain how amplitude and loudness are related.

Properties of Sound

Imagine you are swimming in a neighborhood pool. You hear many different sounds as you float on the water. Some are high, like the laughter of small children, and some are low, like the voices of men. Some sounds are loud, like the *BOING* of the diving board, and some are soft, like the sound of water lapping on the sides of the pool. The differences between the sounds—how high or low and how loud or soft they are—depend on the properties of the sound waves. In this section, you will learn about properties of sound.

The Speed of Sound Depends on the Medium

If two people at the other end of the pool shout at you at the same time, will you hear one person's voice before the other? No—the sounds of their voices will reach you at the same time. The time it takes for the sounds to reach you does not depend on who shouted or how loudly the person shouted. The speed of sound depends only on the medium through which the sound is traveling. Assuming that your head is above water, the sounds of the voices traveled through air to your ears and therefore traveled at the same speed.

Speed Changes When the Medium Changes The speed of sound through any medium is constant if the properties of the medium do not change. The chart at left shows the speed of sound in different media. If the properties of a medium change, the speed of sound through that medium will change. On the next page, you will explore how a change in one property—temperature—affects the speed of sound through air.

Speed of Sound in Different Media at 20°C	
Medium	**Speed (m/s)**
Air	343
Helium	1,005
Water	1,482
Sea water	1,522
Wood (oak)	3,850
Glass	4,540
Steel	5,200

MATH BREAK

Speed of Sound

The speed of sound depends on the medium through which sound is traveling and the medium's temperature. Sound travels at 343 m/s through air that has a temperature of 20°C. How far will sound travel in 3 seconds through air at 20°C?

distance = speed × time

distance = $343 \frac{m}{s} \times 3 \, s$

distance = 1,029 m

Now It's Your Turn

How far does sound travel in 5 seconds through air, water, and steel at 20°C? Use the speeds given in the chart on the previous page.

The Speed of Sound Depends on Temperature In 1947, American pilot Chuck Yeager became the first person to travel faster than the speed of sound. But he was flying at a speed of only 293 m/s! If the speed of sound in air is 343 m/s (as shown in the chart on the previous page), how did Yeager fly faster than the speed of sound? The answer has to do with the temperature of the air.

In general, the cooler the medium, the slower the speed of sound. This happens because particles in cool materials move slower than particles in warmer materials. When the particles move slower, they transmit energy more slowly. Therefore, sound travels more slowly in cold air than in hot air.

Chuck Yeager flew at 12,000 m above sea level. At that height the temperature of the air is so low that the speed of sound is only 290 m/s. So when he flew at 293 m/s, he was flying 3 m/s faster than the speed of sound.

Pitch Depends on Frequency

Think about the guitar you made at the beginning of this chapter. You used two rubber bands of different thicknesses as strings. You probably noticed that the thicker rubber band made a lower sound than the thinner rubber band made. How low or high you perceive a sound to be is the **pitch** of that sound.

The pitch of a sound is determined by the frequency of the sound wave, as shown in **Figure 6.** The *frequency* of a wave is the number of waves produced in a given time. Frequency is expressed in *hertz* (Hz), where 1 Hz = 1 wave per second.

Figure 6 *The longer tuning fork vibrates at a lower frequency. Therefore, it creates a sound with a lower pitch.*

High frequency = high pitch

Low frequency = low pitch

Frequency and Hearing Some people use dog whistles to call their dog. But when you see someone blow a dog whistle, the whistle seems silent to you. That's because the frequency of the sound wave is out of the range of human hearing. But the dog hears a very high pitch from the whistle and comes running! The graph below compares the range of frequencies that humans and animals can hear.

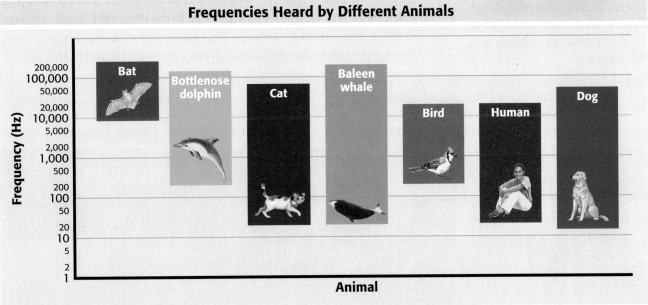

Frequencies You Can Hear The average human ear can detect sounds that have frequencies between 20 Hz and 20,000 Hz. Examples of sounds within this range include the lowest sound a pipe organ can make (about 40 Hz) and the screech of a bat (10,000 Hz or higher). The range of hearing varies from person to person. Young children can often hear sounds with frequencies above this range, while many elderly people have difficulty hearing sounds higher than 8,000 Hz.

Frequencies You Can't Hear Sounds that are outside the range of human hearing have special names. Sounds with frequencies that are lower than 20 Hz are described as **infrasonic.** Sounds with frequencies that are higher than 20,000 Hz are described as **ultrasonic.** The sounds are given these names because *sonic* refers to sound, *infra* means "below," and *ultra* means "beyond."

Ultrasonic waves have a variety of applications. For example, ultrasonic waves are used to clean jewelry and to remove ice from metal. Scientists hope to use this technology to remove ice from airplane wings, car windshields, and freezers. You will learn about other uses of ultrasonic waves in the next section.

Biology
C O N N E C T I O N

Kidney stones—deposits of calcium salts that form inside kidneys—can cause a great deal of pain. Sometimes they are so large that they have to be removed by a doctor. Surgery was once the primary way to remove kidney stones, but now ultrasonic waves can be used to break kidney stones into smaller pieces that can pass out of the body with urine.

The Nature of Sound   **541**

The Doppler Effect Have you ever been passed by a car with its horn honking? If so, you probably noticed the sudden change in pitch—sort of an *EEEEEOOoooowwn* sound— as the car sped past you. The pitch you heard was higher while the car was approaching than it was after the car passed. This is a result of the Doppler effect. For sound waves, the **Doppler effect** is the apparent change in the frequency of a sound caused by the motion of either the listener or the source of the sound. **Figure 7** explains the Doppler effect. Keep in mind that the frequency of the car horn does not really change; it only sounds like it does. The driver of the car always hears the same pitch because the driver is moving with the car.

Figure 7 *The Doppler effect occurs when the source of a sound is moving relative to the listener.*

ⓐ The car moves toward the sound waves in front of it, causing the waves to be closer together and to have a higher frequency.

ⓑ The car moves away from the sound waves behind it, causing the waves to be farther apart and to have a lower frequency.

ⓒ A listener in front of the car hears a higher pitch than a listener behind the car.

Loudness Is Related to Amplitude

If you gently tap a bass drum, you will hear a soft rumbling. But if you strike the drum with a large force, you will hear a loud *BOOM!* By changing the force you use to strike the drum, you change the loudness of the sound that is created. **Loudness** is how loud or soft a sound is perceived to be.

Energy and Vibration The harder you strike a drum, the louder the boom. As you strike the drum harder, you transfer more energy to the drum. The drum moves with a larger vibration and transfers more energy to the surrounding air. This increase in energy causes air particles to vibrate farther from their rest positions.

BRAIN FOOD

The sounds made by booming sands are sometimes so loud that scientists working on the dunes have to shout to hear each other.

Increasing Amplitude When you strike a drum harder, you are increasing the amplitude of the sound waves being created. The *amplitude* of a wave is the maximum distance the particles in a wave vibrate from their rest positions. The larger the amplitude, the louder the sound, and the smaller the amplitude, the softer the sound. **Figure 8** shows one way to increase the loudness of a sound. Do the QuickLab on this page to investigate the loudness and pitch of sounds.

Figure 8 *An amplifier increases the amplitude of the sound generated by an electric guitar.*

Measuring Loudness The most common unit used to express loudness is the **decibel (dB).** The faintest sounds an average human ear can hear are at a level of 0 dB. The level of 120 dB is sometimes called the threshold of pain because sounds at that level and higher can cause your ears to hurt. Continued exposure to sounds above 85 dB causes gradual hearing loss by permanently damaging the hair cells in your inner ear. The chart below shows the decibel levels of some common sounds.

Some Common Decibel Levels

Sound	Decibel level
The softest sounds you can hear	0
Whisper	20
Purring cat	25
Normal conversation	60
Lawn mower, vacuum cleaner, truck traffic	80
Chain saw, snowmobile	100
Sandblaster, loud rock concert, automobile horn	115
Threshold of pain	120
Jet engine 30 m away	140
Rocket engine 50 m away	200

QuickLab

Sounding Board

1. With one hand, hold a **metric ruler** on your desk so that one end of it hangs over the edge.

2. With your other hand, pull the free end of the ruler up a few centimeters and let go.

3. Try pulling the ruler up different distances. How does the distance affect the sounds you hear? What property of the sound wave are you changing?

4. Try changing the length of the part that hangs over the edge. What property of the sound wave is affected?

5. Record your answers and observations in your ScienceLog.

Figure 9 *An oscilloscope can be used to represent sounds.*

"Seeing" Sounds Because sound waves are invisible, their amplitude and frequency is impossible to measure directly. However, technology can provide a way to "see" sound waves. A device called an *oscilloscope* (uh SIL uh SKOHP), shown in **Figure 9,** is used to graph representations of sound waves.

A microphone first converts the sound wave into an electric current. The oscilloscope then converts the electric current into graphs such as the ones shown in **Figure 10.** Notice that the graphs look like transverse waves instead of longitudinal waves. The highest points (crests) of these waves represent compressions, and the lowest points (troughs) represent rarefactions. By looking at the displays on the oscilloscope, you can quickly see the difference in both amplitude and frequency of sound waves.

Figure 10 "Seeing" Sounds

The graph on the right has a **larger amplitude** than the graph on the left. Therefore, the sound represented on the right is **louder** than the one on the left.

The graph on the right has a **lower frequency** than the one on the left. So the sound represented on the right has a **lower pitch** than the one on the left.

REVIEW

1. In general, how does changing the temperature of a medium affect the speed of sound through that medium?

2. What properties of waves affect the pitch and loudness of sound?

3. **Inferring Conclusions** Will a listener notice the Doppler effect if he or she and the source of the sound are traveling toward each other? Explain your answer.

Interactions of Sound Waves

What You'll Do

◆ Explain how echoes are produced, and describe their use in locating objects.
◆ Give examples of constructive and destructive interference of sound waves.
◆ Identify three sound-wave interactions, and give examples of each.

Beluga whales, such as those shown in **Figure 11,** communicate by using a wide variety of sounds, including clicks, chirps, whistles, trills, screeches, and moos. The sounds they make can be heard above and below water. Because of the wide range of sounds they make, belugas have been nicknamed "sea canaries." But belugas use sound for more than just communication—they also use reflected sound waves to find fish, crabs, and shrimp to eat. In this section you'll learn about reflection and other interactions of sound waves.

Figure 11 *Beluga whales depend on sound interactions for survival.*

Reflection of Sound Waves

Reflection is the bouncing back of a wave after it strikes a barrier. You're probably already familiar with a reflected sound wave, otherwise known as an **echo.** The amount a sound wave will reflect depends on the reflecting surface. Sound waves reflect best off smooth, hard surfaces. That's why a shout in an empty gymnasium can produce an echo, but a shout in an empty auditorium usually does not, as shown in **Figure 12.**

Figure 12
Sound Reflection and Absorption

Sound waves easily reflect off the smooth, hard walls of a gymnasium. That's why you hear an echo.

In well-designed auditoriums, echoes are reduced by soft materials that absorb sound waves and by irregular shapes that scatter sound waves.

Echolocation Beluga whales use echoes to find food. The process of using reflected sound waves to find objects is called **echolocation.** Other animals—such as dolphins, bats, and some species of birds—also use echolocation to hunt food and detect objects in their paths. **Figure 13** shows how echolocation works.

Figure 13 *Bats use echolocation to navigate around barriers and to find insects to eat.*

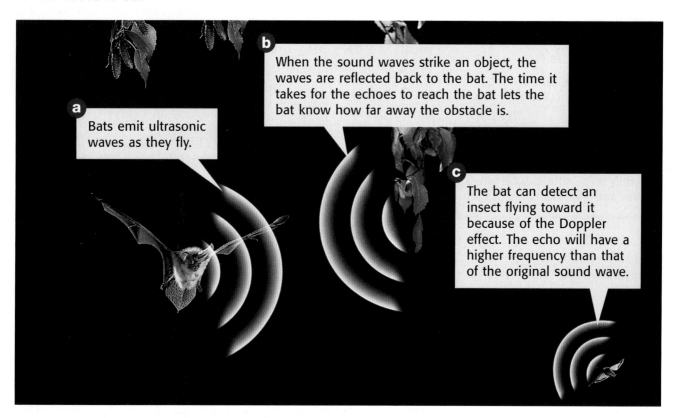

a Bats emit ultrasonic waves as they fly.

b When the sound waves strike an object, the waves are reflected back to the bat. The time it takes for the echoes to reach the bat lets the bat know how far away the obstacle is.

c The bat can detect an insect flying toward it because of the Doppler effect. The echo will have a higher frequency than that of the original sound wave.

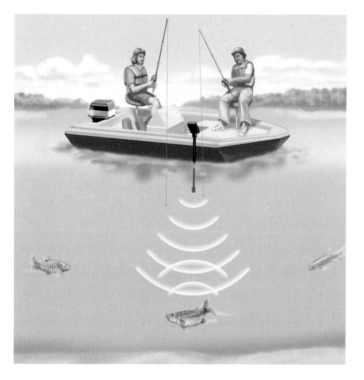

Echolocation Technology Humans use echoes to locate objects underwater and underground by using sonar (**so**und **na**vigation and **r**anging). *Sonar* is a type of electronic echolocation. **Figure 14** shows how sonar works. Ultrasonic waves are used because their short wavelengths provide more details about the objects they reflect off. Sonar can also help navigators on ships detect icebergs and can help oceanographers map the ocean floor.

Figure 14 *A depth finder sends ultrasonic waves down into the water. The time it takes for the echo to return helps the fishermen determine the location of the fish.*

Many people who are blind use a cane to help them detect obstacles while they are walking. Now engineers have developed a sonar cane, shown at right, to help blind people even more. The cane emits and detects sound waves. Based on your knowledge of echolocation, explain how you think this cane works.

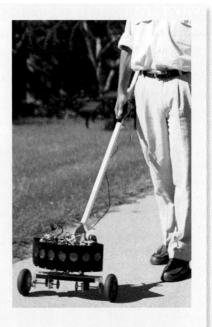

Ultrasonography Another type of electronic echolocation is used in a medical procedure called *ultrasonography*. Ultrasonography uses echoes to "see" inside a patient's body without performing surgery. A device called a transducer produces ultrasonic waves, which reflect off the patient's internal organs. These echoes are then converted into images that can be seen on a television monitor, as shown in **Figure 15.** Ultrasonography is used to examine kidneys, gallbladders, and other abdominal organs and to check the development of an unborn baby in a mother's body. Ultrasonic waves are safer than X rays because sound waves are less harmful to human tissue.

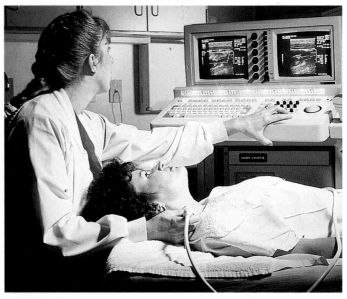

Figure 15 *Images created by ultrasonography are fuzzy, but they are a safe way to see inside a patient's body.*

REVIEW

1. Describe a place in which you would expect to hear echoes.

2. How do bats use echoes to find insects to eat?

3. **Comparing Concepts** Explain how sonar and ultrasonography are similar when used to locate objects.

Interference of Sound Waves

Another interaction of sound waves is interference. **Interference** is the result of two or more waves overlapping. **Figure 16** shows how two sound waves can combine by both constructive and destructive interference.

Figure 16 *Sound waves from two speakers producing sound of the same frequency combine by both constructive and destructive interference.*

Constructive Interference
As the compressions of one wave overlap the compressions of another wave, the sound will be louder because the amplitude is increased.

Destructive Interference
As the compressions of one wave overlap the rarefactions of another wave, the sound will be softer because the amplitude is decreased.

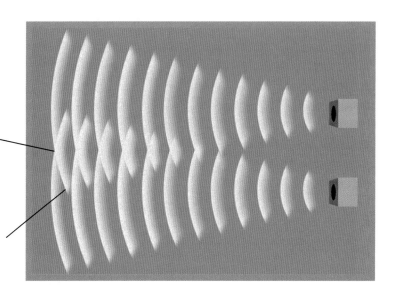

Orchestras and bands take advantage of constructive interference when several instruments play the same notes. The sound waves from the instruments combine by constructive interference to produce a louder sound. But destructive interference may keep you from hearing the concert. "Dead spots" are areas in an auditorium where sound waves reflecting off the walls interfere destructively with the sound waves from the stage. If you are at a concert and you can't hear the orchestra very well, try changing seats before you decide to get your ears checked!

Constructive interference

The Sound Barrier As the source of a sound—such as a jet plane—accelerates to the speed of sound, the sound waves in front of the jet plane compress closer and closer together. **Figure 17** shows what happens as a jet plane reaches the speed of sound.

Figure 17 *When a jet plane reaches the speed of sound, the sound waves in front of the jet combine by constructive interference. The result is a high-density compression that is called the sound barrier.*

Shock Waves and Sonic Booms For the jet in Figure 17 to travel faster than the speed of sound, it must overcome the pressure of the compressed sound waves. **Figure 18** shows what happens as soon as the jet achieves supersonic speeds—speeds faster than the speed of sound. At these speeds, the sound waves trail off behind the jet and combine at their outer edges to form a shock wave.

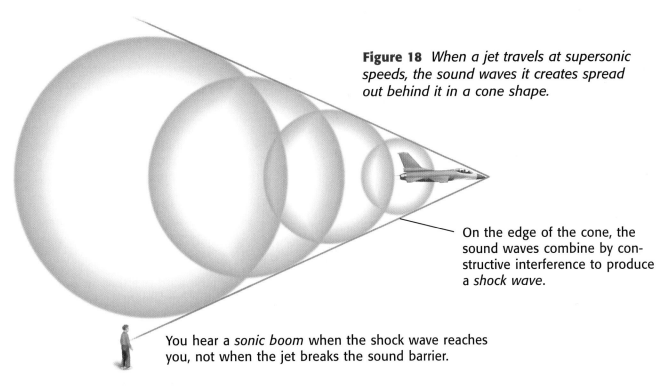

Figure 18 *When a jet travels at supersonic speeds, the sound waves it creates spread out behind it in a cone shape.*

On the edge of the cone, the sound waves combine by constructive interference to produce a *shock wave.*

You hear a *sonic boom* when the shock wave reaches you, not when the jet breaks the sound barrier.

A **sonic boom** is the explosive sound heard when a shock wave reaches your ears. Sonic booms can be so loud that they can hurt your ears and break windows. They can even make the ground shake as it does during an earthquake.

Self-Check

Explain why two people will not hear a sonic boom at the same time if they are standing a block or two apart. *(See page 724 to check your answer.)*

BRAIN FOOD

The cracking sound made by a whip is actually a miniature sonic boom caused by the shock wave formed as the tip of the whip travels faster than the speed of sound!

Standing Waves When you play a guitar, you can make some pleasing sounds and maybe even play a tune. But have you ever watched a guitar string after you've plucked it? You may have noticed that the string vibrates as a standing wave. A **standing wave** is a result of interference in which portions of the wave are at the rest position and other portions have a large amplitude.

Resonant Frequencies Although you can see only one standing wave, the guitar string actually creates several standing waves of different frequencies at the same time. The frequencies at which standing waves are made are called *resonant frequencies*. Resonant frequencies are sometimes called by special names, as shown in **Figure 19.**

Figure 19 *A plucked string vibrates at several resonant frequencies.*

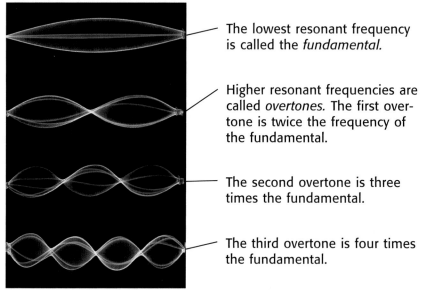

The lowest resonant frequency is called the *fundamental.*

Higher resonant frequencies are called *overtones.* The first overtone is twice the frequency of the fundamental.

The second overtone is three times the fundamental.

The third overtone is four times the fundamental.

A tuning fork and a plastic tube make beautiful music together on page 713 of the LabBook.

Resonance Would you believe that you can make a guitar string make a sound without touching it? You can do this if you have a tuning fork, shown in **Figure 20,** that vibrates at one of the resonant frequencies of the guitar string. Strike the tuning fork, and hold it close to the string. The string will start to vibrate and produce a sound. The effect is the greatest when the resonant frequency of the tuning fork matches the fundamental frequency of the string.

Using the vibrations of the tuning fork to make the string vibrate is an example of resonance. **Resonance** occurs when an object vibrating at or near a resonant frequency of a second object causes the second object to vibrate.

Figure 20 *When struck, a tuning fork can make certain objects vibrate.*

Diffraction of Sound Waves

Have you ever noticed the different sounds of thunder? From a distance, thunder sounds like a low rumbling. From nearby, thunder sounds like a loud *CRACK*! A type of wave interaction called diffraction causes this difference. **Diffraction** is the bending of waves around barriers or through openings. It is how sound waves travel around the corners of buildings and through doorways. The amount of diffraction is greatest when the size of the barrier or the opening is the same size or smaller than the wavelength of the sound waves, as shown in **Figure 21**.

Figure 21 **Determining the Amount of Diffraction**

High-frequency sound waves have short wavelengths and do not diffract very much when they travel through a doorway. Therefore, high pitches can be hard to hear when you are in the next room.

Low-frequency sound waves have longer wavelengths, so they diffract more through doorways. Therefore, you can hear lower pitches better when you are in the next room.

So what about thunder? Thunder consists of both high- and low-frequency sound waves. When lightning strikes nearby, you hear all the sound waves together as a loud cracking noise. But when the lightning strikes far away, buildings, trees, hills, and other barriers stop most of the high-frequency waves. Only the low-frequency waves can diffract around these large objects, and thus you hear only a low rumbling.

REVIEW

1. How is a sound barrier formed?

2. When you are in a classroom, why can you hear voices from the hallway even when you cannot see who is talking?

3. **Inferring Conclusions** Your friend is playing a song on a piano. Whenever your friend hits a certain key, the lamp on top of the piano rattles. Explain why this happens.

internet**connect**

SC**i**LINKS
NSTA

TOPIC: Interactions of Sound Waves
GO TO: www.scilinks.org
*sci*LINKS NUMBER: HSTP520

Sound Quality

Terms to Learn

sound quality
noise

What You'll Do

◆ Define sound quality.
◆ Describe how each family of musical instruments produces sound.
◆ Explain how noise is different from music.

Have you ever been told that some music you really like is just a lot of noise? If you have, you know that people sometimes disagree about the difference between noise and music. You probably think of noise as sounds you don't like and think of music as sounds that are interesting and pleasant to hear. But there is actually a difference between music and noise, and the difference has to do with sound quality.

What Is Sound Quality?

If the same note is played with the same loudness on a piano and on a violin, could you tell the instruments apart without looking? Although the notes played are identical, you probably could tell them apart because the sounds the instruments produce are not the same. The notes sound different because each instrument actually produces several different pitches: the fundamental and several overtones. These pitches are modeled in **Figure 22.** The result of several pitches blending together through interference is **sound quality.** Each instrument has a unique sound quality. **Figure 23** shows how the sound quality differs when two instruments play the same note.

Fundamental

First overtone

Second overtone

Resulting sound

Figure 22 *The top three diagrams represent three different pitches played at the same time. The bottom diagram shows the result when the pitches blend through interference.*

Figure 23 *An oscilloscope shows the difference in sound quality of the same note played on different instruments.*

Piano

Violin

Sound Quality of Instruments

When you listen to an orchestra play you can hear many different kinds of instruments. The difference in sound quality among the instruments comes from the structural differences of the instruments. All instruments produce sound with vibrations. But the part of the instrument that vibrates and how the vibrations are made vary from instrument to instrument. Even so, all instruments fall within three main families: string instruments, wind instruments, and percussion instruments.

✓ Self-Check

Which wave interaction is most important in determining sound quality? *(See page 724 to check your answer.)*

String Instruments Violins, guitars, and banjos are examples of string instruments. They produce sound when their strings vibrate after being plucked or bowed. **Figure 24** shows how two different string instruments produce sounds.

Figure 24 *Cellos and electric guitars are members of the string family.*

a Cellos and guitars have strings of different thicknesses. The thicker the string, the lower the pitch.

b The pitch of the string can be changed by pushing the string against the neck of the instrument to change the string's length. Shorter strings vibrate at higher frequencies.

c A string vibrates when a bow is pulled across it or when the string is plucked.

f Pickups on the guitar convert the vibration of the guitar string into an electrical signal.

d The vibrations in the cello string make the bridge vibrate, which in turn makes the body of the cello vibrate.

e The body of the cello and the air inside it resonate with the string's vibration, creating a louder sound.

g An amplifier converts the electrical signal back into a sound wave and increases the loudness of the sound.

553

Wind Instruments A wind instrument produces sound when a vibration is created at one end of its air column. The vibration creates standing waves in the air column. Wind instruments are sometimes divided into two groups—woodwinds and brass. Examples of woodwinds are saxophones, oboes, and recorders. Brass instruments include French horns, trombones, and tubas. A woodwind instrument and a brass instrument are shown in **Figure 25.**

Figure 25 *Clarinets are woodwind instruments, and trumpets are brass instruments.*

a A trumpet player's lips vibrate when the player blows into a trumpet.

b The reed vibrates back and forth when a musician blows into a clarinet.

c Standing waves are formed in the air columns of the instruments. The pitch of the instrument depends in part on the length of the air column. The longer the column, the lower the pitch.

d The length of the air column in a trumpet is changed by pushing the valves.

e The length of the air column in a clarinet is changed by closing or opening the finger holes.

Percussion Instruments Drums, bells, and cymbals are examples of percussion instruments. They produce sound when struck. Different-sized instruments are used to get different pitches. Usually, the larger the instrument, the lower the pitch. **Figure 26** shows examples of percussion instruments.

Figure 26 *Drums and cymbals in a trap set are examples of percussion instruments.*

The skins of the drums vibrate when struck with drumsticks.

Cymbals vibrate when struck together or when struck with drumsticks.

Each drum in the set is a different size. The larger the drum, the lower the pitch.

Music or Noise?

Most of the sounds we hear are noises. The sound of a truck roaring down the highway, the slamming of a door, and the jingle of keys falling to the floor are all noises. **Noise** can be described as any undesired sound, especially a nonmusical sound, that includes a random mix of pitches. **Figure 27** shows the difference between a musical sound and noise on an oscilloscope.

Figure 27 *A note from a French horn produces a sound wave with a repeating pattern, but noise from a clap produces complex sound waves with no pattern.*

French horn

A sharp clap

Noise Pollution The amount of noise around you can become so great that it is not only bothersome but can cause health problems. When noise reaches a level that causes pain or damages the body, it is considered *noise pollution.*

Noise pollution can damage the inner ear, causing permanent hearing loss. Noise pollution can also contribute to sleeplessness, high blood pressure, and stress. Because of these health concerns, the federal government has set noise exposure limits for people who work in areas with loud noises. Noise pollution also makes the environment less livable for humans as well as wildlife.

Environment
C O N N E C T I O N

The Los Angeles International Airport was built next to the main habitat of an endangered butterfly species called the El Segundo blue. The noise pollution from the airport has driven people and other animals from the area, but the butterflies are not affected because they have no ears!

REVIEW

1. What is the role of interference in determining sound quality?

2. Name the three families of musical instruments, and describe how vibrations are created in each family.

3. **Interpreting Graphics** Look at the oscilloscope screen at right. Do you think the sound represented by the wave on the screen was noise or music? Explain your answer.

internet**connect**

SC*LINKS*
NSTA

TOPIC: Sound Quality
GO TO: www.scilinks.org
*sci*LINKS NUMBER: HSTP525

Chapter Highlights

SECTION 1

Vocabulary

wave *(p. 535)*
medium *(p. 536)*
outer ear *(p. 537)*
middle ear *(p. 537)*
inner ear *(p. 537)*

Section Notes

- All sounds are created by vibrations and travel as longitudinal waves.
- Sound waves require a medium through which to travel.
- Sound waves travel in all directions away from their source.
- The sounds you hear are converted into electrical impulses by your ears and then sent to your brain for interpretation.
- Exposure to loud sounds can cause hearing loss and tinnitus.

SECTION 2

Vocabulary

pitch *(p. 540)*
infrasonic *(p. 541)*
ultrasonic *(p. 541)*
Doppler effect *(p. 542)*
loudness *(p. 542)*
decibel *(p. 543)*

Section Notes

- The speed of sound depends on the medium through which the sound is traveling. Changes in temperature of the medium can affect the speed of sound.
- The pitch of a sound depends on frequency. High-frequency sounds are high-pitched, and low-frequency sounds are low-pitched.
- Humans can hear sounds with frequencies between 20 Hz and 20,000 Hz.

- The Doppler effect is the apparent change in frequency of a sound caused by the motion of either the listener or the source of the sound.
- The loudness of a sound increases as the amplitude increases. Loudness is expressed in decibels.
- An oscilloscope can be used to "see" sounds.

Labs

Easy Listening *(p. 710)*

☑ Skills Check

Math Concepts

THE SPEED OF SOUND The speed of sound depends on the medium through which the sound waves are traveling. The speed of sound through wood at 20°C is 3,850 m/s. The distance sound will travel through wood in 5 seconds can be calculated as follows:

$$\text{distance} = \text{speed} \times \text{time}$$
$$= 3{,}850 \, \frac{\text{m}}{\cancel{\text{s}}} \times 5 \, \cancel{\text{s}}$$
$$= 19{,}250 \text{ m}$$

Visual Understanding

HOW THE HUMAN EAR WORKS The human ear has several parts that are divided into three regions—the outer ear, the middle ear, and the inner ear. Study the diagram on page 537 to review how the ear works.

SECTION 3

Vocabulary

reflection *(p. 545)*

echo *(p. 545)*

echolocation *(p. 546)*

interference *(p. 548)*

sonic boom *(p. 549)*

standing wave *(p. 549)*

resonance *(p. 550)*

diffraction *(p. 551)*

Section Notes

- Echoes are reflected sound waves.

- Some animals use echolocation to find food or navigate around objects. Sonar and ultrasonography are types of echolocation.

- Sound barriers and shock waves are created by interference. You hear a sonic boom when a shock wave reaches your ears.

- Standing waves form at an object's resonant frequencies.

- Resonance occurs when a vibrating object causes a second object to vibrate at one of its resonant frequencies.

- The bending of sound waves around barriers or through openings is called diffraction. The amount of diffraction depends on the wavelength of the waves as well as the size of the opening.

Labs

The Speed of Sound *(p. 712)*

Tuneful Tube *(p. 713)*

The Energy of Sound *(p. 714)*

SECTION 4

Vocabulary

sound quality *(p. 552)*

noise *(p. 555)*

Section Notes

- Different instruments have different sound qualities.

- The three families of instruments are strings, winds, and percussion.

- The sound quality of noise is not pleasing because it is a random mix of frequencies.

internet connect

GO TO: go.hrw.com

Visit the **HRW** Web site for a variety of learning tools related to this chapter. Just type in the keyword:

KEYWORD: HSTSND

GO TO: www.scilinks.org

Visit the **National Science Teachers Association** on-line Web site for Internet resources related to this chapter. Just type in the *sci*LINKS number for more information about the topic:

TOPIC: What Is Sound?   *sci*LINKS NUMBER: HSTP505
TOPIC: The Ear   *sci*LINKS NUMBER: HSTP510
TOPIC: Properties of Sound   *sci*LINKS NUMBER: HSTP515
TOPIC: Interactions of Sound Waves   *sci*LINKS NUMBER: HSTP520
TOPIC: Sound Quality   *sci*LINKS NUMBER: HSTP525

Chapter Review

USING VOCABULARY

To complete the following sentences, choose the correct term from each pair of terms listed below:

1. Humans cannot hear __?__ waves because their frequencies are above the range of human hearing. (*infrasonic* or *ultrasonic*)

2. In the __?__, vibrations are converted to electrical signals for the brain to interpret. (*middle ear* or *inner ear*)

3. The __?__ of a sound wave depends on its amplitude. (*loudness* or *pitch*)

4. Reflected sound waves are called __?__. (*echoes* or *noise*)

5. Two different instruments playing the same note sound different because of __?__. (*echolocation* or *sound quality*)

UNDERSTANDING CONCEPTS

Multiple Choice

6. If a fire engine is traveling toward you, the Doppler effect will cause the siren to sound
   a. higher. **c.** louder.
   b. lower. **d.** softer.

7. The wave interaction most important for echolocation is
   a. reflection. **c.** diffraction.
   b. interference. **d.** resonance.

8. If two sound waves interfere constructively, you will hear
   a. a high-pitched sound.
   b. a softer sound.
   c. a louder sound.
   d. no change in sound.

9. You will hear a sonic boom when
   a. an object breaks the sound barrier.
   b. an object travels at supersonic speeds.
   c. a shock wave reaches your ears.
   d. the speed of sound is 290 m/s.

10. Instruments that produce sound when struck belong to which family?
    a. strings **c.** percussion
    b. winds **d.** none of the above

11. Resonance can occur when an object vibrates at another object's
    a. resonant frequency.
    b. fundamental frequency.
    c. second overtone frequency.
    d. All of the above

12. The amount of diffraction that a sound wave undergoes depends on
    a. the frequency of the wave.
    b. the amplitude of the wave.
    c. the size of the barrier.
    d. Both (a) and (c)

13. A technological device that can be used to "see" sound waves is a(n)
    a. oscilloscope. **c.** transducer.
    b. sonar. **d.** amplifier.

Short Answer

14. Describe how the Doppler effect helps a beluga whale determine whether a fish is moving away from it or toward it.

15. How is interference involved in forming a shock wave?

16. Briefly describe how the three parts of the ear work.

Concept Mapping

17. Use the following terms to create a concept map: sound, sound wave, pitch, loudness, decibel, hertz, frequency, amplitude.

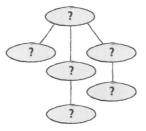

18. An anechoic chamber is a room where there is almost no reflection of sound waves. Anechoic chambers are often used to test sound equipment, such as stereos. The walls of such chambers are usually covered with foam triangles. Explain why this design eliminates echoes in the room.

19. Suppose you are sitting in the passenger seat of a parked car. You hear sounds coming from the stereo of another car parked on the opposite side of the street. You can easily hear the low-pitched bass sounds but cannot hear any high-pitched sounds coming from the parked car. Explain why you think this happens.

20. After working in a factory for a month, a man you know complains about a ringing in his ears. What might be wrong with him? What do you think may have caused his problem? What can you suggest to prevent further hearing loss?

MATH IN SCIENCE

21. How far does sound travel in 4 seconds through water at 20°C and glass at 20°C? Refer to the chart on page 35 for the speed of sound in different media.

INTERPRETING GRAPHICS

Use the oscilloscope screens below to answer the following questions:

22. Which sound is probably noise?

23. Which represents the softest sound?

24. Which represents the sound with the lowest pitch?

25. Which two sounds were produced by the same instrument?

Reading Check-up

Take a minute to review your answers to the Pre-Reading Questions found at the bottom of page 532. Have your answers changed? If necessary, revise your answers based on what you have learned since you began this chapter.

Science, Technology, and Society

Jurassic Bark

Imagine you suddenly hear an incredibly loud honking sound, like a trombone or a tuba. "Must be band tryouts," you think. You turn to find the noise and find yourself face to face with a 10 m long, 2,800 kg dinosaur with a huge tubular crest extending back more than 2 m from its snout. Do you run? No—your musical friend, *Parasaurolophus*, is a vegetarian.

Now there's no way you'll bump into this extinct hadrosaur, a duck-billed dinosaur that existed about 75 million years ago in the late Cretaceous period. But through recent advances in computer technology, you can hear how *Parasaurolophus* might have sounded.

A Snorkel or a Trombone?

Parasaurolophus's crest contained a network of tubes connected to the animal's breathing passages. Some scientists believe the dinosaurs used the distinctive crest to make sounds. Other scientists theorize that the crest allowed *Parasaurolophus* to stay underwater and feed, that it was used to regulate body temperature, or that it allowed the animals to communicate with each other by exhaling strongly through the crest.

The study of the *Parasaurolophus*'s potential sound-making ability really began after a 1995 expedition in northwestern New Mexico uncovered an almost-complete fossil skull of an adult. With this nearly complete skull and some modern technology, scientists tested the noise-making qualities of the crest.

Dino Scan

In Albuquerque, New Mexico, Dr. Carl Diegert of Sandia National Laboratories and Dr. Tom Williamson of the New Mexico Museum of Natural History and Science teamed up to use CT (Computed Tomography). With this scanning system, they created three-dimensional images of the crest's internal structure. The results

▶ *Aside from a role in the* Jurassic Park *movies, the* Parasaurolophus *dinosaur's biggest claim to fame is the enormous crest that extends back from its snout.*

showed that the crest had more tubes than previously thought as well as additional chambers.

Sound That Funky Horn

Once the crest's internal structure was determined, Diegert used powerful computers and special software to produce a sound that *Parasaurolophus* might have made. Since it is not known whether *Parasaurolophus* had vocal cords, Diegert made different versions of the sound by simulating the movement of air through the crest in several ways. Intrigued by Diegert's results, other researchers are trying to reproduce the sounds of other dinosaurs. In time, *Parasaurolophus* might be just one of a band of musical dinosaurs.

On Your Own

▶ *Parasaurolophus* is just one type of hadrosaur recognized for the peculiar bony crest on top of its head. On your own, research other hadrosaurs that had a bony crest similar to that of the *Parasaurolophus*. What are the names of these dinosaurs?

Science Fiction

"Ear"

by Jane Yolen

"Jily put on her Ear and sighed. The world went from awful silence to the pounding rhythms she loved. Without the Ear she was locked into her own thoughts and the few colors her eyes could pick out. But with the Ear she felt truly connected to the world."

Jily and her friends, Sanya and Feeny, live in a time not too far in the future. It is a time when everyone's hearing is damaged. People communicate using sign language—unless they put on their Ear. Then the whole world is filled with sounds. Of course, there are rules. No Ears allowed in school. Ears are only to be worn on the street, at night. Life is so much richer with an Ear, a person would have to be crazy to go without one.

The Low Down, the first club Jily and her friends visit, is too quiet for Jily's tastes. She wants to leave and tries to find Sanya and Feeny. But Sanya is dancing by herself, even though there is no music. When Jily finds Feeny, they notice some Earless kids their own age. Earless people never go to clubs, and Jily finds their presence offensive. But Feeny is intrigued.

Everyone is given an Ear at the age of 12 but has to give it up at the age of 30. Why would these kids want to go out without their Ears before the age of 30? Jily thinks the idea is ridiculous and doesn't stick around to find out the answer to such a question. But, it is an answer that will change her life by the end of the next day.

Read the rest of Jily's story, "Ear" by Jane Yolen, in the *Holt Anthology of Science Fiction.*

Pre-Reading
Questions

1. What is light?
2. How do light waves interact?
3. Why are you able to see different colors?

WHAT ON EARTH...?

What kind of alien life lives on *this* planet? Actually, this isn't a planet at all. It's a photograph of something much, much smaller. Have you guessed yet? It's an ordinary soap bubble! The brightly colored swirls on the surface of this bubble are reflections of light. In this chapter, you will learn more about light, including how waves interact and why you can see different colors like the ones on the surface of this soap bubble.

COLORS OF LIGHT

Is white light really white? In this activity, you will use a spectroscope to answer that question.

Procedure

1. Your teacher will give you a **spectroscope** or instructions for making one.

2. Turn on an **incandescent light bulb.** Look at the light bulb through your spectroscope. In your ScienceLog, write a description of what you see.

3. Repeat step 2 looking at a **fluorescent light.** Again, in your ScienceLog, describe what you see.

Analysis

4. Compare what you saw in step 2 with what you saw in step 3.

5. Both kinds of bulbs produce white light. What did you learn about white light using the spectroscope?

6. Light from the sun is white light. Make inferences about what you would see if you looked at sunlight using a spectroscope.
   Caution: Do NOT use your spectroscope to look at the sun. It does not give enough protection against bright sunlight.

Terms to Learn

electromagnetic wave
radiation

What You'll Do

◆ Explain why electromagnetic waves are transverse waves.
◆ Describe how electromagnetic waves are produced.
◆ Calculate distances traveled by light using the value for speed of light.

What Is Light?

We rely on light from the sun and from electric bulbs to help us see. But what exactly is light? Scientists are still studying light to learn more about its makeup and characteristics. Fortunately, much has already been discovered about light, as you will soon find out. You may even become enlightened!

Light Is an Electromagnetic Wave

Like sound, light is a type of energy that travels as a wave. But unlike sound, light does not require a medium through which to travel. Light is an **electromagnetic wave** (EM wave). An EM wave is a wave that can travel through space or matter and consists of changing electric and magnetic fields. A *field* is a region around an object that can exert a force, a push or pull, on another object without actually touching that object. For example, a magnet is surrounded by a magnetic field that can pull a paper clip toward it. But keep in mind that this field, like all fields, is not made of matter.

Figure 1 shows a diagram of an electromagnetic wave. Notice that the electric and magnetic fields are at right angles—or *perpendicular*—to each other. These fields are also perpendicular to the direction of the wave motion. Because of this arrangement, electromagnetic waves are transverse waves.

Figure 1 *Electromagnetic waves are transverse waves.*

Magnetic field

Electric field

The electric field is perpendicular to the magnetic field.

Direction of travel

How Light Is Produced

An EM wave is produced by the vibration of an electrically charged particle. A particle with an electric charge is surrounded by an electric field. When the particle vibrates, or moves back and forth, the electric field around it vibrates too. When the electric field starts vibrating, a vibrating magnetic field is created. The vibration of an electric field and a magnetic field together produces an EM wave that carries energy released by the original vibration of the particle. The emission of energy in the form of EM waves is called **radiation.**

Sounds complicated, right? To better understand how light is produced, think about the following example. When you turn on a lamp, the electrical energy supplied to the filament in the bulb causes the atoms in the filament to vibrate. Charged particles inside the atoms then vibrate, and light is produced, as shown in **Figure 2.**

Extra! Extra! Read all about how light-producing fireflies save people's lives! Turn to page 590.

Figure 2 The Production of Light

a Electrons (negatively charged particles) in an atom move about the nucleus at different distances depending on the amount of energy they have. When an electron absorbs energy, it can jump to a new position.

b This new position is generally unstable, and the electron may not stay there very long. The electron returns to its original position, releasing the energy it absorbed in a tiny "packet" called a *photon.*

Nucleus
Electron
Energy levels

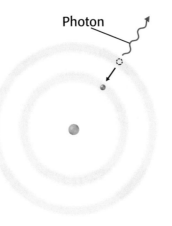

Photon

c The movement of electrons back and forth creates a stream of photons. This stream of photons can be thought of as waves of vibrating electric and magnetic fields. The stream of photons (the EM wave) carries the energy released by the electrons.

The Split Personality of Light

The fact that light is a wave explains certain behaviors of light, but not others. These puzzling behaviors of light are easier to explain if light is thought to consist of particles instead of waves. Scientists think that light has the properties of both a particle and a wave. Albert Einstein was one of many scientists who researched the dual nature of light. The idea that light can act as either particles or waves is known as the *particle-wave theory of light.*

MATH BREAK

Just How Fast Is Light?

To give you an idea of how fast light travels, calculate the time it takes for light to travel from Earth to the moon. The distance from Earth to the moon is 382,000,000 m.

$$speed = \frac{distance}{time}$$

This equation can be rearranged to solve for time:

$$time = \frac{distance}{speed}$$

$$time = \frac{382,000,000 \text{ m}}{300,000,000 \text{ m/s}}$$

$$time = 1.27 \text{ seconds}$$

Now It's Your Turn

The distance from the sun to Earth is 150,000,000,000 m. Calculate the time it takes for light to travel that distance.

internet connect

SCiLINKS
NSTA

TOPIC: Light Energy
GO TO: www.scilinks.org
*sci*LINKS **NUMBER:** HSTP529

The Speed of Light

Scientists have yet to discover anything in the universe that travels faster than light. In the near-vacuum of space, the speed of light is about 300,000,000 m/s. Light travels slightly slower in air, glass, and other types of matter. (Keep in mind that even though EM waves do not require a medium, they can travel through many substances.) Believe it or not, light can travel more than 880,000 times faster than sound! This explains the phenomenon described in **Figure 3.** And if you could run at the speed of light, you could travel around Earth 7.5 times in 1 second.

Figure 3 *Although thunder and lightning are produced at the same time, you usually see lightning before you hear thunder. That's because light travels much faster than sound.*

REVIEW

1. Why are electromagnetic waves transverse waves?

2. How is a sound wave different from an EM wave?

3. How does a charged particle produce an EM wave?

4. **Making Inferences** Explain why EM waves do not require a medium through which to travel.

5. **Doing Calculations** The distance from the sun to Jupiter is 778,000,000,000 m. How long does it take for light from the sun to reach Jupiter?

What You'll Do

◆ Identify how EM waves differ from each other.
◆ Describe some uses for radio waves and microwaves.
◆ Give examples of how infrared waves and visible light are important in your life.
◆ Explain how ultraviolet light, X rays, and gamma rays can be both helpful and harmful.

The Electromagnetic Spectrum

When you look around, you can see objects because light reflects off them. But if a bee looked at the same objects, it would see them differently, as shown in **Figure 4.** This is because bees can see a kind of light that you can't see. This type of light is called ultraviolet light.

It might seem strange to you to call something you can't see *light,* because the light you are most familiar with is visible light. But ultraviolet light is very similar to visible light. Both visible light and ultraviolet light are types of EM waves. In this section you will learn about many other types of EM waves, including X rays, radio waves, and microwaves.

Figure 4 *The petals of the flower on the right look solid yellow to you. But a bee may see dark ultraviolet markings that make the same flower appear quite different to the bee.*

Astronomy
C O N N E C T I O N

Scientists know that all electromagnetic waves in empty space travel at the same speed. If EM waves traveled at different speeds, planets, stars, and galaxies would appear to be in different places depending upon which EM wave was used to view them. For example, using X rays to view a star might make the star appear to be in a different place than if radio waves were used.

Characteristics of EM Waves

Even though there are many types of EM waves, each type of wave travels at the same speed in a vacuum—300,000,000 m/s. How is this possible? Well, the speed of a wave is determined by multiplying its wavelength by its frequency. So EM waves having different wavelengths can travel at the same speed as long as their frequencies are also different. The entire range of EM waves is called the **electromagnetic spectrum.** Categories of waves in the EM spectrum include radio waves, microwaves, and visible light.

Radio Waves

Radio waves cover a wide range of waves in the EM spectrum. Radio waves have some of the longest wavelengths and the lowest frequencies of all EM waves. Therefore, radio waves are low energy waves. They carry enough energy, however, to be used for broadcasting radio signals. **Figure 5** shows how this process works.

Radio stations encode sound information into radio waves by varying either the waves' amplitude or their frequency. Changing amplitude or frequency is called modulation. You probably know that there are AM radio stations and FM radio stations. The abbreviation AM stands for amplitude modulation, and the abbreviation FM stands for frequency modulation. AM radio waves have longer wavelengths than FM radio waves.

Figure 5 *Radio waves cannot be heard, but they carry energy that can be converted into sound.*

1 A radio station converts sound into an electric current. The current produces radio waves that are sent out in all directions by the antenna.

2 A radio receives radio waves and then converts them into an electric current, which is then converted to sound.

Electromagnetic Spectrum

The electromagnetic spectrum is arranged from long to short wavelength or from low to high frequency.

Radio waves	Microwaves	Infrared
All radio and television stations broadcast radio waves.	Despite their name, microwaves are not the shortest EM waves.	*Infrared* means "below red."

AM and FM Radio Waves Although AM radio waves can travel farther than FM waves, as shown in **Figure 6,** many stations—especially those that broadcast mostly music—use FM waves. That's because more information can be encoded by using frequency modulation than by using amplitude modulation. Because FM waves carry more information, music broadcast from FM stations sounds better.

Figure 6 *The difference in the wavelengths of AM and FM radio waves affects how the waves interact with a layer of the atmosphere called the ionosphere.*

AM radio waves can reflect off the ionosphere. This helps AM waves travel long distances.

FM radio waves pass through the ionosphere. Therefore, FM waves cannot travel as far as AM waves.

Decreasing wavelength ⇒

Increasing frequency ⇒

Visible light

Visible light contains all the colors you can see.

Ultraviolet

Ultraviolet means "beyond violet."

X rays

X rays were discovered in the early 1900s.

Gamma rays

Gamma rays are produced by some nuclear reactions.

The Nature of Light **569**

Television and Radio Waves Television signals are also carried by radio waves. Most television stations broadcast radio waves that have shorter wavelengths and higher frequencies than those broadcast by radio stations. However, television signals are still broadcast using amplitude modulation and frequency modulation. Television stations use frequency-modulated waves to carry sound and amplitude-modulated waves to carry pictures.

Some waves carrying television signals are transmitted to satellites around the Earth. The waves are amplified and relayed back to ground antennae and then travel through cables to televisions in homes. This is how cable television works.

Microwaves

Microwaves have shorter wavelengths and higher frequencies than radio waves. Therefore, microwaves carry more energy than radio waves. You are probably familiar with microwaves—they are created in a microwave oven, like the model illustrated in **Figure 7.**

Figure 7 How a Microwave Oven Works

a A device called a magnetron produces microwaves by accelerating charged particles.

b The microwaves reflect off a metal fan and are directed into the cooking chamber.

c Microwaves can penetrate several centimeters into the food.

d The energy of the microwaves causes water molecules inside the food to vibrate. The vibration of the water molecules causes the temperature of the food to increase.

Radar Microwaves are also used in radar. Radar (**ra**dio **d**etection **a**nd **r**anging) is used to detect the speed and location of objects. **Figure 8** shows a police officer using radar to determine the speed of a car. The officer points the radar device at a car and presses a button. The device emits short pulses of microwaves that reflect off the car and return to the device. The rate at which the waves are reflected is used to calculate the speed of the car. Radar is also used to monitor the movement of airplanes and to help ship captains navigate at night or in foggy weather.

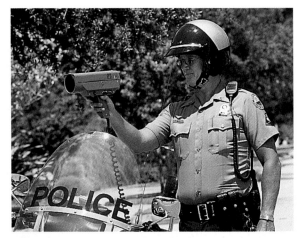

Figure 8 *Police officers use radar to detect cars going faster than the speed limit.*

Infrared Waves

Infrared waves have shorter wavelengths and higher frequencies than microwaves. So infrared waves can carry more energy than microwaves and radio waves carry.

When you sit outside on a sunny summer day, you feel warm because of *infrared waves* emitted by the sun. Infrared waves are absorbed by your skin when they strike your body. The energy of the waves causes the particles in your skin to vibrate faster, and you feel the increased vibration as an increase in temperature.

The sun is not the only source of infrared waves. Objects that emit infrared waves include stars, planets, buildings, trees, and you! The amount of infrared radiation emitted by an object varies depending on the object's temperature. Warmer objects give off more infrared radiation than cooler objects.

Your eyes can't see infrared waves, but there are devices that can detect infrared radiation. For example, infrared binoculars convert infrared radiation into light you can see. Such binoculars can be used to observe animals at night. **Figure 9** shows how certain photographic films are sensitive to infrared radiation.

Figure 9 *In this photograph, brighter colors indicate higher temperatures.*

REVIEW

1. How do infrared waves differ from radio waves in terms of frequency and wavelength?

2. Describe two ways that radio waves are used for transmitting information.

3. **Inferring Relationships** Why do the frequencies of EM waves increase as the wavelengths decrease?

Biology CONNECTION

Visible light provides the energy necessary for photosynthesis—the process by which plants make their own food. Photosynthesis is important to you for two reasons. First, during photosynthesis, plants produce oxygen for you to breathe. Second, the food produced by plants provides your body with energy. When you eat plants, or eat meat from animals that ate plants, you get energy to live from the food produced through photosynthesis.

Visible Light

Visible light is the very narrow range of wavelengths and frequencies in the electromagnetic spectrum that humans can see. Humans see the different wavelengths as different colors, as shown in **Figure 10.** The longest wavelengths are seen as red light, and the shortest wavelengths are seen as violet light. Because violet light has the shortest wavelength, it carries the most energy of the visible light waves.

Figure 10 *White light, such as light from the sun, is actually visible light of all wavelengths combined. You see all the colors of visible light in a rainbow.*

Colors of Light The range of colors is called the *visible spectrum.* When you list the colors, you might use the imaginary name "Roy G. Biv" to help you remember their order. The letters in Roy's name represent the first letter of each color of visible light: **r**ed, **o**range, **y**ellow, **g**reen, **b**lue, **i**ndigo, and **v**iolet. When all the colors of visible light are combined, you see the light as white light. Sunlight and light from incandescent light bulbs and fluorescent light bulbs are examples of white light. You can see the visible spectrum in **Figure 11.**

Figure 11 *The visible spectrum contains all colors of light.*

R   O   Y   G   B   I   V

Ultraviolet Light

Ultraviolet light is another type of electromagnetic wave produced by the sun. Ultraviolet waves have shorter wavelengths and higher frequencies than visible light. Therefore, ultraviolet waves carry more energy than visible light carries. This greater amount of energy affects us in both positive and negative ways.

Positive Effects On the positive side, ultraviolet waves produced artificially by ultraviolet lamps are used to kill bacteria on food and surgical instruments. In addition, limited exposure to ultraviolet light is beneficial to your body. When exposed to ultraviolet light, skin cells produce vitamin D, a substance necessary for the absorption of calcium by the intestines. Without calcium, your teeth and bones would be very weak.

Negative Effects On the negative side, overexposure to ultraviolet light can cause sunburn, skin cancer, damage to the eyes, wrinkles, and premature aging of the skin. Fortunately, much of the ultraviolet light from the sun does not reach the surface of the Earth. But you should still protect yourself against the ultraviolet light that does reach you. To do so, you should use sunscreen with a high SPF (**S**un **P**rotection **F**actor) and wear sunglasses that block out ultraviolet light, like the person on the left in **Figure 12.** You need this protection even on overcast days because ultraviolet light can travel through clouds.

Figure 12 *Sunscreen offers protection against a painful sunburn.*

Blocking the Sun

Sunscreens contain a chemical that prevents ultraviolet light from penetrating your skin. When you look at a bottle of sunscreen, you will see the abbreviation SPF followed by a number. The number is a guide to how long you can stay in the sun without getting a sunburn. For example, if you use a sunscreen with SPF 15 and you normally burn after being in the sun for 10 minutes, you will be able to stay in the sun for 150 minutes without getting burned. Why do you think people who burn easily need a higher SPF?

X Rays and Gamma Rays

X rays and gamma rays have some of the shortest wavelengths and highest frequencies of all EM waves. X rays carry a great deal of energy and easily penetrate a variety of materials. This characteristic makes X rays useful in the medical field, as shown in **Figure 13.** However, too much exposure to X rays can damage or kill living cells. Patients receiving X-ray examinations often wear a lead-lined apron to protect the parts of the body that do not need X-ray exposure.

Figure 13 *If you fall and hurt your arm, a doctor might use an X-ray machine to check for broken bones.*

X rays travel easily through skin and muscle but are absorbed by bones.

The X rays that are not absorbed strike the film.

Bright areas appear on the film where X rays are absorbed by the bones.

Gamma rays carry large amounts of energy and can penetrate materials very easily. Every day you are exposed to small amounts of gamma rays that do not harm you. Because of their high energy, gamma rays are used to treat some forms of cancer. Radiologists focus the rays on tumors inside the body to kill the cancer cells. While this treatment can have positive effects, it often has negative side effects because some healthy cells are also killed.

🖰 internet**connect**

SC*i*LINKS.
NSTA

TOPIC: The Electromagnetic Spectrum
GO TO: www.scilinks.org
*sci*LINKS NUMBER: HSTP530

REVIEW

1. Explain why ultraviolet light, X rays, and gamma rays can be both helpful and harmful.

2. Describe how three different types of electromagnetic waves have been useful to you today.

3. **Comparing Concepts** Compare the wavelengths and frequencies of infrared, ultraviolet, and visible light. How does the energy carried by each type of wave compare with the others?

Interactions of Light Waves

What You'll Do

◆ Compare regular reflection with diffuse reflection.
◆ Describe absorption and scattering of light.
◆ Explain how refraction can create optical illusions and separate white light into colors.
◆ Describe diffraction and interference of light.

Have you ever seen a cat's eyes glow in the dark when light shines on them? Cats have a special layer of cells in the back of their eyes that reflects light. This layer helps the cat see better by giving the eyes another chance to detect the light. Reflection is just one way light waves interact. All types of EM waves interact in several ways. Because we can see visible light, it is easier to explain interactions involving visible light.

Reflection

Reflection occurs when light or any other wave bounces off an object. When you see yourself in a mirror, you are actually seeing light that has been reflected twice—first from you and then from the mirror. Reflection allows you to see objects that don't produce their own light. When light strikes an object, some of the light reflects off of it and is detected by your eyes.

But if light is reflecting off you and off the objects around you, why can't you see your reflection on a wall? To answer this question, you must first learn about the law of reflection.

The Law of Reflection Light reflects off surfaces the same way that a ball bounces off the ground. If you throw the ball straight down against a smooth surface, it will bounce straight up. If you bounce it at an angle, it will bounce away at an angle. The **law of reflection** states that the angle of incidence is equal to the angle of reflection. *Incidence* is the falling of a beam of light on a surface. **Figure 14** illustrates this law.

Figure 14 The Law of Reflection

A line perpendicular to the mirror's surface is called the *normal.*

The beam of light traveling toward the mirror is called the *incident beam.*

The beam of light reflected off the mirror is called the *reflected beam.*

The angle between the incident beam and the normal is called the *angle of incidence.*

The angle between the reflected beam and the normal is called the *angle of reflection.*

Types of Reflection So back to the question, "Why can you see your reflection in a mirror but not in a wall?" The answer has to do with the differences between the two surfaces. If the reflecting surface is very smooth, like a mirror or polished metal, light beams reflect off all points of the surface at the same angle. This is called *regular reflection*. If the reflecting surface is slightly rough, like a wall, light beams will hit the surface and reflect at many different angles. This is called *diffuse reflection*. **Figure 15** illustrates the difference between the two types of reflection.

Figure 15 Regular Reflection Vs. Diffuse Reflection

Regular reflection occurs when light beams are reflected at the same angle. When your eye detects the reflected beams, you can see a reflection on the surface.

Diffuse reflection occurs when light beams reflect at many different angles. You can't see a reflection because not all of the reflected light is directed toward your eyes.

Absorption and Scattering

You have probably noticed that when you use a flashlight, objects that are closer to you appear brighter than objects that are farther away. The light appears to weaken the farther it travels from the flashlight. This happens partially because the beam spreads out and partially because of absorption and scattering.

Absorption of Light The transfer of energy carried by light waves to particles of matter is called **absorption**. When you shine a flashlight in the air, the air particles absorb some of the energy from the light. This causes the light to become dim, as shown in **Figure 16.** The farther the light travels from the flashlight, the more it is absorbed by air particles.

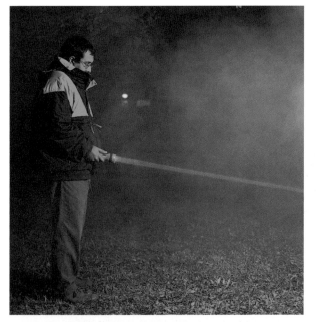

Figure 16 *A beam of light becomes dimmer partially because of absorption and scattering.*

Scattering of Light The release of light energy by particles of matter that have absorbed energy is called **scattering.** When the light is released, it scatters in all directions. Light from a flashlight is scattered out of the beam by air particles. This scattered light allows you to see objects outside of the beam, as shown in Figure 16 on the previous page. However, because light is scattered out of the beam, the beam becomes dimmer.

Scattering makes the sky blue. Light with shorter wavelengths is scattered more than light with longer wavelengths. Sunlight is made up of many different colors of light, but blue light (which has a very short wavelength) is scattered more than any other color. So when you look at the sky, you see a background of blue light. You can learn more about the scattering of light by doing the QuickLab at right.

Refraction

Imagine that you and a friend are at a lake. Your friend wades into the water. You look at her and are startled to see that her feet look like they are separated from her legs! You know her feet did not come off, so how can you explain what you see? The answer has to do with refraction.

Refraction is the bending of a wave as it passes at an angle from one medium to another. Refraction of light waves occurs because the speed of light varies depending on the material through which the waves are traveling. In a vacuum, light travels at 300,000,000 m/s, but it travels more slowly through matter. When a wave enters a new medium at an angle, the part of the wave that enters first begins traveling at a different speed from the rest of the wave. **Figure 17** shows how a light beam is bent by refraction.

Scattering Milk

1. Fill a clear **2 L plastic bottle** with **water.**

2. Turn the lights off, and shine a **flashlight** through the water. Look at the water from all sides of the bottle. Describe what you see in your ScienceLog.

3. Add a few drops of **milk** to the water, and shake the bottle to mix it up.

4. Repeat step 2. Describe any color changes. If you don't see any, add more milk until you do.

5. How is the water-and-milk mixture like air particles in the atmosphere? Write your answer in your ScienceLog.

TRY at HOME

Figure 17 *Light travels more slowly through glass than it does through air. Therefore, light refracts as it passes at an angle from air to glass or from glass to air.*

If light passes into a medium where the speed of light is slower, the light bends away from the boundary between the media.

Light in

If light passes into a medium where the speed of light is faster, the light bends toward the boundary.

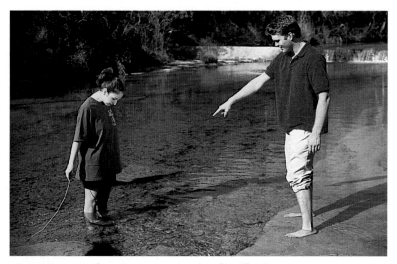

Figure 18 *Refraction can create the illusion that the feet of the person in the water are separated from her legs. Try this for yourself!*

Optical Illusions Normally when you look at an object, the light reflecting off the object travels in a straight line from the object to your eye. Your brain always interprets light as traveling in straight lines. However, when you look at an object that is underwater, the light reflecting off the object does *not* travel in a straight line. Instead, it refracts. **Figure 18** shows how refraction creates an optical illusion.

Refraction and Color Separation You have already learned that white light is actually composed of all the colors of visible light. You also know that the different colors correspond to different wavelengths. When white light is refracted, the amount that the light bends depends on its wavelength. Light waves with short wavelengths bend more than light waves with long wavelengths. Because of this, white light can be separated into different colors during refraction, as shown in **Figure 19.** Color separation during refraction is responsible for the formation of rainbows. Rainbows are created when sunlight is refracted by water droplets.

Figure 19 *A prism is a piece of glass that separates white light into the colors of visible light by refraction.*

Light passing through a prism is refracted twice—once when it enters and once when it exits.

Violet light, which has a short wavelength, is refracted more than red light, which has a long wavelength.

Diffraction

Refraction isn't the only way light waves are bent. **Diffraction** is the bending of waves around barriers or through openings. The diffraction of light waves is not always easy to see. The diffraction of water waves, shown in **Figure 20,** is easier to see. The amount a wave diffracts depends on its wavelength and the size of the barrier or the opening. The greatest amount of diffraction occurs when the barrier or opening is the same size or smaller than the wavelength.

The wavelength of light is very small—about 100 times smaller than the thickness of a human hair! So in order for light to diffract very much, light has to be passing through a slit or some other opening that is very narrow.

Light waves cannot diffract very much around large obstacles, such as buildings. That's why you can't see around corners. But light waves always diffract a small amount. You can observe light waves diffracting if you examine the edges of a shadow. Diffraction causes the edges of shadows to be blurry.

Figure 20 *Water waves are often used to model the behavior of light waves.*

Interference

Interference is a wave interaction that occurs when two or more waves overlap. Overlapping waves can combine by constructive or destructive interference.

Constructive Interference When waves combine by *constructive interference,* the resulting wave has a greater amplitude than the individual waves had. Constructive interference of light waves can be observed when light of one wavelength shines through two small slits onto a screen. The light on the screen will appear as a series of alternating bright and dark bands. The bright bands result from light waves combining through constructive interference to create a light wave with a greater amplitude.

Two lamps are brighter than one, but it's not because of constructive interference. It's because two lamps produce more energy in the form of photons than one lamp. As a result, the light has a greater intensity, which makes the room brighter.

Destructive Interference When waves combine by *destructive interference,* the resulting wave has a smaller amplitude than the individual waves had. Therefore, when light waves interfere destructively, the result will be dimmer light.

You do not see constructive or destructive interference of white light. To understand why, remember that white light is composed of waves with many different wavelengths. The waves rarely line up to combine in total destructive interference. However, if light of only one wavelength is used, both constructive and destructive interference are easily observed, as illustrated in **Figure 21.**

Figure 21 Constructive and Destructive Interference

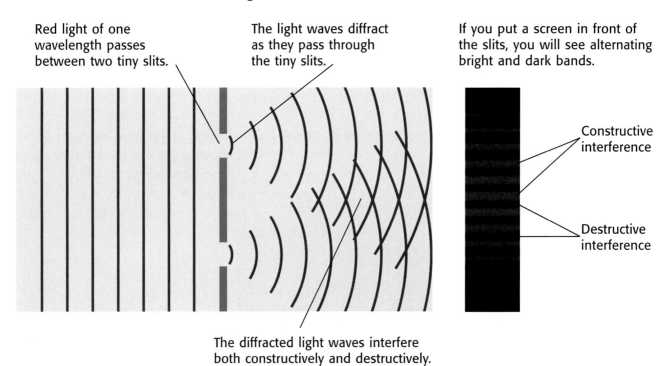

Red light of one wavelength passes between two tiny slits.

The light waves diffract as they pass through the tiny slits.

If you put a screen in front of the slits, you will see alternating bright and dark bands.

Constructive interference

Destructive interference

The diffracted light waves interfere both constructively and destructively.

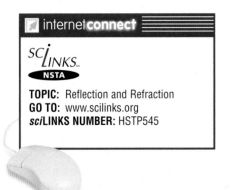

internet**connect**

SCi*LINKS*

NSTA

TOPIC: Reflection and Refraction
GO TO: www.scilinks.org
*sci***LINKS NUMBER:** HSTP545

REVIEW

1. Explain the difference between absorption and scattering.

2. Why does a straw look bent in a glass of water?

3. Why do the edges of shadows seem blurry? Explain your answer.

4. **Applying Concepts** Explain why you can see your reflection on a spoon but not on a piece of cloth.

Light and Color

Terms to Learn

transmission
transparent
translucent
opaque
pigment

What You'll Do

◆ Name and describe the three ways light interacts with matter.
◆ Explain how the color of an object is determined.
◆ Compare the primary colors of light and the primary pigments.

Have you ever wondered what gives an object its color? You already know that white light is made of all the colors of light. But when you see fruit in white light, you see color. For example, strawberries are red and bananas are yellow. Why aren't they all white? And how can a soda bottle be green and let you see through it at the same time? To answer these questions, you must first learn how light interacts with matter. Then you will understand why objects have different colors.

Light and Matter

When light strikes any form of matter, it can interact with the matter in three different ways—it can be reflected, absorbed, or transmitted. You learned about reflection and absorption in the previous section. **Transmission** is the passing of light through matter. You see the transmission of light all the time. All of the light that reaches your eyes is transmitted through air. Light can interact with matter in several ways at the same time, as shown in **Figure 22.**

Figure 22 *Light is transmitted, reflected, and absorbed when it strikes the glass in a window.*

You can see the glass and your reflection in it because light is **reflected** off the glass.

You can see objects outside because light is **transmitted** through the glass.

The glass feels warm when you touch it because some light is **absorbed** by the glass.

Types of Matter Matter through which visible light is easily transmitted is said to be **transparent.** Air, glass, and water are examples of transparent matter. You can see objects clearly when you view them through transparent matter.

Sometimes windows in bathrooms are made of frosted glass. If you try to look through one of these types of windows, you will see only blurry shapes. You can't see clearly through a frosted window because it is translucent. **Translucent** matter transmits light but also scatters the light as it passes through the matter. Wax paper is an example of translucent matter.

Matter that does not transmit any light is said to be **opaque.** You cannot see through opaque objects. Metal, wood, and this book are examples of opaque objects. You can compare transparent, translucent, and opaque matter in **Figure 23.**

Figure 23 What's for Lunch?

Translucent wax paper makes it a little harder to see exactly what's for lunch.

Transparent plastic makes it easy to see what you are having for lunch.

Opaque aluminum foil makes it impossible to see your lunch without unwrapping it.

Colors of Objects

How does the interaction of light with matter determine an object's color? You already know that the color of light is determined by the wavelength of the light wave. Red has the longest wavelength, violet has the shortest wavelength, and other colors have wavelengths in between.

The color that an object appears to be is determined by the wavelengths of light that reach your eyes. Light reaches your eyes after being reflected off an object or after being transmitted through an object. After reaching your eyes, light is converted into electrical impulses and interpreted by your brain as colors.

What's a bean's favorite color? It's not a riddle, it's an experiment on page 716 of the LabBook.

Colors of Opaque Objects When white light strikes a colored opaque object, some colors of light are absorbed and some are reflected. Only the light that is reflected reaches your eyes and is detected. Therefore, the colors of light that are reflected by an opaque object determine the color you see. For example, if your sweater reflects blue light and absorbs all other colors, you will see that the sweater is blue. Another example is shown in **Figure 24.**

✓ Self-Check

If blue light shines on a white sheet of paper, what color does the paper appear to be?

(Turn to page 724 to check your answer.)

Figure 24 *When white light shines on a strawberry, only red light is reflected. All other colors of light are absorbed. Therefore, the strawberry looks red to you.*

If green objects reflect green light and red objects reflect red light, what colors of light are reflected by the cow shown at right? Remember that white light includes all colors of light. So white objects—such as the white hair in the cow's hide—appear white because all the colors of light are reflected. On the other hand, black is the absence of color. When light strikes a black object, all the colors are absorbed.

Colors of Transparent and Translucent Objects
The color of transparent and translucent objects is determined differently from the color of opaque objects. Ordinary window glass is colorless in white light because it transmits all the colors that strike it. However, some transparent objects are colored. When you look through colored transparent or translucent objects, you see the color of light that was transmitted through the material. All the other colors were absorbed, as shown in **Figure 25.**

Figure 25 *This bottle is green because the plastic transmits only green light.*

Mixing Colors of Light

In order to get white light, you need to combine all colors of light, right? Well, that's one way of doing it. You can also get white light by adding just three colors of light together—red, blue, and green—as shown in **Figure 26.** In fact, these three colors can be combined in different ratios to produce all colors of visible light. Red, blue, and green are therefore called the *primary colors of light.*

Color Addition When colors of light combine, more wavelengths of light are present. Therefore, combining colors of light is called color addition. When two primary colors are added together, a *secondary color* is produced. The secondary colors are cyan (blue plus green), magenta (blue plus red), and yellow (red plus green).

Figure 26 *Primary colors—written in white—combine to produce white light. Secondary colors—written in black—are the result of two primary colors added together.*

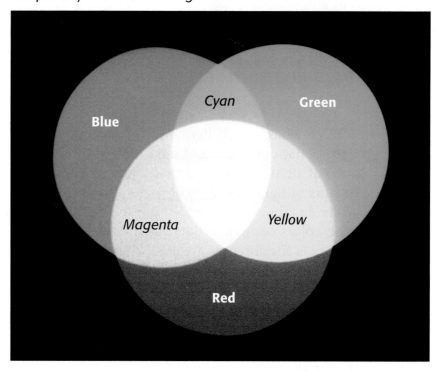

Mixing Colors of Pigment

If you have ever tried mixing paints in art class, you know that you can't make white paint by mixing red, blue, and green paint. The difference between mixing paint and mixing light is due to the fact that paint contains pigments. A **pigment** is a material that gives a substance its color by absorbing some colors of light and reflecting others.

Almost everything contains pigments. In fact, pigments give objects color. Chlorophyll and melanin are two examples of pigments. Chlorophyll gives plants a green color, and melanin gives your skin its color.

Color Subtraction Each pigment absorbs at least one color of light. When you mix pigments together, more colors of light are absorbed, or subtracted. Therefore, mixing colors of pigments is called color subtraction.

The *primary pigments* are yellow, cyan, and magenta. They can be combined to produce any other color. In fact, all the colors in this book were produced by using just the primary pigments and black ink. The black ink was used to provide contrast to the images. **Figure 27** shows how the four pigments combine to produce many different colors.

Geology
C O N N E C T I O N

Minerals are naturally occurring crystalline solids. A blue mineral called azurite was once used by European painters as a pigment in paint. But these painters didn't realize that azurite changes into another mineral over time. The new mineral, malachite, is green. So some paintings that once had beautiful blue skies now have skies that look greenish.

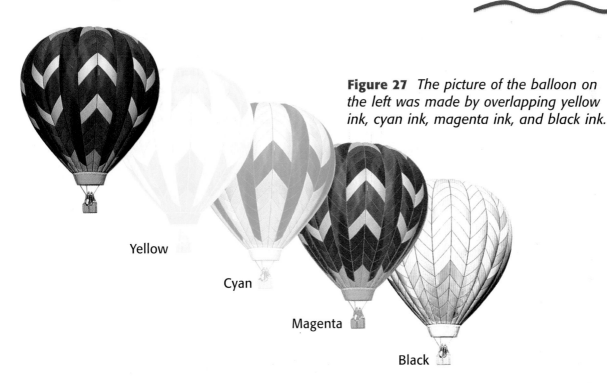

Figure 27 *The picture of the balloon on the left was made by overlapping yellow ink, cyan ink, magenta ink, and black ink.*

Yellow

Cyan

Magenta

Black

REVIEW

1. Describe three different ways light interacts with matter.

2. What are the primary colors of light, and why are they called primary colors?

3. Describe the difference between the primary colors of light and the primary pigments.

4. **Applying Concepts** Explain what happens to the different colors of light when white light shines on a violet object.

internetconnect

*SCi*LINKS
NSTA

TOPIC: Colors
GO TO: www.scilinks.org
*sci*LINKS NUMBER: HSTP550

Chapter Highlights

SECTION 1

Vocabulary

electromagnetic wave *(p. 564)*

radiation *(p. 565)*

Section Notes

- Light is an electromagnetic (EM) wave. An electromagnetic wave is a wave that travels as vibrating electric and magnetic fields. EM waves require no medium through which to travel.

- Electromagnetic waves are produced by the vibration of electrically charged particles.

- The speed of light in a vacuum is 300,000,000 m/s.

SECTION 2

Vocabulary

electromagnetic spectrum *(p. 567)*

Section Notes

- All EM waves travel at the speed of light. EM waves differ only by wavelength and frequency.

- The entire range of EM waves is called the electromagnetic spectrum.

- Radio waves are most often used for communication.

- Microwaves are used for cooking and in radar.

- Infrared waves have shorter wavelengths and higher frequencies than microwaves. The absorption of infrared waves is felt as an increase in temperature.

- Visible light is the very narrow range of wavelengths that humans can see. Different wavelengths are seen as different colors.

- Ultraviolet light is useful for killing bacteria and for producing vitamin D in the body, but overexposure can cause health problems.

- X rays and gamma rays are EM waves that are often used in medicine. Overexposure to these EM waves can damage or kill living cells.

☑ Skills Check

Math Concepts

DISTANCE To calculate the distance that light travels in space, multiply the amount of time light travels by the speed of light in a vacuum. The speed of light in a vacuum is 300,000,000 m/s. If light from a star travels for 192 seconds before reaching a planet, then the distance the light traveled can be calculated as follows:

$$\text{distance} = \text{speed of light} \times \text{time}$$

$$\text{distance} = 300{,}000{,}000 \text{ m/s} \times 192 \text{ s}$$

$$\text{distance} = 57{,}600{,}000{,}000 \text{ m}$$

Visual Understanding

THE PRODUCTION OF LIGHT Light is produced by the vibration of electrically charged particles. Repeated vibrations of these particles, or electrons, release tiny "packets" of energy called photons. Review Figure 2 on page 565 to see how light and other electromagnetic waves are the result of electron movement.

SECTION 3

Vocabulary
reflection *(p. 575)*
law of reflection *(p. 575)*
absorption *(p. 576)*
scattering *(p. 577)*
refraction *(p. 577)*
diffraction *(p. 579)*
interference *(p. 579)*

Section Notes
- Two types of reflection are regular and diffuse reflection.

- Absorption and scattering cause light beams to become dimmer with distance.

- How much a light beam bends during refraction depends on the light's wavelength.

- Light waves diffract more when traveling through a narrow opening.

- Interference of light waves can cause bright and dark bands.

SECTION 4

Vocabulary
transmission *(p. 581)*
transparent *(p. 582)*
translucent *(p. 582)*
opaque *(p. 582)*
pigment *(p. 584)*

Section Notes
- Objects are classified as transparent, translucent, or opaque depending on their ability to transmit light.

- Colors of opaque objects are determined by the color of light they reflect. White opaque objects reflect all colors and black opaque objects absorb all colors.

- Colors of transparent and translucent objects are determined by the color of light they transmit. All other colors are absorbed.

- White light is a mixture of all colors of light. The primary colors of light are red, blue, and green.

- Pigments give objects color. The primary pigments are magenta, cyan, and yellow.

Labs
What Color of Light Is Best for Green Plants? *(p. 716)*
Which Color Is Hottest? *(p. 717)*
Mixing Colors *(p. 718)*

Chapter Review

To complete the following sentences, choose the correct term from each pair of terms listed below:

1. ___?___ is the transfer of energy by electromagnetic waves. *(Radiation or Scattering)*

2. This book is a(n) ___?___ object. *(translucent or opaque)*

3. ___?___ is a wave interaction that occurs when two or more waves overlap and combine. *(Diffraction or Interference)*

4. Light is a type of ___?___. *(electromagnetic wave or electromagnetic spectrum)*

5. Light travels through an object during ___?___. *(absorption or transmission)*

UNDERSTANDING CONCEPTS

Multiple Choice

6. Electromagnetic waves transmit
   a. charges.
   b. fields.
   c. matter.
   d. energy.

7. Objects that transmit light easily are
   a. opaque.
   b. translucent.
   c. transparent.
   d. colored.

8. You can see yourself in a mirror because of
   a. absorption.
   b. scattering.
   c. regular reflection.
   d. diffuse reflection.

9. Shadows have blurry edges because of
   a. diffuse reflection.
   b. scattering.
   c. diffraction.
   d. refraction.

10. Microwaves are often used for
    a. cooking.
    b. broadcasting AM radio.
    c. cancer treatment.
    d. All of the above

11. What color of light is produced when red light is added to green light?
    a. cyan
    b. blue
    c. yellow
    d. white

12. Prisms produce rainbows through
    a. reflection.
    b. refraction.
    c. diffraction.
    d. interference.

13. Which type of electromagnetic wave travels the fastest in a vacuum?
    a. radio waves
    b. visible light
    c. gamma rays
    d. They all travel at the same speed.

14. Electromagnetic waves are made of
    a. vibrating particles.
    b. vibrating charged particles.
    c. vibrating electric and magnetic fields.
    d. electricity and magnetism.

Short Answer

15. Name two ways EM waves differ from one another.

16. Describe how an electromagnetic wave is produced.

17. Why is it difficult to see through glass that has frost on it?

Concept Mapping

18. Use the following terms to create a concept map: light, matter, reflection, absorption, scattering, transmission.

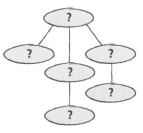

19. A tern is a type of bird that dives underwater to catch fish. When a young tern begins learning to catch fish, it is rarely successful. The tern has to learn that when a fish appears to be in a certain place underwater, the fish is actually in a slightly different place. Explain why the tern sees the fish in the wrong place.

20. Radio waves and gamma rays are both types of electromagnetic waves. Exposure to radio waves does not harm the human body, whereas exposure to gamma rays can be extremely dangerous. What is the difference between these types of EM waves? Why are gamma rays more dangerous?

21. If you look around a parking lot during the summer, you might notice sun shades set up in the windshields of cars. Explain how the sun shades help keep the inside of a car cool.

MATH IN SCIENCE

22. Calculate the time it takes for light from the sun to reach Mercury. Mercury is 54,900,000,000 m away from the sun.

INTERPRETING GRAPHICS

23. Each of the pictures below shows the effects of a wave interaction of light. Identify the interaction involved.

a

b

c

Reading Check-up

Take a minute to review your answers to the Pre-Reading Questions found at the bottom of page 562. Have your answers changed? If necessary, revise your answers based on what you have learned since you began this chapter.

Science, Technology, and Society

Fireflies Light the Way

Just as beams of light from coastal lighthouses warn boats of approaching danger, scientists are using the light of an unlikely source—fireflies—to warn food inspectors of life-threatening bacterial contamination! Thousands of people die each year from meat contaminated with bacteria. The light from fireflies is being used to study several diseases, waste-water treatment, and environmental protection as well!

Nature's Guiding Light

A number of organisms, including some fishes, squids, beetles, and bacteria, emit light. Fireflies, in particular, use this light to attract mates. How do these organisms use energy to emit light?

Remarkably, all of these organisms use one enzyme to make light, an enzyme called *luciferase.* This enzyme breaks down *adenosine triphosphate* (ATP) to create energy. This energy is used to excite electrons to produce light in the form of a glow or flash. Fireflies are very effective light bulbs. Nearly 100 percent of the energy they get from ATP is given off as light. Only 10 percent of energy given off by electrical light bulbs is in the form of light; the other 90 percent is thermal energy!

Harnessing Life's Light

How have scientists harnessed the firefly's ability to produce light to find bacteria? Researchers have found the gene responsible for making luciferase. Scientists have taken the gene from fireflies that makes luciferase and inserted it into a virus that preys on bacteria. The virus isn't harmful to humans and can be mixed into meat to help scientists detect bacteria. When the virus infects the bacteria, it transfers the gene into the genetic machinery of the bacteria. This bacteria then produces luciferase and glows!

▲ *The firefly* (Photuris pyralis) *is helping food inspectors save thousands of lives each year!*

This process is being used to find a number of dangerous bacteria that contaminate foods, including *Salmonella* and *Escherichia coli.* These bacteria are responsible for thousands of deaths each year. Not only is the test effective, it is fast. Before researchers developed this test, it took up to 3 days to determine whether food was contaminated by bacteria. By that time, the food was already at the grocery store!

Think About It!

▶ What color of light would you hypothesize gives plants the most energy? Investigate, and see if your hypothesis is right!

Eureka!

It's a Heat Wave!

Percy L. Spencer never stopped looking for answers. In fact, he patented 120 inventions in his 39 years with the company Raytheon. During a routine visit to one of the Raytheon laboratories in 1946, Spencer found that a candy bar had melted inside his coat pocket. He could have just chalked this up to body heat, but he didn't. Instead, he took a closer look at his surroundings and noticed a nearby magnetron—a tube he designed to produce microwaves for radar systems.

A Popping Test

This made Spencer curious. Did the microwaves from the magnetron melt the candy bar, and if so, could microwaves be used to heat other things? Spencer answered his questions by putting a bag of unpopped corn kernels next to a magnetron. The kernels popped! Spencer had just made the first "microwave" popcorn! The test was a huge success. This simple experiment showed that a magnetron could heat foods with microwaves, and it could heat them quickly. When Spencer patented his invention in 1953, he called it a "High Frequency Dielectric Heating Apparatus."

Perfect Timing!

Spencer originally designed magnetrons for radar machines used in World War II. Discovering another use for them was well timed. After the war, the military had little use for the 10,000 magnetrons a week that Raytheon could manufacture. So Raytheon decided to use the magnetrons to power Spencer's "High Frequency Dielectric

The first microwave ▲ *oven, known as a "Radarange," 1953*

Heating Apparatus." But first the company had to come up with a simpler name! The winning entry in the renaming contest was "Radar Range," which later became one word, *Radarange*.

An Inconvenient Convenience

The first Radaranges had a few drawbacks. For one thing, they were very expensive. They also weighed over 340 kg and were 1.6 m tall. Try fitting that on your kitchen counter! Because the Radarange was so large and expensive, only restaurants, railroad companies, and cruise ships used them. By 1967, improvements in the design made the Radarange compact and affordable, similar to the microwave ovens of today.

Now You're Cooking!

Just how do microwave ovens cook food? It just so happens that microwaves are absorbed by water molecules in the food being cooked. When water molecules throughout the food absorb microwaves, they start to move faster. As a result, the food's temperature increases. Leftovers anyone?

Find Out for Yourself

▶ Microwaves make water molecules in food move faster. This is what increases the temperature of food that is cooked in a microwave. But did you know that most dishes will not heat up in a microwave oven if there is no food on them? To discover why, find out what most dishes are made of. Then infer why empty dishes do not heat up in a microwave.

Light and Our World

Pre-Reading
Questions

1. Name three sources of light.

2. How do mirrors and lenses form images?

3. How does the human eye detect light?

BRIGHT LIGHTS, NEON LIGHTS

Look at the multicolored arcs of light in this photo. These "neon" lights are made by passing electric current through tubes filled with certain gases. Neon, argon, krypton, helium, and mercury gases each light up as a different dazzling color. In this chapter, you will learn how different kinds of light are produced and how images that reflect or focus light are formed. You will also learn how mirrors, lenses, and high-tech instruments focus or transmit light energy.

MIRROR, MIRROR

In this activity, you will explore images formed by plane mirrors.

Procedure

1. **Tape** a sheet of **graph paper** on your desk. Stand a **plane mirror** straight up in the middle of the paper. Hold the mirror in place with small pieces of **modeling clay.**

2. Count four grid squares from the mirror, and place a **pencil** there. Look in the mirror. How many squares behind the mirror is the image of the pencil? Move the pencil farther away from the mirror. How did the image change?

3. Replace the mirror with **colored glass.** Look at the pencil image in the glass. Compare it with the image you saw in the mirror.

4. Use a pencil to draw a square on the graph paper in front of the glass. Looking through the glass, trace the image of the square on the paper behind the glass. Using a **metric ruler,** measure and compare the sizes of the two squares.

Analysis

5. How does the distance from an object to a plane mirror compare with the apparent distance from the mirror to the object's image behind the mirror?

6. In general, how does the size of an object compare with that of its image in a plane mirror?

Light Sources

Terms to Learn

luminous   neon light
illuminated   vapor light
incandescent light
fluorescent light

What You'll Do

◆ Compare luminous and
   illuminated objects.
◆ Name four ways light can be
   produced.

Although visible light represents only a small portion of the electromagnetic spectrum, it has a huge effect on your life. Visible light from the sun gives plants the energy necessary for growth and reproduction. Without plants at the base of the food chain, few other life-forms could exist. And of course, without visible light, you could not see anything. Your eyes are totally useless without sources of visible light.

Light Source or Reflection?

If you look at a television in a bright room, you see the cabinet around the television as well as the image on the screen. But if you look at the same television in the dark, only the image on the screen shows up. The difference is that the screen is a light source, while the cabinet around the television isn't.

You can see a light source even in the dark because its light passes directly into your eyes. Flames, light bulbs, fireflies, and the sun are all light sources. Scientists describe objects that produce visible light as being **luminous** (LOO muh nuhs). **Figure 1** shows examples of luminous objects.

Most of the objects around you are not light sources. But you can still see them because light from a light source reflects off the objects and then travels to your eyes. Scientists describe a visible object that is not a light source as being **illuminated** (i LOO muh NAYT ed).

Astronomy

C O N N E C T I O N

Sometimes the moon shines so brightly that you might think there is a lot of "moonlight." But did you know that moonlight is actually sunlight? The moon does not give off light. You can see the moon because it is illuminated by light from the sun. You see different phases of the moon because light from the sun shines only on the part of the moon that faces the sun.

Figure 1 *Television screens, fires, and fireflies are luminous objects.*

Producing Light

Light sources produce light in many ways. For example, if you heat a piece of metal enough, it will visibly glow red hot. Light can also be produced chemically, like the light produced by a firefly. Light can even be produced by sending an electric current through certain gases.

Incandescent Light If you have ever looked inside a toaster while toasting a piece of bread, you may have seen thin wires or bars glowing red. The wires give off energy as light when heated to a high temperature. Light produced by hot objects is called **incandescent** (IN kuhn DES uhnt) **light. Figure 2** shows a source of incandescent light that you have in your home.

Sources of incandescent light also release a large amount of thermal energy. Sometimes this thermal energy is useful because it can be used to cook food or to warm a room. But often this thermal energy is not used for anything. For example, the thermal energy given off by a light bulb is not very useful.

Halogen lights are another type of incandescent light. They were originally developed for use on the wings of airplanes, but they are now used in homes and in car headlights. **Figure 3** shows how halogen lights work.

Figure 2 *Light bulbs produce incandescent light.*

ⓐ Wires and the filament carry an electric current.

ⓑ Electric current in the tungsten filament causes the filament's temperature to increase.

ⓒ The hot filament gives off visible light and thermal energy.

Figure 3 *The way in which the tungsten from the filament can be used over and over again prevents the bulb from burning out too quickly.*

A tungsten filament, heated to about 3,000°C, glows very brightly and vaporizes.

The tungsten vapor (red particles) travels to the glass wall, where it cools to about 800°C.

At the lower temperature, tungsten combines with a halogen gas (blue particles) to form a new compound.

The new compound travels back to the filament, where it breaks down because of the high temperature. Tungsten from the compound is deposited on the filament and can be used again.

Fluorescent Light The light that comes from the long, cylindrical bulbs in your classroom is called fluorescent light. **Fluorescent** (FLOO uh RES uhnt) **light** is visible light emitted by a phosphor particle when it absorbs energy such as ultraviolet light. Fluorescent light is sometimes called cool light because less thermal energy is produced than with incandescent light. **Figure 4** shows how a fluorescent light bulb works.

Figure 4 Fluorescent Light

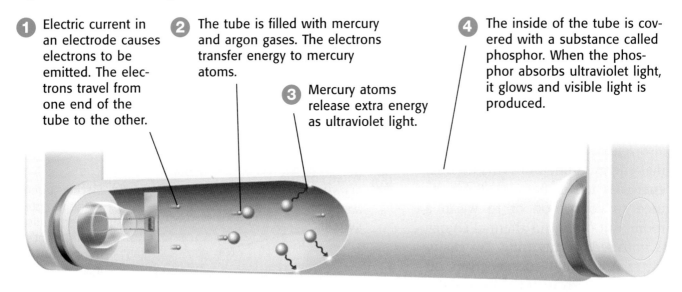

1 Electric current in an electrode causes electrons to be emitted. The electrons travel from one end of the tube to the other.

2 The tube is filled with mercury and argon gases. The electrons transfer energy to mercury atoms.

3 Mercury atoms release extra energy as ultraviolet light.

4 The inside of the tube is covered with a substance called phosphor. When the phosphor absorbs ultraviolet light, it glows and visible light is produced.

Neon Light The visible light emitted by atoms of certain gases, such as neon, when they absorb and then release energy is called **neon light. Figure 5** shows how neon light is produced.

A true neon light—one in which the tube is filled with neon gas—glows red. Other colors are produced when the tubes are filled with different gases. For example, sodium gas produces yellow light, and krypton gas produces purple light. A mixture of argon gas and mercury gas produces blue light.

Figure 5 Neon Light

1 Electric current in an electrode causes electrons to be emitted. The electrons travel from one end of the tube to the other.

2 The tube is filled with gas. The electrons transfer energy to gas particles during collisions.

3 The gas particles release extra energy as visible light.

Vapor Light   Another type of incandescent light, called **vapor light,** is produced when electrons combine with gaseous metal atoms. Street lamps usually contain either mercury vapor or sodium vapor. You can tell the difference by the color of the light. If the light is bluish, the lamp contains mercury vapor. If the light is orange, the lamp contains sodium vapor. Both kinds of vapor lamps produce light in similar ways, as described in **Figure 6.**

Stop! and go read about the invention of traffic lights on page 618.

Figure 6 *Sodium vapor lights are very bright and do not produce much glare.*

1. High-voltage electric current creates an arc of electrons between two electrodes.

2. The arc passes through a gas called xenon, heating the gas to a high temperature.

3. The hot xenon vaporizes sodium in the tube and causes the sodium atoms to lose electrons.

4. When the electrons recombine with sodium, light is produced.

REVIEW

1. Identify five illuminated objects in your classroom, and name the luminous object (or objects) providing the light.

2. Describe places where you might use incandescent light, fluorescent light, neon light, and vapor light.

3. Describe how fluorescent light is similar to neon light.

4. **Applying Concepts**   Halogen bulbs emit bright light from small bulbs. They also emit thermal energy. Would you use a halogen bulb to study by? Why or why not?

internetconnect

SciLINKS
NSTA

TOPIC: Producing Light
GO TO: www.scilinks.org
*sci***LINKS NUMBER:** HSTP555

Mirrors and Lenses

Look at the letters on the front of the ambulance shown at right. Do you notice anything strange about them? Some of the letters are backward, and they don't seem to spell a word.

The letters spell the word AMBULANCE when viewed in a mirror. Images in mirrors are reversed left to right. The word *ambulance* is spelled backward so that people driving cars can read it when they see the ambulance in their rearview mirror. To understand how images are formed in mirrors, you must first learn how to use rays to trace the path of light waves.

Rays Show the Path of Light Waves

Light is an electromagnetic wave. Light waves travel from their source in all directions. If you could trace the path of one wave as it travels away from a light source, you would find that the path is a straight line. Because light waves travel in straight lines, you can use an arrow called a *ray* to show the path and the direction of a light wave. **Figure 7** shows some rays coming from a light bulb.

Rays can also be used to show the path of light waves after the waves have been reflected or refracted. Therefore, rays in ray diagrams are often used to show changes in the direction light travels after being reflected by mirrors or refracted by lenses. You'll learn more about ray diagrams a little later in this section.

Figure 7 *Rays from this light bulb show the path and direction of some light waves produced by the bulb.*

Mirrors Reflect Light

Have you ever looked at your reflection in a metal spoon? The polished metal of the spoon acts like a mirror, but not like the mirror in your bathroom! If you look on one side of the spoon, your face is upside down. But if you look on the other side, your face is right side up. Why?

The shape of a reflecting surface affects the way light reflects from it. Therefore, the image you see in your bathroom mirror differs from the image you see in a spoon. Mirrors are classified by their shape. The different shapes are called plane, concave, and convex.

Plane Mirrors Most mirrors, such as the one in your bathroom, are plane mirrors. A **plane mirror** is a mirror with a flat surface. When you look in a plane mirror, your reflection is upright and is the same size as you are. Images in plane mirrors are reversed left to right, as shown in **Figure 8.**

When you look in a plane mirror, your image appears to be the same distance behind the mirror as you are in front of it. Why does your image seem to be behind the mirror? Because mirrors are opaque objects, light does not travel through them. But when light reflects off the mirror, your brain interprets the reflected light as if it travels in a straight line from behind the mirror. A *virtual image* is an image through which light does not actually travel. The image formed by a plane mirror is a virtual image. The ray diagram in **Figure 9** explains how light travels when you look into a mirror.

Figure 8 *Rearview mirrors in cars are plane mirrors.*

Figure 9 *The rays show how light reaches your eyes. The dotted lines show where the light appears to come from.*

Light reflects off of you and strikes the mirror, where it is reflected again. Some of the light reflecting off the mirror enters your eyes.

Your image appears to be behind the mirror because your brain assumes that the light rays that enter your eyes travel in a straight line from an object to your eyes.

Concave Mirrors Mirrors that are curved inward, such as the inside of a spoon, are called **concave mirrors.** Because the surfaces of concave mirrors are curved, the images formed by concave mirrors differ from the images formed by plane mirrors. To understand how concave mirrors form images, you must learn the terms illustrated in **Figure 10.**

Figure 10 *The image formed by a concave mirror depends on its optical axis, its focal point, and its focal length.*

a A straight line drawn outward from the center of the mirror is called the *optical axis.*

b Light beams entering the mirror parallel to the optical axis are reflected through a single point, called the **focal point.**

c The distance between the mirror's surface and the focal point is called the *focal length.*

You already learned that plane mirrors can form only virtual images. Concave mirrors also form virtual images, but they can form *real images* too. A real image is an image through which light actually passes. A real image can be projected onto a screen; a virtual image cannot. To find out what kind of image a concave mirror forms, you can create a ray diagram. Just remember the following three rules when drawing ray diagrams for concave mirrors:

1 Draw a ray from the top of the object parallel to the optical axis. This ray will reflect through the focal point.

2 If the object is more than one focal length away from the mirror, draw a ray from the top of the object through the focal point. This ray will reflect parallel to the optical axis.

3 If the object is less than one focal length away from the mirror, draw a ray through the top of the object as if it came from the focal point. This ray will reflect parallel to the optical axis.

Is an image real or virtual? Turn to page 720 in the LabBook to see the difference.

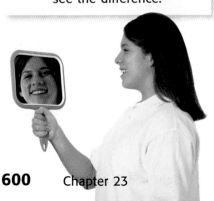

Real or Virtual For each ray diagram, you need to draw only two rays from the top of the object to find what kind of image is formed. If the reflected rays cross in front of the mirror, a real image is formed. The point where the rays cross is the top of the image. If the reflected rays do not cross, trace the reflected rays in straight lines behind the mirror. Those lines will cross to show where a virtual image is formed. Study **Figure 11** to better understand ray diagrams.

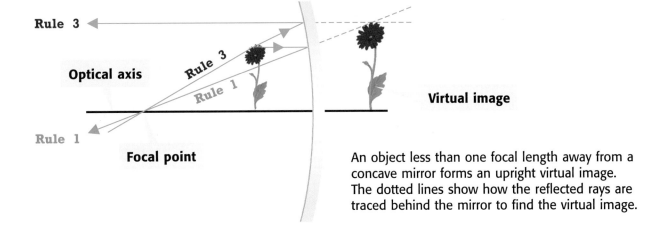

Figure 11 *The type of image formed by a concave mirror depends on the distance between the object and the mirror as well as the focal length.*

An object more than one focal length away from a concave mirror forms an upside-down real image.

An object less than one focal length away from a concave mirror forms an upright virtual image. The dotted lines show how the reflected rays are traced behind the mirror to find the virtual image.

Neither Real Nor Virtual If an object is placed at the focal point of a concave mirror, no image will form. Rule 2 explains why this happens—all rays that pass through the focal point on their way to the mirror will reflect parallel to the optical axis. Because all the reflected rays are parallel, they will never cross in front of or behind the mirror. If you place a light source at the focal point of a concave mirror, the light will reflect outward in a powerful light beam. Therefore, concave mirrors are used in car headlights and flashlights.

Convex Mirrors If you look at your reflection in the back of a spoon, you will notice that your image is right side up and small. The back of a spoon is a **convex mirror**—a mirror that curves out toward you. **Figure 12** shows how an image is formed by a convex mirror. All images formed by convex mirrors are virtual, upright, and smaller than the original object. Convex mirrors are useful because they produce images of a large area. This is the reason convex mirrors are often used for security in stores and factories. Convex mirrors are also used as side mirrors in cars and trucks.

Figure 12 *All images formed by convex mirrors are formed behind the mirror. Therefore, all images formed by convex mirrors are virtual.*

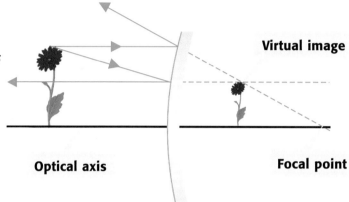

Virtual image

Optical axis

Focal point

 APPLY

Convex Mirrors Help Drivers

The passenger side mirrors of most cars and trucks are convex mirrors. Convex mirrors are used because they help the driver see more of the traffic around the car than a plane mirror would. However, these mirrors are often stamped with the words "Objects in Mirror Are Closer Than They Appear." What property of convex mirrors makes this warning necessary? Why do you think the warning is important for drivers?

REVIEW

1. How is a concave mirror different from a convex mirror?

2. Draw a ray diagram showing how a concave mirror forms a real image.

3. **Applying Concepts** Plane mirrors, concave mirrors, and convex mirrors are useful at different times. Describe a situation in which you would use each type of mirror.

Lenses Refract Light

What do cameras, binoculars, telescopes, and movie projectors have in common? They all use lenses to create images. A **lens** is a curved, transparent object that forms an image by refracting, or bending, light. Like mirrors, lenses are classified by their shape. There are two types of lenses—convex and concave.

Convex Lenses A **convex lens** is thicker in the middle than at the edges. When light rays enter a convex lens, they refract toward the center. Light rays that enter a convex lens parallel to the optical axis are refracted so that they go through a focal point. The amount of refraction and the focal length depend on the curvature of the lens, as shown in **Figure 13.** Light rays that pass through the center of a lens are not refracted.

Convex lenses form many different kinds of images, depending on the focal length of the lens and the position of the object. For example, whenever you use a magnifying glass, you are using a convex lens to form an enlarged, virtual image. **Figure 14** illustrates how a magnifying lens works.

Figure 13 *Light rays refract more through convex lenses with greater curvature than through convex lenses with less curvature.*

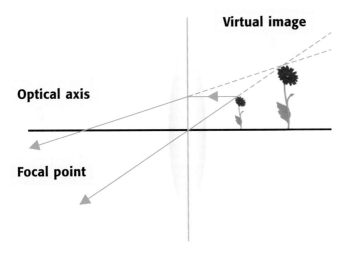

Figure 14 *If an object is less than one focal length away from a convex lens, a virtual image is formed. The image is larger than the object and can be seen only by looking into the lens.*

Convex lenses can also form real images. Movie projectors use convex lenses to focus real images on a screen. Cameras use convex lenses to focus real images on a piece of film. Both types of images are shown in **Figure 15.**

Figure 15 *Convex lenses can also form real images.*

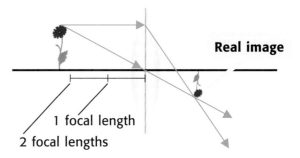

Real image

a If the object is located between one and two focal lengths away from the lens, a real, enlarged image is formed far away from the lens. This is how movie projectors produce images on large screens.

b If the object is located more than two focal lengths away from the lens, a real, reduced image is formed close to the lens. This is how the lens of a camera forms images on the film.

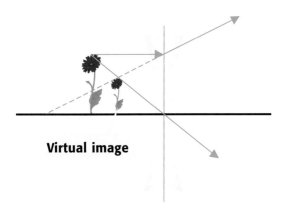

Virtual image

Figure 16 *Concave lenses form reduced virtual images. If you trace the refracted rays in a straight line behind a concave lens, you can determine where the virtual image is formed.*

Concave Lenses A **concave lens** is thinner in the middle than at the edges. Light rays entering a concave lens parallel to the optical axis always bend away from each other toward the edges of the lens; the rays never meet. Therefore, concave lenses can never form a real image. Instead, they form virtual images, as shown in **Figure 16.** Concave lenses are sometimes combined with other lenses in telescopes. The combination of lenses produces clearer images of distant objects. You will read about another, more common use for concave lenses in the next section.

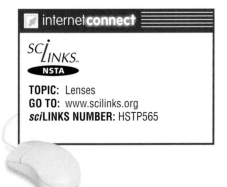

internetconnect

SC*i*LINKS
NSTA

TOPIC: Lenses
GO TO: www.scilinks.org
*sci*LINKS **NUMBER:** HSTP565

REVIEW

1. Draw a ray diagram showing how a magnifying glass forms a virtual image.

2. Explain why a concave lens cannot form a real image.

3. **Applying Concepts** Your teacher sometimes uses an overhead projector to show transparencies on a screen. What type of lens does an overhead projector use?

Light and Sight

Terms to Learn

cornea   iris
pupil   retina

What You'll Do

♦ Identify the parts of the human eye, and describe their functions.
♦ Describe some common vision problems, and explain how they can be corrected.

When you look around, you can see objects both near and far. You can also see the different colors of the objects. You see luminous objects because they produce their own light, which is detected by your eyes. You see all other objects (illuminated objects) because light reflecting off the objects enters your eyes. But how do your eyes work, and what causes people to have problems with their vision? Read on to find out.

How You Detect Light

Visible light is the part of the electromagnetic spectrum that can be detected by your eyes. The process by which your eye gathers light to form the images that you see involves several steps, as shown in **Figure 17.**

Figure 17 How Your Eyes Work

b Light then passes through the **pupil,** the opening to the inside of the eye.

a Light is refracted as it passes through the **cornea** (KOR nee uh), a transparent membrane that protects the eye.

c The size of the pupil is controlled by the **iris,** the colored part of the eye. In low light the pupil is large; in bright light the pupil is small.

d The lens of the eye is convex and refracts light to focus a real image on the back of the eye. Muscles around the lens change the thickness of the lens so that objects at different distances can be seen in focus.

e The back surface of the eye is called the **retina** (RET nuh). The light forming the real image is detected by receptors in the retina called *rods* and *cones.*

Light from a distant object

f Nerves attached to the rods and cones carry information to the brain about the light that strikes the retina.

Common Vision Problems

A person with normal vision can clearly see objects both close up and far away and can distinguish all colors of visible light. However, because the eye is complex, it's no surprise that many people have defects in their eyes that affect their vision. Luckily, some common vision problems can be easily corrected.

Nearsightedness and Farsightedness The lens of a properly working eye focuses light on the retina, so the images formed are always clear. Two common vision problems—nearsightedness and farsightedness—occur when light is not focused on the retina. A nearsighted person can see objects clearly only if the objects are nearby. Objects that are farther away look blurry. A farsighted person can see faraway objects clearly, but objects nearby look blurry. **Figure 18** explains how nearsightedness and farsightedness occur and how they can be corrected.

Figure 18 *Nearsightedness and farsightedness are common vision problems that can be corrected easily with glasses or contact lenses.*

Nearsightedness occurs when the eye is too long and the lens focuses light in front of the retina.

A **concave lens** placed in front of the eye refracts the light outward. The lens in the eye can then focus the light on the retina.

Farsightedness occurs when the eye is too short and the lens focuses light behind the retina.

A **convex lens** placed in front of the eye refracts the light and focuses it slightly. The lens in the eye can then focus the light on the retina.

Color Deficiency Roughly 5 to 8 percent of men and 0.5 percent of women in the world have *color deficiency,* often referred to as colorblindness. True colorblindness, in which a person can see only in black and white, is very rare. The majority of people with color deficiency have trouble distinguishing shades of red and green, or distinguishing red from green.

Color deficiency occurs when the cones in the retina do not receive the right instructions. The three types of cones are named for the colors they detect most—red, green, and blue. Each type of cone reacts to a range of wavelengths of light. A person with normal color vision can see all colors. But in some people, the cones get the wrong instructions and respond to the wrong wavelengths. That person may have trouble seeing certain colors. For example, he or she may see too much red or too much green, and not enough of the other color. **Figure 19** shows one type of test for color deficiency.

Biology
C O N N E C T I O N

Whether a person is colorblind depends on his or her genes. Certain genes give instructions to the cones for detecting certain wavelengths of light. If the genes give the wrong instructions, the person will have a color deficiency. A person needs one set of the genes that give the right instructions. Genes for color vision are on the X chromosome. Women have two X chromosomes, but men have only one. Therefore, men are more likely to be lacking a set of these genes and are more likely than women to be colorblind.

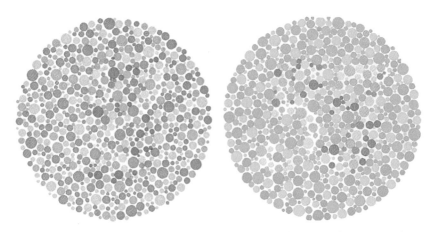

Figure 19 *Doctors use images like these to detect red-green color deficiency. Can you see a number in each image?*

REVIEW

1. Name the parts of the human eye, and describe what each part does.

2. What kind of lens would help a person who is nearsighted? What kind would help someone who is farsighted?

3. **Inferring Conclusions** Why do you think colorblindness cannot be corrected?

4. **Applying Concepts** Sometimes people are both nearsighted and farsighted. They wear glasses with two different kinds of lenses. Why are two lenses necessary?

internet**connect**

*sci*LINKS.
NSTA

TOPIC: The Eye
GO TO: www.scilinks.org
*sci***LINKS NUMBER:** HSTP570

Light Technology

Terms to Learn

laser   hologram

What You'll Do

◆ Explain how optical instruments use lenses and mirrors to form images.
◆ Explain how lasers work and what makes laser light different from non-laser light.
◆ Identify uses for lasers.
◆ Describe how optical fibers and polarizing filters work.

So far in this chapter, you have learned some ways light can be produced, how mirrors and lenses affect light, and some ways that people use mirrors and lenses. In this section, you will learn how different technological devices rely on mirrors and lenses and how mirrors help produce a type of light called laser light.

Optical Instruments

Optical instruments are devices that use arrangements of mirrors and lenses to help people make observations. Some optical instruments help you see objects that are very far away, and some help you see objects that are very small. Some optical instruments record images. The optical instrument that you are probably most familiar with is the camera.

Cameras The way a camera works is similar to the way your eye works. A camera has a lens that focuses light and has an opening that lets in light. The main difference between a camera and the eye is that the film in a camera permanently stores the images formed on it, but the images formed on the retina disappear when you stop looking at an object. **Figure 20** shows the parts of a camera and their functions.

Figure 20 The Parts of a Camera

The shutter opens and closes behind the lens to control how much light enters the camera. The longer the shutter is open, the more light enters the camera.

The film is coated with chemicals that react when they are struck by light. The result is an image stored on the film.

The lens of a camera is a convex lens that focuses light on the film. Moving the lens focuses light from objects at different distances.

The aperture is an opening in the lens that lets light into the camera. The larger the aperture is, the more light enters the camera.

Telescopes Astronomers use telescopes to study objects in space, such as the moon, planets, and stars. Telescopes are classified as either refracting or reflecting. Refracting telescopes use lenses to collect light, while reflecting telescopes use mirrors. **Figure 21** illustrates how simple refracting and reflecting telescopes work.

Figure 21 *Both refracting and reflecting telescopes are used to see objects that are far away.*

A **refracting telescope** has two convex lenses. Light enters through the objective lens and forms a real image. This real image is then magnified by the eyepiece lens. You see this magnified image when you look through the eyepiece lens.

A **reflecting telescope** has a concave mirror that collects and focuses light to form a real image. The light strikes a plane mirror that directs the light to the convex eyepiece lens, which magnifies the real image.

Light Microscopes Simple light microscopes are similar to refracting telescopes. They have two convex lenses—an objective lens, which is close to the object being studied, and an eyepiece lens, which you look through. The difference between microscopes and telescopes is that microscopes are used to see magnified images of tiny, nearby objects rather than images of large, distant objects.

> ✔ **Self-Check**
>
> Explain why the objective lens of a telescope cannot be a concave lens. *(See page 724 to check your answer.)*

Lasers and Laser Light

Have you ever seen a laser light show? Laser light beams flash through the air and sometimes form pictures on surfaces. A **laser** is a device that produces intense light of only one color and wavelength. Laser light is different from non-laser light in many ways. One important difference is that laser light is *coherent*. When light is coherent, light waves move together as they travel away from their source. The crests and troughs of coherent light waves line up, and the individual waves behave as one single wave. Other differences between laser light and non-laser light are shown in **Figure 22,** on the next page.

Figure 22 Laser Light Versus Non-laser Light

Laser light is tightly focused and does not spread out very much over long distances. Laser light contains light waves of only one wavelength and color.

Non-laser light spreads out greatly even over short distances. It may contain light waves of many different wavelengths and colors.

How Lasers Produce Light The word *laser* stands for **l**ight **a**mplification by **s**timulated **e**mission of **r**adiation. You already know what light and radiation are. *Amplification* is the increase in the brightness of the light.

What is stimulated emission? In an atom, an electron can move from one energy level to another. A photon is released when an electron moves from a higher energy level to a lower energy level. This process is called *emission. Stimulated emission* occurs when a photon strikes an atom in an excited state and makes that atom emit another photon. The newly emitted photon is identical to the first photon, and they travel away from the atom together. **Figure 23** shows how stimulated emission works to produce laser light.

Figure 23 A Helium-Neon Laser

a The inside of the laser is filled with helium and neon gases. An electric current in the gases excites the atoms of the gases.

b Excited neon atoms release photons of red light. When these photons strike other excited neon atoms, stimulated emission occurs.

c Plane mirrors on both ends of the laser reflect photons traveling the length of the laser back and forth along the tube.

d Because the photons travel back and forth many times, many stimulated emissions occur, making the laser light brighter.

e One mirror is only partially coated, so some of the photons "leak" out and form a laser light beam.

Holograms Lasers are used to produce holograms. A **hologram** is a piece of film on which an interference pattern produces a three-dimensional image of an object. You have probably seen holograms on magazine covers or baseball cards. **Figure 24** shows how light from a laser is split into two beams. These two beams combine to form an interference pattern on the film, which results in a hologram.

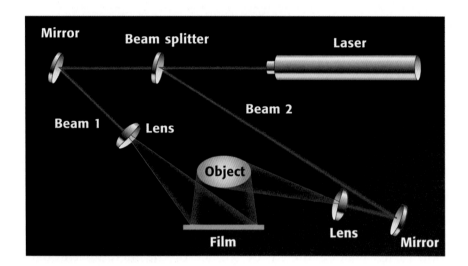

Figure 24 *Light from one beam shines directly on the film, and light from the other beam shines on an object and is reflected onto the film.*

Holograms, like the one shown in **Figure 25,** are similar to photographs because they are images permanently recorded on film. However, unlike photographs, the images you see are not on the surface of the film. They appear either in front of or behind the film. And if you move the image around, you will see it from different angles.

Figure 25 *After the film is developed, the interference pattern reconstructs a three-dimensional image of the object.*

Other Uses for Lasers In addition to making holograms, lasers are used for a wide variety of tasks. For example, lasers are used to cut materials such as metal and cloth. Surgeons sometimes use lasers to cut through human tissue. Laser surgery on the cornea of the eye can correct nearsightedness and farsightedness. And, as you read at the beginning of this chapter, lasers can also be used as extremely accurate rulers. You even use a laser when you listen to music from a CD player.

Fiber Optics

Imagine a glass thread as thin as a human hair that can transmit more than 1,000 telephone conversations at the same time with only flashes of light. It might sound impossible, but such glass threads are at work all over the world. These threads, called *optical fibers,* are thin, flexible glass wires that can transmit light over long distances. Some optical fibers are shown at left. The use of optical fibers is called *fiber optics.* The transmission of information through telephone cables is the most common use of fiber optics. Optical fibers carry information faster and more clearly than older copper telephone cables. Optical fibers are also used to network computers and to allow doctors to see inside patients' bodies without performing major surgery.

Light in a Pipe Optical fibers transmit light over long distances because they act like pipes for light. Just as a good water pipe doesn't let water leak out, a good light pipe doesn't let light leak out. Light stays inside an optical fiber because of total internal reflection. *Total internal reflection* is the complete reflection of light along the inside surface of the medium through which it travels. **Figure 26** shows total internal reflection in an optical fiber.

Figure 26 *As light travels through an optical fiber, it reflects off the sides thousands of times each meter.*

Polarized Light

Next time you go shopping for sunglasses, look for those that have lenses that polarize light. Sunglasses that contain polarizing lenses reduce glare better than sunglasses that do not. *Polarized light* consists of light waves that vibrate in only one plane. **Figure 27** illustrates how light is polarized.

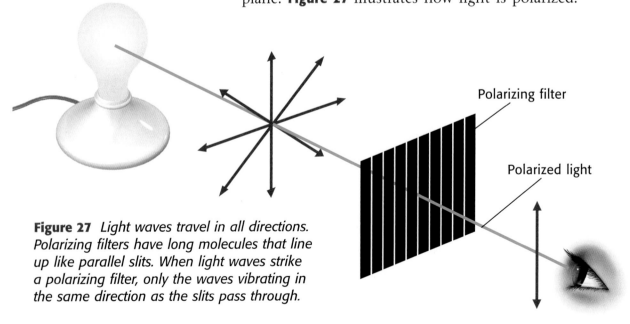

Polarizing filter

Polarized light

Figure 27 *Light waves travel in all directions. Polarizing filters have long molecules that line up like parallel slits. When light waves strike a polarizing filter, only the waves vibrating in the same direction as the slits pass through.*

When light reflects at a certain angle from a smooth surface, it is completely polarized parallel to that surface. If the surface is parallel to the ground, the light is polarized horizontally. This is what causes the bright glare from bodies of water and car hoods.

Polarizing sunglasses reduce glare from horizontal surfaces because the sunglasses have lenses with vertically polarized filters. These filters allow only vertically vibrating light waves to pass through them. So when you wear polarizing sunglasses, the reflected light that is horizontally polarized does not reach your eyes. Polarizing filters are also used by photographers to reduce glare and reflection in their photographs. Examine **Figure 28** to see the effect of a polarizing filter on a camera.

Figure 28 *These two photos were taken by the same camera from the same angle. There is less reflected light in the photo at right because a polarizing filter was placed over the lens of the camera.*

Quick Lab

**Now You See,
Now You Don't**

1. Hold a **lens from a pair of polarizing sunglasses** up to your eye, and look through it. Describe your observations in your ScienceLog.

2. Put a **second polarizing lens** over the first lens. Make sure both lenses are right side up. Look through both lenses, and describe your observations in your ScienceLog.

3. Rotate one lens slowly as you look through both lenses, and describe what happens.

4. Why can't you see through the lenses when they are lined up a certain way? Record your answer in your ScienceLog.

TRY at HOME

REVIEW

1. How is a camera similar to the human eye?

2. What is the difference between a refracting telescope and a reflecting telescope?

3. How is a beam of laser light different from non-laser light?

4. Why are fiber optics useful for transmitting information?

5. **Applying Concepts** Why do you think lasers are used to cut cloth and metal and to perform surgery?

internet connect

SCiLINKS
NSTA

TOPIC: Lasers
GO TO: www.scilinks.org
sciLINKS NUMBER: HSTP575

Chapter Highlights

Vocabulary

luminous (*p. 594*)

illuminated (*p. 594*)

incandescent light (*p. 595*)

fluorescent light (*p. 596*)

neon light (*p. 596*)

vapor light (*p. 597*)

Section Notes

• You see objects either because they are luminous (produce their own light) or because they are illuminated (reflect light).

• Light produced by hot objects is incandescent light. Ordinary light bulbs are a common source of incandescent light.

• Fluorescent light is visible light emitted by a particle when it absorbs ultraviolet light. Little energy is wasted by fluorescent light bulbs.

• Neon light results from an electric current in certain gases.

• Vapor light is produced when electrons combine with gaseous metal atoms.

Vocabulary

plane mirror (*p. 599*)

concave mirror (*p. 600*)

focal point (*p. 600*)

convex mirror (*p. 602*)

lens (*p. 603*)

convex lens (*p. 603*)

concave lens (*p. 604*)

Section Notes

• Rays are arrows that show the path and direction of a single light wave. Ray diagrams can be used to determine where images are formed by mirrors and lenses.

• Plane mirrors produce virtual images that are the same size as the objects. These images are reversed left to right.

☑ Skills Check

Visual Understanding

OPTICAL AXIS, FOCAL POINT, AND FOCAL LENGTH To understand how concave and convex mirrors and lenses work, you need to know what the terms *optical axis*, *focal point*, and *focal length* mean. Figure 10 on page 600 explains these terms.

LASERS Laser light is different from ordinary non-laser light in several ways. Look back at Figure 22 on page 610 to review some differences between the two types of light.

THE EYE Study Figure 17 on page 605 to review the parts of the eye and review the process by which your eye gathers light to form the images that you see.

SECTION 2

- Concave mirrors can produce real images and virtual images. They can also be used to produce a powerful light beam.

- Convex mirrors produce only virtual images.

- Convex lenses can produce real images and virtual images. A magnifying glass is an example of a convex lens.

- Concave lenses produce only virtual images.

Labs

Mirror Images (*p. 720*)

Images from Convex Lenses (*p. 722*)

SECTION 3

Vocabulary

cornea (*p. 605*)

pupil (*p. 605*)

iris (*p. 605*)

retina (*p. 605*)

Section Notes

- Your eye has several parts, such as the cornea, the pupil, the iris, the lens, and the retina.

- Nearsightedness and farsightedness occur when light is not focused on the retina. Both problems can be corrected with glasses or contact lenses.

- Color deficiency is a genetic condition in which cones in the retina are given the wrong instructions. Color deficiency cannot be corrected.

SECTION 4

Vocabulary

laser (*p. 609*)

hologram (*p. 611*)

Section Notes

- Optical instruments, such as cameras, telescopes, and microscopes, are devices that use mirrors and lenses to help people make observations.

- Lasers are devices that produce intense, coherent light of only one wavelength and color. Lasers produce light by a process called stimulated emission.

- Optical fibers can transmit light over long distances because of total internal reflection.

- Polarized light contains light waves that vibrate in only one direction.

---

internetconnect

GO TO: go.hrw.com

Visit the **HRW** Web site for a variety of learning tools related to this chapter. Just type in the keyword:

KEYWORD: HSTLOW

GO TO: www.scilinks.org

Visit the **National Science Teachers Association** on-line Web site for Internet resources related to this chapter. Just type in the *sci*LINKS number for more information about the topic:

TOPIC: Producing Light	*sci*LINKS NUMBER: HSTP555
TOPIC: Mirrors	*sci*LINKS NUMBER: HSTP560
TOPIC: Lenses	*sci*LINKS NUMBER: HSTP565
TOPIC: The Eye	*sci*LINKS NUMBER: HSTP570
TOPIC: Lasers	*sci*LINKS NUMBER: HSTP575

Chapter Review

To complete the following sentences, choose the correct term from each pair of terms listed below:

1. __?__ is commonly used in homes and produces a lot of thermal energy. (*Incandescent light* or *Fluorescent light*)

2. A __?__ is curved inward, like the inside of a spoon. (*convex mirror* or *concave mirror*)

3. You can see an object when light is focused on the __?__ of your eye. (*pupil* or *retina*)

4. A __?__ is a device that produces coherent, intense light of only one color. (*laser* or *lens*)

5. You can see this book because it is a(n) __?__ object. (*luminous* or *illuminated*)

UNDERSTANDING CONCEPTS

Multiple Choice

6. When you look at yourself in a plane mirror, you see a
   a. real image behind the mirror.
   b. real image on the surface of the mirror.
   c. virtual image that appears to be behind the mirror.
   d. virtual image that appears to be in front of the mirror.

7. A vision problem that occurs when light is focused in front of the retina is
   a. nearsightedness.
   b. farsightedness.
   c. color deficiency.
   d. None of the above

8. Which part of the eye refracts light?
   a. iris
   b. cornea
   c. lens
   d. both (b) and (c)

9. Visible light produced when electrons combine with gaseous metal atoms is
   a. incandescent light.
   b. fluorescent light.
   c. neon light.
   d. vapor light.

10. You see less of a glare when you wear certain sunglasses because the lenses
    a. produce total internal reflection.
    b. create holograms.
    c. produce coherent light.
    d. polarize light.

11. What kind of mirrors provide images of large areas and are used for security?
    a. plane mirrors
    b. concave mirrors
    c. convex mirrors
    d. all of the above

12. A simple refracting telescope has
    a. a convex lens and a concave lens.
    b. a concave mirror and a convex lens.
    c. two convex lenses.
    d. two concave lenses.

13. Light waves in a laser beam interact and act as one wave. This light is called
    a. red.
    b. white.
    c. coherent.
    d. emitted.

Short Answer

14. What type of lens should be prescribed for a person who cannot focus on nearby objects? Explain.

15. How is a hologram different from a photograph?

16. Why might a scientist at the North Pole need polarizing sunglasses?

Concept Mapping

17. Use the following terms to create a concept map: lens, telescope, camera, real image, virtual image, optical instrument.

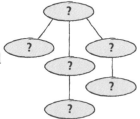

CRITICAL THINKING AND PROBLEM SOLVING

18. Stoplights are usually mounted so that the red light is on the top and the green light is on the bottom. Explain why it is important for a person who has red-green color deficiency to know this arrangement.

19. Some companies are producing fluorescent light bulbs that will fit into sockets on lamps designed for incandescent light bulbs. Although fluorescent bulbs are more expensive, the companies hope that people will use them because they are better for the environment. Explain why fluorescent light bulbs are better for the environment than incandescent light bulbs.

20. Imagine you are given a small device that produces a beam of red light. You want to find out if the device is producing laser light or if it is just a red flashlight. To do this, you point the beam of light against a wall across the room. What would you expect to see if the device is producing laser light? Explain.

INTERPRETING GRAPHICS

21. Examine the ray diagrams below, and identify the type of mirror or lens that is being used and the kind of image that is being formed.

Reading Check-up

Take a minute to review your answers to the Pre-Reading Questions found at the bottom of page 592. Have your answers changed? If necessary, revise your answers based on what you have learned since you began this chapter.

Science, Technology, and Society

Traffic Lights

One day in the 1920s, an automobile collided with a horse and carriage. The riders were thrown from their carriage, the driver of the car was knocked unconscious, and the horse was fatally injured. A man named Garrett Morgan (1877–1963) witnessed this scene, and the accident gave him an idea.

A Bright Idea

Morgan's idea was a signal that included signs to direct traffic at busy intersections. The signal could be seen from a distance and could be clearly understood.

Morgan patented the first traffic signal in 1923. His signal looked very different from those used today. Unlike the small, three-bulb signal boxes that now hang over most busy intersections, the early versions were T-shaped, with the words *stop* and *go* printed on them.

Morgan's traffic signal was operated by a preset timing system. An electric motor turned a system of gears that operated a timing dial. As the timing dial rotated, it turned the switches on and off.

Morgan's invention was an immediate success, and he sold the patent to General Electric Corporation for $40,000—quite a large sum in those days. Since then, later versions of Morgan's traffic signal have been the mainstay of urban traffic control.

Light Technology

The technology of traffic lights continues to improve. For example, in some newer models the timing can be changed, depending on the traffic needs for a particular time of day. Some models have sensors installed in the street to monitor traffic flow. In other models, sensors can be triggered from inside an ambulance so that the light automatically turns green, allowing the ambulance to pass.

More About Morgan

Garrett Morgan, the son of former slaves, was born in Paris, Kentucky. He was one of 11 children, and his formal education ended at the sixth grade. At age 14, with no money and few skills, Morgan left home to work in Cincinnati, Ohio. He soon moved to Cleveland and quickly taught himself enough about sewing machines to get a job repairing them. Morgan saw how important the rest of his education was, so he taught himself and he hired tutors to help him complete his education. By 1907, Morgan opened his own sewing-machine repair shop. He was on his way!

Not only was Morgan an inventor, he was a hero. Gas masks that Morgan invented in 1912 were used in WWI to protect soldiers from chlorine gas fumes. Morgan himself, wearing one of his masks, later helped save several men trapped in a tunnel after a gas explosion.

Think About It

▶ Traffic control is not the only system in which light is used as a signal. What are some other systems that do so, and what makes light so useful for communication?

▲ *Morgan's patent for the first traffic light*

EYE ON THE ENVIRONMENT

Light Pollution

At night, large cities are often visible from far away. Soft light from windows outlines buildings. Bright lights from stadiums and parking lots shine like beacons. Scattered house lights twinkle like jewels. The sight is stunning!

Unfortunately, astronomers consider all these lights a form of pollution. Around the world, light pollution is reducing astronomers' ability to see beyond our atmosphere.

Sky Glow

Twenty years ago, stars were very visible above even large cities. The stars are still there, but now they are obscured by city lights. This glow, called sky glow, is created when light reflects off dust and other particles suspended in the atmosphere. Sky glow affects the entire atmosphere to some degree. Today, even remote locations around the globe are affected by light pollution.

The majority of light pollution comes from outdoor lights such as headlights, street lights, porch lights, and bright parking-lot and stadium lights. Other sources include forest fires and gas burn-offs in oil fields. Air pollution makes the situation worse, adding more particles to the air so that reflection is even greater.

A Light of Hope

Unlike other kinds of pollution, light pollution has some simple solutions. In fact, light pollution can be reduced in as little time as it takes to turn off a light! While turning off most city lights is impractical, several simple strategies can make a surprising difference. For example, using covered outdoor lights keeps the light angled downward, preventing most of the light from reaching particles in the sky. Also, using motion-sensitive lights and timed lights helps eliminate unnecessary light.

▲ *Lights from cities can be seen from space, as shown in this photograph taken from the space shuttle* Columbia. *Bright, uncovered lights (inset) create a glowing haze in the night sky above most cities in the United States.*

Many of these strategies also save money by saving energy.

Astronomers hope that public awareness will help improve the visibility of the night sky in and around major cities. Some cities, including Boston and Tucson, have already made some progress in reducing light pollution. Scientists have projected that if left unchecked, light pollution will affect every observatory on Earth within the next decade.

See for Yourself

▶ With your parents' permission, go outside at night and find a place where you can see the sky. Count the number of stars you can see. Now turn on a flashlight or porch light. How many stars can you see now? Compare your results. How much was your visibility reduced?

Contents

Exploring, inventing, and investigating are essential to the study of science. However, these activities can also be dangerous. To make sure that your experiments and explorations are safe, you must be aware of a variety of safety guidelines.

You have probably heard of the saying, "It is better to be safe than sorry." This is particularly true in a science classroom where experiments and explorations are being performed. Being uninformed and careless can result in serious injuries. Don't take chances with your own safety or with anyone else's.

Following are important guidelines for staying safe in the science classroom. Your teacher may also have safety guidelines and tips that are specific to your classroom and laboratory. Take the time to be safe.

Safety Rules!

Start Out Right

Always get your teacher's permission before attempting any laboratory exploration. Read the procedures carefully, and pay particular attention to safety information and caution statements. If you are unsure about what a safety symbol means, look it up or ask your teacher. You cannot be too careful when it comes to safety. If an accident does occur, inform your teacher immediately, regardless of how minor you think the accident is.

If you are instructed to note the odor of a substance, wave the fumes toward your nose with your hand. Never put your nose close to the source.

Safety Symbols

All of the experiments and investigations in this book and their related worksheets include important safety symbols to alert you to particular safety concerns. Become familiar with these symbols so that when you see them, you will know what they mean and what to do. It is important that you read this entire safety section to learn about specific dangers in the laboratory.

Eye protection	Clothing protection	Hand safety
Heating safety	Electric safety	Chemical safety
Animal safety	Sharp object	Plant safety

Eye Safety

Wear safety goggles when working around chemicals, acids, bases, or any type of flame or heating device. Wear safety goggles any time there is even the slightest chance that harm could come to your eyes. If any substance gets into your eyes, notify your teacher immediately, and flush your eyes with running water for at least 15 minutes. Treat any unknown chemical as if it were a dangerous chemical. Never look directly into the sun. Doing so could cause permanent blindness.

Avoid wearing contact lenses in a laboratory situation. Even if you are wearing safety goggles, chemicals can get between the contact lenses and your eyes. If your doctor requires that you wear contact lenses instead of glasses, wear eye-cup safety goggles in the lab.

Safety Equipment

Know the locations of the nearest fire alarms and any other safety equipment, such as fire blankets and eyewash fountains, as identified by your teacher, and know the procedures for using them.

Be extra careful when using any glassware. When adding a heavy object to a graduated cylinder, tilt the cylinder so the object slides slowly to the bottom.

Neatness

Keep your work area free of all unnecessary books and papers. Tie back long hair, and secure loose sleeves or other loose articles of clothing, such as ties and bows. Remove dangling jewelry. Don't wear open-toed shoes or sandals in the laboratory. Never eat, drink, or apply cosmetics in a laboratory setting. Food, drink, and cosmetics can easily become contaminated with dangerous materials.

Certain hair products (such as aerosol hair spray) are flammable and should not be worn while working near an open flame. Avoid wearing hair spray or hair gel on lab days.

Sharp/Pointed Objects

Use knives and other sharp instruments with extreme care. Never cut objects while holding them in your hands. Place objects on a suitable work surface for cutting.

Heat

Wear safety goggles when using a heating device or a flame. Whenever possible, use an electric hot plate as a heat source instead of an open flame. When heating materials in a test tube, always angle the test tube away from yourself and others. In order to avoid burns, wear heat-resistant gloves whenever instructed to do so.

Electricity

Be careful with electrical cords. When using a microscope with a lamp, do not place the cord where it could trip someone. Do not let cords hang over a table edge in a way that could cause equipment to fall if the cord is accidentally pulled. Do not use equipment with damaged cords. Be sure your hands are dry and that the electrical equipment is in the "off" position before plugging it in. Turn off and unplug electrical equipment when you are finished.

Chemicals

Wear safety goggles when handling any potentially dangerous chemicals, acids, or bases. If a chemical is unknown, handle it as you would a dangerous chemical. Wear an apron and safety gloves when working with acids or bases or whenever you are told to do so. If a spill gets on your skin or clothing, rinse it off immediately with water for at least 5 minutes while calling to your teacher.

Never mix chemicals unless your teacher tells you to do so. Never taste, touch, or smell chemicals unless you are specifically directed to do so. Before working with a flammable liquid or gas, check for the presence of any source of flame, spark, or heat.

Animal Safety

Always obtain your teacher's permission before bringing any animal into the school building. Handle animals only as your teacher directs. Always treat animals carefully and with respect. Wash your hands thoroughly after handling any animal.

Plant Safety

Do not eat any part of a plant or plant seed used in the laboratory. Wash hands thoroughly after handling any part of a plant. When in nature, do not pick any wild plants unless your teacher instructs you to do so.

Glassware

Examine all glassware before use. Be sure that glassware is clean and free of chips and cracks. Report damaged glassware to your teacher. Glass containers used for heating should be made of heat-resistant glass.

DISCOVERY LAB

Exploring the Unseen

Your teacher will give you a box in which a special divider has been created. Your task is to describe this divider as precisely as possible—without opening the box! Your only aid is a marble that is also inside the box. This task will allow you to demonstrate your understanding of the scientific method. Good luck!

Materials

• a sealed mystery box

Ask a Question

1. In your ScienceLog, record the question that you are trying to answer by doing this experiment. (Hint: Read the introductory paragraph again if you are not sure what your task is.)

Form a Hypothesis

2. Before you begin the experiment, think about what's required. Do you think you will be able to easily determine the shape of the divider? What about its texture? its color? In your ScienceLog, write a hypothesis that states how much you think you will be able to determine about the divider during the experiment. (Remember, you can't open the box!)

Test the Hypothesis

3. Using all the methods you can think of (except opening the box), test your hypothesis. Make careful notes about your testing and observations in your ScienceLog.

Analyze the Results

4. What characteristics of the divider were you able to identify? Draw or write your best description of the interior of the box.

5. Do your observations support your hypothesis? Explain. If your results do not support your hypothesis, write a new hypothesis and test it.

6. With your teacher's permission, open the box and look inside. Record your observations in your ScienceLog.

Communicate Results

7. Write a paragraph summarizing your experiment. Be sure to include your methods, whether your results supported your hypothesis, and how you could improve your methods.

Off to the Races!

Scientists often use models—representations of objects or systems. Physical models, such as a model airplane, are generally a different size than the objects they represent. In this lab you will build a model car, test its design, and then try to improve the design.

Procedure

1. Using the materials listed, design and build a car that will carry the load (the eraser or block of wood) down the ramp as quickly as possible. Your car must be no wider than 8 cm, it must have room to carry the load, and it must roll.

2. As you test your design, do not be afraid to rebuild or redesign your car. Improving your methods is an important part of scientific progress.

3. When you have a design that works well, measure the time required for your car to roll down the ramp. Record this time in your ScienceLog. Repeat this step several times.

4. Try to improve your model. Find one thing that you can change to make your model car roll faster down the ramp. In your ScienceLog, write a description of the change.

5. Repeat step 3.

Analysis

6. Why is it important to have room in the model car for the eraser or wood block? (Hint: Think about the function of a real car.)

7. Before you built the model car, you created a design for it. Do you think this design is also a model? Explain.

8. Based on your observations in this lab, list three reasons why it is helpful for automobile designers to build and test small model cars rather than immediately building a full-size car.

9. In this lab you built a model that was smaller than the object it represented. Some models are larger than the objects they represent. List three examples of larger models that are used to represent objects. Why is it helpful to use a larger model in these cases?

Materials

- 2 sheets of typing paper
- glue
- 16 cm clothes-hanger wire
- pliers or wire cutters
- metric ruler
- rubber eraser or wooden block
- ramp (board and textbooks)
- stopwatch

Measuring Liquid Volume

In this lab you will use a graduated cylinder to measure and transfer precise amounts of liquids. Remember, in order to accurately measure liquids in a graduated cylinder, you should read the level at the bottom of the meniscus, the curved surface of the liquid.

Materials

- masking tape
- marker
- 6 large test tubes
- test-tube rack
- 10 mL graduated cylinder
- 3 beakers filled with colored liquid
- small funnel

Procedure

1. Using the masking tape and marker, label the test tubes A, B, C, D, E, and F. Place them in the test-tube rack. Be careful not to confuse the test tubes.

2. Using the 10 mL graduated cylinder and the funnel, pour 14 mL of the red liquid into test tube A. (To do this, first pour 10 mL of the liquid into the test tube and then add 4 mL of liquid.)

3. Rinse the graduated cylinder and funnel between uses.

4. Measure 13 mL of the yellow liquid, and pour it into test tube C. Then measure 13 mL of the blue liquid, and pour it into test tube E.

5. Transfer 4 mL of liquid from test tube C into test tube D. Transfer 7 mL of liquid from test tube E into test tube D.

6. Measure 4 mL of blue liquid from the beaker, and pour it into test tube F. Measure 7 mL of red liquid from the beaker, and pour it into test tube F.

7. Transfer 8 mL of liquid from test tube A into test tube B. Transfer 3 mL of liquid from test tube C into test tube B.

Collect Data

8. Make a data table in your ScienceLog, and record the color of the liquid in each test tube.

9. Use the graduated cylinder to measure the volume of liquid in each test tube, and record the volumes in your data table.

10. Record your color observations in a table of class data prepared by your teacher. Copy the completed table into your ScienceLog.

Analysis

11. Did all of the groups report the same colors? Explain why the colors were the same or different.

12. Why should you not fill the graduated cylinder to the very top?

Coin Operated

All pennies are exactly the same, right? Probably not! After all, each penny was made in a certain year at a specific mint, and each has traveled a unique path to reach your classroom. But all pennies *are* similar. In this lab you will investigate differences and similarities among a group of pennies.

Materials

- 10 pennies
- metric balance
- few sheets of paper
- 100 mL graduated cylinder
- water
- paper towels

Procedure

1. Write the numbers 1 through 10 on a page in your ScienceLog, and place a penny next to each number.

2. Use the metric balance to find the mass of each penny to the nearest 0.1 g. Record each measurement in your ScienceLog.

3. On a table that your teacher will provide, make a mark in the correct column of the table for each penny you measured.

4. Separate your pennies into piles based on the class data. Place each pile on its own sheet of paper.

5. Measure and record the mass of each pile. Write the mass on the paper you are using to identify the pile.

6. Fill a graduated cylinder about halfway with water. Carefully measure the volume, and record it.

7. Carefully place the pennies from one pile in the graduated cylinder. Measure and record the new volume.

8. Carefully remove the pennies from the graduated cylinder, and dry them off.

9. Repeat steps 6 through 8 for each pile of pennies.

Analyze the Results

10. Determine the volume of the displaced water by subtracting the initial volume from the final volume. This amount is equal to the volume of the pennies. Record the volume of each pile of pennies.

11. Calculate the density of each pile. To do this, divide the total mass of the pennies by the volume of the pennies. Record the density in your ScienceLog.

Draw Conclusions

12. How is it possible for the pennies to have different densities?

13. What clues might allow you to separate the pennies into the same groups without experimentation? Explain.

Volumania!

You have learned how to measure the volume of a solid object that has square or rectangular sides. But there are lots of objects in the world that have irregular shapes. In this lab activity, you'll learn some ways to find the volume of objects that have irregular shapes.

Part A: Finding the Volume of Small Objects

Procedure

1. Fill a graduated cylinder half full with water. Read the volume of the water, and record it in your ScienceLog. Be sure to look at the surface of the water at eye level and to read the volume at the bottom of the meniscus, as shown below.

Read volume here

2. Carefully slide one of the objects into the tilted graduated cylinder, as shown below.

3. Read the new volume, and record it in your ScienceLog.

4. Subtract the old volume from the new volume. The resulting amount is equal to the volume of the solid object.

5. Use the same method to find the volume of the other objects. Record your results in your ScienceLog.

Analysis

6. What changes do you have to make to the volumes you determine in order to express them correctly?

7. Do the heaviest objects always have the largest volumes? Why or why not?

Materials

Part A
- graduated cylinder
- water
- various small objects supplied by your teacher

Part B
- bottom half of a 2 L plastic bottle or similar container
- water
- aluminum pie pan
- paper towels
- funnel
- graduated cylinder

Part B: Finding the Volume of Your Hand

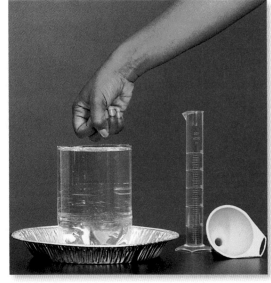

Procedure

8. Completely fill the container with water. Put the container in the center of the pie pan. Be sure not to spill any of the water into the pie pan.

9. Make a fist, and put your hand into the container up to your wrist.

10. Remove your hand, and let the excess water drip into the container, not the pie pan. Dry your hand with a paper towel.

11. Use the funnel to pour the overflow water into the graduated cylinder. Measure the volume. This is the volume of your hand. Record the volume in your ScienceLog. (Remember to use the correct unit of volume for a solid object.)

12. Repeat this procedure with your other hand.

Analysis

13. Was the volume the same for both of your hands? If not, were you surprised? What might account for a person's hands having different volumes?

14. Would it have made a difference if you had placed your open hand into the container instead of your fist? Explain your reasoning.

15. Compare the volume of your right hand with the volume of your classmates' right hands. Create a class graph of right-hand volumes. What is the average right-hand volume for your class?

Going Further

■ Design an experiment to determine the volume of a person's body. In your plans, be sure to include the materials needed for the experiment and the procedures that must be followed. Include a sketch that shows how your materials and methods would be used in this experiment.

■ Using an encyclopedia, the Internet, or other reference materials, find out how the volumes of very large samples of matter—such as an entire planet—are determined.

Determining Density

The density of an object is its mass divided by its volume. But how does the density of a small amount of a substance relate to the density of a larger amount of the same substance? In this lab, you will calculate the density of one marble and of a group of marbles. Then you will confirm the relationship between the mass and volume of a substance.

Materials

- 100 mL graduated cylinder
- water
- paper towels
- 8 to 10 glass marbles
- metric balance
- graph paper

Collect Data

1. Copy the table below in your ScienceLog. Include one row for each marble.

Mass of marble, g	Total mass of marbles, g	Total volume, mL	Volume of marbles, mL (total volume minus 50.0 mL)	Density of marbles, g/mL (total mass of marbles divided by volume of marbles)
DO NOT WRITE IN BOOK			DO NOT WRITE IN BOOK	

2. Fill the graduated cylinder with 50.0 mL of water. If you put in too much water, twist one of the paper towels and use its end to absorb excess water.

3. Measure the mass of a marble as accurately as you can (to at least one-tenth of a gram). Record the marble's mass in the table.

4. Carefully drop the marble in the tilted cylinder, and measure the total volume. Record the volume in the third column.

5. Measure and record the mass of another marble. Add the masses of the marbles together, and record this value in the second column of the table.

6. Carefully drop the second marble in the graduated cylinder. Complete the row of information in the table.

7. Repeat steps 5 and 6, adding one marble at a time. Stop when you run out of marbles, the water no longer completely covers the marbles, or the graduated cylinder is full.

Analyze the Results

8. Examine the data in your table. As the number of marbles increases, what happens to the total mass of the marbles? What happens to the volume of the marbles? What happens to the density of the marbles?

9. Graph the total mass of the marbles (y-axis) versus the volume of the marbles (x-axis). Is the graph a straight line or a curved line?

Draw Conclusions

10. Does the density of a substance depend on the amount of substance present? Explain how your results support your answer.

Going Further

Calculate the slope of the graph. How does the slope compare with the values in the column titled "Density of marbles"? Explain.

Layering Liquids

You have learned that liquids form layers according to their densities. In this lab, you'll discover whether it matters in which order you add the liquids.

Materials

- liquid A
- liquid B
- liquid C
- beaker or other small, clear container
- 10 mL graduated cylinders (3)
- 3 funnels

Make a Prediction

1. Does the order in which you add liquids of different densities to a container affect the order of the layers formed by those liquids?

Conduct an Experiment

2. Using the graduated cylinders, add 10 mL of each liquid to the clear container. Remember to read the volume at the bottom of the meniscus, as shown below. In your ScienceLog, record the order in which you added the liquids.

3. Observe the liquids in the container. In your ScienceLog, sketch what you see. Be sure to label the layers and the colors.

4. Add 10 mL more of liquid C. Observe what happens, and write your observations in your ScienceLog.

5. Add 20 mL more of liquid A. Observe what happens, and write your observations in your ScienceLog.

Analyze Your Results

6. Which of the liquids has the greatest density? Which has the least density? How can you tell?

7. Did the layers change position when you added more of liquid C? Explain your answer.

8. Did the layers change position when you added more of liquid A? Explain your answer.

Communicate Your Results

9. Find out in what order your classmates added the liquids to the container. Compare your results with those of a classmate who added the liquids in a different order. Were your results different? In your ScienceLog, explain why or why not.

Draw Conclusions

10. Based on your results, evaluate your prediction from step 1.

White Before Your Eyes

You have learned how to describe matter based on its physical and chemical properties. You have also learned some clues that can help you determine whether a change in matter is a physical change or a chemical change. In this lab, you'll use what you have learned to describe four substances based on their properties and the changes they undergo.

Materials

- 4 spatulas
- baking powder
- plastic-foam egg carton
- 3 eyedroppers
- water
- stirring rod
- vinegar
- iodine solution
- baking soda
- cornstarch
- sugar

Procedure

1. Copy Table 1 and Table 2, shown on the next page, into your ScienceLog. Be sure to leave plenty of room in each box to write down your observations.

2. Use a spatula to place a small amount (just enough to cover the bottom of the cup) of baking powder into three cups of your egg carton. Look closely at the baking powder, and record observations of its color, texture, etc., in the column of Table 1 titled "Unmixed."

3. Use an eyedropper to add 60 drops of water to the baking powder in the first cup, as shown below. Stir with the stirring rod. Record your observations in Table 1 in the column titled "Mixed with water." Clean your stirring rod.

4. Use a clean dropper to add 20 drops of vinegar to the second cup of baking powder. Stir. Record your observations in the column titled "Mixed with vinegar." Clean your stirring rod.

5. Use a clean dropper to add five drops of iodine solution to the third cup of baking powder. Stir. Record your observations in the column in Table 1 titled "Mixed with iodine solution." Clean your stirring rod.

Caution: Be careful when using iodine. Iodine will stain your skin and clothes.

6. Repeat steps 2–5 for each of the other substances. Use a clean spatula for each substance.

Analysis

7. In Table 2, write the type of change you observed, and state the property that the change demonstrates.

8. What clues did you use to identify when a chemical change happened?

Table 1 Observations				
Substance	Unmixed	Mixed with water	Mixed with vinegar	Mixed with iodine solution
Baking powder				
Baking soda				
Cornstarch				
Sugar				

Table 2 Changes and Properties						
	Mixed with water		Mixed with vinegar		Mixed with iodine solution	
Substance	Change	Property	Change	Property	Change	Property
Baking powder						
Baking soda						
Cornstarch						
Sugar						

DISCOVERY LAB

Full of Hot Air!

Why do hot-air balloons float gracefully above Earth, while balloons you blow up fall to the ground? The answer has to do with the density of the air inside the balloon. Density is mass per unit volume, and volume is affected by changes in temperature. In this experiment, you will investigate the relationship between the temperature of a gas and its volume. Then you will be able to determine how the temperature of a gas affects its density.

Form a Hypothesis

1. How does an increase or decrease in temperature affect the volume of a balloon? Write your hypothesis in your ScienceLog.

Test the Hypothesis

2. Fill an aluminum pan with water about 4 to 5 cm deep. Put the pan on the hot plate, and turn the hot plate on.

3. While the water is heating, fill the other pan 4 to 5 cm deep with ice water.

4. Blow up a balloon inside the 500 mL beaker, as shown. The balloon should fill the beaker but should not extend outside the beaker. Tie the balloon at its opening.

5. Place the beaker and balloon in the ice water. Observe what happens. Record your observations in your ScienceLog.

6. Remove the balloon and beaker from the ice water. Observe the balloon for several minutes. Record any changes.

Materials

- 2 aluminum pans
- water
- metric ruler
- hot plate
- ice water
- balloon
- 250 mL beaker
- heat-resistant gloves

7. Put on heat-resistant gloves. When the hot water begins to boil, put the beaker and balloon in the hot water. Observe the balloon for several minutes, and record your observations.

8. Turn off the hot plate. When the water has cooled, carefully pour it into a sink.

Analyze the Results

9. Summarize your observations of the balloon. Relate your observations to Charles's law.

10. Was your hypothesis for step 1 supported? If not, revise your hypothesis.

Draw Conclusions

11. Based on your observations, how is the density of a gas affected by an increase or decrease in temperature?

12. Explain in terms of density and Charles's law why heating the air allows a hot-air balloon to float.

Can Crusher

Condensation can occur when gas particles come near the surface of a liquid. The gas particles slow down because they are attracted to the liquid. This reduction in speed causes the gas particles to condense into a liquid. In this lab, you'll see that particles that have condensed into a liquid don't take up as much space and therefore don't exert as much pressure as they did in the gaseous state.

Materials

- water
- 2 empty aluminum cans
- heat-resistant gloves
- hot plate
- tongs
- 1 L beaker

Conduct an Experiment

1. Place just enough water in an aluminum can to slightly cover the bottom.

2. Put on heat-resistant gloves. Place the aluminum can on a hot plate turned to the highest temperature setting.

3. Heat the can until the water is boiling. Steam should be rising vigorously from the top of the can.

4. Using tongs, quickly pick up the can and place the top 2 cm of the can upside down in the 1 L beaker filled with room-temperature water.

5. Describe your observations in your ScienceLog.

Analyze the Results

6. The can was crushed because the atmospheric pressure outside the can became greater than the pressure inside the can. Explain what happened inside the can to cause this.

Draw Conclusions

7. Inside every popcorn kernel is a small amount of water. When you make popcorn, the water inside the kernels is heated until it becomes steam. Explain how the popping of the kernels is the opposite of what you saw in this lab. Be sure to address the effects of pressure in your explanation.

Going Further

Try the experiment again, but use ice water instead of room-temperature water. Explain your results in terms of the effects of temperature.

A Hot and Cool Lab

When you add energy to a substance through heating, does the substance's temperature always go up? When you remove energy from a substance through cooling, does the substance's temperature always go down? In this lab you'll investigate these important questions with a very common substance—water.

Part A: Boiling Water

Make a Prediction

1. What happens to the temperature of boiling water when you continue to add energy through heating?

Procedure

2. Fill the beaker about one-third to one-half full with water.

3. Put on heat-resistant gloves. Turn on the hot plate, and put the beaker on the burner. Put the thermometer in the beaker. **Caution:** Be careful not to touch the burner.

Collect Data

4. In a table like the one below, record the temperature of the water every 30 seconds. Continue doing this until about one-fourth of the water boils away. Note the first temperature reading at which the water is steadily boiling.

Time (s)	30	60	90	120	150	180	210	etc.
Temperature (°C)	DO NOT WRITE IN BOOK							

5. Turn off the hot plate.

6. While the beaker is cooling, make a graph of temperature (*y*-axis) versus time (*x*-axis). Draw an arrow pointing to the first temperature at which the water was steadily boiling.

7. After you finish the graph, use heat-resistant gloves to pick up the beaker. Pour the warm water out, and rinse the warm beaker with cool water. **Caution:** Even after cooling, the beaker is still too warm to handle without gloves.

Materials

Part A

- 250 or 400 mL beaker
- water
- heat-resistant gloves
- hot plate
- thermometer
- stopwatch
- graph paper

Part B

- 100 mL graduated cylinder
- water
- large coffee can
- crushed ice
- rock salt
- thermometer
- wire-loop stirring device
- stopwatch
- graph paper

Part B: Freezing Water

Make Another Prediction

8. What happens to the temperature of freezing water when you continue to remove energy through cooling?

Procedure

9. Put approximately 20 mL of water in the graduated cylinder.

10. Put the graduated cylinder in the coffee can, and fill in around the graduated cylinder with crushed ice. Pour rock salt on the ice around the graduated cylinder. Place the thermometer and the wire-loop stirring device in the graduated cylinder.

11. As the ice melts and mixes with the rock salt, the level of ice will decrease. Add ice and rock salt to the can as needed.

Collect Data

12. In a new table, record the temperature of the water in the graduated cylinder every 30 seconds. Stir the water with the stirring device.
Caution: Do not stir with the thermometer.

13. Once the water begins to freeze, stop stirring. Do not try to pull the thermometer out of the solid ice in the cylinder.

14. Note the temperature when you first notice ice crystals forming in the water. Continue taking readings until the water in the graduated cylinder is completely frozen.

15. Make a graph of temperature (*y*-axis) versus time (*x*-axis). Draw an arrow to the temperature reading at which the first ice crystals form in the water in the graduated cylinder.

Analyze the Results (Parts A and B)

16. What does the slope of each graph represent?

17. How does the slope when the water is boiling compare with the slope before the water starts to boil? Why is the slope different for the two periods?

18. How does the slope when the water is freezing compare with the slope before the water starts to freeze? Why is the slope different for the two periods?

Draw Conclusions (Parts A and B)

19. Addition or subtraction of energy leads to changes in the movement of particles that make up solids, liquids, and gases. Use this idea to explain why the temperature graphs of the two experiments look the way they do.

Using Scientific Methods

Flame Tests

Fireworks produce fantastic combinations of color when they are ignited. The different colors are the results of burning different compounds. Imagine that you are the lead chemist for a fireworks company. The label has fallen off one box filled with a compound, and you must identify the unknown compound so that it may be used in the correct fireworks display. To identify the compound, you will use your knowledge that every compound has a unique set of properties.

Make a Prediction

1. Can you identify the unknown compound by heating it in a flame? Explain.

Conduct an Experiment

Caution: Be very careful in handling all chemicals. Tell your teacher immediately if you spill a chemical.

2. Arrange the test tubes in the test-tube rack. Use masking tape to label the tubes with the following names: calcium chloride, potassium chloride, sodium chloride, and unknown.

3. Copy the table below into your ScienceLog. Then ask your teacher for your portions of the solutions.

Test Results	
Compound	**Color of flame**
Calcium chloride	
Potassium chloride	
Sodium chloride	
Unknown	

DO NOT WRITE IN BOOK

Materials

- 4 small test tubes
- test-tube rack
- masking tape
- 4 chloride test solutions
- spark igniter
- Bunsen burner
- wire and holder
- dilute hydrochloric acid in a small beaker
- distilled water in a small beaker

4. Light the burner. Clean the wire by dipping it into the dilute hydrochloric acid and then into distilled water. Holding the wooden handle, heat the wire in the blue flame of the burner until the wire is glowing and it no longer colors the flame. **Caution:** Use extreme care around an open flame.

Collect Data

5. Dip the clean wire into the first test solution. Hold the wire at the tip of the inner cone of the burner flame. In the table, record the color given to the flame.

6. Clean the wire by repeating step 4.

7. Repeat steps 5 and 6 for the other solutions.

8. Follow your teacher's instructions for cleanup and disposal.

Analyze the Results

9. Is the flame color a test for the metal or for the chloride in each compound? Explain your answer.

10. What is the identity of your unknown solution? How do you know?

Draw Conclusions

11. Why is it necessary to carefully clean the wire before testing each solution?

12. Would you expect the compound sodium fluoride to produce the same color as sodium chloride in a flame test? Why or why not?

13. Each of the compounds you tested is made from chlorine, which is a poisonous gas at room temperature. Why is it safe to use these compounds without a gas mask?

A Sugar Cube Race!

If you drop a sugar cube into a glass of water, how long will it take to dissolve? Will it take 5 minutes, 10 minutes, or longer? What can you do to speed up the rate at which it dissolves? Should you change something about the water, the sugar cube, or the process? In other words, what variable should you change? Before reading further, make a list of variables that could be changed in this situation. Record your list in your ScienceLog.

Materials

- water
- graduated cylinder
- 2 sugar cubes
- 2 beakers or other clear containers
- clock or stopwatch
- other materials approved by your teacher

Make a Prediction

1. Choose one variable to test. In your ScienceLog, record your choice, and predict how changing your variable will affect the rate of dissolving.

Conduct an Experiment

2. Pour 150 mL of water into one of the beakers. Add one sugar cube, and use the stopwatch to measure how long it takes for the sugar cube to dissolve. You must not disturb the sugar cube in any way! Record this time in your ScienceLog.

3. Tell your teacher how you wish to test the variable. Do not proceed without his or her approval. You may need additional equipment.

4. Prepare your materials to test the variable you have picked. When you are ready, start your procedure for speeding up the dissolving of

the sugar cube. Use the stopwatch to measure the time. Record this time in your ScienceLog.

Analyze the Results

5. Compare your results with the results obtained in step 2. Was your prediction correct? Why or why not?

Draw Conclusions

6. Why was it necessary to observe the sugar cube dissolving on its own before you tested the variable?

7. Do you think that changing more than one variable would speed up the rate of dissolving even more? Explain your reasoning.

Communicate Results

8. Discuss your results with a group that tested a different variable. Which variable had a greater effect on the rate of dissolving?

Making Butter

A colloid is an interesting substance. It has properties of both solutions and suspensions. Colloidal particles are not heavy enough to settle out, so they remain evenly dispersed throughout the mixture. In this activity, you will make butter—a very familiar colloid—and observe the characteristics that classify butter as a colloid.

Materials

- marble
- small, clear container with lid
- heavy cream
- clock or stopwatch

Procedure

1. Place a marble inside the container, and fill the container with heavy cream. Put the lid tightly on the container.

2. Take turns shaking the container vigorously and constantly for 10 minutes. Record the time when you begin shaking in your ScienceLog. Every minute, stop shaking the container and hold it up to the light. Record your observations.

3. Continue shaking the container, taking turns if necessary. When you see, hear, or feel any changes inside the container, note the time and change in your ScienceLog.

4. After 10 minutes of shaking, you should have a lump of "butter" surrounded by liquid inside the container. Describe both the butter and the liquid in detail in your ScienceLog.

5. Let the container sit for about 10 minutes. Observe the butter and liquid again, and record your observations in your ScienceLog.

Analysis

6. When you noticed the change in the container, what did you think was happening at that point?

7. Based on your observations, explain why butter is classified as a colloid.

8. What kind of mixture is the liquid that is left behind? Explain.

Unpolluting Water

In many cities, the water supply comes from a river, lake, or reservoir. This water may include several mixtures, including suspensions (with suspended dirt, oil, or living organisms) and solutions (with dissolved chemicals). To make the water safe to drink, your city's water supplier must remove impurities. In this lab, you will model the procedures used in real water-treatment plants.

Part A: Untreated Water

Procedure

1. Measure 100 mL of "polluted" water into a graduated cylinder. Be sure to shake the bottle of water before you pour so your sample will include all the impurities.

2. Pour the contents of the graduated cylinder into one of the beakers.

3. Copy the table below into your ScienceLog, and record your observations of the water in the "Before treatment" row.

Materials

- "polluted" water
- graduated cylinder
- 250 mL beakers (4)
- 2 plastic spoons
- small nail
- 8 oz plastic-foam cup (2)
- scissors
- 2 pieces of filter paper
- washed fine sand
- metric ruler
- washed activated charcoal
- rubber band

Observations						
	Color	**Clearness**	**Odor**	**Any layers?**	**Any solids?**	**Water volume**
Before treatment						
After oil separation						
After sand filtration						
After charcoal						

Part B: Settling In

If a suspension is left standing, the suspended particles will settle to the top or bottom. You should see a layer of oil at the top.

Procedure

4. Separate the oil by carefully pouring the oil into another beaker. You can use a plastic spoon to get the last bit of oil from the water. Record your observations.

Part C: Filtration

Cloudy water can be a sign of small particles still in suspension. These particles can usually be removed by filtering. Water-treatment plants use sand and gravel as filters.

Procedure

5. Make a filter as follows:
   a. Use the nail to poke 5 to 10 small holes in the bottom of one of the cups.
   b. Cut a circle of filter paper to fit inside the bottom of the cup. (This will keep the sand in the cup.)
   c. Fill the cup to 2 cm below the rim with wet sand. Pack the sand tightly.
   d. Set the cup inside an empty beaker.

6. Pour the polluted water on top of the sand, and let it filter through. Do not pour any of the settled mud onto the sand. (Dispose of the mud as instructed by your teacher.) In your table, record your observations of the water collected in the beaker.

Part D: Separating Solutions

Something that has been dissolved in a solvent cannot be separated using filters. Water-treatment plants use activated charcoal to absorb many dissolved chemicals.

Procedure

7. Place activated charcoal about 3 cm deep in the unused cup. Pour the water collected from the sand filtration into the cup, and stir for a minute with a spoon.

8. Place a piece of filter paper over the top of the cup, and fasten it in place with a rubber band. With the paper securely in place, pour the water through the filter paper and back into a clean beaker. Record your observations in your table.

Analysis (Parts A–D)

9. Is your unpolluted water safe to drink? Why or why not?

10. When you treat a sample of water, do you get out exactly the same amount of water that you put in? Explain your answer.

11. Some groups may still have cloudy water when they finish. Explain a possible cause for this.

Built for Speed

DESIGN YOUR OWN

Imagine that you are an engineer at GoCarCo, a toy-vehicle company. GoCarCo is trying to beat the competition by building a new toy vehicle. Several new designs are being tested. Your boss has given you one of the new toy vehicles and instructed you to measure its speed as accurately as possible with the tools you have. Other engineers (your classmates) are testing the other designs. Your results could decide the fate of the company!

Materials

- toy vehicle
- meterstick
- masking tape
- stopwatch

Procedure

1. How will you accomplish your goal? Write a paragraph in your ScienceLog to describe your goal and your procedure for this experiment. Be sure that your procedure includes several trials.

2. Show your plan to your boss (teacher). Get his or her approval to carry out your procedure.

3. Perform your stated procedure. Record all data in your ScienceLog. Be sure to express all data in the correct units.

Analysis

4. What was the average speed of your vehicle? How does your result compare with the results of the other engineers?

5. Compare your technique for determining the speed of your vehicle with the techniques of the other engineers. Which technique do you think is the most effective?

6. Was your toy vehicle the fastest? Explain why or why not.

Going Further

Think of several conditions that could affect your vehicle's speed. Design an experiment to test your vehicle under one of those conditions. Write a paragraph in your ScienceLog to explain your procedure. Be sure to include an explanation of how that condition changes your vehicle's speed.

Detecting Acceleration

Have you ever noticed that you can "feel" acceleration? In a car or in an elevator you notice the change in speed or direction—even with your eyes closed! Inside your ears are tiny hair cells. These cells can detect the movement of fluid in your inner ear. When you accelerate, the fluid does, too. The hair cells detect this acceleration in the fluid and send a message to your brain. This allows you to sense acceleration.

In this activity you will build a device that detects acceleration. Even though this device is made with simple materials, it is very sensitive. It registers acceleration only briefly. You will have to be very observant when using this device.

Materials

- scissors
- string
- 1 L container with water-tight lid
- pushpin
- small cork or plastic-foam ball
- modeling clay
- water

Procedure

1. Cut a piece of string that is just long enough to reach three quarters of the way inside the container.

2. Use a pushpin to attach one end of the string to the cork or plastic-foam ball.

3. Use modeling clay to attach the other end of the string to the center of the *inside* of the container lid. Be careful not to use too much string—the cork (or ball) should hang no farther than three-quarters of the way into the container.

4. Fill the container to the top with water.

5. Put the lid tightly on the container with the string and cork (or ball) on the inside.

6. Turn the container upside down (lid on the bottom). The cork should float about three-quarters of the way up inside the container, as shown at right. You are now ready to use your accelerometer to detect acceleration by following the steps on the next page.

7. Put the accelerometer lid side down on a tabletop. Notice that the cork floats straight up in the water.

8. Now gently start pushing the accelerometer across the table at a constant speed. Notice that the cork quickly moves in the direction you are pushing then swings backward. If you did not see this happen, try the same thing again until you are sure you can see the first movement of the cork.

9. Once you are familiar with how to use your accelerometer, try the following changes in motion, and record your observations of the cork's first motion for each change in your ScienceLog.

   a. While moving the device across the table, push a little faster.

   b. While moving the device across the table, slow down.

   c. While moving the device across the table, change the direction that you are pushing. (Try changing both to the left and to the right.)

   d. Make any other changes in motion you can think of. You should only change one part of the motion at a time.

Analysis

10. The cork moves forward (in the direction you were pushing the bottle) when you speed up but backward when you slow down. Why? (Hint: Think about the direction of acceleration.)

11. When you push the bottle at a constant speed, why does the cork quickly swing back after it shows you the direction of acceleration?

12. Imagine you are standing on a corner, watching a car that is waiting at a stoplight. A passenger inside the car is holding some helium balloons. Based on what you observed with your accelerometer, what do you think will happen to the balloons when the car begins moving?

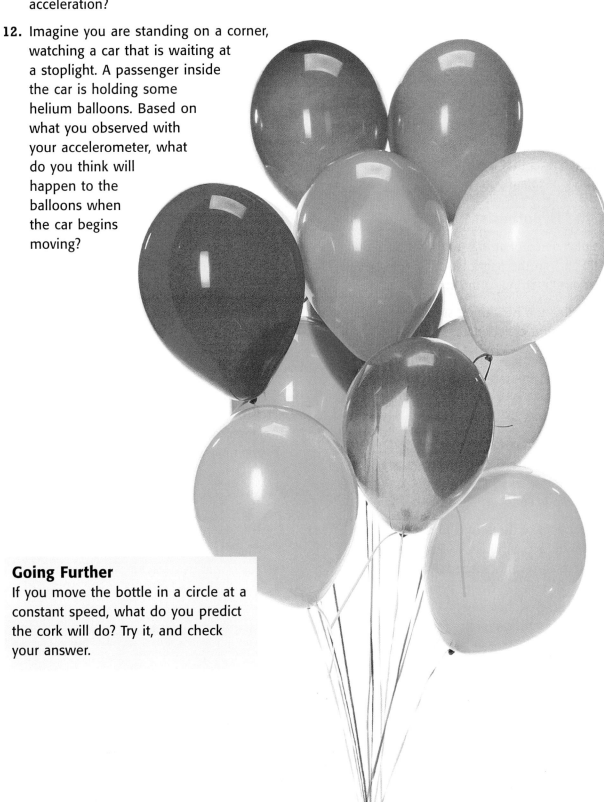

Going Further

If you move the bottle in a circle at a constant speed, what do you predict the cork will do? Try it, and check your answer.

Science Friction

In this experiment, you will investigate three types of friction—static, sliding, and rolling—to determine which is the largest force and which is the smallest force.

Materials

- scissors
- string
- textbook (covered)
- spring scale (force meter)
- 3 to 4 wooden or metal rods

Ask a Question

1. Which type of friction is the largest force—static, sliding, or rolling? Which is the smallest?

Form a Hypothesis

2. In your ScienceLog, write a statement or statements that answer the questions above. Explain your reasoning.

Test the Hypothesis/Collect Data

3. Cut a piece of string, and tie it in a loop that fits in the textbook, as shown below. Hook the string to the spring scale.

4. Practice the next three steps several times before you collect data.

5. To measure the static friction between the book and the table, pull the spring scale very slowly. Record the largest force on the scale before the book starts to move.

6. After the book begins to move, you can determine the sliding friction. Record the force required to keep the book sliding at a slow, constant speed.

7. Place two or three rods under the book to act as rollers. Make sure the rollers are evenly spaced. Place another roller in front of the book so that the book will roll onto it. Pull the force meter slowly. Measure the force needed to keep the book rolling at a constant speed.

Analyze the Results

8. Which type of friction was the largest? Which was the smallest?

9. Do the results support your hypothesis? If not, how would you revise or retest your hypothesis?

Communicate Results

10. Compare your results with those of another group. Are there any differences? Working together, design a way to improve the experiment and resolve possible differences.

Relating Mass and Weight

Why do objects with more mass weigh more than objects with less mass? All objects have weight on Earth because their mass is affected by Earth's gravitational force. Because the mass of an object on Earth is constant, the relationship between the mass of an object and its weight is also constant. You will measure the mass and weight of several objects to verify the relationship between mass and weight on the surface of Earth.

Materials

- metric balance
- small classroom objects
- spring scale (force meter)
- string
- scissors
- graph paper

Collect Data

1. Copy the table below into your ScienceLog.

Mass and Weight Measurements		
Object	Mass (g)	Weight (N)

DO NOT WRITE IN BOOK

2. Using the metric balance, find the mass of five or six small classroom objects designated by your teacher. Record the masses in your ScienceLog.

3. Using the spring scale, find the weight of each object. Record the weights in your ScienceLog. (You may need to use the string to create a hook with which to hang some objects from the spring scale, as shown at right.)

Analyze the Results

4. Using your data, construct a graph of weight (*y*-axis) versus mass (*x*-axis). Draw a line that best fits all your data points.

5. Does the graph confirm the relationship between mass and weight on Earth? Explain your answer.

DISCOVERY LAB

A Marshmallow Catapult

Catapults use projectile motion to launch objects across distances. A variety of factors can affect the distance an object can be launched, such as the weight of the object, how far the catapult is pulled back, and the catapult's strength. In this lab, you will build a simple catapult and determine the angle at which the catapult will launch an object the farthest.

Materials

- plastic spoon
- block of wood, 3.5 cm × 3.5 cm × 1 cm
- duct tape
- miniature marshmallows
- protractor
- meterstick

Form a Hypothesis

1. At what angle, from 10° to 90°, will a catapult launch a marshmallow the farthest?

Test the Hypothesis

2. Copy the table below into your ScienceLog. In your table, add one row each for 20°, 30°, 40°, 50°, 60°, 70°, 80°, and 90° angles.

Angle	Distance 1 (cm)	Distance 2 (cm)	Average distance (cm)
10°	DO NOT WRITE IN BOOK		

3. Attach the plastic spoon to the 1 cm side of the block with duct tape. Use enough tape so that the spoon is attached securely.

4. Place one marshmallow in the center of the spoon, and tape it to the spoon. This serves as a ledge to hold the marshmallow that will be launched.

5. Line up the bottom corner of the block with the bottom center of the protractor, as shown in the photograph. Start with the block at 10°.

6. Place a marshmallow in the spoon, on top of the taped marshmallow. Pull back lightly, and let go. Measure and record the distance from the catapult that the marshmallow lands. Repeat the measurement, and calculate an average.

7. Repeat step 6 for each angle up to 90°.

Analyze the Results

8. At what angle did the catapult launch the marshmallow the farthest? Compare this with your hypothesis. Explain any differences.

Draw Conclusions

9. Does the path of an object's projectile motion depend on the catapult's angle? Support your answer with your data.

10. At what angle should you throw a ball or shoot an arrow so that it will fly the farthest? Why? Support your answer with your data.

Blast Off!

You have been hired as a rocket scientist for NASA. Your job is to design a rocket that will have a controlled flight while carrying a payload. Keep in mind that Newton's laws will have a powerful influence on your rocket.

Procedure

1. When you begin your experiment, your teacher will tape one end of the fishing line to the ceiling.

2. Use a pencil to poke a small hole in each side of the cup near the top. Place a 15 cm piece of string through each hole, and tape down the ends inside.

3. Inflate the balloon, and use the twist tie to hold it closed.

4. Tape the free ends of the strings to the sides of the balloon near the bottom. The cup should hang below the balloon. Your model rocket should look like a hot-air balloon.

5. Thread the fishing line that is hanging from the ceiling through the straw. Tape the balloon securely to the straw.

6. Tape the loose end of the fishing line to the floor.

Collect Data

7. Untie the twist tie while holding the end of the balloon closed. When you are ready, release the end of the balloon. Mark and record the maximum height of the rocket.

8. Repeat the procedure, adding a penny to the cup each time until your rocket cannot lift any more pennies.

Analysis

9. In a paragraph, describe how all three of Newton's laws influenced the flight of your rocket.

10. Draw a diagram of your rocket. Label the action and reaction forces.

Going Further

Brainstorm ways to modify your rocket so that it will carry the most pennies to the maximum height. Select the best design. When your teacher has approved all the designs, each team will build and launch their rocket. Which variable did you modify? How did this variable affect your rocket's flight?

Materials

- tape
- 3 m fishing line
- pencil
- small paper cup
- 15 cm pieces of string (2)
- long, thin balloon
- twist tie
- drinking straw
- meterstick
- pennies

Inertia-Rama!

Inertia is a property of all matter, from small particles of dust to enormous planets and stars. In this lab, you will investigate the inertia of various shapes and types of matter. Keep in mind that each investigation requires you to either overcome or use the object's inertia.

Station 1: Magic Eggs

Procedure

1. There are two eggs at this station—one is hard-boiled (solid all the way through) and the other is raw (liquid inside). The masses of the two eggs are about the same. The eggs are marked so that you can tell them apart.

2. You will spin each egg and then stop it from spinning by placing a finger on its center. Before you do anything to either egg, write some predictions in your ScienceLog: Which egg will be the easiest to spin? Which egg will be the easiest to stop?

3. Spin the hard-boiled egg. Then place your finger on it to make it stop spinning. Record your observations in your ScienceLog.

4. Repeat step 3 with the raw egg.

5. Compare your predictions with your observations. (Repeat steps 3 and 4 if necessary.)

Analysis

6. Explain why the eggs behave differently when you spin them even though they should have the same inertia. (Hint: Think about what happens to the liquid inside the raw egg.)

7. In terms of inertia, explain why the eggs react differently when you try to stop them.

Station 2: Coin in a Cup

Procedure

8. At this station, you will find a coin, an index card, and a cup. Place the card over the cup. Then place the coin on the card over the center of the cup, as shown at right.

Materials

Station 1
- hard-boiled egg
- raw egg

Station 2
- coin
- index card
- cup

Station 3
- spool of thread
- suspended mass
- scissors
- meterstick

9. In your ScienceLog, write down a method for getting the coin into the cup without touching the coin and without lifting the card.

10. Try your method. If it doesn't work, try again until you find a method that does work. When you are done, place the card and coin on the table for the next group.

Analysis

11. Use Newton's first law of motion to explain why the coin falls into the cup when your method is used.

12. Explain why pulling on the card slowly will not work, even though the coin has inertia. (Hint: Friction is a force.)

Station 3: The Magic Thread

Procedure

13. At this station, you will find a spool of thread and a mass hanging from a strong string. Cut a piece of thread about 40 cm long. Tie the thread around the bottom of the mass, as shown at right.

14. Pull gently on the end of the thread. Observe what happens, and record your observations in your ScienceLog.

15. Stop the mass from moving. Now hold the end of the thread so that there is a lot of slack between your fingers and the mass.

16. Give the thread a quick, hard pull. You should observe a very different event. Record your observations in your ScienceLog. Throw away the thread.

Analysis

17. Use Newton's first law of motion to explain why the results of a gentle pull are so different from the results of a hard pull.

Draw Conclusions

18. Remember that both moving and nonmoving objects have inertia. Explain why it is hard to throw a bowling ball and why it is hard to catch a thrown bowling ball.

19. Why is it harder to run with a backpack full of books than with an empty backpack?

Quite a Reaction

Catapults have been used for centuries to throw objects great distances. You may already be familiar with catapults after doing the marshmallow catapult lab. According to Newton's third law of motion (whenever one object exerts a force on a second object, the second object exerts an equal and opposite force on the first), when an object is launched, something must also happen to the catapult. In this activity, you will build a kind of catapult that will allow you to observe the effects of Newton's third law of motion and the law of conservation of momentum.

Conduct an Experiment

1. Glue the cardboard rectangles together to make a stack of three.

2. Push two of the pushpins into the cardboard stack near the corners at one end, as shown below. These will be the anchors for the rubber band.

3. Make a small loop of string.

4. Put the rubber band through the loop of string, and then place the rubber band over the two pushpin anchors. The rubber band should be stretched between the two anchors with the string loop in the middle.

5. Pull the string loop toward the end of the cardboard stack opposite the end with the anchors, and fasten the loop in place with the third pushpin.

6. Place the six straws about 1 cm apart on a tabletop or on the floor. Then carefully center the catapult on top of the straws.

7. Put the marble in the closed end of the V formed by the rubber band.

Materials

- glue
- 10 cm × 15 cm rectangles of cardboard (3)
- 3 pushpins
- string
- rubber band
- 6 plastic straws
- marble
- scissors
- meterstick

8. Use scissors to cut the string holding the rubber band, and observe what happens. (Be careful not to let the scissors touch the cardboard catapult when you cut the string.)

9. Reset the catapult with a new piece of string. Try launching the marble several times to be sure that you have observed everything that happens during a launch. Record all your observations in your ScienceLog.

Analyze the Results

10. Which has more mass, the marble or the catapult?

11. What happened to the catapult when the marble was launched?

12. How far did the marble fly before it landed?

13. Did the catapult move as far as the marble did?

Draw Conclusions

14. Explain why the catapult moved backward.

15. If the forces that made the marble and the catapult move apart are equal, why didn't the marble and the catapult move apart the same distance? (Hint: The fact that the marble can roll after it lands is not the answer.)

16. The momentum of an object depends on the mass and velocity of the object. What is the momentum of the marble before it is launched? What is the momentum of the catapult? Explain your answers.

17. Using the law of conservation of momentum, explain why the marble and the catapult move in opposite directions after the launch.

Going Further
How would you modify the catapult if you wanted to keep it from moving backward as far as it did? (It still has to rest on the straws.) Using items that you can find in the classroom, design a catapult that will move backward less than the original design.

Fluids, Force, and Floating

Why do some objects sink in fluids but others float? In this lab, you'll get a sinking feeling as you determine that an object floats when its weight is less than the buoyant force exerted by the surrounding fluid.

Materials

- large rectangular tank or plastic tub
- water
- metric ruler
- small rectangular baking pan
- labeled masses
- metric balance
- paper towels

Procedure

1. Copy the table below into your ScienceLog.

Measurement	Trial 1	Trial 2
Length (l), cm		
Width (w), cm		
Initial height (h_1), cm		
Initial volume (V_1), cm³ $V_1 = l \times w \times h_1$		
New height (h_2), cm		
New volume (V_2), cm³ $V_2 = l \times w \times h_2$		
Displaced volume (ΔV), cm³ $\Delta V = V_2 - V_1$		
Mass of displaced water, g $m = \Delta V \times 1 \text{ g/cm}^3$		
Weight of displaced water, N (buoyant force)		
Weight of pan and masses, N		

2. Fill the tank or tub half full with water.

3. Measure (in centimeters) the length, width, and initial height of the water. Record your measurements in the table.

4. Using the equation given in the table, determine the initial volume of water in the tank. Record your results in the table.

5. Place the pan in the water, and place masses in the pan, as shown on the next page. Keep adding masses until the pan sinks to about three-quarters of its height. This will cause the water level in the tank to rise. Record the new height of the water in the table. Then use this value to determine and record the new volume of water.

6. Determine the volume of the water that was displaced by the pan and masses, and record this value in the table. The displaced volume is equal to the new volume minus the initial volume.

7. Determine the mass of the displaced water by multiplying the displaced volume by its density (1 g/cm^3). Record the mass in the table.

8. Divide the mass by 100. The value you get is the weight of the displaced water in newtons (N). This is equal to the buoyant force. Record the weight of the displaced water in the table.

9. Remove the pan and masses, and determine their total mass (in grams) using the balance. Convert the mass to weight (N), as you did in step 8. Record the weight of the masses and pan in the table.

10. Place the empty pan back in the tank. Perform a second trial by repeating steps 5–9. This time add masses until the pan is just about to sink.

Analysis

11. In your ScienceLog, compare the buoyant force (the weight of the displaced water) with the weight of the pan and masses for both trials.

12. How did the buoyant force differ between the two trials? Explain.

13. Based on your observations, what would happen if you were to add even more mass to the pan than you did in the second trial? Explain your answer in terms of the buoyant force.

14. What would happen if you put the masses in the water without the pan? What difference does the pan's shape make?

Using Scientific Methods

Density Diver

Crew members of a submarine can control the submarine's density underwater by allowing water to flow into and out of special tanks. These changes in density affect the submarine's position in the water. In this lab, you'll control a "density diver" to learn for yourself how the density of an object affects its position in a fluid.

Materials

- 2 L plastic bottle with screw-on cap
- water
- medicine dropper

Form a Hypothesis

1. How does the density of an object determine whether the object floats, sinks, or maintains its position in a fluid? Write your hypothesis in your ScienceLog.

Test the Hypothesis

2. Completely fill the 2 L plastic bottle with water.

3. Fill the diver (medicine dropper) approximately halfway with water, and place it in the bottle. The diver should float with only part of the rubber bulb above the surface of the water. If the diver floats too high, carefully remove it from the bottle and add a small amount of water to the diver. Place the diver back in the bottle. If you add too much water and the diver sinks, empty out the bottle and diver and go back to step 2.

4. Put the cap on the bottle tightly so that no water leaks out.

5. Apply various pressures to the bottle. Carefully watch the water level inside the diver as you squeeze and release the bottle. Record what happens in your ScienceLog.

6. Try to make the diver rise, sink, or stop at any level. Record your technique and your results.

Analyze the Results

7. How do the changes inside the diver affect its position in the surrounding fluid?

8. What is the relationship between the water level inside the diver and the diver's density? Explain.

Draw Conclusions

9. What relationship did you observe between the diver's density and the diver's position in the fluid?

10. Explain how your density diver is like a submarine.

11. Explain how pressure on the bottle is related to the diver's density. Be sure to include Pascal's principle in your explanation.

12. What was the variable in this experiment? What factors were controlled?

DISCOVERY LAB

LabBook

Taking Flight

MAKING MODELS

When air moves above and below the wing of an airplane, the air pressure below the wing is higher than the air pressure above the wing. This creates lift. In this activity, you will build a model airplane to help you identify how wing size and thrust (forward force provided by the engine) affect the lift needed for flight.

Materials

- sheet of paper

Procedure

1. Fold the paper in half lengthwise and open it again, as shown at right. Make sure to crease all folds well.

2. Fold the right- and left-hand corners toward the center crease.

3. Fold the entire sheet in half along the center crease.

4. With the plane lying on its side, fold the top front edge down so that it meets the bottom edge, as shown.

5. Fold the top wing down again, bringing the top edge to the bottom edge.

6. Turn the plane over, and repeat steps 4 and 5.

7. Raise both wings away from the body to a position slightly above horizontal. Your plane is ready!

Collect Data

8. Point the plane slightly upward, and gently throw it. Repeat several times. Describe your observations in your ScienceLog. **Caution:** Be sure to point the plane away from people.

9. Make the wings smaller by folding them one more time. Gently throw the plane overhand. Repeat several times. Describe your observations in your ScienceLog.

10. Try to achieve the same flight path you saw when the plane's wings were bigger. Record your technique.

Analysis

11. What happened to the plane's flight when you reduced the size of its wings? Explain.

12. What provided your airplane's thrust?

13. From your observations, how does changing the thrust affect the lift?

Using Scientific Methods

A Powerful Workout

Does the amount of work you do depend on how fast you do it? No! But doing work in a shorter amount of time does affect your power—the rate at which work is done. In this lab, you'll calculate your work and power when climbing a flight of stairs at different speeds. Then you'll compare your power with that of an ordinary household object—a 100 W light bulb.

Materials

- flight of stairs
- metric ruler
- stopwatch

Ask a Question

1. How does your power when climbing a flight of stairs compare with the power of a 100 W light bulb?

Form a Hypothesis

2. In your ScienceLog, write a hypothesis that answers the question in step 1. Explain your reasoning.

3. Copy Table 1 into your ScienceLog.

Table 1 Data Collection				
Height of step (cm)	Number of steps	Height of stairs (m)	Time for slow walk (s)	Time for quick walk (s)
		DO NOT WRITE IN BOOK		

Test the Hypothesis

4. Measure the height of one stair step. Record the measurement in Table 1.

5. Count the number of stairs, including the top step, and record this number in Table 1.

6. Calculate the height (in meters) of the stairs by multiplying the number of steps by the height of one step. Record your answer. (You will need to convert from centimeters to meters.)

7. Using a stopwatch, measure how many seconds it takes you to walk slowly up the flight of stairs. Record your measurement in Table 1.

8. Now measure how many seconds it takes you to walk quickly up the flight of stairs. Be careful not to overexert yourself.

Analyze the Results

9. Copy Table 2 into your ScienceLog.

Table 2 Work and Power Calculations			
Weight (N)	Work (J)	Power for slow walk (W)	Power for quick walk (W)
DO NOT WRITE IN BOOK			

10. Determine your weight in newtons by multiplying your weight in pounds (lb) by 4.45 N/lb. Record it in Table 2.

11. Calculate and record your work done to climb the stairs using the following equation:

$$\text{Work} = \text{Force} \times \text{distance}$$

Remember that 1 N•m is 1 J. (Hint: Remember that force is expressed in newtons.)

12. Calculate and record your power for each trial (the slow walk and the quick walk) using the following equation:

$$\text{Power} = \frac{\text{Work}}{\text{time}}$$

Remember that the unit for power is the watt (1 W = 1 J/s).

Draw Conclusions

13. In step 11 you calculated your work done in climbing the stairs. Why didn't you calculate your work for each trial?

14. Look at your hypothesis in step 2. Was your hypothesis supported? Write a statement in your ScienceLog that describes how your power in each trial compares with the power of a 100 W light bulb.

15. The work done to move one electron in a light bulb is very small. Write down two reasons why the power is large. (Hints: How many electrons are in the filament of a light bulb? Why was more power used in your second trial?)

Communicate Results

16. Write your average power in a class data table. Calculate the average power for the class. How many light bulbs would it take to equal the power of one student?

Where is work done in a light bulb?
Electrons in the filament move back and forth very quickly. These moving electrons do work by heating up the filament and making it glow.

Inclined to Move

In this lab, you will examine a simple machine—an inclined plane. Your task is to compare the work done with and without the inclined plane and to analyze the effects of friction.

Materials

- string
- small book
- spring scale
- meterstick
- wooden board
- blocks
- graph paper

Collect Data

1. Copy the table below into your ScienceLog.

2. Tie a piece of string around a book. Attach the spring scale to the string. Use the spring scale to slowly lift the book to a height of 50 cm. Record the output force (the force needed to lift the book). The output force is constant throughout the lab.

3. Use the board and blocks to make a ramp 10 cm high at the highest point. Measure and record the ramp length.

4. Keeping the spring scale parallel to the ramp, as shown below, slowly raise the book. Record the input force (the force needed to pull the book up the ramp).

5. Increase the height of the ramp by 10 cm. Repeat step 4. Repeat this step for each ramp height up to 50 cm.

Analyze the Results

6. The *real* work done includes the work done to overcome friction. Calculate the real work at each height by multiplying the ramp length (converted to meters) by the input force. Graph your results, plotting work (*y*-axis) versus height (*x*-axis).

7. The *ideal* work is the work you would do if there were no friction. Calculate the ideal work at each height by multiplying the ramp height (m) by the output force. Plot the data on your graph.

Force vs. Height			
Ramp height (cm)	Output force (N)	Ramp length (cm)	Input force (N)
10			
20			
30		DO NOT WRITE	
40		IN BOOK	
50			

Draw Conclusions

8. Does it require more or less force and work to raise the book using the ramp? Explain, using your calculations and graphs.

9. What is the relationship between the height of the inclined plane and the input force?

10. Write a statement that summarizes why the slopes of the two graphs are different.

Building Machines

You are surrounded by machines. Some are simple machines, such as ramps for wheelchair access to a building. Others are compound machines, like elevators and escalators, that are made of two or more simple machines. In this lab, you will design and build several simple machines and a compound machine.

Procedure

1. Use the listed materials to build a model of each simple machine: inclined plane, lever, wheel and axle, pulley, screw, and wedge. Describe and draw each model in your ScienceLog.

2. In your ScienceLog, design a compound machine using the materials listed. You may design a machine that already exists, or you may invent your own machine—be creative!

3. After your teacher approves your design, build your compound machine.

Analysis

4. List a possible use for each of your simple machines.

5. Compare your simple machines with those created by your classmates.

6. How many simple machines are in your compound machine? List them.

7. Compare your compound machine with those created by your classmates.

8. What is a possible use for your compound machine? Why did you design it as you did?

9. A compound machine is listed in the Materials list. What is it?

Materials

- bottle caps
- cardboard
- craft sticks
- empty thread spools
- glue
- modeling clay
- paper
- pencils
- rubber bands
- scissors
- shoe boxes
- stones
- straws
- string
- tape
- other materials available in your classroom that are approved by your teacher

Going Further

Design a compound machine that has all the simple machines in it. Explain what the machine will do and how it will make work easier. With your teacher's approval, build your machine.

Wheeling and Dealing

A wheel and axle is one type of simple machine. A crank handle, such as that used in pencil sharpeners, ice-cream makers, and water wells is one kind of wheel and axle. In this lab, you will use a crank handle to find out how a wheel and axle helps you do work. You will also determine what effect the length of the handle has on the operation of the machine.

Materials

- wheel and axle assembly
- meterstick
- large mass
- spring scale
- handles
- 0.5 m string
- 2 C-clamps

Procedure

1. Copy Table 1 into your ScienceLog.

2. Measure the radius (in meters) of the large dowel in the wheel and axle assembly. Record this in Table 1 as the axle radius, which remains constant throughout the lab. (Hint: Measure the diameter and divide by two.)

3. Using the spring scale, measure the weight of the large mass. Record this in Table 1 as the output force, which remains constant throughout the lab.

4. Use two C-clamps to secure the wheel and axle assembly to the table, as shown at right.

Collect Data

5. Measure the length (in meters) of handle 1. Record this as a wheel radius in Table 1.

6. Insert the handle into the hole in the axle. Attach one end of the string to the large mass and the other end to the screw in the axle. The mass should hang down and the handle should turn freely.

7. Turn the handle to lift the mass off the floor. Hold the spring scale upside down, and attach it to the end of the handle. Measure the force (in newtons) as the handle pulls up on the spring scale. Record this as the input force.

Table 1 Data Collection				
Handle	Axle radius (m)	Output force (N)	Wheel radius (m)	Input force (N)
1				
2				
3				
4				

DO NOT WRITE IN BOOK

8. Remove the spring scale, and lower the mass to the floor. Remove the handle.

9. Repeat steps 5 through 8 with the other three handles. Record all data in Table 1.

Analyze the Results

10. Copy Table 2 into your ScienceLog.

						Table 2 Calculations	

Handle	Axle distance (m)	Wheel distance (m)	Work input (J)	Work output (J)	Mechanical efficiency (%)	Mechanical advantage
1						
2						
3						
4						

DO NOT WRITE IN BOOK

11. Calculate the following for each handle using the equations given. Record your answers in Table 2.

   a. Distance axle rotates =
   $2 \times \pi \times$ axle radius

   Distance wheel rotates =
   $2 \times \pi \times$ wheel radius

   (Use 3.14 for the value of π.)

   b. Work input =
   input force $\times$ wheel distance

   Work output =
   output force $\times$ axle distance

   c. Mechanical efficiency =
   $\dfrac{\text{work output}}{\text{work input}} \times 100$

   d. Mechanical advantage =
   $\dfrac{\text{wheel radius}}{\text{axle radius}}$

Draw Conclusions

12. What happens to work output and work input as the handle length increases? Why?

13. What happens to mechanical efficiency as the handle length increases? Why?

14. What happens to mechanical advantage as the handle length increases? Why?

15. What will happen to mechanical advantage if the handle length is kept constant and the axle radius gets larger?

16. What factors were controlled in this experiment? What was the variable?

Finding Energy

When you coast down a big hill on a bike or skateboard, you may notice that you pick up speed. Because you are moving, you have kinetic energy—the energy of motion. Where does that energy come from? In this lab you will find out!

Materials

- 2 or 3 books
- wooden board
- masking tape
- meterstick
- metric balance
- rolling cart
- stopwatch

Form a Hypothesis

1. Where does the kinetic energy come from when you roll down a hill? Write your hypothesis in your ScienceLog.

Conduct an Experiment

2. Copy Table 1 into your ScienceLog.

<table>
<tr><td colspan="8" align="center">Table 1 Data Collection</td></tr>
<tr><td rowspan="2">Height of ramp (m)</td><td rowspan="2">Length of ramp (m)</td><td rowspan="2">Mass of cart (kg)</td><td rowspan="2">Weight of cart (N)</td><td colspan="3">Time of trial (s)</td><td rowspan="2">Average time (s)</td></tr>
<tr><td>1</td><td>2</td><td>3</td></tr>
<tr><td colspan="8" align="center">DO NOT WRITE IN BOOK</td></tr>
</table>

3. Make a ramp with the books and board.

4. Use masking tape to make a starting line. Be sure the starting line is far enough from the top so the cart can be placed behind the line.

5. Place a strip of masking tape at the bottom of the ramp to mark the finish line.

6. Determine the height of the ramp by measuring the height of the starting line and subtracting the height of the finish line. Record the height of the ramp in meters in Table 1.

7. Measure the distance in meters between the starting and the finish lines. Record this distance as the length of the ramp in Table 1.

8. Use the metric balance to find the mass of the cart in grams. Convert this to kilograms by dividing by 1,000. Record the mass in kilograms in Table 1.

9. Multiply the mass by 10 to get the weight of the cart in newtons. Record the weight in Table 1.

Collect Data

10. Set the cart behind the starting line, and release it. Use the stopwatch to time how long it takes for the cart to reach the finish line. Record the time in Table 1.

11. Repeat step 10 twice more, and average the results. Record the average time in Table 1.

Analyze the Results

12. Copy Table 2 into your ScienceLog.

Table 2 Calculations			
Average speed (m/s)	Final speed (m/s)	Kinetic energy at bottom (J)	Gravitational potential energy at top (J)
	DO NOT WRITE IN BOOK		

13. Calculate and record the following quantities for the cart in Table 2 using your data and the equations below:

a. Average speed = $\dfrac{\text{length of ramp}}{\text{average time}}$

b. Final speed = 2 × average speed
(This equation works because the cart accelerates smoothly from 0 m/s.)

c. Kinetic energy = $\dfrac{\text{mass} \times (\text{final speed})^2}{2}$
(Remember that $1\ \text{kg} \cdot \text{m}^2/\text{s}/\text{s} = 1\ \text{J}$, the unit used to express energy.)

d. Gravitational potential energy = weight × height
(Remember that $1\ \text{N} = 1\ \text{kg} \cdot \text{m}/\text{s}/\text{s}$, so $1\ \text{N} \times 1\ \text{m} = 1\ \text{kg} \cdot \text{m}^2/\text{s}/\text{s} = 1\ \text{J}$.)

Draw Conclusions

14. How does the cart's gravitational potential energy at the top of the ramp compare with its kinetic energy at the bottom? Does this support your hypothesis? Explain your answer.

15. You probably found that the gravitational potential energy of the cart at the top of the ramp was close but not exactly equal to the kinetic energy of the cart at the bottom. Explain this finding.

16. While riding your bike, you coast down both a small hill and a large hill. Compare your final speed at the bottom of the small hill with your final speed at the bottom of the large hill. Explain your answer.

Energy of a Pendulum

A pendulum clock is a compound machine that uses stored energy to do work. A spring stores energy, and with each swing of the pendulum, some of that stored energy is used to move the hands of the clock. In this lab you will take a close look at the energy conversions that occur as a pendulum swings.

Materials

- 1 m of string
- 100 g hooked mass
- marker
- meterstick

Collect Data

1. Make a pendulum by tying the string around the hook of the mass. Use the marker and the meterstick to mark points on the string that are 50 cm, 70 cm, and 90 cm away from the mass.

2. Hold the string at the 50 cm mark. Gently pull the mass to the side, and release it without pushing it. Observe at least 10 swings of the pendulum.

3. In your ScienceLog, record your observations. Be sure to note how fast and how high the pendulum swings.

4. Repeat steps 2 and 3 while holding the string at the 70 cm mark and again while holding the string at the 90 cm mark.

Analyze the Results

5. In your ScienceLog, list similarities and differences in the motion of the pendulum during all three trials.

6. At which point (or points) of the swing was the pendulum moving the slowest? the fastest?

Draw Conclusions

7. In each trial, at which point (or points) of the swing did the pendulum have the greatest potential energy? the smallest potential energy? (Hint: Think about your answers to question 6.)

8. At which point (or points) of the swing did the pendulum have the greatest kinetic energy? the smallest kinetic energy? Explain your answers.

9. Describe the relationship between the pendulum's potential energy and its kinetic energy on its way down. Explain.

10. What improvements might reduce the amount of energy used to overcome friction so that the pendulum would swing for a longer period of time?

Eggstremely Fragile

All moving objects have kinetic energy. The faster an object is moving, the more kinetic energy it has. When a falling object hits the floor, the law of conservation of energy requires that the energy be transferred to another object or changed into another form of energy.

When an unprotected egg hits the ground from a height of 1 m, most of the kinetic energy of the falling egg is transferred to the pieces of the shell—with messy results. In this lab you will design a protection system for an egg.

Materials

- raw egg
- empty half-pint milk carton
- assorted materials provided by your teacher

Conduct an Experiment

1. Using the materials provided by your teacher, design a protection system that will prevent the egg from breaking when it is dropped from heights of 1, 2, and 3 m. Keep the following points in mind while developing your egg-protection system:

   a. The egg and its protection system must fit inside the closed milk carton. (Note: The milk carton will not be dropped with the egg.)

   b. The protective materials don't have to be soft.

   c. The protective materials can surround the egg or can be attached to the egg at various points.

2. In your ScienceLog, explain why you chose your materials.

3. You will perform the three trials at a time and location specified by your teacher. Record your results for each trial in your ScienceLog.

Analyze the Results

4. Did your egg survive all three trials? If it did not, why did your egg-protection system fail? If your egg did survive, what features of your egg-protecting system transferred or absorbed the energy?

Draw Conclusions

5. How do egg cartons like those you find in a grocery store protect eggs from mishandling?

Feel the Heat

Heat is the transfer of energy between objects at different temperatures. Energy moves from objects at higher temperatures to objects at lower temperatures. If two objects are left in contact for a while, the warmer object will cool down, and the cooler object will warm up until they eventually reach the same temperature. In this activity, you will combine equal masses of water and iron nails at different temperatures to determine which has a greater effect on the final temperature.

Materials

- rubber band
- 10–12 nails
- metric balance
- 30 cm of string
- 9 oz plastic-foam cups (2)
- hot water
- 100 mL graduated cylinder
- cold water
- thermometer
- paper towels

Make a Prediction

1. When you combine substances at two different temperatures, will the final temperature be closer to the initial temperature of the warmer substance or of the colder substance, or halfway in between? Write your prediction in your ScienceLog.

Conduct an Experiment/Collect Data

2. Copy the table below into your ScienceLog.

		Data Collection Table			
Trial	**Mass of nails (g)**	**Volume of water that equals mass of nails (mL)**	**Initial temp. of water and nails (°C)**	**Initial temp. of water to which nails will be transferred (°C)**	**Final temp. of water and nails combined (°C)**
1					
2					

DO NOT WRITE IN BOOK

3. Use the rubber band to bundle the nails together. Find and record the mass of the bundle. Tie a length of string around the bundle, leaving one end of the string 15 cm long.

4. Put the bundle of nails into one of the cups, letting the string dangle outside the cup. Fill the cup with enough hot water to cover the nails, and set it aside for at least 5 minutes.

5. Use the graduated cylinder to measure enough cold water to exactly equal the mass of the nails (1 mL of water = 1 g). Record this volume in the table.

6. Measure and record the temperature of the hot water with the nails and the temperature of the cold water.

7. Use the string to transfer the bundle of nails to the cup of cold water. Use the thermometer to monitor the temperature of the water-nail mixture. When the temperature stops changing, record this final temperature in the table.

8. Empty the cups, and dry the nails.

9. For Trial 2, repeat steps 3 through 8, but switch the hot and cold water. Record all of your measurements.

Analyze the Results

10. In Trial 1, you used equal masses of cold water and nails. Did the final temperature support your initial prediction? Explain.

11. In Trial 2, you used equal masses of hot water and nails. Did the final temperature support your initial prediction? Explain.

12. In Trial 1, which material—the water or the nails—changed temperature the most after you transferred the nails? What about in Trial 2? Explain your answers.

Draw Conclusions

13. The cold water in Trial 1 gained energy. Where did the energy come from?

14. How does the energy gained by the nails in Trial 2 compare with the energy lost by the hot water in Trial 2? Explain.

15. Which material seems to be able to hold energy better? Explain your answer.

16. Specific heat capacity is a property of matter that indicates how much energy is required to change the temperature of 1 kg of a material by 1°C. Which material in this activity has a higher specific heat capacity (changes temperature less for the same amount of energy)?

17. Would it be better to have pots and pans made from a material with a high specific heat capacity or a low specific heat capacity? Explain your answer. (Hint: Do you want the pan or the food in the pan to absorb all of the energy from the stove?)

Communicate Results

18. Share your results with your classmates. Discuss how you would change your prediction to include your knowledge of specific heat capacity.

Save the Cube!

The biggest enemy of an ice cube is the transfer of thermal energy—heat. Energy can be transferred to an ice cube in three ways: conduction (the transfer of energy through direct contact), convection (the transfer of energy by the movement of a liquid or gas), and radiation (the transfer of energy through matter or space). Your challenge in this activity is to design a way to protect an ice cube as much as possible from all three types of energy transfer.

Materials

- small plastic bag
- ice cube
- assorted materials provided by your teacher
- empty half-pint milk carton
- metric balance
- small plastic or paper cup

Procedure

1. Follow these guidelines: Use a plastic bag to hold the ice cube and any water from its melting. You may use any of the materials to protect the ice cube. The ice cube, bag, and protection must all fit inside the milk carton.

2. Describe your proposed design in your ScienceLog. Explain how your design protects against each type of energy transfer.

3. Find the mass of the empty cup, and record it in your ScienceLog. Then find and record the mass of an empty plastic bag.

4. Place an ice cube in the bag. Quickly find and record their mass together.

5. Quickly wrap the bag (and the ice cube inside) in its protection. Remember that the package must fit in the milk carton.

6. Place your protected ice cube in the "thermal zone" set up by your teacher. After 10 minutes, remove the package from the zone and remove the protective material from the plastic bag and ice cube.

7. Open the bag. Pour any water into the cup. Find and record the mass of the cup and water together.

8. Find and record the mass of the water by subtracting the mass of the empty cup from the mass of the cup and water.

9. Use the same method to find and record the mass of the ice cube.

10. Find the percentage of the ice cube that melted using the following equation:

$$\% \text{ melted} = \frac{\text{mass of water}}{\text{mass of ice cube}} \times 100$$

11. Record this percentage in your ScienceLog and on the board.

Analysis

12. Compared with other designs in your class, how well did your design protect against each type of energy transfer? How could you improve your design?

13. Why is a white plastic-foam cooler so useful for keeping ice frozen?

Counting Calories

Energy transferred by heat is often expressed in units called calories. In this lab, you will build a model of a device called a calorimeter. Scientists often use calorimeters to measure the amount of energy that can be transferred by a substance. In this experiment, you will construct your own calorimeter and test it by measuring the energy released by a hot penny.

Materials

- small plastic-foam cup with lid
- thermometer
- large plastic-foam cup
- water
- 100 mL graduated cylinder
- tongs
- heat source
- penny
- stopwatch

Procedure

1. Copy the table below into your ScienceLog.

Data Collection Table									
Seconds	0	15	30	45	60	75	90	105	120
Water temp. (°C)									

DO NOT WRITE IN BOOK

2. Place the lid on the small plastic-foam cup, and insert a thermometer through the hole in the top of the lid. (The thermometer should not touch the bottom of the cup.) Place the small cup inside the large cup to complete the calorimeter.

3. Remove the lid from the small cup, and add 50 mL of room-temperature water to the cup. Measure the water's temperature, and record the value in the first column (0 seconds) of the table.

4. Using tongs, heat the penny carefully. Add the penny to the water in the small cup, and replace the lid. Start your stopwatch.

5. Every 15 seconds, measure and record the temperature. Gently swirl the large cup to stir the water, and continue recording temperatures for 2 minutes (120 seconds).

Analysis

6. What was the total temperature change of the water after 2 minutes?

7. The number of calories absorbed by the water is the mass of the water (in grams) multiplied by the temperature change (in °C) of the water. How many calories were absorbed by the water? (Hint: 1 mL of water = 1 g of water)

8. In terms of heat, explain where the calories to change the water temperature came from.

Made to Order

Imagine that you are a new employee at the Elements-4-U Company, which custom builds elements. Your job is to construct the atomic nucleus for each element ordered by your clients. You were hired for the position because of your knowledge about what a nucleus is made of and your understanding of how isotopes of an element differ from each other. Now it's time to put that knowledge to work!

Materials

- 4 protons (white plastic-foam balls, 2–3 cm in diameter)
- 6 neutrons (blue plastic-foam balls, 2–3 cm in diameter)
- 20 strong-force connectors (toothpicks)
- periodic table

Procedure

1. Copy the table below into your ScienceLog. Be sure to leave room to expand the table to include more elements.

	Hydrogen-1	Hydrogen-2	Helium-3	Helium-4	Lithium-7	Beryllium-9	Beryllium-10
No. of protons							
No. of neutrons							
Atomic number							
Mass number							

DO NOT WRITE IN BOOK

2. Your first assignment: the nucleus of hydrogen-1. Pick up one proton (a white plastic-foam ball). Congratulations! You have just built a hydrogen-1 nucleus, the simplest nucleus possible.

3. Count the number of protons and neutrons in the nucleus, and fill in rows 1 and 2 for this element in the table.

4. Use the information in rows 1 and 2 to determine the atomic number and mass number of the element. Record this information in the table.

5. Draw a picture of your model in your ScienceLog.

6. Hydrogen-2 is an isotope of hydrogen that has one proton and one neutron. Using a strong-force connector, add a neutron to your hydrogen-1 nucleus. (Remember that in a nucleus, the protons and neutrons are held together by the strong force, which is represented in this activity by the toothpicks.) Repeat steps 3–5.

7. Helium-3 is an isotope of helium that has two protons and one neutron. Add one proton to your hydrogen-2 nucleus to create a helium-3 nucleus. Each particle should be connected to the other two particles so they make a triangle, not a line. Protons and neutrons always form the smallest arrangement possible because the strong force pulls them together. Repeat steps 3–5.

8. For the next part of the lab, you will need to use information from the periodic table of the elements. Look at the illustration at right. It shows the periodic table entry for carbon, one of the most abundant elements on Earth. For your job, the most important information in the periodic table is the atomic number. You can find the atomic number of any element at the top of its entry on the table. In the example, the atomic number of carbon is 6.

9. Use the information in the periodic table to build models of the following isotopes of elements: helium-4, lithium-7, beryllium-9, and beryllium-10. Remember to put the protons and neutrons as close together as possible—each particle should attach to at least two others. Repeat steps 3–5 for each isotope.

Atomic number

6

C

Carbon

12.0

Analyze the Results

10. What is the relationship between the number of protons and the atomic number?

11. If you know the atomic number and the mass number of an isotope, how could you figure out the number of neutrons in its nucleus?

12. Look up uranium on the periodic table.
    a. What is the atomic number of uranium?
    b. How many neutrons does the isotope uranium-235 have?

Communicate Results

13. Compare your model with the models of other groups. How are they similar? How are they different?

Going Further
Working with another group, combine your models. Identify the element (and isotope) you have created.

Create a Periodic Table

You probably have classification systems for many things in your life, such as your clothes, your books, and your CDs. One of the most important classification systems in science is the periodic table of the elements. In this lab you will develop your own classification system for a collection of ordinary objects. You will analyze trends in your system and compare your system with the periodic table of the elements.

Materials

- bag of objects
- 20 squares of paper, each 3 × 3 cm
- metric balance
- metric ruler
- 2 sheets of graph paper

Procedure

1. Your teacher will give you a bag of objects. Your bag is missing one item. Examine the items carefully. Describe the missing object in as many ways as you can in your ScienceLog. Be sure to include the reasons why you think the missing object has these characteristics.

2. Lay the paper squares out on your desk or table so that you have a grid of five rows of four squares each.

3. Arrange your objects on the grid in a logical order. (You must decide what order is logical!) You should end up with one blank square for the missing object.

4. In your ScienceLog, describe the basis for your arrangement.

5. Measure the mass (g) and diameter (mm) of each object, and record your results in the appropriate square. Each square (except the empty one) should have one object and two written measurements on it.

6. Examine your pattern again. Does the order in which your objects are arranged still make sense? Explain.

7. Rearrange the squares and their objects if necessary to improve your arrangement. Describe the basis for the new arrangement in your ScienceLog.

8. Working across the rows, number the squares 1 to 20. When you get to the end of a row, continue numbering in the first square of the next row.

9. Copy your grid into your ScienceLog. In each square, be sure to list the type of object and label all measurements with appropriate units.

Analyze the Results

10. Make a graph of mass (y-axis) versus object number (x-axis). Label each axis, and title the graph.

11. Now make a graph of diameter (y-axis) versus object number (x-axis).

Communicate Results

12. Discuss each graph with your classmates. Try to identify any important features of the graph. For example, does the graph form a line or a curve? Is there anything unusual about the graph? What do these features tell you? Write your answers in your ScienceLog.

Draw Conclusions

13. How is your arrangement of objects similar to the periodic table of the elements found in this textbook? How is your arrangement different from that periodic table?

14. Look back at your prediction about the missing object. Do you think it is still accurate? Try to improve your description by estimating the mass and diameter of the missing object. Record your estimates in your ScienceLog.

15. Mendeleev created a periodic table of elements and predicted characteristics of missing elements. How is your experiment similar to Mendeleev's work?

Covalent Marshmallows

A hydrogen atom has one electron in its outer energy level, but two electrons are required to fill its outer level. An oxygen atom has six electrons in its outer energy level, but eight electrons are required to fill its outer level. In order to fill their outer energy levels, two atoms of hydrogen and one atom of oxygen can share electrons, as shown below. Such a sharing of electrons to fill the outer level of atoms is called covalent bonding. When hydrogen and oxygen bond in this manner, a molecule of water is formed. In this lab you will build a three-dimensional model of water in order to better understand the covalent bonds formed in a water molecule.

Materials

- marshmallows (2 of one color, 1 of another color)
- toothpicks

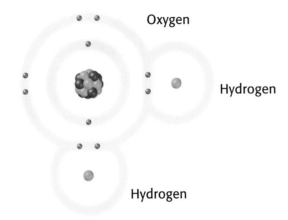

Oxygen

Hydrogen

Hydrogen

A Model of a Water Molecule

Procedure

1. Using the marshmallows and toothpicks, create a model of a water molecule. Use the diagram above for guidance in building your model.

2. Draw a sketch of your model in your ScienceLog. Be sure to label the hydrogen and oxygen atoms on your sketch.

3. Draw an electron-dot diagram of the water molecule in your ScienceLog. (Refer to the chapter text if you need help drawing an electron-dot diagram.)

Analysis

4. What do the marshmallows represent? What do the toothpicks represent?

5. Why are the marshmallows different colors?

6. Compare your model with the picture above. How might your model be improved to more accurately represent a water molecule?

7. Hydrogen in nature can covalently bond to form hydrogen molecules, H_2. How could you model this using the marshmallows and toothpicks?

8. Draw an electron-dot diagram of a hydrogen molecule in your ScienceLog.

9. Which do you think would be more difficult to create—a model of an ionic bond or a model of a covalent bond? Explain your answer.

Going Further

Create a model of a carbon dioxide molecule, which consists of two oxygen atoms and one carbon atom. The structure is similar to the structure of water, although the three atoms bond in a straight line instead of at angles. The bond between each oxygen atom and the carbon atom in a carbon dioxide molecule is a "double bond," so use two connections. Do the double bonds in carbon dioxide appear stronger or weaker than the single bonds in water? Explain your answer.

Finding a Balance

Usually, balancing a chemical equation involves just writing in your ScienceLog. But in this activity, you will use models to practice balancing chemical equations, as shown below. By following the rules, you will soon become an expert equation balancer!

Materials

• envelopes, each labeled with an unbalanced equation

Example

$$\_H_2 + \_O_2 \rightarrow \_H_2O$$

Balanced Equation

$$2H_2 + O_2 \rightarrow 2H_2O$$

Procedure

1. The rules:
   a. Reactant-molecule models may be placed only to the left of the arrow.
   b. Product-molecule models may be placed only to the right of the arrow.
   c. You may use only complete molecule models.
   d. At least one of each of the reactant and product molecules shown in the equation must be included in the model when you are finished.

2. Select one of the labeled envelopes. Copy the unbalanced equation written on the envelope into your ScienceLog.

3. Open the envelope, and pull out the molecule models and the arrow. Place the arrow in the center of your work area.

4. Put one model of each molecule that is a reactant on the left side of the arrow and one model of each product on the right side.

5. Add one reactant-molecule or product-molecule model at a time until the number of each of the different-colored squares on each side of the arrow is the same. Remember to follow the rules.

6. When the equation is balanced, count the number of each of the molecule models you used. Write these numbers as coefficients, as shown in the balanced equation above.

7. Select another envelope, and repeat the steps until you have balanced all of the equations.

Analysis

8. The rules specify that you are only allowed to use complete molecule models. How is this similar to what occurs in a real chemical reaction?

9. In chemical reactions, energy is either released or absorbed. In your ScienceLog, devise a way to improve the model to show energy being released or absorbed.

DISCOVERY LAB

Cata-what? Catalyst!

Catalysts increase the rate of a chemical reaction without being changed during the reaction. In this experiment, hydrogen peroxide, H_2O_2, decomposes into oxygen, O_2, and water, H_2O. An enzyme present in liver cells acts as a catalyst for this reaction. You will investigate the relationship between the amount of the catalyst and the rate of the decomposition reaction.

Ask a Question

1. How does the amount of a catalyst affect reaction rate?

Form a Hypothesis

2. In your ScienceLog, write a statement that answers the question above. Explain your reasoning.

Test the Hypothesis

3. Put a small piece of masking tape near the top of each test tube, and label the tubes 1, 2, and 3.

4. Create a hot-water bath by filling the beaker half-full with hot water.

5. Using the funnel and graduated cylinder, measure 5 mL of the hydrogen peroxide solution into each test tube. Place the test tubes in the hot-water bath for 5 minutes.

6. While the test tubes warm up, grind one liver cube with the mortar and pestle.

7. After 5 minutes, use the tweezers to place the cube of liver in test tube 1. Place the ground liver in test tube 2. Leave test tube 3 alone.

Make Observations

8. Observe the reaction rate (the amount of bubbling) in all three test tubes, and record your observations in your ScienceLog.

Materials

- 10 mL test tubes (3)
- masking tape
- 600 mL beaker
- hot water
- funnel
- 10 mL graduated cylinder
- hydrogen peroxide solution
- 2 small liver cubes
- mortar and pestle
- tweezers

Analyze Your Results

9. Does liver appear to be a catalyst? Explain your answer.

10. Which type of liver (whole or ground) produced a faster reaction? Why?

11. What is the purpose of test tube 3?

Draw Conclusions

12. How do your results support or disprove your hypothesis?

13. Why was a hot-water bath used? (Hint: Look in your book for a definition of activation energy.)

Putting Elements Together

A synthesis reaction is a reaction in which two or more substances combine to form a single compound. The resulting compound has different chemical and physical properties than the substances from which it is composed. In this activity, you will synthesize, or create, copper(II) oxide from the elements copper and oxygen.

Materials

- metric balance
- evaporating dish
- weighing paper
- copper powder
- ring stand and ring
- wire gauze
- Bunsen burner or portable burner
- spark igniter
- tongs

Conduct an Experiment/Collect Data

1. Copy the table below into your ScienceLog.

Data Collection Table	
Object	**Mass (g)**
Evaporating dish	
Copper powder	
Copper + evaporating dish after heating	
Copper(II) oxide	

2. Use the metric balance to measure the mass (to the nearest 0.1 g) of the empty evaporating dish. Record this mass in the table.

3. Place a piece of weighing paper on the metric balance, and measure approximately 10 g of copper powder. Record the mass (to the nearest 0.1 g) in the table.
   Caution: Wear protective gloves when working with copper powder.

4. Use the weighing paper to place the copper powder in the evaporating dish. Spread the powder over the bottom and up the sides as much as possible. Discard the weighing paper.

5. Set up the ring stand and ring. Place the wire gauze on top of the ring. Carefully place the evaporating dish on the wire gauze.

6. Place the Bunsen burner under the ring and wire gauze. Use the spark igniter to light the Bunsen burner.
Caution: Use extreme care when working near an open flame.

7. Heat the evaporating dish for 10 minutes.

8. Turn off the burner, and allow the evaporating dish to cool for 10 minutes. Use tongs to remove the evaporating dish and place it on the balance to determine the mass. Record the mass in the table.

9. Determine the mass of the reaction product—copper(II) oxide—by subtracting the mass of the evaporating dish from the mass of the evaporating dish and copper powder after heating. Record this mass in the table.

Analyze the Results

10. What evidence of a chemical reaction did you observe after the copper was heated?

11. Explain why a change in mass occurred.

12. How does the change in mass support the idea that this is a synthesis reaction?

Draw Conclusions

13. Why was powdered copper used rather than a small piece of copper? (Hint: How does surface area affect the rate of the reaction?)

14. Why was the copper heated? (Hint: Look in your book for the discussion of *activation energy*.)

15. The copper bottoms of cooking pots can turn black when used. How is that similar to the results you obtained in this lab?

Going Further

Rust, shown below, is iron(III) oxide—the product of a synthesis reaction between iron and oxygen. How does painting a car help prevent this type of reaction?

Speed Control

The reaction rate (how fast a chemical reaction happens) is an important factor to control. Sometimes you want a reaction to take place rapidly, such as when you are removing tarnish from a metal surface. Other times you want a reaction to happen very slowly, such as when you are depending on a battery as a source of electrical energy. In this lab, you will discover how changing the surface area and concentration of the reactants affects reaction rate. In this lab, you can estimate the rate of reaction by observing how fast bubbles form.

Part A—Surface Area

Ask a Question

1. How does changing the surface area of a metal affect reaction rate?

Form a Hypothesis

2. In your ScienceLog, write a statement that answers the question above. Explain your reasoning.

Test the Hypothesis

3. Use three identical strips of aluminum. Put one strip into a test tube. Place the test tube in the test-tube rack.
   Caution: The strips of metal may have sharp edges.

4. Carefully fold a second strip in half and then in half again. Use a text book or other large object to flatten the folded strip as much as possible. Place the strip in a second test tube in the test-tube rack.

5. Use scissors to cut a third strip of aluminum into the smallest possible pieces. Place all of the pieces into a third test tube, and place the test tube in the test-tube rack.

Materials

- 30 mL test tubes (6)
- 6 strips of aluminum, approximately 5 × 1 cm each
- test-tube rack
- scissors
- 2 funnels
- 10 mL graduated cylinders (2)
- acid A
- acid B

6. Use a funnel and a graduated cylinder to pour 10 mL of acid A into each of the three test tubes.
   Caution: Hydrochloric acid is corrosive. If any acid should spill on you, immediately flush the area with water and notify your teacher.

Make Observations

7. Observe the rate of bubble formation in each test tube. Record your observations in your ScienceLog.

Analyze the Results

8. Which form of aluminum had the greatest surface area? Which had the smallest?

9. In the three test tubes, the amount of aluminum and the amount of acid were the same. Which form of the aluminum seemed to react the fastest? Which form reacted the slowest? Explain your answers.

10. Do your results support the hypothesis you made in step 2? Explain.

Draw Conclusions

11. Would powdered aluminum react faster or slower than the forms of aluminum you used? Explain your answer.

Part B—Concentration

Ask a Question

12. How does changing the concentration of acid affect the reaction rate?

Form a Hypothesis

13. In your ScienceLog, write a statement that answers the question above. Explain your reasoning.

Test the Hypothesis

14. Place one of the three remaining aluminum strips in each of the three clean test tubes. (Note: Do not alter the strips.) Place the test tubes in the test-tube rack.

15. Using the second funnel and graduated cylinder, pour 10 mL of water into one of the test tubes. Pour 10 mL of acid B into the second test tube. Pour 10 mL of acid A into the third test tube.

Make Observations

16. Observe the rate of bubble formation in the three test tubes. Record your observations in your ScienceLog.

Analyze the Results

17. In this set of test tubes, the strips of aluminum were the same, but the concentration of the acid was different. Acid A is more concentrated than acid B. Was there a difference between the test tube with water and the test tubes with acid? Which test tube formed bubbles the fastest? Explain your answers.

18. Do your results support the hypothesis you made in step 13? Explain.

Draw Conclusions

19. Explain why spilled hydrochloric acid should be diluted with water before it is wiped up.

Cabbage Patch Indicators

Indicators are weak acids or bases that change color due to the pH of the substance to which they are added. Red cabbage contains a natural indicator that turns specific colors at specific pHs. In this lab you will extract the indicator from red cabbage and use it to determine the pH of several liquids.

Materials

- distilled water
- 250 mL beaker
- red cabbage leaf
- hot plate
- beaker tongs
- masking tape
- test tubes
- test-tube rack
- eyedropper
- sample liquids provided by teacher
- litmus paper

Procedure

1. Copy the table below into your ScienceLog. Be sure to include one line for each sample liquid.

Data Collection Table			
Liquid	Color with indicator	pH	Effect on litmus paper
Control			

DO NOT WRITE IN BOOK

2. Put on protective gloves. Place 100 mL of distilled water in the beaker. Tear the cabbage leaf into small pieces, and place the pieces in the beaker.

3. Use the hot plate to heat the cabbage and water to boiling. Continue boiling until the water is deep blue. **Caution:** Use extreme care when working near a hot plate.

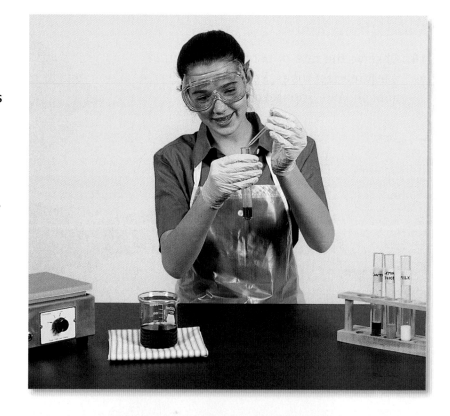

4. Use tongs to remove the beaker from the hot plate, and turn the hot plate off. Allow the solution to cool for 5–10 minutes.

5. While the solution is cooling, use masking tape and a pen to label the test tubes for each sample liquid. Label one test tube as the control. Place the tubes in the rack.

6. Use the eyedropper to place a small amount (about 5 mL) of the indicator (cabbage juice) in the test tube labeled as the control. Pour a small amount (about 5 mL) of each sample liquid into the appropriate test tube.

7. Using the eyedropper, place several drops of the indicator into each test tube and swirl gently. Record the color of each liquid in the table. Use the chart below to determine and record the pH for each sample.

pH 1   2   3   4   5   6   7   8   9   10 11 12 13 14

8. Litmus paper is an indicator that turns red in an acid and blue in a base. Test each liquid with a strip of litmus paper, and record the results.

Analysis

9. What purpose does the control serve? What is the pH of the control?

10. What colors are associated with acids? with bases?

11. Why is red cabbage juice considered a good indicator?

12. Which do you think would be more useful to help identify an unknown liquid—litmus paper or red cabbage juice? Why?

Going Further

Unlike distilled water, rainwater has some carbon dioxide dissolved in it. Is rainwater acidic, basic, or neutral? To find out, place a small amount of the cabbage juice indicator (which is water-based) in a clean test tube. Use a straw to gently blow bubbles in the indicator. Continue blowing bubbles until you see a color change. What can you conclude about the pH of your "rainwater?" What is the purpose of blowing bubbles in the cabbage juice?

Making Salt

A neutralization reaction between an acid and a base produces water and a salt. In this lab, you will react an acid with a base and then let the water evaporate. You will then examine what is left for properties that tell you that it is indeed a salt.

Procedure

1. Put on protective gloves. Carefully measure 25 mL of hydrochloric acid in a graduated cylinder, then pour it into the beaker. Carefully rinse the graduated cylinder with distilled water to clean out any leftover acid.
   Caution: Hydrochloric acid is corrosive. If any should spill on you, immediately flush the area with water and notify your teacher.

2. Add three drops of phenolphthalein indicator to the acid in the beaker. You will not see anything happen yet because this indicator won't show its color unless too much base is present.

3. Measure 20 mL of sodium hydroxide (base) in the graduated cylinder, and add it slowly to the beaker with the acid. Use the stirring rod to mix the substances completely.
   Caution: Sodium hydroxide is also corrosive. If any should spill on you, immediately flush the area with water and notify your teacher.

4. Use an eyedropper to add more base to the acid-base mixture in the beaker a few drops at a time. Be sure to stir the mixture after each few drops. Continue adding drops of base until the mixture remains colored after stirring.

5. Use another eyedropper to add acid to the beaker, one drop at a time, until the color just disappears after stirring.

Materials

- hydrochloric acid
- 100 mL graduated cylinder
- 100 mL beaker
- distilled water
- phenolphthalein solution in a dropper bottle
- sodium hydroxide
- glass stirring rod
- 2 eyedroppers
- evaporating dish
- magnifying lens

6. Pour the mixture carefully into an evaporating dish, and place the dish where your teacher tells you to allow the water to evaporate overnight.

7. The next day, examine your evaporating dish and study the crystals that were left with a magnifying lens. Identify the color, shape, and other properties that the crystals have.

Analysis

8. The equation for the reaction above is:

$$HCl + NaOH \longrightarrow H_2O + NaCl.$$

NaCl is ordinary table salt and forms very regular cubic crystals that are white. Did you find white cubic crystals?

9. The phenolphthalein indicator changes color in the presence of a base. Why did you add more acid in step 5 until the color disappeared?

Going Further

Another neutralization reaction occurs between hydrochloric acid and potassium hydroxide, KOH. The equation for this reaction is as follows:

$$HCl + KOH \longrightarrow H_2O + KCl$$

What are the products of this neutralization reaction? How do they compare with those you discovered in this experiment?

Domino Chain Reactions

Fission of uranium-235 is a process that relies on neutrons. When a uranium-235 nucleus splits into two smaller nuclei, it releases two or three neutrons that can cause neighboring nuclei to undergo fission. This can result in a nuclear chain reaction. In this lab you will build two models of nuclear chain reactions using dominoes.

Materials

- 15 dominoes
- stopwatch

Conduct an Experiment

1. For the first model, set up the dominoes as shown below. Each domino should hit two dominoes in the next row when pushed over.

2. Measure the time it takes for all of the dominoes to fall. To do this, start the stopwatch as you tip over the front domino. Stop the stopwatch when the last domino falls. Record this time in your ScienceLog.

3. If some of the dominoes do not fall, repeat steps 1 and 2. You may have to adjust the setup a few times.

4. For the second model, set up the dominoes as shown at right. The domino in the first row should hit both of the dominoes in the second row. Beginning with the second row, only one domino from each row should hit both of the dominoes in the next row.

5. Repeat step 2. Again, you may have to adjust the setup a few times to get all the dominoes to fall.

Analyze Your Results

6. Which model represents an uncontrolled chain reaction? Which represents a controlled chain reaction? Explain your answers.

7. Imagine that each domino releases a certain amount of energy as it falls. Compare the total amount of energy released in the two models.

8. Compare the time needed to release the energy in the models. Which model was longest? Which model was shortest?

Draw Conclusions

9. In a nuclear power plant, a chain reaction is controlled by using a material that absorbs neutrons. Only enough neutrons to continue the chain reaction are allowed to produce further fission of uranium-235. Explain how your model of a controlled nuclear chain reaction modeled this process.

10. Why must uranium nuclei be close to each other in order for a nuclear chain reaction to occur? (Hint: What would happen in your model if the dominoes were too far apart?)

Stop the Static Electricity!

Imagine this scenario: Some of your clothes cling together when they come out of the dryer. This annoying problem is caused by static electricity—the buildup of electric charges on an object. In this lab, you'll discover how this buildup occurs.

Materials

- 30 cm thread
- plastic-foam packing peanut
- tape
- rubber rod
- wool cloth
- glass rod
- silk cloth

Ask a Question

1. How do electric charges build up on clothes in a dryer?

Form a Hypothesis

2. Write a statement that answers the question above. Explain your reasoning.

Test the Hypothesis

3. Tie a piece of thread approximately 30 cm in length to a packing peanut. Hang the peanut by the thread from the edge of a table. Tape the thread to the table.

4. Rub the rubber rod with the wool cloth for 10–15 seconds. Bring the rod near, but do not touch, the peanut. Observe the peanut and record your observations. If nothing happens, repeat this step.

5. Touch the peanut with the rubber rod. Pull the rod away from the peanut, and then bring it near again. Record your observations.

6. Repeat steps 4 and 5 with the glass rod and silk cloth.

7. Now rub the rubber rod with the wool cloth, and bring the rod near the peanut again. Record your observations.

Analyze the Results

8. What caused the peanut to act differently in steps 4 and 5?

9. Did the glass rod have the same effect on the peanut as the rubber rod did? Explain how the peanut reacted in each case.

10. Was the reaction of the peanut the same in steps 5 and 7? Explain.

Draw Conclusions

11. Based on your results, was your hypothesis correct? Explain your answer, and write a new statement if necessary.

Communicate Results

12. Explain why the rubber rod and the glass rod affected the peanut.

Going Further

Do some research to find out how a dryer sheet helps stop the buildup of electric charges in the dryer.

Potato Power

Have you ever wanted to look inside a D cell from a flashlight or an AA cell from a portable radio? All cells include the same basic components, as shown below. There is a metal "bucket," some electrolyte (a paste), and a rod of some other metal (or solid) in the middle. Even though the construction is simple, companies that manufacture cells are always trying to make a product with the highest voltage possible from the least expensive materials. Sometimes they try different pastes, and sometimes they try different combinations of metals. In this lab, you will make your own cell. Using inexpensive materials, you will try to produce the highest voltage you can.

Materials

- labeled metal strips
- potato
- metric ruler
- voltmeter

Procedure

1. Choose two metal strips. Carefully push one of the strips into the potato at least 2 cm deep. Insert the second strip the same way, and measure how far apart the two strips are. (If one of your metal strips is too soft to push into the potato, push a harder strip in first, remove it, and then push the soft strip into the slit.) Record the two metals you have used and the distance between the strips in your ScienceLog. **Caution:** The strips of metal may have sharp edges.

2. Connect the voltmeter to the two strips, and record the voltage.

3. Move one of the strips closer to or farther from the other. Measure the new distance and voltage. Record your results.

4. Repeat steps 1 through 3, using different combinations of metal strips and distances until you find the combination that produces the highest voltage.

Analysis

5. What combination of metals and distance produced the highest voltage?

6. If you change only the distance but use the same metal strips, what is the effect on the voltage?

Metal "bucket"

Electrolyte

Metal or carbon rod

D cell

7. One of the metal strips tends to lose electrons, while the other tends to gain electrons. What do you think would happen if you used two strips of the same metal?

Circuitry 101

You have learned that there are two basic types of electrical circuits. A series circuit connects all the parts in a single loop, and a parallel circuit connects each of the parts on separate branches to the power source. If you want to control the whole circuit, the loads and the switch must be wired in series. If you want parts of the circuit to operate independently, the loads must be wired in parallel.

No matter how simple or complicated a circuit may be, Ohm's law (current equals voltage divided by resistance) applies. In this lab, you will construct both a series circuit and a parallel circuit. You will use an ammeter to measure current and a voltmeter to measure voltage. With each circuit, you will test and apply Ohm's law.

Materials

- power source—dry cell(s)
- switch
- 3 light-bulb holders
- 3 light bulbs
- insulated wire, cut into 15 cm lengths with both ends stripped
- ammeter
- voltmeter

Part A—Series Circuit

Procedure

1. Construct a series circuit with a power source, a switch, and three light bulbs. **Caution:** Always leave the switch open when constructing or changing the circuit. Close the switch only when you are testing or taking a reading.

2. Draw a diagram of your circuit in your ScienceLog.

3. Test your circuit. Do all three bulbs light up? Are they all the same brightness? What happens if you carefully unscrew one light bulb? Does it make any difference which bulb you unscrew? Record your observations in your ScienceLog.

4. Connect the ammeter between the power source and the switch. Close the switch, and record the current with a label on your diagram in your ScienceLog. Be sure to show where you measured the current and what the value was.

5. Reconnect the circuit so the ammeter is between the first and second bulbs. Record the current, as you did in step 4.

6. Move the ammeter so it is between the second and third bulbs, and record the current again.

7. Remove the ammeter from the circuit, and connect the voltmeter to the two ends of the power source. Record the voltage with a label on your diagram.

8. Use the voltmeter to measure the voltage across each bulb. Label the voltage across each bulb on your diagram.

Part B—Parallel Circuit

Procedure

9. Take apart your series circuit, and reassemble the same power source, switch, and three light bulbs so that the bulbs are wired in parallel. (Note: The switch must remain in series with the power source to be able to control the whole circuit.)

10. Draw a diagram of your parallel circuit in your ScienceLog.

11. Test your circuit, and record your observations, as you did in step 3.

12. Connect the ammeter between the power source and the switch. Record the reading on your diagram.

13. Reconnect the circuit so that the ammeter is right next to one of the three bulbs. Record the current on your diagram.

14. Repeat step 13 for the two remaining bulbs.

15. Remove the ammeter from your circuit, and connect the voltmeter to the two ends of the power source. Record this voltage.

16. Measure and record the voltage across each light bulb.

Analysis—Parts A and B

17. Was the current the same at all places in the series circuit? Was it the same everywhere in the parallel circuit?

18. For each circuit, compare the voltage at each light bulb with the power source.

19. What is the relationship between the voltage at the power source and the voltages at the light bulbs in a series circuit?

20. Use Ohm's law and the readings for current (*I*) and voltage (*V*) at the power source for both circuits to calculate the total resistance (*R*) in both the series and parallel circuits.

21. Was the total resistance for both circuits the same? Explain your answer.

22. Why did the bulbs differ in brightness?

23. Based on your results, what do you think might happen if too many electric appliances are plugged into the same series circuit? the same parallel circuit?

Magnetic Mystery

Every magnet is surrounded by a magnetic field. Magnetic field lines show the shape of the magnetic field. These lines can be modeled by using iron filings. The iron filings are affected by the magnetic field, and they fall into lines showing the field. In this lab, you will first learn about magnetic fields, and then you will use this knowledge to identify a mystery magnet's shape and orientation based on observations of the field lines.

Materials

- 2 magnets, different shapes
- sheet of clear acetate
- iron filings
- shoe box
- masking tape

Collect Data

1. Lay one of the magnets flat on a table.

2. Place a sheet of clear acetate over the magnet. Sprinkle some iron filings on the acetate to see the magnetic field lines.

3. In your ScienceLog, draw the magnet and the magnetic field lines.

4. Remove the acetate, and pour the iron filings back into the container.

5. Place your magnet so that one end is pointing up. Repeat steps 2 through 4.

6. Place your magnet on its side. Repeat steps 2 through 4.

7. Repeat steps 1 through 6 with the other magnet.

Conduct an Experiment

8. Create a magnetic mystery for another lab team by removing the lid from a shoe box, and taping a magnet underneath the lid. Orient the magnet so that determining the shape of the magnetic field and the orientation of the magnet will be challenging. Once the magnet is secure, place the lid on the box.

9. Exchange boxes with another team.

10. Without opening the box, use the sheet of acetate and the iron filings to determine the shape of the magnetic field of the magnet in the box.

11. Make a drawing of the magnetic field lines in your ScienceLog.

Draw Conclusions

12. Use your drawings from steps 1 through 7 to identify the shape and orientation of the magnet in your magnetic mystery box. Draw a picture of your conclusion.

Going Further

Examine your drawings. Can you identify the north and south poles of a magnet from the shape of the magnetic field lines? Design a procedure that would allow you to determine the poles of a magnet.

DISCOVERY LAB

Electricity from Magnetism

You use electricity every day. But did you ever wonder where it comes from? Some of the electrical energy you use is converted from chemical energy in cells or batteries. But what about when you plug a lamp into a wall outlet? In this lab, you will see how electricity can be generated from magnetism.

Ask a Question

1. How can electricity be generated from magnetism?

Form a Hypothesis

2. Write a statement to answer question 1.

Test the Hypothesis

3. Sand the enamel off of the last 2 or 3 cm of each end of the magnet wire. Wrap the magnet wire around the tube to make a coil as illustrated below. Attach the bare ends of the wire to the galvanometer using the insulated wires.

4. While watching the galvanometer, move a bar magnet into the coil, hold it there for a moment, and then remove it. Record your observations in your ScienceLog.

5. Repeat step 4 several times, moving the magnet at different speeds. Observe the galvanometer carefully.

6. Hold the magnet still, and pass the coil over the magnet. Record your observations.

Analyze the Results

7. How does the speed of the magnet affect the size of the electric current?

Materials

- sandpaper
- 150 cm of magnet wire
- cardboard tube
- commercial galvanometer
- 2 insulated wires with alligator clips, each approximately 30 cm long
- strong bar magnet

8. How is the direction of the electric current affected by the motion of the magnet?

9. Examine your hypothesis. Is your hypothesis accurate? Explain. If necessary, write a new hypothesis to answer question 1.

Draw Conclusions

10. Would an electric current still be generated if the wire were broken? Why or why not?

11. Could a stationary magnet be used to generate an electric current? Explain.

12. What energy conversions occur in this investigation?

Communicate Results

13. Write a short paragraph that explains the requirements for generating electricity from magnetism.

Build a DC Motor

Electric motors can be used for many things. Hair dryers, CD players, and even some cars and buses are powered by electric motors. In this lab, you will build a direct current electric motor— the basis for the electric motors you use every day.

Procedure

1. To make the armature for the motor, wind the wire around the cardboard tube to make a coil like the one shown below. Wind the ends of the wire around the loops on each side of the coil. Leave about 5 cm free on each end.

2. Hold the coil on its edge. Sand the enamel from only the top half of each end of the wire. This acts like a commutator, except that it blocks the electric current instead of reversing it during half of each rotation.

3. Partially unfold the two paper clips from the middle. Make a hook in one end of each paper clip to hold the coil, as shown at right.

4. Place two disk magnets in the bottom of the cup, and place the other magnets on the outside of the bottom of the cup. The magnets should remain in place when the cup is turned upside down.

5. Tape the paper clips to the sides of the cup. The hooks should be at the same height, and should keep the coil from hitting the magnet.

6. Test your coil. Flick the top of the coil lightly with your finger. The coil should spin freely without wobbling or sliding to one side.

7. Make adjustments to the ends of the wire and the hooks until your coil spins freely.

8. Use the alligator clips to attach one wire to each paper clip.

9. Attach the free end of one wire to one terminal of the battery.

Materials

- 100 cm of magnet wire
- cardboard tube
- sandpaper
- 2 large paper clips
- 4 disk magnets
- plastic-foam cup
- tape
- 2 insulated wires with alligator clips, each approximately 30 cm long
- 4.5 V battery
- permanent marker

Coil

Paper clip

Paper clip

Disc magnet

Alligator clip

Tape

Cup

Wire

Collect Data

10. Connect the free end of the other wire to the second battery terminal and give your coil a gentle spin. Record your observations.

11. Stop the coil and give it a gentle spin in the opposite direction. Record your observations.

12. If the coil does not keep spinning, check the ends of the wire. Bare wire should touch the paper clips during half of the spin, and only enamel should touch the paper clips for the other half of the spin.

13. If you removed too much enamel, color half of the wire with a permanent marker.

14. Switch the connections to the battery and repeat steps 10 and 11.

Analyze the Results

15. Did your motor always spin in the direction you started it? Explain.

16. Why was the motor affected by switching the battery connections?

17. Some electric cars run on solar power. Which part of your model would be replaced by the solar panels?

Draw Conclusions

18. Some people claim that electric-powered cars are cleaner than gasoline-powered cars. Explain why this might be true.

19. List some reasons that electric cars are not ideal. (Hint: What happens to batteries?)

20. How could your model be used to help design a hair dryer?

21. Make a list of at least three other items that could be powered by an electric motor like the one you built.

Tune In!

You probably have listened to radios many times in your life. Modern radios are complicated electronic devices. However, radios do not have to be so complicated. The basic parts of all radios include: a diode, an inductor, a capacitor, an antenna, a ground wire, and an earphone (or a speaker and amplifier on a large radio). In this activity, you will examine each of these components one at a time as you build a working model of a radio-wave receiver.

Materials

- diode
- 2 m of insulated wire
- 2 cardboard tubes
- tape
- scissors
- aluminum foil
- sheet of paper
- 7 connecting wires, 30 cm each
- 3 paper clips
- cardboard, 20 × 30 cm
- antenna
- ground wire
- earphone

Procedure

1. Examine the diode. Describe it in your ScienceLog.

2. A diode carries current in only one direction. Draw the inside of a diode in your ScienceLog, and illustrate how this might occur.

3. An inductor controls the amount of electric current due to the resistance of the wire. Make an inductor by winding the insulated wire around a cardboard tube approximately 100 times. Wind the wire so that all the turns of the coil are neat and in an orderly row, as shown below. Leave about 25 cm of wire on each end of the coil. The coil of wire may be held on the tube using tape.

4. Now you will construct the variable capacitor. A capacitor stores electrical energy when an electric current is applied. A variable capacitor is a capacitor in which the amount of energy stored can be changed. Cut a piece of aluminum foil to go around the tube but only half the length of the tube, as shown on the next page. Keep the foil as wrinkle-free as possible as you wrap it around the tube, and tape the foil to itself. Now tape the foil to the tube.

5. Use the sheet of paper and tape to make a sliding cover on the tube. The paper should completely cover the foil on the tube with about 1 cm extra.

6. Cut another sheet of aluminum foil to wrap completely around the paper. Leave approximately 1 cm of paper showing at each end of the foil. Tape this foil sheet to the paper sleeve. If you have done this correctly, you have a paper/foil sheet which will slide up and down the tube over the stationary foil. The two pieces of foil should not touch.

7. Stand your variable capacitor on its end so that the stationary foil is at the bottom. The amount of stored energy is greater when the sleeve is down than when the sleeve is up.

8. Use tape to attach one connecting wire to the stationary foil at the end of the tube. Use tape to attach another connecting wire to the sliding foil sleeve. Be sure that the metal part of the wire touches the foil.

9. Hook three paper clips on one edge of the cardboard, as shown below. Label one paper clip A, another B, and the third one C.

10. Lay the inductor on the piece of cardboard, and tape it to the cardboard.

11. Stand the capacitor next to the inductor, and tape the tube to the cardboard. Be sure not to tape the sleeve—it must be free to slide.

Capacitor

Partially Completed Model Receiver

12. Use tape to connect the diode to paper clips A and B. The cathode should be closest to paper clip B. (The cathode end of the diode is the one with the dark band.) Make sure that all connections have good metal-to-metal contact.

13. Connect one end of the inductor to paper clip A, and the other end to paper clip C. Use tape to hold the wires in place.

14. Connect the wire from the sliding part of the capacitor to paper clip A. Connect the other wire (from the stationary foil) to paper clip C.

15. The antenna receives radio waves transmitted by a radio station. Tape a connecting wire to your antenna. Then connect this wire to paper clip A.

16. Use tape to connect one end of the ground wire to paper clip C. The other end of the ground wire should be connected to an object specified by your teacher.

A Completed Model Receiver!

Earphone

Antenna

Ground wire

17. The earphone will allow you to detect the radio waves you receive. Connect one wire from the earphone to paper clip B and the other wire to paper clip C.

18. You are now ready to begin listening. With everything connected, and the earphone in your ear, slowly slide the paper/foil sheet of the capacitor up and down. Listen for a very faint sound. You may have to troubleshoot many of the parts to get your receiver to work. As you troubleshoot, check to be sure there is good contact between all the connections.

Analysis

19. Describe the process of operating your receiver.

20. Considering what you have learned about a diode, why is it important to have the diode connected the correct way?

21. A function of the inductor on a radio is to "slow the current down." Why does the inductor you made slow the current down more than does a straight wire the length of your coil?

22. A capacitor consists of any two conductors separated by an insulator. For your capacitor, list the two conductors and the insulator.

23. Explain why the amount of stored energy is increased when you slide the foil sleeve down and decreased when the sleeve is up.

24. In your ScienceLog, make a list of ways that your receiver is similar to a modern radio. Make a second list of ways that your receiver is different from a modern radio.

DISCOVERY LAB

Wave Energy and Speed

If you threw a rock into a pond, waves would carry energy away from the point of origin. But if you threw a large rock into a pond, would the waves carry more energy away from the point of origin than waves created by a small rock? And would a large rock create waves that move faster than waves created by a small rock? In this lab you'll answer these questions.

Materials

- shallow pan, approximately 20 × 30 cm
- newspaper
- small beaker
- water
- 2 pencils
- stopwatch

Ask a Question

1. In this lab you will answer the following questions: Do waves created by a large disturbance carry more energy than waves created by a small disturbance? Do waves created by a large disturbance travel faster than waves created by a small disturbance?

Form a Hypothesis

2. In your ScienceLog, write a few sentences that answer the questions above.

Test the Hypothesis

3. Place the pan on a few sheets of newspaper. Using the small beaker, fill the pan with water.

4. Make sure that the water is still. Tap the surface of the water near one end of the pan with the eraser end of one pencil. This represents the small disturbance. In your ScienceLog, record your observations about the size of the waves that are created and the path they take.

5. Repeat step 4. This time, use the stopwatch to measure the time it takes for one of the waves to reach the other side of the pan. Record your data in your ScienceLog.

6. Repeat steps 4 and 5 using two pencils at once. This represents the large disturbance. (Try to use the same amount of force to tap the water as you did with just one pencil.)

Analyze the Results

7. Compare the appearance of the waves created by one pencil with that of the waves created by two pencils. Were there any differences in amplitude (wave height)?

8. Compare the amount of time required for the waves to reach the side of the pan. Did the waves travel faster when two pencils were used?

Draw Conclusions

9. Do waves created by a large disturbance carry more energy than waves created by a small disturbance? Explain your answer using your results to support your answer. (Hint: Remember the relationship between amplitude and energy.)

10. Do waves created by a large disturbance travel faster than waves created by a small disturbance? Explain your answer.

Going Further

A tsunami is a giant ocean wave that can reach a height of 30 m. Tsunamis that reach land can cause injury and enormous property damage. Using what you learned in this lab about wave energy and speed, explain why tsunamis are so dangerous. How do you think scientists can predict when tsunamis will reach land?

Wave Speed, Frequency, and Wavelength

Wave speed, frequency, and wavelength are three related properties of waves. In this lab you will make observations and collect data to determine the relationship among these properties.

Part A—Wave Speed

Procedure

1. Copy Table 1 into your ScienceLog.

Materials

- coiled spring toy
- meterstick
- stopwatch

Table 1 Wave Speed Data			
Trial	**Length of spring (m)**	**Time for wave (s)**	**Speed of wave (m/s)**
1			
2			
3			
Average			

DO NOT WRITE IN BOOK

2. On the floor or a table, two students should stretch the spring to a length of 2 to 4 m. A third student should measure the length of the spring. Record the length in Table 1.

3. One student should pull part of the spring sideways with one hand, as shown at right, and release the pulled-back portion. This will cause a wave to travel down the spring.

4. Using a stopwatch, the third student should measure how long it takes for the wave to travel down the length of the spring and back. Record this time in Table 1.

5. Repeat steps 3 and 4 two more times.

Analyze Your Results

6. Calculate and record the wave speed for each trial. (Hint: Speed equals distance divided by time; distance is twice the spring length.)

7. Calculate and record the average time and the average wave speed.

Part B—Wavelength and Frequency

Procedure

8. Keep the spring the same length that you used in Part A.

9. Copy Table 2 into your ScienceLog.

Table 2 Wavelength and Frequency Data				
Trial	Length of spring (m)	Time for 10 cycles (s)	Wave frequency (Hz)	Wavelength (m)
1				
2				
3				
Average				

DO NOT WRITE IN BOOK

10. One of the two students holding the spring should start shaking the spring from side to side until a wave pattern appears that resembles one of those shown below.

11. Using the stopwatch, the third group member should measure and record how long it takes for 10 cycles of the wave pattern to occur. (One back-and-forth shake is one cycle.) Keep the pattern going so that measurements for three trials can be made.

Analyze Your Results

12. Calculate the frequency for each trial by dividing the number of cycles (10) by the time. Record the answers in Table 2.

13. Determine the wavelength using the equation at right that matches your wave pattern. Record your answer in Table 2.

14. Calculate and record the average time and frequency.

Draw Conclusions—Parts A and B

15. To discover the relationship among speed, wavelength, and frequency, try multiplying or dividing any two of them to see if the result equals the third. (Use the average speed, wavelength, and average frequency from your data tables.) In your ScienceLog, write the equation that shows the relationship.

16. Reread the definitions for *frequency* and *wavelength* in the chapter titled "The Energy of Waves." Use these definitions to explain the relationship that you discovered.

Wave Patterns

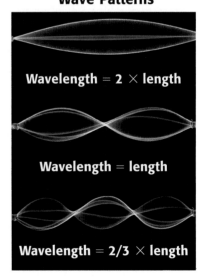

Wavelength = 2 × length

Wavelength = length

Wavelength = 2/3 × length

Easy Listening

Pitch describes how low or high a sound is. A sound's pitch is related to its frequency—the number of waves per second. Frequency is expressed in hertz (Hz), where 1 Hz equals one wave per second. Most humans can hear frequencies from 20 Hz to 20,000 Hz. However, not everyone detects all pitches equally well at all distances. In this activity you will collect data to see how well you and your classmates hear different frequencies at different distances.

Materials

- 4 tuning forks of different frequencies
- pink rubber eraser
- meterstick
- graph paper

Ask a Question

1. Do students in your classroom hear low-, mid-, or high-frequency sounds better?

Form a Hypothesis

2. In your ScienceLog, write a hypothesis that answers the question above. Explain your reasoning.

Test the Hypothesis

3. Choose one member of your group to be the sound maker. The others will be the listeners.

4. Copy the data table below into your ScienceLog. Be sure to include a column for every listener in your group.

Data Collection Table				
	Distance (m)			
Frequency	Listener 1	Listener 2	Listener 3	Average
1 (___Hz)				
2 (___Hz)				
3 (___Hz)				
4 (___Hz)				

DO NOT WRITE IN BOOK

5. Record the frequency of one of the tuning forks in the top row of the first column of the data table.

6. The listeners should stand in front of the sound maker with their backs turned.

7. The sound maker will create a sound by striking the tip of the tuning fork gently with the eraser.

8. The listeners who hear the sound should take one step away from the sound maker. The listeners who do not hear the sound should stay where they are.

9. Repeat steps 7 and 8 until none of the listeners can hear the sound or the listeners reach the edge of the room.

10. Using the meterstick, the sound maker should measure the distance from his or her position to each of the listeners. All group members should record this data in their tables.

11. Repeat steps 5 through 10 with a different tuning fork.

12. Continue until all four tuning forks have been tested.

Analyze the Results

13. Calculate the average distance for each frequency. Share your group's data with the rest of the class to make a data table for the whole class.

14. Calculate the average distance for each frequency for the class.

15. Make a graph of the class results, plotting average distance (*y*-axis) versus frequency (*x*-axis).

Draw Conclusions

16. Was everyone in the class able to hear all frequencies equally? (Hint: Was the average distance for each frequency the same?)

17. If the answer to question 16 is no, which frequency had the largest average distance? Which frequency had the smallest average distance?

18. Based on your graph, do your results support your hypothesis? Explain your answer.

19. Do you think your class sample is large enough to confirm your hypothesis for all humans of all ages? Explain your answer.

The Speed of Sound

In the chapter titled "The Nature of Sound," you learned that the speed of sound in air is 343 m/s at 20°C (approximately room temperature). In this lab you'll design an experiment to measure the speed of sound yourself—and you'll determine if you're "up to speed"!

Materials

- materials of your choice, approved by your teacher

Procedure

1. Brainstorm with your teammates to come up with a way to measure the speed of sound. Consider the following as you design your experiment:

   a. You must have a method of making a sound. Some simple examples include speaking, clapping your hands, and hitting two boards together.

   b. Remember that speed is equal to distance divided by time. You must devise methods to measure the distance that a sound travels and to measure the amount of time it takes for that sound to travel that distance.

   c. Sound travels very rapidly. A sound from across the room will reach your ears almost before you can start recording the time! You may wish to have the sound travel a long distance.

   d. Remember that sound travels in waves. Think about the interactions of sound waves. You might be able to include these interactions in your design.

2. Discuss your experimental design with your teacher, including any equipment you need. Your teacher may have questions that will help you improve your design.

Conduct an Experiment

3. Once your design is approved, carry out your experiment. Be sure to perform several trials. Record your results in your ScienceLog.

Draw Conclusions

4. Was your result close to the value given in the introduction to this lab? If not, what factors may have caused you to get such a different value?

5. Why was it important for you to perform several trials in your experiment?

Communicate Your Results

6. Compare your results with those of your classmates. Determine which experimental design provided the best results. In your ScienceLog, explain why you think this design was so successful.

Tuneful Tube

If you have seen a singer shatter a crystal glass simply by singing a note, you have seen an example of resonance. For this to happen, the note has to match the resonant frequency of the glass. A column of air within a cylinder can also resonate if the air column is the proper length for the frequency of the note. In this lab you will investigate the relationship between the length of an air column, the frequency, and the wavelength during resonance.

Materials

- 100 mL graduated cylinder
- water
- plastic tube, supplied by your teacher
- metric ruler
- 4 tuning forks of different frequencies
- pink rubber eraser
- graph paper

Procedure

1. Copy the data table below into your ScienceLog.

Data Collection Table			
Frequency (Hz)			
Length (cm)			

DO NOT WRITE IN BOOK

2. Fill the graduated cylinder with water.

3. Hold a plastic tube in the water so that about 3 cm is above the water.

4. Record the frequency of the first tuning fork. Gently strike the tuning fork with the eraser, and hold it so that the prongs are just above the tube, as shown at right. Slowly move the tube and fork up and down until you hear the loudest sound.

5. Measure the distance from the top of the tube to the water. Record this length in your data table.

6. Repeat steps 3–5 using the other three tuning forks.

Analysis

7. Calculate the wavelength (in centimeters) of each sound wave by dividing the speed of sound in air (343 m/s at 20°C) by the frequency and multiplying by 100.

8. Make the following graphs: air column length versus frequency and wavelength versus frequency. On both graphs, plot the frequency on the x-axis.

9. Describe the trend between the length of the air column and the frequency of the tuning fork.

10. How are the pitches you heard related to the wavelengths of the sounds?

The Energy of Sound

In the chapter titled "The Nature of Sound," you learned about various properties and interactions of sound. In this lab you will perform several activities that will demonstrate that the properties and interactions of sound all depend on one thing—the energy carried by sound waves.

Part A—Sound Vibrations

Procedure

1. Lightly strike a tuning fork with the eraser. Slowly place the prongs of the tuning fork in the plastic cup of water. Record your observations in your ScienceLog.

Analysis

2. How do your observations demonstrate that sound waves are carried through vibrations?

Part B—Resonance

Procedure

3. Strike a tuning fork with the eraser. Quickly pick up a second tuning fork in your other hand and hold it about 30 cm from the first tuning fork.

4. Place the first tuning fork against your leg to stop its vibration. Listen closely to the second tuning fork. Record your observations, including the frequencies of the two tuning forks.

5. Repeat steps 3 and 4, using the remaining tuning fork as the second tuning fork.

Analysis

6. Explain why you can hear a sound from the second tuning fork when the frequencies of the tuning forks used are the same.

7. When using tuning forks of different frequencies, would you expect to hear a sound from the second tuning fork if you strike the first tuning fork harder? Explain your reasoning.

Materials

- 2 tuning forks of the same frequency and one of a different frequency
- pink rubber eraser
- small plastic cup filled with water
- rubber band
- 50 cm string

Part C—Interference

Procedure

8. Using the two tuning forks that have the same frequencey, place a rubber band tightly over the prongs near the base of one tuning fork, as shown at right. Strike both tuning forks against the eraser. Hold the stems of the tuning forks against a table, 3 to 5 cm apart. If you cannot hear any differences, move the rubber band up or down the prongs. Strike again. Record your observations in your ScienceLog.

Analysis

9. Did you notice the sound changing back and forth between loud and soft? A steady pattern like this is called a beat frequency. Explain this changing pattern of loudness and softness in terms of interference (both constructive and destructive).

Part D—The Doppler Effect

Procedure

10. Your teacher will tie the piece of string securely to the base of one tuning fork. Your teacher will then strike the tuning fork and carefully swing the tuning fork in a circle overhead. Record your observations in your ScienceLog.

Analysis

11. Did the tuning fork make a different sound when your teacher was swinging it than when he or she was holding it? If yes, explain why.

12. Is the actual pitch of the tuning fork changing? Explain.

Draw Conclusions— Parts A–D

13. Explain how your observations from each part of this lab verify that sound waves carry energy from one point to another through a vibrating medium.

14. Particularly loud thunder can cause the windows of your room to rattle. How is this evidence that sound waves carry energy?

DISCOVERY LAB

What Color of Light Is Best for Green Plants?

Plants grow well outdoors under natural sunlight. However, some plants are grown indoors under artificial light. A wide variety of colored lights are available for helping plants grow indoors. In this experiment, you'll test several colors of light to discover which color best meets the energy needs of green plants.

Ask a Question

1. What color of light is the best for growing green plants?

Form a Hypothesis

2. In your ScienceLog, write a hypothesis that answers the question above. Explain your reasoning.

Test the Hypothesis

3. Use the masking tape and marker to label the side of each Petri dish with your name and the type of light you will place the dish under.

4. Place a moist paper towel in each Petri dish. Place five seedlings on top of the paper towel. Cover each dish.

5. Record your observations of the seedlings, such as length, color, and number of leaves, in your ScienceLog.

6. Place each dish under the appropriate light.

7. Observe the Petri dishes every day for at least 5 days. Record your observations in your ScienceLog.

Analyze the Results

8. Based on your results, which color of light is the best for growing green plants? Which color of light is the worst?

Materials

- masking tape
- marker
- Petri dishes and covers
- water
- paper towels
- bean seedlings
- variety of colored lights, supplied by your teacher

Draw Conclusions

9. Remember that the color of an opaque object (such as a plant) is determined by the colors the object reflects. Use this information to explain your answer to question 8.

10. Would a purple light be good for growing purple plants? Explain.

Communicate Results

11. Write a short paragraph summarizing your conclusions.

Which Color Is Hottest?

Will a navy blue hat or a white hat keep your head warmer in cool weather? Colored objects absorb energy, which can make the objects warmer. How much energy is absorbed depends on the object's color. In this experiment you will test several colors under a bright light to determine which colors absorb the most energy.

Materials

- tape
- squares of colored paper
- thermometer
- light source
- cup of room-temperature water
- paper towels
- graph paper
- colored pencils or pens

Procedure

1. Copy the table below into your ScienceLog. Be sure to have one column for each color of paper you have and enough rows to end at 3 minutes.

Data Collection Table				
Time (s)	White	Red	Blue	Black
0				
15				
30				
45				
etc.				

DO NOT WRITE IN BOOK

2. Tape a piece of colored paper around the bottom of a thermometer and hold it under the light source. Record the temperature every 15 seconds for 3 minutes.

3. Cool the thermometer by removing the piece of paper and placing the thermometer in the cup of room-temperature water. After 1 minute, remove the thermometer, and dry it with a paper towel.

4. Repeat steps 2 and 3 with each color, making sure to hold the thermometer at the same distance from the light source.

Analyze the Results

5. Prepare a graph of temperature (*y*-axis) versus time (*x*-axis). Plot all data on one graph using a different colored pencil or pen for each set of data.

6. Rank the colors you used in order from hottest to coolest.

Draw Conclusions

7. Compare the colors based on the amount of energy each absorbs.

8. In this experiment a white light was used. How would your results be different if you used a red light? Explain.

9. Use the relationship between color and energy absorbed to explain why different colors of clothing are used for different seasons.

Mixing Colors

When you mix two colors, like red and green, you create a different color. But what color do you create? And is that new color brighter or darker? The color and brightness you see depend on the light that reaches your eye, and that depends on whether you are performing color addition (combining wavelengths by mixing colors of light) or color subtraction (absorbing light by mixing colors of pigments). In this experiment, you will try both types of color formation and see the results firsthand!

Part A—Color Addition

Procedure

1. Place a colored filter over each flashlight lens. Use masking tape to hold the filters in place.

2. In a darkened room, shine the red light on a sheet of clean white paper. Then shine the blue light next to the red light. You should see two circles of light, one red and one blue, next to each other.

3. Move the flashlights so that the circles overlap by about half their diameter. Examine the three areas of color, and record your observations. What color is formed in the mixed area? Is the mixed area brighter or darker than the single-color areas?

4. Repeat steps 2 and 3 with the red and green lights.

5. Now shine all three lights at the same point on the sheet of paper. Examine the results, and record your observations.

Analysis

6. In general, when you mixed two colors, was the result brighter or darker than the original colors?

7. In step 5, you mixed all three colors. Was the resulting color brighter or darker than mixing two colors? Explain your answer in terms of color addition. (Hint: Read the definition of color addition in the introduction.)

8. Based on your results, what do you think would happen if you mixed all the colors of light? Explain.

Materials

Part A
- 3 flashlights
- colored filters—red, green, and blue
- masking tape
- white paper

Part B
- masking tape
- 2 small plastic or paper cups
- water
- paintbrush
- watercolor paints
- white paper
- metric ruler

Red   ?   Green

Part B—Color Subtraction

Procedure

9. Place a piece of masking tape on each cup. Label one cup "Clean" and the other cup "Dirty." Fill both cups approximately half full with water.

10. Wet the paintbrush thoroughly in the "Clean" cup. Using the watercolor paints, paint a red circle on the white paper. The circle should be approximately 4 cm in diameter.

11. Clean the brush by rinsing it first in the "Dirty" cup and then in the "Clean" cup.

12. Paint a blue circle next to the red circle. Then paint half the red circle with the blue paint.

13. Examine the three areas: red, blue, and mixed. What color is the mixed area? Does it appear brighter or darker than the red and blue areas? Record your observations in your ScienceLog.

14. Clean the brush. Paint a green circle 4 cm in diameter, and then paint half the blue circle with green paint.

15. Examine the green, blue, and mixed areas. Record your observations.

16. Now add green paint to the mixed red-blue area, so that you have an area that is a mixture of red, green, and blue paint. Clean your brush.

17. Record your observations of this new mixed area.

Analysis

18. In general, when you mixed two colors, was the result brighter or darker than the original colors?

19. In step 16, you mixed all three colors. Was the result brighter or darker than mixing two colors? Explain your answer in terms of color subtraction. (Hint: Read the definition of color subtraction in the introduction.)

20. Based on your results, what do you think would happen if you mixed all the colors of paint? Explain.

Mirror Images

When light actually passes through an image, the image is a real image. When light does not pass through the image, the image is a virtual image. Recall that plane mirrors produce only virtual images because the image appears to be behind the mirror where no light can pass through it.

In fact, all mirrors can form virtual images, but only some mirrors can form real images. In this experiment, you will explore the virtual images formed by concave and convex mirrors, and you will try to find a real image using both types of mirrors.

Materials

- convex mirror
- concave mirror
- candle
- jar lid
- modeling clay
- matches
- index card

Part A—Finding Virtual Images

Make Observations

1. Hold the convex mirror at arm's length away from your face. Observe the image of your face in the mirror.

2. Slowly move the mirror toward your face, and observe what happens to the image. Record your observations in your ScienceLog.

3. Move the mirror very close to your face. Record your observations in your ScienceLog.

4. Slowly move the mirror away from your face, and observe what happens to the image. Record your observations.

5. Repeat steps 1 through 4 with the concave mirror.

Analyze Your Results

6. For each mirror, did you find a virtual image? How can you tell?

7. Describe the images you found. Were they smaller, larger, or the same size as your face? Were they upright or inverted?

Draw Conclusions

8. Describe at least one use for each type of mirror. Be creative, and try to think of inventions that might use the properties of the two types of mirrors.

Part B—Finding a Real Image

Make Observations

9. In a darkened room, place a candle in a jar lid near one end of a table. Use modeling clay to hold the candle in place. Light the candle.
Caution: Use extreme care around an open flame.

10. Use more modeling clay to make a base to hold the convex mirror upright. Place the mirror at the other end of the table, facing the candle.

11. Hold the index card between the candle and the mirror but slightly to one side so that you do not block the candlelight, as shown below.

12. Move the card slowly from side to side and back and forth to see whether you can focus an image of the candle on it. Record your results in your ScienceLog.

13. Repeat steps 10–12 with the concave mirror.

Analyze Your Results

14. For each mirror, did you find a real image? How can you tell?

15. Describe the real image you found. Was it smaller, larger, or the same size as the object? Was it upright or inverted?

Draw Conclusions

16. Astronomical telescopes use large mirrors to reflect light to form a real image. Based on your results, would a concave or convex mirror be better for this instrument? Explain your answer.

DISCOVERY LAB

Images from Convex Lenses

A convex lens is thicker in the center than at the edges. Light rays passing through a convex lens come together at a point. Under certain conditions, a convex lens will create a real image of an object. This image will have certain characteristics, depending on the distance between the object and the lens. In this experiment you will determine the characteristics of real images created by a convex lens—the kind of lens used as a magnifying lens.

Materials

- index card
- modeling clay
- candle
- jar lid
- matches
- convex lens
- meterstick

Ask a Question

1. What are the characteristics of real images created by a convex lens? How do these characteristics depend on the location of the object and the lens?

Conduct an Experiment

2. Copy the table below into your ScienceLog.

	Data Collection			
Image	Orientation (upright/inverted)	Size (larger/smaller)	Image distance (cm)	Object distance (cm)
1				
2				
3				

3. Use some modeling clay to make a base for the lens. Place the lens and base in the middle of the table.

4. Stand the index card upright in some modeling clay on one side of the lens.

5. Place the candle in the jar lid, and anchor it with some modeling clay. Place the candle on the table so that the lens is halfway between the candle and the card. Light the candle. **Caution:** Use extreme care around an open flame.

Collect Data

6. In a darkened room, slowly move the card and the candle away from the lens while keeping the lens exactly halfway between the card and the candle. Continue until you see a clear image of the candle flame on the card. This is image 1.

7. Measure and record the distance between the lens and the card (image distance) and between the lens and the candle (object distance).

8. Is image 1 upright or inverted? Is it larger or smaller than the candle? Record this information in the table.

9. Slide the lens toward the candle to get a new image (image 2) of the candle on the card. Leave the lens in this position.

10. Repeat steps 7 and 8 for image 2.

11. Move the lens back to the middle, and then move the lens toward the card to get a third image (image 3).

12. Repeat steps 7 and 8 for image 3.

Analyze Your Results

13. Describe the trend between image distance and image size.

14. What are the similarities between the real images formed by a convex lens?

Draw Conclusions

15. The lens of your eye is a convex lens. Use the information you collected to describe the image projected on the back of your eye when you look at an object.

16. Convex lenses are used in film projectors. Explain why your favorite movie stars are truly "larger than life" on the screen in terms of the image distance and the object distance.

Communicate Your Results

17. Write a paragraph to summarize your answer to the question in step 1. Be sure to include the roles that image distance and object distance have in determining the characteristics of the images.

Self-Check Answers

Chapter 1—The World of Physical Science
Page 16: flapping rate

Chapter 2—The Properties of Matter
Page 41: approximately 30 N

Chapter 3—States of Matter
Page 64: The pressure would increase.

Page 70: endothermic

Chapter 4—Elements, Compounds, and Mixtures
Page 87: No, the properties of pure water are the same no matter what its source is.

Page 93: Copper and silver are solutes. Gold is the solvent.

Chapter 5—Matter in Motion
Page 110: Numbers 1 and 3 are examples of velocity.

Page 117: 2 N north

Page 122: sliding friction

Page 126: Gravity is a force of attraction between objects that is due to the masses of the objects.

Chapter 6—Forces in Motion
Page 140: A leaf is more affected by air resistance.

Page 147: This can be answered in terms of either Newton's first law or inertia.

Newton's first law: When the bus is still, both you and the bus are at rest. The bus started moving, but no unbalanced force acted on your body, so your body stayed at rest.

Inertia: You have inertia, and that makes you difficult to move. As a result, when the bus started to move, you didn't move with it.

Chapter 7—Forces in Fluids
Page 175: Air travels faster over the top of a wing.

Chapter 8—Work and Machines
Page 189: Pulling a wheeled suitcase is doing work because the force applied and the motion of the suitcase are in the same direction.

Chapter 9—Energy and Energy Resources

Page 223: A roller coaster has the greatest potential energy at the top of the highest hill (usually the first hill) and the greatest kinetic energy at the bottom of the highest hill.

Chapter 10—Heat and Heat Technology

Page 259: Two substances can have the same temperature but different amounts of thermal energy because temperature, unlike thermal energy, does not depend on mass. A small amount of a substance at a particular temperature will have less thermal energy than a large amount of the substance at the same temperature.

Page 261: Steam can cause a more severe burn than boiling water because steam contains more energy per unit mass than does boiling water.

Chapter 11—Introduction to Atoms

Page 285: The particles Thomson discovered had negative charges. Because an atom has no charge, it must contain positively charged particles to cancel the negative charges.

Chapter 12—The Periodic Table

Page 312: It is easier for atoms of alkali metals to lose one electron than for atoms of alkaline-earth metals to lose two electrons. Therefore, alkali metals are more reactive than alkaline-earth metals.

Chapter 13—Chemical Bonding

Page 333: neon

Page 337: 1. 6 **2.** In a covalent bond, electrons are shared between atoms. In an ionic bond, electrons are transferred from one atom to another.

Chapter 14—Chemical Reactions

Page 353: 2 sodium atoms, 1 sulfur atom, and 4 oxygen atoms

Page 355: $CaBr_2 + Cl_2 \rightarrow Br_2 + CaCl_2$

        reactants: $CaBr_2$ and Cl_2

        products: Br_2 and $CaCl_2$

Chapter 15—Chemical Compounds

Page 381: a soft drink

Chapter 16—Atomic Energy

Page 400: alpha particles

Chapter 17—Introduction to Electricity

Page 425: Plastic wrap is charged by friction as it is pulled off the roll.

Page 438: $E = P \times t$; $E = 200\,\text{W} \times 2\,\text{h} = 400\,\text{Wh}$

Students will have to use data from the table on page 438 to answer this question.

Page 441: Yes; a microwave oven is an example of a load because it uses electrical energy to do work.

Chapter 18—Electromagnetism

Page 464: No; an electromagnet is produced when the magnetic field of the coil of wire causes the domains in the core to line up. Wood does not contain domains and therefore cannot be the core of an electromagnet.

Chapter 19—Electronic Technology

No self-check question for this chapter.

Chapter 20—The Energy of Waves

Page 512: Mechanical waves require a medium; electromagnetic waves do not.

Page 521: A light wave will not refract if it enters a new medium perpendicular to the surface because the entire wave enters the new medium at the same time.

Chapter 21—The Nature of Sound

Page 549: A person hears a sonic boom when a shock wave reaches his or her ears. If two people are standing a block or two apart, the shock wave will reach them at different times, so they will hear sonic booms at different times.

Page 553: Interference is the most important wave interaction for determining sound quality.

Chapter 22—The Nature of Light

Page 583: The paper will appear blue because only blue light is reflected from the paper.

Chapter 23—Light and Our World

Page 602: Concave lenses do not form real images. Only a real image can be magnified by another lens, such as the eyepiece lens.

CONTENTS

Concept Mapping: A Way to Bring Ideas Together

What Is a Concept Map?

Have you ever tried to tell someone about a book or a chapter you've just read and found that you can remember only a few isolated words and ideas? Or maybe you've memorized facts for a test and then weeks later discovered you're not even sure what topics those facts covered.

In both cases, you may have understood the ideas or concepts by themselves but not in relation to one another. If you could somehow link the ideas together, you would probably understand them better and remember them longer. This is something a concept map can help you do. A concept map is a way to see how ideas or concepts fit together. It can help you see the "big picture."

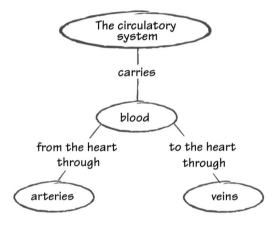

How to Make a Concept Map

❶ Make a list of the main ideas or concepts.

It might help to write each concept on its own slip of paper. This will make it easier to rearrange the concepts as many times as necessary to make sense of how the concepts are connected. After you've made a few concept maps this way, you can go directly from writing your list to actually making the map.

❷ Arrange the concepts in order from the most general to the most specific.

Put the most general concept at the top and circle it. Ask yourself, "How does this concept relate to the remaining concepts?" As you see the relationships, arrange the concepts in order from general to specific.

❸ Connect the related concepts with lines.

❹ On each line, write an action word or short phrase that shows how the concepts are related.

Look at the concept maps on this page, and then see if you can make one for the following terms:

plants, water, photosynthesis, carbon dioxide, sun's energy

One possible answer is provided at right, but don't look at it until you try the concept map yourself.

SI Measurement

The International System of Units, or SI, is the standard system of measurement used by many scientists. Using the same standards of measurement makes it easier for scientists to communicate with one another.

SI works by combining prefixes and base units. Each base unit can be used with different prefixes to define smaller and larger quantities. The table below lists common SI prefixes.

SI Prefixes			
Prefix	**Abbreviation**	**Factor**	**Example**
kilo-	k	1,000	kilogram, 1 kg = 1,000 g
hecto-	h	100	hectoliter, 1 hL = 100 L
deka-	da	10	dekameter, 1 dam = 10 m
		1	meter, liter
deci-	d	0.1	decigram, 1 dg = 0.1 g
centi-	c	0.01	centimeter, 1 cm = 0.01 m
milli-	m	0.001	milliliter, 1 mL = 0.001 L
micro-	μ	0.000 001	micrometer, 1 μm = 0.000 001 m

SI Conversion Table		
SI units	**From SI to English**	**From English to SI**
Length		
kilometer (km) = 1,000 m	1 km = 0.621 mi	1 mi = 1.609 km
meter (m) = 100 cm	1 m = 3.281 ft	1 ft = 0.305 m
centimeter (cm) = 0.01 m	1 cm = 0.394 in.	1 in. = 2.540 cm
millimeter (mm) = 0.001 m	1 mm = 0.039 in.	
micrometer (μm) = 0.000 001 m		
nanometer (nm) = 0.000 000 001 m		
Area		
square kilometer (km^2) = 100 hectares	1 km^2 = 0.386 mi^2	1 mi^2 = 2.590 km^2
hectare (ha) = 10,000 m^2	1 ha = 2.471 acres	1 acre = 0.405 ha
square meter (m^2) = 10,000 cm^2	1 m^2 = 10.765 ft^2	1 ft^2 = 0.093 m^2
square centimeter (cm^2) = 100 mm^2	1 cm^2 = 0.155 $in.^2$	1 $in.^2$ = 6.452 cm^2
Volume		
liter (L) = 1,000 mL = 1 dm^3	1 L = 1.057 fl qt	1 fl qt = 0.946 L
milliliter (mL) = 0.001 L = 1 cm^3	1 mL = 0.034 fl oz	1 fl oz = 29.575 mL
microliter (μL) = 0.000 001 L		
Mass		
kilogram (kg) = 1,000 g	1 kg = 2.205 lb	1 lb = 0.454 kg
gram (g) = 1,000 mg	1 g = 0.035 oz	1 oz = 28.349 g
milligram (mg) = 0.001 g		
microgram (μg) = 0.000 001 g		

Temperature Scales

Temperature can be expressed using three different scales: Fahrenheit, Celsius, and Kelvin. The SI unit for temperature is the kelvin (K).

Although 0 K is much colder than 0°C, a change of 1 K is equal to a change of 1°C.

Three Temperature Scales

	Fahrenheit	Celsius	Kelvin
Water boils	212°	100°	373
Body temperature	98.6°	37°	310
Room temperature	68°	20°	293
Water freezes	32°	0°	273

Temperature Conversions Table

To convert	Use this equation:	Example
Celsius to Fahrenheit °C ⟶ °F	$°F = \left(\frac{9}{5} \times °C\right) + 32$	Convert 45°C to °F. $°F = \left(\frac{9}{5} \times 45°C\right) + 32 = 113°F$
Fahrenheit to Celsius °F ⟶ °C	$°C = \frac{5}{9} \times (°F - 32)$	Convert 68°F to °C. $°C = \frac{5}{9} \times (68°F - 32) = 20°C$
Celsius to Kelvin °C ⟶ K	$K = °C + 273$	Convert 45°C to K. $K = 45°C + 273 = 318\ K$
Kelvin to Celsius K ⟶ °C	$°C = K - 273$	Convert 32 K to °C. $°C = 32\ K - 273 = -241°C$

Measuring Skills

Using a Graduated Cylinder

When using a graduated cylinder to measure volume, keep the following procedures in mind:

1 Make sure the cylinder is on a flat, level surface.

2 Move your head so that your eye is level with the surface of the liquid.

3 Read the mark closest to the liquid level. On glass graduated cylinders, read the mark closest to the center of the curve in the liquid's surface.

Using a Meterstick or Metric Ruler

When using a meterstick or metric ruler to measure length, keep the following procedures in mind:

1 Place the ruler firmly against the object you are measuring.

2 Align one edge of the object exactly with the zero end of the ruler.

3 Look at the other edge of the object to see which of the marks on the ruler is closest to that edge. **Note:** Each small slash between the centimeters represents a millimeter, which is one-tenth of a centimeter.

Using a Triple-Beam Balance

When using a triple-beam balance to measure mass, keep the following procedures in mind:

1 Make sure the balance is on a level surface.

2 Place all of the countermasses at zero. Adjust the balancing knob until the pointer rests at zero.

3 Place the object you wish to measure on the pan. **Caution:** Do not place hot objects or chemicals directly on the balance pan.

4 Move the largest countermass along the beam to the right until it is at the last notch that does not tip the balance. Follow the same procedure with the next-largest countermass. Then move the smallest countermass until the pointer rests at zero.

5 Add the readings from the three beams together to determine the mass of the object.

6 When determining the mass of crystals or powders, use a piece of filter paper. First find the mass of the paper. Then add the crystals or powder to the paper and re-measure. The actual mass of the crystals or powder is the total mass minus the mass of the paper. When finding the mass of liquids, first find the mass of the empty container. Then find the mass of the liquid and container together. The mass of the liquid is the total mass minus the mass of the container.

Scientific Method

The series of steps that scientists use to answer questions and solve problems is often called the **scientific method.** The scientific method is not a rigid procedure. Scientists may use all of the steps or just some of the steps of the scientific method. They may even repeat some of the steps. The goal of the scientific method is to come up with reliable answers and solutions.

Six Steps of the Scientific Method

Ask a Question

1 **Ask a Question** Good questions come from careful **observations.** You make observations by using your senses to gather information. Sometimes you may use instruments, such as microscopes and telescopes, to extend the range of your senses. As you observe the natural world, you will discover that you have many more questions than answers. These questions drive the scientific method.

Questions beginning with *what, why, how,* and *when* are very important in focusing an investigation, and they often lead to a hypothesis. (You will learn what a hypothesis is in the next step.) Here is an example of a question that could lead to further investigation.

Question: How does acid rain affect plant growth?

Form a Hypothesis

2 **Form a Hypothesis** After you come up with a question, you need to turn the question into a **hypothesis.** A hypothesis is a clear statement of what you expect the answer to your question to be. Your hypothesis will represent your best "educated guess" based on your observations and what you already know. A good hypothesis is testable. If observations and information cannot be gathered or if an experiment cannot be designed to test your hypothesis, it is untestable, and the investigation can go no further.

Here is a hypothesis that could be formed from the question, "How does acid rain affect plant growth?"

Hypothesis: Acid rain causes plants to grow more slowly.

Notice that the hypothesis provides some specifics that lead to methods of testing. The hypothesis can also lead to predictions. A **prediction** is what you think will be the outcome of your experiment or data collection. Predictions are usually stated in an "if . . . then" format. For example, **if** meat is kept at room temperature, **then** it will spoil faster than meat kept in the refrigerator. More than one prediction can be made for a single hypothesis. Here is a sample prediction for the hypothesis that acid rain causes plants to grow more slowly.

Prediction: If a plant is watered with only acid rain (which has a pH of 4), then the plant will grow at half its normal rate.

3 **Test the Hypothesis** After you have formed a hypothesis and made a prediction, you should test your hypothesis. There are different ways to do this. Perhaps the most familiar way is to conduct a **controlled experiment.** A controlled experiment tests only one factor at a time. A controlled experiment has a **control group** and one or more **experimental groups.** All the factors for the control and experimental groups are the same except for one factor, which is called the **variable.** By changing only one factor, you can see the results of just that one change.

Sometimes, the nature of an investigation makes a controlled experiment impossible. For example, dinosaurs have been extinct for millions of years, and the Earth's core is surrounded by thousands of meters of rock. It would be difficult, if not impossible, to conduct controlled experiments on such things. Under such circumstances, a hypothesis may be tested by making detailed observations. Taking measurements is one way of making observations.

Test the Hypothesis

4 **Analyze the Results** After you have completed your experiments, made your observations, and collected your data, you must analyze all the information you have gathered. Tables and graphs are often used in this step to organize the data.

Analyze the Results

5 **Draw Conclusions** Based on the analysis of your data, you should conclude whether or not your results support your hypothesis. If your hypothesis is supported, you (or others) might want to repeat the observations or experiments to verify your results. If your hypothesis is not supported by the data, you may have to check your procedure for errors. You may even have to reject your hypothesis and make a new one. If you cannot draw a conclusion from your results, you may have to try the investigation again or carry out further observations or experiments.

Draw Conclusions

Do they support your hypothesis?

No

Yes

6 **Communicate Results** After any scientific investigation, you should report your results. By doing a written or oral report, you let others know what you have learned. They may want to repeat your investigation to see if they get the same results. Your report may even lead to another question, which in turn may lead to another investigation.

Communicate Results

Scientific Method in Action

The scientific method is not a "straight line" of steps. It contains loops in which several steps may be repeated over and over again, while others may not be necessary. For example, sometimes scientists will find that testing one hypothesis raises new questions and new hypotheses to be tested. And sometimes, testing the hypothesis leads directly to a conclusion. Furthermore, the steps in the scientific method are not always used in the same order. Follow the steps in the diagram below, and see how many different directions the scientific method can take you.

Ask a question

START

Form a hypothesis

Make observations

Test the hypothesis

Perform experiments

Analyze the results

YES

NO

Do Observations and Experiments Support Hypothesis?

YES

NO

Draw conclusions

Was process faulty?

Communicate results

Making Charts and Graphs

Circle Graphs

A circle graph, or pie chart, shows how each group of data relates to all of the data. Each part of the circle represents a category of the data. The entire circle represents all of the data. For example, a biologist studying a hardwood forest in Wisconsin found that there were five different types of trees. The data table at right summarizes the biologist's findings.

Wisconsin Hardwood Trees	
Type of tree	Number found
Oak	600
Maple	750
Beech	300
Birch	1,200
Hickory	150
Total	3,000

How to Make a Circle Graph

❶ In order to make a circle graph of this data, first find the percentage of each type of tree. To do this, divide the number of individual trees by the total number of trees and multiply by 100.

$$\frac{600 \text{ oak}}{3,000 \text{ trees}} \times 100 = 20\%$$

$$\frac{750 \text{ maple}}{3,000 \text{ trees}} \times 100 = 25\%$$

$$\frac{300 \text{ beech}}{3,000 \text{ trees}} \times 100 = 10\%$$

$$\frac{1,200 \text{ birch}}{3,000 \text{ trees}} \times 100 = 40\%$$

$$\frac{150 \text{ hickory}}{3,000 \text{ trees}} \times 100 = 5\%$$

❷ Now determine the size of the pie shapes that make up the chart. Do this by multiplying each percentage by 360°. Remember that a circle contains 360°.

20% × 360° = 72°	25% × 360° = 90°
10% × 360° = 36°	40% × 360° = 144°
5% × 360° = 18°	

❸ Then check that the sum of the percentages is 100 and the sum of the degrees is 360.

20% + 25% + 10% + 40% + 5% = 100%

72° + 90° + 36° + 144° + 18° = 360°

❹ Use a compass to draw a circle and mark its center.

❺ Then use a protractor to draw angles of 72°, 90°, 36°, 144°, and 18° in the circle.

❻ Finally, label each part of the graph, and choose an appropriate title.

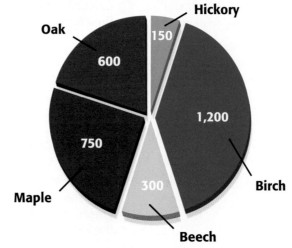

A Community of Wisconsin Hardwood Trees

Hickory 150 — Oak 600 — Maple 750 — Beech 300 — Birch 1,200

Line Graphs

Population of Appleton, 1900–2000	
Year	Population
1900	1,800
1920	2,500
1940	3,200
1960	3,900
1980	4,600
2000	5,300

Line graphs are most often used to demonstrate continuous change. For example, Mr. Smith's science class analyzed the population records for their hometown, Appleton, between 1900 and 2000. Examine the data at left.

Because the year and the population change, they are the *variables*. The population is determined by, or dependent on, the year. Therefore, the population is called the **dependent variable**, and the year is called the **independent variable.** Each set of data is called a **data pair.** To prepare a line graph, data pairs must first be organized in a table like the one at left.

How to Make a Line Graph

1 Place the independent variable along the horizontal (x) axis. Place the dependent variable along the vertical (y) axis.

2 Label the x-axis "Year" and the y-axis "Population." Look at your largest and smallest values for the population. Determine a scale for the y-axis that will provide enough space to show these values. You must use the same scale for the entire length of the axis. Find an appropriate scale for the x-axis too.

3 Choose reasonable starting points for each axis.

4 Plot the data pairs as accurately as possible.

5 Choose a title that accurately represents the data.

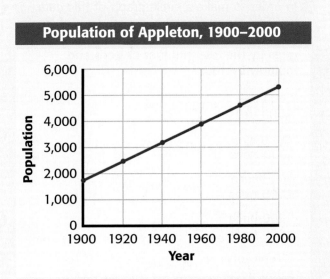

How to Determine Slope

Slope is the ratio of the change in the y-axis to the change in the x-axis, or "rise over run."

1 Choose two points on the line graph. For example, the population of Appleton in 2000 was 5,300 people. Therefore, you can define point a as (2000, 5,300). In 1900, the population was 1,800 people. Define point b as (1900, 1,800).

2 Find the change in the y-axis.
(y at point a) − (y at point b)
5,300 people − 1,800 people = 3,500 people

3 Find the change in the x-axis.
(x at point a) − (x at point b)
2000 − 1900 = 100 years

4 Calculate the slope of the graph by dividing the change in y by the change in x.

$$\text{slope} = \frac{\text{change in } y}{\text{change in } x}$$

$$\text{slope} = \frac{3,500 \text{ people}}{100 \text{ years}}$$

$$\text{slope} = 35 \text{ people per year}$$

In this example, the population in Appleton increased by a fixed amount each year. The graph of this data is a straight line. Therefore, the relationship is **linear.** When the graph of a set of data is not a straight line, the relationship is **nonlinear.**

Using Algebra to Determine Slope

The equation in step 4 may also be arranged to be:

$$y = kx$$

where *y* represents the change in the *y*-axis, *k* represents the slope, and *x* represents the change in the *x*-axis.

$$\text{slope} = \frac{\text{change in } y}{\text{change in } x}$$

$$k = \frac{y}{x}$$

$$k \times x = \frac{y \times x}{x}$$

$$kx = y$$

Bar Graphs

Bar graphs are used to demonstrate change that is not continuous. These graphs can be used to indicate trends when the data are taken over a long period of time. A meteorologist gathered the precipitation records at right for Hartford, Connecticut, for April 1–15, 1996, and used a bar graph to represent the data.

Precipitation in Hartford, Connecticut April 1–15, 1996

Date	Precipitation (cm)	Date	Precipitation (cm)
April 1	0.5	April 9	0.25
April 2	1.25	April 10	0.0
April 3	0.0	April 11	1.0
April 4	0.0	April 12	0.0
April 5	0.0	April 13	0.25
April 6	0.0	April 14	0.0
April 7	0.0	April 15	6.50
April 8	1.75		

How to Make a Bar Graph

❶ Use an appropriate scale and a reasonable starting point for each axis.

❷ Label the axes, and plot the data.

❸ Choose a title that accurately represents the data.

Precipitation in Hartford, Connecticut, April 1–15, 1996

Math Refresher

Science requires an understanding of many math concepts. The following pages will help you review some important math skills.

Averages

An **average,** or **mean,** simplifies a list of numbers into a single number that *approximates* their value.

Example: Find the average of the following set of numbers: 5, 4, 7, and 8.

Step 1: Find the sum.

$$5 + 4 + 7 + 8 = 24$$

Step 2: Divide the sum by the amount of numbers in your set. Because there are four numbers in this example, divide the sum by 4.

$$\frac{24}{4} = 6$$

The average, or mean, is **6.**

Ratios

A **ratio** is a comparison between numbers, and it is usually written as a fraction.

Example: Find the ratio of thermometers to students if you have 36 thermometers and 48 students in your class.

Step 1: Make the ratio.

$$\frac{36 \text{ thermometers}}{48 \text{ students}}$$

Step 2: Reduce the fraction to its simplest form.

$$\frac{36}{48} = \frac{36 \div 12}{48 \div 12} = \frac{3}{4}$$

The ratio of thermometers to students is **3 to 4,** or $\frac{3}{4}$. The ratio may also be written in the form 3:4.

Proportions

A **proportion** is an equation that states that two ratios are equal.

$$\frac{3}{1} = \frac{12}{4}$$

To solve a proportion, first multiply across the equal sign. This is called cross-multiplication. If you know three of the quantities in a proportion, you can use cross-multiplication to find the fourth.

Example: Imagine that you are making a scale model of the solar system for your science project. The diameter of Jupiter is 11.2 times the diameter of the Earth. If you are using a plastic-foam ball with a diameter of 2 cm to represent the Earth, what diameter does the ball representing Jupiter need to be?

$$\frac{11.2}{1} = \frac{x}{2 \text{ cm}}$$

Step 1: Cross-multiply.

$$\frac{11.2}{1} \diagdown\!\!\!\!\diagup \frac{x}{2}$$

$$11.2 \times 2 = x \times 1$$

Step 2: Multiply.

$$22.4 = x \times 1$$

Step 3: Isolate the variable by dividing both sides by 1.

$$x = \frac{22.4}{1}$$

$$x = 22.4 \text{ cm}$$

You will need to use a ball with a diameter of **22.4 cm** to represent Jupiter.

Percentages

A **percentage** is a ratio of a given number to 100.

Example: What is 85 percent of 40?

Step 1: Rewrite the percentage by moving the decimal point two places to the left.

$$0.85$$

Step 2: Multiply the decimal by the number you are calculating the percentage of.

$$0.85 \times 40 = 34$$

85 percent of 40 is **34.**

Decimals

To **add** or **subtract decimals,** line up the digits vertically so that the decimal points line up. Then add or subtract the columns from right to left, carrying or borrowing numbers as necessary.

Example: Add the following numbers: 3.1415 and 2.96.

Step 1: Line up the digits vertically so that the decimal points line up.

$$\begin{array}{r} 3.1415 \\ + \ 2.96 \\ \hline \end{array}$$

Step 2: Add the columns from right to left, carrying when necessary.

$$\begin{array}{r} 1\ 1 \\ 3.1415 \\ + \ 2.96 \\ \hline 6.1015 \end{array}$$

The sum is **6.1015.**

Fractions

Numbers tell you how many; **fractions** tell you *how much of a whole.*

Example: Your class has 24 plants. Your teacher instructs you to put 5 in a shady spot. What fraction does this represent?

Step 1: Write a fraction with the total number of parts in the whole as the denominator.

$$\frac{?}{24}$$

Step 2: Write the number of parts of the whole being represented as the numerator.

$$\frac{5}{24}$$

$\frac{5}{24}$ of the plants will be in the shade.

Reducing Fractions

It is usually best to express a fraction in simplest form. This is called *reducing* a fraction.

Example: Reduce the fraction $\frac{30}{45}$ to its simplest form.

Step 1: Find the largest whole number that will divide evenly into both the numerator and denominator. This number is called the greatest common factor (GCF).

factors of the numerator 30: 1, 2, 3, 5, 6, 10, **15,** 30

factors of the denominator 45: 1, 3, 5, 9, **15,** 45

Step 2: Divide both the numerator and the denominator by the GCF, which in this case is 15.

$$\frac{30}{45} = \frac{30 \div 15}{45 \div 15} = \frac{2}{3}$$

$\frac{30}{45}$ reduced to its simplest form is $\frac{2}{3}$.

Adding and Subtracting Fractions

To **add** or **subtract fractions** that have the **same denominator,** simply add or subtract the numerators.

Examples:

$$\frac{3}{5} + \frac{1}{5} = ? \quad \text{and} \quad \frac{3}{4} - \frac{1}{4} = ?$$

Step 1: Add or subtract the numerators.

$$\frac{3}{5} + \frac{1}{5} = \frac{4}{} \quad \text{and} \quad \frac{3}{4} - \frac{1}{4} = \frac{2}{}$$

Step 2: Write the sum or difference over the denominator.

$$\frac{3}{5} + \frac{1}{5} = \frac{4}{5} \quad \text{and} \quad \frac{3}{4} - \frac{1}{4} = \frac{2}{4}$$

Step 3: If necessary, reduce the fraction to its simplest form.

$\frac{4}{5}$ cannot be reduced, and $\frac{2}{4} = \frac{1}{2}$.

To **add** or **subtract fractions** that have **different denominators,** first find the least common denominator (LCD).

Examples:

$$\frac{1}{2} + \frac{1}{6} = ? \quad \text{and} \quad \frac{3}{4} - \frac{2}{3} = ?$$

Step 1: Write the equivalent fractions with a common denominator.

$$\frac{3}{6} + \frac{1}{6} = ? \quad \text{and} \quad \frac{9}{12} - \frac{8}{12} = ?$$

Step 2: Add or subtract.

$$\frac{3}{6} + \frac{1}{6} = \frac{4}{6} \quad \text{and} \quad \frac{9}{12} - \frac{8}{12} = \frac{1}{12}$$

Step 3: If necessary, reduce the fraction to its simplest form.

$\frac{4}{6} = \frac{2}{3}$, and $\frac{1}{12}$ cannot be reduced.

Multiplying Fractions

To **multiply fractions,** multiply the numerators and the denominators together, and then reduce the fraction to its simplest form.

Example:

$$\frac{5}{9} \times \frac{7}{10} = ?$$

Step 1: Multiply the numerators and denominators.

$$\frac{5}{9} \times \frac{7}{10} = \frac{5 \times 7}{9 \times 10} = \frac{35}{90}$$

Step 2: Reduce.

$$\frac{35}{90} = \frac{35 \div 5}{90 \div 5} = \frac{7}{18}$$

Dividing Fractions

To **divide fractions,** first rewrite the divisor (the number you divide *by*) upside down. This is called the reciprocal of the divisor. Then you can multiply and reduce if necessary.

Example:

$$\frac{5}{8} \div \frac{3}{2} = ?$$

Step 1: Rewrite the divisor as its reciprocal.

$$\frac{3}{2} \rightarrow \frac{2}{3}$$

Step 2: Multiply.

$$\frac{5}{8} \times \frac{2}{3} = \frac{5 \times 2}{8 \times 3} = \frac{10}{24}$$

Step 3: Reduce.

$$\frac{10}{24} = \frac{10 \div 2}{24 \div 2} = \frac{5}{12}$$

Scientific Notation

Scientific notation is a short way of representing very large and very small numbers without writing all of the place-holding zeros.

Example: Write 653,000,000 in scientific notation.

Step 1: Write the number without the place-holding zeros.

653

Step 2: Place the decimal point after the first digit.

6.53

Step 3: Find the exponent by counting the number of places that you moved the decimal point.

6̰53000000

The decimal point was moved eight places to the left. Therefore, the exponent of 10 is positive 8. Remember, if the decimal point had moved to the right, the exponent would be negative.

Step 4: Write the number in scientific notation.

$$6.53 \times 10^8$$

Area

Area is the number of square units needed to cover the surface of an object.

Formulas:
Area of a square = side × side
Area of a rectangle = length × width
Area of a triangle = $\frac{1}{2}$ × base × height

Examples: Find the areas.

Triangle
Area = $\frac{1}{2}$ × base × height
Area = $\frac{1}{2}$ × 3 cm × 4 cm
Area = **6 cm²**

3 cm · 4 cm

Rectangle
Area = length × width
Area = 6 cm × 3 cm
Area = **18 cm²**

3 cm · 6 cm

Square
Area = side × side
Area = 3 cm × 3 cm
Area = **9 cm²**

3 cm · 3 cm

Volume

Volume is the amount of space something occupies.

Formulas:
Volume of a cube =
side × side × side

Volume of a prism =
area of base × height

Examples:
Find the volume
of the solids.

Cube
Volume = side × side × side
Volume = 4 cm × 4 cm × 4 cm
Volume = **64 cm³**

4 cm · 4 cm · 4 cm

4 cm · 3 cm · 5 cm

Prism
Volume = area of base × height
Volume = (area of triangle) × height
Volume = $\left(\frac{1}{2} \times 3\ \text{cm} \times 4\ \text{cm} \right)$ × 5 cm
Volume = 6 cm² × 5 cm
Volume = **30 cm³**

Physical Science Refresher

Atoms and Elements

Every object in the universe is made up of particles of some kind of matter. **Matter** is anything that takes up space and has mass. All matter is made up of elements. An **element** is a substance that cannot be separated into simpler components by ordinary chemical means. This is because each element consists of only one kind of atom. An **atom** is the smallest unit of an element that has all of the properties of that element.

Atomic Structure

Atoms are made up of small particles called subatomic particles. The three major types of subatomic particles are **electrons, protons,** and **neutrons.** Electrons have a negative electric charge, protons have a positive charge, and neutrons have no electric charge. The protons and neutrons are packed close to one another to form the **nucleus.** The protons give the nucleus a positive charge. Electrons are most likely to be found in regions around the nucleus called **electron clouds.** The negatively charged electrons are attracted to the positively charged nucleus. An atom may have several energy levels in which electrons are located.

Atomic Number

To help in the identification of elements, scientists have assigned an **atomic number** to each kind of atom. The atomic number is the number of protons in the atom. Atoms with the same number of protons are all the same kind of element. In an uncharged, or electrically neutral, atom there are an equal number of protons and electrons. Therefore, the atomic number equals the number of electrons in an uncharged atom. The number of neutrons, however, can vary for a given element. Atoms of the same element that have different numbers of neutrons are called **isotopes.**

Periodic Table of the Elements

In the periodic table, the elements are arranged from left to right in order of increasing atomic number. Each element in the table is in a separate box. An atom of each element has one more electron and one more proton than an atom of the element to its left. Each horizontal row of the table is called a **period.** Changes in chemical properties of elements across a period correspond to changes in the electron arrangements of their atoms. Each vertical column of the table, known as a **group,** lists elements with similar properties. The elements in a group have similar chemical properties because their atoms have the same number of electrons in their outer energy level. For example, the elements helium, neon, argon, krypton, xenon, and radon all have similar properties and are known as the noble gases.

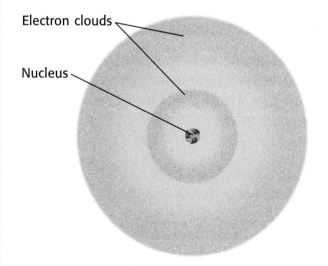

Electron clouds

Nucleus

Molecules and Compounds

When two or more elements are joined chemically, the resulting substance is called a **compound.** A compound is a new substance with properties different from those of the elements that compose it. For example, water, H_2O, is a compound formed when hydrogen (H) and oxygen (O) combine. The smallest complete unit of a compound that has the properties of that compound is called a **molecule.** A chemical formula indicates the elements in a compound. It also indicates the relative number of atoms of each element present. The chemical formula for water is H_2O, which indicates that each water molecule consists of two atoms of hydrogen and one atom of oxygen. The subscript number is used after the symbol for an element to indicate how many atoms of that element are in a single molecule of the compound.

Acids, Bases, and pH

An ion is an atom or group of atoms that has an electric charge because it has lost or gained one or more electrons. When an acid, such as hydrochloric acid, HCl, is mixed with water, it separates into ions. An **acid** is a compound that produces hydrogen ions, H^+, in water. The hydrogen ions then combine with a water molecule to form a hydronium ion, H_3O^+. A **base,** on the other hand, is a substance that produces hydroxide ions, OH^-, in water.

To determine whether a solution is acidic or basic, scientists use pH. The **pH** is a measure of the hydronium ion concentration in a solution. The pH scale ranges from 0 to 14. The middle point, pH = 7, is neutral, neither acidic nor basic. Acids have a pH less than 7; bases have a pH greater than 7. The lower the number is, the more acidic the solution. The higher the number is, the more basic the solution.

Chemical Equations

A chemical reaction occurs when a chemical change takes place. (In a chemical change, new substances with new properties are formed.) A chemical equation is a useful way of describing a chemical reaction by means of chemical formulas. The equation indicates what substances react and what the products are. For example, when carbon and oxygen combine, they can form carbon dioxide. The equation for the reaction is as follows: $C + O_2 \longrightarrow CO_2$.

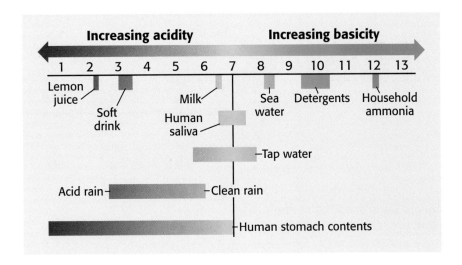

Periodic Table of the Elements

Each square on the table includes an element's name, chemical symbol, atomic number, and atomic mass.

Atomic number	6
Chemical symbol	C
Element name	Carbon
Atomic mass	12.0

The background color indicates the type of element. Carbon is a nonmetal.

The color of the chemical symbol indicates the physical state at room temperature. Carbon is a solid.

Background
Metals
Metalloids
Nonmetals

Chemical symbol
Solid
Liquid
Gas

Period 1

1
H
Hydrogen
1.0

Group 1 · **Group 2**

Period 2

3	4
Li	**Be**
Lithium	Beryllium
6.9	9.0

Period 3

11	12
Na	**Mg**
Sodium	Magnesium
23.0	24.3

Group 3 · **Group 4** · **Group 5** · **Group 6** · **Group 7** · **Group 8** · **Group 9**

Period 4

19	20	21	22	23	24	25	26	27
K	**Ca**	**Sc**	**Ti**	**V**	**Cr**	**Mn**	**Fe**	**Co**
Potassium	Calcium	Scandium	Titanium	Vanadium	Chromium	Manganese	Iron	Cobalt
39.1	40.1	45.0	47.9	50.9	52.0	54.9	55.8	58.9

Period 5

37	38	39	40	41	42	43	44	45
Rb	**Sr**	**Y**	**Zr**	**Nb**	**Mo**	**Tc**	**Ru**	**Rh**
Rubidium	Strontium	Yttrium	Zirconium	Niobium	Molybdenum	Technetium	Ruthenium	Rhodium
85.5	87.6	88.9	91.2	92.9	95.9	(97.9)	101.1	102.9

Period 6

55	56	57	72	73	74	75	76	77
Cs	**Ba**	**La**	**Hf**	**Ta**	**W**	**Re**	**Os**	**Ir**
Cesium	Barium	Lanthanum	Hafnium	Tantalum	Tungsten	Rhenium	Osmium	Iridium
132.9	137.3	138.9	178.5	180.9	183.8	186.2	190.2	192.2

Period 7

87	88	89	104	105	106	107	108	109
Fr	**Ra**	**Ac**	**Rf**	**Db**	**Sg**	**Bh**	**Hs**	**Mt**
Francium	Radium	Actinium	Rutherfordium	Dubnium	Seaborgium	Bohrium	Hassium	Meitnerium
(223.0)	(226.0)	(227.0)	(261.1)	(262.1)	(263.1)	(262.1)	(265)	(266)

A row of elements is called a period.

A column of elements is called a group or family.

Lanthanides

58	59	60	61	62
Ce	**Pr**	**Nd**	**Pm**	**Sm**
Cerium	Praseodymium	Neodymium	Promethium	Samarium
140.1	140.9	144.2	(144.9)	150.4

Actinides

90	91	92	93	94
Th	**Pa**	**U**	**Np**	**Pu**
Thorium	Protactinium	Uranium	Neptunium	Plutonium
232.0	231.0	238.0	(237.0)	244.1

These elements are placed below the table to allow the table to be narrower.

Group 18

| | | | | | | 2
He
Helium
4.0 |

This zigzag line reminds you where the metals, nonmetals, and metalloids are.

Group 13	Group 14	Group 15	Group 16	Group 17	
5 **B** Boron 10.8	6 **C** Carbon 12.0	7 **N** Nitrogen 14.0	8 **O** Oxygen 16.0	9 **F** Fluorine 19.0	10 **Ne** Neon 20.2
13 **Al** Aluminum 27.0	14 **Si** Silicon 28.1	15 **P** Phosphorus 31.0	16 **S** Sulfur 32.1	17 **Cl** Chlorine 35.5	18 **Ar** Argon 39.9

Group 10	Group 11	Group 12					
28 **Ni** Nickel 58.7	29 **Cu** Copper 63.5	30 **Zn** Zinc 65.4	31 **Ga** Gallium 69.7	32 **Ge** Germanium 72.6	33 **As** Arsenic 74.9	34 **Se** Selenium 79.0	35 **Br** Bromine 79.9	36 **Kr** Krypton 83.8
46 **Pd** Palladium 106.4	47 **Ag** Silver 107.9	48 **Cd** Cadmium 112.4	49 **In** Indium 114.8	50 **Sn** Tin 118.7	51 **Sb** Antimony 121.8	52 **Te** Tellurium 127.6	53 **I** Iodine 126.9	54 **Xe** Xenon 131.3
78 **Pt** Platinum 195.1	79 **Au** Gold 197.0	80 **Hg** Mercury 200.6	81 **Tl** Thallium 204.4	82 **Pb** Lead 207.2	83 **Bi** Bismuth 209.0	84 **Po** Polonium (209.0)	85 **At** Astatine (210.0)	86 **Rn** Radon (222.0)
110 **Uun** Ununnilium (271)	111 **Uuu** Unununium (272)	112 **Uub** Ununbium (277)						

The names and symbols of elements 110–112 are temporary. They are based on the atomic number of the element. The official name and symbol will be approved by an international committee of scientists.

63 **Eu** Europium 152.0	64 **Gd** Gadolinium 157.3	65 **Tb** Terbium 158.9	66 **Dy** Dysprosium 162.5	67 **Ho** Holmium 164.9	68 **Er** Erbium 167.3	69 **Tm** Thulium 168.9	70 **Yb** Ytterbium 173.0	71 **Lu** Lutetium 175.0
95 **Am** Americium (243.1)	96 **Cm** Curium (247.1)	97 **Bk** Berkelium (247.1)	98 **Cf** Californium (251.1)	99 **Es** Einsteinium (252.1)	100 **Fm** Fermium (257.1)	101 **Md** Mendelevium (258.1)	102 **No** Nobelium (259.1)	103 **Lr** Lawrencium (262.1)

A number in parentheses is the mass number of the most stable isotope of that element.

Physical Science Laws and Principles

Law of Conservation of Energy

The law of conservation of energy states that energy can be neither created nor destroyed.

The total amount of energy in a closed system is always the same. Energy can be changed from one form to another, but all the different forms of energy in a system always add up to the same total amount of energy, no matter how many energy conversions occur.

Law of Universal Gravitation

The law of universal gravitation states that all objects in the universe attract each other by a force called gravity. The size of the force depends on the masses of the objects and the distance between them.

The first part of the law explains why a bowling ball is much harder to lift than a table-tennis ball. Because the bowling ball has a much larger mass than the table-tennis ball, the amount of gravity between the Earth and the bowling ball is greater than the amount of gravity between the Earth and the table-tennis ball.

The second part of the law explains why a satellite can remain in orbit around the Earth. The satellite is carefully placed at a distance great enough to prevent the Earth's gravity from immediately pulling it down but small enough to prevent it from completely escaping the Earth's gravity and wandering off into space.

Newton's Laws of Motion

Newton's first law of motion states that an object at rest remains at rest and an object in motion remains in motion at constant speed and in a straight line unless acted on by an unbalanced force.

The first part of the law explains why a football will remain on a tee until it is kicked off or until a gust of wind blows it off.

The second part of the law explains why a bike's rider will continue moving forward after the bike tire runs into a crack in the sidewalk and the bike comes to an abrupt stop until gravity and the sidewalk stop the rider.

Newton's second law of motion states that the acceleration of an object depends on the mass of the object and the amount of force applied.

The first part of the law explains why the acceleration of a 4 kg bowling ball will be greater than the acceleration of a 6 kg bowling ball if the same force is applied to both.

The second part of the law explains why the acceleration of a bowling ball will be larger if a larger force is applied to it.

The relationship of acceleration (a) to mass (m) and force (F) can be expressed mathematically by the following equation:

$$\text{acceleration} = \frac{\text{force}}{\text{mass}}, \text{ or } a = \frac{F}{m}$$

This equation is often rearranged to the form:

$$\text{force} = \text{mass} \times \text{acceleration},$$
$$\text{or}$$
$$F = m \times a$$

Newton's third law of motion states that whenever one object exerts a force on a second object, the second object exerts an equal and opposite force on the first.

This law explains that a runner is able to move forward because of the equal and opposite force the ground exerts on the runner's foot after each step.

Law of Reflection

The law of reflection states that the angle of incidence is equal to the angle of reflection. This law explains why light reflects off of a surface at the same angle it strikes the surface.

A line perpendicular to the mirror's surface is called the *normal.*

The beam of light reflected off the mirror is called the *reflected beam.*

The beam of light traveling toward the mirror is called the *incident beam.*

The angle between the incident beam and the normal is called the *angle of incidence.*

The angle between the reflected beam and the normal is called the *angle of reflection.*

Charles's Law

Charles's law states that for a fixed amount of gas at a constant pressure, the volume of the gas increases as its temperature increases. Likewise, the volume of the gas decreases as its temperature decreases.

If a basketball that was inflated indoors is left outside on a cold winter day, the air particles inside of the ball will move more slowly. They will hit the sides of the basketball less often and with less force. The ball will get smaller as the volume of the air decreases. If a basketball that was inflated outdoors on a cold winter day is brought indoors, the air particles inside of the ball will move more rapidly. They will hit the sides of the basketball more often and with more force. The ball will get larger as the volume of the air increases.

Boyle's Law

Boyle's law states that for a fixed amount of gas at a constant temperature, the volume of a gas increases as its pressure decreases. Likewise, the volume of a gas decreases as its pressure increases.

This law explains why the pressure of the gas in a helium balloon decreases as the balloon rises from the Earth's surface.

Pascal's Principle

Pascal's principle states that a change in pressure at any point in an enclosed fluid will be transmitted equally to all parts of that fluid.

When a mechanic uses a hydraulic jack to raise an automobile off the ground, he or she increases the pressure on the fluid in the jack by pushing on the jack handle. The pressure is transmitted equally to all parts of the fluid-filled jacking system. The fluid presses the jack plate against the frame of the car, lifting the car off the ground.

Archimedes' Principle

Archimedes' principle states that the buoyant force on an object in a fluid is equal to the weight of the volume of fluid that the object displaces.

A person floating in a swimming pool displaces 20 L of water. The weight of that volume of water is about 200 N. Therefore, the buoyant force on the person is 200 N.

Bernoulli's Principle

Bernoulli's principle states that as the speed of a moving fluid increases, its pressure decreases.

Bernoulli's principle explains how a wing gives lift to an airplane or even how a Frisbee® can fly through the air. Because of the shape of the Frisbee, the air moving over the top of the Frisbee must travel farther than the air below the Frisbee in the same amount of time. In other words, the air above the Frisbee is moving faster than the air below it. This faster-moving air above the Frisbee exerts less pressure than the slower-moving air below it. The resulting increased pressure below exerts an upward force, pushing the Frisbee up.

Useful Equations

Average speed

$$\text{Average speed} = \frac{\text{total distance}}{\text{total time}}$$

Example: A bicycle messenger traveled a distance of 136 km in 8 hours. What was the messenger's average speed?

$$\frac{136 \text{ km}}{8 \text{ h}} = 17 \text{ km/h}$$

The messenger's average speed was **17 km/h.**

Average acceleration

$$\text{Average acceleration} = \frac{\text{final velocity} - \text{starting velocity}}{\text{time it takes to change velocity}}$$

Example: Calculate the average acceleration of an Olympic 100 m dash sprinter who reaches a velocity of 20 m/s south at the finish line. The race was in a straight line and lasted 10 s.

$$\frac{20 \text{ m/s} - 0 \text{ m/s}}{10 \text{ s}} = 2 \text{ m/s/s}$$

The sprinter's average acceleration is **2 m/s/s south.**

Net force

Forces in the Same Direction

When forces are in the same direction, add the forces together to determine the net force.

Example: Calculate the net force on a stalled car that is being pushed by two people. One person is pushing with a force of 13 N northwest and the other person is pushing with a force of 8 N in the same direction.

$$13 \text{ N} + 8 \text{ N} = 21 \text{ N}$$

The net force is **21 N northwest.**

Forces in Opposite Directions

When forces are in opposite directions, subtract the smaller force from the larger force to determine the net force.

Example: Calculate the net force on a rope that is being pulled on each end. One person is pulling on one end of the rope with a force of 12 N south. Another person is pulling on the opposite end of the rope with a force of 7 N north.

$$12 \text{ N} - 7 \text{ N} = 5 \text{ N}$$

The net force is **5 N south.**

Work

Work is done by exerting a force through a distance. Work has units of joules (J), which are equivalent to Newton-meters.

$$W = F \times d$$

Example: Calculate the amount of work done by a man who lifts a 100 N toddler 1.5 m off the floor.

$$W = 100 \text{ N} \times 1.5 \text{ m} = 150 \text{ N} \bullet \text{m} = 150 \text{ J}$$

The man did **150 J** of work.

Power

Power is the rate at which work is done. Power is measured in watts (W), which are equivalent to joules per second.

$$P = \frac{W}{t}$$

Example: Calculate the power of a weightlifter who raises a 300 N barbell 2.1 m off the floor in 1.25 s.

$$W = 300 \text{ N} \times 2.1 \text{ m} = 630 \text{ N} \bullet \text{m} = 630 \text{ J}$$
$$P = \frac{630 \text{ J}}{1.25 \text{ s}} = 504 \text{ J/s} = 504 \text{ W}$$

The weightlifter has **504 W** of power.

Pressure

Pressure is the force exerted over a given area. The SI unit for pressure is the pascal, which is abbreviated Pa.

$$\text{Pressure} = \frac{\text{force}}{\text{area}}$$

Example: Calculate the pressure of the air in a soccer ball if the air exerts a force of 10 N over an area of 0.5 m^2.

$$\text{Pressure} = \frac{10 \text{ N}}{0.5 \text{ m}^2} = 20 \text{ N/m}^2 = 20 \text{ Pa}$$

The pressure of the air inside of the soccer ball is **20 Pa.**

Density

$$\text{Density} = \frac{\text{mass}}{\text{volume}}$$

Example: Calculate the density of a sponge with a mass of 10 g and a volume of 40 mL.

$$\frac{10 \text{ g}}{40 \text{ mL}} = 0.25 \text{ g/mL}$$

The density of the sponge is **0.25 g/mL.**

Concentration

$$\text{Concentration} = \frac{\text{mass of solute}}{\text{volume of solvent}}$$

Example: Calculate the concentration of a solution in which 10 g of sugar is dissolved in 125 mL of water.

$$\frac{10 \text{ g of sugar}}{125 \text{ mL of water}} = 0.08 \text{ g/mL}$$

The concentration of this solution is **0.08 g/mL.**

Glossary

A

absolute zero the lowest possible temperature (0 K, −273°C) (249)

absorption the transfer of energy carried by light waves to particles of matter (576)

acceleration (ak SEL uhr AY shuhn) the rate at which velocity changes; an object accelerates if its speed changes, if its direction changes, or if both its speed and its direction change (112)

acid any compound that increases the number of hydrogen ions when dissolved in water and whose solution tastes sour and can change the color of certain compounds; acids turn blue litmus red, react with metals to produce hydrogen gas, and react with limestone or baking soda to produce carbon dioxide gas (377)

activation energy the minimum amount of energy needed for substances to react (362)

active solar heating a solar-heating system consisting of solar collectors and a network of pipes that distributes energy from the sun throughout a building (265)

alkali (AL kuh LIE) **metals** the elements in Group 1 of the periodic table; they are the most reactive metals; their atoms have one electron in their outer level (310)

alkaline-earth metals the elements in Group 2 of the periodic table; they are reactive metals but are less reactive than alkali metals; their atoms have two electrons in their outer level (311)

alloys solid solutions of metals or nonmetals dissolved in metals (93)

alpha decay the release of an alpha particle from a nucleus (399)

alpha particle a type of nuclear radiation consisting of two protons and two neutrons emitted by the nucleus of a radioactive atom; identical to the nucleus of a helium atom (399)

alternating current (AC) electric current in which the charges continually switch from flowing in one direction to flowing in the reverse direction (434)

amplitude the maximum distance a wave vibrates from its rest position (516, 543)

analog (AN uh LAHG) **signal** a signal whose properties, such as amplitude and frequency, can change continuously according to changes in the original information (489)

Archimedes' (ahr kuh MEE deez) **principle** the principle that states that the buoyant force on an object in a fluid is an upward force equal to the weight of the volume of fluid that the object displaces (168)

area a measure of how much surface an object has (26)

atmospheric pressure the pressure caused by the weight of the atmosphere (163)

atom the smallest particle into which an element can be divided and still be the same substance (280)

atomic mass the weighted average of the masses of all the naturally occurring isotopes of an element (292)

atomic mass unit (amu) the SI unit used to express the masses of particles in atoms (288)

atomic number the number of protons in the nucleus of an atom (290)

average speed the overall rate at which an object moves; average speed can be calculated by dividing total distance by total time (109)

B

balanced forces forces on an object that cause the net force to be zero; balanced forces do not cause a change in motion or acceleration (118)

base any compound that increases the number of hydroxide ions when dissolved in water and whose solution tastes bitter, feels slippery, and can change the color of certain compounds; bases turn red litmus blue (379)

battery a device that is made of several cells and that produces an electric current by converting chemical energy into electrical energy (430)

Bernoulli's (buhr NOO leez) **principle** the principle that states that as the speed of a moving fluid increases, its pressure decreases (173)

beta decay the release of a beta particle from a nucleus (400)

beta particle an electron or positron emitted by the nucleus of a radioactive atom (400)

bimetallic (BIE muh TAL ik) **strip** a strip made by stacking two different metals in a long thin strip; because the different metals expand at different rates, a bimetallic strip can coil and uncoil with changes in temperature; bimetallic strips are used in devices such as thermostats (250)

binary (BIE neh ree) two; binary numbers contain only the digits 1 and 0 (490)

biochemicals organic compounds made by living things (384)

biomass organic matter, such as plants, wood, and waste, that contains stored energy (236)

bit the name for each of the digits in a binary number (497)

block and tackle a fixed pulley and a movable pulley used together; it can have a large mechanical advantage if several pulleys are used (204)

boiling vaporization that occurs throughout a liquid (70)

boiling point the temperature at which a liquid boils and becomes a gas (70)

Boyle's law the law that states that for a fixed amount of gas at a constant temperature, the volume of a gas increases as its pressure decreases (65)

buoyant force the upward force that fluids exert on all matter; buoyant force opposes gravitational force (168)

byte a unit in which computers store and process information; equal to eight bits (497)

C

calorie the amount of energy needed to change the temperature of 0.001 kg of water by 1°C; 1 calorie is equivalent to 4.184 J (258)

calorimeter (KAL uh RIM uht uhr) a device used to determine the specific heat capacity of a substance (258)

carbohydrates biochemicals composed of one or more simple sugars bonded together that are used as a source of energy and for energy storage (384)

catalyst (KAT uh LIST) a substance that speeds up a reaction without being permanently changed (365)

cathode-ray tube (CRT) a special vacuum tube in which a beam of electrons is projected onto a screen (493)

cell a device that produces an electric current by converting chemical energy into electrical energy (430)

central processing unit (CPU) the physical area in which a computer performs tasks (496)

centripetal (sen TRIP uht uhl) **acceleration** the acceleration that occurs in circular motion; an object traveling in a circle is constantly changing directions, so acceleration occurs continuously (114)

change of state the conversion of a substance from one physical form to another (68, 261)

characteristic property a property of a substance that is always the same whether the sample observed is large or small (48)

Charles's law the law that states that for a fixed amount of gas at a constant pressure, the volume of a gas increases as its temperature increases (66)

chemical bond a force of attraction that holds two atoms together (328)

chemical bonding the joining of atoms to form new substances (328)

chemical change a change that occurs when one or more substances are changed into entirely new substances with different properties; cannot be reversed using physical means (49, 262)

chemical energy the energy of a compound that changes as its atoms are rearranged to form a new compound; chemical energy is a form of potential energy (218)

chemical equation a shorthand description of a chemical reaction using chemical formulas and symbols (354)

chemical formula a shorthand notation for a compound or a diatomic element using chemical symbols and numbers (352)

chemical property a property of matter that describes a substance based on its ability to change into a new substance with different properties (47)

chemical reaction the process by which one or more substances undergo change to produce one or more different substances (350)

circuit a complete, closed path through which electric charges flow (440)

circuit board a collection of hundreds of tiny circuits that supply electric current to the various parts of an electronic device (482)

coefficient (KOH uh FISH uhnt) a number placed in front of a chemical symbol or formula; used to balance a chemical equation (356)

colloid (KAWL OYD) a mixture in which the particles are dispersed throughout but are not heavy enough to settle out (97)

combustion the burning of fuel; specifically, the process in which fuel combines with oxygen in a chemical change that produces thermal energy (266)

compound a pure substance composed of two or more elements that are chemically combined (86)

compound machine a machine that is made of two or more simple machines (204)

compression a region of higher density or pressure in a wave (514, 534)

computer an electronic device that performs tasks by processing and storing information (494)

concave lens a lens that is thinner in the middle than at the edges (604)

concave mirror a mirror that is curved inward like the inside of a spoon (600)

concentration a measure of the amount of solute dissolved in a solvent (94, 364)

condensation the change of state from a gas to a liquid (71)

condensation point the temperature at which a gas becomes a liquid (71)

conduction (electrical) a method of charging an object that occurs when electrons are transferred from one object to another by direct contact (425)

conduction (thermal) the transfer of thermal energy from one substance to another through direct contact; conduction can also occur within a substance (253)

conductor (electrical) a material in which charges can move easily (427)

conductor (thermal) a substance that conducts thermal energy well (254)

constructive interference interference that results in a wave that has a greater amplitude than that of the individual waves (523, 548, 579)

convection the transfer of thermal energy by the movement of a liquid or a gas (254)

convection current the circular motion of liquids or gases due to density differences that result from temperature differences (254)

convex lens a lens that is thicker in the middle than at the edges (603)

convex mirror a mirror that is curved outward like the back of a spoon (602)

cornea a transparent membrane that protects the eye and refracts light (605)

covalent (KOH VAY luhnt) **bond** the force of attraction between the nuclei of atoms and the electrons shared by the atoms (336)

covalent compounds compounds that are composed of elements that are covalently bonded; these compounds are composed of independent molecules, tend to have low melting and boiling points, do not usually dissolve in water, and form solutions that do not conduct an electric current when they do dissolve (375)

crest the highest point of a transverse wave (513)

crystal lattice (LAT is) a repeating three-dimensional pattern of ions (335)

current a continuous flow of charge caused by the motion of electrons; the rate at which charge passes a given point; expressed in amperes (A) (433)

D

data any pieces of information acquired through experimentation (16)

decibel (dB) the most common unit used to express loudness (543)

decomposition reaction a reaction in which a single compound breaks down to form two or more simpler substances (359)

density the amount of matter in a given space; mass per unit volume (27, 44, 165)

destructive interference interference that results in a wave that has a smaller amplitude than that of the individual waves (523, 548, 579)

diffraction the bending of waves around a barrier or through an opening (521, 551, 579)

digital signal a series of electrical pulses that represents the digits of binary numbers (490)

diode (DIE OHD) an electronic component that allows electric current in only one direction (484)

direct current (DC) electric current in which the charges always flow in the same direction (434)

doping (DOHP eeng) the process of replacing a few atoms of a semiconductor with a few atoms of another substance that have a different number of valence electrons (483)

Doppler effect the apparent change in the frequency of a sound caused by the motion of either the listener or the source of the sound (refers to sound only) (542)

double-replacement reaction a reaction in which ions in two compounds switch places (360)

drag the force that opposes or restricts motion in a fluid; drag opposes thrust (176)

ductility (duhk TIL uh tee) the ability of a substance to be drawn or pulled into a wire (44, 340)

E

echo a reflected sound wave (520, 545)

echolocation the process of using reflected sound waves to find objects (546)

electrical energy the energy of electric charges (219, 430)

electric discharge the loss of static electricity as charges move off an object (428)

electric field the region around a charged particle that can exert a force on another charged particle (423)

electric force the force between charged objects (423)

electric motor a device that changes electrical energy into kinetic energy (466)

electric power the rate at which electrical energy is used to do work; expressed in watts (W) (437)

electrode the part of a cell through which charges enter or exit (430)

electrolyte in a cell, a mixture of chemicals that carries an electric current (430)

electromagnet a magnet that consists of a solenoid wrapped around an iron core (464)

electromagnetic induction the process by which an electric current is produced by a changing magnetic field (469)

electromagnetic spectrum the entire range of electromagnetic waves (567)

electromagnetic wave a wave that can travel through space or matter and consists of changing electric and magnetic fields (492, 512, 564)

electromagnetism the interaction between electricity and magnetism (463)

electron clouds the regions inside an atom where electrons are likely to be found (286)

electrons the negatively charged particles found in all atoms; electrons are involved in the formation of chemical bonds (283)

element a pure substance that cannot be separated or broken down into simpler substances by physical or chemical means (82)

endothermic the term used to describe a physical or a chemical change in which energy is absorbed (69, 362)

energy the ability to do work (214)

energy conversion a change from one form of energy into another (222)

energy efficiency (e FISH uhn see) a comparison of the amount of energy before a conversion and the amount of useful energy after a conversion (228)

energy resource a natural resource that can be converted by humans into other forms of energy in order to do useful work (232)

evaporation (ee VAP uh RAY shuhn) vaporization that occurs at the surface of a liquid below its boiling point (70)

exothermic the term used to describe a physical or a chemical change in which energy is released or removed (69, 361)

external combustion engine a heat engine that burns fuel outside the engine, such as a steam engine (266)

F

fiber optics the use of optical fibers (thin, flexible glass wires) to transmit light over long distances (612)

fixed pulley a pulley that is attached to something that does not move; fixed pulleys change the direction of a force but do not increase the force (203)

fluid any material that can flow and that takes the shape of its container (162)

fluorescent light visible light emitted by a phosphor particle when it absorbs energy such as ultraviolet light (596)

focal length the distance between a mirror or lens and its focal point (600)

focal point the point on the axis of a mirror or lens through which all incident parallel light rays are focused (600)

force a push or a pull; all forces have both size and direction (115)

fossil fuels nonrenewable energy resources that form in the Earth's crust over millions of years from the buried remains of once-living organisms (232)

free fall the condition an object is in when gravity is the only force acting on it (141)

freezing the change of state from a liquid to a solid (69)

freezing point the temperature at which a liquid changes into a solid (69)

frequency the number of waves produced in a given amount of time (518, 540)

friction a force that opposes motion between two surfaces that are touching (119, 229)

fulcrum the fixed point about which a lever pivots (198)

fundamental the lowest resonant frequency (550)

G

gamma decay the release of gamma rays from a nucleus (400)

gamma rays EM waves with very high energy and no mass or charge; they are emitted by the nucleus of a radioactive atom (400, 574)

gas the state in which matter changes in both shape and volume (63)

generator a device that uses electromagnetic induction to convert kinetic energy into electrical energy (470)

geothermal energy energy resulting from the heating of the Earth's crust (236)

gravitational potential energy energy due to an object's position above the Earth's surface (216)

gravity a force of attraction between objects that is due to their masses (39, 125)

greenhouse effect the natural heating process of a planet, such as the Earth, by which gases in the atmosphere trap thermal energy (255)

group a column of elements on the periodic table (309)

H

half-life the amount of time it takes for one-half of the nuclei of a radioactive isotope to decay (404)

halogens the elements in Group 17 of the periodic table; they are very reactive nonmetals, and their atoms have seven electrons in their outer level (316)

hardware the parts or equipment that make up a computer (496)

heat the transfer of energy between objects that are at different temperatures; energy is always transferred from higher-temperature objects to lower-temperature objects until thermal equilibrium is reached (251); *also* the amount of energy that is transferred between objects that are at different temperatures (257)

heat engine a machine that uses heat to do work (266)

hertz (Hz) the unit used to express frequency; one hertz is one cycle per second (518, 540)

heterogeneous (HET uhr OH JEE nee uhs) **mixture** a combination of substances in which different components are easily observed (96)

hologram a piece of film on which an interference pattern produces a three-dimensional image of an object (611)

homogeneous (HOH moh JEE nee uhs) **mixture** a combination of substances in which the appearance and properties are the same throughout (92)

hydraulic (hie DRAW lik) **device** a device that uses liquids to transmit pressure from one point to another (167)

hydrocarbons organic compounds that are composed of only carbon and hydrogen (388)

hypothesis a possible explanation or answer to a question (14)

I

ideal machine a machine that has 100 percent mechanical efficiency (197)

illuminated the term describing visible objects that are not a light source (594)

incandescent light light produced by hot objects (595)

inclined plane a simple machine that is a straight, slanted surface; a ramp (200)

induction a method of charging an object that occurs when charges in an uncharged object are rearranged without direct contact with a charged object (425)

inertia the tendency of all objects to resist any change in motion (42, 147)

infrared waves EM waves that are between microwaves and visible light in the electromagnetic spectrum (571)

infrasonic the term describing sounds with frequencies lower than 20 Hz (541)

inhibitor a substance that slows down or stops a chemical reaction (365)

inner ear the part of the ear where vibrations created by sound are changed into electrical signals for the brain to interpret (537)

input the information given to a computer (494)

input device a piece of hardware that feeds information to the computer (496)

input force the force applied to a machine (193)

insulation a substance that reduces the transfer of thermal energy (264)

insulator (electrical) a material in which charges cannot easily move (427)

insulator (thermal) a substance that does not conduct thermal energy well (254)

integrated (IN tuh GRAYT ed) **circuit** an entire circuit containing many transistors and other electronic components formed on a single silicon chip (486)

interference a wave interaction that occurs when two or more waves overlap (522, 548, 579)

internal combustion engine a heat engine that burns fuel inside the engine; for example, an automobile engine (267)

Internet a huge computer network consisting of millions of computers that can all share information with one another (499)

ionic (ie AHN ik) **bond** the force of attraction between oppositely charged ions (332)

ionic compounds compounds that contain ionic bonds; composed of ions arranged in a crystal lattice, they tend to have high melting and boiling points, are solid at room temperature, and dissolve in water to form solutions that conduct an electric current (374)

ions charged particles that form during chemical changes when one or more valence electrons transfer from one atom to another (332)

iris the colored part of the eye (605)

isotopes atoms that have the same number of protons but have different numbers of neutrons (290, 400)

J

joule (J) the unit used to express work and energy; equivalent to the newton-meter (N•m) (190)

K

kilocalorie the unit of energy equal to 1,000 calories; the kilocalorie can also be referred to as the Calorie, which is the unit of energy listed on food labels (258)

kinetic (ki NET ik) **energy** the energy of motion; kinetic energy depends on speed and mass (215)

L

laser a device that produces intense light of only one wavelength and color (609)

law a summary of many experimental results and observations; a law tells how things work (19)

law of conservation of energy the law that states that energy is neither created nor destroyed (230, 362)

law of conservation of mass the law that states that mass is neither created nor destroyed in ordinary chemical and physical changes (357)

law of electric charges the law that states that like charges repel and opposite charges attract (423)

law of reflection the law that states that the angle of incidence is equal to the angle of reflection (575)

law of universal gravitation the law that states that all objects in the universe attract each other through gravitational force; the size of the force depends on the masses of the objects and the distance between them (126)

lens a curved, transparent object that forms an image by refracting light (603); *also* the part of the eye that refracts light to focus an image on the retina (605)

lever a simple machine consisting of a bar that pivots at a fixed point, called a fulcrum; there are three classes of levers, based on where the input force, output force, and fulcrum are placed in relation to the load: first class levers, second class levers, and third class levers (198)

lift an upward force on an object (such as a wing) that opposes the downward pull of gravity; differences in pressure above and below the object contribute to lift (174)

light energy the energy produced by the vibrations of electrically charged particles (220)

lipids biochemicals that do not dissolve in water; their functions include storing energy and making up cell membranes; waxes, fats, and oils (385)

liquid the state in which matter takes the shape of its container and has a definite volume (62)

load a device that uses electrical energy to do work (440)

longitudinal wave a wave in which the particles of the medium vibrate back and forth along the path that the wave travels (514)

loudness how loud or soft a sound is perceived to be (542)

lubricant (LOO bri kuhnt) a substance applied to surfaces to reduce the friction between them (123)

luminous the term describing objects that produce visible light (594)

M

machine a device that helps make work easier by changing the size or direction (or both) of a force (192)

magnet any material that attracts iron or materials containing iron (454)

magnetic field the region around a magnet in which magnetic forces can act (456)

magnetic force the force of repulsion or attraction between the poles of magnets (455)

malleability (MAL ee uh BIL uh tee) the ability of a substance to be pounded into thin sheets (44, 340)

mass the amount of matter that something is made of (26, 38, 129)

mass number the sum of the protons and neutrons in an atom (291, 399)

matter anything that has volume and mass (7, 36)

mechanical advantage a number that tells how many times a machine multiplies force; can be calculated by dividing the output force by the input force (196)

mechanical efficiency (e FISH uhn see) a comparison—expressed as a percentage—of a machine's work output with the work input; can be calculated by dividing work output by work input and then multiplying by 100 (197)

mechanical energy the total energy of motion and position of an object (217)

medium a substance through which a wave can travel (511, 536)

melting the change of state from a solid to a liquid (69)

melting point the temperature at which a substance changes from a solid to a liquid (69)

memory the location where a computer stores information (494)

meniscus (muh NIS kuhs) the curve at a liquid's surface by which you measure the volume of the liquid (37)

metallic bond the force of attraction between a positively charged metal ion and the electrons in a metal (339)

metalloids elements that have properties of both metals and nonmetals; sometimes referred to as semiconductors (85)

metals elements that are shiny and are good conductors of thermal energy and electric current; most metals are malleable and ductile (85)

meter (m) the basic unit of length in the SI system (25)

microprocessor an integrated circuit that contains many of a computer's capabilities on a single silicon chip (495)

microwaves EM waves that are between radio waves and infrared waves in the electromagnetic spectrum (570)

middle ear the part of the ear where the amplitude of sound vibrations is increased (537)

mixture a combination of two or more substances that are not chemically combined (90)

model a representation of an object or system (20, 283)

modem a piece of computer hardware that allows computers to communicate over telephone lines (497)

molecule (MAHL i KYOOL) a neutral group of atoms held together by covalent bonds (336)

momentum a property of a moving object that depends on the object's mass and velocity (152)

motion an object's change in position over time when compared with a reference point (108)

movable pulley a pulley attached to the object being moved; movable pulleys increase force (203)

N

negative acceleration acceleration in which velocity decreases; also called deceleration (113)

neon light light emitted by atoms of certain gases, such as neon, when they absorb and then release energy (596)

net force the force that results from combining all the forces exerted on an object (116)

neutrons the particles of the nucleus that have no charge (288)

newton (N) the SI unit of force (41, 115)

noble gases the unreactive elements in Group 18 of the periodic table; their atoms have eight electrons in their outer level (except for helium, which has two electrons) (316)

noise any undesired sound, especially nonmusical sound, that includes a random mix of pitches (555)

nonmetals elements that are dull and are poor conductors of thermal energy and electric current (85)

nonrenewable resource a natural resource that cannot be replaced or that can be replaced only over thousands or millions of years (232)

nuclear (NOO klee uhr) **chain reaction** a continuous series of nuclear fission reactions (407)

nuclear energy the form of energy associated with changes in the nucleus of an atom (221)

nuclear fission the process in which a large nucleus splits into two smaller nuclei (235, 406)

nuclear fusion the process in which two or more nuclei with small masses join together, or fuse, to form a larger, more massive nucleus (410)

nuclear radiation high-energy particles and rays that are emitted by the nuclei of some atoms; alpha particles, beta particles, and gamma rays are types of nuclear radiation (398)

nucleic acids biochemicals that store information and help to build proteins and other nucleic acids; made up of subunits called nucleotides (387)

nucleus (NOO klee uhs) the tiny, extremely dense, positively charged region in the center of an atom; made up of protons and neutrons (285)

O

observation any use of the senses to gather information (12)

Ohm's law the law that states the relationship between current (I), voltage (V), and resistance (R); expressed by the equation $I = \frac{V}{R}$ (437)

opaque the term describing matter that does not transmit any light (582)

optical axis a straight line drawn outward from the center of a mirror or lens (600)

organic compounds covalent compounds composed of carbon-based molecules (383)

oscilloscope (uh SIL uh SKOHP) a device used to graph representations of sound waves (544)

outer ear the part of the ear that acts as a funnel to direct sound waves into the middle ear (537)

output the result of processing that is the final result or the proof of the task performed by a computer (494)

output device a piece of hardware on which a computer shows the results of performing a task (497)

output force the force applied by a machine (193)

overtones resonant frequencies that are higher than the fundamental (550)

P

parallel circuit a circuit in which different loads are on separate branches (443)

pascal (Pa) the SI unit of pressure; equal to the force of 1 N exerted over an area of one square meter (162)

Pascal's principle the principle that states that a change in pressure at any point in an enclosed fluid is transmitted equally to all parts of that fluid (167)

passive solar heating a solar-heating system that relies on thick walls and large windows to use energy from the sun as a means of heating (265)

period a horizontal row of elements on the periodic table (309)

periodic having a regular, repeating pattern (302)

periodic law the law that states that the chemical and physical properties of elements are periodic functions of their atomic numbers (303)

perpendicular at right angles (513, 564)

perpetual (puhr PECH oo uhl) **motion machine** a machine that runs forever without any additional energy input; perpetual motion machines are impossible to create (231)

pH a measure of hydronium ion concentration in a solution; a pH of 7 is neutral; a pH less than 7 is acidic; a pH greater than 7 is basic (380)

photocell the part of a solar panel that converts light into electrical energy (432)

photon a tiny "packet" of energy that is released by an electron that moves to a lower energy level in an atom (565)

physical change a change that affects one or more physical properties of a substance; many physical changes are easy to undo (48, 261)

physical property a property of matter that can be observed or measured without changing the identity of the matter (43)

physical science the study of matter and energy (7)

pigment a material that gives a substance its color by absorbing some colors of light and reflecting others (584)

pitch how high or low a sound is perceived to be (540)

plane mirror a mirror with a flat surface (599)

plasma the state of matter that does not have a definite shape or volume and whose particles have broken apart; plasma is composed of electrons and positively charged ions (67)

polarized light consists of light waves that vibrate in only one plane (one direction) (612)

poles the parts of a magnet where the magnetic effects are strongest (454)

positive acceleration acceleration in which velocity increases (113)

positron a beta particle with a charge of 1+ and a mass of almost 0 (400)

potential difference energy per unit charge; specifically, the difference in energy per unit charge as a charge moves between two points in an electric circuit (same as voltage); expressed in volts (V) (431)

potential energy the energy of position or shape (216)

power the rate at which work is done (191)

pressure the amount of force exerted on a given area; expressed in pascals (Pa) (64, 162)

primary colors of light red, blue, and green; these colors of light can be combined in different ratios to produce all colors of light (584)

primary pigments yellow, cyan, and magenta; these pigments can be combined to produce any other pigment (585)

products the substances formed from a chemical reaction (354)

projectile (proh JEK tuhl) **motion** the curved path an object follows when thrown or propelled near the surface of the Earth (143)

proteins biochemicals that are composed of amino acids; their functions include regulating chemical activities, transporting and storing materials, and providing structural support (386)

protons the positively charged particles of the nucleus; the number of protons in a nucleus is the atomic number that determines the identity of an element (288)

pulley a simple machine consisting of a grooved wheel that holds a rope or a cable (203)

pupil the opening to the inside of the eye (605)

pure substance a substance in which there is only one type of particle; includes elements and compounds (82)

R

radiation the transfer of energy through matter or space as electromagnetic waves, such as visible light and infrared waves (255, 565)

radioactive decay the process in which the nucleus of a radioactive atom releases nuclear radiation (399)

radioactivity the ability of some elements to give off nuclear radiation (398)

radio waves EM waves with long wavelengths and low frequencies (568)

RAM (random-access memory) computer memory that stores information only while that information is being used (497)

rarefaction (RER uh FAK shuhn) a region of lower density or pressure in a wave (514, 534)

reactants (ree AK TUHNTS) the starting materials in a chemical reaction (354)

real image an image through which light passes (600)

reference point an object that appears to stay in place in relation to an object being observed for motion (108)

reflection the bouncing back of a wave after it strikes a barrier or an object (520, 545, 575)

refraction the bending of a wave as it passes at an angle from one medium to another (521, 577)

renewable resource a natural resource that can be used and replaced over a relatively short time (235)

resistance the opposition to the flow of electric charge; expressed in ohms (Ω) (435)

resonance what occurs when an object vibrating at or near a resonant frequency of a second object causes the second object to vibrate (524, 550)

resonant frequencies the frequencies at which standing waves are made (524, 550)

resultant velocity the combination of two or more velocities (111)

retina the back surface of the eye (605)

ROM (read-only memory) computer memory that cannot be added to or changed (497)

S

salt an ionic compound formed from the positive ion of a base and the negative ion of an acid (382)

saturated hydrocarbon a hydrocarbon in which each carbon atom in the molecule shares a single bond with each of four other atoms; an alkane (388)

saturated solution a solution that contains all the solute it can hold at a given temperature (94)

scattering the release of light energy by particles of matter that have absorbed energy (577)

scientific method a series of steps that scientists use to answer questions and solve problems (11)

screw a simple machine that is an inclined plane wrapped in a spiral (201)

secondary color cyan, magenta, and yellow; a color of light produced when two primary colors of light are added together (584)

semiconductor (SEM i kuhn DUHK tor) a substance that conducts electric current better than an insulator but not as well as a conductor (483)

series circuit a circuit in which all parts are connected in a single loop (442)

signal something that represents information, such as a command, a sound, or a series of numbers and letters (488)

simple machines the six machines from which all other machines are constructed: a lever, an inclined plane, a wedge, a screw, a wheel and axle, and a pulley (198)

single-replacement reaction a reaction in which an element takes the place of another element in a compound; this can occur only when a more-reactive element takes the place of a less-reactive one (359)

software a set of instructions or commands that tells a computer what to do; a computer program (498)

solenoid a coil of wire that produces a magnetic field when carrying an electric current (463)

solid the state in which matter has a definite shape and volume (61)

solubility (SAHL yoo BIL uh tee) the ability to dissolve in another substance; more specifically, the amount of solute needed to make a saturated solution using a given amount of solvent at a certain temperature (44, 94)

solute the substance that is dissolved to form a solution (92)

solution a mixture that appears to be a single substance but is composed of particles of two or more substances that are distributed evenly amongst each other (92)

solvent the substance in which a solute is dissolved to form a solution (92)

sonar (**so**und **na**vigation and **r**anging) a type of electronic echolocation (546)

sonic boom the explosive sound heard when a shock wave from an object traveling faster than the speed of sound reaches a person's ears (549)

sound energy the energy caused by an object's vibrations (220)

sound quality the result of several pitches blending together through interference (552)

specific heat capacity the amount of energy needed to change the temperature of 1 kg of a substance by 1°C (256)

speed the rate at which an object moves; speed depends on the distance traveled and the time taken to travel that distance (109)

standing wave a wave that forms a stationary pattern in which portions of the wave do not move and other portions move with a large amplitude (524, 549)

states of matter the physical forms in which a substance can exist; states include solid, liquid, gas, and plasma (60, 260)

static electricity the buildup of electric charges on an object (427)

sublimation (SUHB luh MAY shuhn) the change of state from a solid directly into a gas (72)

subscript a number written below and to the right of a chemical symbol in a chemical formula (352)

surface tension the force acting on the particles at the surface of a liquid that causes the liquid to form spherical drops (63)

surface wave a wave that occurs at or near the boundary of two media and that is a combination of transverse and longitudinal waves (515)

suspension a mixture in which particles of a material are dispersed throughout a liquid or gas but are large enough that they settle out (96)

synthesis (SIN thuh sis) **reaction** a reaction in which two or more substances combine to form a single compound (358)

T

technology the application of knowledge, tools, and materials to solve problems and accomplish tasks; technology can also refer to the objects used to accomplish tasks (11)

telecommunication the sending of information across long distances by electronic means (488)

temperature a measure of how hot (or cold) something is; specifically, a measure of the average kinetic energy of the particles in an object (26, 246)

terminal velocity the constant velocity of a falling object when the size of the upward force of air resistance matches the size of the downward force of gravity (140)

theory a unifying explanation for a broad range of hypotheses and observations that have been supported by testing (19, 280, 328)

thermal energy the total energy of the particles that make up an object (218, 252)

thermal equilibrium the point at which two objects reach the same temperature (252)

thermal expansion the increase in volume of a substance due to an increase in temperature (248)

thermal pollution the excessive heating of a body of water (269)

thermocouple a device that converts thermal energy into electrical energy (432)

thrust the forward force produced by an airplane's engines; thrust opposes drag (175)

tinnitus hearing loss resulting from damage to the hair cells and nerve endings in the cochlea (538)

tracer a radioactive element whose path can be followed through a process or reaction (405)

transformer a device that increases or decreases the voltage of alternating current (472)

transistor an electronic component that can be used as an amplifier or a switch (485)

translucent the term describing matter that transmits light but also scatters the light as it passes through the matter (582)

transmission the passing of light through matter (581)

transparent the term describing matter through which light is easily transmitted (582)

transverse wave a wave in which the particles of the wave's medium vibrate perpendicular to the direction the wave is traveling (513)

trough the lowest point of a transverse wave (513)

turbulence an irregular or unpredictable flow of fluids that can cause drag; lift is often reduced by turbulence (176)

U

ultrasonic the term describing sounds with frequencies higher than 20,000 Hz (541)

ultrasonography a medical procedure that uses echoes from ultrasonic waves to "see" inside a patient's body without performing surgery (547)

ultraviolet light EM waves that are between visible light and X rays in the electromagnetic spectrum (573)

unbalanced forces forces on an object that cause the net force to be other than zero; unbalanced forces produce a change in motion or acceleration (117)

unsaturated hydrocarbon a hydrocarbon in which at least two carbon atoms share a double bond (an alkene) or a triple bond (an alkyne) (388)

V

valence (VAY luhns) **electrons** the electrons in the outermost energy level of an atom; these electrons are involved in forming chemical bonds (329)

vapor light light produced when electrons combine with gaseous metal atoms (597)

vaporization the change of state from a liquid to a gas; includes boiling and evaporation (70)

velocity (vuh LAHS uh tee) the speed of an object in a particular direction (110)

vibration the complete back-and-forth motion of an object (534)

virtual image an image through which light does not actually pass (599)

viscosity (vis KAHS uh tee) a liquid's resistance to flow (63)

visible light the very narrow range of wavelengths and frequencies in the electromagnetic spectrum that humans can see (572)

voltage the difference in energy per unit charge as a charge moves between two points in an electric circuit (same as potential difference); expressed in volts (V) (434)

volume the amount of space that something occupies or the amount of space that something contains (25, 36)

W

watt (W) the unit used to express power; equivalent to joules per second (J/s) (191)

wave a disturbance that transmits energy through matter or space (510, 535)

wavelength the distance between one point on a wave and the corresponding point on an adjacent wave in a series of waves (517)

wave speed the speed at which a wave travels (519)

wedge a simple machine that is a double inclined plane that moves; a wedge is often used for cutting (201)

weight a measure of the gravitational force exerted on an object, usually by the Earth (40, 128)

wheel and axle a simple machine consisting of two circular objects of different sizes; the wheel is the larger of the two circular objects (202)

work the action that results when a force causes an object to move in the direction of the force (188)

work input the work done on a machine; the product of the input force and the distance through which it is exerted (193)

work output the work done by a machine; the product of the output force and the distance through which it is exerted (193)

X

X rays high-energy EM waves that are between ultraviolet light and gamma rays in the electromagnetic spectrum (574)

Spanish Glossary

A

absolute zero/cero absoluto la temperatura más baja posible (0° K, -273° C) (249)

absorption/absorción la transferencia de energía de las ondas luminosas a las partículas de materia (576)

acceleration/aceleración la proporción a que cambia la velocidad; un objeto se acelera si cambia su velocidad, si cambia su dirección, o si cambian su velocidad y su dirección (112)

acid/ácido cualquier compuesto que aumenta de número de iones de hidrógeno cuando se lo disuelve en agua, y cuya solución tiene sabor amargo y puede cambiar el color de ciertos compuestos; los ácidos hacen que el papel de tornasol azul se vuelva rojo, reaccionan con los metales para producir gas hidrógeno, y reaccionan con cal o con bicarbonato de sodio para producir gas dióxido de carbono (377)

activation energy/energía de activación la cantidad mínima de energía que requieren las sustancias para tener una reacción (362)

active solar heating/calefacción solar activa sistema que consiste de colectores de energía solar y una red de tubos que distribuyen la energía solar por un edificio (265)

alkali metals/metales alcalinos los elementos en el Grupo 1 de la tabla periódica; son los metales más reactivos; sus átomos tienen un electrón en su nivel exterior (310)

alkaline-earth metals/metales alcalinotérreos los elementos en el Grupo 2 de la tabla periódica, son metales reactivos pero son menos reactivos que los metales alcaloides; sus átomos tienen dos electrones en su nivel exterior (311)

alloys/aleaciones soluciones sólidas de metales, o de no metales disueltos en metales (93)

alpha decay/desintegración alfa la liberación de una partícula alfa de un núcleo (399)

alpha particle/partícula alfa tipo de radiación nuclear que consiste de dos protones y de dos neutrones emitidos por el núcleo de un átomo radioactivo; es idéntica al núcleo de un átomo de helio (399)

alternating current/corriente alterna corriente eléctrica en la cual las cargas continuamente cambian de fluir en una dirección a fluir en otra (434)

amplitude/amplitud la distancia máxima a la que vibra una onda a partir de su posición de descanso (516, 543)

analog signal/señal analogica es una señal cuyas propiedades, tales como amplitud y frecuencia, pueden cambiar continuamente según los cambios en la información original; las señales de radio son señales análogas de ondas sonoras (489)

Archimedes' principle/principio de Arquímedes el principio que establece que la fuerza de flotación sobre un objeto en un fluido es una fuerza hacia arriba igual al peso del volumen de fluido desplazado por el objeto (168)

area/área la medida de la superficie que ocupa un objeto (26)

atmospheric pressure/presión atmosférica la presión causada por el peso de la atmósfera (163)

atom/átomo la partícula más pequeña en la que puede ser dividido un elemento y seguir siendo la misma sustancia (280)

atomic mass/masa atómica el peso promedio de las masas de todos los isótopos de un elemento que ocurren de manera natural (292)

atomic mass unit (amu)/unidad de masa atómica la unidad del SI (estándar internacional) usada para expresar las masas de las partículas en los átomos (288)

atomic number/número atómico el número de protones en el núcleo de un átomo; el número atómico es el mismo para todos los átomos de un elemento (290)

average speed/velocidad promedio la velocidad general a que se mueve un objeto; la velocidad promedio puede calcularse dividiendo la distancia total por el tiempo total (109)

B

balanced forces/fuerzas equilibradas las fuerzas que actúan sobre un objeto, que hacen que la fuerza neta sea cero; las fuerzas equilibradas no hacen que haya un cambio en el movimiento o la aceleración (118)

base/base cualquier compuesto que aumenta el número de iones hidroxilos cuando se disuelven en agua, y cuya solución tiene sabor amargo, es viscosa, y puede cambiar el color de ciertos compuestos; las bases hacen que el papel de tornasol rojo se vuelva azul (379)

battery/batería un aparato formado por varias células que produce una corriente eléctrica al convertir energía química en energía eléctrica (430)

Bernoulli's principle/principio de Bernoulli el principio que declara que cuando aumenta la velocidad de un fluido en movimiento, disminuye la presión (173)

beta decay/desintegración beta cuando una partícula beta se libera de un núcleo (400)

beta particle/partícula beta un electrón o positrón emitido por el núcleo de un átomo radioactivo (400)

bimetallic strip/tira bimetálica una tira formada al poner dos metales diferentes uno sobre otro en una tira larga y fina; como los metales diferentes se expanden a velocidades diferentes, una tira bimetálica puede enrollarse y desenrollarse con los cambios en la temperatura; las tiras bimetálicas se usan en aparatos como los termostatos (250)

binary/binario dos; los números binarios contienen sólo los dígitos 1 y 0 (490)

biochemicals/bioquímicos compuestos orgánicos formados por cosas vivas (384)

biomass/biomasa materia orgánica como plantas, madera, y desechos que contienen energía almacenada (236)

bit/bit el nombre para cada uno de los dígitos en un número binario (497)

block and tackle/aparejo de poleas una polea fija y una móvil que se usan juntas, puede tener una gran ventaja mecánica si se usan varias poleas (204)

boiling/ebullición vaporización que ocurre en la totalidad de un líquido (70)

boiling point/punto de ebullición la temperatura a que un líquido hierve y se transforma en gas (70)

Boyle's law/ley de Boyle la ley que declara que para una cantidad fija de gas a una temperatura constante, el volumen del gas aumenta al disminuir la presión (65)

buoyant force/fuerza boyante la fuerza ascendente que los fluidos ejercen sobre toda materia; la fuerza de flotación se opone a la fuerza de gravedad (168)

byte/byte unidad en que las computadoras almacenan y procesan información; es igual a ocho bits (497)

C

calorie/caloría la cantidad de energía que se necesita para cambiar la temperatura de 0.001 kg de agua en 1°C; una caloría es equivalente a 4.184 J (258)

calorimeter/calorímetro aparato usado para determinar la capacidad específica de una sustancia para calor (258)

carbohydrates/carbohidratos sustancias bioquímicas compuestas por un azúcar simple o más, enlazados, que se usan como fuente de energía y para almacenar energía (384)

catalyst/catalizador una sustancia que, sin cambiar en forma permanente, aumenta la velocidad a que ocurre una reacción (365)

cathode-ray tube CRT/tubo de rayo catódico un tubo especial de vacío en el que un rayo de electrones es proyectado en una pantalla; el rayo de electrones produce las imágenes en una pantalla de televisión (493)

cell/célula aparato que produce una corriente elécrica al convertir energía química en energía eléctrica (430)

central processing unit CPU/unidad central procesadora el área física en la que la computadora lleva a cabo el trabajo (496)

centripetal acceleration/aceleración centrípeta la aceleración que ocurre en un movimiento circular; un objeto que se mueve en un círculo cambia de dirección constantemente, por lo que la aceleración ocurre continuamente (114)

change of state/cambio de estado la conversión de una sustancia de una forma física a otra (68, 261)

characteristic property/propiedad característica propiedad de una sustancia que es siempre la misma sin importar si la muestra en observación es pequeña o grande (48)

Charles's law/ley de Charles ley que declara que para una cantidad fija de gas a una presión constante, el volumen del gas aumenta al aumentar su temperatura (66)

chemical bond/lazo químico la fuerza de atracción que une a dos átomos (328)

chemical bonding/enlace químico la unión de los átomos para formar nuevas sustancias (328)

chemical change/cambio químico cambio que ocurre cuando una o más sustancias se transforman en sustancias completamente nuevas, con propiedades diferentes; no puede revertirse usando medios físicos (49, 262)

chemical energy/energía química la energía en un compuesto que cambia cuando sus átomos se vuelven a alinear para formar un nuevo compuesto; la energía química es una forma de energía potencial (218)

chemical equation/ecuación química descripción resumida de una reacción química, expresada con fórmulas y símbolos químicos (354)

chemical formula/fórmula química nota resumida para un compuesto o un elemento diatómico, expresada con símbolos químicos y números (352)

chemical property/propiedad química propiedad de la materia que describe a una sustancia en base a su capacidad de convertirse en una nueva sustancia con propiedades diferentes (47)

chemical reaction/reacción química proceso por el cual una o más sustancias sufren un cambio para producir una o más sustancias diferentes (350)

circuit/circuito una trayectoria completa y cerrada a través de la cual se mueven las cargas eléctricas (440)

circuit board/placa de circuito una colección de cientos de circuitos muy pequeños que proveen corriente eléctrica a las varias partes de un aparato electrónico (482)

coefficient/coeficiente número que se pone antes de un símbolo químico o una fórmula; se usa para equilibrar la ecuación química (356)

colloid/coloide mezcla en la que las partículas se dispersan pero no tienen el peso suficiente para asentarse (97)

combustion/combustión quemar combustible; específicamente, el proceso en el cual el combustible se combina con el oxígeno en un cambio químico que produce energía térmica (266)

compound/compuesto una sustancia pura compuesta de dos o más elementos que están combinados químicamente (86)

compound machine/máquina compuesta máquina formada por dos máquinas simples o más (204)

compression/compresión región de mayor densidad o presión en una onda (514, 534)

computer/computadora aparato electrónico que realiza trabajos procesando y almacenando información (494)

concave lens/lente cóncava lente que es más fina en el medio que en los bordes (604)

concave mirror/espejo cóncavo espejo que se curva hacia el centro, como la parte interior de una cuchara (600)

concentration/concentración medida de la cantidad de un soluto disuelto en un solvente (94, 364)

condensation/condensación cambio de estado de gas a líquido (71)

condensation point/punto de condensación temperatura a la cual un gas se vuelve líquido (71)

conduction (electrical)/conducción (eléctrica) método de cargar un objeto que ocurre cuando los electrones se transfieren de un objeto a otro por contacto directo (425)

conduction (thermal)/conducción (térmica) transferencia de energía térmica de una sustancia a otra por contacto directo; la conducción también puede ocurrir dentro de una sustancia (253)

conductor (electrical)/conductor (eléctrico) un material en el cual se pueden mover fácilmente las cargas (427)

conductor (thermal)/conductor (térmico) sustancia que conduce bien la energía termal (254)

constructive interference/interferencia constructiva interferencia que resulta en una onda con una amplitud más grande quela de las ondas individuales (523, 548, 579)

convection/convección la transferencia de energía térmica por el movimiento de un líquido o un gas (254)

convection current/corriente de convección el movimiento circular de líquidos o gases causado por las diferencias en densidad que resultan de las diferencias en temperatura (254)

convex lens/lente convexa lente que es más gruesa en el medio que en los bordes (603)

convex mirror/espejo convexo espejo que se curva hacia afuera, como la parte de afuera de una cuchara (602)

cornea/córnea membrana transparente que protege el ojo y refracta la luz (605)

covalent bond/enlace covalente la fuerza de atracción entre los núcleos de los átomos y los electrones que los átomos comparten (336)

covalent compounds/compuestos covalentes compuestos formados por elementos que están enlazados de forma covalente; estos compuestos están formados por moléculas independientes, tienden a fundirse y a hacer ebullición a puntos bajos, en general no se disuelven en agua, y, cuando se disuelven, forman soluciones que no conducen corrientes eléctricas (375)

crest/cresta el punto más alto de una onda transversal (513)

crystal lattice/estructura cristalina diseño tridimensional de iones, que se repite (335)

current/corriente un fluir continuo de carga causado por el movimiento de electrones; la velocidad a la que la carga pasa un punto dado; se expresa en amperes (A) (433)

D

data/dato información recopilada mediante experimentación (16)

decibel/decibelio la unidad más común usada para expresar volumen de sonido (543)

decomposition reaction/reacción de descomposición reacción en la cual un compuesto individual se descompone para formar dos o más sustancias más simples (359)

density/densidad la cantidad de materia en un espacio dado; masa por unidad de volumen (27, 44, 165)

destructive interference/interferencia destructiva interferencia que resulta en una onda con una amplitud menor que la de las ondas individuales (523, 548, 579)

diffraction/difracción cuando las ondas se doblan alrededor de una barrera o a través de una apertura (521, 551, 579)

digital signal/señal digital serie de pulsos eléctricos que representan los dígitos de números binarios (490)

diode/diodo componente electrónico que permite que la corriente eléctrica pase en una sola dirección (484)

direct current/corriente directa corriente eléctrica en que las cargas siempre fluyen en la misma dirección (434)

doping/adulteración el proceso de remplazar algunos átomos de un semiconductor con algunos átomos de otra sustancia que tienen un número diferente de electrones de valencia; al implantar se cambia la disposición de los electrones en el semiconductor (483)

Doppler effect/efecto de Doppler el cambio aparente en el tono de un sonido, causado por el movimiento del que lo escucha o de la fuente del sonido (sólo se refiere a sonido) (542)

double-replacement reaction/reacción de sustitución doble reacción en la que los iones en dos compuestos cambian de lugar; con frecuencia, uno de sus productos es un gas o un precipitado (360)

drag/draga la fuerza que se opone al movimiento en un líquido o que lo restringe; el arrastre se opone al impulso (176)

ductility/ductilidad la capacidad de una sustancia de ser arrastrada o atraída al interior de un cable (44, 340)

E

echo/eco una onda sonora reflejada (520, 545)

echolocation/ecolocación proceso de usar ondas sonoras reflejadas para encontrar objetos (546)

electrical energy/energía eléctrica la energía de los electrones en movimiento (219)

electric discharge/descarga eléctrica cuando las cargas se retiran de un objeto (428)

electric field/campo eléctrico la región alrededor de una partícula con carga que puede ejercer una fuerza sobre otra partícula con carga (423)

electric force/fuerza eléctrica la fuerza entre los objetos con carga (423)

electric motor/motor eléctrico aparato que cambia la energía eléctrica a energía cinética (466)

electric power/fuerza eléctrica la velocidad a la que se usa la energía eléctrica para hacer trabajo; se expresa en vatios (437)

electrode/electrodo la parte de una pila a través de la cual entran o salen las cargas (430)

electrolyte/electrolito en una pila, la mezcla de sustancias químicas que conducen la corriente eléctrica (430)

electromagnet/electroimán un imán que consiste de un solenoide que envuelve un centro de hierro (464)

electromagnetic induction/inducción electromagnética el proceso por el cual se produce una corriente eléctrica al cambiar un campo magnético (469)

electromagnetic spectrum/espectro electromagnético la gama completa de ondas electromagnéticas (567)

electromagnetic wave/onda electromagnética onda que puede viajar a través del espacio o de la materia y que consiste de campos eléctricos y magnéticos que cambian (492, 512, 564)

electromagnetism/electromagnetismo la interacción entre la electricidad y el magnetismo (463)

electron clouds/nubes de electrones regiones dentro de un átomo donde es probable encontrar electrones (286)

electrons/electrones las partículas con carga negativa que se encuentran en todos los átomos; los electrones intervienen en la formación de enlaces químicos (283)

element/elemento sustancia pura que no puede separarse o dividirse en sustancias más simples por medios físicos o químicos (82)

endothermic/endotérmico término usado para describir un cambio físico o químico en el que se absorbe la energía (69, 362)

energy/energía la capacidad de hacer trabajo (214)

energy conversion/conversión de energía cambio de una forma de energía a otra; cualquier forma de energía puede convertise en otra forma de energía (222)

energy efficiency/eficiencia energética comparación de la cantidad de energía antes de una conversión y la cantidad de energía útil luego de la conversión (228)

energy resource/recurso energético recurso natural que los seres humanos pueden convertir en otras formas de energía para hacer trabajo útil (232)

evaporation/evaporación vaporización que ocurre en la superficie de un líquido antes de llegar a su punto de ebullición (70)

exothermic/exotérmico término usado para describir un cambio físico o químico en el que se libera o se extrae energía (69, 361)

external combustion engine/motor de combustión externa un motor a calor que quema combustible fuera del motor, como un motor a vapor (266)

F

fiber optics: transmisión por fibra óptica el uso de fibras ópticas (alambres de metal finos y flexibles) para transmitir luz a través de largas distancias (612)

fixed pulley/polea fija una polea que está unida a algo que no se mueve; las poleas fijas cambian la dirección de la fuerza pero no aumentan la fuerza (203)

fluid/fluido cualquier material que puede fluir y que toma la forma del recipiente que lo contiene (162)

fluorescent light/luz fluorescente luz visible emitida por una partícula de fósforo cuando absorbe energía, como la luz ultravioleta (596)

focal length/distancia focal la distancia entre un espejo o una lente y su punto de foco (600)

focal point/punto focal el punto en el eje de un espejo o una lente a través del cual se enfocan todos los rayos incidentes de luz paralela (600)

force/fuerza lo que empuja o arrastra; todas las fuerzas tienen tamaño y dirección (115)

fossil fuels/combustibles fósiles recursos energéticos no renovables que se formaron a través de millones de años en la corteza terrestre de los restos enterrados de organismos que en algún momento estuvieron vivos (232)

free fall/caída libre la condición en que está un objeto cuando la gravedad es la única fuerza que actúa sobre él (141)

freezing/congelación cambio de estado de líquido a sólido (69)

freezing point/punto de congelación la temperatura a la que un líquido se transforma en sólido (69)

frequency/frecuencia el número de ondas producido en un período de tiempo dado (518, 540)

friction/rozamiento fuerza que se opone al movimiento entre dos superficies que se tocan (119, 229)

fulcrum/punto de apoyo el punto fijo alrededor del cual rota una palanca (198)

fundamental/vibración fundamental la frecuencia de resonancia más baja (550)

G

gamma decay/desintegración gamma la liberación de rayos gamma de un núcleo (400)

gamma rays/rayos gamma ondas electromagnéticas con energía muy alta y sin masa ni carga; estos rayos son emitidos por el núcleo de un átomo radioactivo (400, 574)

gas/gaseoso estado en que la materia cambia en forma y en volumen (63)

generator/generador aparato que usa la inducción electromagnética para convertir la energía cinética en energía eléctrica (470)

geothermal energy/energía geotérmica energía que resulta del calentamiento de la corteza de la Tierra (236)

gravitational potential energy/energía potencial de gravedad energía que se debe a la posición de un objeto sobre la superficie de la Tierra (216)

gravity/gravedad fuerza de atracción entre objetos que se debe a sus masas (39, 125)

greenhouse effect/efecto invernadero el proceso natural de calentamiento de un planeta, como la Tierra, en el que los gases en la atmósfera atrapan energía térmica (255)

group/grupo columna de elementos en la tabla periódica (309)

H

half-life/vida media el tiempo que le lleva a la mitad de los núcleos de un isótopo radioactivo para desintegrarse (404)

halogens/halógenos los elementos en el Grupo 17 de la tabla periódica; son metaloides muy reactivos, y sus átomos tienen siete electrones en su nivel externo (316)

hardware/hardware el conjunto de elementos físicos que forman una computadora (496)

heat/calor la tranferencia de energía entre objetos que tienen temperaturas diferentes; la energía siempre se transfiere de los objetos que tienen temperatura más alta a los que la tienen más baja hasta que se llega al equilibrio térmico; (251) también es la cantidad de energía que se transfiere entre objetos a diferentes temperaturas (257)

heat engine/motor térmico una máquina que usa calor para funcionar (266)

hertz/hertzio la unidad usada para expresar frecuencia; un herzio es un ciclo por segundo (518, 540)

heterogeneous mixture/mezcla heterogénea combinación de sustancias en la que los diferentes componentes se pueden observar con facilidad (96)

hologram/holograma trozo de película en el que un diseño de interferencia produce la imagen tridimensional de un objeto (611)

homogeneous mixture/mezcla homogénea combinación de sustancias en que la apariencia y las propiedades son iguales en toda la mezcla (92)

hydraulic device/aparato hidráulico aparato que usa líquidos para transmitir presión de un punto a otro (167)

hydrocarbons/hidrocarburos componentes orgánicos que están compuestos solamente de carbón e hidrógeno (388)

hypothesis/hipótesis posible explicación o respuesta para una pregunta (14)

I

ideal machine/máquina ideal una máquina 100 por ciento eficiente (197)

illuminated/iluminado término que describe objetos visibles que no son fuentes de luz (594)

incandescent light/luz incandescente luz producida por objetos calientes (595)

inclined plane/plano inclinado una máquina simple formada por una superficie plana, inclinada; una rampa (200)

induction/inducción método de cargar un objeto; ocurre cuando, en un objeto sin carga, las cargas se vuelven a ordenar sin contacto directo con un objeto con carga (425)

inertia/inercia la tendencia de todos los objetos de resistir los cambios en su movimiento (42, 147)

infrared waves/ondas infrarrojas ondas electromagnéticas que existen en el espectro electromagnético entre las microondas y la luz visible (571)

infrasonic/infrasónico término que describe los sonidos con frecuencias más bajas que 20 hertzios (541)

inhibitor/inhibidor sustancia que detiene o hace más lenta una reacción química (365)

inner ear/oído interno la parte del oído en que las vibraciones creadas por el sonido se cambian en señales eléctricas que el cerebro puede interpretar (537)

input/datos entrados la información que se da a una computadora (494)

input device/unidad de entrada la parte de la computadora que le proporciona la información (496)

input force/fuerza de entrada la fuerza que se aplica a una máquina (193)

insulation/aislamiento sustancia que reduce la transferencia de energía térmica (264)

insulator (electrical)/aislante (eléctrico) material en el que las cargas no se pueden mover con facilidad (427)

insulator (thermal)/aislante (térmico) material que no es buen conductor de energía térmica (254)

integrated circuit/circuito integrado circuito completo que contiene muchos transistores y otros componentes electrónicos en un chip de silicona único (486)

interference/interferencia interacción de ondas que ocurre cuando dos o más ondas se superponen (522, 548, 579)

internal combustion engine/motor de combustión interna un motor de calor que quema combustible dentro del motor, como por ejemplo, un motor de automóvil (267)

Internet/Internet una red gigante de computadoras, que consiste de millones de computadoras que pueden compartir información una con otra (499)

ionic bond/enlace iónico la fuerza de atracción entre iones con cargas opuestas (332)

ionic compounds/compuestos iónicos compuestos que contienen enlaces iónicos; están formados por iones dispuestos en una estructrura cristalina, tienden a tener puntos de fusión y de ebullición altos, son sólidos a temperatura ambiente, y se disuelven en agua para formar soluciones conductoras de corriente eléctrica (374)

ions/iones partículas con carga que se forman durante cambios químicos cuando uno o más electrones de valencia pasan de un átomo a otro (332)

iris/iris la parte coloreada del ojo (605)

isotopes/isótopos átomos que tienen el mismo número de protones pero un número diferente de neutrones (290, 400)

J

joule/joule la unidad usada para expresar trabajo y energía; es equivalente al newton-metro (N.m) (190)

K

kilocalorie/kilocaloría la unidad de energía igual a 1,000 calorías; la kilocaloría también se conoce como la Caloría, que es la unidad de energía que aparece en las etiquetas de los alimentos (258)

kinetic energy/energía cinética la energía del movimiento; depende de la velocidad y la masa (215)

L

laser/láser un aparato que produce luz intensa de sólo un color y una longitud de onda (609)

law/ley un resumen de muchos resultados y observaciones de experimentos; la ley dice cómo funcionan las cosas (19)

law of conservation of energy/ley de conservación de energía la ley que establece que la energía no se crea ni se destruye (230, 362)

law of conservation of mass/ley de conservación de materia la ley que establece que la masa ni se crea ni se destruye con los cambios químicos y físicos comunes (357)

law of electrical charges/ley de cargas eléctricas la ley que establece que las cargas iguales se repelen y las opuestas se atraen (423)

SPANISH GLOSSARY

law of reflection/ley de reflexión la ley que establece que el ángulo de incidencia es igual al ángulo de reflexión (575)

law of universal gravitation/ley de gravitación universal la ley que establece que todos los objetos en el universo se atraen mutuamente por la fuerza de gravedad; el tamaño de la fuerza depende de la masa de los objetos y de la distancia entre ellos (126)

lens/lente un objeto curvo, transparente, que forma una imagen al refractar la luz (603); también es la parte del ojo que refracta la luz } para enfocar una imagen en la retina (605)

lever/palanca una máquina simple que consiste en una barra que rota alrededor de un punto fijo, llamado punto de apoyo; hay tres clases de palancas, dependiendo de dónde se encuentran la fuerza de entrada, la fuerza de salida y el punto de apoyo con respecto a la carga: palancas de primera clase, de segunda clase, y de tercera clase (198)

lift/elevación fuerza ascendente sobre un objeto (como un ala), causada por diferencias en la presión arriba y abajo del objeto; la elevación se opone al arrastre de la gravedad (174)

light energy/energía de la luz la energía producida por las vibraciones de las partículas cargadas con electricidad (220)

lipids/lípidos sustancias bioquímicas que no se disuelven en agua; sus funciones incluyen almacenar energía y formar membranas celulares; los lípidos incluyen las ceras, las grasas, y los aceites (385)

liquid/líquido el estado en que la materia toma la forma de su recipiente y tiene un volumen definido (62)

load/cargador aparato que usa energía eléctrica para funcionar (440)

longitudinal wave/onda longitudinal una onda en que las partículas del medio vibran hacia adelante y hacia atrás en la trayectoria de la onda (514)

loudness/sonoridad la percepción de si un sonido es fuerte o suave (542)

lubricant/lubricante una sustancia que se aplica a las superficies para reducir la fricción entre ellas (123)

luminous/luminoso término que describe los objetos que producen luz visible (594)

M

machine/máquina un aparato que ayuda a hacer que el trabajo sea más fácil al cambiar el tamaño y/o la dirección de una fuerza (192)

magnet/imán cualquier material que atrae al hierro o a los materiales que contienen hierro (454)

magnetic field/campo magnético región alrededor de un imán sobre la que actúan las fuerzas magnéticas (456)

magnetic force/fuerza magnética la fuerza de repulsión o de atracción entre los polos de los imanes (455)

malleability/maleabilidad la capacidad de una sustancia de ser martillada y convertida en hojas finas (44, 340)

mass/masa la cantidad de materia de que está hecho algo; su valor no cambia con la situación del objeto en el universo (26, 38, 129)

mass number/número de masa la suma de los protones y neutrones en un átomo (291, 399)

matter/materia cualquier cosa que tenga volumen y masa (7, 36)

mechanical advantage/ventaja mecánica un número que indica las veces que una máquina multiplica la fuerza; se puede calcular dividiendo la fuerza de salida por la fuerza de entrada (196)

mechanical efficiency/eficiencia mecánica comparación del rendimiento de salida de una máquina y su rendimiento de entrada, expresada como porcentaje, se puede calcular dividiendo el rendimiento de salida por el rendimiento de entrada y luego multiplicando por 100 (197)

mechanical energy/energía mecánica la energía total del movimiento y posición de un objeto (217)

medium/medio sustancia a través de la cual puede viajar una onda (511, 536)

melting/fusión cambio de estado de sólido a líquido (69)

melting point/punto de fusión la temperatura a la cual una sustancia cambia de sólido a líquido (69)

memory/memoria el lugar donde una computadora almacena información (494)

meniscus/menisco la curvatura en la superficie de un líquido por la que se mide el volumen del líquido (37)

metallic bond/enlace metálico la fuerza de atracción entre un ion metálico con carga positiva y los electrones en un metal (339)

metalloids/metaloides elementos que tienen propiedades tanto de los metales como de los no metales; algunas veces se los llama semiconductores (85)

metals/metales elementos que brillan y que son buenos conductores de energía térmica y corriente eléctrica; la mayoría de los metales son maleables y dúctiles (85)

meter/metro la unidad básica de longitud en el sistema SI (25)

microprocessor/microprocesador un circuito integrado que contiene muchas de las capacidades de una computadora en un solo chip de silicona (495)

microwaves/microondas ondas electromagnéticas que se encuentran entre las ondas de radio y las ondas infrarrojas en el espectro electromagnético (570)

middle ear/oído medio la parte del oído donde se aumenta la amplitud de las vibraciones de sonido (537)

mixture/mezcla la combinación de dos o más sustancias que no están combinadas químicamente (90)

model/modelo representación de un objeto o sistema (20, 283)

modem/modem parte física de una computadora que permite que las computadoras se comuniquen por líneas telefónicas (497)

molecule/molécula grupo neutral de átomos que se mantienen unidos por enlaces covalentes (336)

momentum/momento propiedad de un objeto en movimiento que depende de la masa y velocidad del objeto (152)

motion/movimiento el cambio de posición de un objeto a través del tiempo cuando se lo compara con un punto de referencia (108)

movable pulley/polea móvil una polea fijada al objeto que se mueve; las poleas móviles aumentan la fuerza (203)

N

negative acceleration/aceleración negativa aceleración en la que la velocidad disminuye, también se llama deceleración (113)

neon light/luz de neón luz emitida por los átomos de ciertos gases como el neón, cuando absorben y luego liberan energía (596)

net force/fuerza resultante la fuerza que resulta al combinar todas las fuerzas ejercidas sobre un objeto (116)

neutrons/neutrones las partículas del núcleo que no tienen carga (288)

newton/newton la unidad de fuerza del SI (41, 115)

noble gases/gases nobles los elementos no rectivos en el Grupo 18 de la tabla periódica; sus átomos tienen ocho electrones en su nivel exterior (excepto el helio, que tiene dos electrones) (316)

noise/ruido cualquier sonido no deseado, especialmente un sonido no musical, que incluye una mezcla accidental de tonos (555)

nonmetals/no metales elementos que son inactivos y malos conductores de energía térmica y corriente eléctrica (85)

nonrenewable resource/recursos no renovables recursos naturales que no se pueden remplazar o que pueden remplazarse sólo luego del paso de miles o millones de años (232)

nuclear chain reaction/reacción nuclear en cadena una serie continua de reacciones de fisión nuclear (407)

nuclear energy/energía nuclear la forma de energía asociada con los cambios en el núcleo de un átomo, un recurso de energía alternativa (221)

nuclear fission/fisión nuclear el proceso en que un núcleo grande se divide en dos núcleos más pequeños (235, 406)

nuclear fusion/fusión nuclear el proceso en que dos o más núcleos con poca masa se unen, o se funden, para formar un núcleo más grande y más masivo (410)

nuclear radiation/radiación nuclear partículas y rayos de alta energía emitidos por el núcleo de algunos átomos; las partículas alfa, las partículas beta, y los rayos gamma son tipos de radiación nuclear (398)

nucleic acids/ácidos nucleicos sustancias bioquímicas que almacenan información y ayudan a formar proteínas y otros ácidos nucleicos; formadas por subunidades llamadas nucleótidos (387)

nucleus: núcleo la pequeña región extremadamente densa y con carga positiva en el centro de un átomo; formada por protones y neutrones (285)

O

observation/observación cualquier uso de los sentidos para reunir información (12)

Ohm's law/ley de Ohm la ley que establece la relación entre corriente (I), voltaje (V) y resistencia (R); expresada con la ecuación I=V/R (437)

opaque/opaco término que describe la materia que no trasmite ninguna luz (582)

optical axis/eje óptico línea recta trazada hacia afuera desde el centro de un espejo o lente (600)

organic compounds/compuestos orgánicos compuestos covalentes formados por moléculas con base de carbono (383)

oscilloscope/osciloscopio aparato usado para representar gráficamente las ondas sonoras (544)

outer ear/oído externo la parte del oído que actúa como embudo para dirigir las ondas sonoras hacia el oído medio (537)

output/salida el resultado final del procesamiento o la prueba del trabajo realizado por una computadora (494)

output device/unidad de salida parte de la computadora en que se muestran los resultados de hacer un trabajo (497)

output force/fuerza de salida la fuerza aplicada por una máquina (193)

overtones/armónicos frecuencias resonantes que son más altas que las fundamentales (550)

P

parallel circuit/circuito en paralelo circuito en el cual las diferentes cargas están en ramas separadas (443)

pascal/pascal la unidad SI de presión (Pa); es igual a la fuerza de un newton ejercida sobre un área de un metro cuadrado (162)

Pascal's principle/principio de Pascal principio que establece que un cambio en presión en cualquier punto de un fluido se trasmite a todas las partes de ese fluido por igual (167)

passive solar heating/calefacción solar pasiva sistema de calefacción solar que depende de paredes gruesas y ventanas grandes para usar la energía del sol como medio de calefacción (265)

period/período una hilera horizontal de elementos en la tabla periódica (309)

periodic/periódico que tiene una configuración regular que se repite (302)

periodic law/ley periódica la ley que establece que las propiedades químicas y físicas de los elementos son funciones periódicas de sus números atómicos (303)

perpendicular/perpendicular a ángulos rectos (513, 564)

perpetual motion machine/máquina de movimiento perpetuo máquina que funciona permanentemente sin que se le entre energía adicional; su rendimiento de energía sería igual a su entrada de energía; las máquinas de movimiento perpetuo son imposibles de crear (231)

pH/pH una medida de la concentración de ion de hidronio en una solución; un pH de 7 es neutro; un pH menor que 7 es ácido; y un pH mayor que 7 es básico (380)

photocell/fotocélula la parte de un panel solar que convierte la luz en energía eléctrica (432)

photon/fotón un "paquete" de energía muy pequeño liberado por un electrón que se mueve a un nivel de energía más bajo en un átomo (565)

physical change/cambio físico un cambio que afecta una o más de las propiedades físicas de una sustancia, los cambios físicos con frecuencia son fáciles de hacer (48, 261)

physical property/propiedad física una propiedad de la materia que se puede observar o medir sin cambiar la identidad de la materia (43)

physical science/ciencia física el estudio de la materia y la energía (7)

pigment/pigmento un material que le da su color a una sustancia al absorber algunos colores de la luz y reflejar otros (584)

pitch/tono cómo se percibe un sonido, si es grave o agudo (540)

plane mirror/espejo plano un espejo con una superficie plana (599)

plasma/plasma el estado de la materia que no tiene una forma o un volumen definido y cuyas partículas se han separado; el plasma está compuesto de electrones y iones con carga positiva (67)

polarized light/luz polarizada consiste de ondas de luz que vibran en sólo un plano (una dirección) (612)

poles/polos las partes de un imán en que los efectos magnéticos son más fuertes (454)

positive acceleration/aceleración positiva la aceleración en que la velocidad aumenta (113)

positron/positrón partícula beta con una carga de 1+ y una masa de casi 0 (400)

potential difference/diferencia potencial energía por unidad de carga; específicamente, la diferencia en energía por unidad de carga al moverse la carga entre dos puntos en un circuito eléctrico (lo mismo que el voltaje); se expresa en voltios (431)

potential energy/energía potencial la energía de posición o forma (216)

power/poder la proporción a la que se hace el trabajo (191)

pressure /presión la cantidad de fuerza que se ejerce en un área determinada; la unidad SI para la presión es el pascal (64, 162)

primary colors of light/colores primarios de la luz rojo, azul, y verde; estos colores de la luz se pueden combinar en proporciones diferentes para producir todos los colores del espectro (584)

primary pigments/pigmentos primarios amarillo, cian, y magenta; estos pigmentos se pueden combinar para producir cualquier otro pigmento (585)

products/productos las sustancias formadas por una reacción química (354)

projectile motion/movimiento proyectil el movimiento curvo que sigue un objeto cuando es lanzado cerca de la superficie de la Tierra (143)

proteins/proteínas sustancias bioquímicas que están compuestas de aminoácidos; sus funciones incluyen regular las actividades químicas, transportar y almacenar materiales, y dar apoyo estructural (386)

protons/protones las partículas con carga positiva del núcleo; el número de protones en un núcleo es el número atómico que determina la identidad de un elemento (288)

pulley/polea una máquina simple que consiste de una rueda con ranuras que sostiene una cuerda o un cable; hay dos clases de poleas, las fijas y las móviles (203)

pupil/pupila la apertura hacia el interior del ojo (605)

pure substance/sustancia pura una sustancia en la que hay solamente una clase de partícula; incluye elementos y compuestos (82)

R

radiation/radiación la transferencia de energía térmica a través del espacio en forma de ondas electromagnéticas, como la luz visible y las ondas infrarrojas (255, 565)

radioactive decay/desintegración radioactiva el proceso en el cual el núcleo de un átomo radioactivo libera radiación nuclear (399)

radioactivity/radioactividad la capacidad de algunos elementos de despedir radiación nuclear (398)

radio waves/ondas de radio ondas electromagnéticas con longitud de onda larga y frecuencias cortas (568)

RAM (random-access memory)/RAM (memoria de acceso aleatorio) memoria de la computadora que almacena la información solamente cuando esa información está en uso (497)

rarefaction/rarefacción una región de densidad o presión más baja en una onda (514, 534)

reactants/reactivos los materiales que dan comienzo a una reacción química (354)

real image/imagen real imagen a través de la cual pasa la luz (600)

reference point/punto de referencia un objeto que parece estar inmóvil en relación a otro objeto que se observa en movimiento (108)

reflection/reflexión momento en que una onda rebota luego de chocar contra una barrera o un objeto (520, 545, 575)

refraction/refracción cuando una onda se dobla al pasar de un medio a otro (521, 577)

renewable resource/recurso renovable un recurso natural que puede usarse y ser remplazado en un período de tiempo corto (235)

resistance/resistencia la oposición al flujo de cargas eléctricas; se expresa en ohms (435)

resonance/resonancia lo que ocurre cuando un objeto que vibra en la frecuencia resonante de un segundo objeto o cerca de él, hace que el segundo objeto vibre también (524, 550)

resonant frequencies/frecuencias de resonancia las frecuencias a que se hacen las ondas estacionarias (524, 550)

resultant velocity/velocidad resultante la combinación de dos o más velocidades (111)

retina/retina la superficie de atrás del ojo (605)

ROM (read-only memory)/ROM (memoria sin acceso directo) la memoria que no se puede aumentar ni cambiar en una computadora (497)

S

salt/sal un compuesto iónico formado del ion positivo de una base y del ion negativo de un ácido (382)

saturated hydrocarbon/hidrocarburo saturado un hidrocarburo en que cada átomo de carbono en la molécula comparte un enlace simple con uno de otros cuatro átomos; un alcano (388)

saturated solution/solución saturada solución que contiene todo el soluto que puede contener a una temperatura dada (94)

scattering/dispersión cuando las partículas de materia que han absorbido energía despiden luz como energía (577)

scientific method/método científico serie de pasos que los científicos usan para responder preguntas y resolver problemas (11)

screw/tornillo una máquina simple que es un plano inclinado envuelto en un espiral (201)

secondary color/color secundario cian, magenta, y amarillo; un color producido al combinar dos colores primarios (584)

semiconductor/semiconductor sustancia que conduce la corriente eléctrica mejor que un aislante pero no tan bien como un conductor (483)

series circuit/circuito en serie circuito en que todas las partes están conectadas en un lazo simple (442)

signal/señal algo que representa información, como una orden, un sonido, o una serie de números y letras (488)

simple machines/máquinas simples las seis máquinas con las que se construyen todas las otras: una palanca, un plano inclinado, una cuña, un tornillo, una rueda y eje, y una polea (198)

single-replacement reaction/reacción de sustitución simple reacción en la que un elemento toma el lugar de otro en un compuesto; puede ocurrir solamente cuando un elemento más reactivo toma el lugar de otro menos reactivo (359)

software/software serie de instrucciones u órdenes que le dicen a una computadora qué debe hacer (498)

solenoid/solenoide un espiral de alambre que produce un campo magnético cuando lleva una corriente eléctrica (463)

solid/sólido el estado en que la materia tiene forma y volumen definidos (61)

solubility/solubilidad la capacidad de disolverse en otra sustancia; más específicamente, la cantidad de soluto que se necesita para hacer una solución saturada usando una cierta cantidad de solvente a una cierta temperatura (44, 94)

solute/substancia por disolver la sustancia que se disuelve para formar una solución (92)

solution/solución mezcla que parece una sustancia simple, pero está compuesta de las partículas de dos o más sustancias que se distribuyen igualmente entre sí (92)

solvent/solvente la sustancia en la cual se disuelve un soluto para formar una solución (92)

sonar (sound navigation and ranging)/sonar un tipo de detección electrónica por ultrasonido (546)

sonic boom/estruendo sónico el sonido explosivo que se oye cuando la onda de choque producida por un objeto que viaja a más velocidad que la velocidad del sonido alcanza los oídos de una persona (549)

sound energy/energía de sonido la energía causada por las vibraciones de un objeto (220)

sound quality/cualidad del sonido el resultado de varios tonos que se mezclan a través de interferencia (552)

specific heat capacity/capacidad de calor específico la cantidad de energía que se necesita para cambiar la temperatura de 1 kg de una sustancia en 1°C; la capacidad para calor específico es una propiedad característica de una sustancia (256)

speed/velocidad la velocidad a que se mueve un objeto; la velocidad depende de la distancia a que se viaja y del tiempo que lleva recorrer esa distancia (109)

standing wave/onda estacionaria onda que forma un diseño estacionario en el que ciertas partes de la onda no se mueven y otras partes se mueven con una amplitud grande (524, 549)

states of matter/estados de la materia las formas físicas en que puede existir una sustancia; los estados incluyen sólido, líquido, gas, y plasma (60, 260)

static electricity/electricidad estática la acumulación de cargas eléctricas en un objeto (427)

sublimation/sublimación el cambio de estado de sólido directamente a un gas (72)

subscript/subíndice el número que se escribe debajo y a la derecha de un símbolo químico en una fórmula química (352)

surface tension/tensión de la superficie la fuerza que actúa sobre las partículas en la superficie de un líquido, que causa que el líquido forme gotas esféricas (63)

surface wave/onda superficial onda que ocurre cerca de o en el límite de dos medios y que es una combinación de ondas transversales y longitudinales (515)

suspension/suspensión mezcla en la cual las partículas de un material se dispersan a través de un líquido o gas, pero como son lo suficientemente grandes, se asientan (96)

synthesis reaction/reacción de síntesis reacción en la cual dos o más sustancias se combinan para formar un compuesto único (358)

T

technology/tecnología la aplicación de conocimiento, instrumentos, y materiales para resolver problemas y realizar tareas; la tecnología también se puede referir a los objetos usados para realizar tareas (11)

telecommunication/telecomunicación enviar información a través de grandes distancias por medios electrónicos (488)

temperature/temperatura medida de cuán caliente o frío es algo; específicamente, la medida de la energía cinética promedio de las partículas en un objeto (26, 246)

terminal velocity/velocidad terminal la velocidad constante de un objeto que cae cuando la magnitud de la fuerza ascendente de la resistencia del aire es igual a la magnitud de la fuerza de gravedad hacia abajo (140)

theory/teoría la explicación que unifica una gran variedad de hipótesis y observaciones que han sido apoyadas por la experimentación (19, 280, 328)

thermal energy/energía térmica totalidad de la energía cinética de las partículas que forman un objeto (218, 252)

thermal equilibrium/equilibrio térmico punto en el cual dos objetos llegan a la misma temperatura; cuando se está en equilibrio térmico no ocurre ninguna transferencia neta de energía térmica (252)

thermal expansion/expansión termal el aumento en volumen de una sustancia debido a un aumento en temperatura (248)

thermal pollution/polución térmica el calentamiento excesivo de una extensión de agua (269)

thermocouple/par térmico aparato que convierte la energía térmica en energía eléctrica (432)

thrust/empuje la fuerza hacia adelante producida por los motores de un avión; el impulso se opone al arrastre (175)

tinnitus/tinnitus pérdida de audición que resulta por el daño a las células capilares y a las terminaciones nerviosas en la cóclea (538)

tracer/indicador radioactivo un elemento radioactivo cuya trayectoria se puede seguir a través de un proceso o reacción (405)

transformer/transformador aparato que aumenta o disminuye el voltaje de corriente alterna (472)

transistor/transistor componente electrónico que se puede usar como amplificador o interruptor (485)

translucent/translúcido término que describe la materia que transmite luz pero que la desparrama cuando la luz la atraviesa (582)

transmission/transmisión cuando la luz pasa por la materia (581)

transparent/transparente término que describe la materia a través de la cual la luz se transmite con facilidad (582)

transverse wave/onda transversa onda cuyas partículas del medio vibran perpendicularmente a la dirección en que se desplaza la onda (513)

trough/seno la parte más baja de una onda transversal (513)

turbulence/turbulencia un fluir de líquidos irregular o impredecible que puede causar arrastre; la elevación con frecuencia es reducida por la turbulencia (176)

U

ultrasonic/ultrasónico el término que describe los sonidos con frecuencias más altas que 20,000 Hz (541)

ultrasonography/ultrasonograma procedimiento médico que usa ecos de ondas ultrasónicas para "ver" el interior del cuerpo del paciente sin hacer cirugía (547)

ultraviolet light/luz ultravioleta ondas electromagnéticas que están ubicadas entre la luz visible y los rayos X en el espectro electromagnético (573)

unbalanced forces/fuerzas en desequilibrio fuerzas que actúan sobre un objeto, que causan que la fuerza neta sea diferente de cero; las fuerzas en desequilibrio producen un cambio en el movimiento o la aceleración (117)

unsaturated hydrocarbon/hidrocarburo no saturado un hidrocarburo en el cual por lo menos dos átomos de carbono comparten un enlace doble (un alqueno) o un enlace triple (un alquino) (388)

V

valence electrons/electrones de valencia electrones en el nivel de energía exterior en un átomo; estos electrones toman parte en la formación de enlaces químicos (329)

vapor light/luz de vapor luz que se produce cuando los electrones se combinan con átomos gaseosos de metal (597)

vaporization/vaporización el cambio de estado de líquido a gas, incluye la ebullición y la evaporación (70)

velocity/velocidad vectorial la velocidad de un objeto en una dirección específica (110)

vibration/vibración el movimiento completo de un objeto hacia adelante y hacia atrás (534)

virtual image/imagen virtual imagen a través de la cual en realidad no pasa la luz (599)

viscosity/viscosidad la resistencia de un líquido a fluir (63)

visible light/luz visible la extensión muy pequeña de longitud y frecuencias de onda en el espectro electromagnético que los humanos pueden ver (572)

voltage/voltaje la diferencia en energía por unidad de carga cuando la carga se mueve entre dos puntos en un circuito eléctrico (lo mismo que la diferencia potencial); se expresa en voltios (434)

volume/volumen la cantidad de espacio ocupada o contenida por algo (25, 36)

W

watt/vatio la unidad que se usa para expresar electricidad (W); es equivalente a joules por segundo (J/s) (191)

wave/onda una alteración que transmite energía a través de la materia o del espacio (510, 535)

wavelength/longitud de onda la distancia entre un punto en una onda y el punto correspondiente en una onda adyacente en una serie de ondas (517)

wave speed/velocidad de onda la velocidad a que viaja una onda (519)

wedge/cuña una máquina simple formada por un plano inclinado doble que se mueve; con frecuencia se usa para cortar (201)

weight/peso medida de la fuerza de gravedad ejercida sobre un objeto, usualmente por la Tierra (40, 128)

wheel and axle/rueda y eje una máquina simple que consiste de dos objetos circulares de diferentes tamaños; la rueda es la más grande de los dos (202)

work/trabajo la acción que resulta cuando una fuerza hace que un objeto se mueva en la dirección de la fuerza (188)

work input/trabajo aplicado el trabajo que se hace en una máquina; el producto de la fuerza de entrada y la distancia a través de la que se ejerce (193)

work output/trabajo resultante el trabajo hecho por una máquina; el producto de la fuerza de salida y la distancia a través de la que se ejerce (193)

X

x rays/rayos X ondas electromagnéticas de alta energía que están entre las onda ultravioletas y las gamma en el espectro electromagnético (574)

Index

INDEX

X

Y

Z

Credits

Abbreviations used: (t) top, (c) center, (b) bottom, (l) left, (r) right, (bkgd) background

ILLUSTRATIONS

All illustrations, unless noted below, by Holt, Rinehart and Winston.

Table of Contents Page v(bl), Kristy Sprott; vii(tl), ix(tr), Stephen Durke/Washington Artists; ix(bl), Keith Locke/Suzanne Craig; xi(tr), Stephen Durke/Washington Artists; xi(tl), Terry Kovalcik; xii(tl), Stephen Durke/Washington Artists; xii(bl), Blake Thornton/Rita Marie; xiii(bl), Stephen Durke/Washington Artists; xiv(tl), Blake Thornton/Rita Marie; xv(cr), Sidney Jablonski; xv(bl), Marty Roper/Planet Rep; xvi(t), Annie Bissett.

Chapter One Page 6, 9, Rainey Kirk/The Neis Group; 13, John Huxtable/Black, Inc.; 14, Will Nelson/Sweet Reps; 16, Preface, Inc.; 17, Terry Guyer; 18(b), Brian White; 20(tr), Kristy Sprott; 20(bl) Morgan Cain & Associates; 21(t), Stephen Durke/Washington Artists; 21(c), Keith Locke/Suzanne Craig; 21(b) Gary Antonetti/Ortelius Design; 22(cl), Kristy Sprott; 22(b), Blake Thornton/Rita Marie; 23(t), Stephen Durke/Washington Artists and Preface, Inc.; 24(all), Stephen Durke/Washington Artists; 26(t), Morgan Cain & Associates; 29, Blake Thornton/Rita Marie; 31(tl), David Merrell/Suzanne Craig.

Chapter Two Page 38(t), 39, Stephen Durke/Washington Artists; 42(l), Gary Locke/Suzanne Craig; 43, Blake Thornton/Rita Marie; 50, 51, 53, Marty Roper/Planet Rep; 55(lc), Terry Kovalcik; 57(tc), Daniels & Daniels.

Chapter Three Page 60(t), Mark Heine; 60(b), 61, 62, 63, 64, 65, 66(cl,cr), Stephen Durke/Washington Artists; 66(bl), Preface, Inc.; 68, David Schleinkofer/Mendola Ltd.; 70(t), Marty Roper/Planet Rep; 70(b), Mark Heine; 73, David Schleinkofer/Mendola Ltd. and Preface, Inc.; 74(t), Stephen Durke/Washington Artists; 74(b), Preface, Inc.; 75, Marty Roper/Planet Rep; 77(cr), Preface, Inc.

Chapter Four Page 82, Marty Roper/Planet Rep; 84(b), Preface, Inc.; 88, Blake Thornton/Rita Marie; 95, Preface, Inc.

Chapter Five Page 109, Preface, Inc.; 111, Marty Roper/Planet Rep; 112, Gary Locke/Suzanne Craig; 113(t), Mike Carroll/Steve Edsey & Sons; 114(cr), Preface, Inc.; 119(t), Blake Thornton/Rita Marie; 119(b), 120, 122, Gary Ferster; 126, Doug Henry/American Artists; 127, Stephen Durke/Washington Artists; 128, Craig Attebery/Frank & Jeff Lavaty; 129, Terry Guyer; 130(br), Stephen Durke/Washington Artists; 131, Terry Guyer; 133(r), Preface, Inc.

Chapter Six Page 139, 140, Gary Ferster; 142, Craig Attebery/Frank & Jeff Lavaty; 144(tl), Mike Carroll/Steve Edsey & Sons; 146, Marty Roper/Planet Rep; 148, Charles Thomas; 151(tr), Gary Ferster; 154(br), Craig Attebery/Frank & Jeff Lavaty; 155, Marty Roper/Planet Rep; 158, James Pfeffer.

Chapter Seven Page 160, Rainey Kirk/The Neis Group; 162, 163, Stephen Durke/Washington Artists; 164, 165, Rainey Kirk/The Neis Group; 166, Christy Krames; 167, Mark Heine; 168, Preface, Inc.; 169, Will Nelson/Sweet Reps; 171, Preface, Inc.; 172, Sam Collins/Art & Science; 174(cr), Craig Attebery/Frank & Jeff Lavaty; 174(bl), Will Nelson/Sweet Reps; 176(l), Marty Roper/Planet Rep; 177, Terry Guyer; 178, Craig Attebery/Frank & Jeff Lavaty; 181(tr), Jared Schneidman/ Wilkinson Studios; 181(bl), Keith Locke/Suzanne Craig.

Chapter Eight Page 189(tr), Blake Thornton/Rita Marie; 190, John White/The Neis Group; 195(l), Annie Bissett; 195(r), John White/The Neis Group; 196, Keith Locke/Suzanne Craig; 198(l), 199(tl, bl), Annie Bissett; 201(cl), Preface, Inc.; 203(t), Gary Ferster; 203(c,b), 204, John White/The Neis Group; 206, Blake Thornton/Rita Marie.

Chapter Nine Page 215(b), Dave Joly; 216, John White/The Neis Group; 218, Stephen Durke/Washington Artists; 219(t), Kristy Sprott; 219(b), Stephen Durke/Washington Artists; 220(t), Gary Ferster; 224, Will Nelson/Sweet Reps; 225, Dan Stuckenschneider/Uhl Studios Inc.; 226(t), Blake Thornton/Rita Marie; 227, Dan Stuckenschneider/Uhl Studios Inc.; 229, Dan McGeehan/Koralik Associates; 230(t), Marty Roper/Planet Rep; 230(b), 232(b), Dan Stuckenschneider/Uhl Studios Inc.; 233(r), Preface, Inc.; 234, Patrick Gnan/Deborah Wolfe; 235(br), Michael Moore; 236(cr), Dan Stuckenschneider/Uhl Studios Inc.; 237(b), Preface, Inc.; 241(b), Dave Joly.

Chapter Ten Page 246, Blake Thornton/Rita Marie; 247, Stephen Durke/Washington Artists; 248, Terry Guyer; 249(tr), Dave Joly; 250, Dan Stuckenschneider/Uhl Studios Inc.; 252, 253, Stephen Durke/Washington Artists; 254(bl), Mark Heine; 255, Jared Schneidman/Wilkinson Studios; 258, 260, Stephen Durke/Washington Artists; 261, Preface, Inc.; 263, 264, 265, 266, 268, 269, Dan Stuckenschneider/Uhl Studios Inc.; 270(c), Dave Joly; 272(br), Dan Stuckenschneider/Uhl Studios Inc.; 273(cr), Preface, Inc.; 275, Stephen Durke/Washington Artists.

Unit Four Page 276(cr), Stephen Durke/Washington Artists.

Chapter Eleven Page 281(c), Preface, Inc.; 282, Mark Heine; 283, Stephen Durke/Washington Artists; 284(c), Mark Heine; 284(b), Preface, Inc.; 285(t), Stephen Durke/Washington Artists; 286, 288, 289(t,b), Stephen Durke/Washington Artists; 289(cr), Terry Kovalcik; 290, 291(b), 293, 294(br), Stephen Durke/Washington Artists; 295, Terry Kovalcik; 296, Mark Heine; 297(r), Stephen Durke/Washington Artists.

Chapter Twelve Page 302, Michael Jaroszko/American Artists; 304, 305, Kristy Sprott; 306(tr), 307, Stephen Durke/Washington Artists; 309, 310(bc), 311(bl), 312(t), 313(t), 314(tc, b), Preface, Inc.; 314(l), Gary Locke/Suzanne Craig; 315, 316, 317(lc), Preface, Inc.; 319, Gary Locke/Suzanne Craig; 321(tr), Preface, Inc.; 321(bl), Keith Locke/Suzanne Craig; 321(br), Annie Bissett; 323(l), Dan Stuckenschneider/Uhl Studios Inc.

Unit Five Page 324(cr), Kristy Sprott.

Chapter Thirteen Page 329, Stephen Durke/Washington Artists; 330, Preface, Inc.; 331, 333, 334, Stephen Durke/Washington Artists; 335(t), Keith Locke/Suzanne Craig; 335(br), Kristy Sprott; 336(c), 337(tl), Stephen Durke/Washington Artists; 337(tr,c), Preface, Inc.; 338(tr,br), Kristy Sprott; 338(bl), Stephen Durke/Washington

Artists; 339, Kristy Sprott; 340(cl), 341(tc), Kristy Sprott; 341(br), Preface, Inc.; 342(t), Keith Locke/Suzanne Craig; 342(b), Stephen Durke/Washington Artists; 343, Kristy Sprott; 344(b), Stephen Durke/Washington Artists; 346, Kristy Sprott.

Chapter Fourteen Page 352(t), 356, Kristy Sprott; 358(b), 359(c,b), 360(t), Blake Thornton/Rita Marie; 363(t), 365(b), Preface, Inc.; 366, Blake Thornton/Rita Marie; 367, Kristy Sprott; 369(cr), Preface, Inc.

Chapter Fifteen Page 380(t), Dave Joly; 380(b), 383, Preface, Inc.; 384, 385(b), Morgan Cain & Associates; 388, 389(t), 393(tr), Preface, Inc.

Chapter Sixteen Page 399, 400, Stephen Durke/Washington Artists; 401, Gary Ferster; 402, 403, Stephen Durke/Washington Artists; 404, Preface, Inc.; 406, 407, Stephen Durke/Washington Artists; 408, Patrick Gnan/Deborah Wolfe Ltd.; 410(c), 412(br), 414, Stephen Durke/Washington Artists; 415(tr), Preface, Inc.

Chapter Seventeen Page 422(t), Blake Thornton/Rita Marie; 422(b), Stephen Durke/Washington Artists; 423, John White/The Neis Group; 425(l), Stephen Durke/Washington Artists; 428, Dan Stuckenschneider/Uhl Studios Inc.; 430, 432, Mark Heine; 433, 434, Geoff Smith/Scott Hull; 436, Will Nelson/Sweet Reps; 439(cr), Boston Graphics; 444, Dan McGeehan/Koralik Associates.

Chapter Eighteen Page 456, 457, 458, Stephen Durke/Washington Artists; 459, Mark Persyn; 460(b), Stephen Durke/Washington Artists; 462, 463, 465, Sidney Jablonski; 466, Patrick Gnan/Deborah Wolfe Ltd.; 467, Stephen Durke/Washington Artists; 468, Mark Heine; 469, 470(t), Mark Persyn; 470(b), 471(t), David Fischer; 471(b), John Francis, 472, Tony Randazzo; 473, Dan Stuckenschneider/Uhl Studios Inc.; 474(l), Sidney Jablonski; 474(r), Mark Persyn; 475, David Fischer; 477, Stephen Durke/Washington Artists.

Chapter Nineteen Page 483, 484(c), Stephen Durke/Washington Artists; 484(b), Gary Ferster; 485, Blake Thornton/Rita Marie; 486, Gary Ferster; 489, 490(tl), Dan Stuckenschneider/Uhl Studios Inc.; 490(b), 491(tr), Gary Ferster; 491(b), Stephen Durke/Washington Artists; 492, Blake Thornton/Rita Marie; 493, Dan Stuckenschneider/Uhl Studios Inc.; 494, Preface, Inc.; 499, Blake Thornton/Rita Marie; 500(bl), Stephen Durke/Washington Artists; 500(br), Blake Thornton/Rita Marie; 502(cl), 503(tr), Gary Ferster.

Chapter Twenty Page 508(t), Gary Antonetti/Ortelius Design; 510, Will Nelson/Sweet Reps; 513(tr), Preface, Inc.; 513(b), 514(t,c), John White/The Neis Group; 514(b), Sidney Jablonski; 515(tl), Stephen Durke/Washington Artists; 515(r), Jared Schneidman/Wilkinson Studios; 516(t), Marty Roper/Planet Rep; 516(b), 517, 518, Sidney Jablonski; 518(cl, cr), 519(cl,cr), Mike Carroll/Steve Edsey & Sons; 519, 521, Will Nelson/Sweet Reps; 523(tl,t,c,r,cl,c,cr), John White/The Neis Group; 523(br), Terry Guyer; 526(b), John White/The Neis Group; 529(r), Sidney Jablonski.

Chapter Twenty-one Page 534, Annie Bissett; 535(l), Gary Ferster; 535(br), Terry Kovalcik; 536(tl), David Merrell/Suzanne Craig; 537, Keith Kasnot; 538 (tl), Terry Kovalcik; 539, Keith Locke/Suzanne Craig; 540, Annie Bissett; 541, Will Nelson/Sweet Reps (dolphin, cat, dog), Rob Wood (whale), Michael Woods (bat, bird), John White/The Neis Group (girl), and Preface, Inc.; 542, Gary Ferster; 544, Annie Bissett; 545(b), John White/The Neis Group; 546(t), Gary Ferster; 546(b), Terry Guyer; 548(t), Gary Ferster; 548(b), 549, Terry Guyer; 551, 552(c), Gary Ferster; 552(b), 555, Annie Bissett; 556(br), Keith Kasnot; 559(r), Annie Bissett; 560, Barbara Hoopes-Ambler.

Chapter Twenty-two Page 564, Sidney Jablonski; 565(tr), Blake Thornton/Rita Marie; 565(b), Stephen Durke/Washington Artists; 568(t), Blake Thornton/Rita Marie; 568(b), Preface, Inc.; 569(tl,tr), Terry Guyer; 569 (b), Preface, Inc.; 570, Dan Stuckenschneider/Uhl Studios Inc.; 572, Preface, Inc.; 573, Blake Thornton/Rita Marie; 574, 575, 576, Dan Stuckenschneider/Uhl Studios Inc.; 578, Stephen Durke/Washington Artists; 580, Preface, Inc.; 582, Dave Joly; 583, Preface, Inc.; 586, Stephen Durke/Washington Artists.

Chapter Twenty-three Page 595, 596, 597, Dan Stuckenschneider/Uhl Studios Inc.; 598, Stephen Durke/Washington Artists; 599, Preface, Inc.; 601, 602, 603, 604, Will Nelson/Sweet Reps (flowers) and Preface Inc.; 605, Keith Kasnot; 606, Keith Kasnot and Preface Inc.; 608, 609, Dan Stuckenschneider/Uhl Studios Inc.; 610(t), Digital Art; 610(b), Stephen Durke/Washington Artists; 611, Digital Art; 612, Stephen Durke/Washington Artists; 614(t), Dan Stuckenschneider/Uhl Studios Inc.; 614(b), Keith Kasnot; 617, Stephen Durke/Washington Artists (rulers) and Preface, Inc.

LabBook Page 642, Blake Thornton/Rita Marie; 661, Preface, Inc.; 665(l), John White/The Neis Group; 669, Dan McGeehan/Koralik Associates; 671, Marty Roper/Planet Rep.; 674, Dave Joly; 677(r), Preface, Inc.; 680, Stephen Durke/Washington Artists; 689, Preface, Inc.; 695(tr), Gary Ferster; 695(br), Dave Joly; 712, Blake Thornton/Rita Marie; 716, Terry Guyer; 718, Stephen Durke/Washington Artists; 721, 722, John White/The Neis Group.

Appendix Page 727, Blake Thornton/Rita Marie; 730(t), Terry Guyer; 734(b), Mark Mille/Sharon Langley Artist Rep.; 735, 736, 737, Preface, Inc.; 742, Stephen Durke/Washington Artists; 743(tl,c), Kristy Sprott; 743(b), Bruce Burdick; 744, 745, Kristy Sprott; 747(t), Dan Stuckenschneider/Uhl Studios Inc.

PHOTOGRAPHY

Front Cover (tl) Ed Young/Science Photo Library/Photo Researchers, Inc.; (tr) FPG International; (bl) Henry Kaiser/Leo de Wys; (br) Firefly Productions/The Stock Market (also on title page); (cr) Stephen Dalton/Photo Researchers, Inc.; owl (front cover, back cover, spine and title page) Kim Taylor/Bruce Coleman, Inc.

Table of Contents Page v(tr), Robert Daemmrich/Tony Stone Images; (br), Peter Van Steen/HRW Photo; vi(cl), Richard Megna/Fundamental Photographs; (bl), Joseph Drivas/Image Bank; vii(bl), Richard Megna/Fundamental Photographs; viii(tr), James Balog/Tony Stone Images; (cl), Sergio Purtell/FOCA; (bl) NASA; ix(tl), T. Mein/N&M Mischler/Tony Stone Images; x(tr), NASA; xiii(br), Dr. E.R. Degginger/Color-Pic, Inc.; xiv(t), Stephanie Morris/HRW Photo; xv(inset), Archive Photos; xvi(bl), Leonard Lessin/Peter Arnold, Inc.; xvii(tr), Harry Rogers/Photo Researchers, Inc.; xxi(t), Robert Wolf; xxi(br), Superstock.

Feature Borders Unless otherwise noted below, all images ©2001 PhotoDisc/HRW: "Across the Sciences" Pages 56, 135, 242, 267, 322, 370, 418, 448, all images by HRW; "Careers" 32, 159, 243, 323, 395, 509, sand bkgd and saturn, Corbis Images, DNA, Morgan Cain & Associates, scuba gear, ©1997 Radlund & Associates for Artville; "Eureka" 79, 158, 182, 211, 371, ©2001 PhotoDisc/HRW; "Eye on the

Megna/Fundamental Photographs; 361(c), HRW Photo by Peter Van Steen; 361(r), Tom Stewart/The Stock Market; 361(l), HRW photo by Victoria Smith; 364(t), 364(bl), 364(br), Richard Megna/Fundamental Photographs; 365, Dorling Kindersley, LTD, courtesy of the Science Museum, London; 368(t), 369, Richard Megna/Fundamental Photographs.

Chapter Fifteen Page 372(b), SuperStock; 374(t), Yoav Levy/Phototake; 375(t,bl,bl), 376, Richard Megna/Fundamental Photographs; 377(b), Charles D. Winters/Timeframe Photography Inc.; 381(t), Runk/Schoenberger/Grant Heilman Photography Inc.; 381(b), Peter Arnold Inc., NY; 382, Miro Vinton/Stock Boston/PNI; 382(b), John Deeks/Photo Researchers, Inc.; 386(br), Hans Reinhard/Bruce Coleman Inc.; 387, David M. Phillips/Visuals Unlimited; 388(br), Charles D. Winters/Timeframe Photography Inc.; 390, Runk/Schoenberger/Grant Heilman Photography Inc.; 392(b), Charles D. Winters/Timeframe Photography Inc.; 392(t), Richard Megna/Fundamental Photographs; 394, Sygma; 395(t), Tom McHugh/Photo Researchers, Inc.; 395(b), Dennis Kunkel, University of Hawaii.

Chapter Sixteen Page 396(b), Dave Steel/NASA; 396(t), NASA; 398(b), Henri Becquerel/The Granger Collection; 398(t), Dr. E.R. Degginger/Color-Pic, Inc.; 403, Sygma; 405(b), Tim Wright/Corbis; 405(t), Custom Medical Stock Photo; 407, Emory Kristof/National Geographic Image Collection; 409(t), Shone/Liaison International; 409(b), Michael Melford/The Image Bank; 410, Roger Rossmeyer/Corbis Bettmann; 412(c), Dr. E.R. Degginger/Color-Pic, Inc.; 413, Emory Kristof/National Geographic Image Collection; 415(r), Science Photo Library/Photo Researchers, Inc.; 416(l), Sauder/Gamma Liason; 416(t), Cameramann International; 417(b), Charles O'Rear/Corbis ; 417(t), Courtesy of Micheal Atzmon.

Unit Six Page 418(b), Enrico Tedeschi; 418(t), AKG London; 418(c), Peter Southwick/AP Wide World; 419(b), Ilkka Uimonen/Sygma; 419(c), Enrico Tedeschi; 419(tl), Hulton Getty; 419(tr), property of AT&T Archives. Printed with permission of AT&T.

Chapter Seventeen Page 420(t), Norbert Wu; 420(b), Norbert Wu; 421(tr), NASA; 421(tl), Corbis ; 421(br), ESA/Sygma; 421(bl), Anglo-Australian Observatory ; 424(l,r), HRW photo by Victoria Smith; 426(b), HRW photo by Stephanie Morris; 427(b), HRW Photo by Peter Van Steen; 429, Paul Katz/Index Stock Imagery/Picture Quest; 435(t), Patricia Ceisel/Visuals Unlimited; 435(b), David R. Frazier Photolibrary; 436, Takeshi Takahara/Photo Researchers, Inc.; 437, Science Photo Library/Photo Researchers, Inc.; 438(br), HRW photo by Richard Hanes; 439, Visuals Unlimited; 440(l), Richard T. Nowitz/Photo Researchers, Inc.; 445(t), Paul Silverman/Fundamental Photographs; 448(t), HRW photo by Victoria Smith; 450(t), Corbis-Bettmann; 450(b), Bill Ross/ Corbis; 451(l), Daniel Osborne, University of Alaska/Detlev Ban Ravenswaay/Science Photo Library/Photo Researchers, Inc.; 451(r), STARLab, Stanford University.

Chapter Eighteen Page 452(t), Photo Researchers, Inc.; 452(b), Courtesy Dr. Andre Geim; 453, HRW photo by Victoria Smith; 455(bl,bc,br), 456, Richard Megna/Fundamental Photographs; 461(l), Pekka Parviainen/Photo Researchers Inc; 463, SuperStock; 464, Tom Tracy/The Stock Shop; 478, The Image Bank; 479, Howard Sochurek.

Chapter Nineteen Page 480(t), MZTV; 480(inset), Archive Photos; 488, Dr. E.R. Degginger/Color-Pic, Inc.; 489, Yoav Levy/PhotoTake; 493 (inset), Corbis Images; 495(l), Corbis/Bettmann; 495(r), 501, SuperStock; 504, HRW Photo by Peter Van Steen.

Unit Seven Page 506(t), Fotos International/Archive Photos; 506(b), courtesy of Hughes Research Laboratories; 507(tl), David Parker/Science Photo Library/Photo Researchers; 507(tr), Dr. E.R. Degginger/Color-Pic, Inc.; 507(c), Photofest; 507(br), HRW Photo by Victoria Smith; 507(bl), Brook/Gamma Liaison.

Chapter Twenty Page 508, AP/Wide World Photos; 511(t), Phil Degginger/Color-Pic, Inc.; 511(b), Emil Muench/Photo Researchers, Inc.; 512, Norbert Wu; 520(b), Erich Schrempp/Photo Researchers, Inc. ; 520, Don Spiro/Tony Stone Images; 522(tl,tr,), Richard Megna/Fundamental Photographs; 522(b), Richard Hamilton Smith/Corbis-Bettmann; 524(t), Richard Megna/Fundamental Photographs; 525, AP/Wide World Photos; 526, Norbert Wu; 528, Richard Megna/Fundamental Photographs; 529, Martin Bough/Fundamental Photographs; 530, Pete Saloutos/The Stock Market; 531, Betty K. Bruce/Animals Animals/Earth Scenes.

Chapter Twenty-one Page 532(c), SuperStock; 532(t), The Granger Collection, NY; 532(b), Mark Newman/Photo Researchers, Inc,; 538(c), Michael A. Keller/The Picture Cube; 543(cl), Art Wolfe/ Tony Stone Images; 543(b), Tom Hannon/Picture Cube; 544, Charles D. Winters/Timeframe Photography Inc.; 545, Dr. E.R. Degginger/Color-Pic, Inc.; 546, Stephen Dalton/Photo Researchers, Inc.; 547(b), Matt Meadows/Photo Researchers, Inc.; 547(t), courtesy of Johann Borenstein; 550(b,c), Richard Megna/Fundamental Photographs; 553(l), 554(c), Image Club Graphics © 1998 Adobe Systems; 554(tl,tr,br), Bob Daemmrich/HRW Photo; 558, Ross Harrison Koty/Tony Stone Images; 559, Dick Luria/Photo Researchers, Inc.

Chapter Twenty-two Page 562(t), Cindy Roesinger/Photo Researchers, Inc.; 562(b), Visuals Unlimited; 565, Photo Researchers, Inc.; 566, A.T. Willet/The Image Bank; 567(r,l), Leonard Lessing/Photo Researchers, Inc.; 567(c), Michael Fogden and Patricia Fogden/Corbis; 568(l), Robert Wolf; 569(c), Hugh Turvey/Science Photo Library/Photo Researchers, Inc.; 569(r), Blair Seitz/Photo Researchers, Inc.; 569(l), Leonide Principe/Photo Researchers, Inc.; 571(t), Bachmann/Photo Researchers, Inc.; 571(b), The Stock Market; 572, Cameron Davidson/Tony Stone Images; 574, Michael English/Custom Medical Stock Photo; 577, Richard Megna/Fundamental Photographs; 578, Robert Wolf; 579(t), Fundamental Photographs; 581(t), Robert Wolf; 581(b), HRW photo by Stephanie Morris; 583(t), Image copyright 2001 PhotoDisc, Inc.; 583(c), Renee Lynn/Davis/Lynn Images; 583(b), Robert Wolf; 584, Leonard Lessing/Peter Arnold, Inc.; 585, Index Stock Photography; 586, Leonard Lessing/Photo Researchers, Inc.; 587, Robert Wolf; 589(tr), Charles Winters/Photo Researchers, Inc.; 589(cr), Mark E. Gibson; 589(br), Richard Megna/Fundamental Photographs; 590(t,b), Dr. E.R. Degginger/Color-Pic, Inc.; 591, courtesy of the Raytheon Company.

Chapter Twenty-three Page 592(b), NASA; 592(t), Roger Ressmeyer/Corbis Media WA; 594(b), Harry Rogers/Photo Researchers, Inc.; 594(r), Kindra Clinett/The Picture Cube; 596, HRW Photo by Peter Van Steen; 597, Alan Schein/The Stock Market; 598(tr), Yoav Levy/Phototake; 599(tr), HRW Photo by Stephanie Morris; 600(c), Richard Megna/Fundamental Photographs; 602, 603(b), Robert Wolf; 603(t,c), Dr. E.R. Degginger/Color-Pic, Inc.; 607(l,r), Leonard Lessing/Peter Arnold, Inc.; 612, Don

Mason/The Stock Market; 613(l,r), Ken Lax; 616, James L. Amos/National Geographic Society; 618(b), US Patent and Trade Office; 618(t), Private collection of Garrett Morgan Family; 619(b), NASA; 619(t), SuperStock.

LabBook "LabBook Header": "L," Corbis Images, "a," Letraset Phototone "b" and "B," HRW, "o" and "k," images ©2001 PhotoDisc/HRW; 623(c), HRW photo by Michelle Bridwell; 623(br), Image copyright © 2001 PhotoDisc, Inc.; 624(r), HRW photo by Victoria Smith; 624(bl), HRW photo by Stephanie Morris; 625(tl), Patti Murray/Animals Animals; 625(tr), HRW photo by Jana Birchum; 625(b), HRW photo by Peter Van Steen; 626, HRW photo by Victoria Smith; 631, NASA; 638, 639(t), HRW Photo by Victoria Smith; 640, Stuart Westmoreland/Tony Stone Images; 644, Gareth Trevor/Tony Stone Images; 649, copyright 2001 Photo Disc/HRW Photo; 653, NASA; 662, HRW photo by Stephanie Morris; 663, Paul Dance/Tony Stone Images; 665(l,r), Robert Wolf; 670, 673, 676, HRW photo by Victoria Smith; 685, Rob Boudreau/Tony Stone Images; 687, 690, 697, HRW photo by Victoria Smith; 701, David Young-Wolf/PhotoEdit; 706, James H. Karales/Peter Arnold Inc., NY; 709(t,c,b), 710, Richard Megna/Fundamental Photographs; 714, HRW Photo.

Appendix Page 727(t), 727(b), 731(b), HRW photo by Sam Dudgeon; 731(t), HRW photo by Peter Van Steen; 748, HRW photo by Sam Dudgeon.

Sam Dudgeon/HRW Photo Page vii(tl,tr,br); xi,(bl); xiv(bl); xv(tr,tl); xvi(cl); xviii-xx; T6(tl,tr); T11(br); T12(bl); T15(tr); 2(cr); 5(b); 8(tl,tr); 9(bl); 12(t,c); 22(cl); 23(t); 30(all); 31(l); 37(bl); 59(b); 61(bl); 64(r); 66; 76(b); 81(tr); 85(tl,tr,c); 87(r); 90(t); 91(cl); 93(t); 94(bl); 96(t,b); 99; 100(b); 101(br); 106(tr); 107; 112(b); 114(b); 116(t); 118(c); 124(bl); 132; 137(b); 157(r); 161; 177(t); 180; 182(b); 187(b); 195(c); 198; 199(bl); 213; 215; 217; 220; 238; 240(t); 244-45; 251; 256; 279; 282-283; 303; 306; 307(c,tl); 308; 311(b); 312(tl,b); 315; 318(t); 336(b); 338; 339(l); 345; 347; 349; 350(bl); 356; 373; 374(b); 378(b); 386(l); 388(t); 393; 397; 408; 411; 431(b); 432; 438(t,bl,bc); 440(b,c); 445(b); 447; 449(b); 454; 455(t); 457; 458; 460; 476-477; 480(t); 481; 482; 484-487; 490; 494-495; 496; 497; 500; 502; 506(c); 509; 518; 527; 533(b); 535(b); 536; 538(r); 541(t); 550(t); 552; 556-557; 563; 568(c); 588; 593; 594(t); 600(b); 611; 620(cl,t,b); 622; 623(b); 624(br,t); 628; 630; 632-633; 634; 636-637; 639(b); 641; 643; 645-648; 650-652; 654-657; 659-661; 664; 675; 676; 677; 678; 681-684; 688; 692-694; 698-700; 702; 703-705; 707-708; 711; 713; 715; 717; 719-720; 723; 727; 731; 748; 723.

John Langford/HRW Photo Page v(cr); vi(tr); x(tl,bl); xii(br); xiii(tr,cl); T7(r); T8(bl); T12(tr); 6(l); 10(tl,c); 20(cl); 21; 22(tr); 28(bl); 31(t); 35; 36(t); 37(t); 38-39; 41(b); 42; 52(l); 54(all); 64(l); 91(bl,bc,br); 95(all); 145; 188-189; 191; 193; 195(t); 199(t); 201(l); 205(tr); 206; 207; 208(b); 209(tr); 218(l); 219; 220(b); 223(b); 224; 226; 233(cl,r,bl); 235(cr); 247; 252-255; 257; 258; 260-261; 264; 270; 301; 327-328; 332(r); 336(t); 341; 348(b); 354; 355(c); 362-363; 368(b); 372(t); 377(t); 378(t); 379; 388(bl); 389; 415; 421; 425; 426(tl,tr); 427(t); 431(t); 438(tl); 440(r); 441; 442; 443; 444; 446; 448(b); 449(t); 524(b); 535(t);542; 543(t,bc); 553(r); 568(r); 573; 576; 579(b); 582; 594(inset); 599(b); 600(tl); 601(b); 617; 623(t); 631(t); 665(b); 666; 679; 691; 696.

Scott Van Osdol/HRW Photo Page T17(br); 61(br); 62(all); 63(b); 67(r); 69(b); 71-72; 163; 163: 166; 175(br); 194; 196; 199(br); 351(bl); 384; 385; 386(t); 391; 589; 627; 629.